HISTORY
of the
LAND TITLES
in
HUDSON COUNTY NEW JERSEY

- 1608-1871 -

By: Charles H. Winfield

Southern Historical Press, Inc.
Greenville, South Carolina

This volume was reproduced from
a personal copy located in the
Publisher's private library
Greenville, South Carolina

All rights reserved. No part of this publication may be reproduced, stored in a retieval system, Transmitted in any form, posted on to the web in any form or by any means without the prior permission of the publisher.

Please direct ALL correspondence and book orders to:
www.southernhistoricalpress.com
or
Southern Historical Press, Inc.
PO Box 1267
Greenville, SC 29602-1267
southernhistoricalpress@gmail.com

Originally published: New York, NY   1872
ISBN #978-1-63914-036-7
All Rights Reserved
Printed in the United States of America

Entered according to Act of Congress, in the year 1872, by
CHARLES H. WINFIELD,
In the office of the Librarian of Congress at Washington.

TO THE

Freeholders of Hudson County,

NEW JERSEY,

WHO MAY BE INTERESTED IN KNOWING THE PAST HISTORY

OF

THEIR PRESENT REAL POSSESSIONS,

THIS VOLUME

IS

RESPECTFULLY DEDICATED.

CONTENTS.

	PAGE.
CHAPTER I.—TITLES UNDER THE DUTCH,	1
" II.—TITLES UNDER THE KING,	10
" III.—HISTORY OF THE COMMON LANDS,	15
" IV.—FIELD-BOOK AND NOTES,	27
" V.—SECAUCUS COMMONS,	285
" VI.—NEW FIELD-BOOK AND NOTES,	311
" VII.—NEW BARBADOES NECK,	324
" VIII.—MARRIAGES, BIRTHS, AND DEATHS,	329

MAPS AND DIAGRAMS.

1. VAN PURMERENT'S PATENT,	43
2. STOFFELSEN'S PATENT,	46
3. COS'S PATENT,	49
4. DE BACKER'S PATENT,	51
5. HARTMAN'S FIRST PATENT,	54
6. HARTMAN'S SECOND PATENT,	55
7. PARTITION OF MERSELIS'S PROPERTY (GREENVILLE),	63
8. PARTITION BETWEEN VREELAND AND VAN WINKLE (PAMREPAW),	66
9. PARTITION OF GARRET VREELAND'S PROPERTY (PAMREPAW),	67
10. PARTITION OF VAN BUSKIRK'S PROPERTY (BAYONNE),	71
11. PARTITION OF VREELAND'S PROPERTY (CENTREVILLE),	72
12. PARTITION OF CONSTABLE'S HOOK,	75
13. PARTITION OF PRIOR'S PROPERTY (BERGEN),	125
14. DUNHAM'S MAP OF BERGEN POINT,	136
15. CHURCH AND MECHANICS' LOTS,	146
16. SCHOOL LOT,	148
17. HARING'S MAP OF BAYARD'S COMMONS,	152
18. PARTITION OF BRINKERHOFF'S LOT (GREENVILLE),	160
19. LOTS AT SLONGA,	163
20. MAP A, NEW FIELD-BOOK,	311
21. MAP B, NEW FIELD-BOOK,	314
22. PARTITION OF GAUTIER'S PROPERTY (NEAR FIVE CORNERS),	316

PREFACE.

THE FIELD-BOOK, which is the foundation of this volume, comprises the boundaries of the old township of Bergen and of the several lots therein patented to individuals, and of the common lands allotted and partitioned by the Commission of 1764. It is the manuscript record of a survey which, though intricate, is accurate, exhaustive, and authoritative; while the adjudications of ownership, as therein contained, have never been questioned. On questions of title it has always been held in high estimation,—in fact, final and conclusive. From much use, the maps are becoming somewhat defaced, and the book worn and confused through the inaccurate copying, ignorant arrangement, and careless binding of several leaves which had become separated from the work. Impressed with these facts, the Board of Chosen Freeholders decided to do something for the preservation of these important documents. After mature reflection, the plan of simple reproduction, which at first suggested itself, was abandoned, and the following commendable action taken by the Board on the 12th of January, 1871 :—

Whereas, The greatly increased values of land in the County are directing closer attention than formerly to titles ; and,

Whereas, The FIELD-BOOK and MAPS made under the direction of the Commission of 1764 are regarded as quite conclusive upon questions of title up to that time, and are, from their great age and continual use, in such a ruinous condition that this Board should take prompt action for their preservation before it is too late ; and,

Whereas, It would be of great value to the public generally, and land-owners in the County particularly, that the same should be edited and published in book form, instead of being copied; therefore,

Resolved, That a committee of three be appointed, with power to secure the services of some competent person to edit and publish the FIELD-BOOK, and MAPS accompanying the same, in book form.

The committee, consisting of Jeremiah B. Cleveland, Henry D. Van Nostrand, and John M. Wilson, appointed under these resolutions, requested the undersigned to undertake the work. This request was acceded to, with a full appreciation of the magnitude of the task, and with the consciousness that, if properly performed, the result would be of great utility, though it might not be pecuniarily profitable, nor in a general sense popular.

It cannot be denied that the tenacity with which, until a recent period, the descendants of the original owners had retained their ancestral acres, has rendered the work easier than it otherwise would have been. Nevertheless, the subject has grown much beyond what was originally contemplated. New matter has been found, unrecorded deeds and unproved wills have been brought from their hiding-places, and even a NEW FIELD-BOOK and MAPS, complete and in good preservation, which, in their quiet sleep in the old garret, had outlived the memory of man, are now given to the inspection of the curious. Of the great assistance they will be to the conveyancer there can be no doubt.

Much care has been taken to reproduce the text of the FIELD-BOOK without the slightest variation, even in orthography or punctuation. The original paging has been preserved in the margin of this volume, and all references in the body of the work are to the marginal pages. The object, from the beginning, has been to make the volume one of accuracy and usefulness, rather than of display of antiquarian research. The opening chapters give a brief history of the titles under the Dutch, the King, and Lords Proprietors, as well as the disputes concerning the common lands which led to the intervention of the Legislature, and their allotment. The greater part of the labor performed in the preparation of the work has been expended in notes to the several lots described in the FIELD-BOOK.

Though not within the scope of the original plan, it has been deemed advisable to insert a chapter on the early acquisition and ownership of New Barbadoes Neck, so far as the same now lies within the townships of Harrison and Kearney.

As, until a recent period, most of the transfers of lands in the old township of Bergen were by devise or descent, the conveyancer will find the record of MARRIAGES, BIRTHS, AND DEATHS, herein for the first time published, of great use in his investigations. It is taken from the RECORDS of the Old Bergen Reformed Church, and for the most part translated form the Dutch. These records begin in 1664, and as here published contain the marriages down to 1830, the births to 1825, and the deaths to 1850.

The article of Mr. Delos E. Culver on the magnetic needle will be useful to surveyors and interesting to the general reader. In connection therewith it may be well to insert here what should have been inserted in another place :

" Latitude and Longitude of Hudson County Court-House, North Bergen, New Jersey :—

```
        Latitude,              -  40° 43' 50" N.
        Longitude in time,  -     4h. 56m. 14s. 7t.
                                                 3
                                  ────────────────
                                  14  48  44    1
                                                 5
                                  ────────────────
        West from Greenwich -  -  74  03  40   5
    Variation of Compass in 1841,  5°  52'.
                                    W. C. WETMORE,
        July 7, 1846.                   U. S. Navy."
```

In the foot-notes, brief sketches of the patentees have, in most instances, been given. In some cases these sketches have been purposely omitted for more appropriate insertion in the " History of Hudson County," which is now in course of preparation. In these foot-notes to the several patents, allotments, and subdivisions, has been concentrated all the information which could be obtained concerning each lot laid down and numbered on the map. For this information the records at Albany, Perth Amboy, Trenton, Hackensack, and those in the office of the Clerk of the Common Council of New York, have been searched. But few references to authorities have been given, for the reason that such references would have occupied no inconsiderable portion of the volume. Dates have, in nearly all instances, been given; and these, it is hoped, will be a sufficient guide in the investigations of titles.

It ought not to be expected, in a work of this character, to find an abstract of every title in the County. Whoever looks for that may as well leave these pages unread, for he will be disappointed. Yet there has been gathered here, and so arranged as to bear upon each lot, a mass of facts and dates which, it is hoped, will make the book a necessity to lawyers and conveyancers, and a source of gratification to land-owners.

There can hardly be a doubt but that errors of commission and omission will be discovered, of which the author hopes to be informed. The few typographical errors in the book the reader will readily detect, and they need not, therefore, be pointed out.

A number of small maps have been prepared and inserted in the text, for the purpose of showing the location or partition of lots. More would have been inserted could they have been obtained. Considerable trouble was taken to discover Haring's Map of the Bayard Commons. Failing in that, it has, with the assistance of Richard D. Dodge, been reproduced. The MAPS which accompany this work have been prepared, with much labor and expense, by the firm of Mallory & Miller (Franklin J. Mallory and William W. Miller), city surveyors of Jersey City. They are intended to be, and, it is believed, are, fac-similes of the originals. They will be enduring monuments to the ability and accuracy of those enterprising gentlemen. On the FIELD MAP have been traced certain roads, railways, and prominent objects, for the purpose of aiding in the location of property. These, with the descriptions of lots given in the foot-notes, will, it is thought, be sufficient for that purpose.

In conclusion, it may be well to remind the critical reader that this volume was prepared mostly at night, and its materials were gathered in moments taken from the hours of business. It is now twelve months since the work was begun, and the labor in its preparation has been to the author a labor of love. During this time he has, as it were, lived among the memories of a bygone age. The uncouth names of the original settlers have become familiar as household words; and their signatures are as well known to him as his own. With this goodly company he must now part for a time, committing them, with their honest simplicity, and the book with its imperfections, to the tender mercies of the reader, who may be assured, that, if the work meet the approval of those whose experience enables them to appreciate the magnitude of the undertaking, and whose profession and learning qualify them to judge of its merits, the author can hope for no more.

C. H. W.

HILLSIDE, Feb. 6, 1872.

LAND TITLES
IN
HUDSON COUNTY,
NEW JERSEY.

CHAPTER I.

UNDER THE DUTCH.

BETWEEN 1609 and 1614 this part of the American Continent was visited only by occasional traders. On the 27th of March, 1614, the States-General, in compliance with the wishes of some Holland merchants, made an octroy,* giving to those who should discover new lands a monopoly of trade with the same for four voyages. Immediately some merchants of Amsterdam and Hoorn fitted out five ships, three of which came to the Great River of the Manhattans, and thence passed through the Sound and along the coast as far east as Cape Cod. When the report of these voyages was made at home, the merchants interested in the vessels obtained from the States-General, October 11, 1614, a monopoly of the trade with "New Netherland" for four voyages within a period of three years, dating from January 1, 1615. They assumed the name of "The United New Netherland Company." On the expiration of the charter, January 1, 1618, the company did not obtain a renewal thereof, but the individual members of the company, by special license, continued to control the trade of which they previously had the monopoly.

"The Dutch West India Company" was chartered June 3, 1621. Its powers of government were vested in five chambers, but its general supervision was lodged in nineteen delegates from the five chambers known as the "Assembly of XIX." It was not, however, until 1623 that any movement was made looking to

---
* A grant.

an active and systematized trade with this country. In 1624 Peter Minuit came out as Director-General. From this time until 1629 the company made no attempt to establish permanent settlements, but bent every energy to build-up a profitable trade with the natives. On June 7, 1629, an earnest effort was put forth to induce persons to settle in the country, and measures adopted at the same time to secure the advantages of such settlements to the directors of the company. The "Assembly of XIX." agreed upon what they called,

"FREEDOMS AND EXEMPTIONS,

granted by the 'Assembly of XIX.' of the Privileged West India Company, to all such as shall plant any colonies in New Netherland."

Among other articles, not necessary to be mentioned here, were the following:

III.—All such shall be acknowledged Patroons of New Netherland who shall, within the space of four years next after they have given notice to any of the Chambers of the Company here, or to the Commander or Council there, undertake to plant a colonie there of fifty souls, upwards of fifteen years old; one-fourth part within one year, and within three years after the sending of the first, making together four years, the remainder, to the full number of fifty persons, to be shipped from hence, on pain, in case of wilful neglect, of being deprived of the privileges obtained. * *

V.—The Patroons, by virtue of their power, shall and may be permitted, at such places as they shall settle their colonies, to extend their limits four miles* along the shore, that is, on one side of a navigable river, or two miles on each side of a river, and so far into the country as the situation of the occupiers will permit. * *

VI.—They shall forever possess and enjoy all the lands lying within the aforesaid limits, together with the fruits, rights, minerals, rivers, and fountains thereof; as also the chief command and lower jurisdictions, fishing, fowling, and grinding, to the exclusion of all others, to be holden from the Company as a perpetual inheritance, without it ever devolving again to the Company, and in case it should devolve, to be redeemed and repossessed with twenty guilders per colony, to be paid to this Company, at the Chamber here, or to their Commander there, within a year and six weeks after the same occurs, each at the Chamber where he originally sailed from.

* * * * * * *

XXVI.—Whosoever shall settle any colonie out of the limits of the Manhattes Island shall be obliged to satisfy the Indians for the land they shall settle upon, and they may extend or enlarge the limits of their colonies if they settle a proportionate number of colonists thereon.

° Equal to sixteen English miles. These articles may be found *in extenso* in O'Cal N. N., i. 112.

The directors were not slow, in fact some of them did not wait for the ratification of this charter, to secure the advantages here held out. Godyn and Bloemmaert took up a large tract near Cape Henlopen, also a tract sixteen miles square at Cape May. Kiliaen van Rensselaer secured the territory near Fort Orange. The Director-General and Council of New Netherland, acting for Burgomaster Michael Pauw, Lord of Achtienhoven, obtained the following deeds for lands in this county :

We, Director and **Council** of **New Netherland**, residing on the **Island** of **Manahatas** and the Fort Amsterdam, under the authority of their **High Mightinesses** the Lords States-General of this **United Netherlands** and the **Incorporated West India Company**, at their Chambers at Amsterdam, do hereby witness and declare that on this day, the date hereof underwritten, before us in their proper persons appeared and showed themselves, to wit : **Arommeauw, Tekwappo**, and **Sackwomeck**, inhabitants and joint owners of the land called **Hobocan Hackingh**, lying over against (opposite) the aforesaid **Island Manhatas**, who both for themselves and *rato cavern*, for the remaining joint owners of the same land, declared that for and in consideration of a certain quantity of merchandize, which they acknowledged to have received into their own hands, power, and possession, before the passing of these presents in a right, true, and free ownership, have sold, transported, ceded, conveyed, and made over, and by these presents they do transport, cede, and convey to and for the behoof of **Mr. Michiel Pauw**, absent, and for whom we, *ex-officio*, accept under suitable stipulations, viz. : the aforesaid lands by us named **Hobocan Hackingh**, extending on the South side, Ahasimus; Eastward, the **River Mauritius**, and on the West side surrounded by a valley (marsh) and morass, through which the boundaries of said land can be seen with sufficient clearness, and be distinguished; and that, with all the jurisdiction, right, and equity, to them, the grantors, in their quality aforesaid, belonging : Constituting and putting in their place and stead the already mentioned **Mr. Pauw**, in the real and actual possession thereof, and at the same time giving full and irrevocable power, authority, and special command to the said Mr. Pauw peaceably to enjoy, occupy, cultivate, have and hold the aforesaid land, *tanquam actor et procurator in rem suam acpropriam;* and also to do with and dispose of the same as he might do with his own lands to which he has a good and lawful title; without their, the grantors, in their quality aforesaid, saving or reserving any part, right, action, or authority thereto in the least, either of ownership or jurisdiction; but altogether to the behoof as aforesaid, henceforth, forever, wholly, and finally desisting, renouncing, and quit-claiming; promising hereby, moreover, not only to keep, maintain, and fulfil this their grant, and whatever shall be done by virtue thereof, inviolable and irrevocable forever, but also to keep and maintain the same land against all persons free from any claim, challenge, or incumbrance to be made thereon by any person; as also to cause this sale and grant to be approved of and held valid by the remaining joint owners as they are by right obligated to do; all in good faith without fraud or deceit.

In witness whereof these presents are confirmed with our usual signature and with our seal thereto affixed.

Done at the aforesaid Island of Manahatas, in Fort Amsterdam, this 12th July, 1630.*

We, the **Director** and **Council** of **New Netherland,** residing on the **Island** of **Manahatas,** under the jurisdiction of their High Mightinesses the Lords, the States-General of the **United Netherlands,** and the **General Incorporated West India Company,** do, by these presents publish and declare, that on this day, the date underwritten, before us in their own proper persons, came and appeared, **Kikitoauw** and **Aiarouw, Virginians,** Inhabitants and joint owners of the land named **Ahasimus** and the peninsula **Aressick,** as well for themselves as, *rato caverende,* for **Mingm, Wathkath** and **Cauwins,** joint proprietors of the same parcels of land, and declared in the same quality that for and in consideration of certain parcels of goods, which they the appearers acknowledged before the passing of these presents to their full gratitude and satisfaction to have received into their possession, hands, and power in their right and free (unincumbered) ownership, and by virtue of the title and article of sale, they have sold, transported, ceded, and delivered, and by these presents they do transport, cede, and deliver to and for the behoof of the **Noble Lord Michiel Pauw** (absent), and for whom we, *ex-officio,* accept the same with suitable stipulations, namely, the aforesaid land **Ahasimus** and **Aressick,** by us named the **Whores Corner,** extending along the river **Mauritius** and the **Island** of the **Manahatas** on the east side, and the **Island Hoboken Hackingh** on the north side, surrounded by swamps, which are sufficiently distinct boundaries, and that with all the action, right, and equity to them in their quality aforesaid appertaining, constituting and substituting the said grantee as the attorney for the said **Mr. Pauw,** in their stead and state, in the real and actual possession of the same, and at the same time giving him full and irrevocable power, authority, and special license, to the said **Mr. Pauw;** and to his successors, *tanquam in rem suam,* the aforesaid land and its appurtenances peaceably to enter upon, possess, inhabit, farm, occupy, use, and to do therewith and thereon, trade and dispose as he the cedentee, may do with his own lands and domains honestly and legally obtained, without their, the **Grantors,** in their aforesaid quality, having thereto or any part thereof, any part, right, action, or jurisdiction in the least, without reserving or saving any ownership, command, or jurisdiction, but to the behoof aforesaid from henceforth and forever, wholly and absolutely desisting, relinquishing, and renouncing by these **Presents.** Promoting, moreover, not only this their conveyance, and all that may be done by virtue thereof, to keep forever firm, inviolable, and irrevocable, but also the said land to deliver and keep from all demands, challenge, or incumbrances, any and every one that may thereto make any pretense; and, moreover, this purchase and conveyance to cause to be approved and made valid by the other joint owners, as in equity they are bound to do, standing thereto in all good faith without fraud or deceit. **Witness** our several signatures and confirmed by our seal appended thereto.

Done at **Manahattas** in the **Fort Amsterdam** this 22d day of Nov., in the year 1630.†

---

* Land Papers (Albany), G. G. 1.   † Land Papers (Albany,) G. G. 8.

Thus Pauw became the owner of all the land east of the hill and the mill creek, lying between the kil of Hoboken on the north and Communipaw Bay on the south. These bounds are sufficiently expressed and are well known. Yet he seems to have been the owner of "Gemoenepaen," and it was in his colony. By what right, we do not know. There is no record that he bought of the Indians any land besides Hoboken, Ahasimus, and Aressick; and yet, for all we know, he may have claimed, without extinguishing the Indian title, the whole peninsula down to the kills, as he certainly extended his ownership over to Staten Island.* His own name was given to his possessions, and the district was known as Pavonia.

The directors who had failed to become patroons and owners of large and valuable tracts became jealous of those who had been successful, and soon raised dissensions. This caused the patroons to share their advantages with others of the directors. Pauw alone refused to divide. He held on with great tenacity to his valuable territory, yet does not seem to have complied with Article III. of the " Freedoms and Exemptions " in its settlement. After a prolonged controversy with the XIX., he finally transferred to the company all of his right and title to Pavonia for 26,000 florins. This probably took place in 1637, certainly before July, 1638.†

During the next twenty-six years a number of grants of land in this county were made, but, in order to preserve a connected history of the general title, we will leave the particular grants for "Notes to the Field Book."

Notwithstanding the deeds to Pauw, Gov. Stuyvesant was not satisfied that the title of the Dutch to all the land in this county, east of the Hackensack River, was perfect. In order, therefore, as well to quiet the minds of the Indians as to secure the land not covered by Pauw's deed, he obtained the following deed :

"This day, the date hereunder written, appeared before the Honorable Director-General, Petrus Stuyvesant, and the gentlemen of the Council of New Netherlandt, at the Council Chamber, in the Fort Amsterdam, in New Netherlandt, Therincques, Wawapehack, Saghkins, Kogkhennigh, Bomokan, Memiwokan, Sames, Wewenatokwee, for them-

---

* Land Papers (Albany) G. G. 6: Thus was Staten Island a part of the colonie of Pauw, as it should have remained. † Col. Hist. of N. Y., i. 432.

selves and in the name of Moikopes, Pepoghon, Parsoihques, and others, partners of the lands hereafter mentioned. Who declare to be the right owners of the lands lying on the West side of the North River, in New Netherlandt, beginning by the great Rock above Wiehacken, and from thence cross through the lands, till above the Islandt Siskakes, and from thence along the Channel side till Constable's Hook. And from Constable's Hook again, till the aforementioned Rock, above Wiehacken, with all the lands, islands, channels, valleys, therein comprehended, in such manner as the aforementioned parcel of lands are surrounded and encompassed by the North River, the Kill van Koll, and the aforesaid direct line from the Rock above Wiehacken, till above Siskakes, where it is divided by the Channel. Which lands they offer absolutely, to sell unto the Director-General and Council, upon which the General and Council on the one side, and the aforesaid Indians, for themselves and them that are absent, have accorded and agreed in the manner following, in the presence of the hereafter mentioned Christian and Indian witnesses: The aforesaid Indians do acknowledge to have sold, resigned, and transported, as they do, by these presents, all the lands heretofore mentioned, to the aforesaid Director-General and Council and their successors, for eighty fathom of wampum, twenty fathom of cloth, twelve kettles, six guns, two blankets, one double kettle, and one half-barrel of strong beer. Which effects they hereby acknowledge to have enjoyed and received before the passing and signing of this.

Wherefore they do declare, for themselves and them which are absent, to resign and transport the lands before mentioned, to the above-mentioned General and Council, in full, free, and perfect propriety, desisting of all actions and claims, which they could or might pretend, to the lands before mentioned—the transporters promise now or hereafter, not to make any pretensions thereon; but to keep and hold this transport firm, sure, and inviolable. Promising also, to the said Director and Council, to free and warrant the said lands against all claims any other Indians might pretend to, and if it should happen that in future times, any of the Dutch, by any Indians, should be damaged on pretension they were not fully paid for the lands aforesaid, they, the sellers, do promise to repair and satisfy the damages. It is also stipulated and agreed, the aforesaid Indians shall depart and remove by the first convenient opportunity, off the lands aforesaid; and that none of their nation shall come and continue to dwell upon it, without knowledge and consent of the Director-General and Council. Thus done at the fort Amsterdam, and signed with the marks of the Indians, after the cargoes were delivered to their hands, on the 30th day of January, Anno Domino 1658.

T, { the mark of Therincques made by himself.

t, { the mark of Saghkow.

J, the mark of Sames.

t, { the mark of Koghkenningh. Wairimus Couwee.

J, { the mark of Wawapehack.

J, { the mark of Bomokan.

t, { the mark of Wewenatokwee.

J, { the mark of Memirvokan.

J, { the mark of Sames, as witness, otherwise called Job.

"We, the Subscribers, witnesses hereunto, desired by the Director-General and Council, do certifye and declare, by this present, that the above bargain for the lands before mentioned, is so made before us, and the lands, by the sellers transported to the Director-General and Council; on the conditions and terms comprehended in the bill of sale, the conditions and substance plainly told, acquainted and declared to the sellers by the interpreters Govert Loocquermans, Peter Wolphertson van Cowenhoven, and Claas Carstensen, and also by Wharimes van Couwe, formerly an owner of the lands aforesaid; and whereupon, the sellers have consented to the bargain, transported the lands, and received the mentioned cargoes and wampums, signed the conditions, with the above marks.

In witness hereof, have we subscribed this, the day and year aforesaid, at the fort Amsterdam, in New Netherlandt in the Council Chamber.

JOH. MEGAPOLENSIS,   PETRUS STUYVESANT,
SAMUEL DRISIUS,   NICASIUS DE SILLE,
OLOFF HERENSIN,   PITER TOUNEMAN,
GOVERT LOOCQUERMANS, PIETER COWENHOVEN,
MACHIEL YANSEN,   JAN EVERTSEN BOUT,
F, the mark of CLAAS,
CARSTENSEN NOORMAN,
      T' Present,

CORNELIUS VAN RUYVEN, *Secr.*" *

In connection with the above deed it is proper to insert a certificate of Governor Stuyvesant and his secretary:

"We, underwritten, the late Director-General and Council of New Netherlandt, hereby certify and declare, that in the year one thousand six hundred and sixty-one, by us underwritten, in quality as aforesaid, have given and granted to the inhabitants of the village of Bergen, the lands, with the meadows thereunto annexed, situate on the West side of the North River in Pavonia, in the same manner as the same was by us underwritten, purchased of the Indians, and as the same was to us delivered, by the said Indians, pursuant to an instrument of sale and delivery thereof, being under the date of the 30th of January, A. D. one thousand six hundred and fifty-eight; with this express condition and promise, that the aforesaid inhabitants, of the before named village, shall not be prejudiced in their outdrift, by means of any private collective dwellings (saving only the right of the then already cultivated farms at Gemoenepan). But that all such who have any lands within the district of the before named village, and especially at Pemrepogh, and Mingackque, all such owners shall be obliged to remove their dwellings and place them in the village or town of Bergen, or by or about the neighborhood of Gemoenepan before named. Conditioned, how-

---

* N. Y. Col. MSS., viii. 707. It may be well to note here that the Indians, in the conference held at Easton, October 23, 1758, gave to Governor Bernard two deeds, releasing all their rights in and to the soil of New Jersey, for which they received £1,000.—*Smith's Hist. of N. J.*, 479. These deeds were afterwards, at the request of Governor Franklin, ratified by the Six Nations at a conference held at Fort Stanwix (Rome), October 24, 1768. —*Col. Hist. of N. Y.*, viii. 112.

ever, that the aforesaid owners, (in case they should desire the same), should be permitted to share, and divide with the inhabitants of the before named village or town, in the common lands of the said town, and in the place and stead of their lands lying at Pemrepogh and Mingackquie before named. (And especially that the meadows laying near the village or town of Bergen, where the same begins, at the West side along Kill van Kol, should be and belong to and for the use of the before named inhabitants of Bergen.)

And further, we the underwritten, certify and declare, that Michael Jansen, deceased, (before or about the time that the aforesaid village or town was laid out), for himself, as also for and in behalf of his brother-in-law, Nicholas Jansen Barker, did, in our presence, renounce all the right they had to the pasture ground, laying behind Gemoenepan, for a common outdrift and pasture between the aforesaid village or town, and the neighborhood of Gemoenepan, before named.

And lastly, that no more lands were given or granted to Dirck Clausen, than Rightpocques, with the meadows thereunto belonging, as by the ground-brief thereof may further appear.

In testimony of the truth, we have signed these with our own hands, in New York, the 26th of October, A. D.

P. STUYVESANT,
NICASIUS DE SILLE."[*]

By what instrument the lands herein referred to were granted to the inhabitants of Bergen we do not know. Such grant is not to be found in the Ordinance of September 5, 1661, and it is worthy of notice that many grants from the Dutch Government to individuals are to be found bearing a later date; yet the Governor must have understood the Ordinance of 1661 to contain such a grant, or else the grant to which he refers has been lost. Whatever the fact about the grant may be, it is quite probable that this certificate went far towards satisfying Governor Carteret that the freeholders of Bergen were entitled to all the unpatented lands. In this light the charter of 1668 was only a confirmation of the rights which the " Freeholders, Inhabitants of Bergen," possessed under the Dutch Government.

The village of Bergen was laid out in 1660. It was laid out in a square, surrounded by narrow streets, yet in existence, along which were erected the palisades. Within this enclosure all the inhabitants in the township were obliged to gather, except such

---

[*] Taylor's Annals, 50 : "The year when this certificate was given, is not intelligible in the original instrument. But as they certify as former Governor and Council, it must have been after August, 1664, when the English conquered the country.

"New York, February 20th, 1764. Translated from the Dutch, by Abm Lott, Jun'r."

as collected within the fortifications at Communipaw. The land within the town plot was laid out into building plots by Jacques Cortelyou, Town Surveyor, and numbered on the map. The land surrounding the town was laid out into larger lots, for garden or farm purposes, and also numbered on a map. The land outside of the town plot was known as *Buyten Tuyn*—i. e., outside gardens. It still retains its original name. I have not been able to find these maps. The lots within and without the town were freely given to those who desired them. Many, it seems, did not trouble themselves to have their lands surveyed and staked out, or ask for a grant thereof. This made confusion, and caused the following Ordinance :

"ALL Inhabitants of *New Netherland*, and especially those of the Village of *Bergen*, on the West side of the North River; also all others who have or claim any Lands thereabout, are Ordered and commanded that they, within the space of three months after the date hereof, at latest, before the first of January next, shall have all the cultivated and uncultivated Lands which they claim, surveyed by the sworn Surveyor, and set off and designated by proper marks, and on the exhibition of the Return of survey thereof, apply for and obtain a regular Patent as proof of property, on pain of being deprived of their right, to the end that the Director-General and Council may dispose, as they may deem proper, of the remaining Lands which, after the survey, may happen to fall outside of the Patents, for the accommodation of others. All are hereby warned against loss and after complaints.

"Thus done in *Fort Amsterdam* in *New Netherland*, the 15 September, 1661." *

A few lots within the town were taken by persons who resided in New Amsterdam, and possibly elsewhere. They erected no buildings, and of course provided no occupant of their property. Those who resided in the town were forced to contribute to the defence thereof, and thus protected the property of non-residents while securing their own. They felt this to be an unjust burden, and their complaints called forth the following Ordinance, passed November 15, 1663 :

"On the repeated complaints of the majority of the Inhabitants of the Village of *Bergen*, that some continue to neglect to occupy the Lots they obtained in said Village, and to keep thereon a man fit to bear arms ; also that some absent themselves without providing for their Watch, whereby the people of said Village are so much fatigued that they cannot any longer stand at their posts, and are unwilling to go any

---

* N. Y. Col. MSS. IX. 888.

longer on guard unless the others, who have vacant Lots, keep for the guard one man with them for each Lot; the Director-General and Council, in order to prevent this confusion, resolve that all those who claim any Lots in the aforesaid Village shall, within 24 hours after the service hereof, furnish and continually maintain for each Lot one man able to bear arms, and to keep watch and ward, on pain of having the Lots with the Lands thereunto appertaining, as surveyed by the Surveyor, immediately given and granted in propriety to others. Let every one be hereby warned for the last time." *

The Dutch grants were made without pecuniary consideration. There were, however, conditions annexed to them, a sample of which may be found in the Note to the Weehawken Patent.

CHAPTER II.

TITLE UNDER THE KING AND LORDS PROPRIETORS.

NOTWITHSTANDING the occupancy of the country by the Dutch for over half a century, the English had never yielded the claim which they based on the fact that Cabot, in the employ of some Englishmen, in 1498, sailed along our coast, but whether in sight or out of sight they scorned to demonstrate. And with the fact before us that this claim was made good by the irresistible logic of a successful war, it is not worth while to dispute its validity. We will, therefore, proceed to trace the general title from the King of Great Britain: †

On March 12, 1664, Charles II. granted unto his "dearest brother JAMES, Duke of *York*, his Heirs and Assigns," *inter alia*, " all the Lands from the West side of *Connecticut*, to the East side of *Delaware* Bay," with powers of government.‡ On the 23d and 24th of June, 1664, by lease and release, the Duke conveyed to John, Lord Berkeley, Baron of Stratton, and one of the Privy Council, and Sir George Carteret of Saltrum, Knight, and Member of the Privy Council, " All that Tract of Land adjacent to *New-*

---

* N. Y. Col. MSS. X., part ii. 389.

† I give no attention to the claim of Sir Edmund Ployden to all the lands between Long Island Sound and Cape May, who professed to erect it into a free county palatine, and called it New Albion. His pretensions never disturbed the regular current of title. ‡ Leaming & Spicer, 3.

England, and lying and being to the Westward of *Long-Island* and *Manhitas* Island, and bounded on the East part by the main sea, and part by *Hudson's* River, and hath upon the West *Delaware* Bay or River, and extendeth Southward to the Main Ocean as far as *Cape May* at the Mouth of *Delaware* Bay; and to the Northward as far as the Northermost Branch as the said Bay or River of *Delaware*, which is forty-one Degrees and forty Minutes of Latitude, and crosseth over thence in a straight Line to *Hudson's* River in forty-one Degrees of Latitude; which said Tract of Land is hereafter to be called by the Name or Names of *Nova Ceaserea* or *New-Jersey*."*

The war between England and Holland was followed by the Treaty of July 21, 1667; but in 1672 it again broke out, and the Dutch recaptured the country, August 9, 1673. By the Treaty of February 9, 1674, the country was for the second time confirmed to the English.†

While the war was in progress, and on March 18, 1673, Lord Berkley sold his interest in the Province to John Fenwick, in trust for Edward Billinge, for £1,000. Billinge had failed in business; Berkley was his particular friend, and advised him to invest in New Jersey lands for the purpose of retrieving his fortune. He was pleased with the proposition, borrowed the money from his friends, and purchased the land in the name of John Fenwick, who was to have one-tenth of the same. Fenwick managed the purchase so well that, it is said, he would soon have stripped the other of all, but means were employed to compel him to be satisfied with his tenth.‡ Billinge assigned his interest, less Fenwick's tenth, to William Penn, Gawn Laurie, and Nicholas Lucas, February 9 and 10, 1674, in trust for his creditors. Fenwick sold his interest to John Eldridge and Edmond Warren, who sold to Penn, Laurie, and Lucas. §

To clear up any shadow which the recent occupation by the Dutch might have cast upon former grants, Charles II. made a second grant to the Duke, June 29, 1674 .‖ This was followed by the Duke, July 29, 1674, with a grant to Sir George Carteret of what was afterwards known as East Jersey. On July 1,

---

* Leaming & Spicer, 10.   † Valentine's Hist. of N. Y., 175.
‡ Long Isl. Hist. Soc., i. 243.   § Gordon, 72.   ‖ Ibid, 41.

1676, by the "Quintipartite Deed," the State was divided, and Sir George received the eastern portion in severalty.* Sir George, by will dated December 5, 1678, appointed his wife, Elizabeth, sole executrix, and Earl Sandwich, Earl Bath, Lord Grenville, Sir Thomas Crew, Sir Robert Atkins, and Edward Atkins, Trustees, to whom he devised his interest in New Jersey, to be sold for the payment of his debts.† On the 5th and 6th of March, 1680, East Jersey was conveyed to Thomas Cremer and Thomas Pocock, but the transfer does not seem to have been completed. On the 6th of the following August, the Duke indulged in a second grant to Penn and his associates of West Jersey, and Gordon says he also gave one to the representatives of Carteret on March 14, 1682. This has not been discovered, but the following warrant therefor exists:

"These are to direct and require you to prepare for my signature a Deed or fitting Instrument (agreeable to yt. I have already executed unto Edward Billing and others) whereby I may release and confirm unto Sir George Carteret, ye heire of Sir George Carteret (lately deceased) his moyty of New Jersey (called East New Jersey) in America. For wch ys shal be yor Warrt, Provided it be entred wt my Auditor Genll wthin two months of its date. Given undr my hand at Windsor ye 6th day of September. (80).

"To Sir John Churchill Knt my Atturney Genll or to Sir George Jeffreys Knt my Sollicte Genll." ‡

These Releases were given in consequence of an opinion of Sir William Jones, dated July 28, 1680. The Duke's Governor of New York had claimed jurisdiction over both of the Jerseys, and insisted on his right, in behalf of the Duke, to collect duties upon importations therein. These pretensions were resisted with much spirit, until finally the Duke referred the subject to Sir William Jones for an opinion. His decision was that the Duke could not legally demand any duty from the inhabitants of the Jerseys. The Duke gracefully yielded, and gave his third and final Release of East Jersey.§

On the 20th of February, 1681, Earl Sandwich released his interest in East Jersey to his associate trustees, and they again sought to negotiate a sale of the Province. Failing to find a

---

* This division was confirmed by the General Assembly in 1719.
† *Vide* Will, Perth Amboy, Liber, C², 17.
‡ Col. Hist. of N.Y., iii. 2&5. § Ibid.

purchaser at even the sum of five or six thousand pounds, it was sold at public sale to William Penn, Robert West, Thomas Rudyard, Samuel Broome, Thomas Hart, Richard Mew, Ambrose Riggs, John Haywood, Hugh Hartshorne, Clement Plumstead, and Thomas Cooper, all Quakers. The Lease and Release were dated February 1 and 2, 1682, and the consideration was £3,400. To avoid any doubt which might arise by reason of the prior sale to Cremer and Pocock, they joined in the conveyance. The associates then—June 1, 1682—executed a declaration that there should be no benefit of survivorship among themselves. They held the Province for nearly a year, but they were Quakers, and therefore unpopular. To quiet opposition on this ground, they severally conveyed, in 1683, an undivided moiety of their respective interest to twelve others—viz., Robert Barclay, Edward Billinge, Robert Turner, James Braine, Arent Sonmans, William Gibson, Gawn Lauric, Thomas Barker, Thomas Warne, James, Earl of Perth, Robert Gordon, and John Drummond. These associates were afterwards known as the "Twenty-four Proprietors." On the 14th of March, 1683, the Duke confirmed the sale of the Province to the twenty-four proprietors.* Under all of these different owners of the soil of the Province, the rights and powers of Government had always attached to the ownership. The seat of Government was at Perth Amboy, where it was required to record all surveys and transfers of land.†

Many patents for land in this county, east of the Hackensack, had been taken out before the fall of the Dutch power. By the third article in the capitulation, " all people were permitted to enjoy their lands, houses, and goods, and dispose of them at pleasure." Under this article they felt secure until the treaty of Breda, dated July 25, 1667. Then the freeholders in this county took out confirmatory grants from the proprietors subject to a quitrent of half-penny per acre. To this burden much of the lands

---

* East Jersey, 88.
† In the earlier days, deeds were recorded in the "Towne Book of Bergen," which, unhappily, seems to be lost. Then, as stated in the text, they were for a time recorded in the Secretary's office at Amboy. Then they were for a time recorded indifferently at Amboy or Hackensack, the county seat; then exclusively at Hackensack, until Hudson County was set off from Bergen, in 1840. It is well to note, however, that many deeds for land in this county have never been recorded, but not those of modern date.

in East Jersey is yet subject, though years have gone by since its collection was enforced. Whether it was to avoid the granting of particular tracts to individuals, or because the Dutch government had already granted to the town and freeholders all of the unappropriated lands in the old township, we do not know, but it is worthy of notice that the proprietors never gave to an individual an original patent for land in the township of Bergen. On the 22d of September, 1667, Philip Carteret and his Council granted to the town and freeholders of Bergen as follows :

"*Imprimis*.—The Bounds and Limitts of the aforesaid Towne and Corporation of Bergen is to begin at the North end thereof, from a place called Mordanis Meadow, lying upon the West side of Hudson's river, from thence to run upon a N. W. lyne by a Three rail fence that is now standing, to a place called Espatin, and from thence to a little Creek surrounding N.N.W. till it comes into Hackinsack river, containing in Bredth from the top of the Hill 1½ miles, or 120 chains, from thence it runs along the said Hackinsack river upon S.S.W. lyne till it comes to the Point or neck of Land that is over against Staten Island and Shooter's Island in Arthur Cull Bay, containing in length about 12 miles, from thence to run Eastward along the River called Kill van Cull, that parts Staten Island and the Maine to a point or neck of Land called Constable's Point or Constable's Houck, and from thence to run up Northward all along the Bay up into Hudson's river till it comes to Mordanis Meadow aforesaid; So that the whole track of upland and Meadow property belonging to the Jurisdiction of the said Town and Corporation of Bergen, is bounded at the North end by a tract of Land belonging to Capt.ⁿ Nicho. Verlett and Mr. Samuel Edsall. On the East side, by Hudson's river, on the South end by the Kill van Cull, that parts Staten Island and the Maine, and on the West side by Arthur Cull Bay and Hackinsack river, as it is more plainer demonstrated by a draught thereof made by the Surveyor-General, hereunto annexed. The whole, both of upland and Meadows, and Waist land containing according to the Survey 11,520 Acres English measure," * * *
" to continue and remain within the Jurisdiction, Corporation or Township of the said Towne of Bergen from the day of the date hereof forever" * * * "To be holden by them, the said Corporation or Towneship, their heirs and successors, as of the Manor of East Greenwich, in free and common Socage."

" 2ndly. That all the Freeholders of said Corporation or Towneship are hereby jointly and severally obliged to pay or Cause to be paid to the said Lords Proprietors, their heirs and Successors, or to their Receivers-General, within the said Province, on every 25th day of March, according to the English Accompt, the sum of Fifteen Pounds Sterling, of good and Lawful money of England, or the Value thereof, in good and Current pay of the Country, as a quit-rent due to them for the whole said tract of Land above mentioned, in lieu of the ½d. Pr. acre mentioned in the concessions, which payment is to begin on the 25th day of March, which shall be in the Year of Our Lord 1670, and so to continue forever without any charge, to the said Lords Proprietors or their Agent; and that all Pattents for land herebefore Granted, or to be Granted within the said Limitts, are to be accompted upon the aforesaid Rent of Fifteen Pounds Sterling pr annum."

In the course of time the payment of the reserved quit-rent was neglected, and finally refused. Hereupon a controversy arose between the proprietors and the freeholders of Bergen. Finally, Cornelius van Rypen, a freeholder, in the township, was arrested for the debt. A compromise was then agreed upon, and the freeholders of Bergen received a general release upon paying $1,500. This release was dated October 5, 1809.

CHAPTER III.

COMMON LANDS.

HAVING thus, in a general way, glanced at the history of the title to the patented lands in this county east of the Hackensack river; let us now trace the history of the common lands. Carteret's grant calls for 11,520 acres. This, of course, included all the lands in the old township of Bergen. It is quite impossible to say how much of this had already been appropriated by individual grants, but it must have been about 3,500 acres, as about 8,000 acres yet lay in common when the Commissioners undertook the allotment. The patent lands lay in different parts of the township, and generally consisted of small tracts, while the unappropriated lands were used in common. Difficulties, however, soon arose concerning these lands. The owners of private grants encroached upon the common domain, while unauthorized persons pastured their cattle thereon and wasted the timber. For this there did not seem to be any remedy, owing to defects in their charter. Thereupon, the freeholders, in their corporate capacity, petitioned Governor Hunter for relief, and in answer to their petition, they received a new charter, known as Queen Anne's Charter, January 14, 1714. In this they were empowered "to Give Grant, Bargain, Allott, Lett, Dispose of any of the Land belonging or appertaining to ye said Community, and as yett unappropriated, either for one, two, or three lives, for term of years or in fee." While it is not known that any grants were ever made under this charter, it is well known that it did not accomplish what was sought. Encroachments and waste continued as before. In 1743, the freeholders quietly attempted to protect the common lands by the following:

"**Articles** of Agreement Entered into, made, Concluded and agreed upon this Sixteenth day of June, in the Sixteenth year of the reign of our Sovereign Lord King George the Second, Annoq Dom. 1743, **Between** Daniel van Winckell, of the first part, Zacharias Sickells of the second part, Cornelius Blinkerhoof, the third part, Casparus Pryor of the fourth part, Dirck Kadmus, of the fifth part, Michael Cornelisse Vreelandt, of the sixth part, Jacob Van Wagena, of the seventh part, Cornelius Gerrebrant, of the eighth part, Hendrick Vanderhoof, of the ninth part, Abraham Diedericks, of the tenth part, Gerret Newkerck, of the eleventh part, Andries van Boskirk, of the twelfth part, Marten Wenen, of the 13th part, Ido Sip, of the fourteenth part, Johannis Gerritse, of the 15th part, Antje Pietersen, of the sixteenth part, Hendrick Sickelse, of the 17th part, Arent Tores, of the 18th part, Morgan, of the 19th part, Geret Roose, of the 20th part, Johannis Van Houte, of the one and twentieth part, Catharine Van Newkirk, of the two and twentieth, Johannis Vreeland, of the three and twentieth part, Altie Diedericks, of the four and twentieth part, Abraham Sickells, of the 25th part, Myndert Gerbrants, of the 26th part, Johannis Diedericks, of the 27th part, Hendrick Van Winckel, of the 28th part, Peter Marselise, of the 29th part, Laurens Van Boskerck, of the 30th part, Jacob Van Horne, of the 31 part, which parties to these presents above are all Residents, Freeholders and in **Commons** of the County of Bergen, in the Province of East New Jersey.

Whereas the Town and Corporation of Bergen, in East New Jersey, is an antient Township, and for a long time hath enjoyed sundry privileges, And

Whereas Philip Carteret, Esq'r late Governour of the Province of Nova Cesarea, or New-Jersey, and his Councill—to wit: Samuel Edsall, Robert Bond, Nicholas Varlet, Wm. Pardon, Robert Van Quillon, James Bollen—by a certain Grant, Charter or Patent, under the Seal of the said Province, signed by the said Governour and Council, and bearing date the twenty-second day of September, in the year of our Lord, 1668, did thereby grant that the bounds and limits of the town and Corporation of Bergen should begin at the North end thereof from a place called Mordavis Meadow, lying upon the West side of Hudson's River, from thence to run upon a North-West line by a three-railed fence that was then standing to a place called Espatin, and from thence to run to a little Creek surrounding North-North-West till it comes into the Hackensack River, containing in breadth from the top of the hill One and a half miles, or One hundred and twenty chaines, then it runs along the said Hackensack River upon a South-South-West line till it comes to Point or Neck of Land that is over against Staten-Island, and Shooter's Island, in after Cull Creek, containing in Length about twelve miles, from thence running Eastward along the River called Kill Van Cull that parts Staten-Island & the Maine to a point or neck called Constables

Hook, from thence to run Northward all along the Bay up into Hudson's River till it comes into Mordavis Meadow, properly belonging to the jurisdiction of the said Town and Corporation of Bergen. AND he, the said Governour & Council, by the Charter and Grant aforementioned, did give and grant unto the said Freeholders and Inhabitants of the said Town and Corporation of Bergen divers and sundry liberties, powers, franchises, privilidges and Immunities, and particularly that the Freeholders, or the major part of them, sho'd have power to divide proportions of what was within their bounds and Limitts that was not then already appropriated and patended by particular persons before the day of the date of the said Charter & Grant, as.in and by the said Charter & Grant Remaining upon Record in the Secretary's office of the Province of New-Jersey, among other things therein Contained it doth and may more fully and at large appear.

And Whereas since the making of the said Charter and Grant sundry of the said Freeholders have, at sundry times, surveyed, taken, and used and Improved to their own Use and benefit sundry Lotts, pieces and parcells of the common and undivided Lands Lying and being within the said Township and Corporation of Bergen without any Warrant, power, or authority for so doing, and without the Consent of the major part of the Freeholders of the said Township for that purpose first had and obtained, and have used and enjoyed the same with their patented Lands by means whereof it is not known how much of the said Commons have been taken in by the said Freeholders, nor can the same be found out or Discovered without a particular Survey of such patents to which said Common Lands have been taken in & added to, wherefore the said parties have agreed as followeth:

Imprimis. It is agreed by and between all & every the parties to these presents that whatever part of the Common & Undivided Lands have been by them, or either of them, at any time heretofore taken up, used, or claimed & added to their patented or purchased lands shall forever hereafter be deemed, taken, & adjudged, and shall Remain & Continue in Comon, till a division be made of the said Comons & Undivided Lands.

Item 2d. That in order to find out what and how great part of the said Comon and Undivided Lands have, at any time, been taken in by any or either of the parties, It is agreed that every particular grant under wch the parties to these presents do hold their patented Lands, be run Surveyed and Laid out by Cornelius Corsen, Surveyor, whom they the parties, have and by these presents do mutually Elect, Chuse, and Appoint to be the Surveyor thereof, and that he Survey the same within the space and time of Eighty months next coming after the date hereof.

Item. ffor the more Easy and regular Surveying and laying out the said patented Lands, Each of the parties above mentioned, for himself, his heirs, Executors and Administrators, Doth Covenant and Agree, with the other of them, his heires, Executors and Adm^{rs} that they & each of them will, at the request & demand of the said Surveyor, produce and show unto him their Several deeds, Writings, & grants by which they hold their respective farms, and that neither of the said parties shall nor will in any wise Obstruct, molest, or in any wise hinder or Disturb the said Surveyor in Surveying and laying out the same nor Comence, Sue or promote any Action or Suite against him or any, he shall employ to assist him in the doing thereof, and that each party whose Lott or tract shall be so run out and surveyed, shall and will pay for running out the same.

Myndert M Gerrebrat. (His Mark.)
Cornelis Van X Neuwkerk. (His Mark.)
Abraham Diederick.
Cornelus K Gerrebrants. (His Mark.)
Jacobus Van Buskirk.
Andries Van Boskerck.
Lowrens Van Buskirk.
Cornelius C. B. Blinkeroff. (His Mark.)
Jacob Gerre I. G. Van Wagener. (His Mark.)
Jacob I Van Horne. (His Mark.)
Daniel Van Winkle.
Abraham Sickels.
Hendrick Van Winckell.
Johannis Gerre Van Wagenen.

Johannis Van Houten.
Zacharias Sickelse.
Michael Cor'e M Vreeland. (His Mark.)
John Van Horne.
Ido I Sip. (His Mark.)
Hendrick V Sicgels. (His Mark.)
Cornelius Van Woorst.
Jacob I. B. Brower. (His Mark.)
Peter Marcelise.
Hendrick H. S. Spier. (His Mark.)
Arent Toers.
Gerret Roos.
Henderick Vanderoef.
Leveynis Winnen. (His Mark.)

Sealed and delivered in the presence of

JOHANNIS VREELANDT.
DIRCK KADMUS.

So far as we can now learn the measures contemplated by this agreement were not pursued. Matters growing worse, the people petitioned the Legislature for relief. This petition resulted in the following:

An Act appointing Commissioners for finally settling and determining the several Rights, Titles & Claims to the Common Lands of the Township of Bergen; and for making a Partition thereof in just & equitable Proportions, among them who shall be adjudged by the said Commissioners, to be intitled to the same.

Whereas sundry Persons claiming to be Inhabitants and Freeholders within the Township of Bergen aforesaid, by their Petition, presented to the General-Assembly of this Colony, do set forth, that Philip Carteret, Esq' Governor of this Colony of Nova Cesarea, or New Jersey, under the Right Honorable Lord John Berkley, and Sir George Carteret the former Proprietors thereof, by a certain Deed or Instrument in writing purporting to be a Charter granted to the Town and Freeholders of Bergen, and to the Villages and Plantations thereunto belonging, bearing Date the twenty-second Day of September in the year of our Lord one thousand six hundred and sixty-eight, did therein and thereby with the Consent of his Council, grant and declare among other Things therein contained, that the Bounds and Limits of the aforesaid Town and Corporation of Bergen was and is to begin at the North End of

Mordani's Meadow, lying upon the West Side of Hudson's River, from thence to run upon a Northwest Line by a three Rail Fence that was then standing, to a place called Espatin, & from thence to a little Creek surrounding North North-West till it comes into Hackinsack River, containing in Breadth from the Top of the Hill one Mile and a Half or one hundred & twenty Chains From thence it runs alongst the said Hackinsack River upon a South South-West Line till it comes to the Point or Neck of Land that is over against Staten-Island and Shooter's Island in Arthur Cull Bay, containing in Length about twelve Miles, from thence to run Eastward, along the River called Kill Van Cull that parts Staten-Island and the Main, to a Point or Neck of Land called Constable's Point or Constable's Hook, and from thence to run up Northward all along the Bay up into Hudson's River till it comes to Mordani's Meadow aforesaid, so that the whole Tract of Upland and Meadow property belonging to the Jurisdiction of the said Town and Corporation of Bergen, is bounded at the North End by a Tract of Land belonging to Cap^{tn} Nicholas Verlet and Mr. Samuel Edsall, on the East Side by Hudsons River, on the South End by the Kill Van Cull that parts Staten-Island and the Main, and on the West Side by Arthur Cull Bay and Hackinsack River; And did also among other things therein mentioned grant and declare that the Freeholders aforesaid, or the major Part of them, should have Power to chuse their own Magistrates to be Assistants to the President or Judge of the Court and for the ordering all public Affairs within the said Jurisdiction And that the Freeholders aforesaid, or the major Part of them, should have Power to admit of their own Inhabitants and to divide all Proportions of Lands as are within the Bounds and Limits aforesaid, that were not then already appropriated and patented by particular Persons before the Day of the Date thereof, according to their Allotments and Estates, as the Justices & Magistrates should in their Wisdoms think fit, which Land being so divided every Man's Proportion should be surveyed, butted and bounded by the Surveyor, and recorded by the Secretary and Recorder General of this Colony and after two Years in Possession, should not be subject to any Re-Survey or Alteration, but should remain according to the first Survey forever, as by the said Charter more fully and at large may appear. And the said Petitioners further set forth that altho' certain Letters-Patent of her late Majesty Queen Anne, issued under the Great Seal of this Colony, bearing Date the fourteenth Day of January in the twelfth Year of her Reign, confirming the aforesaid Incorporation of the said Township of Bergen; and altho' the said Letters-Patent were confirmed by an Act of the Governor, Council and General Assembly of this Colony, passed the twenty-ninth Day of January in the Year of our Lord one thousand seven hundred thirteen, intituled an Act for Confirmation of a Patent or Charter granted by His Excellency Robert Hunter, Esqr Captain-General and Governor-in-Chief in and over the Provinces of New Jersey and New York, and all the Territories and Tracts of Land depending thereon in America, and Vice-Admiral of the same for the Incorporation of the Town of Bergen in the Eastern Division of the Province of Nova Cesarea or New Jersey: Yet neither the said Letters-Patent nor the said Act do prescribe any Method for the Division of the Common Lands of the said Township of Bergen, but leave the same subject to such Method as is above mentioned to be prescribed by the aforesaid Charter of Governor Philip Carteret: And that altho' the Petition of the said Common Lands, is by the aforesaid Charter of Governor Philip Carteret directed to be made by the said Freeholders, in such Manner as the Justices and Magistrates shall think fit, yet that elective Magistrates having been a Provision in the Infancy of this Colony, and having long since been disused except in some particular Incorporations, among which the said Township of Bergen is not to be ranked, a Partition of the aforesaid Common Lands in the Manner directed by the said Charter, is for that Reason become absolutely impossible; That besides, the Petitioners are not only at some Variance among themselves, as well concerning what particular Tracts of Land patented before the Grant of the said Charter, are included within the above recited Bounds of the said Township of Bergen, and consequently concerning the Persons who may properly be deemed Freeholders of the said Township; And who the Freeholders within the said Township are or are not intitled to Shares of the said Common Lands But it is also disputed among them in what Proportions the said Common Lands ought by Virtue of the said Charter to be divided among those who undoubtedly are Freeholders within the Bounds of the said Township and are Intituled to Shares of the said Common Lands, which Reasons together with the great Number of the Persons Interested and the Infancy, Coverture and Absence beyond Seas of many of them render a Partition of the said Common Lands Impracticable by the Course of the Common Law and Feasible only by Commissioners to be appointed by Act of Legislature as well for settling the several Claims to the Commons as the Respective Proportions in which the same ought to be Divided and that by Reason of the present Undivided State of the said Commons great and Unnecessary Waste is daily Committed by destroying the Timber growing on the same, By which means if the same be not prevented by a Speedy Partition of the said Commons, they will be rendered of Little Value, and the Township of Bergen be reduced to great Distress for want of Timber and Fuel, the Petitioners therefore pray Relief in the Premises as by the said Petition may appear.

Be it therefore enacted By his Excellency the Governor, the Council and General Assembly of this Colony, And it is hereby Enacted by the Authority of the same That Jacob Spicer of Cape May, Charles Clinton of Ulster County, William Donnaldson and Azariah Dunham of New Brunswick, John Berrien of Rocky Hill, Samuel Willis of Long Island, and Abraham Clark, Junr of Elizabethtown, be and hereby are appointed Commissioners for Making Partition of the Common Lands of the Township of Bergen aforesaid, And are hereby Authorized and Required to Divide the same in the Manner hereinafter Directed.

And be it further enacted By the Authority aforesaid That the said Commissioners be and hereby are Impowered and required previous to any Partition of the said Common Lands to give at Least Four Weeks Public Notice in the New York Gazette and Mercury of the Time when and the Place where they will meet to Survey, run out, and ascertain as well the Bounds and Limits of the said Township of Bergen as the Bounds of Each and Every Patent and Grant Contained within the Bounds and Limits of the said Township. And the said Commissioners are hereby Impowered to go with their necessary Attendants and Implements upon and Across any Lands or Meadow contained within the Bounds of the Township of Bergen aforesaid or Adjacent thereto in Order to make the said Survey or Surveys And the Partitions hereinafter

Mentioned Doing as Little Damage as may be to the Owners thereof, without being Liable to any Action for the same, Which said Survey of the said Township of Bergen and of the several Patents or Grants contained within the Bounds and Limits thereof when made, shall Conclude all Persons whomsoever claiming under the said Township of Bergen or any Patent or Patents, Grant or Grants contained within the Bounds and Limits thereof.

And be it enacted By the Authority aforesaid That as soon as the said several Patents or Grants shall be Surveyed And the Bounds and Limits of the same ascertained as aforesaid, the said Commissioners shall set apart so much of the said Common Lands as they think will be sufficient to defray the Charges of Making a General Partition of the said Common Lands, And shall then proceed to make a General Partition of All the Residue of the said Common Lands and lay out and allot to such of the several Patents or Grants Contained within the Bounds and Limits of the Township of Bergen aforesaid as they shall Judge to be Intituled to the same, Such Proportions of the said Common Lands as they shall judge right, having Regard to the Right and Allotments due to the Church and Free-School as in said Charter specified.

And whereas The Freeholders Inhabitants of the Town of Bergen claim a Large Part of the said Common Lands by Virtue of a purchase from the Indians bearing Date the Thirtieth day of January in the Year of our Lord One Thousand Six Hundred and Fifty-Eight And a Patent or Grant from Governor Stuyvesant in the Year of our Lord One Thousand Six Hundred and Sixty One And divers other Disputes and Controversies have Arisen and may Arise as well between the Freholders Inhabitants of the said Township of Bergen relating to their several Rights to the said Common Lands in Virtue to their Several Patents or Grants as between the Freholders of some of the Patents or Grants Contained within the Bounds and Limits of the Township of Bergen aforesaid, For the settling and Determining thereof.

Be it enacted By the Authority aforesaid That the said Commissioners shall and hereby are Authorized and required in a Summary Way to hear and finally Determine According to their discretion the said Claim of the said Freholders Inhabitants of the Town of Bergen, founded on the said Indian Purchase and Governor Stuyvesant's Patent or Grant aforesaid, and All other Disputes and Controversies arisen or which may arise as well between the Freholders Inhabitants of the Township of Bergen aforesaid, Relating to their Several Rights to the said Common Lands in Virtue of their several Patents or Grants as between the Fre holders of each particular Patent or Grant Contained within the Bounds and Limits of the Township of Bergen aforesaid Which Determination of the said Commissioners shall be Final & Conclude all persons whomsover Claiming Under the said Township of Bergen or Under any Patents or Grants Contained within the Bounds and Limits of the said Township.

And be it further enacted by the Authority aforesaid, that the said Commissioners shall within three months next after the said general Partition shall be completed, proceed to sell the said Lands so set apart to defray the Charges of the said general Partition as aforesaid, at public Vendue to the highest Bidder giving at least six Weeks Notice of such Sale, by Advertisement to be affixed on the Court-House in Hackinsack and the Church in Bergen: And the Deed of the said Commissioners to the Purchaser and Purchasers shall pass a good Title, both in Law and Equity to such Purchaser or Purchasers for the separate Enjoyment of the said Lands in Fee Simple, against all Persons whomsover claiming under the said Township of Bergen, or any Patent or Grant contained within the Bounds and Limits of the said Township: And the said Commissioners shall keep and state a particular Account of the whole Charge attending the said general Partition and lay the same before the Justices of the Sessions for the County of Bergen, who are hereby authorized and required to appoint by a Rule to be entered in the Minutes of the said Court of Sessions, Persons to audit the said Account: And the said Persons so appointed shall after fourteen Days Notice given by the said Commissioners, or any one or more of them, in Writing, to any three Persons interested in the said general Partition, of the Time and Place of auditing the same Account that all Persons interested may be heard in objecting to the same, proceed to the auditing of said Account: And out of the Monies arising from such Sale the s^d Commissioners shall detain in their Hands so much as the said Auditors shall report to be due for their Services and Disbursements in compleating the said general Partition And the Surplus, if any be, shall be paid to the Trustees of the Freholders, Inhabitants of the Township of Bergen for the Use of the said Corporation, and their Receipt for the same shall be a sufficient Discharge to the said Commissioners.*

And be it further enacted by the Authority aforesaid that after the said general Partition shall be made the said Commissioners shall proceed to make a Partition and Division of the said Common Lands allotted to each respective Patent or Grant within the Bounds and Limits of the said Township of Bergen to which a Share of the Common Lands shall have been allotted as aforesaid. And for that Purpose they are hereby authorized and required to give at least twelve Weeks Notice, by Advertisements to be published in one or more of the New York News-Papers, of their meeting to proceed upon the Partition or Division of each and every of the said Tracts of Common Lands allotted to each of the said Patents or Grants respectively; By which said Advertisements all Persons interested in the said particular Tracts respectively shall be required to produce their Titles and make out their Claims to the same, Copies of which Advertisements shall be affixed on the Court House in Hackinsack and the Church in Bergen; And when the said Commissioners shall have informed themselves in manner aforesaid of the Rights of the respective Persons claiming Interests in the said Common Lands allotted to such particular Patents or Grants respectively, they shall proceed to make a fair and equitable Partition and Division thereof among all the Persons whom they may adjudge to be interested in such Proportions as they may think Just and reasonable And in like Manner the said Commissioner shall proceed to make a Partition and Subdivision of each and every of the said Tracts of Common Lands allotted to each

---

* The Commissioners submitted their accounts for dividing the Common Lands, to the Court at Hackensack, on the first Tuesday in October, 1764. They were referred to Peter Sobriske, Tunis Day, and Johannis Demarest for audit, with directions to send in their report at the next Term. In January Term, 1765, the Commissioners submitted their accounts for subdividing the Common Lands. They were referred to the same persons for audit. I have not been successful in finding the accounts or reports thereon.

and every of the said Patents or Grants within the Bounds & Limits of the Township of Bergen aforesaid respectively to which a Share of the said Common Lands shall have been allotted as aforesaid: And the Charges of every of such Partition and Subdivision shall be defrayed, and the Accounts of the same respectively kept, stated and audited in the same manner as hereinbefore directed upon the general Partition aforesaid, provided always that the Overplus of the Moneys arising from the Sale of the respective Lands set apart to defray the Charges of each of the said particular Partitions and Subdivisions respectively, if any be shall upon Demand be paid to the respective Persons interested in such particular Tracts, or Proportions to their several Rights.

And be it further enacted by the Authority aforesaid that the said Commissioners shall cause two several Field-Books and Maps to be made both of the general and of each particular Partition and Division of the said Common Lands, specifying the Bounds of the general Partition and of each and of every Lott of each particular Partition and Division respectively and to whom allotted particularly; Which said Maps and Field-Books shall be signed by the said Commissioners and their Surveyor or Surveyors, And one of the said Maps and Field-Books shall be filed in the Secretary's Office at Perth-Amboy and the other in the office of the Clerk of the County of Bergen to remain and be kept as Evidence, and shall be and hereby are made conclusive Evidence, of such Partition which said Partitions and Divisions and each and every of them shall be and hereby is and are declared good and valid in Law to divide and separate the said Lands.

And be it further enacted By the Authority aforesaid That the said Commissioners and their Surveyor shall be allowed each twenty shillings a Day, while actually employed in the said Service, And to each of the Chain-Bearers six shillings a Day, And to the Persons who audit the Accounts of the said Commissioners ten shillings for auditing the accounts of each of the said Partitions and Divisions, And for such other Charges as may accrue on the Service aforesaid the said Auditors may allow a reasonable Sum, And all Persons who shall be employed in the Service aforesaid shall also be provided with all Necessaries usually provided on such Occasions out of the Monies to arise by the Sale of the Land set apart for defraying the Charges of the said Partitions respectively—

Provided always and be it further enacted by the Authority aforesaid, That no Person whomsoever, who shall be employed upon the Service aforesaid, or any other in Trust for him or them, shall become Purchasers of the Lands to be sold by Virtue of this Act or any Part thereof—Provided also, and be it further enacted by the Authority aforesaid, That such of the said Commissioners as may take upon them the Execution of this Act, and their Surveyor or Surveyors whom they are hereby authorized to appoint, shall severally be sworn before one of the Justices of the Supreme Court, or before one of the Judges of the Court of Common Pleas, for the County of Bergen, to execute and perform the Trust and Services required of them severally by this Act fairly and impartially according to the Directions thereof, and the best of their Skill and Judgment, And a Certificate of their being so sworn from the Person administering the Oath be filed in the Office of the Clerk of the County of Bergen.

And be it further enacted by the Authority aforesaid, That as well all & singular as any or either of the Powers hereby vested in the said Commissioners shall and may be executed by the Majority of them and the Survivors and Survivor of them and the Majority of such Survivors.— **Provided always** That Nothing Contained in this Act shall be Deemed, Construed or Understood to Affect or destroy any Claim Right or Title of the General Proprietors of the Eastern Division of this Province to the premises or to any part thereof and Saving Also to His Majesty his Heirs and Successors all his Rights therein as if this Bill had not passed.

COUNCIL CHAMBER.

December 7th, 1763. This Bill having been Three Times Read in Council Resolved that the same do pass By Order of the House
L. M. ASHFIELD.

November 29th, 1763. This Bill having been Three Times Read in the House of Representatives Resolved That the same do pass By Order of the House
ROBERT OGDEN,
Speaker.

December 7th, 1763. I Assent to this Bill Enacting the same & Order it to be Enrolled
WM. FRANKLIN.

The Commissioners appointed by the foregoing act caused to be surveyed every foot of land lying east of the Hackensack in this county, and the result is recorded with great care and particularity in their Field Book and Maps, which were filed, as directed in the seventh section of the above act. By an act of the Legislature approved March 3, 1848, the Field Book and Maps on file in the Clerk's office of Bergen County were required to be filed in the office of the Clerk of Hudson County. They were so filed. But the copy in the Secretary of State's office being in better preservation, and of no particular utility in that place, there was a general desire among the people of the county to secure it, whereupon by an act of the Legislature, approved March 3, 1853, the Clerk of Hudson County returned the one then in his office to the Clerk of Bergen County, and received and filed the one then in the office of the Secretary of State.

NOTE 1.—The reader is indebted to Delos E. Culver, of Jersey City, for the following observations on terrestrial magnetism and its effect on the magnetic needle. His long experience and well-known ability as a practical surveyor and civil engineer make him an authority on the subject. He says:

"Paradoxical as it may appear, many surveyors do not understand the action of the magnetic current upon the needle, and many others but imperfectly. In order to make the needle useful, the laws which govern its movements should be known.

"The magnetic fluid or current sweeps continually from the south to the north magnetic pole, sometimes increasing in intensity, at others decreasing over the earth and beneath its surface on waving meridian lines. The direction of this current at any given point is the magnetic meridian.

"The magnetic poles, however, are constantly moving around the true poles, changing the direction of the current, and with it the direction of the needle, thus accounting for its secular declination. There is also an annular declination of the needle, caused by the revolution of the earth upon its axis, which is completed every day, and another declination, superimposed upon the others, caused apparently by the earth's nearing and receding from the sun each year, its maximum effect being exhibited in January when the earth is nearest the sun.

"Of course, so far as land surveying with the needle is concerned, the secular declination only need be observed. The following extract from the American Encyclopædia of observations made in London and Paris will illustrate this, showing how the north end of the needle travelled eastward at London until the year 1657: "From that time (1657) the westerly declination began, and continued until it began to be thought it would ever move in that direction, until it pointed south. In Paris the easterly declination did not disappear until 1663, and there also the needle travelled westerly until 1814, when it pointed $22\frac{1}{2}°$ towards the west. It then began to flag, and in 1817 the needle began to return towards the north. The same result was not noted in London until the year 1819, when the needle pointed N., 25° W.;" this time, of about 162 years, marking one-half the period of the revolution of the magnetic pole around the true pole. There are two lines passing over the earth's surface upon its opposite sides, on which the needle will point due north and south. Such a line, at the present time, passes very near the City of Detroit in Michigan, and is steadily moving westward. On the east side of this line the variation of the needle is to the west, increasing in amount with the distance from it. On the other side of the line of no variation the declination of the needle is towards the east. So, it will be seen that at any locality the course of the needle will not be exactly the same after the day upon which it is taken until about 160 years have passed by.

"In Hudson County, according to my experience, and from the average of many surveys made from the monuments and courses laid down on the map and field-book, made by the Commissioners in 1764, I determined, to my satisfaction, that here the easterly declination of the needle terminated in the year 1810, and that the average yearly movement before that time was at the rate of 3 3-10 minutes per annum. I found exceptional cases where it would require as much as 4 minutes per annum correction to make the courses agree with the monuments, and others again where less than two minutes would do it. But allowance must be made for imperfections of instruments, local attraction, errors made in observing or recording bearings, etc.

"I would advise surveyors and others, where the title of valuable land is to pass by description based upon needle courses, to carefully note the date of the survey, and have the same go into the instrument conveying the title. The importance of this will at once be seen when it is stated that a variation of 3 3-10 minutes per year will swing the lines of a piece of land of 100 rods long in ten years 16 feet out of its former position unless the proper correction for the time since the survey was made, is made. From an observation of the position of the North Star, made on the evening of May 29, 1871, at Jersey City, the declination of the needle from the true meridian was shown to be 7° 55', the course of a true north line being N., 7° 55', W."

NOTE 2.—The land in these grants was measured by the *Morgen*. containing nearly two acres. An explanation of this measure as it prevailed in the olden time may be useful for a full understanding of the Dutch Patents. A Rhineland rod was the Dutch measure for land. It contains 12 feet and 4¾ inches, English measure. Five of these made a Dutch chain, which consequently contained 61 feet and 11¾ inches. Twenty-five such rods in length and twenty-four in breadth makes a Morgen, which consists of 600 square Dutch rods.—*Moulton's Hist. of N. Y.*, i. 334.

NOTE 3.—The *rod* spoken of in the Notes to the Field Book is the Dutch rod.

THIS IS ONE OF THE FIELD BOOKS

Both of the GENERAL & of each PARTICULAR Partition and Division

of the COMMON LANDS of the TOWNSHIP of

BERGEN

In Two Parts.

The FIRST com- { The General Bounds and Limits of the } From
prehends the { Township, the Location of the Patents } Page
FIELD WORK of { and Grants, & The GENERAL PAR- } 1 to 121.
{ TITION of the COMMON LANDS. }

The SECOND comprehends the FIELD WORK of the PAR- } From
TITION and DIVISION (or SUBDIVISION) of the COM- } Page
MON LAND allotted to the respective PATENTS or } 121 to 221.
GRANTS.

Filed in the Secretary's office at Perth Amboy, March 2d, 1765.

JOHN SMYTH, Reg'r.

Filed in the office of the Clerk of Hudson County, March 15, 1853.

R. GILCHRIST, Cl'k.

As a caution to all who may hereafter be imployed in surveying within the Township of Bergen, the Commissioners have thought it necessary to *Note* that they found an *attraction* more or less in most Parts of the Township, and more especially towards the Northern Bounds, where they found it in some Places near five Degrees.

Part First.

THIS IS ONE OF THE FIELD-BOOKS

Of the General PARTITION of the COMMON LANDS of the Township of BERGEN

Made in pursuance of a LAW of the Province of New Jersey in America pass'd in the fourth Year of the Reign of his present Majesty King George the third, entitled

"An Act appointing Commissioners for finally setling and determining the several Rights, Titles and Claims to the Common Lands of the Township of Bergen, and for making a partition thereof in just and equitable Proportions among those who shall be adjudged by the said Commissioners to be entitled to the same."

The General Partition by the said Act directed was performed by Six of the Seven Commissioners therein named, to wit, Jacob Spicer, Charles Clinton, William Donnaldson, Azariah Dunham, John Berrien and Abraham Clark Junr; Samuel Willis the Seventh Commissioner declined and did not attend the Service.* Those Six Commissioners who

---

* It is worthy of observation that not one of these commissioners lived in the county where the lands to be surveyed lay. Two of them were from Essex County; two from Middlesex; one from Somerset; and two, with the surveyor, George Clinton, Governor of New York during the Revolutionary war, were from the State of New York.

JACOB SPICER,

The son of Col. Jacob Spicer, was born in Cape May County, in 1716. In 1744 he became a member of the General Assembly, which position he held for twenty-one years. He married (1st), Judith, daughter of Humphrey Hughes; (2) Deborah, widow of Christopher Leaming. In 1756 he purchased the interest of the West Jersey Society in Cape May County, constituting what has since been known as the Vacant Right. He was appointed with Aaron Leaming to revise the laws of the State. The result of their labors may be found in " Leaming and Spicer's Collection," published without date, " Printed at Philadelphia, by W. BRADFORD, Printer to the King's Most Excellent Majesty for the Province of *New Jersey*." He was a merchant and surveyor, a man of exemplary habits, and strictly faithful in his business relations. He died in 1765, and was buried at Cold Spring.

CHARLES CLINTON

Was born in the County of Longford, Ireland, in 1690; died November 19, 1773, in the town of New Windsor, then in Ulster, now Orange Co., New York. His grand-

took upon them the execution of the said Act, were severaly duly sworn before one of the Justices of the Supreme Court to exercise and perform the Trust and Services required of them severaly by that Act fairly and impartially according to the Directions thereof; and the best of their Skill & Judgment; as may appear by the certificates filed in the Office of the Clerk of the County of Bergen; true copy's whereof are in the Words following, to wit,

"These are to certify that on the Eighteenth Day of January one thousand seven hundred and sixty four personally appeared before me Samuel Nevill, Esqr, Second Justice of the Supreme Court of Judicature for the Province of New Jersey, William Donnaldson, Azariah Dunham, John Berrien, and Abraham Clark Junr, four of the Commissioners named and appointed by an Act of the General Assembly of the Province of New Jersey; pass'd the last sessions at Burlington, Entitled— an Act appointing Commissioners for finally setling and determining the several Rights, Titles and Claims to the Common Land of the Township of Bergen, and for making a Partition thereof in just and equitable Proportions among those who shall be adjudged by the said Commissioners, to be entitled to the same."

---

father was an adherent of Charles I., and after the defeat of the Royalists fled to the north of Ireland. His mother was the daughter of a captain in the Parliamentary army. He and a number of his friends chartered a ship and sailed for America, May 20, 1729. This company in 1731 selected a place for a permanent settlement, and called it "Little Britain," in New Windsor. He was a farmer and land surveyor, and was appointed Surveyor-General, and Judge of the Common Pleas in Ulster. In 1756 he was appointed lieutenant-colonel in the militia, and served under General Bradstreet in the expedition against Fort Frontenac (now Kingston), Canada. His sons James (father of DeWitt Clinton) and George accompanied him in this expedition. *Vide Appleton's Encyclopædia and Eager's History of Orange County.*

WILLIAM DONNALDSON.

Concerning William Donnaldson nothing whatever has been learned, except (if he was the man) that he kept a tavern, and resided on the road between New Brunswick and Princeton, at the junction of the Rocky Hill road. This is ascertained by the map of the survey of the county line, made by Az. Dunham.

AZARIAH DUNHAM.

Col. Azariah Dunham was born in the township of Piscataway, N. J., in the early part of the eighteenth century. His family settled in the township as early as 1670. He married Mary Ford, of Morristown, and settled at New Brunswick, where he built a mansion on what was originally known as Main, then Burnet, and still later as Little Burnet or Water street. He was a very prominent man, and enjoyed a large share of the public confidence. He was rigidly just, extremely accurate, and highly intelligent. At an early day his name often appears in the minutes of the Courts of Middlesex County as arbitrator to settle matters in dispute or litigation. He was a civil engineer, in which capacity his services were in great demand, both by private parties and public bodies. June 20, 1765, he was appointed by the Legislature one of the commissioners " to view the grounds and make a straight and perfect survey from Bordentown to Kingston, and from Trenton as near as may be, through Princeton, Kingston, New Brunswick, Elizabethtown, and Newark to Second River; also from New Brunswick to Perth Amboy, and from Perth Amboy to

And each of them took an Oath to the following Purport,—That, they and each of them would execute and perform the Trust and Services required of them severally by the said Act fairly and impartially according to the Directions thereof, and the best of their Skill and Judgment. In Witness whereof I have hereunto set my Hand * the *2 Day and Year above mentioned:—Signed Samuel Nevill.

These are to certify that on the Seventh Day of March one thousand seven hundred and sixty-four personally appeared before me John Berrien Esq' third Justice of the Supreme Court of Judicature for the Province of New Jersey Charles Clinton one of the Commissioners named & appointed by an Act of General Assembly of the Province of New Jersey Entitled,

"An Act appointing Commissioners for finally setling and determining the several Rights, Titles and Claims to the Common Lands of the Township of Bergen, and for making a Partition thereof in just and equitable Proportions among those who shall be adjudged by the said Commissioners to be entitled to the same,"

And took An Oath, that, he would execute and perform the Trust and Services required by the said Act fairly and impartialy according

---

Elizabethtown." May 20, 1765, he was selected by the Justices and Freeholders of Middlesex to run the division line between Somerset and Middlesex, which had become "dubious." I have seen a copy of the map of this survey completed May 9, 1766. It was accompanied by a field-book ; and the two accurately described the line and the public highway from New Brunswick to the Province line, west of Princeton. They preserve the names of all the inhabitants living along the road, and note the exact locality of their farms and houses; and also exhibit the extent of Princeton and New Brunswick at that day.

In May, 1775, he was elected to the General Assembly. In the autumn of that year he and other patriotic members of the Assembly absented themselves to meet and confer with patriots from the several colonies in the city of New York. Their absence was noticed by Governor Wm. Franklin, who sent a message to the Assembly complaining of it. Accordingly, November 17, 1775, the House passed the following resolution :

"Several members of the House being absent, whereby the Public Business has been greatly retarded, Ordered, That the Sergeant at Arms do give Notice forthwith to Benjamin Holmes, Robert Friend Price, John Combs, John Wetherill, Azariah Dunham, and William Winds, Esquires, to attend their Service here immediately."

The patriotic members of the Assembly were aware of, and sympathized with the causes which led to their absence ; and a few days later voted a leave of absence to them.

In 1775-6 Colonel Dunham was a member of the Provincial Congress of this State, and by that body was appointed one of the Committee of Safety, which sat, with extraordinary powers, during its recess. He was an active member of the Provincial Congress, and was on committees to draft various important measures : among others, a "resolution respecting apprehending deserters from the Continental troops ;" an "ordinance to compel payment of tax of £10,000 in 1775, from such persons as have refused to pay the same ;" also an "ordinance for emitting £30,000 of credit," and for the purchase of saltpetre, etc., in 1775. He was one of the Masters to review companies raised in the Province in 1775-6 ; and one of the committee "to adjust and settle the accounts of powder furnished to Earl Sterling by Somerset, Brunswick, Woodbridge, and Elizabeth" in 1775. In 1776 he was Lieut.-Colonel of the 2d Batto the Directions thereof, and the best of his Skill and Judgment. In Witness whereof I have hereunto set my Hand the Day and Year aforesaid. Signed John Berrien.

These are to certify that on the fifth Day of April one thousand seven hundred & sixty-four personally appeared before me John Berrien third Justice of the Supreme Court of Judicature for the Province of New Jersey Jacob Spicer one of the Commissioners named and appointed by an Act of General Assembly of the Province of New Jersey pass'd the last Sessions at Burlington—Entitled,

" An Act appointing Commissioners for finaly setling and determining the several Rights, Titles and Claims to the Common Lands of the Township of Bergen and for making a Partition thereof in just and equitable Proportions among those who shall be adjudged by the said Commissioners to be entitled to the same," and took an Oath to the following Purport, That, he would execute and perform the Trust and Services required of him by the said Act fairly and impartially according to the Directions thereof, and the best of his Skill and Judgment. In Witness whereof, I have hereunto set my Hand the Day and Year above mentioned. Signed John Berrien.

---

talion Middlesex Militia; but resigned in order to devote himself to the duties of "Superintendent of Purchases" for the Province, and of " Commissioner to raise troops"—positions to which he had been appointed by the Provincial Congress, and which he held until the close of the war. He was appointed one of the signers of the Jersey Bills of Credit for the Eastern Department of the State. He embarked a large part of his ample means in the cause of his country, and died at a ripe old age in 1790.

JOHN BERRIEN,

The grandfather of the late John McPherson Berrien, of Georgia, was appointed Associate Justice of the Supreme Court of the Province, February 20, 1764. He was a surveyor, as appears by the following sneer of the Tory historian of New York, William Smith. Referring to the death of Chief-Justice Morris, he says: " Franklin has put Charles Read in his place upon the bench, and filled up Read's with one John Berrien, a babbling country surveyor, not fit to be a deputy to any sheriff in England."—*Contributions to East Jersey History*, 180. Notwithstanding Smith's opinion, there can be no doubt that he was a man of integrity and ability, or the Legislature would not have associated him with such high-toned gentlemen as composed the Commission. He died in the latter part of April, 1772, leaving a widow and six children.

ABRAHAM CLARK

Was born at Elizabethtown, February 15, 1726. He was the only child of Alderman Thomas Clark. He married Sarah Hetfield in 1743. In early life his particular studies were mathematics and law, which fitted him for surveying and giving legal advice. He was not by profession a lawyer, but gave advice gratuitously. This procured for him the honorable title of the " poor man's counsellor." His services were frequently sought as arbitrator in questions concerning land titles. Under the Colonial Government he was High Sheriff of Essex, and Clerk of the Assembly. At the breaking out of the Revolution he became a member of the Committee of Public Safety. He was appointed a Delegate to the Provincial Congress, June 21, 1776. A few days after his appointment he affixed his name to the Declaration of

And We the said William Donnaldson, Azariah Dunham, John Berrien and Abraham Clark, Junr the four Commissioners first sworn as aforesaid did immediately thereafter make and subscribe a Notice in the Words following, to-wit,

"**To** all whom these Presents may concern and particularly to such as claim any Interest in the Common Lands of the Township of Bergen in the County of Bergen in the Eastern Division of the Province of New Jersey.

Whereas by a late Law of the said Province—Entitled an Act appointing Commissioners for finally setling and determining the several Rights, Titles and Claims to the Common Lands of the Township of Bergen and for making a Partition thereof in just and equitable Proportions among those who shall be adjudged by the said Commissioners to be entitled to the same, Certain Persons are therein named as Commissioners of whom we, the subscribers are the Major Part; And Whereas we have severally taken the Oath by the said Act required; **Now therefore** towards the Execution of the Trust in the said Commissioners or the Major Part of them reposed; we the (*) Subscribers Do hereby give public Notice that at ten o'clock in the Forenoon of Tuesday the Sixth Day of March next at the House of Stephen Bourdett at Wehawken in the said Township of Bergen; we or a Majority of the said Commissioners will meet to survey, run out and ascertain as well the Bounds and Limits of the said Township of Bergen as the Bounds of each and every Patent and Grant contained within the Bounds & Limits of the said Township; And we do also request all Persons concerned or claiming Lands within the said Township to produce to us some or one of us their original Patents, Deeds or Grants or true attested Copies thereof within all convenient speed that we may be truly informed of their Rights and Claims in due Season, And also copies of all such Title Deeds whereon any Claims are grounded against the Extent of the General Bounds of the said Township; And all these we desire to have on or before the twenty-first Day of February next. Given under our Hands

*3

Independence. He was elected to the Provincial Congress of New Jersey, November 30, 1776, and with the exception of 1779, was annually re-elected until 1783. In 1788 he again had a seat in the National Legislature. In the mean time he was a frequent member of the State Legislature. While in this position he became known, though unjustly, as the "Father of the Paper Currency." In 1787 he was appointed a member of the State Convention which ratified the Constitution of the United States, but owing to ill health did not take his seat. In 1789 he was appointed a Commissioner to settle the accounts of the State with the United States. At the next election he was again chosen as representative in Congress, which position he held until a short time before his death. He retired from public life on the adjournment of Congress, June 9, 1794. He died in the autumn of 1794 from the effects of *coup de soleil*, and was buried in the churchyard at Rahway. Over his grave is the following inscription:

> Firm and decided as a patriot,
> Zealous and faithful as a friend to the public,
> He loved his country,
> And adhered to her cause
> In the darkest hour of her struggles
> Against oppression.

the Eighteenth Day of January in the Year of our Lord one thousand seven hundred and sixty-four.

Signed { WILL. DONNALDSON, Az. DUNHAM, JOHN BERRIEN, ABR^A CLARK, JUN^R

As by the same original Notice filed in the Office of the Clerk of the County of Bergen may appear, a true copy of which said Notice was printed and published in two of the public News Papers commonly called the New York Gazette and Mercury, to wit, in the Gazette Numbers 267, 268, 269, 270, and in the Mercury Numbers 639, 640, 641, 642 as by the same News Papers refference being thereunto had may appear; And the said Commissioners so qualified having met pursuant to said notice did appoint Jonathan Hampton of Elizabeth Town in New Jersey and George Clinton* of Ulster County in the Province of New York to be Surveyors of the Lands so to be divided, and they were accordingly severally sworn to execute and perform the Trusts and Services required of them by the said Act in due Form of Law before Mr. Justice Berrien as may appear by the Certificates thereof filed in the office of the Clerk of the said County of Bergen true copies whereof are in the Words following, to wit,

"These are to certify that on the ninth Day of March one thousand "seven hundred and sixty four personally appeared before me John Ber-"rien Esqr. third Justice of the Supreme Court of Judicature for the "Province of New Jersey, Jonathan Hampton one of the Surveyors "appointed by the Commissioners named and appointed by an Act of the "General Assembly of the Province of New Jersey pass'd the last Ses-"sions at Burlington entitled 'An Act appointing Commissioners for "finally setling and determining the several Rights, Titles and Claims to "the Common Lands of the Township of Bergen; and for making a "Partition thereof in just and equitable Proportions among those who "shall be adjudged by the said Commissioners to be entitled to the

---

* GEORGE CLINTON

Was the youngest son of Charles Clinton, one of the Commissioners for dividing the Common Lands. He was born in Ulster Co. (Little Britain), N. Y., July, 26, 1739, died at Washington, April 20, 1812. He joined his father in the expedition against Fort Frontenac, in the French war. He was a lawyer, and was elected to the Colonial Assembly in 1768. Here he soon became head of the Whigs. He was elected to the Continental Congress in 1775, voted for the Declaration of Independence, was appointed Brigadier-General in 1777, and in the same year, at the first election under the Constitution of N. Y., was chosen both Governor and Lieutenant-Governor. He held the office for eighteen years, being chosen at six successive elections. He was energetic, and rendered his country great service during the revolution. In 1788 he was President of the State Convention to consider the Federal Constitution, to the adoption of which he was opposed, not deeming it sufficiently decided in favor of the sovereignty of each State. In 1792, at Washington's second election, Clinton received fifty votes for the Vice-presidency. In 1801 he was again elected Governor, and in 1804 Vice-president of the United States. In 1808 he received six electoral votes for President, in opposition to Madison, but was continued as Vice-president. By his casting vote in the senate, Jan. 24, 1811, the National Bank was not rechartered.

JONATHAN HAMPTON, though sworn did not serve.

" same'—And took an Oath to the following purport that he would exe-
" cute and perform the Trust and Services required of him as Surveyor
" fairly and impartially according to the Directions which he shall from
" Time to Time receive from the said Commissioners pursuant (*) to the *4
" said Act to the best of his Skill and Judgment. In Witness whereof I
" have hereunto set my Hand the Day and Year above mentioned.
                " Signed   JOHN BERRIEN."

" These are to certify that on the twenty Sixth Day of March one
" thousand seven hundred and sixty four personally appeared before me
" John Berrien Esqr. third Justice of the Supreme Court of Judicature for
" the Province of New Jersey George Clinton one of the Surveyors
" appointed by the Commissioners named and appointed by an Act of
" the General Assembly of the Province of New Jersey pass'd the last
" Sessions at Burlington entitled ' An Act appointing Commissioners for
" finally setling and determining the several Rights, Titles and Claims to
" the Common Lands of the Township of Bergen and for making a Par-
" tition thereof in just and equitable Proportions among those who shall
" be adjudged by the said Commissioners to be entitled to the same '—
" And took an Oath to the following Purport, that he would execute and
" perform the Trust and Services required of him as Surveyor fairly and
" impartially according to the Directions which he shall from Time to
" Time receive from the said Commissioners pursuant to the said Act to
" the best of his Skill and Judgment.
" In Witness whereof I have hereunto set my Hand the Day and Year
" above mentioned.
                " Signed   JOHN BERRIEN."

And we the said Commissioners so qualified with our said Surveyors proceeded then to the Survey of the said Township of Bergen as by the said Act directed; And we the said Commissioners do adjudge the Bounds and Limits thereof to be as follows, to wit,

The **Bounds** and **Limits** of the said Township of Bergen **Begins** at the Northeastermost Corner thereof at a **Chessnutt=Tree** standing on the Easterly End of a small narrow high Ridge of land, the said **Tree** is marked on the Northwest side thereof with a Blaze and three Notches and on its Southwest Side with the Letter B and the said Tree on a Course (from it) South forty nine Degrees East is thirty five Links distant from the Northwesterly Side of Mordainis Meadow; and on a Course (from it) North Sixty Eight Degrees West is Seventy Seven Links distant from a large Rock mark'd with these four Figures 1764; And on a Course (from it) Southwest is fifty Links from the middle of a small Run of Water in a large Gully near the Head of a Creek; and from which said **Tree** these several **Objects** on the East Side of Hudson's River have the following Bearings, to wit, the Southermost Chimney of Humphreys Jones's House bears South sixty two Degrees and five Minutes East; The single Chimney of Dennis Hicks's House bears South fifty Degrees and five Minutes East; the Door in the Middle of Charles Ward Apthorp's New House bears South forty Degrees and fifty Minutes East; And the Northeastermost Chimney of Bloomingdaal House (late Mr. Oliver Delancey's) bears South seventeen Degrees East;—And from the said **Chesnutt=Tree** running upon a Course North forty nine Degrees West ninety seven Chains (by a Line of mark't

Trees) to a stake (mark't E & B) Standing by the side of the Eastermost Branch of a small Creek, and about one Chain and a Half from the Head of the said Branch, at or near a Place called Espatin—Thence running down the said Creek Northerly, Westerly and Southwesterly as the same Creek runs, till it comes into Hackensack River—Thence (*) along Hackinsack River Southwesterly as the same River runs till it comes into New Ark or After Cul Bay—Thence Southwesterly along said New Ark Bay to Kill Van Cul (which parts Staten Island from the Main) —Thence Easterly along Kill Van Cull to New York Bay—Then Northerly along New York Bay to the Mouth of Hudson's River— —Then Northerly up along Hudson's River to the Southermost Point of Mordainis Meadow aforesaid—Then Northerly along the Edge of said Mordainis Meadow or Marsh where the same joins the Upland 'til it comes to bear South forty nine Degrees East from the aforesaid **Ches=nutt Tree**—Thence North forty nine Degrees west thirty five Links to the said **Chesnutt Tree** the Place of Beginning.

Having thus run out and ascertained the **General Bounds** and **Limits** of the said Township of Bergen we proceeded next to a Survey of the several Patents and Grants contain'd within the same which are many, and we have thought fit to enumerate them in the following Order.

First inserting the Grantors Name, The Grantees Name and date of each Patent and Grant; and then the Bounds and Limits thereof as by us discovered, survey'd and ascertain'd. A Work attended with much Difficulty and setled upon a due Attention, as well to the Words, and Descriptions in the Patents and Grants themselves as to antient Possession, and the Allegations and Proofs suggested & produced upon the Spot. The stating of all which we conceived to be unnessessary and expensive, and it is therefore omitted. **But** we do hereby declare once for all, That, the **Limits** mentioned in our Survey immediately after the Grantor and Grantees Names and Date of each Patent and Grant hereinafter inserted are the **Limits** which we **Do** adjudge, assign, and ascertain for such Patent and Grant.

We begin with

> The Patent of Wiehaken granted by William Kieft to Maryn Adrianse dated the Eleventh Day of May one thousand six hundred and forty seven, and confirm'd by Patent from Philip Carteret to said Maryn Adrianse dated the Eighteenth Day of April one thousand six hundred and seventy.

Our Survey whereof shews, and we do adjudge it to be a **tract** which on the Map is mark'd No. 1.*

---

* Adriaensen was born in 1600, *N. Y. Col. MSS.* i. 249, came from Veere to this country in 1631 and settled in Rensselaer Wyck, *O'Cal. N. N.* i. 434. For the terrible massacres of 1643 he was greatly responsible. The accusation of this was more than he could bear, and armed with a cutlass and pistol he one day rushed up to the Director-General and said, "What devillish lies are these you have been telling of me," at the same time attempting to shoot. He was seized and committed to prison. *O'Cal. N. N.* i. 273. In March 1643 he was sent in irons to Holland for trial. He returned and obtained a patent for Awiehaken. He was a bad man; a noted freebooter, *O'Cal. N.N.* i. 434; a drunkard, *N.Y. Col. MSS.* i. 200; and a slanderer, *Ibid* iv. 94. His wife's name was Lysbet Tysen. She survived him and married Geerlief Michielsen, May 3, 1654, *New Amst. Rec.* i. 448.

Beginning at the Mouth of Hobocken Creek (which parts Wiehaken from Hobocken) and from thence running up Hudson's River as the same River runs to the Mouth of a small Creek at Wiehaken Ferry, Then up the same Creek to a Stone planted in the Mouth of the first Gully and Run of Water that runs from the Westward into said Creek (which Stone is North thirty seven Degrees and a half East thirty Eight Chains and sixty seven Links from the Mouth of said Hobocken Creek) and from the said Stone North fifty two Degrees and a Half West twenty seven Chains

---

The following is a copy of the Dutch grant:

" We William Kieft the Director-General and the Council in the behalf of the High and Mighty Lords, the States General of the United Netherlands, his Highness (the Prince) of Orange and the Noble Lords, the Managers of the Incorporated West India Company in New Netherland residing, by these presents do publish and declare that **We** on this day of the date underwritten have given and granted unto **Maryn Adriaensen** a certain piece of land known by the name of **Awiehaken**, situated on the West side of the North River, bounded on the North by the Kil of Hoboken, and from thence North till to the next Kil, and with the same breadth into the woods till containing fifty Morgens of land: with the express condition and terms that he the said **Maryn Adriaensen** or they who by virtue of these presents to his action may hereafter succeed, shall acknowledge the noble Lords the managers aforesaid as his Lords and Patroons under the sovereignty of the High and Mighty Lords the States General, and unto their Director and Council here, shall in all things be conformed, as all good inhabitants are in duty bound: Provided also that he shall be further subject to all such burdens and imposts as already by the Noble Lords have been enacted, or such as may yet hereafter be enacted, constituting therefore the said **Maryn Adriaensen** in our stead in the real and actual possession of the aforesaid piece of land, giving unto him by these presents the full might, authority and special license, the aforesaid land to enter, cultivate, inhabit and occupy in like manner as he may lawfully do with other his patrimonial lands and effects, without our the Grantor's in the quality as aforesaid thereunto any longer having reserving or saving any part, action or controul whatever, but to the behoof as aforesaid from all desisting from this time forth and forever more.

Promising moreover this Transport firmly, inviolably and irrevocably to maintain fulfil and execute, and finally to do all that in equity we are bound to do. Witness these presents by us undersigned and confirmed with our Seal. Done in the Fort New Amsterdam in New Netherland this 11th day of May A.D. 1647.

WILLEM KIEFT.

By the order of the Noble Lords, the Director General and the Council of New Netherland.

CORNELIS VAN TIENHOVEN, SECY."

Land Papers (Albany) G. G. 217.

It is well to note that all confirmations of the Dutch grants were made by Patent signed by the Governor and major part of his Council and under the seal of the Province. Preceding such patent, however, was a warrant signed in the same manner, directed to the Surveyor General who made his return of the survey. Both survey and patent were recorded by the register. This system continued until the surrender, when the governor ceased to be an officer of the proprietors and they no longer had control of the great seal.—*Nixon's Digest,* 838.

When and how Nicholas Bayard obtained this tract I do not know, but it was at an early date. On June 10, 1678, Governor Carteret with the consent of the Free-

and seventy five Links to a Heap of Stones (ten Links North from a black Oak Tree mark'd on its North side W B) Then South thirty seven Degrees & a Half West thirty seven Chains and sixty seven Links to
*6 another Heap of Stones (Eighteen (*) Links Northwesterly from a large flat Rock) Then South fifty two Degrees and a Half East to the aforesaid Hobocken Creek, thence down along the said Creek to the Mouth thereof on Hudson's River the Place of Beginning.—Next,

holders of Bergen granted to him "full power and authority to Build erect and set up on the Water Run of Wiehaken a saw and Corn Mill." He was not to cut any trees within 200 Rods of the upper fence by Espatin, nor within the same distance of the lower fence of Wiehaken, and was to keep only three cows, for which he was to pay to Bergen six guilders a head, and for horses nine guilders, "which horses are to be working horses and none other without consent."

By his will, dated May 7, 1707, proved April 19, 1711, he left his real estate including Weehawken to his son Samuel.

The following, in connection with this tract, will be interesting to the curious reader:

"At a meeting of the trustees of the Township of Bergen the 5th day of June 1721,

Present, John Sipp, Ruth Van Hoorne, Wander Diedricks, Hendrick Kuypers, Johannis Gerritsen, Matthias DeMott.

Whereas the Trustees of this Corporation, did on the 15th day of April 1718, by order of this Corporation grant unto Samuel Bayard and to every one of the Proprietors of Particular tracts of Land Lying within the Limitts and bounds of the Township of Bergen having always Payd their Proportional Part of the Towne Quit rents charges of the Pattent for Incorporation of the said Township and other cost and Charges of the said Township, that each and every of them have on their own cost and Charge a Graunt of this Corporation under the Common Seale of the Corporation for Leave, Lycence and Libberty for their Respective Lands of having Cutting, Carting of and from and out of the Common Woodlands and Swamps of said Township of Bergen all manner of Post Rayles, fencing stof, Timber, Polls, and other Timber necessary for the use of their Respective Lands and Meadows and in case of a Divident of the said Common Lands and Meadowes an equitable Proportion [several words obliterated] several and respective tracts of Lands and Meadowes.

The Trustees being aprehensief that that graunt might hereafter prove Inconvenient, do Order that neither the said Samuel Bayard nor any other of the Proprietors of Particular Lands within the Limmitts and bounds of the said Township of Bergen have any graunt of this Corporation Pursuant to said order of the 15th April 1718."

Stephen Bayard, the son of Samuel, inherited this lot, and by will dated January 31, 1753, proved February 9, 1757, gave it, along with the ferry grant, to his son Robert. It was confiscated as the property of William, and sold by the agent of Forfeited Estates to Jacobus J. Bogert, May 11, 1784, and by him to John Stevens, May 1, 1788.

The following is the title of the act under which this property was confiscated. Chapter CXXII.

"An Act for forfeiting to, and vesting in, the State of New Jersey, the Real Estates of certain Fugitives and Offenders, and for directing the Mode of determining and satisfying the lawful Debts and Demands which may be due from, or made against, such Fugitives and Offenders; and for other purposes herein mentioned."

Passed December 11, 1778. *Wilson's Laws*, 67.

The Patent of Hobocken, granted by Petrus Stuyvesant to Nicholas Varlett Esqr. dated the fifth Day of February one thousand six hundred and sixty three and confirm'd by Patent from Philip Carteret to said Nicholas Varlett dated the twelfth Day of May one thousand six hundred sixty eight.

Our Survey whereof shews, and we adjudge it to be a **Tract** which on the Map is mark'd No. 2.*

ᵃ Nicholas Varleth or Varlet, was a man of note. The first his name appears in the records of New Netherlands is December 9, 1652. From this time his success was remarkable. October 14, 1656, having lost his wife, he married Anna, the sister of Governeur Stuyvesant, and widow of Samuel Bayard. April 7, 1657, he was appointed Commissary of Imports and Exports; April 17, 1657, he was admitted to the rights of a small burgher; April 23, 1658, became "collector," also "Farmer of Duties on Exports and Imports to and from New England and Virginia." In the same year being "an old and suitable person," he was invested with the "Great Burgher Right," and appointed "Searcher and Inspector," and " Commissary of the Company's Stores." February 27, 1660, he was sent with Brian Newton as ambassador to Virginia, "to condole the death of Gov. Matthews, to propose a league offensive and defensive against the Indians, to conclude a commercial treaty, and to request permission to enlist" men for the New Netherland army.—*N. Y. Col. MSS.*, ix. 101; was named a commissioner to agree on terms of capitulation, September 6, 1664; appointed captain of the militia in Bergen, Gamoenepan, Ahasimus, and Hooboocken, October 6, 1665; on the same day a member of the court at Bergen, and on the first of November following a member of Carteret's Council. These positions he continued to hold for several years. He died in the summer of 1675.

In the patent from Cartaret, this tract is said to contain 276 acres. At what time Varlet obtained possession of it is not known, but it was previous to March, 1656, *N. Y. Col. MSS.*, vi. 347. He received a patent for it, said to contain 138 morgens, February 5, 1663.

He left two children, *Abraham* and *Susanna*. *Abraham*, born 1650; was Clerk in the Office of the Secretary of the Province in 1673, and a commissioner to administer the oath of allegiance to the inhabitants of the towns in Achter Col (New Jersey) in 1673. He left the Province in 1675; entered the Dutch East India Company's service, and afterwards died in the city jail at Ceylon. I have heard that Prof. Dodd, of Princeton, discovered a deed from him to Samuel Bayard among the Bayard papers. *Susanna* married Jan or Johannis DeForest, June 8, 1673. In a controversy which arose between the widow of Varlet and her two children in 1676, Samuel Edsell and Peter Stoutenburgh acted as agents for *Abraham*, then absent. Oloffe Stevenson Van Courtlandt, William Beekman, Francis Rombout, and Gulian Ver Planck acted as arbitrators. Their award, dated August 22, 1676, was that after satisfying the four children by her former husband, Samuel Bayard, according to the terms of their will out of Varlet's property, the residue should belong to her and the two Varlet children. *Susanna* had four children, viz.: Nicholas, born February 4, 1675; Susanna, born January 4, 1677; Sara, born April 10, 1678; and Sara, born March 12, 1680. The only one who survived the age of childhood was Susanna, who married Robert Hickman. Hickman et ux, sold Hoboken to Samuel Bayard for £500, June 19, 1711; deed acknowledged before Judge Pinhorne. He left it to his son Stephen, who by his will dated Jan. 31, 1753, proved Feb.

Beginning at the Mouth of the Creek that Parts Hobocken from Wiehaken (being the Place of Beginning also of Wiehaken Patent) and from thence running up said Creek as it runs to a stake at the Foot of the Hill (which stake stands North fifty two Degrees & a Half West Eighteen Chains and sixty three Links from the Mouth of said Creek) Then from the said stake Westerly along the foot of the Hill One hundred and thirteen Chains and a Half on a streight Line to a stake by a Creek which Parts Hobocken from the Meadows lying North of Horsimus (from which stake the said Creek runs about twelve Chains on a course South Sixty Six Degrees and a Half East) Then down said Creek as it runs to Hudson's River, then up along Hudson's River as it runs to the Place of Beginning.

> The Patent granted by Philip Carterett to Ide Cornelison Van Voost dated the thirtieth Day of March one thousand six hundred and sixty Eight for sundry Parcels of Land lying at Horsimus.

Our Survey whereof shews and we do adjudge them to be two **Tracts** first a House Lot which on the Map is mark'd No. 3.*

9, 1757, gave it to his son *William*. William Bayard went to the British during the Revolution, and it was confiscated to the State. He joined the army of the King, May 1, 1777, as per inquisition made at the house of Stephen Bogert, near the Pond Church, Oct. 21, 1779. Thereupon a writ dated Jan. 30, 1784, issued out of the Common Pleas of Bergen, directed to Cornelius Haring, Agent of Forfeited Estates in Bergen County, to sell and dispose of all the land belonging to Bayard. He sold the tract in question to John Stevens, Junior, of New York, March 16, 1784, for £18,360. The deed of Haring to Stevens was dated July 26, 1784, and conveyed 564 acres. In 1804 the upland was mapped out, and the map entitled, "A Map of the New City Hoboken," made by Charles Loss. Stevens bought from John Dey 30 acres of meadow, Feb. 4, 1792, and 10 acres June 5, 1795. This was lot 133. *Vide Note to Van Purmerent's Patent* p. 7. He sold to Samuel Swartwout 327 acres of meadow, April 15, 1814. This Swartwout mortgaged to John G. Coster, Dec. 6, 1827. The mortgage was foreclosed, decree dated July 15, 1840, and Robert Van Arsdale, Master's deed, dated Oct. 24, 1840, to John G. Coster, who died seized, Aug. 8, 1844. His will dated April 9, 1842, proved in New York Sept. 6, 1844; in Hudson County, March 23, 1849.

* Gov. Stuyvesant gave to Van Vorst a "lot at Ahasimus S. W. of the wagon road," April 5, 1664.—*Land Papers (Albany) H. H.* 136. This was his home lot, and the Patent therefor was destroyed by fire. Carteret's patent adds to the original grant, and describes the two lots:

Lot No 3, lying at Haasemus on the N.E. side of Class Jansen, S.W. of the cart way in size 16 rods on the S. E. and N. W. side; 22 rods 19 feet on the N. E. side; 21 rods on the S. W. side.

Lot No. 6, between Hassemus and Jan de Lacher's Point or Neck, beginning at the little Creek, 140 rods to the Creek of the High Woodland, 100 rods in width=25 morgens.

This property was inherited by his only son Cornelius. By the will of Cornelius 3d, dated June 13, 1733, proved Aug. 15, 1753, his son Cornelius 4th, received all his real estate. From him it passed to his son Cornelius 5th, known as "Faddy." "Faddy" by will dated Sept. 19, 1814, gave to his son John the homestead at Harsimus and one half of his lands at Showhank and Slonga. To his grandson Cornelius

Beginning South seventy one Degrees and a Half East fifteen Links from the Northeast Corner of Cornelius Van Vost (the present Possessor) his Stable; and thence running along the Road North seventy one Degrees and a Half West four Chains and twenty nine Links to the Corner of Land in Possession of Michael De Mott (being Jacob Stoffelsen's Patent mark'd on the Map No. 9). Thence South seventeen Degrees and a Half West three Chains and one Link to the Northwest Corner of Hendrick Kuyper's House Lott (being the House Lott in Class Jansen Van Purmerant's Patent mark'd No. 4); Thence South seventy one Degrees and a Half East four Chains and nineteen Links to the Northeast Corner of said Cuyper's House Lot, and from thence North thirty one Degrees and Twenty Minutes East three Chains and four Links, to the Place of Beginning—Together with all the Land lying in the Front of said Lot down to Low Water Mark.

Second a Tract of Upland and Meadow (which on the Map is mark'd No. 6).

* **Beginning** at the Mouth of a small Creek on the Southwest side *7 of Paulus Hook, and runs North twenty seven Degrees and forty Minutes East twenty two chains and thirty Links, Then North Eight Degrees West twelve Chains and ninety five Links to a stake near Hudson's River, Then South sixteen Degrees and forty Minutes West five Chains and seventy Links to the Corner of the Fence in the Meadow, Then North sixty four Degrees and forty Minutes West Ten Chains and fifty five Links to the middle Causeway leading across the Meadow to Paulus Hook where the s'd Causeway joins the Upland of Horsimus, Then South Eighty Seven Degrees West five Chains and ninety four Links along the Fence, Then North sixty one Degrees West twenty nine Chains along said Fence; Then North sixty four Degrees and twenty Minutes West sixteen Chains to a stake standing on the East side of Horsimus Creek, that divides Horsimus from Bergen and Communipan (being the first Creek that said Line meets with) which stake stands seventy two links northeast from the upper side of the Causeway or solid Bridge that crosses said Creek; Thence Southerly down along said Creek as it runs to Hudson's River or the Bay (leaving a small Island of Meadow to the southwestward) Then up said River or Bay Northeastward to the Place where it first Began at the Mouth of the little Creek aforesaid.

The Patent granted by Petrus Stuyvesant to Claas Jansen Van Purmerant dated the thirty first day of January, one thousand six hundred and sixty two, and confirm'd by Patent

---

7th he gave "the land between Hassemus and Jan de Lacher's Hook." This devisee mapped out the property June, 1835, and since his death, Jan. 3, 1852, this land has become the finest part of Jersey City. His children partitioned in chancery Oct 16, 1869. John died seized Jan. 30, 1832, of what he received by his father's will. His land at Harsimus lay N. of Newark Ave, W. of Warren St. to Grove, then N. to South 9th, then E. to Prospect, then N. to near South 5th, then W. to De Mott's line near Grove, then N. to South 4th. He left children *Ann Eliza*, wife of J. Dickinson Miller, *Cornelia*, wife of Henry Augustus Booraem, *Sarah Frances* whose first husband was Charles B. C. Bacot, and now wife of Michael Lienau, and *John*. *Vide Note to Lot No.* 211, p. 77.

from Philip Carteret to said Class Jansen Van Purmerant, dated this thirtieth Day of March one thousand six hundred and sixty Eight for sundry Parcels of Land lying at and near Horsimus.

Our survey whereof shews and we adjudge them to be four **Tracts**, first, a House Lot (which on the Map is mark'd No. 4.)*

---

* This patentee came from Purmerent, a town about twelve miles from Amsterdam. He was sometimes called Claas Jansen Van Purmerent. In 1638 he leased from Planck one morgen of land on Paulus Hook for a tobacco plantation. He was residing there in 1643. He was sometimes known by the name of Jan Pottagie, *anglicé* "Soup Johnny." His first wife was Pietersje, daughter of —— Brackhoengie, by whom he had three children. Through his wife he inherited certain lands at Gowanus. He was well versed in the Indian language, and therefore able occasionally to communicate important facts to the Dutch Government. Previous to 1656 his wife died, for on Nov. 11, 1656, he married Annetje Van Vorst, daughter of Pauw's old "commander," and defendant in the *cause celebré*, Cock *vs.* Van Vorst, *New Amst. Rec.*, i. 123, 148, 449, 463. He then went to reside in "Ahasymus," and in Oct., 1664, took the oath of allegiance to the English government. He was elected Schepen for "Ahasymus" in the Bergen court, Aug. 31, 1674; took an active part with his neighbors in annoying the occupants of the Duke's Farm; was appointed by the General Assembly of New Jersey in 1682, one of the Surveyors of Highways in Bergen County, and is named in the Act, "Clause Jansen Van Sarmarant."—*Leaming and Spicer*, 257.

The Patent describes those lots as follows:

Lot No. 4, lying N. E. of the house where Jacob Stoffelsen dwelt, S. W. of Ide Cornellisen Van Voorst; in size, 20 rods on S. E. and N. W. sides and 21 rods on N. E. side.

Lot No. 7 was 25x100 rods in garden and orchard.

Lot No. 8 was a farm lot, lying N. E. of the cart way. In size it was 12 3-10 rods along the cart way, 19 rods on the E. side, 18 3-10 rods on W. side, and 17 3-10 rods on N. W. side.

Lot No. 133, lying "between Haassemus and Hoboocken," S. of a small creek, in size 30x190 rods=25 morgens; the four lots containing, as per patent, 45 acres.

These lots (except No. 133) were taken out of the West India Company's Farm. Among the patentee's children were *Cornelis*, born March 21, 1659, and *Hendrick*, born May 10, 1676. Long before his death, he abandoned the name of "Van Purmerent," and was known as "Kuyper," probably from his being a cooper. This name his children retained until his family became extinct. He died intestate, Nov. 30, 1688, and his property was inherited by his eldest son Cornelius. On June 12, 1714, Jansen's widow (who signed her name "Annetje Cornelis," though in the body of the deed named "Anna Cooper,") and her son *Cornelius* for £220 sold to her son *Hendrick* along with other lands, *vide Note to Van Ostrum's Patent*, p. 63, and *Note to Lot* 240, p. 78, these four tracts, three of which, 4, 7 and 8, were then said to contain 25 acres. Hendrick Kuyper died March 16, 1756. By will dated Sept. 16, 1754, proved July 24, 1764, he gave to his only son *Hendrick* all his lands. His daughters were *Catherine*, wife of Garret Newkirk; *Geertje*, wife of John Van Dalson; *Jenneke, Marytje*, wife of Roelof Van der Linden, and *Elizabeth*, wife of William Sickles. Kuyper conveyed Lot 133 to John Dey, Jan. 1, 1780, who conveyed to John Stevens, Feb. 14, 1792, and June 5, 1795. Stephens sold part of it to Jacob Newkirk, Sept. 21,

Beginning at the Southeast Corner of Ide Cornelison Van Vost's House Lott (being the House Lot mentioned in the immediate foregoing Patent and mark'd on the Map No. 3) And runs North seventy one Degrees and a Half West four Chains and nineteen Links to the Southwest Corner of s'd Ide Cornelison Van Vost's House Lot, Then South Seventeen Degrees and a Half West One Chain and sixty six Links to a stake (being the southerly Corner of Jacob Stoffelsen's Patent mark'd No. 9), Then South seventy one Degrees & a Half East, Three Chains and ninety seven Links to a stake standing forty one Links on a Course south forty three Degrees and a Half East from the south East Corner of the said Class Jansen Van Purmirant (now Hendrick Kuyper's) House; And from thence North thirty one Degrees a Half East one Chain and sixty nine Links to the Place of Beginning. Together with all the Land lying in the Front of said Lot down to low Water mark.

Second, a Garden and Orchard Lot (which on the Map is mark'd No. 7.)

Beginning at a stake standing North thirty eight Degrees and Ten Minutes East One Chain and twenty seven Links from the Northeast Corner of Ide Cornelison Van Vost's House Lot (being the House Lot mark'd on the Map No. 3 as mentioned in the * preceeding Patent And from the said Stake runs along the Road on the North side thereof North seventy four Degrees and thirty Minutes West three Chains and fifty Eight Links, Thence North Eight Degrees East three Chains and thirty Links, Thence south Seventy Degrees and ten Minutes East three Chains and forty three Links, Thence south four Degrees and forty Minutes West three Chains and thirty Links to the Place of Beginning.

*8

1795. Newkirk died seized, June 9, 1818. By will dated April 6, 1817, proved Aug. 26, 1818, he gave the same to his sons *Garret* and *John J.* Garret died, and the lot was partitioned between his children and John J. in 1819; they taking the S. half and he the N. half, which he sold to Henry Traphagen, May 7, 1835; by whose children it is yet owned. The other lots passed to the Van Vorst family, but how I have not learned. By the will of Cornelius Van Vorst, dated Sept. 19, 1814, proved Oct. 7, 1818, lot 8 was given to his daughter Neeltje, wife of Henry Traphagen. She died in 1826, and her husband died in 1860, leaving children *Anna V. H., Cornelius V. V., Hannah Maria,* wife of William G. Post, and *Henry M.* These still hold in common what has not been sold.

Kuyper died and his widow Catherine was appointed his administratrix, Sept. 4, 1783.

This diagram shows the location of lot No. 8.

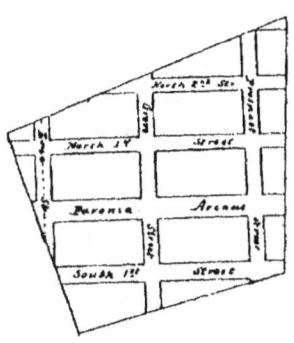

Third, a Farm Lot (which on the Map is mark'd No. 8.)

Beginning at a stake standing North twenty five Degrees East, twelve chains and Eighty six Links from the Northeast Corner of said Ide CornelisonVan Vost's House Lot (being the House Lot mark'd on the Map No 3 as mentioned in the preceeding Patent) and from the said stake runs South eighty nine Degrees and forty Minutes West fourteen Chains and fifteen Links, Thence North five Degrees and fifty five Minutes West fourteen Chains and thirty two Links, Thence North Eighty five Degrees and thirty five Minutes East twenty Chains and forty eight Links, Thence South seventeen Degrees and ten Minutes West sixteen Chains and sixty one Links to the Place of Beginning.

Fourth, a Piece of Meadow (which on the Map is mark'd No. 133).

Beginning at the Easterly End of a Ditch (that was formerly cut for a Fence from the Creek called Horsimus Creek, to a small Creek that runs up out of a Bay between Horsimus and Hobocken Creek) And from the said Easterly End of the said Ditch running as said Ditch runs Westward about four Chains 'till it comes to the Creek of Horsimus aforesaid, Thence runing up said Horsimus Creek as the same runs Northwardly following the Northward Branch of the same to a stake standing north fifteen Degrees and ten Minutes West fourteen Chains and sixty four Links from the Easterly End of the first mentioned Ditch the Place of Beginning (which stake is the southerly Corner of Meadow late possess'd by Sir Peter Warren) and from said stake running North sixty nine Degrees and ten Minutes East thirty four Chains and fifty two Links to said Hobocken Creek, Thence down the said Creek as the same runs to the Mouth thereof at the Bay; Thence southwesterly along the said Bay to the Mouth of the second Creek above mentioned, Thence running up the same to the Place of Beginning.

The Patent of Philip Carterett to Abraham Isaacson Plank dated the twelfth Day of May One thousand six hundred and sixty Eight for a Neck of Land call'd Paulus Hook.

Our Survey whereof shews, and we adjudge to be a Tract (which on the Map is markt No. 5.)*

---

* The history of the title to this tract is brief. The Dutch West India Company conveyed it as per following deed:

"This day, date underwritten, before me Cornelis Van Tienhoven, Secretary of New Netherland, appeared the Honorable, wise and prudent Mr. William Kieft Director-General of New Netherland (on the one part) and Abraham Isaacsen Planck on the other part, and mutually agreed and contracted for the purchase of a certain parcel of land called *Pouwels Hook*, situate Westward of the Island Manhates and eastward of Ahasims, extending from the North River unto the valley [marsh] which runs around it there. Which land Mr. Kieft hath sold to Abraham Planck, who also acknowledges to have bought the aforesaid land for the sum of Four Hundred and fifty Guilders calculated at 20 stivers the guilder, which sum aforesaid Abraham Isaacsen Planck promises to pay to the Honble Mr. Kieft, or his order, in three installments, the first at the Fair A° 1638, 2d A° 1639, and the third and last installment on the Fair A° 1640; and in case he remains in default of payment, Jacob Albertsen Planck, Sheriff

Beginning at the Mouth of a small Creek on the south west side of said Hook and runs up the Creek north twenty seven Degrees and forty Minutes East twenty two Chains and thirty Links, Thence North eight Degrees West twelve Chains and ninety * five links to Hudson's River, Thence down said River Easterly, Southerly and Westerly round said Paulus Hook to the Mouth of said Creek the place of Beginning.

*9

---

in the Colonie of Renselaers Wyck substitutes himself as bail and principal for the purchaser, promising to pay the aforesaid fl. 450 free of costs and charges; For all which aforesaid, the purchaser and bondsman aforesaid pledge their persons and property real and personal, present and future, without any exception, submitting to the Provincial Court of Holland, and to all other Courts, Judges and Justices, and in acknowledgment and token of the truth, these presents are signed by the parties respectively, and 2 copies hereof are made of the same tenor.

Done on the Island Manhates in Fort Amsterdam this first of May, 1638.

[signatures: Abram Isaack Planck / Jacob Planck]

Carteret confirmed this patent for "all of a neck of land, heretofore granted unto him by the Dutch Governor Kieft, lying and being on the West side of Hudson River, and called by the Dutch Powlus Houck, separated from Aharsimus by a small creek to have and to hold the said neck of land and meadow," &c., &c., "as of the manner of East Greenwich in free and common socage." The patentee married Maria Ross, widow, daughter of Guleyn Vigné. His children were *Abigail*, wife of Adrian Van Laer, *Geleyn, Catelyn*, wife of David Pietersen Schuyler, *Isaac, Susanna*, wife of Marten Van Waert, *Jacamyntje, Ariantje, Hillegond* and *Isaac*. Planck died about 1680. The Hook remained in the possession of his family until Aug. 2, 1699, when John Abeel, Attorney in fact of Planck's heirs, conveyed it to Cornelius Van Vorst. This deed is now in the possession of John Van Vorst. It has never been recorded. It was proved before Rynier Van Giesen, "one of his Majesties Judges," May 30, 1754. It was signed in presence of Brandt Schuyler and William Huddleston. The place remained in possession of the Van Vorst family until March 26, 1804. *Vide Note to Van Vorst's Patent*, p. 6. Then Cornelius Van Vorst sold it to Anthony Dey for an annuity of "Six thousand Spanish milled Dollars." This annuity was given in his will to his son John, who assigned it to Richard Varick, March 12, 1824. By him it was assigned to the Associates Nov. 18, 1830. Dey conveyed the tract to Abraham Varick, April 18, 1804; and he to Richard Varick, Jacob Radcliff and Anthony Day, April 20, 1804. They mapped out the place and entitled the Map "A Map of that part of the town of Jersey commonly called Powles Hook." "The Associates of the Jersey Company" were incorporated Nov. 10, 1804. To this body Varick, Radcliff and Dey conveyed the Hook, Feb. 1, 1805. From this company comes the title to the lots in old Jersey City. They were at first sold subject to a quit-rent. Only a few lots remain subject to this rent, the title to most of them having been perfected by payment of a sum in gross.

𝕿𝖍𝖊 𝖕𝖆𝖙𝖊𝖓𝖙 of Petrus Stuyvesant to Jacob Stoffelsen dated the Seventh Day of May One thousand six hundred and sixty four for a Piece of Land lying at Horsimus.

𝕺𝖚𝖗 𝕾𝖚𝖗𝖛𝖊𝖞 whereof shews and we adjudge it to be a **𝕿𝖗𝖆𝖈𝖙** (which on the Map is mark'd No. 9.)*

---

* Stoffelsen was born in 1601, *Col. Hist. of N. Y.*, i. 194, came from Zirickzee, the chief city of the Island of Schowen, and the oldest city of Zeeland, to this country at an early date.—*Powers of Atty. New Amst.* 39. In 1633 he was "Commissary of Stores," *New Neth. Register*, 30, and overseer of the Company's negroes, *N. Y. Col. MSS.*, i. 84; chosen one of the "Twelve" in 1641, *Col. Hist. of N. Y.*, i. 415; one of the "Eight" in 1645, in the same year one of the Directors' Council, *pro hac vice*, to consult on Indian affairs, *New Neth. Register*, 15. In 1656 he hired the Company's Bouwerie at Ahassimus, where he continued to reside until his death in 1677. In 1639 he married the widow of Cornelis Van Voorst, and in 1657, being a widower, married Tryntje, the widow of Jacob Walingen Van Hoorn, *Val. Man.* 1861, 648, by whom he had two children, viz., Stoffel and Jacobus.—*Ibid.* 1863, 813. In the same year he was admitted to the rights of a Small Burgher, *New Neth. Register*, 183. He was an uneducated man, but greatly respected, and of considerable influence with the Indians.

This tract was taken out of the West India Company's Farm. It was irregular in shape, but this diagram will show its location. The lines between Hiram Gilbert, its then owner, and Cole's estate were straightened, Aug. 26, 1838, by an exchange of property.

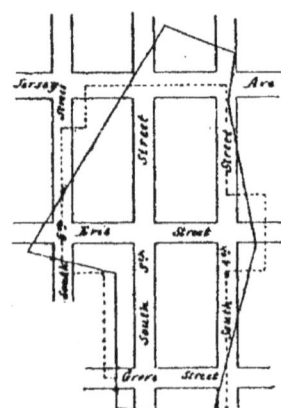

It was laid out, Sept. 20, 1677, and confirmed Nov. 10, 1677, to Casper Steinmets in right of Trintje Walings, his lately deceased wife, formerly widow of Jacob Stoffelsen, as land for a garden and orchard at Horsemus, in length 15 chains, width in the middle 5 chains, at the ends 4 chains, bounded N. by a rail fence, E. by Van Vorst and Van Purmerent, S. & W. by the West India Company's Farm, "now belonging to the Lords Proprietors"=6 acres.

At an early date Mattys De Mott became the owner, and by will, dated Dec. 13, 1755, proved June 8, 1756, gave it to his sons Michael and Joris, who held as joint tenants. Michael married Claesje Winne, but died Nov. 16, 1799, intestate, and without issue. His widow, by will dated the May 17, 1787, proved Jan. 27, 1789, gave to the children of her brother John Winne one-half of her property, and the other half to the children of her brother Levinus. What realty passed by her will I do not know. George died Sept. 9, 1800, unmarried. By will dated April 5, 1794, codicil Aug. 26, 1800, proved Oct. 9, 1804, he gave to Michael, son of his brother Hendrick of Pompton, all his real estate in the Township of Bergen.

This devisee died seized, May 27, 1832. By will dated May 10, 1831, proved May 19, 1845, he gave this tract to his children, *Garret, George, Jane* the wife of Peter Merselis, *Margaret* the wife of Richard Vreeland, *Maria* the wife of James Cadmus, *Catherine* the wife of Richard Cadmus, and *Henry* (dead before his father, leaving two sons, *Henry B.* and *Michael H.*, and three daughters). These heirs and devisees by five several deeds in 1835, conveyed the same to Hiram Gilbert, Cyrus S. Browning, and Caleb E. Draper. By several deeds in 1838 the title passed to Gilbert, who mapped it out. *Vide Note to Harmensen's Patent*, p. 50. *Note to Post's Patent*, p. 23.

Beginning at the Northwest Corner of Ide Corneleson Van Vost's House Lot (which on the Map is mark'd No. 3) Thence running south seventeen Degrees and thirty minutes West four Chains and sixty seven Links along the Rear of said Van Vost's & Van Purmerant's House Lots, Thence North seventy eight Degrees and forty Minutes West six Chains and fifty two Links, Then south twenty seven Degrees and Thirty Minutes West four Chains and forty two Links, Thence North forty six Degrees West twelve Chains and sixty Links, thence North twenty nine Degrees and thirty Minutes East three Chains and fifty one Links, Then south seventy one Degrees and forty Minutes East two Chains and fifty three Links, Thence South eighty six degrees East seven chains, thence South sixty six degrees, East eight Chains and fifty Links to the Place of Beginning.

> **The Patent** of Philip Carterett to Petrus Stuyvesant dated the thirty first Day of July One thousand six hundred and sixty nine for a Piece of Meadow at Horsimus.

Our Survey whereof shews & we adjudge it to be a Tract (which on the map is mark'd No. 10.)*

Beginning at a stake standing on the East side of Horsimus Creek (being South eighty nine Degrees and twenty Minutes East Eight chains and ninety Links from the Northwest Corner of Ide Corneleson Van Vost's Farm Lot mark'd on the Map No. 6); And from the said stake runs South forty six Degrees and thirty Minutes East One Chain & sixty Links to the Upland, Thence North fifty two Degrees and twenty Minutes East three Chains and twenty one Links along the Upland, Thence North sixty five Degrees east Eight Chains and eighty Links along said Upland, Thence South forty seven Degrees east One Chain and Eighteen Links across a Ditch to the Head of a small Creek, Thence down the said small Creek as the same runs to where the said Creek empties into the first mentioned Horsimus Creek, Thence down the same as it runs to the Place of Beginning.

> **The Patent** of Phillip Carteret to Claess Comptah (alias Claas Pieterson Cors) dated the third Day of June One thousand six hundred and seventy One for a Parcell of Upland and Meadow lying at Comunipan.

Our Survey whereof shews and we adjudge it to be a Tract which on the Map is mark'd No. 11.†

---

* "A lot of Meadow N. of the upland Hahasemes, butting on the W. side of Communipaw Creek, N. and E. side by a small creek,=4 morgens, 288 rods." This was Governor Stuyvesant. The tract lies S. of Newark avenue, at the foot of the hill, and N. of the Point of Rocks. The title seems to have descended until we find it in Peter Stuyvesant in 1764. He died Aug. 10, 1770. By will dated July 7, 1767, proved Sept. 29, 1770, he gave all his realty to his son Peter, whose will was dated Nov. 20, 1821; proved Jan. 9, 1822. It is probable that he disposed of it during his lifetime. *Vide Note to Varlet's Patent*, p. 62.

Was this an original patent, or had the governor some private claim to it previous to the surrender? Again, have these Stuyvesants been recognized as among the governor's descendants? I think not. Who, then, was the *Petrus Stuyvesant* of 1764, and how came he by the land as well as the name?

† This patentee was born in 1619. He came hither a soldier in the service of the West India Company. For an assault on Robert Pinnoyer he was, Sept. 29, 1644,

*10 ***Beginning** at a stone (on the Northwest side of York Bay or Hudson's River) in the Middle of a Road (which stone stands ninety seven Links from the South Corner of Myndert Garabrant's House on as

fined 50 guilders, and sentenced to "ride the wooden horse during parade."—*Alb. Rec.*, iii.

This patent calls for 182 acres, beginning " at ye Corner of his House Lott, running along ye Highway 200 Rodds to a black oak burnt stump, thence N. 30 chains, N. E. and E. to ye corner stake of Nicholas, the Baker, then E. along a small Creek to another creek where the Mill of Hossemus stands 30 chains, thence running as ye Creek between Hossemus & Communican Runs 45 Chains to the Mouth of the Creek, thence to the first mentioned Corner 24 Chains: Bounded on the Highway that goeth to Bergen, on the North by Nicholas, the Baker's Land, on the East by the Creek that parteth Hossemus and Comunipan, on the South by Hudson's River." Its N. extremity was " where the Mill of Hossemus stands," afterwards known as " Prior's Mill;" and the house lot referred to was S. of Communipaw avenue and fronting the river. It was afterwards owned by the Brinkerhoffs. *Vide Hartman's 1st Patent*, p. 11. This is a part of the tract given to Jan Evertse Bout by the Dutch West India Company, and by him sold to the patentee prior to 1657; for on Jan. 23, 1657, Cos pledged it as security for the support of his daughter by his first wife, " to teach her reading & writing, sewing & some trade & give her 200 florins out of her mother's estate." Cos paid to Bout 1,444 guilders for the tract. By a survey made by James Alexander, Feb. 15, 1723, the "black oak burnt stump" was found to be 26 rods beyond the 200 rods named in the patent. In this survey the place is called " Pannonia alias Communipan." Cos's second wife was Grietje Maes, widow of Claas Teunissen, whom he married Dec. 31, 1656. By her he had no children, and at his death his property went to *Maritje*, his only child by his first wife, Neeltje Engels. *Maritje* married Gerbrand Claesen, the founder of the Garrabrants family, Aug. 2, 1674. He died intestate June 19, 1703. She died October, 1714. By will dated Jan. 7, 1714, proved Feb. 3, 1715, she gave this tract to her sons *Cornelius* and *Myndert;* Cornelius taking all east of a line not far from Pine street, and Myndert all lying west of that line. We will first trace the share of Cornelius.

Cornelius, by will dated Feb. 13, 1767, proved March 4, 1774, gave all his lands to his son Cornelius, who, by will dated April 16, 1814, gave this tract to his sons *Cornelius* and *Peter*. Cornelius took the N. part, bounded S. by the narrow meadow extending from the present engine-house of the Central Railroad Company, W. to about Pine street. Peter took that part lying between said meadow and Communipaw avenue.

Peter sold 11¼ acres to Garret Van Horne, March 20, 1822, bounded N.W. by Myndert Garrabrants, N.E. and S.E. by Cornelius Garrabrants, S.W. by Communipaw road.

Van Horne died intestate, and the lot was partitioned among his children, viz.: *Margaret, Hartman V.* and *Garret*, Aug. 14, 1848, and in 1856 sold to William Keenney and John R. Halladay. The balance of Peter's lands (except the house lot on the shore) he sold to his brother Cornelius and John Van Horne, June 8, 1821. These grantees resold to Peter. He sold 16 76-100 acres lying N. of Communipaw avenue, and E. of Garret Van Horn, to Jane, widow of Cornelius Garrabrants, March 20, 1822. Cornelius left one child, *Jane*, who married Cornelius Van Horne. She inherited and yet owns the most of her parent's estate.

Myndert died May 5, 1781. By will dated Oct. 10, 1772, proved May 28, 1783, he gave to his son *Garrabrant* the use of one-third of his farm for life. The

Course south Fifteen Degrees and thirty Minutes East, and ninety six Links from the East Corner of Cornelius Brinkerhooff's House on a Course south forty nine Degrees and thirty Minutes East); And from the said Stone runs along the Road or Highway North thirty one Degrees and ten Minutes West seventeen Chains, Then along the said

rest of his land, with the remainder in this tract he gave to his son *Myndert*. Garrabrant died March 29, 1791. Myndert 2d (generally known as Myndert 1st), had three children, *Trintje*, wife of Garret Van Horne; *Hannah*, wife of Michael Vreeland; and *Myndert*. To his two daughters he gave the land between Van Horne street and the Mill Road and Brinkerhoff's land, and N. of Communipaw avenue. This deed was dated June 10, 1805. The grantees partitioned; Van Horne getting that portion lying between Van Horne street and the lane leading to the zinc works, and Vreeland all between that lane and the old mill road and Brinkerhoff's land. The deed of June 10, 1805, extended the boundaries N. of Communipaw avenue, a sufficient distance to include 30 acres. On a division of the lands between *John G.* and *Myndert*, sons of Garret Van Horne, April 14, 1838, Garret's part of this tract went to Myndert.

Myndert Garrabrant 2nd sold the balance of his property to his son *Myndert 3d* (generally known as Myndert 2nd), Aug. 20, 1805. Myndert 3rd sold in trust for his son *Myndert* 4th (known as Myndert 3d), all his property, including his share of the tract in question, and a lot at Slonga to his father-in-law, John Van Houten, and brother-in-law Helmigh Van Houten, Aug. 10, 1807. This deed was set aside in Chancery, Sept. 9, 1808, and another executed in accordance with the Decree, March 15, 1809. On Aug. 14, 1835, Myndert 4th sold to Merselis J. Merselis 15 or 16 acres in the N. end of the patent, lying in the meadow S. of the N. J. R. R. near the Point of Rocks. He conveyed all his lands and meadow at "Swane Punt" to John G. and Mindert Van Horne, Feb. 9, 1837. (I think this conveyance was in trust.) The same was partitioned between Effie Van Buskirk and Mary Elizabeth, afterwards wife of Charles G. Sisson; report confirmed June Term, 1845. Myndert 2d died Sept. 20, 1814. Myndert 3d died Sept. 3, 1846. Myndert 4th died May 1, 1837, leaving two children, *Effie*, wife of James Van Buskirk, and *Mary Elizabeth*, wife of Charles G. Sisson. To these two John Van Houten, et al. conveyed, May 17, 1852, according to the provisions of the trust deed of March 15, 1809. They partitioned, June 25, 1853. Van Buskirk et ux. sold to Keeney and Halliday, April 29, 1856, and this purchase with the land bought of the heirs of Garret Van Horne was laid out into lots in 1856, and the map entitled "Map of Lafayette." The most of the land which fell to Mrs. Sisson lay at Swane Punt, and was sold by Jacob Weart, her trustee, in 1870. She died in 1871. *Vide Price* vs. *Sisson*, 2 *Beasley*, 168.

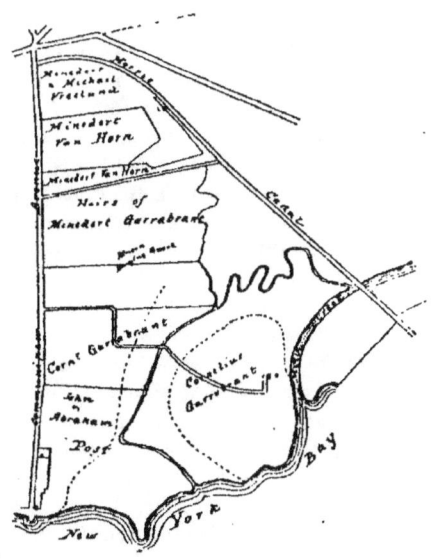

Road North thirty seven Degrees West twenty seven Chains and seventy three Links, Then along said Road North thirty nine Degrees and forty Minutes West Seventeen Chains to a stake standing on the Easterly side of a Brook, Thence North forty two Degrees and fifteen Minutes East, twenty four Chains to a Stake set in a small Creek and near the Head thereof, Then down along the said small Creek as it runs (leaving a small Island of Meadow to the Northeastward) till it comes into Horsimus Creek (which Horsimus Creek divides Horsimus from Comunipan) Then down said Horsimus Creek as it runs to Hudson's River or York Bay, Then along said River or Bay Southwesterly to the Place of Beginning.

The Patent of Philip Carteret to Nicholas Jansen Baker dated the twelfth Day of May One thousand six hundred and sixty eight for two Parcels of Land lying at Comunipan.

Our Survey whereof shews and we adjudge them to be two Tracts, **First a Tract** (which on the Map is mark'd No. 12).*

Beginning at a Stake standing on the Easterly side of a Brook (which Stake is the Westerly Corner of the immediate preceeding Patent of Class Pieterson Cors) thence running North forty nine Degrees and forty five Minutes West thirty nine Chains to a Stake (standing in the Line of the Lot of Jacob Luby mark'd on the Map No. 56) and from the said Stake runs north forty one Degrees and forty five Minutes East twenty five Chains to a Stake, Thence South forty nine Degrees and forty five Minutes East thirty nine Chains and forty eight Links to a

---

* This patentee lived in Pearl Street, N. Y., but never in this county. He was a baker by trade, hence his name—Claes Jansen de Backer. He married Annetje, the sister of Fitje Hartmans named in the next Patent.

Lot No. 12 was upland, extending from the junction of Communipaw Ave. and the Bergen Point Plank Road, N. E. 120x200 Dutch rods=40 morgens. For this he received a Patent Nov. 27, 1654. *Land Papers (Albany) H. H.* 26.

Lot No. 13 was 30x140 Dutch rods=7 morgens, lying behind Swane Punt, and along the foot of the hill N. of Hudson Ave.

This lot was included in the gift of the Dutch West India Company to Jan Evertse Bout, and in his deed to Michael Jansen. *Vide Note to Hartman's 1st Patent*, p. 11. Jansen's widow, Fitje Hartmans, sold it to de Backer, Dec. 20, 1667. In this deed was a clause that the grantee should not alienate without giving the grantor the preference of repurchasing. De Backer sold the whole tract to Hendrick George, May 30, 1677. My opinion is that the grantee was none other than Hendrick Joris (*anglicé* George) Van Blinkerhoef. He conveyed it to his son *Cornelius*, Feb. 24, 1708, who by will dated Sept. 22, 1755, proved Oct. 25, 1770, gave to his son *Hendrick* these lots and a farm at "Pembrepog," also all his lands in the township.

Hendrick was a bachelor. By will dated Sept. 22, 1792, he gave to Hendrick, son of his brother Hartman, the lots in question; also a wood lot at Slonga, the Cedar Swamp and meadow at Secaucus; land and meadow near Brown's Ferry; a lot of woodland at Bergen Point, and the woodland and meadow adjudged to him for the Patent of Secaucus, at a place called the Maize Land. This devisee had one son, *Hartman*, who died before his father, leaving three sons, *Henry, Cornelius*, and *John*. By Hendrick's will, dated Feb. 12, 1834, proved March 28, 1838, he gave to his grandson Henry the farm at Communipaw (in Hartman's first Patent) and a strip through this lot adjoining E. side of Monticello Ave., and to his grandsons Cornelius and John he gave the remainder of the tract in question.

Stake standing near a small Creek (which Stake on a Course North forty two Degrees and fifteen Minutes East is One Chain distant from where the Line of said Claas Pieterson Cors meets the said Creek near the Head thereof); And from said Stake South forty two Degrees and fifteen Minutes West twenty five Chains to the Place of Beginning

Second a Tract (which on the Map is mark'd No. 13.)

Beginning at the Northeasterly Corner of the foregoing first Tract, Thence running along the Line of the said first Tract North forty nine Degrees and forty five Minutes West seven Chains and fifty Links to a Stake planted on the Upland near the Foot of the Hill, Thence North forty Degrees and fifteen Minutes * East twenty Six Chains and twenty five Links to a Stake in the Meadow, Thence South forty nine Degrees and forty five Minutes East Seven Chains to a Stake by a small Creek, Then down the same as it runs South Sixteen Degrees West Six Chains and thirty Links on a streight Line to where it empties into a Creek which is the Northwesterly Bounds of Claas Pieterson Cors aforesaid, then up the last mentioned Creek as it runs to the Place of Beginning. *11

The first **Patent** of Phillip Carterett to Fytje Hartman dated the twelfth Day of May One thousand Six hundred and sixty Eight, for a Tract of Land lying at Comunipan.

Our Survey whereof shews and we adjudge it to be a Tract (which on the Map is mark'd No. 14.)*

This diagram will show the division and what was sold of Lots No. 12 and 13. Henry sold his share of the "bush lot" to David B. Wakeman May 1, 1852. The division among the brothers being imperfect, a decree in chancery was obtained in 1852, confirming the same. Aaron Tuers owned a house lot in the S. side of Cornelius' share. Cornelius died seized and intestate June 13, 1851. His executors sold 6 92-100 acres out of the N. side of his share W. of Palisade Ave. (marked A) to Bernhard Vetterlein. This sale was confirmed by the Orphan's Court, Oct. Term, 1857. The residue was divided between his two children *Cornelius* and *Eleanor C.* (now wife of Wm. H. Speer). Cornelius took Nos. 2, 3, 6, 8, 9. Eleanor C. took Nos. 1, 4, 5, 7, 11.

This partition was made in 1857, by commissioners, report confirmed Oct. Term, 1857.

Out of the N. W. corner of the tract adjoining the school lot Henry Brinkerhoff sold to Casparus Prior, June 29, 1829, 4 32-100 acres. This on a partition of his estate fell to his grandson Michael, who sold to Jacob M. Merselis. *Vide Note to Varlet's Patent*, p. 62. About the same date he sold the front along Bergen Ave. to other parties. These sales included all the land between Bergen and Monticello Aves.

* This lot was a part of the farm sold by Jan Evertse Bout to the patentee's husband, Michael Jansen, for 8,000 Florins, and for which a deed was given Sept. 9, 1656.

FITJE HARTMAN.

Beginning at a Stone (on the Northwest side of York Bay or Hudson's River which is also the Place of Beginning of Claas Pietersen Cors's Patent); which Stone stands in the Middle of a Road and is ninety seven Links from the south Corner of Myndert Garabrants's

Bout's title came by the following Patent. I give a translation; the original is in the possession of John C. Van. Horne:

"We William Kieft, Governor General and Council under the High and Mighty Lords, States General of the United Netherlands, His Highness of Orange and the Honble. the Directors of the authorized West India Company, residing in New Netherlands, make known and declare that on this day here underwritten, we have given and granted Jan. Everse Bout, a piece of land lying on the North River westward from Fort Amsterdam, before these, pastured and tilled by Jan Everse, named Gamoenepaen and Jan de Lacher's Houck, with the meadows as the same lay within the post and rail fence, containing eighty-four morgens.

In testimony whereof is these by us signed and with our Seal confirmed in Fort Amsterdam in New Netherlands, the which land Jan Everse took possession of in Anno 1638, and began then to plow and sow it.

WILLEM KIEFT,
By Order of the Honble. Gov'r Genl

[L. S.]   and Council of New Netherland.

CORNELIS VAN TIENHOVEN, Sec'y."

No date appears in the deed, but it must have been given about 1641. It was a free gift to him from the Company. Jansen bought about 1647, and paid for his purchase in installments. He and Bout agreed concerning the balance due, June 9, 1655, and it was not until the whole consideration was paid that he received his deed. The tract lay S. of Communipaw Ave. and extended to the creek which yet empties into the bay on the S. side of the Abattoir. The Patent called for 107 acres. The patentee died seized Oct. 17, 1697.

By will she left all of her lands to her children, *Elias, Enoch, Johannis, Hartman, Cornelis, Jannetje,* and *Pryntje.* These partitioned, June 26, 1701, but owing to the uncertainties of the boundaries it is impossible to give the location of the several allotments.

Enoch Vreeland, son of the above-named Enoch, sold, May 7, 1710, to Rutgert Van Horne, then living at Pembrepogh, a lot at Communipaw, but where located, or of what size, is not stated. But it seems to have been the allotment of Enoch in the general partition, and by him sold to his son. The consideration in the deed of Enoch to Van Horne was *one pepper corn,* when demanded by his father Enoch Michielse of Pembrepogh. Jannetje married Dirck Teunissen Van Vechten. Her son Michael sold to Rutgert Van Horne (then living at Communipaw) April 14, 1715, the portion which in the division fell to his mother. It is described as "extending up to the Brook commonly called the Off-fall, then through the meadow along said Brook to Grawss Point." This I take to be the tract on which John G. Van Horne recently lived.

Elias died seized of his lot obtained in the general partition. The children, *Michael, Jacob, Fitje,* wife of John Thomas, of Elizabethtown, and *Rachel,* sold the same, together with a house lot and other lands, to Lawrence Van Galen, June 24, 1707. The deed limited the fee to the grantee, his wife, and the heirs of their bodies. He sold the same to Rutgert Van Horne, March 24, 1710. His children, *Catherine* wife of ———— Loofborrow, and *Margaret* wife of Thomas Hadden, quit-claimed their interest therein to George Ross, of Elizabethtown, and Isaac Ogden, of Newark, Feb.

House on a Course South fifteen Degrees and thirty Minutes East; And is ninety six Links from the East Corner of Cornelius Brinkerhooff's House on a Course South forty nine Degrees and thirty Minutes East; And from said Stone runs along the Road or Highway North thirty one

---

27, 1764. On the 22d day of May following, Ebenezer Foster and Catherine Loofborrow sold the same to John Van Horne.

Pryntje married Andries Claesen, and had three sons, *Michael, Abraham,* and *Claas,* who inherited their mother's share in the partition. Michael and Abraham sold their interest therein to Claas, who sold to Rutgert Van Horne, Aug. 29, 1721, the "House, home lot and garden on the W. side of the road," also land and meadow, "beginning at the road on the N. W. bounds of Cornelis Michielse, and so along said bounds to the great Creek, then along said Creek to stones laid by said Claas and Cornelius Hendricksen Van Blinkerhoff, so along said Stones to the road, then along said road to the Beginning."

These several deeds seem to me to vest in Rutgert Van Horne title to all the land S. of Communipaw Ave., from Brinkerhoff's line on the E., to the Off-fall brook on the W. By Van Horne's will, dated June 6, 1740, proved June 8, 1741, he gave to his only son *John* all his lands at Communipaw. John, by his will dated Dec. 6, 1757, proved Dec. 29, 1757, gave to his son *John* the same lands. This devisee, by will dated Sept. 22, 1786, proved Jan. 23, 1787, gave the same to his two sons, *John* and *Garret,* except the dwelling-house which he gave to his son *John.* Garret died seized April 7, 1808, leaving his property to his two children, *John G.* and *Myndert.* These two and their uncle John partitioned Dec. 13, 1827, they taking the land lying adjoining the Off-fall, and he the land lying between their tract and Washington Ave., and what lay in the rear of Brinkerhoff's land. In a partition between John G. and Myndert, April 14, 1838, John G. received most of the land left to them by their father lying in this Patent adjoining Communipaw Ave., and Myndert a lot S. of John G. John (the uncle) died Aug. 29, 1843. By will dated Aug. 12, 1843, he gave his property to his son *John*, and grandchildren, *Agnes* wife of Garret Van Horne, and *Jane* wife of Peter V. B. Vreeland, children of his son *Peter.* John took the land lying east of John G. Van Horne, and extending from Communipaw Ave. S. Jane took what lay S. of John and W. of Washington Ave. Agnes took what lay S. of Brinkerhoff and E. of Washington Ave. Jane died seized in 1871. Agnes sold to James Stevens, William W. Edwards, and Andrew McKnight.

Lawrence Van Galen sold to Cornelius Blinckerhofe, May 22, 1710, a house lot on the S. W. corner of Communipaw Ave. and the Bay. It remained in the family until Jan. 5, 1831, when Henry sold it to Nicholas J. Prior. The Brinkerhoff lot was bought at an early date. It was sold by Hendrick to his son *Cornelius,* Feb. 24, 1708, and was then bounded N. by the "wagon or cartway of Gemonipa, E. and W. by Fitje Hartmans, and S. by the creek "behind the Swan's Point." Cornelius, by his will dated Sept. 22, 1755, gave this lot to his son *Hendrick,* who devised it to his nephew Hendrick, who devised it to his grandson Henry, who died seized, leaving one son, Garret. *Vide Note to De Backer's Patent,* p. 10.

Paul Douwesse sold to Rutgert Van Horne, May 18, 1702, a lot on the shore= 15 morgens, S. W. of Cornelius Vreeland. Michael Vreeland, of Stony Point, sold to Johannis Vreeland, of Communipaw, July 1, 1771, in exchange for land on "Rackpogas," the land in the rear of the house lots from the avenue down to the creek, as per deed of June 26, 1701. Of this Johannis died seized and intestate. It was inherited by his only child Antje, wife of Johannis Van Wagenen, of Teaneck, who sold 12¾ acres to John Van Horne, Dec. 7, 1790. *Vide Note to Lot* 303, p. 133. This I take to be the

Degrees and ten Minutes West Seventeen Chains, then along said Road North thirty seven Degrees West twenty seven Chains and seventy three Links, Thence along said Road North thirty nine Degrees and forty Minutes West Seventeen Chains to a Stake standing on the Easterly side of a Brook (which Stake is the West Corner of Claas Pietersen Cors's Patent) thence down the said Brook or Creek as it runs to a Ditch cut out of the same to the Eastward opposite to the Southermost Corner of a Piece of Meadow (patented to Henderick Tunisse which on the Map is mark'd No. 73) Then Easterly along said Ditch 'till it comes into a small Creek (which small Creek is the Northeast Boundary of Dirck Claasen's Patent mark'd on the map No. 16) Then Southeasterly along the last mentioned Creek as it runs to the Mouth thereof on Hudson's River, or York Bay; then up the said Bay or River Northeasterly to the Place of Beginning.

The second Patent of Phillip Carteret to Fytje Hartman, dated the twelfth Day of May, One thousand Six hundred and sixty Eight, for a Tract of Land lying behind Communipan.

Our Survey whereof shews and we adjudge it to be a Tract (which on the Map is mark'd No. 15.)*

---

land bought by the New Jersey Stock Yard and Market Company of Jacob Van Horne in 1866. Abraham Sickles (who married an Outwater) sold to Peter Garrabrants, May 1, 1811, 3 4-100 acres in the rear of the Communipaw lots, being one-half of what was allotted to the heirs of Guilliam Outwater. The heirs of Lozier sold to John Van Horne 6 35-100 acres W. of Brinkerhoff's lot, E. of Outwater, and S. of Communipaw Ave., April 28, 1817, and to Garret M. Vreeland 5¼ acres and 28 perches of meadow S. W. of Van Horne and Brinkerhoff, April 2, 1817.

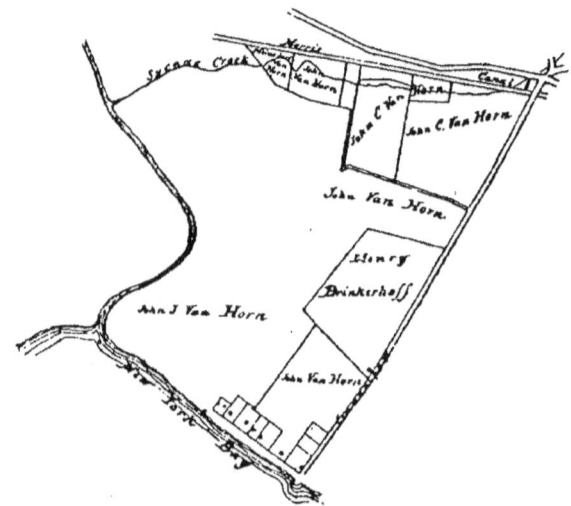

The village of Communipaw--older than Bergen--lies within this Patent. A number of small lots on the shore were sold to different persons, who here huddled within the stockades for protection. Among these early owners was Dirk Claesen, the owner of Raccocus and Cavan Point. In the division of his property this house lot fell to his son-in-law, Hartman Michielse Vreeland, who left it to his son *Michael*, who left it to his son *Claas*, who left it to his grandsons *Nicholas* and *Garret*. Garret took the S. W. half and sold to David Bush, May 15, 1820, and Nicholas took the N. E. half, and sold to Daniel Welsh, Nov. 16, 1822. *Vide Note to Claasen's 1st Patent*, p. 12. It was a double house, and Bush took down his part. The part owned by Welsh is yet standing and inhabited.

º This lot was 80x200 Dutch rods=21¼ morgens. Carteret's Patent calls for 61¼ acres. It was bounded generally N. by Communipaw Lane, E. by the Off-full

FITJE HARTMAN.

Beginning at a Stake standing on the easterly Side of a Brook which * Stake is the Westerly Corner of Claas Pieterson Corss's Patent, mark'd on the Map No. 11, and the Northerly Corner of Fytje Hartman's foregoing Patent, mark'd on the Map No. 14), And from the said Stake runs North forty nine Degrees and forty five minutes West, thirty

*12

---

brook, S. by Bramhall Ave., W. by lots 56, 57, and 58, a little E, of the old road leading to Bergen Point. This diagram will show its subsequent divisions. It may not be accurate, but, I trust, sufficiently so for practical purposes.

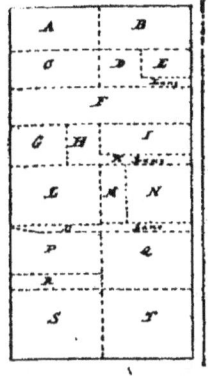

Lawrence Van Galen, who married Fitje Vreeland, granddaughter of the patentee, inherited a part of the tract. His children, *Catherine*, wife of —— Loofborrow, and *Margaret*, widow of Thomas Hadden, with one Ebenezer Foster, *vide Note to Hartman's 1st Patent*, p. 11, sold to Joseph Waldron Nov. 7, 1761, a lot in the N. W. corner of the Patent, said to contain 4 192-1000 acres. Waldron owned lot A, B, C, D, and E, which was more land than called for in Van Galen's deed. It is probable that Waldron sold A. B. to John Kelly prior to 1800. Kelly sold A to Walter Clendenny, June 10, 1801, and B to John Kelly, Jr., July 20, 1815. A part of this, Kelly, Jr., sold to Benjamin F. Welsh, June 10, 1819, who sold to Stephen Garretson, Aug. 16, 1849. Waldron sold C to Cornelius Garrabrant, May 23, 1769, who, by will dated April 16, 1814, proved July 30, 1814, gave it to his sons, *Cornelius* and *Peter*. It contained 2¼ acres. Peter sold to Daniel Vreeland, May 28, 1817. Cornelius did not convey, but his only child, Jane, widow of Cornelius Van Horne, released to Andrew Clerk, June 9, 1851. Waldron sold D =1¼ acres, to Daniel Sickles, June 28, 1766 (deed unrecorded). Sickles died Oct. 23, 1813. By his will, dated March 6, 1798 (unproved), he gave his property to the children of his only child, *Geertje*, wife of Michael Vreeland, viz: *Nicholas, Garret, Catherine,* wife of Henry Van Horne, *Ann,* wife of Jacob D. Van Winkle (who sold to Daniel Vreeland, June 16, 1715), *Abraham,* and *Cornelius* (who sold to Daniel Vreeland, Jan. 1, 1851). It is probable that Waldron sold E to Capt. Thomas Brown, as it was at one time in possession of his widow, who sold to Samuel Ten Eyck Gautier, Jan. 6, 1818. A colored servant of the Captain, known as Jack (John) Brown, received it as a gift from Samuel T. Gautier, Dec. 13, 1828.

Michael Hartman Vreeland, grandson of the patentee, owned part of this tract in 1764. His will was dated March 19, 1762, proved Feb. 4, 1768. While there is not in it any particular devise of his interest in this lot to his son Claas, yet it is certain that Claas claimed and was in possession of F, O, P, Q, R, S, T. By his will dated July 23, 1801, proved May 21, 1803, he gave F to his grandson Daniel, who sold to Stephen Garretson, Oct. 22, 1844. To his grandsons Garret and Nicholas, he gave P, Q, R, S, T. They partitioned, June 1, 1832; Garret taking P, R, T, and Nicholas taking Q, S.

Michael Cornelise Vreeland sold M to John Vreeland (son of Helmus), June 8, 1776. (He and John held a release for this from Michael Vreeland, of Aquacknonck, dated June 25, 1737). It is probable that John Vreeland sold it to James Collerd.

John Van Horne sold G, H, I, K to Joseph Waldron, Nov. 1, 1803. What interest Peter Stuyvesant had therein I do not know, but whatever it was he quit-claimed it to Waldron, Oct. 31, 1803. Waldron sold C to John E. Post, May 11, 1813.

James Collerd died seized, Aug. 11, 1791. By will dated Nov. 27, 1790, proved Dec. 6, 1791, he gave all his realty to his son John, who sold L to Post, April 4, 1776

nine Chains to a Stake (standing in the Line of the Lot of Jacob Luby mark'd on the Map No. 56) being the West Corner of a Lot in Nicholas Jansen Baker's Patent, mark'd on the Map No. 12; And from said Stake runs South thirty five Degrees West Sixteen Chains and fifty Links to a Stake, Then South forty nine Degrees and twenty Minutes East forty two Chains and eighty four Links to the Brook or Creek first mentioned, Then up the same as it runs to the Place of Beginning.

The first Patent of Phillip Carteret to Dick Claasen, dated the twelfth Day of May, One thousand Six hundred and sixty Eight, for a Tract of Upland and Meadow called Kewan.

Our Survey whereof shews and we adjudge it to be a Tract (which on the Map is mark'd No. 16.)*

Garret Vreeland sold O to Post, March 21, 1823. Post sold G, L, O, to Dr. Valentine Mott, July 19, 1826. Waldron sold H to Mott, Aug. 7, 1827, and I, K, Feb. 3, 1830. Mott sold G, H, I, K, L, O to Sarah Munns, Feb. 6, 1835, who sold G, H, K, L, O to Robert L. Smith, Oct. 15, 1835. Munns sold I to Mott, Jan. 1, 1850, and Mott to Jeremiah Jackson, Jan. 12, 1850. John Collerd sold M, N, to Jacob G. Outwater, April 1, 1810, who sold to Peter Van Horne, May 15, 1824, who sold to Robert L. Smith, April 20, 1836. Garret Vreeland sold P to Smith, Aug. 10, 1836. Smith sold G, H, K, L, N, O, P, Q to Jacob Brinkerhoff, May 1, 1843, who sold G, H, L, M, O, P, and half of K, to Jeremiah Jackson, June 10, 1844.

* This patentee after the death of Teunisen received a lease from Kieft of Hoboken, in about 1646. He shortly after abandoned it. *Col. Hist. of N. Y.*, i. 329. He was at one time skipper of the Sloop *Union*, from which he was dismissed April 20, 1658, for disobedience of orders. *N. Y. Col. MSS.*, viii. 851. He was one of the commissioners to fortify "Gemoenepa" in 1663. *New Neth. Reg.* 159.

The first grant of this tract was from Gov. Kieft to Egbert Woutersen, a soldier in the service of the company, and the old occupant of Jan de Lacher's Houck, May 10, 1647. *Land Papers (Albany)* G. G. 16. It was then known by the Indian name Apopcalyck, and "extended from Dirck the paver's Kil to Gemoenepaen or Jan Evertz Kil." It is probable that Claasen purchased it from Woutersen. In Carteret's Patent it is called Kewan, and its boundaries begin at the mouth of Sycan's Creek, which was the probable intention in Kieft's Patent. It included all the upland and meadow S. of Communipaw Creek and E. of Sycan's Creek=141 acres. The N. part was known as Reckpokus (now Raccocus) and the S. part as Kewan (now Cavan Point).

Claasen's full name was Dirck Claasen Braecke. He had three daughters, viz: *Marijte*, who married Hartman Michielse Vreeland, *Claesje*, who married Johannis Michielse Vreeland, and *Metje*, who married Cornelis Michielse Vreeland. Dirck Claasen died seized, March 26, 1693. His daughters inherited his property, and with their consent the same was divided among their husbands, Sept. 1, 1696, as follows:

Hartman received the part beginning in the "meadow in the byte by a poynt commonly called fish point at a small creek as it is staked out up to the upland of the island where it is divided by a fence, and running over said Island into a certain pond a little way from said Island, and from thence something S. to the E. edge of the great Kewan, and from thence W. to the river side, then E. and N. along said river side to the Beginning." Hartman's widow for £450, July 13, 1723, sold to her youngest son Michael Hartmanse Vreeland, the same tract, including the "Home

Beginning at the Mouth of Sycan's Creek, lying Northwest of Kewan Point (which Creek is the Northeasterly and Northerly Bounds of the Piece of Meadow in the Patent of Dick Sycan, mark'd on the Map No. 18); and then up along the said Creek the several courses thereof as it runs to the Southermost Point of Hendrick Tunisess Meadow, mark'd on the Map No. 73; Then Easterly along a Ditch and small Creek (which is the Southerly Bounds of Fytje Hartman's Patent, mark'd on the Map No. 14), to the Mouth thereof on Hudson's River or York Bay; Then Southwesterly round said Kewan Point; Then Northwesterly to the Mouth of the first mentioned Creek, the Place of Beginning.

The Second **Patent** of Phillip Carteret to Dick Claasen, dated the twelfth Day of May, One thousand Six hundred and sixty Eight, for a Tract of Land called Stony Point.

Our Survey whereof shews and we adjudge it to be a Tract (which on the Map is mark'd No. 17).*

Lott, Farme and Farme House, wherein she now lives called Reckpokus." Michael by will dated March 19, 1762, proved Feb. 4, 1768, gave the same "on the south side of Regpokes Island" to his son Nicholas. Nicholas by will dated July 23, 1801 proved May 21, 1803, gave to his son Stephen the whole of his land lying upon the Island Right-Coakkuss. Stephen died Aug. 31, 1865. His interest in this tract he had previously given to his sons *Nicholas S.* and *Stephen B.* The balance of his lands he conveyed to Mundet Van Horne June 25, 1858, in trust to be divided in accordance with his will previously executed. He executed another will Oct. 8, 1860. Controversies arose among his heirs after his death, and compromise was effected March 27, 1866.

Johannis received by the following description: The N. side is divided from the S. side in manner aforesaid until it come to the water side or river, thence W. and N. W. and sometimes N. along said river side and great (Sycan's) Creek to a small creek emptying into the great creek over against the brook or fall emptying into the great creek by Enoch Michielse's Stony Point.

* This Patent calls for 59 acres 4 perches. It extended from Sycan's Creek, 100 rods W. to a Great Swamp (Ocean Ave.) In the division of Dirck Claasen's lands, as mentioned in the note to the preceding Patent, this tract was allotted to Cornelius Michielse Vreeland by the description: "The wood or bush land is divided from the other two parts; on the S. W. by Enoch Michielse, W. and N. by the Commons, with the upland and meadow = 25 morgens, to which is added a piece of meadow beginning at a small creek over against the brook of Enoch Michielse's Stony Point, and along said creek, runs to the Edge of the Island, and along said Island until it comes to the bounds of Fitje Hartman's at the dam or double ditch, and so along her lands as far as it reaches." This is lot 73. *Vide Note to Hartman's First Patent,* p. 11, and *Note to Teunise's Patent,* p. 54. The "Stony Point" here referred to, is the bluff on which Garret R. Vreeland now lives, where the Central R. R. crosses the Morris Canal. The tract was inherited by Cornelius's son *Michael,* who owned it in 1764. From him it went to his younger son *Johannis.* He by deed, Dec. 18, 1795, gave to his son Michael the west half of his farm = 40 acres, and on April 25, 1820, gave him the whole of it, with all his land at Raekpokus and the salt meadow belonging to the farm, and his wood lots at Slonga (204, 301). By his will dated Nov. 20, 1817, proved Sept. 27, 1823, he gave to his son Michael all his lands in the township. Michael, by will dated Oct. 30, 1824, proved March 18, 1828, gave the S. third of his

Beginning at a Stake (which Stake stands at the Edge of the Upland bearing North fifty-three Degrees East two Chains and eighty-four Links from the East Corner of a large Rock before Michael Vreeland's Door; The Chimney of the Island Hospital bears from said Stake South forty Seven Degrees and fifteen Minutes East); And from the said Stake running South twenty Eight Degrees West twenty five Chains and ninety five Links, to the Mouth of a small Creek putting into a Creek called Sycans Creek, Thence North twenty seven Degrees and thirty Minutes West twenty four Chains and seventeen Links up into the Woods to a Stake, Thence North twenty * Eight Degrees East, thirty nine Chains and twenty Links to a Stake then South twenty seven Degrees and thirty Minutes East twenty two Chains and thirty two Links to the Edge of the Meadow and Upland, Thence along Meadow Edge to the first mentioned Stake the Place of Beginning.

13

The first **Patent** of Philip Carteret to Dirck Sycan dated the twelfth Day of May, One thousand Six hundred and sixty Eight for a Tract of Upland and Meadow lying at Mingackqua.

Our Survey whereof shews, and we adjudge it to be a Tract (which on the Map is mark'd No. 18).*

---

farm to his son John M. The other two-thirds he gave to his sons Myndert and Michael, who had not formally partitioned before selling to Edmund C. Bramhall in 1852. This joint tract is now known as Claremont, and bounded generally N. by Forest St., E. by the Morris Canal, S. by Myrtle Ave., W. by Ocean Ave. The share of John M. lay between Myrtle Ave. on the N. and "the brook of Enoch Michielse's Stony Point," or Richard Vreeland's line on the S. He sold the S. half of his share to Capt. George W. Howe, and it is yet held by his heirs. He gave to his son *Michael J.* 12¼ acres, bounded N. by Myrtle Ave., who sold to Samuel Bostwick in March, 1859.

* Seickan or Sycan was a soldier in the service of the company, and for insolence was sentenced to be shot, Feb. 21, 1647. He afterwards was pardoned and became a farmer, and lived in N. Y. in 1664; was admitted to the rights of a small burgher, April 26, 1657.

This lot consisted of two tracts; 1st, beginning at a creek coming out of the woods (this was Straatmaker's creek a little N. of the line of Chestnut Ave. in Greenville), extending 100 Dutch rods up into the woods (to Ocean Ave.), and 300 rods along the river = 50 morgens; 2d, a lot adjoining on the W. N. W. and N. E. to the creek still coming from the swamp and emptying into the Morris Canal by Enoch Michielse's Stony Point = 15 1-6 morgens. Dirck Straatmaker was the owner of this tract previous to 1643. He probably had his house on the bluff by the Central R. R. bridge, from which point he could see the field of the Communipaw massacre, where he was slain in February of that year. After his death the land probably reverted to the Dutch West India Company. It was given by Gov. Stuyvesant to Dirck Sycan, June 16, 1654. He sold it to Enoch Michielse Vreeland, Feb. 13, 1679, for 4,900 guilders. There must have been some claim, however, set up by the heirs of Dirck Straatmaker, for on March 18, 1698, Vreeland obtained from Jan Dircksen Straatmaker, the son of Dirck, a quit-claim of all his interest in the tract, for £20. The tract was known by the Indian name *Najacksick* or *Neyonsick*, to which sometimes was added "*alias* Pembrepogh."

Vreeland, by will dated April 12, 1715, proved April 9, 1720, gave the tract to his

Beginning at the Mouth of a small Creek (putting into a Creek called Sycan's Creek, which small Creek is the Southeasterly Corner of Dirck Claasen's Patent mark'd on the Map No. 17); Thence North twenty seven Degrees and thirty Minutes West twenty four Chains and seventeen Links to a Stake (being the Westerly Corner of said Dirck Claasen's Patent mark'd on the Map No. 17), Thence South forty two Degrees West sixty Chains and forty Links to a Gum Sapling mark'd with a Blaze and three Notches on four sides and V on East side (which Sapling stands in the Line of Lawrence Andrieses's Patent mark'd on the Map No. 19) And from said Sapling runs South twenty seven Degrees and thirty Minutes East twenty nine Chains and forty eight Links to the Mouth of Straatamaker s Creek on Hudsons River or York Bay; Then along the said Bay or River Northeasterly to the Mouth of Sycan s Creek (the Mouth of which Creek is the place of beginning of Dirck Claasens Patent mark'd on the Map No. 16) then up the said Creek the several Courses thereof to the Mouth of the first mentioned Creek the Place of Beginning.

The Patent of William Keift to Claas Carstensen Norman dated the twenty-fifth Day of March, One thousand six hundred and forty Seven, and confirm'd (with an addition of Land) by Patent from Phillip Carteret to Lawrence Andriesen dated the twenty Sixth Day of March, One thousand six hundred & Sixty Seven for a Parcell of Land lying at Mingackqua.

Our Survey whereof shews and we adjudge it to be a Tract (which on the Map is mark'd No. 19).*

---

sons *Jacob* and *George*. His widow, Aagtje, gave to Jacob and George a deed for the same, bounded S. W. by Andries Van Buskirk and up to near "Stoon Pint," while to her sons Elias and Benjamin she gave 320 acres on the Raritan River, June 12, 1731. George's will, dated May 4, 1793, proved Aug. 14, 1795, he gave to his son John the S. W. half of the tract = 149 acres 3 roods 33 perches, which John afterwards by will gave to his nephew, Col. Jacob, son of Garret, by whom it was in part sold to the New York Bay Cemetery Company. He also conveyed the old homestead E. of the Canal to Benjamin H. Broomhed, April 16, 1849. After several transfers the same came to Geo. W. Howe, by four deeds, in Oct. and Nov., 1854. Howe conveyed the S. corner to Clement D. Hancox, Dec. 1, 1860 and July 7, 1863; he to Joseph W. Hancox, Jan 11, 1866; he to Elizabeth G , wife of John N. Harriman, Aug. 25, 1868. Garret received the N. E. half of the tract = 165 acres 2 roods 33 perches. By will Garret gave to his son *Jacob* that part which lies S. of Woodlawn Ave.; the balance he gave to his sons *George* and *Richard*.

Jacob sold to Matthew Armstrong, April 1, 1836, 16 acres S. of Woodlawn Ave., and 6 acres to Abraham Becker, Nov. 12, 1839, lying S. of Armstrong, part of which Becker sold to Henry D. Van Nostrand. George took the N. E. part which he sold to his brother Richard, July 22, 1833, who still owns what he took under his father's will and what he bought from his brother George, extending from Woodlawn Ave. to the N E. bounds of the Patent; except a small lot E. of the plank road, sold to Geo. W. Robeson, now owned by the heirs of Matthew Armstrong.

*The Patent calls for 170 Acres. The first owner was Barent Jansen. This fact is recited in the Norman's Patent *Land Papers (Albany) G. G.* 197. Claas Carstensen the Norman (sometimes called Van Saut) after Jansen's death, received a

Beginning at a Stake on the Northwest side of Hudson's River or York Bay (from which Stake the most Easterly Corner of Jacob Van Wagenen's House bears South Seventy Six Degrees and forty Minutes West Seven Chains and eighty Eight Links) And from the said Stake runs North twenty seven Degrees and thirty Minutes West Eighty two

grant for it, May 25, 1647. He was a soldier in the service of the company. It is not known if he purchased from Jansen, or if Jansen abandoned it. It then contained 50 morgens. The Norman sold it to Jan Vinge Jan. 19, 1655. Vinge sold it to the " Virtuous Annetje Dircksen, widow of Pieter Cock," who owned it in 1662. *Register of Van Der Veen, N. Y.* 34. It is probable that she sold it to Lawrens Andriesen, who added to it 18 morgens as mentioned in his patent, It was probably added to by previous owners, so that with the 18 morgens, it now contained 170 acres. It was the first tract going S. which extended from bay to bay on which it lay "elbow ways." This peculiar position was caused by the course of Straatmakers Creek to which the lines of the several Patents from this point S. were made to conform. Streets have been laid to suit property lines, property lines were laid to suit Straatmakers Creek, hence the absence of right angles—all of which it may be well for " Map Commissions" to bear in mind.

By Andriesen's will dated Aug. 29, 1679, his sons *Pieter* and *Thomas* received this tract. In what manner Thomas' interest became vested in Pieter I do not know, but Pieter became the sole owner, and by will dated Jan. 20, 1735, proved Sept. 8, 1738, left it to his sons *Lawrence* and *Andries*. I find a deed from Andries Van Buskirk to Michael Andriesen of Communipaw, dated March 12, 1718, for a small lot adjoining Gerrit G. Van Wagenen, described as bounded at the middle by the division fence. By the same description Andriesen sold it to Cornelius Brinkerhoff by two deeds, March 1, 1729, and June 30, 1740. Whatever passed by these deeds lay within this patent and Brinkerhoff yet owned it in 1764, *page* 143. When or how the title thereto passed out of Brinkerhoff I have not discovered. Andries released to his brother Lawrence his interest in the farm, Oct. 14, 1723.

The date of this deed seems to indicate that the two brothers owned the farm prior to their father's will, probably by gift. The father lived at Constable's Hook. This deed was proved before Robert Lettis Hooper, Chief Justice of New Jersey, April 7, 1731.

Lawrence died, seized Dec. 13, 1752, leaving him surviving five children, viz: *Cornelius*, *Metje*, wife of Johannis La Grange, *Jannetje*, wife of Jacob Van Horne, *Fitje*, wife of John Roll, and *Anna*, wife of Thomas Brown. By his will dated Nov. 7, 1750, codicil May 27, 1752, proved April 22, 1753. Cornelius received all his father's real estate. He died, seized Feb. 4, 1754, intestate and without issue. His four sisters inherited the tract in question in common. But Mrs. Brown being then dead her interest had passed to her only child Lawrence.

Thomas Brown bought the interest of Metje, March 13, 1757. from her two children, *John* and *Fitje*. Jacob Van Horne et ux. sold an undivided quarter to George Vreeland, April 1, 1758. This quarter was afterwards located next to his own land and lay between the " middle of the mouth of Straatmaker's Creek" and the present Chestnut Ave. A deed for this purpose was given to Vreeland by Thomas Brown et ux., and John Roll et ux., June 5, 1758. It was said to contain 85 acres and extended from N. Y. Bay, 95 chains to Swampy Creek. This quarter east of the new Bergen road, went to John Vreeland under his father's will. *Vide Note to Sycan's Patent p.* 13, and from John to his nephew Col. Jacob, and from him in part to the New York Bay Cemetery Company. Garret received all W. of the new Bergen road by the par-

Chains and fifty Links, to New Ark Bay. Then * up along said New Ark *14
Bay until it comes to the Mouth of a small Creek (that parts this Land from
Meadow patented to Barnt Christian which is mark'd on the Map No.
122) Then up said Creek North forty Seven Degrees and fifty Minutes
East four Chains and fifty four Links, Then South eighty nine Degrees

---

tition of Feb. 5, 1796, *Vide Note to Lot* 212 *p*, 86. By Garret's will this was left to his sons *George* and *Richard*, who held in common until they sold to Samuel C. Nelson. John Roll et ux. took the quarter adjoining S. W. the quarter sold to George Vreeland. He died Feb. 2, 1761, and his widow married Andries Segaerd, a mariner. By will dated July 14, 1784, proved April 7, 1801, Fitje Segaerd gave this property to her grand daughter, Mary, wife of Thomas Cubberly, for life and after the testatrix's death to Cubberly's children, viz: *Jacob, Elizabeth*, wife of Paul Salter, *Gitty*, wife of Jacob Ackerman, *Ann*, wife of Joseph Van Winkle, and *Maria*; who sold to George Vreeland, July 22, 1833, that part of Fitje Segaerd's quarter lying E. of the old Bergen road, and also five acres of meadow at Droyer's Point. This quarter lay between Chestnut Ave. and Linden Ave.

Thomas Brown et ux. had one child, viz: Lawrence, who was born May 18, 1751 and died July 4, 1767, intestate and unmarried. His father then purchased the interest of his son's three aunts, who had inherited his quarter. This gave him one half of the Patent. He married for his second wife, Mary, daughter of Samuel Ten Eyck, Jan. 23, 1756. By this marriage was one child, *Mary*, born Oct. 17, 1756, married Andrew Gautier, Oct. 6, 1772. Capt. Brown died seized Oct. 30, 1782. By will dated Sept. 21, 1782, he gave all of his property to his two grandson's *Thomas* and *Daniel Gautier*; to Thomas his N. Y. property and to Daniel his N. J. property. Daniel was born Feb. 7, 1776 and died Jan. 7, 1791, intestate and without issue. His property was inherited by his brother Thomas, who married Elizabeth, daughter of John Leary, April 28, 1796, and died, Oct. 17, 1802, leaving his widow and children, *Thomas B., Helen D.* and *Samuel T.*

To carry the out will of Mary, the widow of Thomas Brown, (who died Dec. 8, 1818) the widow Elizabeth, Thomas B. and Helen D. released to Samuel T. that part of the patent lying S. of Linden Ave (owned by Capt. Brown) and 30 acres of meadow held in Common with the Cubberlys and the Vreelands, May 17, 1823. Samuel mortgaged to Thomas B. Gautier, May 8, 1824. This mortgage was foreclosed and the property sold by John Blanvelt, Sheriff, to his mother, Elizabeth Gautier, Feb. 27, 1829. She sold to George Vreeland Aug. 19, 1829, all lying E. of the old road. Vreeland conveyed as follows: to John Syms, 22 84-100 acres Jan. 2, 1837, bounded N. by Chestnut Ave. E. by the Plank road, S. by Linden Ave. and W. by old Bergen road. That part of this tract which lies between Danforth and Linden Avenues, Syms conveyed to Matthew Armstrong, June 25, 1838, (Armstong died seized and his executors sold in lots at public auction in 1868) Syms sold a small part of his purchase lying N. of Danforth Ave. March 7, 1850 to Henry Rosencamp (now owned by Thomas Musgrove) and a small lot' to; Gilbert C. Smith. The residue Syms conveyed to Nicholas D. Danforth, Oct 6, 1855. Danforth mortgaged; the mortgages were foreclosed, the property sold and (the most of it) purchased by the mortgagee, Jane Brinkerhoff. It is now owned in parcels by Julia A. wife of J. Otto Seymour, John Kennell, Matthew Armstrong, Thomas Cary, Emma wife of Frederick M. Lockwood, Jacob J. Detwiller and Mr. Danforth (father of said N. D.)

Vreeland conveyed to Peter Julius Lignot, John Jacobs, Cortlandt Smith and another all lying between the Plank road, Ocean Ave. Linden Ave. and the S. bounds of the patent. All between Ocean Ave. and the old Bergen road, is now owned in small

East three chains & eighty five Links, Then South thirty two Degrees East five chains and thirty six Links. Then North eighty three Degrees and thirty Minutes East nine Chains and ninety Seven Links to a stake standing in the said Creek (where it is called a Swampy Creek) And from the said Stake South twenty Seven Degrees and thirty Minutes East ninety three Chains and ninety four Links to the Mouth of Straatamakers Creek on said Hudson's River or York Bay; Then Southwesterly along said Bay or River to the Place of Beginning.

The Patent of Petrus Stuyvesant to Lubert Gilbertse dated the fifth Day of December One thousand six hundred and fifty four, for a piece of Land lying at Mingackqua.

Our Survey whereof shews and we adjudge it to be a Tract (which on the Map is mark'd No. 20.)*

---

plots. To the Central R. R. Company of New Jersey, Vreeland conveyed all lying between the Bergen Point plank road and the E. line of the Railroad and Chestnut Ave. and Edwin J. Brown's line, except a small strip owned by the heirs of Henry Vreeland. The R R. Company mapped out this tract. They sold, July 15, 1866, to Harriet M. Winfield, eight lots on the S. E. Corner of Danforth Ave. and the plank road, and to Charles H. Winfield, June 10, 1867, eight lots on the N. E. corner of Linden Ave. and the plank road. The remainder of the land (except the right of way for the R. R. and a depot plot) they sold to the Hudson County Land Improvement Company, June 10, 1867. What lies E. of the Railroad is yet owned by the Vreeland family except a small plot given by George Vreeland to his son-in-law —Smith and by him sold to Cornelius Vreeland.

What lay West of the old road belonging to Mrs. Gautier was mapped by Adolph Loss in 1822 and sold in parcels as per Loss' Map; to William Anderson 15 acres Oct. 22 1831, and 13 acres Aug. 16, 1832; to Thomas and John Jackson six acres Oct. 22, 1831; and to John E. Post 15 acres, Oct 22, 1831. This last tract is now in possession of John Wauters and Dennis McCarron, (Lessee). A ten acre tract lying next N. of Post, Mrs. Gautier conveyed to Ephraim Morris, who conveyed to Andrew Van Horne, Feb. 6, 1834. He died seized, leaving *Jacob G., David L., John A.* and *Dorcas*, wife of James Kells. His executors, Henry R. Welsh and David L. Van Horne conveyed to these heirs, Dec. 31, 1859, who, on the same day, conveyed to Nelson B. Pearsall about 8 acres. Pearsall mapped, Aug. 5, 1864, and on Sept. 20, 1864, conveyed to George W. Dilloway six lots. David L. Van Horne owns the N. E. corner of the tract.

Fitje Segaerd's lands W. of the old Bergen road were sold by her heirs, viz: Jacob Cubberly, et al. in parcels, viz: to Jacob Ackerman 6 65-100 July 3, 1833; (Ackerman to Peter Rowe, March 4, 1841; Rowe to Samuel Wescott, May 9, 1850, Wescott to Gustavus A. Lilliendahl); to Walter Woods a little over six acres July 3, 1833; (Woods to Peter Rowe, Aug. 23, 1851, and Rowe to Agnes, wife of John Morrell, Sept. 4 1868); to Stephen Vreeland 11 91-100 acres, July 3, 1833, (now in part owned by his son Nicholas S. *Vide Note to Claesen's 1st Patent p.* 12

In addition to the above tract the Patent included a strip of land lying on the W. side 12 rods wide=5 Morgens; also a lot of Meadow "between Constable's Hook and Pembrepock" adjoining Barent Christian's land=12 Morgens.

*There is an error in the name of the patentee as here given. It should be Lubert Gysbertsen. The explanation may, however, be found in the fact that Gilbert is the English of Dutch Gysbert. By this name he received the Patent for this tract, bounded N. by Jan Vinge and S. by Jan Cornelisen Buys. It was 90x333½ rods =

Beginning at a Stake on the Northwest Side of Hudson's River or York Bay, (from which Stake the most easterly corner of Jacob Van Wagenen's House bears South Seventy Six Degrees and forty Minutes

---

50 morgens. There is a patent, *Land Papers (Albany) H.H.* 34, *Dec.* 5, 1654, to Jan Vinge, which answers the description, in size, given in Carteret's patent. This seems to be the only tract of such a shape. I have not seen any Dutch grant to Gilbertse. The same tract, at least 40 acres of it, seems to have been included in another Patent. *Vide Note to Jacobse's Patent*, p. 46. Van Wagenen received part of the commons allotted to Jacobe's Patent. p. 196,.

Gysbertsen died seized and intestate, leaving one son and two daughters. The son dying without issue, the land passed to the two daughters, *Anna* and *Gysbertje*, who, by two deeds dated Sept. 17, 1729, and April 24, 1730, sold the same to Charles Dorland, son of Gysbertje. Dorland sold the same for £50 to Jacob Van Wagenen, Dec. 14, 1730. He built and occupied the Point Breeze House, now owned by John H. Midmer.

Several of the heirs of Jacob Van Wagenen quit-claimed their interest in the testator's property, to Jacob Merselis; Henry Austin and Isabella, ux, March 16, 1816; Henry Heyzer and Elizabeth, ux, July 20, 1816, and Mary Merselis, Oct. 27, 1818. Van Wagenen died seized Jan. 27, 1783, and his surviving executor, Jacob Van Wagenen, *vide Note to Spier's Patent*, p. 15, sold it to Jacob Merselis and Merselis J. Merselis, June 22, 1824. It was then described as lying between the two bays, Samuel Gautier on the N. E. and Robert Thomson on the S. W. These grantees sold the right of way to the Morris Canal, Feb. 2, 1835. Merselis J. Merselis died March 21, 1837. By his will dated March 20, 1837, he gave his realty to his four children, viz: *Jacob M.*, *Susan*, wife of Thomas Anderson, *Catherine*, wife of Garret Vreeland, and *Mary*, wife of Stephen B. Vreeland, equally. These devisees then owned an undivided half with their grandfather Jacob. The property was partitioned by decree, dated June 18, 1838, as per annexed sketch. Jacob conveyed to his grandson, Jacob M. lots 1 and 2, June 21, 1838, on the grantee executing an agreement to quit claim to his sisters all his interest in Lots 3 and 4. This he afterwards did, the deed to Mrs.

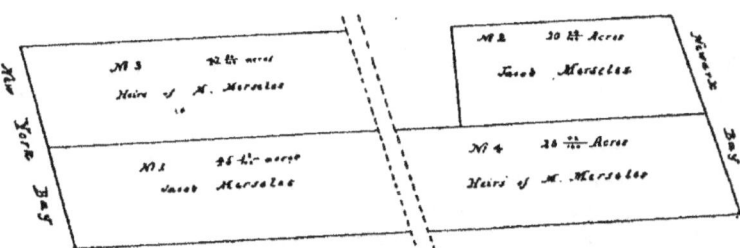

Anderson being dated, March 27, 1841, That part of lot No. 1, which lies S. E. of the Plank road, he sold to Edwin J. Brown, who sold a plot in the S. corner to John H. Midmer. That part of the lot which lies between the Plank road and the old Bergen road he mapped, (map filed June 29, 1866) and sold in lots to several people among whom are Michael Smith, Robert Drake, James Fleming, Matthew Armstrong and John Cadmus. His sisters partitioned lots 3 and 4, report confirmed, Dec. Term, 1841; Lot 3 in annexed sketch was divided into two parts, the N.=19 acres fell to Mary, the S.=22 88-100 acres fell to Catherine; Lot 4 fell to Susan, except 22-100 of an acre in the S. E. corner, which fell to Catherine. Catherine sold the E. end of her lot to Noah D. and Thomas Taylor in 1868.

West Seven Chains and Eighty Eight Links being the Southerly Corner and Place of Beginning of the immediate foregoing Patent) And from said Stake runs North twenty Seven Degrees and thirty Minutes West Sixty eight Chains and Sixty four Links to a Stake, Thence South Sixty two Degrees and thirty Minutes West eighteen Chains and fifty Six Links to a Stake standing below the Bank on New Ark Bay ; Thence South twenty Seven Degrees and thirty Minutes East Seventy one Chains and forty five Links to a stake on the Bank of said Hudson's River or York Bay ; Thence up along said River or Bay Northeastward to the Place of Beginning.

The Patent of Philip Carteret to Severin Laurens dated the twelfth Day of May One thousand Six hundred and sixty eight for a Piece of Land at Mingackqua formerly granted by a Dutch Patent to Jan Cornelison Buys.

Our Survey whereof shews and we adjudge it to be a Tract (which on the Map is mark'd No. 21.) *

*15 **Beginning** at a Mulberry Tree standing on the Edge of a High Bank on the Northwest Side of Hudson's River or York Bay (being the easternmost Corner of the immediate subsequent Patent of Hendrick Jansen Spier) And from said * Tree runs North twenty seven Degrees and thirty Minutes West fifty four Chains and Fifty Links to a stake ; Thence North Sixty two Degrees and Thirty Minutes East twelve Chains and twenty five Links to a Stake, Thence South twenty Seven Degrees and Thirty Minutes East fifty one Chains and twenty Eight Links to said Hudson's River or York Bay ; Then along said River or Bay Southwesterly to the Place of Beginning.

The Patent of Philip Carteret to Hendrick Jansen Speir dated the twelfth Day of May one thousand Six hundred and sixty eight for a Piece of Land lying at Mingackqua.

° This tract was originally granted to Jan Cornelissen Buys.—*Land Papers (Albany)*, H. H. 20. Buys, known as "Jan the Soldier," *vide Note to Jacobse's Patent*, p. 46, probably sold it to Severyn Laurensen, who seems to have been a wayward fellow. He was a lance-corporal in the service of the West India Company. His views upon *meum et tuum* were not accurate, hence he was, April 12,' 1658, sentenced to be stripped of his arms and publicly flogged and branded for theft. Awaiting execution, he was put in jail in charge of Corporal Simon Wautersen, but escaped. This caused the degradation of Simon to the ranks. Laurensen was re-arrested, but pardoned, May 12, 1658, with permission to live on Long Island. He then opened a tap-room, sold liquor "during divine service," for which he was prosecuted, May 11, 1662 ; and afterwards fined for permitting persons to play nine-pins in his place on Sunday. He was twice married, the last time to Grietje Hendricks, Aug. 5, 1671. He sold the tract in question to Hendrick Jansen Spier, who died seized, leaving his widow, Madeline Hanse (who married Jan Aertsen Van der Bilt, Dec. 10, 1681), and *Jan, Hans*, and *Barent*. To pay off the debts of Spier, the above-named parties sold this tract to Gerrit Gerritse (Van Wagenen, jr.,), April 10, 1694 This grantee gave it to his son *Jacob*. *Vide Note to Gerritse's Patent*, p. 58, and *Note to Spier's Patent*, p. 15. It now forms the N. part of Currie s estate.

Our Survey whereof shews and we adjudge it to be a Tract (which on the map is mark'd No. 22).*

Beginning at the Westermost Point of a large Rock in the Water at the Eastermost Side of the Mouth of a small Creek and thence runs through a Piece of salt Meadow up into the Woods North twenty Seven Degrees and thirty Minutes West forty three Chains and twelve Links to a Stake; Thence North Sixty two Degrees & thirty Minutes East Sixteen Chains and fifty five Links to a small Cedar Tree mark'd I. S. Thence South twenty Seven Degrees and thirty Minutes East thirty Seven Chains to a Mulberry Tree (being the southerly Corner of the immediate foregoing Patent of Jan Cornelison Buys) Thence continuing same course to Hudson's River or York Bay, and thence Southwesterly along said River of Bay to the Place of Beginning.

The second **Patent** of Philip Carteret to Dirck Sycan dated the twelfth Day of May One thousand Six hundred & sixty Eight for two Parcels of Land lying at Pembrepogh.

Our Survey whereof shews and we adjudge them to be two Tracts.

The First whereof (mark'd on the Map No. 23).†

---

* This patentee, with his wife and two children, arrived in New Amsterdam in the ship *Faith*, Dec., 1659.

This tract was originally granted to Jan Lubbertsen, Dec. 5, 1654. *Land Papers (Albany)*, H. H., 30. He probably sold it to the Patentee Spier. The Patent describes it in size 80x187¼ rods = 25 morgens, same as in the Dutch grant. This and the lot of Common land No. 23) allotted to the Patent now belongs to the estate of James Currie, dec'd. It remained in the patentee's family until May 1, 1768, when they sold it and lot No. 239 to Jacob Van Wagenen, by the following description: "The home lot, bounded N. W. by Newark Bay, N. E. by Jacob G. Van Wagenen, S. E. by Hudson's River, S. W. by the widow Van Winkel," = 100 acres. Van Wagenen died, Jan. 28, 1783, without issue. His will was dated Dec. 19, 1782, proved March 24, 1785. He named as executors, Effie his widow, Garret Vreeland his brother-in-law, Jacob Van Wagenen his nephew, and Guilliam Outwater. Jacob Van Wagenen, the surviving executor, sold to Robert Thomson the above described tract, together with the adjoining Patent, to Severin Lawrence, May 6, 1824. Thomson died seized, Dec. 14, 1841. By will dated Sept. 15, 1841, proved Jan. 5, 1842, he gave the land so purchased to his nephew, James Currie, who died seized, Feb. 3, 1870.

Jacob Van Wagenen sold to his grandson, Cornelius Van Buskirk, son of his daughter Beelitje, Dec. 10, 1774, three acres near the Bockie (on the point at Fiddler's Elbow), which he sold to Paul Salter, and by him sold to James Currie, and so again joined to the Spier Patent. By the same deed, Van Buskirk also received a lot one chain and 25 links wide out of the S. W. corner of the Patent, extending from the Plank road W. to Newark Bay, now owned by the estate of Michael Cadmus ; also a five-acre lot, bounded S. by Henry Fielding, W. by Newark Bay, N. by Van Wagenen, E. by the old road. One acre of this last tract he sold to Michael G. Vreeland, July 1, 1812. He died seized of the 4 acres, March 2, 1814.

By his will, dated July 10, 1793, proved May 14, 1814, he gave all his property to his wife Antje. The strip, one chain and 25 links in width, she sold to Col. Jasper Cadmus, Dec. 29, 1821.

† Lot No. 23 was 40x375 rods = 25 morgens. It was granted to Gerrit Pietersen, Dec. 5, 1654. *Land Papers (Albany)*, H. H., 33.

Begins at the westermost Point of a large Rock in the Water at the Eastermost Side of the Mouth of a small Creek (being the Southermost Corner and Place of Beginning of the immediate preceeding Patent of Hendrick Jansen Spier) And from thence runs North twenty Seven

---

Lot No. 24 was of the same size. It was granted to Jan Cornelissen, the shoemaker, Dec. 5, 1654. *Land Papers (Albany), H. H.*, 32. These two patentees sold to Claas Jansen Van Purmerent, Aug. 20, 1655, and he to Dirck Sycan, Sept. 18, 1658. Sycan's wife, Jannetje Tonis, died in 1659, leaving two children, viz.: Jan, aged six years, and Teunis, aged two years. When Sycan was about to marry again, he agreed with the Orphan's Court in New Amsterdam that, when these children became of age, they should each receive 400 guilders and jointly this tract at Pemmerpoock. As security he pledged his house in New Amsterdam, where Harman Smeeman formerly resided. *Orphan's Court, New Amst.*, 90. Yet he and his second wife, Geertje Jansen, sold it to William Douglas, May 31, 1674, for "one negro boy by name Emanuel."

Lot No. 25 (first Patent to Thomas Davison) was granted to Jan Gerritsen Van Imme, Dec 5, 1654.—*Land Papers (Albany), H. H.*, 31.

By him it was sold to the deacons of the Church in N. Y., and by them to Thomas Davison (Tames Davitson), July 14, 1665; by him to William Douglas, May 10, 1671. Douglas, being now the owner of the two lots in the Patent to Sycan and Davison's first Patent = 75 morgens, sold the same to Cornelis Michielse Vreeland, March 7, 1696, for £600. He received from the Proprietors, April 27, 1696, a confirmatory deed for the same, said to contain 150 acres, bounded N. by Jan Artse Van der Bilt,

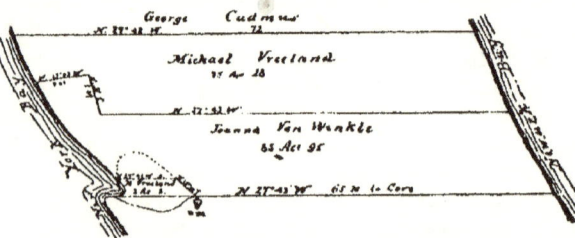

E. by Hudson's River, S. by Paul Douwesse, W. by Newark Bay.

By will, dated Oct. 12, 1713, Vreeland gave his lands to his children, viz.: *Fitje*, wife of Lawrence Van Buskirk; *Metje*, wife of Rynier Van Giesen *Aagtje*, wife of Roelof Van Houte; *Johanna*, wife of Daniel Van Winkle, and *Michael*. These agreed, Sept. 6, 1723, to sell the same to the highest bidder among themselves. It was bought, Nov. 29, 1723, by Michael Vreeland and Daniel Van Winkle, for £1,000.

Daniel Van Winkle died, Jan. 10, 1757. His widow and her brother Michael partitioned, Aug. 20, 1768. Johanna took the N. E. part, next to Van Wagenen's = 85 95-100 acres. Michael took the S. W. part = 75 28-100 acres, lying between his sister's and Joris Cadmus' (now Richard's) line. Michael took also about two acres on the N. Y. Bay shore at the Bockie. The sketch here inserted shows the lines of division. The map from which it is taken was made by Jonathan Hampton and Ephraim Terril of Elizabethtown, Aug. 1, 1768. By Daniel Van Winkle's will, dated June 3, 1751, his wife, Johanna, received this property for life. Then it went to her daughter *Antje*, wife of Henry Fielding. She sold, June 18, 1785, to Egbert Post a lot = 32 acres, 1 rood, 20 perches, lying W. of the present plank road, and including all her land there. She sold to Michael Vreeland, June 18, 1785, one acre on N. Y. Bay, at or near where Gunther's house now is. She sold, March 27, 1787, to Michael Vreeland, all the rest of her land lying E. of the plank road. Michael now owned all the land E. of the plank road, from Cadmus' line to

Degrees and thirty Minutes West seventy Chains and thirty one Links to a stake standing by the Edge of New Ark Bay Then along said New Ark Bay South thirty one Degrees and thirty Minutes West nine Chains and Seventy Links to a Stake standing on the Bank by the Edge of said New Ark Bay; Thence South twenty Seven Degrees and thirty Minutes East Sixty nine Chains and Sixty five Links to a small Heap of Stones by the Side of York Bay (from which said Heap of Stones the Easterly Corner * of Henry Fielding's Stone Kitchin is distant one Chain and twenty Links on a Course south fifty three Degrees and ten Minutes West) and from said Heap of Stones running Northerly along said York Bay as the same runs to the Place of Beginning.

*16

Currie's line, and the S. W. half of the farm W. of the plank road. By his will, dated July 16, 1802, proved Jan. 26, 1805, he gave all this land to his sons *George* and *John*. They partitioned, John taking the S. half, lying between Cadmus' line and Salter's lane. George taking from Salter's lane to Currie's line. They also partitioned the lot W. of the plank road. John held his half in tail; and died July, 1830, without issue, when the remainder vested in the heirs of George, who was dead. These heirs conveyed this land to Paul and David Salter, June 15, 1832. Paul quit-claimed to David, Nov. 16, 1835. George, by will, dated Nov. 6, 1822, proved Aug. 9, 1824, directed that his land E. of the plank road should be divided into four equal parts. 52d street (before right angling) became the division line N. E. and S. W. His son *Michael* received the W. quarter, also the S. half of the lot W. of the plank road. *Hartman* received the N. quarter, also the N. half of the lot W. of the plank road. *Garret* received the S. quarter, also three acres of salt meadow near the Bockie, now owned by John Post. Garret died seized, Feb. 10, 1852, and his quarter was partitioned

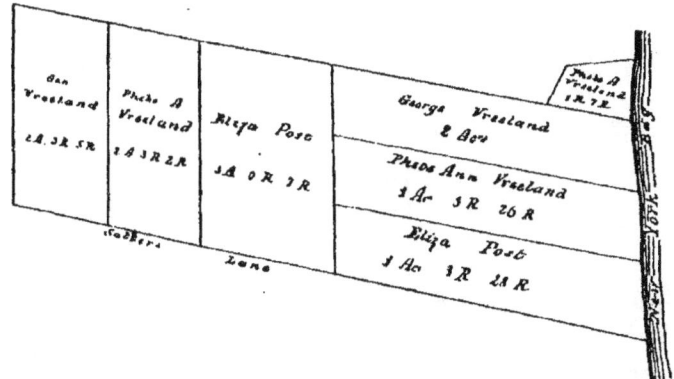

among his children, as per annexed sketch. *John* received the E. quarter, excepting the three acres of salt meadow. Hartman bought the E. and W. quarters, March, 1836. The land W. of the plank road, belonging to Egbert Post, was by him sold, Dec. 15, 1821, to Jasper Cadmus, excepting one acre which he gave to his daughter, the wife of Merseles Waters, where the mansion house lately stood. Cadmus sold the S. portion to Hartman Vreeland. By will, dated April 23, 1864, proved Feb. 17, 1868, Hartman gave to his adopted son, Hartman Vreeland, all his land between N. Y. Bay and the back road. The N. part, = 21 47/100 acres, Cadmus sold to William C. Vreeland, Sept. 17, 1836, who sold to Andrew Clerk, May 1 1854, who sold to the Hudson County Land Improvement Company, June, 1, 1867.

The second **Tract** (mark'd on the Map No. 24).

Begins at a small Heap of Stones (which said Heap of Stones is distant from the easterly Corner of Henry Fielding's Stone Kitchin One Chain and twenty Links on a Course North fifty-three Degrees and ten Minutes East, and is the Southerly Corner of the last mentioned Lot) And from said Heap of Stones Runs North twenty Seven Degrees and thirty Minutes West Sixty nine Chains and sixty five Links to a Stake standing on the Bank of New Ark Bay; Thence South forty Six Degrees and twenty Minutes West Eight Chains and sixty Links along the Edge of said Bay to a Stake standing in a small Gully; Thence South twenty Seven Degrees and thirty Minutes East Seventy two Chains and twenty one Links to a Stake standing on the side of York Bay; Then Northeasterly along said York Bay as the same runs to the Place of Beginning.

> **The** first **Patent** of Phillip Carteret to Thomas Davison dated the twenty second Day of December One thousand Six hundred & sixty nine for a Parcel of Land lying at Pembrepogh.

Our Survey whereof shews and we adjudge it to be a Tract (which is mark'd on the Map No. 25).*

Beginning at a Stake Standing on the side of York Bay (which Stake is the Southerly Corner of the Second Tract of the last recited Patent of Dirck Sycan) and from said stake runs North twenty seven Degrees and Thirty Minutes West seventy two Chains and twenty one Links to a stake standing in a small Gully by the Edge of New Ark Bay; Thence down along said Bay South thirty six Degrees and forty five Minutes West nine Chains and eighteen Links to a Stake standing between a Black Beech & a white Oak Bush on the Bank of said Bay; Then South twenty Seven Degrees and thirty Minutes East seventy two Chains and twenty Seven Links to a Rock mark'd C IV at the Edge of New York Bay; Thence Northeasterly along said York Bay as the same runs to the Place of Beginning.

> **The** second **Patent** of Philip Carteret to Thomas Davison dated the twelfth Day of December One thousand Six hundred and sixty nine for a parcell of Land lying at Pembrepogh.

Our Survey whereof shews and we adjudge it to be a Tract (which on the Map is mark'd No. 26).†

---

* Davison was an Englishman. In 1661 he purchased a sloop, and with a negro slave to assist him, did a freighting business between New Amsterdam and Albany. He lived in N. Y., and died in 1688. *Vide Note to Sycan's Patent*, p. 15.

† This tract was first given to Jan Cornelisen Crynnen, Dec. 5, 1654. Its only description was, as was the description of each Patent in this vicinity, "between Gemoenepaen and Kil von Kol." Crynnen sold it to Isaac DeForest, who received a Patent for it, April 17, 1664. The size was 40 x 375 rods. He sold it to Thomas Davison, of New York, April 15, 1665. Davison sold to Sjoert Olphertz, of Hooboocken, Feb. 11, 1670, a strip 20 rods wide out of the S. W. side of the tract, which Olphertz sold to Cornelis Steenwyck, July 29, 1681, and by him to Bartel Claesen, Oct. 5, 1681, and by Bartel Jacobs to Rutgert Van Horne, March, 1702. *Vide Note to Slott's Patent*, p. 17. The N. E. half of the tract Davison sold to Jan

* **Beginning** at a Rock mark'd G/V on the West Side of York Bay (being the Southerly Corner of the immediate preceeding Patent) and from said Rock runs North twenty Seven Degrees and Thirty Minutes West Seventy two Chains and twenty seven Links to a Stake standing between a black Beach and a white Oak Bush on the Bank of New Ark Bay, Then down along the Edge of said Bay South forty two Degrees and thirty Minutes West Eight Chains and seventy six Links to a stake in a Gully; Thence South twenty seven Degrees and thirty Minutes East seventy one Chains and fifty Eight Links to a stake by the Edge of York Bay; Thence Northeasterly along said York Bay as it runs to the Place of Beginning.

The Patent of Petrus Stuyvesant to Peter Jansen Slaat dated the fifth Day of December One thousand Six hundred and fifty four confirm'd by Patent from Philip Carteret to said Slaat dated the twelfth Day of May one thousand six hundred and sixty Eight, for a parcel of Land lying at Pembrepogh.

Our Survey whereof shews and we adjudge it to be a Tract (which on the Map is mark'd No. 27).*

Loosdregh, of Communipaw, May 6, 1670, who sold to Simon Jansen Romeyn, attorney of Poulesse Cornelisen, formerly of Pembrepock, Dec. 14, 1680, who sold to Jan Van der Lynden five morgens, May 31, 1681, who sold to Cornelis Steenwyck, July 29, 1681. Romeyn sold the balance of his purchase to Poules Douwesse, of Pembrepock, Dec. 6, 1682, who sold to Rutgert Van Horne, March 18, 1702. The history of this tract henceforth is connected with that of the next Patent.

° This tract was first granted to Gysbert Lubbertse, Dec. 5, 1654. *Land Papers* (*Albany*), *H. H.*, 36, and not to Peter Jansen Slott as mentioned in the text. It may have been granted to Lubbertse by mistake, for on the original Patent which I have seen was endorsed, "This Patent must be in the name of Pieter Jansen Slott, by mee, Guysbert Lubbertse, May 14, 1657." By both it was treated as if made to Slott. The tract was 40x375 rods. Slott sold it to Joost Van der Linden, Jan. 30, 1671. Van der Linden's heirs, viz.: his children, *Jan, Roelof, Jannetje, Hendrickje*, and sons-in-law, Albert Zabbristke, and Laurens Laurens sold it to Cornelis Steenwyck, July 29, 1681. On the same day Jan Van der Linden sold to Steenwyck the five morgens belonging to the preceding Patent, bought of Romeyn, May 31, 1681, also a piece of meadow lying between Constable's Hook and Bergen Point, bought by him of Samuel Edsall. *Vide Map in Note to Lot* 418, p. 155; also a house built by him on the land sold by Sjoert Olphertz to Steenwyck. Steenwyck sold this land and meadow and part of the preceding Patent bought of Olphertz to Bartel Claesen, of Middewout, L. I., Oct. 5, 1681, for 5,000 guilders of wampum, "in good and clean Long Island wheat or other winter wheat to be grown hereabout," deed to be given on date of first payment, Dec. 1682. It is probable that Claesen sold to Bartel Jacobs, the son-in-law of William Douglas, who sold, March 1702, to Rutgert Van Horne, a cordwainer, the land in Slott's Patent, also the five morgens of the preceding Patent, also the piece of meadow between Constable's Hook and Bergen Point, also the ten morgens formerly belonging to Olphertz.

It is probable that Van Horne was attracted hither from Hackensack by the widow of Jan Van der Linden, whom he married, April 25, 1697. When he purchased the whole of Davison's 2d Patent I do not know, but it was probably in 1702. He purchased the Van Schalckwyck Patent, in 1735. *Vide Note to Van Schalckwyck's*

Beginning at a Stake by the Edge of York Bay (being the Southerly Corner of the last recited Patent) and from said stake runs North twenty seven Degrees and thirty Minutes West Seventy one Chains and fifty Eight Links to a Stake standing in a Gully at the Edge of New Ark Bay; Thence along the Edge of said Bay South thirty six Degrees West ten Chains and twenty Links to a Stake; Thence South twenty seven Degrees and thirty Minutes East Sixty five Chains and fifty Eight Links to a Stake standing by the Edge of York Bay, Thence Northeasterly along said York Bay as it runs to the Place of Beginning.

The Patent of Petrus Stuyvesant to Hendrick Jansen Van Schalckwyck dated the fifth Day of December one thousand six hundred and fifty four, confirm'd by Patent from Philip Carteret to Hessel Veygerse dated the thirtieth Day of March One thousand Six hundred and Seventy five, for a Parcel of Land lying at Pembrepogh.

Our Survey whereof shews and we adjudge it to be a Tract (which on the Map is mark'd No. 28).*

Patent, p. 17. He sold to his son-in-law, Dederick Cadmus, Nov. 17, 1740, a lot 32x375 rods, bounded S. W. by Jacob Barentzen Van Horne, N. E. by land of grantor. This strip extended from bay to bay, and was within Van Schalckwyck's Patent. By will dated June 13, 1740, he gave to his daughter Jannetje, wife of said Cadmus, all his farm at Pamrepogh. In this farm was included all of the land in Davison's 2d Patent, and the Slott and Van Schalckwyck Patents, except what he had sold to said Cadmus. Cadmus had one son Joris or George, and two daughters. George received from his mother, by deed dated July 20, 1747, the lands bought from and devised by his grandfather Van Horne. It must have been to clear up some doubt that he received a deed from his uncle, John Van Horne, July 19, 1747, for a strip across the neck 40x375 rods (Van Schalckwyck's Patent), and also a piece of meadow (in Constable's Hook Patent), reserving, however, the right to the common lands which had been given to him by his father, by deed, dated Aug. 12, 1738.

This explains why the common land allotted to Van Schalckwyck's Patent was adjudged to Van Horne when he did not own the Patent. The allotments to these three Patents were likely to cause trouble between Van Horne and Cadmus. By an agreement in writing between them, dated Feb. 9, 1765, they bound themselves in effect to accept the allotments adjudged to each, and so avoided legal controversy.

By will dated June 27, 1779, proved April 14, 1786, George Cadmus gave all his lands at Pembrepock and Bergen Point to his sons *Dirck* or Richard, and *Caspar* or Jasper. Richard was a bachelor and sold to his brother Jasper March 12, 1819, all his interest in this tract. Jasper Cadmus, by will dated May 26, 1824, unproved, gave to his son *Richard* the S. W. half of his tract, and to his son *Andrew* the N. E. half. But Andrew dying before his father the devise was changed, so that Richard received the N. E. half, and still owns it. The S. E. half was given to the sons of Andrew in tail.

° The original Patent calls for 40x375 rods=25 morgens, *Land Papers* (*Albany*), H. H., 37, while the confirmatory Patent calls for 20 morgens; lying N. of Cornelis Abrahamsen and S. of Joost Van der Linden. Viggertse (Vygerse or Wiggersen) conveyed the same to his "friend Douwe Aukins of Schenectady Sept. 16, 1696. (This man arrived in this country in the Sloop, *Stetin*, Sept. 1663.) It was a gift; "Provided always in case the sayd Hessel Wiggersen should happen during his naturall Life to want naturall Sustenance, that then the said Douwe Aukins doth oblige

CATHARINE WALLINGEN VAN HORNE.   71

Beginning at a Stake standing by the edge of York Bay (being the Southerly Corner of the last recited Patent) And from said Stake runs North twenty Seven Degrees and thirty Minutes West Sixty five Chains and fifty Eight Links to a Stake standing by the Edge of New Ark Bay; Thence South thirty * two Degrees and twenty Minutes West, Ten Chains and twenty Links along the Edge of said Bay to a Stake between two Cedar Bushes (the Southermost of which is mark'd C) Thence South twenty Seven Degrees and thirty Minutes East Sixty four Chains and Seventy Eight Links to a Stake by the Edge of York Bay; Then Northeasterly along said York Bay as it runs to the Place of Beginning.

*18

The Patent of Philip Carteret to Catharine formerly the Widow of Jacob Wallingen Van Horne then the Widow of Jacob Stoffelsen dated the thirty first Day of March One thousand Six hundred and Sixty Eight for a Parcel of Land lying at Pembrepogh.

Our Survey whereof shews and we adjudge it to be a Tract (which on the Map is mark'd No. 29).*

---

himself to maintain & keep the sayd Hessel Wiggersen during his naturall Life in meate, Drinke, apparel, Washing & Lodging & to give a good & handsome funerall or buryall." Aukins sold the same to Cornelis Aresmith or Asmet of Schenectady, March 18, 1729, who sold to Rutgert Van Horne, Oct. 29, 1735, who gave the same to his son John, Aug. 17, 1738, with one third of the Common right belonging to his other lands at Pembrepogh. From this time its history is connected with *Slott's Patent*, p. 17.

* This tract was first granted to Jacob Wallingen from Hoorn, Oct. 23, 1654. *Land Papers (Albany), H. H.*, 28 = 25 morgens. *Wallingen* came over with Capt. De Vries in 1635, and was admitted to the rights of a Small Burgher, April 17, 1657. This patent was confirmed for the same amount, in size 45x333½ rods. It was in possession of Jacob Barentzen Van Horne in 1740. *Vide Note to Slott's Patent*, p. 17, whom I take to be a grandson of Barnt Christian, named in the next Patent. He died seized, April 14, 1775, leaving two sons, *Cornelius* and *John*. I have not seen his will though he left one, but his son *John* owned this tract, and prior to 1790, sold it to David Baldwin. Lot 276 of the commons and the N. end of lot 277, and the N. end of Barent Christian's Patent (number 30 on the field map), passed with the Patent in this sale to Baldwin, making a total of 115 or 120 acres. Baldwin sold the same to Cornelius Van Buskirk of Saddle River, taking in exchange land at the latter place, Sept. 13, 1792. Cornelius died, May 29, 1819. By will, dated May 3, 1803, unproved, he gave to his sons *Abraham, David, Cornelius,* and *James,* all his land equally. They divided as per this sketch. Cornelius' lot W. of the plank

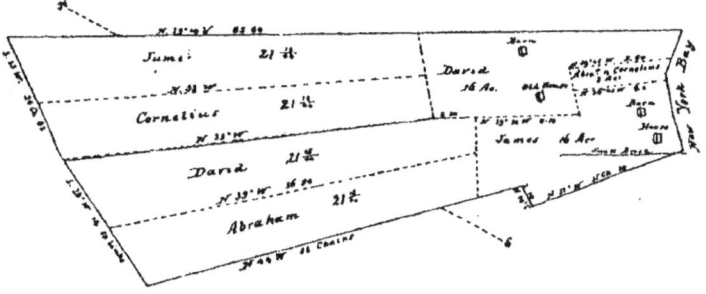

Beginning at a Stake by the Edge of York Bay (being the Southerly Corner of the last recited Patent); And from said stake runs North twenty Seven Degrees and thirty Minutes West Sixty four Chains and Seventy eight Links to a Stake standing between two Cedar Bushes at the Edge of New Ark Bay (the Southermost of which Bushes is mark'd C) Thence South forty Six Degrees and thirty Minutes West Ten Chains and thirty Links along said Bay to a Stake; Thence South twenty seven Degrees and thirty Minutes East Sixty Chains and twenty Links to a stake standing by the Edge of York Bay on the Easterly Side of a small Creek; Thence Northeasterly along said York Bay as it runs to the Place of Beginning.

The Patent of Phillip Carteret to Barnt Christian dated the twenty Sixth Day of March One thousand Six hundred and sixty seven for a Parcel of Land lying at Pembrepogh, and a Piece of Meadow lying at New Ark Bay.

Our Survey whereof shews and we adjudge them to be two Tracts.

The First whereof being a parcel of Upland mark'd on the Map No. 30.*

Begins at a Stake standing by the Edge of York Bay on the Easterly Side of a small Creek (which Stake is the Southerly Corner of the last recited Patent) and from said Stake runs North twenty Seven Degrees and thirty Minutes West fourteen Chains and ninety Seven Links to a Stake, Thence South twenty Eight Degrees and thirty Minutes West fifty five Chains and twenty nine Links to a Stake, Thence South twenty Seven Degrees and thirty Minutes East fifteen Chains and Sixty five Links to a Stake standing on the Edge of the Salt Meadow, Thence along the Edge of the said Meadow betwixt the Meadow and Upland to York Bay, Then Northerly along said York Bay to the Place of Beginning.

---

road was bought May 3, 1824, by James and David. Abraham's lot W. of the plank road was bought, and is now owned by John Serrel. His lot E. of the plank road is owned by the Elsworths. David died without issue. By will dated Jan. 4, 1865, proved March 1, 1866, he gave his property to his brother James and the children of his brothers Cornelius and Abraham, entailed.

º Lot No. 30 was bounded N. by Jacob Wallen's land, 44x200 rods=55 acres.

Lot No. 122, at Droyer's Point, was described as lying at the "north end of the lake that runs in towards Kil von Kul,"=30 acres.

Lot 30 lay about parallel with the meadow, and extended from the S. boundary of the preceding Patent to near the Constable's Hook Road. The accompanying sketch showing partition among the heirs of Cornelius Vreeland, includes a portion of this lot and of Lot 271, lying N. of the Constable's Hook Road.

Lot No. 122 was at an early day annexed to Andriesen's Patent, and was owned by the holders of that Patent in 1764. *Vide*

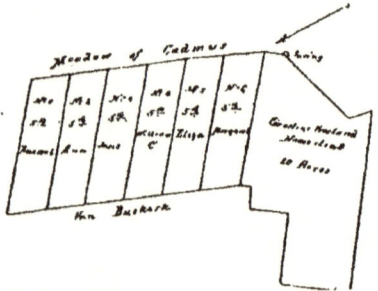

Note to Andriesen's Patent, p. 13.

* **The Second** of the said Tracts being a Piece of Meadow *19 (mark'd on the Map No. 122).

Begins at the Mouth of a small Creek near the Head of New Ark Bay (which Creek is the Northerly Bounds of the Patent of Lawrence Andrise (mark'd on the Map No. 19) and from the Mouth of said Creek runs across the salt Meadow North forty Degrees East twelve Chains and forty eight Links to a Red Oak Tree mark'd standing on the Upland near the Meadow; Then along the Edge of the Meadow North forty Degrees and thirty Minutes West two Chains and fifty nine Links, Then continuing along the Edge of the Meadow North Six Degrees West five Chains and ten Links to a Stake mark'd C V near the head of a Ditch or small Creek; Then down said Ditch or Creek as the same runs North thirty five Degrees and thirty Minutes West Eight Chains and Seventy Links; Then continuing running down said Creek as the same runs Northwesterly till it comes into Hackinsack River, Then down along said River as the same runs Westerly, Southerly and Southeasterly round the Meadows to the Place of Beginning.

The Patent of Richard Nicoll's to Nicholas Jansen and Samuel Edsall dated the twenty Sixth Day of October, One thousand Six hundred and Sixty four, for a Neck of Land call'd Nip Nickson lying at the Mouth of Kil Van Kul.

Our Survey whereof shews, and we adjudge it to be a Tract (which on the Map is mark'd No. 31).*

º Edsall was a native of Reading, in Berkshire, England, and a hatter. In 1655 he married Jannetje Wessels, a great belle in New Amsterdam, whose mother kept a tavern in Pearl Street celebrated for Burgomasters' dinners. In April, 1657, he was admitted to the rights of a small Burgher. He was appointed Ensign in the Esopus war of 1663. In 1664 he was the owner of a farm in Bergen and sent over four men to do his share in the defence of the place. *N. Y. Col. MSS.*, x., part iii., 67. After the surrender he swore allegiance to the British Government. He moved from Newtown, L. I., to Bergen, " in Col. Nicoll's time." He was a member of Carteret's Council from 1668 to 1672; appointed one of a Commission to assess and raise a tax to resist invasion, and treasurer of the same when raised in 1668; joined James Bollen and John Berry in petitioning the Dutch Government that the books and papers concerning the "Province called New Yarsie" be delivered to Secretary Bayard, Sept. 12, 1673; and was one one of the commissioners sent by Bergen to the same government. He moved to New York in 1689, became an active adherent of Leisler, a member of the Committee of Safety, of the Council, and of the Court of Exchequer. He now became an object of love and hatred, as he was considered by the friends or enemies of Leisler. The former called him "loyal," "honest," &c.; the latter thought him an "insipid mobile," "most wicked and poorest of the sons of men," "a base villian." He was involved in the fall of his chief, put upon trial for high treason, and acquitted. In 1699 he was living in Queens County, L. I. His daughter Anna married William Lawrence, of N. Y., and Julia married Benjamin Blagg, of Plymouth, England. To these two sons-in-law he gave all his lands in the lower part of Bergen County. It is said that he had two sons, Richard and John, who settled at Hackensack. John died in 1774, aged 54 years, leaving two sons, Samuel and John. *Annals of New-town.* 341.

This tract was known by its Indian name *Nipnichsen*, and was (at least 115 morgens of it) granted by William Kieft to Jacob Jacobsen Roy. *Land Papers (Albany)*,

Beginning at a Stone planted at the Southwest Point of a large Salt Marsh or Meadow at a Place call'd the Northeast Harbour where

G. G., 141. He was the *Konstapel*, or *gunner*, at Fort Amsterdam; hence the name. This grant was made in 1646. When the English came in 1664 the place seems to have been unoccupied and unclaimed. Therefore Gov. Nicolls made the following grant:

"The Governors Graunt to Nicholas
Johnson and Samuel Edsall.

To all to whome these presents shall come I Richard Nicolls Governor under his Royall Highness the Duke of Yorke of his Territoryes in America Send Greeting Whereas there is a Parcell of Land within my Government Commonly called or Known by the name of Nip Nickson upon the Maine which is not Inhabited or Planted but lyeth unmanured upon the request of Nicholas Jansen and Sam'll Edsall who have Purchased the said Lands from the Native Proprietors and for other good causes and Consideracons mee thereunto moving I do hereby Give, Confirm and Graunt unto the said Nicholas Johnson and Samuel Edsall the said Parcell of Land called Nip Nickson aforesaid containing by Estimacon five hundred acres or thereabout, being bounded with a Meadow on the North side extending to the wood Land and on the east with the North River on the South side with Kill Van Koll Together with all Meadowes, Woods, Pastures and appurtenances whatsoever thereunto belonging or *appertaining*. **To Have & to Hold** the said Parcell of Land called Nip Nickson and the Appurtenances unto the said Nicholas Johnson and Samuel Edsall their Heirs, Executors, Administrators and Assignes they planting and manuring the same within the usual time Allotted, And rendering and Paying to his Royall Highness, the Duke of York or his Assignes the accustomed Rent of the Country for the first Planters of Lands therein.

In Witnesse Whereof I have hereunto sett my hand and Seale at ffort James in New Yorke on the Island of Manhatans this 26th Day of October in ye yeare of our Lord 1664.

RICHARD NICOLLS."

On this Patent was endorsed the following:

Memorandum, That I Oratum Sagamore of Hackingsack Do hereby acknowledge to have received full Satisfaction of Nicholas Jansen and Sam'll Edsall for a Neck of Land about four hundred Acres lying and being on the Maine neare the Kill Van Cull agst the North side of Staten Island Comoñly called Nip Nickson with a Meadow on the North side of it And do herby acquitt them the said Nicholas Johnson and Sam'll Edsall for the same.

In Testimony whereof I have hereunto sett my hand this 6th day of October 1664 in N. Yorke on Manhatans Island.

Signed & Delivered in ye pr sence of	The Mark of
MATTHIAS NICOLLS, SECT.	X
FFRANCIS WALSALL."	Oratum.

The Johnson here referred to was Claas Jansen de Backer. *Vide Note to de Backer's Patent*, p 10. His interest in the tract was sold by Nicholas Bayard at Public Auction in N. Y., Sept. 22, 1670, to Samuel Edsall for 4620 Guilders, wampum value. Edsall sold to Jan Van der Linden a piece of meadow lying between the Hook and Bergen Point. This I take to be the piece of meadow adjoining the upland S. of the Constable's Hook road. *Vide Note to Slott's Patent*, p 17. It was owned by the Cadmus family in 1764, and even to a much later date. *Vide Note to Lot* 418, p 155.

the said Marsh or Meadow joins the Upland and Kill Van Kull; and from the said Stone runs Northerly along the West Side of the said salt

---

Edsall sold the balance of the tract to Hans Harmanse of Long Island, Feb. 20, 1694, for £562.10. Harmanse died Oct. 26, 1700. By his will dated Nov. 12, 1694, his daughter *Trintje*, wife of Peter Van Boskerk and his grandson Hartman, son of his deceased daughter *Annetje*, wife of Claas Vreeland, received the tract in common. Hartman Claasen sold his interest to his uncle Peter Van Boskerk, Dec. 17, 1730. By his will dated Jan. 20, 1735, proved Sept. 8, 1738, Van Boskerk gave to his sons *Johannis* and *Lawrence* 600 acres of land near Hackensack; to *Andries* 60 acres out of the tract in question, bordering on the Kills; the remainder of the tract to his son *Jacobus*. Jacobus and the widow of Andries were yet living in 1764. The four sons bound themselves in writing, Nov. 30, 1736, to divide the estate according to their father's will. Deeds of release for this purpose were executed July 20, 1738. By will dated May 24, 1762, proved Dec. 23, 1762, Andries gave his realty to his wife Margaret for life, then to be sold and the proceeds divided among his children. Helmus Vreeland and William Douglas were named executors. Vreeland the surviving executor sold the 60 acres of Andries to Israel Oakley, April 10, 1784; Oakley to Abraham Van Buskirk, Jan. 3, 1797. In 1798 Van Buskirk sold it to Thomas Hazard, deed unrecorded. There seems to have been an exchange of land between Van Buskirk and Hazard, the former receiving a lot in Frankfort st., N. Y. City, for his land at the Hook. Hazard sold 12 9-10 acres of Lot 270 to Andrew Van Horn Sept. 21, 1797 (Abraham Van Buskirk was a subscribing witness to this deed). This lot lay E. of the Plank road and N. of Constable's Hook road. Van Horn sold 5 9-10 acres to Michael B. Terhune in 1805, (deed acknowledged May 7, 1805,) and Terhune to Thomas E. Davis, Aug. 30, 1836. Davis mortgaged and the mortgages were afterwards foreclosed. Jacobus Van Buskirk died Jan. 3, 1767. By his will dated Sept. 14, 1765, proved Feb. 18, 1767, he divided his interest in the tract between his two sons *Peter* and *John*. The lot of Common land No. 418, adjudged to him for this Patent, he gave to them in common. Peter died June, 1819. By will dated April 1, 1816, he gave all his property to the children of his daughters, *Elizabeth*, wife of Cornelius Vreeland, and *Rachel*, wife of William Vreeland. These children were *Margaret*, wife of Henry Vreeland, *Eliza*, wife of Stephen Terhune, *Jane*, wife of Garret J. Vreeland, *Rachel*, wife of Henry J. Mandeville, *Anne*, wife of Michael M. Vreeland, *William C.*, *Cornelius*, and *Peter*. Among these the estate was partitioned June 3, 1830, and the proceedings confirmed in June term 1831. This sketch shows the partition.

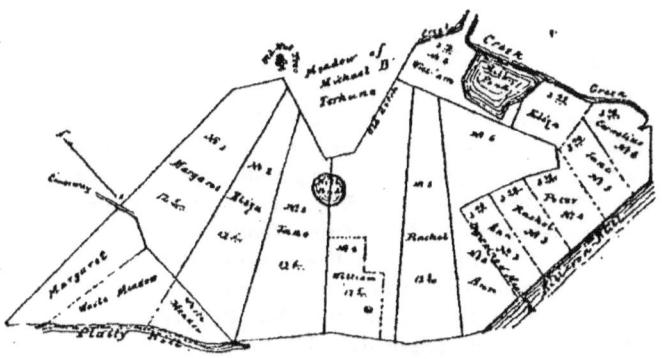

Marsh or Meadow where the same joins the Upland till it comes to York Bay near the House of Jacob Van Horne, Then running Southeasterly along said York Bay as the same runs to the Mouth of Kill Van Kull then running Westerly along Kill Van Kull as the same runs to the Place of Beginning.

The Patent of Philip Carteret to Mark Noble and Samuel Moore dated the twentieth Day of July One thousand Six hundred and sixty nine for sundry Parcels of Land lying in and about the Town of Bergen.

Our Survey whereof shews and we adjudge them to be three Tracts

*20   * **The First** is a Lot in the Town (mark'd on the Map No. 59.)*

Beginning at a Stake near the Northerly Corner of Peter Hessel

---

By several deeds from 1834 to 1836, the interest of these children became vested in Thomas E. Davis.

John left his interest in the tract to his only son Jacobus, who died Aug. 12, 1832. By will dated Sept. 28, 1823, proved Dec. 27, 1823, he gave all his realty to his sons *John, Nicholas* and *James*, on condition that they should not sell but divide it among their children. They partitioned, and the map is now on file in the county clerk's office. James' will was dated July 14, 1854, proved Sept. 4, 1856. *Vide Note to Lots* 418 and 419, p. 155.

° These lots were sold to the patentees by Samuel Edsall, July 15, 1669. They were merchants in Barbadoes.

Lot No. 59 lay in the N. W. corner of the town plot. On it was a kitchen, barn, and brew-house.

Lots No. 32 *and* 33 : One lay on the N. W. side of the town adjoining the N. W. gate; the other on the N. E. side, adjoining the highway.

Lot No. 39 was composed of two wood lots, each 14 rods wide, bounded S. W. by the N. E. lane "that goes into the woods."

Lot No. 64. The five upland lots were wood lots, each 19x150 rods. The five meadow lots adjoined the N. W. end of the five wood lots, and extended to the Hackensack river. Joseph Hawkins owned part of this lot, and died seized. Casparus Prior died seized of part of it, which he gave to his grandchildren by will. *Vide Note to Varlet's Patent*, p. 62. Jasper received this in the partition of his grandfather's estate, and sold 20 acres, extending from the E. end of the lot to a ditch to Peter Bentley and Stephen D. Harrison, March 1, 1856, the present owners. The balance of the upland was sold to Peter Bentley, Nov. 1, 1853, by the commissioners to divide the estate of Richard Van Rypen.

Roelof Van Houten and Maritje ux, sold, May 2, 1745, to Cornelius Brinkerhoff a part of this Patent, = 19 acres, 1 rood, 16 rods of upland, and 9¼ acres of meadow, lying between Zacharias Sickles and Hendrick Vanderhoof. This I take to be a part of *Lot* 64, afterwards known as Brinkerhoff's "Brown's Ferry Lot." *Vide Note to Backers Patent*, p. 10. It is probable that Johannis Van Rypen purchased Lot 39 shortly after 1764. His son, Garret—"Long Gat"—inherited it, and divided it by deed, Dec. 14, 1836 (vide also May 9, 1835), between his sons-in-law, viz.: *John G. Van Horne*, who received the N. W. quarter; *Daniel Van Rypen*, who received the quarter next S. E. of Van Horne; *John Van Buskirk*, who received the quarter next S. E. of Van Rypen, which he sold to Aaron Sergeant, April 1, 1837; and *Cornelius Van Winkle*, who received the S. E. quarter. Van Rypen's daughter, *Catlyntje*, wife of Helmigh Van Houten, died before her father.

Peterse's House (being the North Corner of the Town) and from said Stake runs along the Street on the Northeast Side of the Town South forty two Degrees East three Chains and twenty nine Links, Then South forty eight Degrees West two Chains and ninety three Links, Then North forty two Degrees West three Chains and twenty nine Links to the Street on the Northwest Side of the Town, Then along said Street North forty Eight Degrees East two Chains and ninety three Links to the Place of Beginning.

The Second Tract comprehends two Out Garden Plotts near the Town mark'd on the Map No. 32 & 33 Also two Lotts of Land adjoining together mark'd on the Map No. 39; Which Garden Plotts and Wood Lotts lying and adjoining together are comprehended in one Survey.

Beginning at a stake on the Northerly Corner of the town bearing from the most Northerly Corner of Peter Hessel Peterse's House North three Degrees and fifty Minutes West Seventy four Links; and from said Stake runs South forty eight Degrees West five Chains and fifty Links along the Street to a Road (commonly call'd the Middle Road) Thence along the said Road North eight Degrees West three Chains and ten Links, Then along said Road North five Degrees East Seven Chains and Sixty one Links to a Stake, Thence South Seventy five Degrees and fifty Minutes East twenty Eight Chains and Sixty Six Links to a Stake (standing in the Road that leads from the Town to the English Neighbourhood); Thence South forty one Degrees and thirty Minutes West Six Chains and forty Seven Links along said Road to a Stake (at the turn of the Road leading into the Town); Thence along said Road North Seventy four Degrees and thirty Minutes West Eighteen Chains and Sixty three Links to a Stake, Thence South forty Degrees West two Chains and sixty four Links to the Street, Then along the said Street North forty two Degrees West three Chains and Seventy Six Links to the Place of Beginning.

The Third Tract comprehends five Lotts of Upland and five Lotts of Meadow; which several Lotts lying and adjoining together are comprehended in our Survey (mark'd on the Map No. 64).

Beginning at a Stake standing in a Road (which Stake is the Southerly Corner of one of the Lots of Dow Harmanse's Patent mark'd on the Map No. 65) And from said Stake runs North fifty four Degrees and ten Minutes West seventy Seven Chains and ninety Links to Hackinsack River, Then returning to the Stake the Place of Beginning and running from thence South thirty Seven Degrees * West Seventeen Chains and eighty Six Links along said Road to a Stake (being the Easterly Corner of one or the Lots of Fredrick Phillipse's Patent mark'd on the Map No. 63) And from said Stake running North fifty four Degrees and ten Minutes West Seventy one Chains and fifty Links to said Hackinsack River, Then up alongsaid River as it runs till it reaches the first mentioned Line *21

The first **Patent** of Philip Carteret to Casper Stymats dated the twelfth Day of May, One thousand Six hundred and sixty Eight for two Parcels of Land and Meadow near the town of Bergen.

Our Survey whereof shews and we adjudge them to be two Tracts

The First whereof is a Tract of Upland (mark'd on the Map No. 34).*

Beginning at a stake (standing in the Road that leads from the Town of Bergen to the English Neighbourhood, which Stake is the Easterly Corner of the Lott of Mark Noble and Samuel Moore mark'd on the Map No. 39) And from said Stake runs along said Road North thirty one Degrees East seven Chains to a Stake Thence North seventy five Degrees and fifty Minutes West thirty one Chains and eighty four Links to a Stake by the Middle Road, Thence South four Degrees West Six Chains and Seventy nine Links to the Northerly Corner of the said Lott of Noble and Moore, Thence South Seventy five Degrees and fifty Minutes East twenty eight Chains and sixty Six Links (along the Northerly Bounds of the Lott of said Noble and Moore) to the Place of Beginning.

The second is a **Tract** of **Meadow** (mark'd on the Map No. 137).

Beginning at a stake (which is the Northerly Corner of a Lot of Meadow in Guert Garritse's Patent mark'd on the Map No. 136) and from said stake runs North fifty one Degrees and fifty Minutes West seventeen Chains and seventy three Links to Pinhornes Creek, Thence returning to the Stake the Place of Beginning and running from thence South thirty eight Degrees and twenty Minutes West eight Chains and ten Links to a Stake in the Westerly Corner of the said Lott of Guert Garritse, thence North forty eight Degrees West eleven Chains and two Links to Hackinsack River, Then up along said River as it runs to the Mouth of Pinhornes Creek, Then up along said Creek the several Courses thereof as it runs till it reaches the first mentioned Line.

---

* At what time Steinmets came to this country does not appear. In the spring of 1652, having lost his first wife, he married Jannekin Gerrits, of Zutphen, probably living at Harsimus at that time. For his third wife, he married Tryntje, the widow of Jacob Stoffelsen. He resided at Harsimus, and was driven out by the Indians in 1655. He went to New Amsterdam, where, on Feb. 22, 1656, he was licensed to tap beer and wine for the "accommodation of the Burghery and Strangers." *New Amst. Rec.*, ii., 85. He was admitted to the rights of a small burgher, April 11, 1657. *New Neth. Reg.*, 175. On the 21st of June he was appointed lieutenant of the Bergen militia. *N. Y. Col. MSS.*, x., 149; and on the 4th of September, 1673, was made captain. *Col. Hist. of N. Y.*, ii., 597. In 1674 he was a deputy from Bergen in the Council of New Orange, *Ibid*, 702; and a representative from Bergen in the first and second General Assembly in New Jersey. *Leaming & Spicer*, 77, 85. After his marriage with Stoffelsen's widow, he took possession of the West India Company's farm at Harsimus, and, as was always the case with the possessors of that farm, became involved in trouble with his neighbors, Van Vorst and others. *Col. Hist. of N. Y.*, ii., 704, 716. He died in 1702. His descendants, at one time, were quite numerous in this county, but they have long since died out.

Lot No. 34 was in the old maize land, 36x160 rods = 9 morgens, 360 rods.

Lot No. 137 adjoined Geurt Gerritsen's, and extended from Gerritsen's to the Creek = 6 morgens. This Patent was owned by Peter Merselis in 1764, who died April 1, 1770.

CASPAR STEINMETS. 79

The second **Patent** of Philip Carteret to Casper Stymats, dated the twelfth Day of May, One thousand six hundred and Sixty eight, for sundry Parcels of Land in and about the Town of Bergen.

* **Our Survey** whereof shews and we adjudge them to be five *[22] Tracts.

The first whereof (being a Tract of Upland and Meadow mark'd on the Map No. 81).*

Begins at a Stake standing by the Middle Road (being the easterly Corner of a Lot of Dow Harmanse's Patent mark'd on the Map No. 80); And from said Stake runs North Sixty Six Degrees and Thirty Minutes West to Hackinsack River, Then returning to said Stake the Place of Beginning and running thence along the said Road North twenty four Degrees East three Chains and Sixty one Links to a Stake (being the Southerly Corner of a Lot in Hendrick Teunise's Patent mark'd on the Map No. 82); And from said Stake runs North Sixty four Degrees and Ten Minutes West Sixty Chains and Sixty Links to said Hackinsack River, Then down said River as it runs 'til it reaches the first mentioned Line.

The second (being also a Tract of Upland and Meadow mark'd on the Map No. 66).

Begins at a Stake standing by a Road (being the Easterly Corner of a Lot in Dow Harmanse's Patent mark'd on the Map No. 65), and from said Stake runs North fifty four Degrees and ten Minutes, West Seventy Eight Chains to Hackinsack River, Then returning to said Stake the Place of Beginning, and from thence runs along said Road North thirty nine Degrees East Seven Chains and thirteen Links to a Stake (being the Southerly Corner of a Lot in Varlett and Bayard's Patent mark'd on the Map No. 68), and from said Stake runs North fifty four Degrees and Ten Minutes West Eighty Chains and eighty three Links to said Hackinsack River, Then down said River as it runs till it reaches the first mentioned Line.

---

a *Lot No.* 81 was in the new maize land, between Douwe Harmensen and Hendrick de Backer, was 20 rods wide, and extended from the road to the river = 10 morgens.

Lot No. 66 was a wood lot, between Douwe Harmensen and Nicholas Varlet, 38 rods wide from the road to the creek = 17¼ morgens, owned by Johannis Van Houten in 1764. *Vide Note to Lot No. 25, New Field Book.*

Lot No. 101 was a wood lot, and with meadow No. 5 in the original allotment = 16 morgens. It was sold by Steinmets to Elias Michielse Vreeland, May 2, 1678. Captain Thomas Brown owned this lot in 1764. *Vide Note to Andriesen's Patent,* p. 13.

Lot No. 116 composed of two lots: 1st, a lot adjoining Harman Edwards, 7¼x12¼ rods; 2d, a lot between Frederick Philipsen and Douwe Harmensen, 5x15 rods.

Lot No. 95 was 8x20 rods, between Dirck Teunisen and Geurt Coerten. The whole = 100 acres.

Lots 81, 95 *and* 116, were sold by the patentee to Siba Epsa Banta, and by him to Elias Michielse Vreeland, April 6th, 1693, and by him to Mattys De Mott, April 19, 1707. *Vide Note to Sloffelsen's Patent,* p. 9, *and Note to Harmansen's Patent,* p. 50. Michael DeMott sold Lot 95 to Cornelius G. Van Rypen. *Vide Note to Coerten's 1st Patent,* p. 25.

The Third (being also a **Tract** of Upland and Meadow mark'd on the Map No. 101).

Begins at a Stake standing by the Side of the Highway leading from the Town to Bergen Point (which Stake is the Easterly Corner of a Lot in Guert Garritse's Patent mark'd on the Map No. 102) And from said Stake runs North fifty Degrees and ten Minutes West twenty three Chains and Sixty five Links, Then North fifty four Degrees and ten Minutes West Sixty four Chains and sixty Links to Hackinsack River, Then returning to said Stake the Place of Beginning and from thence runs along said Highway North forty three Degrees and thirty Minutes East four Chains and Eighty Links to a Stake, Thence North fifty Degrees and ten Minutes West twenty three Chains and fifty three Links to a Stake in a Road (which Stake is the Southerly Corner of a Lot in Jacob Luby's Patent mark'd on the Map No. 62) and from said Stake runs North fifty four Degrees and ten Minutes West Sixty Six Chains and Seventy Links to said Hackinsack River Then down along said River as it runs 'till it reaches the first mentioned Line that runs to said River.

*23   * **The** fourth **Tract** (comprehends two Lots in the Town which being adjoining together are comprehended in one Survey mark'd on the Map No. 116.)

Beginning at a Stake (standing on the Northwesterly Side of the Street near the Southerly Corner of Michael DeMott's new Barn); and from said Stake runs North forty two Degrees West three Chains and forty two Links, Thence North forty eight Degrees East two Chains and ninety two Links to a Street, Thence South forty two Degrees East ninety seven Links along said Street, Thence South forty eight Degrees West One Chain and forty six Links, Thence South forty two Degrees East two Chains and forty five Links to the first mentioned Street, Thence South forty eight Degrees West one Chain and forty Six Links to the Place of Beginning.

The fifth **Tract** (being an Out Garden Lot near the Town mark'd on the Map No. 95.)

Begins at a Stake (standing on the Northwesterly Side of a Street South fifty Degrees West four Chains and Eight Links from a Stake; which last Stake stands thirty Links from the Easterly Corner of the Widow Van Riper's House on a Course South fifty eight Degrees and thirty Minutes East); And from the first mentioned Stake runs North forty one Degrees and thirty Minutes West, four Chains and eighty Links to a Stake, Thence South forty nine Degrees and thirty Minutes West One Chain and twenty seven Links to a Stake, Then South forty Degrees East four Chains and eighty Links to the Street, Then along the Street North fifty Degrees East One Chain and thirty nine Links to the Place of Beginning.

> **The Patent** of Philip Carteret to Adrian Post dated the twelfth Day of May, One thousand Six hundred and Sixty eight for sundry Parcels of Land lying in and about the Town of Bergen.

Our Survey whereof shews and we adjudge them to be five Tracts.

𝕿𝖍𝖊 𝕱𝖎𝖗𝖘𝖙 whereof (mark'd on the Map No. 35).*

𝕭𝖊𝖌𝖎𝖓𝖘 at a Stake (standing on the West Side of the Road that leads from the Town to the English Neighbourhood, which Stake is the easterly Corner of a Lot of Casper Stymat's first Patent mark'd on the Map No. 34) and from said Stake runs North seventy five Degrees and fifty Minutes West thirty one Chains and Eighty four Links to a Stake standing by the Middle Road, Thence North nine Degrees & forty five Minutes East Seven Chains and fifty five Links along said Road to a Stake, Thence South Seventy * five Degrees and fifty Minutes East, *24 Thirty two Chains and Eighteen Links to the first mentioned Road, Then along said Road South twelve Degrees and twenty Minutes West seven Chains and fifty one Links to the Place of Beginning.

𝕿𝖍𝖊 Second 𝕿𝖗𝖆𝖈𝖙 (mark'd on the Map No. 55).

𝕭𝖊𝖌𝖎𝖓𝖘 at a Stake (which Stake is the Southerly Corner of one of the Lots of Guert Coerten's first Patent mark'd on the Map No 54). And from said Stake runs North fifty five Degrees West twenty nine Chains and ten Links to a Stake by a Road, Thence running along said Road South thirty nine Degrees West three Chains and sixty seven Links to a Stake, Thence South fifty five Degrees East, twenty nine Chains to

---

° Post was agent of the Baron van der Capellen, and in charge of his colonie on Staten Island, when the place was destroyed by the Indians in 1655. *Col. Hist. of N. Y.*, i. 638. In October of that year he was appointed to treat with the Hackensack Indians for a release of prisoners, *New Neth. Reg.* 153, and ensign in the Bergen Militia, Sept. 4, 1673. He was the ancestor of the Post family, and died Feb. 28, 1677.

Lot No. 35, between Geurt Coerten and what did belong to Laurens Andriesen, 40x160 rods = 10⅔ morgens. This lot was owned by Cornelius G. Van Rypen in 1764. From him it passed to his son Daniel, then to his grandson Cornelius, then to his great-grandsons, Daniel and Cornelius, who yet own part of it. *Vide Note to Lot* 411 p. 166.

Lot No, 55: A wood lot, between Geurt Coerten and Jacob Luby, 10x150, rods = 4¾ morgens. This lot was owned by the De Motts in 1764. *Vide Note to Stoffelsen's Patent,* p. 9, *and Note to Harmensen's Patent,* p. 50. Michael DeMott conveyed to Peter Bently, March 29, 1850, and he conveyed a part of his purchase to Stephen D. Harrison, Sept. 7th, 1850. They yet own it. *Vide Note to Luby's 1st Patent,* p. 42.

Lot No. 117 was meadow lot No. 1 in the original allotment. 48 rods wide, stretching to the river = 21 acres. The patentee sold this lot to Jacob Jacobse Van Winckel, who sold it to Jan A. Sip, Oct. 16, 1707. *Vide Note to Coerten's 1st Patent,* p. 25.

Lot No. 164, on the corner by the N. W. gate, 7½x12½ rods : the whole = 55 acres. It was sold at an early date by the patentee to Cornelis Steenwyck, who sold it to Gerrit Gerritse, Dec. 2, 1681, who died seized Feb. 28, 1697, and by his will left it to his son Johannis. *Vide Note to Gerritsen's Patent,* p. 58. It remains in the family, and is part of the homestead of Hartman Van Wagenen.

Lot No. 100 was on the N. W. side of the town, on the corner S. of the wagon way. The patent calls for 55 acres in all. *Vide Note to Spiers Patent,* p. 15 ; *Note to Stoffelsen's Patent,* p. 9. Lot 100 belonged to Garret Van Rypen in 1764. He died seized, and his son George, of Saddle River, conveyed to Peter Sip, Sept. 5, 1836. It is now the homestead lot of Col. Garret Sip's family.

a Red Oak Tree mark'd D. T. Thence North forty one Degrees and forty five Minutes East three Chains and sixty seven Links to the Place of Beginning.

The Third (which is a Tract of Meadow mark'd on the Map No. 117).

Begins at a Stake standing by the Edge of Hackinsack River (which Stake is the West Corner of a Lot of Guert Garritse's Patent mark'd on the Map No. 102) and from said Stake runs South fifty four Degrees and ten Minutes East eighteen Chains to the Edge of the Upland, Thence South thirty Degrees West nine Chains and five Links along the Edge of the Upland to a Stake, Thence North fifty four Degrees and ten Minutes West eleven Chains and fifty Links to said Hackinsack River, Thence up said River as it runs to the Place of Beginning.

The Fourth (which is a Lot in the Town mark'd on the Map, No. 164).

Begins at a Stake (being the West Corner of the North Quarter of the Town and is two Chains and eighty five Links Distant on a Course South forty eight Degrees West from the West corner of the House Lot of Noble and Moore mark'd on the Map No. 59,) and from said Stake runs South forty two Degrees East two Chains and thirty two Links along the street, Thence North forty eight Degrees East One Chain and forty three Links, Thence North forty two Degrees West two Chains and thirty two Links to a Street, Thence South forty eight Degrees West One Chain and forty three Links to the Place of Beginning.

The Fifth (which is an Out Garden near the said Town mark'd on the Map No. 100).

Begins at a Stake (standing South fifty eight Degrees and thirty Minutes East thirty Links from the easterly Corner of the Widow Van Riper's House) and from said Stake runs South fifty Degrees West ninety three Links along a Street to a Stake, Thence North forty eight Degrees West four Chains and ninety Links to a Stake, Thence North forty nine Degrees and thirty Minutes East One Chain and twenty four Links to a Stake, Thence South Seventy two Degrees East three Chains and nine-
*23 teen Links to a * Stake by the Middle Road, Then along said Road South seven Degrees and thirty five Minutes East two Chains and fifty six Links to the Place of Beginning.

The first **Patent** of Philip Carteret to Guert Corten dated the twelfth Day of May, One thousand six hundred and sixty eight for sundry Parcels of Land lying in, and about the Town of Bergen.

Our Survey whereof shews, and we adjudge them to be Seven Tracts.

The First whereof (mark'd on the Map No. 36).*

---

* As early as 1646 this patentee obtained a lease of Van Twiller's farm on Manhatten Island, He was a soldier, and a member of the Burgher Corps in 1653. He was admitted to the rights of a Small Burgher, April 17, 1657.

Lot No. 36 was 28x160 rods=7 morgens, 28 rods. This lot lies on the S. side of Newark Ave., and extends from the Five Corners W. The N. part of the lot belonged

Begins at a Stake by the Road that leads from the Town to the English Neighbourhood (which Stake is the Easterly Corner of a Lot in Adrian Post's Patent mark'd on the Map No. 35) and from said Stake runs North seventy five Degrees and fifty Minutes West thirty two Chains and eighteen Links to a Stake standing by the Middle Road, Thence North twenty three Degrees and thirty Minutes East five Chains and

---

to Garret, from whom it descended to George Van Rypen, who sold 12 acres to Abel I. and Job Smith, Sep. 1, 1830. It extended W. to the back road from Riker's house at the "Five Points." The Smiths laid out their purchase into lots, and sold to different parties in 1836 and 1838. The S. part of the lot belonged to Altje Van Winkle, from whom it passed to her eldest son *Jeremiah*, then to his eldest son *Garret*, then to his eldest son Daniel G., who owned it subsequent to 1840.

Lot No. 48 was in the old Maize land, 14x150 rods=3¼ morgens.

Lot No. 54, a wood lot, 19x150=4¾ morgens. Owned by Altje Van Winkle in 1764. She had three children, viz., *Jeremiah, Catrintje*, wife of Jacob Merseles, and *Henry D.* Jeremiah purchased from his mother this lot, and gave it to his son *John G.*, who died seized Jan. 8, 1846. His executors sold to Jacob Van Winkle, who sold to Dr. Magaw, who sold to George Gifford.

Lot No. 91, E. of Samuel Edsall, butting on the Creupel Bosch, with the meadow =27 acres. Owned by Garret Van Rypen in 1764, from whom it descended to his son George, who sold it to Garret H. Newkirk. *Vide Teunisen's Patent*, p. 57.

Lot No. 94 formerly belonged to Dirck Teunisen, 8x26 rods. *Vide Teunisen's Patent*, p. 57.

Lot No. 97 was a garden plot, between Christian Pietersen and Geurt Gerritsen, 8x26 rods; owned by Cornelius G. Van Rypen in 1764.

Lot No. 147 was 7½x12½ rods. The whole=77 acres.

By his will dated Feb. 5, 1671, recorded June 1, 1671, the patentee gave to Thomas Juriansen (Van Rypen) his land next to Douwe Harmensen (i.e. lot 147), and two out gardens, one between Harmensen and Casper Steinmets (i.e. lot 94), the other between Steinmets and Harmen Coerten. Garret Juriansen by will dated March 14, 1745, proved April 8, 1749, gave to the children of his son Juriaen, viz.: *Gerrit, Aeltje, Beelitje*, one half of his three lots. To his son *Cornelius*, he gave the other half, also an out garden formerly belonging to Geurt Coerten; to his son *Johannis* (i.e. Beelitje's Haus, p. 170), he gave the lot and meadow formerly belonging to Balthus Bayard. The children of Thomas Juriansen, viz.: *Thomas, Garret, Johannis, Harman, Maritje*, wife of Claas Garrabrant, and *Christyntje*, wife of Cornelius Van Dine, sold to their sister Aeltje lots 147 and 94, May 15, 1722, who sold to her nephew *Cornelius*, the son of Gerrit, May 13, 1746. Cornelius by will dated Aug. 29, 1767, proved May 4, 1772, gave to his son *Garret* the dwelling-house and three lots adjoining, and the land N. of Pieter Merselis, also the meadow N. of the Bergen Mill, and 19 acres of woodland at Crommel's Point, also one half of all his other lands except what he gave to his son Daniel. To his son *Daniel* he gave the lot S. W. of Garret Newkirk, and the remainder of the woodland at Crommel's Point, and one half of all his other lands, except what he gave to Garret. How he came to own it I do not know, but Hendrick Van Ostrum sold to Jan A. Sip, May 20, 1711, one third of the out plantations of Geurt Coerten and Nicholas Varlet. *Vide Hendrick Teunise's Patent*, p. 54. Garret died seized Aug. 30, 1795. By will dated Feb. 11, 1795, proved Oct. 12, 1795, he gave all his realty to his brother Daniel, who divided his property between his sons *Cornelius* and *Richard*, giving lots 94, 96, 97, and 147 to Cornelius, who gave them to his son *Cornelius*. *Vide Note to Lot* 411, p. 166.

twenty six Links along said Road to a Stake, Thence South seventy five Degrees and fifty Minutes East thirty One Chains to the first mentioned Road, Then along said Road south ten degrees and fifteen Minutes West five Chains and twenty six Links to the Place of Beginning.

The Second (mark'd on the Map No. 48).

Begins at a stake (being the Southerly Corner of a Lot of Fredrick Philipse's Patent mark'd on the Map No. 47) and from said stake runs North fifty six Degrees and twenty Minutes West twenty nine Chains and sixty Links to a stake by a Road, Thence South thirty three Degrees West two Chains and fifty three Links along said Road to a Stake, Thence South fifty six Degrees and twenty Minutes East, twenty nine Chains and ninety Links to a Stake, Thence North thirty Degrees East two Chains and fifty three Links to the Place of Beginning.

The Third (mark'd on the Map No. 54).

Begins at a Stake (being the Easterly Corner of a Lot of Adrian Post's Patent mark'd on the Map No. 55) and from said Stake runs North fifty five Degrees West twenty nine Chains and ten Links to a Stake by a Road, Thence North thirty nine Degrees East three Chains and sixty Links along said Road to a Stake, Thence South fifty four Degrees and fifty Minutes East twenty nine Chains and thirty Links to a Stake, Thence South forty one Degrees and forty five Minutes West three Chains and sixty Links to the Place of Beginning.

*26   * **The Fourth** (being a Tract of Upland and Meadow and mark'd on the Map No. 91).

Begins at a Stake near the Road leading from the Town to the English Neighbourhood (being the southerly Corner of a Lot of Arent Lawrence's Patent mark'd on the Map No. 92) and from said Stake runs North sixty seven Degrees and thirty Minutes West nine Chains and twentyfour Links, Then North forty three Degrees West thirty two Chains and forty seven Links to Bridge Creek, Then returning to said Stake the Place of Beginning and runs from thence South sixteeen Degrees and five Minutes East five Chains and sixty eight Links along the Road to a Stake, Thence South ten Degrees West eight Chains and sixty one Links along said Road to a Stake, Then South fifty one Degrees West seven Chains and ninety five Links to a Stake, Then South eighty four Degrees and fifteen Minutes West three Chains to a Stake, Then North sixty three Degrees West seven Chains and seventy five Links to a Stake, Then South eighty eight Degrees and twenty Minutes West four Chains and eighty seven Links to a Stake standing near a small Brook Thence North four Degrees East one Chain and six Links to a Stake on the Top of a Hill, Then North nine Degrees and Thirty Minutes West sixteen Chains and thirty Links to a Stake standing in the Edge of the Meadow, Thence North forty four Degrees and twenty Minutes West fourteen Chains and fifty three Links to said Bridge Creek, Then up along said Creek the several Courses thereof as it runs till it comes to the other Line that strikes said Creek.

The Fifth (being an Out Garden Plott on the Northwest Side of the Town mark'd on the Map No. 94).

Begins at a Stake (standing on the Northwesterly Side of a Street south fifty Degrees West two Chains and sixty eight Links from a Stake which last Stake stands thirty Links from the Easterly Corner of the Widow Van Riper's House on a Course south fifty eight Degrees and thirty Minutes East) and from the first mentioned Stake runs North forty one Degrees and thirty Minutes West four Chains and Eighty Links to a Stake, Thence South forty nine Degrees and thirty Minutes West One Chain and thirty nine Links to a Stake, Thence South forty one Degrees and thirty Minutes East four Chains and eighty Links to said Stake, Thence North fifty Degrees East one Chain and forty Links to the Place of Beginning.

The Sixth (being also an Out-Garden-Plott on the Northwest Side of the Town mark'd on the Map No. 97).

Begins at a Stake (standing South fifty Degrees West two Chains and seventy three Links from the southerly Corner of the Garden Plott No. 94 last above describ'd) and from said Stake runs North forty Degrees West four Chains and Eighty Links to a Stake, Thence south forty nine Degrees and thirty Minutes West one Chain and * twenty Links to *27 a Stake, Thence south thirty nine Degrees and twenty Minutes East four Chains and eighty Links to the Street, Thence North fifty Degrees East One Chain and thirty five Links to the Place of Beginning.

The Seventh (being a Lot in the Town of Bergen mark'd on the Map No. 147).

Begins at a stake standing on the southerly Side of a Street (which Stake is two Chains and eighty two Links distant from the Easterly Corner of Widow Van Riper's House on a Course south thirty three Degrees West) and from said Stake runs south forty eight Degrees West One Chain and forty six Links along said Street to a Stake, Thence South forty two Degrees East two Chains and thirty two Links to a Stake, Thence North forty eight Degrees East one Chain and forty six Links to a Stake. Thence North forty two Degrees West two Chains and thirty two Links to the Place of Beginning.

The (second) **Patent** of Philip Carteret to Guert Coerten dated the twelfth Day of May, One thousand six hundred and sixty Eight for sundry Parcels of Land lying in and about the Town of Bergen.

Our Survey whereof shews and we adjudge them to be three Tracts.

The First whereof (mark'd on the Map No. 124).*

Begins at a Stake (being the Easterly Corner of a Lot of John Berry's Patent mark'd on the Map No. 125) and from said Stake runs South thirty eight Degrees and forty five Minutes East fifteen Chains to the Edge of the Meadow, Then returning to said Stake the Place of Beginning, and from thence, running South fifty one Degrees and fifteen

---

o *Lot No.* 124 was 48x92 rods = 7 morgens, 216 rods.

Lot No. 148, bounded N. E. by Guert Coerten ; S. W. by Pieter Rudolphus ; 7½ x12¼ rods.

Lot No. 96, lay "without the land port," 8x25 rods. The whole = 22 acres. This lot belonged to Beelitje's Hans, *alias* Johannis Van Rypen, in 1764, and must have been sold by him to Cornelius G. Van Rypen. It is now owned by Cornelius C. Van Rypen. *Vide Note to Coerten's 1st Patent*, p. 25.

Minutes West nine Chains and ninety Links to a Stake, Thence South thirty Eight Degrees and forty five Minutes East nineteen Chains to the Edge of the Meadow, Thence along the Edge of said Meadow and Upland as far as reaches the first Line.

The Second being a Lot in the Town of Bergen (mark'd on the Map No. 148).

Begins at a Stake on the Southeasterly Side of a Street (which Stake is four Chains and twenty three Links distant from the Easterly Corner of the Widow Van Riper's House on a Course south thirty eight Degrees and fifteen Minutes West) And from said Stake runs South forty eight Degrees West One Chain and forty one Links along said Street to a Stake, Thence South forty two Degrees East two Chains & thirty two Links to a Stake, Thence North forty eight Degrees East One Chain and forty *28 one * Links to a Stake, Then North forty two Degrees West, two Chains and thirty two Links to the Place of Beginning.

The Third being an Out-Garden-Plot on the Northwesterly Side of the Town (mark'd on the Map No. 96).

Begins at a Stake (being the Easterly Corner of the Garden Plott in Guert Coerten's first Patent mark'd on the Map No. 97) and from said Stake runs North forty Degrees West four Chains and eighty Links to a Stake, Thence North forty nine Degrees and thirty Minutes East one Chain and thirty four Links to a Stake, Thence South forty Degrees East four Chains and eighty Links to the Street, Thence south fifty Degrees West One Chain and thirty four Links along said Street to the Place of Beginning.

The (third) **Patent** of Philip Carteret to Guert Coerten, dated the twenty first Day of March One thousand Six hundred and seventy for a Piece of Meadow lying Northerly of Town (mark'd on the Map No. 139).*

Our Survey whereof shews and we adjudge it to be a Tract.

Beginning at a Stake standing on the Northwest Side of Bridge Creek (which Stake is the eastermost Corner of a Meadow Lot in Angleburt Stienhuysen's Patent mark'd on the Map No. 138) and from said Stake runs North fifty one Degrees and fifty Minutes West forty Chains and ten Links to a Stake by a very small Creek or Worm, Thence North fifty eight Degrees and forty Minutes East eleven Chains and seventy eight Links to a Stake, Thence North two Degrees and fifteen Minutes East four Chains and ninety one Links to a Stake, Thence South forty three Degrees and forty five Minutes East thirty five Chains and fifty Links to said Bridge Creek, Thence down along said Bridge Creek as it runs to the Place of Beginning.

The Patent of Philip Carteret to Fredrick Philipse dated the twelfth Day of May one thousand six hundred and sixty eight for sundry Parcels of Land lying in and about the Town of Bergen.

º Beginning at the N. W. Corner of Steenhuysen's meadow, then along the Creek 15 chains, then S. E. 30 chains to another Creek, then along said Creek 12 chains. then N. W. 32 chains to the beginning=40 acres.

FREDERICK PHILLIPSE.

Our Survey whereof shews and we adjudge them to be twelve Tracts.

The First whereof (mark'd on the Map No. 37).*

---

* *Phillipse* was one of the richest men in the country. His name first appears in 1655. He was largely engaged in the Indian fur trade. He married 1st Margaret Van Hardenbrook, widow of Pieter Rudolphus; 2d Catherine, daughter of Oloff Stevenson Van Courtlandt, widow of John Dervall. He died on his estate at Tarrytown in 1702.

Lot No. 37, between Guert Coerten and Paulus Pieterse, 20 rods wide=5¼ morgens, bounded S. by Newark Ave.

Lot No. 74, between Jan Scholten and Adrian Hendricksen, 6 rods wide=4 morgens. This lot was owned by Abraham Diedricks in 1764.—*Vide Note to Lot* 404, p. 174.

Lot No. 63, between same parties, 18 rods wide, with the meadow=7 morgens, owned by Garret Newkirk in 1764. This lot is now in part owned by the heirs of Nathaniel C. Slaight.

Lot No. 60, a triangle between Jan Scholten and the out gardens=3¼ morgens. The S. half of this lot was owned by Peter Merselis and the N. half by Cornelius and Garret Sip, sons of Ide, in 1764. The N. half yet remains in the Sip family, and was the homestead of the late Col. Garret. *Vide Note to Van Vorst's Patent*, p. 60. The S. half descended in the Merselis family until after 1840, when it was owned by Altje Merselis, daughter of John, and wife of James Parks. *Vide Note to Lot* 11, *New Field Book.*

Lot No. 47, in the old maize land, between Guert Coerton and Paulus Pietersen, 1 rods wide=3¼ morgens, owned by Garret Newkirk in 1764. This lot and lot 46 in Pieterse's Patent in the partition of Newkirk's property fell to Hendrick. He gave the two=15 acres, with his other lands, to his sons *Garret H.* and *George*. On partition between them, July 24, 1835, George released them to Garret who conveyed in trust this and other property to George Newkirk and Hartman Van Wagenen, Sept. 14, 1835. George conveyed an undivided half to Van Wagenen, July 17, 1861. Van Wagenen to John N. Carnes, July 25, 1866, who declared a trust to John Anness and Edward F. C. Young for two-thirds, Sept. 13, 1838. Carnes et al. filed a map of nine plots, bounded N. by Church Street, March 16, 1869. Carnes, Young, et al. reside on Lot 46; James S. De Mott et al. on Lot 47.

Lot No. 53, a wood lot between the same parties, 19 rods wide=4¾ morgens, owned by Garret Newkirk in 1764. *Vide Note to Pieterse's Patent*, p 40. This was the lot which Aaron took in the division, and sold to his daughter Catherine, wife of Cornelius M. Vreeland, July 1, 1832, as mentioned in that Note.

Lot No. 86, a wood lot between Jan Scholten and Adrian Hendricksen, 19 rods wide=10 morgens, owned by Peter Merselis in 1764. It remained in his descendants until after 1840.

Lot No. 142, a piece of meadow over the Creek towards Snake Hill.

Lots Nos. 149 and 151, one between Harman Edwards and Thomas De Cuyper, the other between De Cuyper and Guert Coerten, each 7½x12¼ rods.

Lot No. 150, adjoining Casper Steinmets, 5½x7½ rods, owned by Cornelius Diedricks in 1764. He had one child, *Aeltje* who married Johannis Winne, Dec. 10, 1758. *Vide Note to Lot* 406, p 175. Under Cornelius' will his nephew Daniel seems to have obtained this lot. He died seized April 8, 1822, and his widow Effie conveyed it to Abraham Collerd, May 3, 1822. *Vide Note to Lot* 358, p 179.

Begins at a Stake by the Road that leads from the Town to the English Neighbourhood (which Stake is the Easterly Corner of a Lot in Guert Coerten's Patent * mark'd on the Map No. 36) and from said Stake runs North seventy five Degrees and fifty Minutes West thirty one Chains to a Stake standing by the Middle Road, Thence North twenty five Degrees and thirty Minutes East three Chains and eighty two Links along said Road to a Stake, Thence South seventy five Degrees and fifty Minutes East thirty Chains and forty Links to the first mentioned Road, Thence South fourteen Degrees and ten Minutes West three Chains and Seventy five Links along said Road to the Place of Beginning.

*29

The Second (which is mark'd on the Map No. 74).

Begins at a Stake standing on the Westerly Side of the Middle Road (which Stake is the Easterly Corner of a Lot in Jacob Luby's Patent mark'd on the Map No. 61). And from said Stake runs North sixty nine Degrees and ten Minutes West forty nine Chains and eighty Links to a Stake by the Edge of a Meadow, Then North thirty eight Degrees East three Chains and forty Links along said Meadow Edge to a Stake, Thence South sixty eight Degrees and forty Minutes East forty eight Chains to a Stake by said Middle Road, Thence South four Degrees West two Chains and eighty eight Links along said Road to the Place of Beginning.

The Third (which is a Tract of Upland and Meadows mark'd on the Map No. 63).

Begins at a Stake standing by a Road (being the southerly Corner of the Lott in Noble and Moore's Patent. mark'd on the Map No. 64) and from said Stake runs North fifty four Degrees and ten Minutes West seventy one Chains fifty Links to Hackinsack River ; and then returning to said Stake the Place of Beginning, and thence running south forty Degrees West three Chains and sixty Links along said Road to a Stake, Thence North fifty four Degrees and ten Minutes West seventy Chains to said Hackinsack River, Thence up along said River as it runs till it reaches the first mentioned Line.

The Fourth (mark'd on the Map No. 60).

Begins at a Stake standing by a Road (being the Westerly Corner of a Garden Plott in Arent Lawrence's Patent mark'd on the Map No. 99) and from said Stake runs North fifty six Degrees and forty Minutes West seventeen Chains & thirty six Links to a Stake standing in the Corner of said Road, Thence North twenty eight Degrees and fifty Minutes East six Chains and thirty Links to a Stake, Thence south sixty nine Degrees and ten Minutes East twenty one Chains and sixty Links to a

---

* Lot No. 41, a double garden plot adjoining De Cuyper, 16x20 rods. The whole= 98 acres.

So far I as have discovered the patentee died seized. By his will dated Oct. 16, 1700, Phillip French of London, then of New Brunswick, who had married his daughter, Annetje, July 8, 1694, became the owner of all his lands in Bergen. French sold to Ide Sip, June 4, 1752, a house lot in the town and a large out garden=15 acres. My opinion is that the house lot referred to was lot No. 151 on the N. W. corner of Bergen Square, which the Sips afterwards sold to the church, by whom it is now owned. Vide Note to Van Vorst's Patent, p 60, and Note to Lot 285, p 109.

Stake, Thence south forty nine Degrees and thirty Minutes West eleven Chains and thirty two Links to the Place of Beginning.

* The Fifth (mark'd on the Map No. 47) *30

Begins at a Stake (being the Easterly Corner of a Lot in Guert Coerten's first Patent Mark'd on the Map No. 48) and from said Stake runs North fifty six Degrees and twenty Minutes West twenty nine Chains and seventy five Links to a Stake by a Road, Thence North thirty six Degrees and twenty Minutes East two Chains & fifty five Links along said Road to a Stake, Thence South fifty six Degrees and forty Minutes East twenty nine Chains and sixty Links to a Stake, Thence South thirty Degrees West two Chains and seventy two Links to the Place of Beginning.

The Sixth (mark'd on the Map No. 53)

Begins at a Stake (being the Easterly Corner of a Lott in Guert Coerten's first Patent mark'd on the Map No. 54). And from said Stake runs North fifty four Degrees and fifty Minutes West, twenty nine Chains and thirty Links to a Stake in a Road, Thence North thirty nine Degrees East three Chains and sixty seven Links along said Road to a Stake, Thence South fifty four Degrees and fifty Minutes East twenty nine Chains and forty six Links to a Stake, Thence South forty one Degrees and forty five Minutes West three Chains and sixty eight Links to the Place of Beginning.

The Seventh (being a Tract of Upland and Meadow mark'd on the Map No. 86)

Begins at a Stake by the Middle Road (which Stake is the Southerly Corner of a Lot of Jacob Luby's Patent marked on the Map No. 87) And from said Stake runs North forty eight Degrees West sixty eight Chains and fifty Links to Hackinsack River to a Stake standing South thirty six Degrees and twenty Minutes East nine Chains and eighty six Links from the Mouth of Pinhorne's Creek, Then returning to said Stake the Place of Beginning and from thence running South twenty one Degrees and thirty Minutes West five Chains and seventy three Links along said Road to a Stake, Thence North forty eight Degrees West sixty one Chains and twenty Links to said Hackinsack River, Then up along said River as it runs as far as reaches the first mentioned Line.

The Eighth (being a Tract of Meadow mark'd on the Map No. 142)

Begins at Pinhornes Creek at the Northwesterly End of a Ditch which communicates from said Pinhornes Creek to Bridge Creek to prevent the Catle running into the Patented Meadows And from thence runs along said Ditch South forty two Degrees East forty eight Chains and thirty eight Links to said Bridge Creek, Then down said Creek as it runs to a Stake standing South twenty one Degrees and thirty Minutes West three Chains and forty six Links from the southeasterly End of said Ditch, and from said * stake runs North forty three Degrees and forty five Minutes West thirty five Chains and fifty Links to a Stake, *31 Thence North two degrees and fifteen Minutes East one Chain to the Easterly Corner of a Lot of Meadow in the Patent of Thomas De Cuper (mark'd on the Map No. 141), Thence North forty two Degrees West fourteen Chains and twenty nine Links along the Line of said De Cuyper's

Meadow to Pinhorne's Creek, then up along Pinhorne's Creek as it runs to the Place of Beginning.

The Ninth (being a Lot in the Town of Bergen mark'd on the Map No. 149)

Begins at a Stake on the Southeasterly Side of a Street (which Stake is five Chains and Sixty five Links distant from the Easterly Corner of the Widow Van Riper's House on a Course south forty Degrees and forty five Minutes West,) and from said Stake runs South forty eight Degrees West one Chain and forty one Links along said Street to a Stake at the West Corner of the Town, Thence South forty two Degrees East two Chains and thirty two Links along another Street to a Stake, Thence North forty eight Degrees East one Chain and forty one Links to a Stake, Thence North forty two Degrees West two Chains and thirty two Links to the Place of Beginning.

The Tenth (being another Lot in the Town mark'd on the Map No. 150)

Begins at a Stake standing South forty two Degrees East ninety seven Links from the Easterly Corner of a Town Lot in the Patent of Dow Harmense mark'd on the Map No. 161), And from said Stake runs South forty two Degrees East One Chain and sixty one Links along the Street to the Town Square, Thence South forty eight Degrees West One Chain and forty six Links to a Stake, Thence North forty two Degrees West One Chain and Sixty one Links to a Stake, Then North forty eight Degrees East One Chain and forty six Links to the Place of Beginning.

The Eleventh (being another Lott in the Town mark'd on the Map No. 151)

Begins at a Stake (standing in the Square of the Town North forty Eight Degrees East sixty three Links from the Easterly Corner of the last described Town Lot No. 150) and from said Stake runs North forty eight Degrees East one Chain and forty six Links along said Square to a Stake, Thence North forty two Degrees West one Chain and fifty eight Links to a Stake Thence South forty eight Degrees West One Chain and forty six Links to the Street, Thence South forty two Degrees East One Chain and fifty eight Links along said Street to the Place of Beginning.

The Twelfth (being an Out Garden Plot on the Southwest Corner of the Town mark'd on the Map No. 41)

32* * **Begins** at a Stake standing by a Street (which Stake is the Northerly Corner of an Out Garden Plot in the Patent of Thomas De Cuyper mark'd on the Map No. 42) and from said Stake runs North forty three Degrees West three Chains and six Links to the Corner of a Road, Thence South forty four Degrees and forty Minutes West, three Chain and three Links to a Stake, Thence South fifty five Degrees and ten Minutes East two Chains and ninety three Links to a Stake, Thence North forty eight Degrees East two Chains and forty four Links to said Street the Place of Beginning.

> **The Patent** of Philip Carteret to Englebert Steinheysen dated the twenty second Day of July One thousand six hundred and seventy for sundry Parcels of Land in and about the Town of Bergen.

𝕺ur 𝖘urvey whereof shews and we adjudge them to be seven Tracts.

𝕿he 𝕱irst whereof (mark'd on the Map No. 38)*

---

* This patentee was a tailor by trade, and came from Soest, the second city in Westphalia; arrived in New Amsterdam in the ship *Moesman,* April 25, 1659. He has the honor of being the first schoolmaster in Bergen, having been licensed by the Director-General, Oct. 6, 1662. *New Neth. Reg.,* 133; *N. Y. Col. MSS.,* x., pt. 2, 439. He was made schepen in Bergen, Oct. 13, 1662, and Aug. 31, 1674. With Harman Smeeman he represented Bergen in the "Landtag" in 1634. *Broadhead,* i., 729.

Lot No. 38, in the new maize land, 40x160 = 10⅘ morgens, owned by Hendrick Van Winkle in 1764. *Vide Note to Teunise's Patent,* p. 54.

Lot No. 40 was of same size, N. W. of Tielman Van Vleck = 21¼ acres.

Lot No. 89, N. W. of the highway, S. E. of a swamp, 90x83 rods = 13 1-5 morgens. Lots 40 and 89 belonged to Daniel Diedricks in 1764. *Vide Note to Lot* 317, p. 176 *Note to Diedricks' Patent,* p. 56. Charles E. Newham recently occupied the old Sickles house, close by the reservoir. Daniel Simonson conveyed all his interest in the Diedricks farm to Elizabeth Harding, March 2, 1840, who conveyed to Hartman Vreeland and David M. Demarest, March 4, 1840.

Lot No. 90, a farm that was Samuel Edsall's = 10 morgens, 130 rods, owned by Johannis Van Wagenen in 1764. *Vide Note to Gerritse's Patent,* p. 58. By Jacob's will this lot was given to the children of his son *John,* viz.: Cornelius, Jacob, and Christiana. It adjoins the reservoir.

Lot No. 138, meadow adjoining Geurt Coerten = 20 morgens.

Lot No. 152, a house lot between Derrick Gerritse and the "Plain." Sold by William Day to Mattys De Mott Dec. 2, 1708. *Vide Note to Stoffelsen's Patent,* p. 9.

Lot No. 139 does not seem to be included in the Patent, although the Commissioners so adjudge. The whole = 150 acres *Vide New Field Book and Map B.*

Steenhuysen died seized, leaving a widow and three sons, viz.: *Stephen, Joost,* and *Pieter.* By his will, dated Dec. 13, 1677, proved April 9, 1678, Claas and Jan Arentse Toers were named executors with power to sell. In his lifetime the patentee had sold a house and planter's lot = 1½ lots to Laurent Arentse Toers, who sold the same to Jacob Jacobsen Van Winckel, who sold to Jan A. Sip. This sale was confirmed to Sip by the executors, May 22, 1711. It lay adjacent to the lot sold to Sip by Van Voorst, 7¾x17½ rods. Frederick Thomase sold to Hendrick Sickles "land in and about the town," Oct. 10, 1732. Whatever passed by this sale, I think, must have been within this Patent. Sickles, by will, dated June, 22, 1776, proved May 12, 1783, gave to his sons, *Derrick* and *John,* all his lands.

Wander Diedericks bought, Dec. 16, 1710, of the executors of the patentee, 5 morgens in the S. E. corner of lot 138, of which he died seized and intestate. *Vide Note to Diedericks' Patent,* p. 56. It was partitioned, as per *Note to Lot* 317, p. 176, the wife of Simonson taking the S. half, and the heirs of Cellerd the N. half.

Claas Arentse Toers died seized of a part of this Patent, leaving his widow, Jacomyntje, and children, *Arent, Judith,* wife of Gerrit Roos, and *Petertje.* His widow's will was dated May 26, 1730; proved Jan. 9, 1744. His son, Arent, received his property. The following facts relating to the Toers (or Tuers) family may assist in tracing title to some of the lands owned by that family. Claes Arentse Toers m. Jacomyntje Van Neste, July 6, 1684, d. Oct. 10, 1724. Arent, named in his mother's will, was b. June 10, 1699; m. Annetje Spier, July 19, 1730. He had three daughters and one son—Nicholas, b. March 23, 1737; m. Jannetje Van Rypen, May 11, 1766.

Begins at a Stake standing by the Road that leads from the Town to the English Neighbourhood which Stake is the Easterly Corner of a Lot in Fredrick Philipse's Patent (mark'd on the Map No. 37) and from said Stake runs North Seventy five Degrees and fifty Minutes West thirty Chains & forty Links to a Stake by the Middle Road, Then North twenty five Degrees and twenty five Minutes East seven Chains and sixty four Links along said Road to a Stake, Thence south seventy five Degrees and fifty Minutes East twenty eight Chains and ninety Links to the first mentioned Road, Thence south fourteen Degrees and ten Minutes West seven Chains and fifty Links to the Place of Beginning.

The Second (mark'd on the Map No. 40)

Begins at a Stake standing by the Road that leads from the Town to the English Neighbourhood which stake stands North fourteen Degrees and ten Minutes East seven Chains and Eighty seven Links from the Easterly Corner of the foregoing first Tract (mark'd on the Map No. 38) and from said Stake runs North seventy five Degrees and fifty Minutes West twenty eight Chains and five Links to a Stake by the Middle Road, Thence North thirty two Degrees and twenty three Minutes East eight Chains and eighty nine Links along said Road to a Stake, Thence south seventy five Degrees and fifty Minutes East twenty nine Chains and sixty nine Links to a Stake by the first mentioned Road, Thence south forty one Degrees West nine Chains and fifty Links to the Place of Beginning.

The Third (mark'd on the Map No. 89)

*33 **Begins** at a Stake standing by the Road leading from the Town to the English Neighbourhood being the Easterly Corner of the last mentioned Tract (mark'd on * the Map No. 40) and from said Stake runs North seventy five Degrees and fifty Minutes West twenty nine Chains and sixty nine Links to a Stake by the Middle Road, Thence North thirty one Degrees East One Chain and fifty nine Links along said Road to a Stake, Then south fifty one Degrees and ten Minutes East three Chains and Eighty Links along said Road to a Stake, Thence North twenty eight Degrees East three Chains and thirty two Links along said Road to a Stake, Thence North fifteen Degrees East five Chains and seventy three Links along said Road to a Stake, Thence North twenty

---

Had children—Annetje (in another place written *Aeltje*), b. April 3, 1770; and Arent (or Aaron), b. Jan. 27, 1784. Annetje m. Edo Winne, Nov. 6, 1790, and had children—*Annatje*, b. Nov. 30, 1794, d. Nov. 17, 1811; *Jannetje*, b. June 8, 1797, m. Garret Vreeland, July 21, 1814; *Antje*, b Dec. 17, 1799, m. John H. Zabriskie, April 1, 1820; and *Nicholas*, Feb. 1, 1809. Zabriskie's wife had *Hannah*, who m. John De Mott, and *Margavet*, who m. Garret Z. Demarest. Nicholas Tuers conveyed to his son Arent all of his land E. of Bergen Ave., May 2, 1814, who conveyed to John Van Horne, Garret Vreeland, and Isaac Van Winkle, June 15, 1835, all his property in trust, for his own use. Arent (or Aaron) Tuers m. Effie Van Winkle, Nov. 30, 1826; and by will, dated June 20, 1835, proved March 16, 1836, gave to his only son, *Nicholas*, all his homestead. Nicholas m , and died seized and intestate, leaving his widow, Jane, and an infant son, who died at three or four years of age. The property was partitioned, Jan. 3, 1853, among the heirs of Edo Winne, viz.: Jane, wife of Garret Vreeland; Nicholas, and Hannah, wife of De Mott; and Margaret, wife of Demarest. The last two representing their mother Antje, wife of John H. Zabriskie, then dead. Lot 130 was of doubtful ownership in 1764. *Vide Lot* 356, p. 180.

one degrees and thirty Minutes East five Chains and twenty three Links along said Road to a Stake, Then south seventy six Degrees and thirty Minutes East thirty two Chains and twenty five Links to the first mentioned Road, Thence south forty four Degrees and thirty Minutes West seventeen Chains and twelve Links to the Place of Beginning.

The Fourth (mark'd on the Map No. 90)

Begins at a Stake standing by the Road that leads from the Town to the English Neighbourhood being the Easterly Corner of the last describ'd Tract (mark'd on the Map No. 89) and from said Stake runs North seventy six Degrees and thirty Minutes West thirty two Chains and twenty five Links to a Stake by the Middle Road, Thence North twenty one Degrees and thirty Minutes East fifty Links along said Road to a Stake, Thence North thirty four Degrees and fifteen Minutes East twelve Chains and sixty one Links along said Road to a Stake, Thence North four Degrees East one Chain and seventy five Links to a Stake near a small Brook, Thence North eighty eight Degrees and twenty Minutes East four Chains and eighty seven Links, Thence South sixty three Degrees East seven Chains and seventy five Links, Then North eighty four Degrees and fifteen Minutes East three Chains, Then North fifty one Degrees East seven Chains and ninety five Links to the first mentioned Road, Thence South four Degrees East nine Chains and seventy five Links along said Road to a Stake, Thence South twenty six Degrees and forty Minutes East eight Chains and eighty one Links along said Road to a Stake, Thence South sixteen Degrees West four Chains and twenty two Links along said Road to the Place of Beginning.

The Fifth being a Tract of Medow (mark'd on the Map No. 138)

Begins at a Stake (standing North sixty eight Degrees East five Chains and seventy five Links from the Mouth of Pinhorne's Creek which Stake is the Northerly Corner of a Lott of Meadow in Caspar Stymats first Patent mark'd on the Map No. 137) and from said Stake runs South fifty one Degrees and fifty Minutes East thirty five Chains and fifty three Links to Bridge Creek, Then returning to said Stake the Place of Beginning; and from thence running North seventy four Degrees and thirty Minutes East four Chains and four Links along said Pinhorne's Creek, Then North twenty Degrees and thirty Minutes East three Chains * along said Pinhorne's Creek, Then North twenty three *34 Degrees and thirty five Minutes West five Chains and seventy five Links along said Pinhorne's Creek to the Mouth of a very small Creek or Worm, Then North sixty eight Degrees and thirty Minutes East five Chains and seventy four Links along said Worm, Then South eighty eight Degrees & thirty Minutes East six Chains and sixteen Links to a Stake standing by said Worm, Then South fifty one Degrees and fifty Minutes East forty Chains and Ten Links to a Stake by said Bridge Creek, Then down said Bridge Creek the several Courses thereof as it runs as far as 'till it meets the first mentioned Line.

The Sixth being a Lot in the Town of Bergen (mark'd on the Map No. 142)

Begins at a Stake being the Northerly Corner of said Lot (which Stake bears from a Stake standing nearly about the Middle of the Square south forty Degrees and thirty Minutes West one Chain and ninety nine

Links; and which said Stake standing in the Square bears from the Easterly Corner of Bergen Church North forty seven Degrees East six Chains and fifty three Links) And from the first mentioned Stake runs South forty two Degrees East two Chains and forty one Links to a Stake, Thence South forty eight Degrees West, One Chain and forty four Links to a Stake, Thence North forty two Degrees West two Chains and forty one Links to the Street, Then North forty eight Degrees East One Chain and forty four Links along said Street to the Place of Beginning.

The Seventh (mark'd on the Map No. 130)

Begins at a Stake (being the Northerly Corner of a Lott in Nicholas Varlet's Patent mark'd on the Map No. 127) and from said Stake runs South fifty Degrees East seventeen Chains to Horsimus Creek, and then returning to said Stake the Place of Beginning and from thence running North thirty two Degrees East fourteen Chains and fifty Links to a Stake, Thence South fifty Degrees East thirty one Chains and seventy seven Links to said Horsimus Creek, Then down said Creek the several Courses thereof as it runs 'til it meets the first mentioned Line.

The Patent of Philip Carteret to Thomas Fredrick alias De Cuyper dated the tenth Day of November, One thousand six hundred and seventy seven for sundry Parcels of Land about the Town of Bergen.

Our Survey whereof shews and we adjudge them to be four Tracts.

The First whereof being a Tract of Upland and Meadow mark'd on the Map No. 62)*

*35   * **Begins** at a Stake standing by a Road (which Stake is the southerly Corner of a Lot in Fredrick Philipse's Patent mark'd on the Map No. 63) and from said Stake runs North fifty four Degrees and ten Minutes West Seventy Chains to Hackinsack River, and then returning to said Stake the Place of Beginning; and runs from thence South forty Degrees West four Chains and fifteen Links along said Road to a Stake, Thence North fifty four Degrees and Ten Minutes West sixty six Chains and seventy Links to said Hackinsack River, Then up along said River 'til it meets the first mentioned Line.

The Second (mark'd on the Map No. 45)

Begins at a Stake (which Stake is the southerly Corner of a Lot in Guert Garritse's Patent mark'd on the Map No. 44) and from said Stake runs North fifty six Degrees and forty Minutes West twenty eight Chains

---

* In the Patent he is named Thomas Fredrick Cooper.

Lot No. 62, 3½x27 chains, bounded S. E. by a highway = 9½ acres.

Lot No. 45, 2½x27 chains = 6½ acres, bounded N. W. by the road leading to Bergen Point.

Lot No. 141, 8x16 chains = 13 acres, bounded N. W. by Pinhorne's Creek.

Lot No. 42. = 1¼ acres, bounded S. E. and N. E. by a highway. *Vide Note to Stoffelsen's Patent*, p. 9, and *Note to Harmensen's Patent*, p. 50.

Johannis Tomasen (whom I take to be a son of the patentee), a weaver, sold this land to Mattys De Mott, blacksmith, June 25, 1714.

The Patent calls for 10 acres of meadow, which I do not find in the text. This, with the other lots, makes 40½ acres.

and eighty Links to a Road. Then South thirty six Degrees and twenty Minutes West two Chains & fifty eight Links along said Road to a Stake, Thence south fifty six Degrees and forty Minutes East twenty nine Chains to a Stake, Thence North thirty Degrees East two Chains and Sixty one Links to the Place of Beginning.

The Third (being a Tract of Meadow mark'd on the Map No. 141).

Begins at a Stake standing by Pinhorne's Creek (which Stake is the Westerly Corner of a Lot of Meadow in Fredrick Philipse's Patent mark'd on the Map No. 142) And from said Stake runs south forty two Degrees East fourteen Chains and twenty nine Links to a Stake at the End of a very small Creek or Worm, Then South two degrees and fifteen Minutes West five Chains and ninety one Links along said Worm to a Stake, Thence South fifty eight Degrees and forty minutes West three Chains and ninety eight Links along said Worm to the Easterly Corner of a Lot of Meadow in Jacob Luby's Patent mark'd on the Map No. 140), Thence North forty Degrees and forty five Minutes West Eighteen Chains and seventy eight Links to said Pinhorne's Creek, Then up along said Creek the several Courses thereof as it runs to the Place of Beginning.

The Fourth (being an Out-Garden-Plott mark'd on the Map No. 42.)

Begins at a Stake by the Street (which Stake is the Easterly Corner of a Garden Plott in Fredrick Philipse's Patent mark'd on the Map No. 41) And from said Stake runs south forty one Degrees and forty five Minutes East two Chains and Eighty five Links along the Street to the Northerly Corner of the Church Yard, Then South forty Degrees and twenty Minutes West four Chains and fifty one Links to a Stake being the Easterly Corner of a Lot in Guert Garritse's Patent mark'd on the Map No. 44), Thence North fifty six Degrees and forty Minutes West two Chains and fifty six * Links to a Stake, Thence North thirty Degrees East two Chains and ninety Links to a Stake, Thence North forty eight Degrees East two Chains and forty four Links to the Place of Beginning.

*36

The Patent of Petrus Stuyvesant to Harman Edward, dated the fourteenth Day of September, One thousand Six hundred and sixty two, For sundry Parcels of Land lying in and about the Town of Bergen.

Our Survey whereof shews and we adjudge them to be six Tracts.

The First whereof (mark'd on the Map No. 43)*

---

* This patentee was one of the Commissioners to fortify Bergen in 1663. He and Joost Van der Linden, Hendrick Janse Spier and Hendrick de Backer, June 15, 1674, petitioned the government for land on Staten Island at the mouth of the Kill Van Koll. *Col. Hist. of N. Y.* ii. 721.

Lot No. 43, in the old maize land, was No. 28 in the original allotment, 14x150 rods=3¼ morgens.

Lot No. 50, a wood lot, 19x150 rods=4¾ morgens.

Lot No. 69, a wood lot between Captain Varlet and Samuel Edsall, 19x150 rods with the meadow=9 morgens.

Lot No. 153, 7½x12½ rods.

Begins at a Stake (Which Stake is the Westerly Corner of a Lot in Thomas Fredrick alias De Cuyper's Patent mark'd on the Map No 42) And from said Stake runs North fifty six Degrees and forty Minutes West twenty five Chains and ninety five Links to a Stake by a Road, Thence North thirty six Degrees and twenty Minutes East two Chains and eighty two Links along said Road to a Stake standing in the Turn of said Road, Thence South fifty six Degrees and forty Minutes East twenty six Chains along said Road in Part and Part along the Line of Fredrick Philipse's Garden Plot mark'd on the Map No. 41, to a Stake, Thence South thirty nine Degrees West two Chains and ninety Links to the Place of Beginning.

The Second (mark'd on the Map No. 50)

Begins at a Stake (which Stake is the Southerly Corner of a Lot in Dirck Garritse's Patent mark'd on the Map No. 49) And from said Stake runs North fifty four Degrees and fifty Minutes West thirty Chains and sixty Links to a Stake by a Road, Thence South thirty three Degrees West three Chains and seventy six Links along said Road to a Stake, Thence South fifty-five Degrees East thirty Chains and ninety Links to a Stake, Thence North forty one Degrees and forty five Minutes East fifty Links, Then North thirty Degrees East three Chains and thirty two Links to the Place of Beginning.

The Third (being a Tract of Upland and Meadow mark'd on the Map No. 69)

Begins at a Stake by a Road (which Stake is the Southerly Corner of a Lot in John Berry's Patent mark'd on the Map No. 70) and from said Stake runs North fifty four Degrees and ten Minutes West eighty one Chains and forty nine Links to Hackinsack River and then returning to said Stake the Place of Beginning, and from thence runs South thirty three Degrees West three Chains and fifty six Links [*] along said Road to a Stake, Thence North fifty four Degrees and ten Minutes West eighty one Chains and forty nine Links to said Hackinsack River, Then up along said River 'til it meets the first mentioned Line.

[*37]

The Fourth (being a Lot in the Town of Bergen mark'd on the Map No. 153)

Begins at a Stake standing on the Northwest side of a Street (which Stake is the Southerly Corner of a Town Lot in Caspar Stymat's second Patent mark'd on the Map No. 116) And from said Stake runs North forty two Degrees West two Chains and forty five Links to a Stake, Thence South forty eight Degrees West One Chain and forty one Links to a Stake, Thence South forty two Degrees East two Chains and forty five Links to said Street, Then North forty eight Degrees East one Chain and forty one Links along said Street to the Place of Beginning.

The Fifth being an out Garden Plot (mark'd on the Map No. 111)

Begins at a Stake standing by the Road that leads from the Town to Bergen Point (which Stake is the Westerly Corner of a Garden Plot in Hans Dedrick's Patent mark'd on the Map No. 110) And from said

---

Lot No. 111, extended from the highway to the swamp, 12 rods wide.

Lot No. 118, was No. 2 in the original allotment, 40 rods wide from the woods to the river. The whole=69 acres. *Vide Teunise's Patent*, p. 54.

Stake runs South forty Degrees East nine Chains and sixty Links to a Stake, Thence South forty four Degrees West two Chains and sixty Links to a Stake, Thence North forty Degrees West eight Chains and six Links to a Stake by said Road, Thence North nineteen Degrees East one Chain and fifty-three Links along said Road, Then North fourteen Degrees and twenty Minutes East one Chain and sixty Links along said Road to the Place of Beginning.

The Sixth being a Piece of Meadow on Hackinsack River (mark'd on the Map No. 118)

Begins at a Stake standing by the Edge of the Upland (which Stake is the Southerly Corner of a Piece of Meadow in Adrian Post's Patent mark'd on the Map 117) And from said Stake runs North fifty four Degrees and Ten Minutes West Eleven Chains and fifty Links to Hackinsack River; and Then returning to said Stake the Place of Beginning and from thence runs South thirty Degrees West seven Chains and fifty five Links along the Edge of the Upland to a Stake, Thence North fifty four Degrees and Ten Minutes West nine Chains and fifty Links to said Hackinsack River, Then up along the said River 'till it meets the first mentioned Line.

* **The Patent** of Philip Carteret to Guert Garritse, dated the twenty second Day of July One thousand Six hundred and seventy for sundry Parcels of Land lying in and about the Town of Bergen. *38

Our Survey whereof shews and we adjudge them to be six Tracts.

The First whereof (mark'd on the Map No. 44)*

Begins at a Stake standing by a Road (which Stake is the Westerly Corner of a Lot in Harman Edward's Patent mark'd on the Map No. 43) and from said Stake runs South fifty six Degrees and forty Minutes East twenty eight Chains and fifty Links to a Stake standing at the southerly Corner of an Out-Garden Plot in Thomas Fredrick alias De Cuyper's Patent mark'd on the No. 42 and from thence runs South thirty Degrees West two Chains and sixty seven Links to a Stake, Then North fifty six Degrees and forty Minutes West twenty eight Chains

---

* *Lot No.* 44, upland in the old maize land, 14x150 rods=3¼ morgens; owned by Cornelius and Garret Sip in 1764. *Vide Van Vorst's Patent*, p. 60.

Lot No. 51, two wood lots, 38x150 rods=9¼ morgens. It was sold by the patentee to Hendrick Janse Ostrum, and by him to Beelitje Dircks, daughter of Dirck Janse Van Osten, March 17, 1668; and it was owned by her son Hans, or Johannis Van Rypen in 1764. He died seized Aug. 24, 1776. It was probably sold by Hans to Cornelius G. Van Rypen.

Lot No. 102 extended from the road to the river, and, with the meadow No. 6 in the original allotment=22 morgens. John DeBow sold to Jacob Van Wagenen, May 18, 1767, a lot of upland and meadow in this Patent, which from the description I think is part of this lot.

Lot No. 136 was over the Creek=18 morgens.

Lot No. 107, between Hendrick de Backer and Jacob Sergeant, 8x20 rods.

Lot No. 154, between the same parties, 7¼x12¼ rods. The whole=100 acres. The W. part of Lot 102 was in doubtful ownership in 1764. *Vide Lot* 325, p 186.

and eighty Links to the said Road, Then North thirty six Degrees and twenty Minutes East two Chains and sixty seven Links along said Road to the Place of Beginning.

The Second Tract (being comprehensive of two Lots of Land lying together under one Boundary in the Patent) mark'd on the Map No. 51

Begins at a Stake (which Stake is the Southerly Corner of a Lot in Harman Edward's Patent mark'd on the Map No. 50) and from said Stake runs North fifty five Degrees West thirty Chains and ninety Links to a Stake by a Road, Thence South thirty three Degrees West seven Chains and thirty four Links along said Road to a Stake, Thence South fifty five Degrees East, twenty nine Chains and eighty Links to a Stake, Thence North forty one Degrees and forty five Minutes East, seven Chains and forty two Links to the Place of Beginning.

The Third being a Tract of Upland and Meadow (mark'd on the Map No. 102)

Begins at a Stake standing by a Road (which Stake is the Southerly Corner of a Lot in Caspar Stymat's Second Patent mark'd on the Map No. 101) and from said Stake runs North fifty Degrees and Ten Minutes West twenty three Chains and sixty five Links to a Stake, Thence North fifty four Degrees and Ten Minutes West sixty four Chains and sixty Links to Hackinsack River; and then returning to the first mentioned Stake the Place of Beginning; And from thence runs South forty three Degrees and thirty Minutes West nine Chains along said Road to a Stake, Thence North fifty Degrees and ten Minutes West twenty three Chains and sixty *39 five Links* to a Stake, Then North fifty four Degrees and ten Minutes West fifty three Chains to said Hackinsack River, Then up along said River 'til it meets the first mentioned Line that comes to the River.

The Fourth (being a Tract of Meadow mark'd on the Map No. 136)

Begins at a Stake (which Stake is the Southerly Corner of a Lot of Meadow in Caspar Stymat's Patent mark'd on the Map No. 137) and from said Stake runs South forty eight Degrees East nineteen Chains and twenty Links to a Stake standing by the Westerly side of Bridge Creek opposite to the Westerly Corner of a Lot in Jacob Luby's first Patent mark'd on the Map No. 87) and then returning to the first mentioned Stake at the Place of Beginning; And from thence runs North thirty Eight Degrees and twenty Minutes East eight Chains and ten Links to a Stake, Thence South fifty one Degrees and fifty Minutes East seventeen Chains & eighty Links to said Bridge Creek, Then down along the said Creek the several Courses thereof 'til it comes to the first mentioned Line.

The Fifth (being an Out-Garden Plot near the Town mark'd on the Map No. 107)

Begins at a Stake (which Stake is the Westerly Corner of an Out-Garden Plot in Hendrick Teunise's Patent mark'd on the Map No. 106) and from said Stake runs South forty one Degrees East six Chains and ninety Links, to a Stake, Thence South forty eight Degrees West One Chain and forty two Links to a Stake, Thence North forty Degrees West six

Chains and ninety Links to the Street, Thence North forty eight Degrees East One Chain fifty Links along said Street to the Place of Beginning.

The Sixth (being a Lot in the Town of Bergen mark'd on the Map No. 154)

Begins at a Stake (which Stake is the Easterly Corner of a Town Lot in Paulus Peterse's Patent mark'd on the Map No. 155) and from said Stake runs South forty two Degrees East two Chains and forty one Links to the Street, Then North forty eight Degrees East One Chain and thirty eight Links along said Street to a Stake, Thence North forty two Degrees West two Chains and forty one Links to a Stake, Thence South forty eight Degrees West One Chain and thirty eight Links to the Place of Beginning.

* **The Patent** of Petrus Stuyvesant to Paulus Pieterse dated *40 the Seventh Day of March One thousand six hundred and sixty three and confirm'd to said Pieterse by Patent from Philip Carteret dated the twelfth Day of May, One thousand six hundred and sixty eight for sundry Parcels of Land lying in and about the Town of Bergen.

Our Survey whereof shews, and we adjudge them to be five Tracts.

The First whereof (mark'd on the Map No. 41)*

Begins at a Stake (which Stake is the Southerly Corner of a Lot in Thomas Fredrick alias De Cuyper's Patent mark'd on the Map No. 45) And from said Stake runs North fifty six Degrees and forty Minutes West

---

o This patentee was one of the commissioners to fortify Bergen in 1663. *New Neth. Reg.*, 158.

Lot No. 46, 14x150 rods = 3¼ morgens. This lot fell to Newkirk's son, *Hendrick*, and on partition between his sons, to his eldest son, *Garret H.*, who died a bachelor Oct. 21, 1860.

Lot No. 152, 39x150 rods = 9¼ morgens.

Lot No. 120, meadow No, 4 in the original allotment, extending from the woods to the river, 48 rods wide.

Lot No. 155, consisted of two lots : 1st, 7¼x12¼ rods ; 2d, 5x7¼ rods.

Lot No. 103 was 16 rods and 4 feet wide. This lot fell to Hendrick. On partition of his property between his sons, *Garret H.* and *George*, it went to his son, Garret H., who sold it to his brother George and brother-in-law Hartman Van Wagenen, Sept. 14, 1835. It was known as the Orchard.

The whole = 37 acres, owned by Garret Newkirk in 1764. Newkirk died seized, April 23, 1785. By his will he gave all his realty to his two sons, *Mathevis* and *Hendrick*, who partitioned by deed, July 7, 1795. Lots 52 and 53 were then as one lot, called the "large pasture." Hendrick took the N. E. half, and gave it to his sons, *Garret H.* and *George.* Garret H. conveyed to George, Oct. 20, 1836, who sold to William Jewett, the present owner, Oct. 20, 1836. Mathevis took the S. W. half, and gave all his realty to his two sons, *Garret* and *Aaron.* On division between them, this lot (No. 53) fell to Aaron, who gave part of it to his daughter *Catherine*, wife of Cornelius M. Vreeland, July 1, 1832. The deed of partition between him and his brother having been lost, the children of Garret released to Catherine, May 1, 1852. *Vide Note to Philipse's Patent,* p. 28, and *Note to Berry's Patent,* p. 51.

twenty nine Chains and twenty Links to a Stake by a Road, Thence South thirty six Degrees and twenty Minutes West two Chains and eighty Links along said Road to a Stake, Then South fifty six Degrees and forty Minutes East twenty nine Chains & sixty Links to a Stake, Thence North thirty Degrees East, two Chains and eighty Links to the Place of Beginning.

The Second Tract (being comprehensive of a double or two Lots of Land lying together under one Boundary in the Patent) mark'd on the Map No. 52

Begins at a Stake (which Stake is the Southerly Corner of a Lot in Guert Garritse's Patent mark'd on the Map No. 51) And from said Stake runs North fifty five Degrees West twenty nine Chains and eighty Links to a Stake in a Road, Thence South thirty nine Degrees West Seven Chains and thirty three Links along said Road to a Stake, Thence South fifty five Degrees East twenty nine Chains and forty six Links to a Stake, Thence North forty one Degrees and forty five Minutes East seven Chains and thirty four Links to the Place of Beginning.

The Third (being a piece of Meadow mark'd on the Map No. 120)

Begins at a Stake standing by the Edge of the Upland (which Stake is the Southerly Corner of a Lot of Meadow in Jan Lubertse's Patent mark'd on the Map No. 119) And from said Stake runs North fifty four Degrees and ten Minutes West twelve Chains to Hackinsack River, Then returning to the first mentioned Stake the Place of Beginning; And from thence runs South twenty two Degrees West nine Chains *41 and twenty five Links along the Edge of the Upland to * a Stake, Thence North fifty four Degrees and ten Minutes West eleven Chains and twenty Links to said Hackinsack River, Then up along said River 'til it meets the first mentioned Line.

The Fourth (Comprehends two Lots in the Town of Bergen mark'd on the Map No. 155 which two Lots being adjoining together are comprehended in one Survey)

Beginning at a Stake (which Stake stands North sixty nine Degrees East one Chain and thirty-four Links from the Easterly Corner of Bergen Church) and from said Stake runs South forty two Degrees East three Chains and thirty seven Links along the Street to a Stake, Thence North forty eight Degrees East one Chain and forty six Links to a Stake, Thence North forty two Degrees West three Chains and thirty seven Links to another Street, Then South forty eight Degrees West One Chain and forty six Links along said other Street to the Place of Beginning.

The Fifth (being an Out-Garden Plot near the Town mark'd on the Map No. 103)

Begins at a Stake (standing South eleven Degrees and forty Minutes West sixty nine Links from the Westerly Corner of the Lot in Town last above describ'd) And from said Stake runs South forty two Degrees East four Chains and twelve Links along a Street to a Stake being the Northerly Corner of the Old Burying Ground, Thence South thirty nine Degrees West three Chains and two Links to a Stake, Thence North fifty three Degrees and fifty Minutes West two Chains & thirty Links to the Road leading from the Town to Bergen Point; Then North fourteen Degrees and twenty Minutes East four Chains and fifteen Links along said Road to the Place of Beginning.

The Patent of Philip Carteret to Dirck Garretse dated the twelfth Day of May One thousand six hundred and sixty eight for sundry Parcels of Land lying in and about the Town of Bergen.

Our Survey whereof shews, and we adjudge it to be three Tracts.

The First whereof (being a Tract of Upland mark'd on the Map No. 49)*

Begins at a Stake (which Stake is the Southerly Corner of a Lot in Guert Coerten's first Patent mark'd on the Map No. 48) and from said Stake runs North fifty six Degrees and twenty Minutes West twenty nine Chains and ninety Links to a Stake * in a Road, Thence South thirty three Degrees West ten Chains and fifty Links along said Road to a Stake, Thence South fifty four Degrees and fifty Minutes East thirty Chains and sixty Links to a Stake, Thence North thirty Degrees East eleven Chains and twenty-two Links to the Place of Beginning. *42

The Second (being a Piece of Meadow mark'd on the Map No. 67)

Begins at a Stake standing by Hackinsack River (which Stake is the Northerly Corner of a Lot of Upland and Meadow in Caspar Stymat's Second Patent Mark'd on the Map No. 66) And from said Stake runs South fifty four Degrees and ten Minutes East forty three Chains and seventy five Links to a Stake by the Edge of the Upland, Thence North fifty two Degrees East three Chains and seventy Links along the Edge of the Upland to a Stake, Thence North fifty four Degrees and ten Minutes West forty four Chains and seventy five Links to said Hackinsack River, Then down along the said River to the Place of Beginning.

---

* The Dutch Patent was dated Sept. 14, 1662.

Lot No. 49, in the old maize land, 50x150 rods=25 acres.

Lot No. 67, 19 rods wide from the woods to the river=11¼ acres.

Lot No. 156, 7½x12¼ rods.

Previous to his death the patentee sold to Baltus Barentsen Van Kleek. Gerritse received the money, but before the transfer was completed he died, leaving a widow and one son. The widow, Gerten Hoppe, and son, Garret Van Dien, then living in Hackensack, carried out the sale of Gerritse, Oct. 13, 1686. Van Dien confirmed this deed by another, dated Oct. 12, 1700. Barentsen sold to Andries Preyer, a weaver, May 8, 1697. William Day seems to have been a partner of Preyer in this purchase, as appears by his affidavit, dated Oct. 15, 1737. The two partitioned, Preyer taking the orchard, and Day an equivalent strip from Preyer's land.

Lot 156 Day sold to Mattys De Mott, Dec. 2, 1708. *Vide Note to Stoffelsen's Patent*, p. 9. It remained in his heirs until a recent period. Daniel Van Rypen owned lot 49 in 1764. He sold 21 acres of the N. side to his son *Richard*, Oct. 9, 1809. His grandson Daniel (son of Richard) yet owns part of it.

Andries Prior died Nov. 16, 1698, leaving all his lands to his son Casparus, who died Feb. 26, 1755, and by will dated Nov. 22, 1753, proved March 16, 1659, gave his lands to his wife Saertje for life, then in fee to his son *Nicholas*. She died Aug. 25, 1774. Nicholas left him surviving, *Casparus*, who married Antje, daughter of Garret Van Wagnenen, of Saddle River. By will he gave all his lands to the children of his son Nicholas. *Vide Note to Varlet's Patent*, p. 62.

The Third (being a Lot in the Town of Bergen mark'd on the Map No. 156)

Begins at a Stake standing by a Street (which Stake is the Northerly Corner of the Town Lots in Paulus Pieterse's Patent mark'd on the Map No. 155) and from said Stake runs South forty two Degrees East, two Chains and forty one Links to a Stake, Thence North forty eight Degrees East one Chain and thirty eight Links to a Stake, Thence North forty two Degrees West two Chains and forty one Links to a Stake by said Street, Thence South forty eight Degrees West One Chain and thirty eight Links along said Street to the Beginning.

The Patent of Petrus Stuyvesant to Jacob Luby dated the fourteenth Day of September, One thousand six hundred and Sixty two for sundry Parcels of Land lying in and about the Town of Bergen.

Our Survey whereof shews and we adjudge them to be Six Tracts.

The First whereof (mark'd on the Map No. 56)*

Begins at a Red Oak Tree mark'd D T (which Tree is the Southerly Corner of a Lot in Adrian Post's Patent mark'd on the Map No. 55) and from said Red Oak Tree runs North fifty five Degrees West twenty nine Chains to a Stake by a Road, Thence South thirty seven Degrees West nine Chains and seventy five Links along said Road to a Stake, Thence South fifty one Degrees East twenty eight Chains and ninety Links to a

---

° Luby was a sergeant in the army of the West India Company. On his own petition he was discharged from service Feb. 15, 1656. *N. Y. Col. MSS.*, vi. 281. He was one of the commissioners to fortify Bergen in 1663, *New Neth. Reg.*, 158, and died June 11, 1691.

Lot No. 56, 57x150 rods=14¼ morgens, owned by Arent Tuers in 1764. *Vide Note to Steenhuysen's Patent*, p. 32. Aaron Tuers conveyed to John Welsh the N. part of this lot, May 17, 1830, who conveyed the front part of his purchase to James W. Welsh, Sept. 17, 1836; James to John Mead, Jan. 20, 1852; Mead to Levi Decker, March 29, 1853. John Welsh conveyed the rear part of his purchase to Alexander C. Mulford, Oct. 20, 1836; who reconveyed to Welsh, April 16, 1839; who conveyed to Benjamin F. Welsh, Jr., Dec. 21, 1852; they both conveyed to Levi Decker, June 12, 1854. Decker sold part of his purchase to John S. Sutphen, March 3, 1859; who conveyed to George W. Helm, Sept. 24, 1866. Bentley Av. is laid about 15 feet N. of the N. line of this lot, and through lot 55. *Vide Note to Post's Patent*, p. 23. It extended S. to about Oxford Ave.

Lot No. 140, "in the new Indian corn field or new maize land,"=8 morgens.

Lot No. 61, was part of lot No. 1 in the original allotment=3¾ morgens, sold by the patentee to John Van Giesen, March 24, 1697, and by him to Jan A. Sip, April 19, 1698. This last deed was confirmed, June 13, 1712, by Claas and Jan Arentse Toers. *Vide Note to Van Vorst's Patent*, p. 60.

Lot No. 87, extended from the road to the Kill=12 morgens, 350 rods.

Lot No. 108, was a garden between Jan Swaen and Capt. Varlet, 7x25 rods. Owned by Johannis Van Houten in 1764. *Vide Note to Lot 25 New Field Book.*

Lot No. 157 was 7½x12½ rods.

Besides these there was a piece of woodland mentioned in the Patent, S. of Phillipsen. 19 rods=9 morgens, 250 rods; the whole=94 acres.

Stake, Thence North thirty five Degrees East seven Chains and seventy one Links to a Stake, Thence North forty one Degrees and forty five Minutes East four Chains & two Links to the Place of Beginning.

* **The Second** (being a Lot of Meadow mark'd on the Map No. *43 140)

Begins at a Stake (standing at the Mouth of a very small Creek or Worm which empties into Pinhorne's Creek) And from said Stake runs North sixty eight Degrees & thirty Minutes East five Chains and seventy four Links along said Worm, Thence South eighty eight Degrees and thirty Minutes East six Chains and sixteen Links along said Worm to a Stake (standing in the West Corner of a Lot of Meadow in Guert Coertens third Patent mark'd on the Map No. 139) Thence North fifty eight Degrees and forty Minutes East Seven Chains and eighty Links along said Worm to a Stake (standing in the Southerly Corner of a Lot of Meadow in Thomas Fredrick alias De Cuyper's Patent mark'd on the Map No. 141,) Thence North forty Degrees and forty five Minutes West eighteen Chains and seventy eight Links to Pinhorne's Creek, Then down along the Creek as it runs to the Beginning.

The Third (mark'd on the Map No. 61)

Begins at a Stake standing by the Middle Road (which Stake is the Northeast Corner of an Out Garden Plot in Adrian Post's Patent mark'd on the Map No. 100) and from said Stake runs North two Degrees East two Chains and eighty nine Links along said Road to a Stake, Thence North sixty nine Degrees and ten Minutes West twenty three Chains and forty four Links to a Stake, Thence South twenty eight Degrees and fifty Minutes West two Chains and ninety six Links to a Stake, Thence South Sixty nine Degrees and ten Minutes East twenty one Chains and Sixty Links to a Stake, Thence South Seventy two Degrees East three Chains and nineteen Links to the Place of Beginning.

The Fourth (being a Tract of Upland and Meadow mark'd on the Map No. 87)

Begins at a Stake by the Middle Road (which Stake is the Easterly Corner of a Lot in Fredrick Philipse's Patent mark'd on the Map No. 86) And from said Stake runs North forty eight Degrees West, thirty nine Chains and forty seven Links to Bridge Creek, and then returning to said Stake the Place of Beginning; and from thence runs North thirty four Degrees and fifteen Minutes East five Chains and seventy five Links along said Road to a Stake, Thence North forty four Degrees and twenty Minutes West thirty four Chains and twenty Links to said Bridge Creek, Then down along the said Creek the several Courses thereof as it runs 'til it meets the first mentioned Line.

The Fifth (being an Out Garden Plot near the Town mark'd on the Map No. 108)

Begins at a Stake standing by a Street (which Stake is the Westerly Corner of an* Out-Garden Plot in Guert Garretse's Patent mark'd on *44 the Map No. 107) and from said Stake runs South forty Degrees East six Chains and ninety Links to a Stake, Thence South forty four Degrees West one Chain and thirty five Links to a Stake, Thence North forty Degrees West seven Chains to a Stake by said Street, Thence North forty eight Degrees East one Chain and thirty four Links along said Street to the Place of Beginning.

The Sixth (being a Lot in the Town of Bergen mark'd on the Map No. 157)

Begins at a Stake standing by a Street (which Stake is the Southerly Corner of the Town Lots in Paulus Pieterse's Patent mark'd on the Map No. 155) And from said Stake runs South forty two Degrees East two Chains and forty one Links along said Street to a Stake, Thence North forty eight Degrees East one Chain and forty six Links along another Street to a Stake, Thence North forty two Degrees West two Chains and forty one Links to a Stake, Thence South forty eight Degrees West One Chain and forty Six Links to the Place of Beginning.

The Patent of Philip Carteret to Jacob Luby dated the tenth Day of November, One thousand six hundred and Seventy Seven for sundry Parcels of Land lying at and near Wiehaken in the Township of Bergen.

Our Survey whereof shews and we adjudge them to be Two small Lots of Upland near Wiehaken which lying and adjoining together we have comprehended in one Survey as mark'd on the Map No 144)*

Beginning at a Stone planted in the Mouth of the first Gully and Run of Water that runs from the Westward into the Creek at Wiehaken Ferry (which Stone is North thirty seven Degrees and a Half East thirty eight Chains and sixty seven Links from the Mouth of Hoboken Creek) and from said Stake runs South thirty Degrees East four Chains and eighty six Links along said Ferry Creek to Hudson's River, Then North fifty eight Degrees and fifty Minutes East five Chains and sixty eight Links along said River, Then North three Degrees East, three Chains and eighty Links along said River, Then North seventy Degrees East three Chains and seventy eight Links along said River to a large Chessnut Tree mark'd on four sides, Thence North twenty six Degrees West four Chains and twenty four Links, Then North forty one Degrees and thirty Minutes West three Chains and fifty two Links to a Red Oak Tree mark'd on four sides standing on the East side of a Brook that empties into said Ferry Creek, Thence South fifty nine Degrees West thirteen Chains and twenty one Links to the North Line of Wiehaken Patent, Then South fifty two Degrees & thirty Minutes East five Chains & sixty seven Links to the Place of Beginning.

*45   * It is to be observed, that, this Patent farther grants a Piece of Upland said to contain twenty three Acres; also a Piece of Meadow said to contain Sixteen Acres. These were purchased by Luby of Maryn Adrianse and are confirm'd to Luby by this Patent from Philip Carteret, But as

---

* This Patent calls for three lots

1st. Along the foot of the hill 22 chains, running N. E. and S. W. in width; at the S. end 18 chains, at the N. end 4 chains. Bounded S. by his own meadow, E. by Hudson's River, N. by a small brook, W. by the mountain = 23 acres.

2d. Upland between two hills, lying on the side of the brook, 20x40 rods = 4 acres.

3d. Meadow bounded W. by the hills, E. by Hudson's River, S. by a small creek, N. by his own land = 16 acres.

At an early day this land was owned by Samuel Bayard. *Vide Note to Varlet's Patent,* p. 6.

they are Part of, and were comprehended in the Original Patent of Wiehaken granted by William Kieft to said Maryn Adrianse dated the Eleventh Day of May, One thousand six hundred and forty seven ; and confirm'd to said Adrianse by Patent from Philip Carteret dated the Eighteenth Day of April One thousand six hundred and seventy, we have included them in our survey of Wiehaken (mark'd on the Map No. 1) under the original Patent to said Maryn Adrianse.

  The Patent of Philip Carteret to Jan Lubertse dated the twelfth Day of May One thousand six hundred and sixty eight for sundry Parcels of Land lying in and about the Town of Bergen.

  Our Survey whereof shews and we adjudge them to be five Tracts.

  The First whereof (mark'd on the Map No. 71)*

  Begins at a Stake standing by a Road (which Stake is the Easterly Corner of a Lot in John Berry's Patent mark'd on the Map No. 70) and from said Stake runs North fifty four Degrees and Ten Minutes West, Thirty Chains to a Stake at the Edge of the Meadow, Thence North thirty six Degrees and twenty Minutes East five Chains and seventy four Links along the Meadow Edge to a Stake, Thence South fifty four Degrees and Ten Minutes West, thirty Chains to said Road, Then South thirty six Degrees and twenty Minutes West five Chains and seventy four Links along said Road to the Place of Beginning.

---

* This patentee was appointed a clerk in the Secretary's office, Sept 8, 1654. *N. Y. Col. MSS.*, v., 371; licensed "to teach reading, writing, and cyphering," in New Amsterdam, Aug. 13, 1658, *Ibid*, viii., 939 ; and appointed one of the commissioners to fortify Bergen in 1663. *New Neth. Reg.*, 158.

Lot No. 71 was a double lot, consisting of Nos. 4 and 6 in the original allotment, 31x160 rods = 8 morgens 160 rods.

Lot No. 57 was a wood lot 19x150 rods = 4¾ morgens; owned by the heirs of Walter Clendenny in 1840. I think the E. end of this lot was conveyed to Peter Adolph by Arent Toers, June 10, 1754, and by Adolph to Andries Prior, Oct. 27, 1858. *Vide* Note to Lot 367, p. 194. The lot lies a little S. of the Newark plank road.

Lot No. 119 was meadow No. 3 in the original allotment, 48 rods wide from the woods to the river. This lot was owned by Gysbert Van Blarcom, of Aquacknonk, in 1764. By his will, dated April 14, 1760, proved March 3, 1764, it was given to his son *John*, who sold it to Michael Vreeland, Sept. 18, 1770. In March, 1784, Helmus Vreeland, of Staten Island, John Vreeland, of Stony Point, Derrick Vreeland and Cornelius Vreeland, of English Neighbourhood, conveyed the same to Michael Vreeland.

Lot No. 158 was between the school-house and Hans Diedrick's, 5x15 rods. This and lot No. 115 were sold by Gysbert Van Blerteum, weaver, (probably a son of the patentee), to Martin Winne, mason, Aug. 20, 1714. He also sold, at the same time, a lot = 90 acres, extending from the road to the Hackensack river. This was *Lot No.* 71. It lay W. of the town. Winne died seized, July 8, 1737. His son Levinus owned it in 1764, and died May 31, 1802. *Vide* Note to *Van Vleck's Patent*, p. 53, and *Note to Lot* 363, p. 192. The lots seem to have been considerably cut up before 1764. Lot 158 remained in the Winner family until quite a recent period. Robert McFarland was at one time owner, then Daniel Clark, whose widow, Helen, purchased it at Sheriff's sale, Nov., 1837, and sold it to John Romaine, June 7, 1840.

The Second (mark'd on the Map No. 57)

Begins at a Stake (which Stake is the Southerly Corner of a Lot in Jacob Luby's first Patent mark'd on the Map No. 56), and from said Stake runs North fifty one Degrees West twenty eight Chains and ninety Links to a Stake by a Road, Thence South thirty seven Degrees West three Chains and twenty five Links along said Road to a Stake, Thence South forty nine Degrees and thirty Minutes East twenty nine Chains to a Stake, Thence North thirty five Degrees East three Chains and ninety three Links to the Place of Beginning.

*46   * **The Third** (being a Piece of Meadow on Hackinsack River mark'd on the Map No. 119)

Begins at a Stake by the Edge of the Upland (which Stake is the Southerly Corner of a Lot of Meadow in Harman Edward's Patent mark'd on the Map No. 118) and from said Stake runs North fifty four Degrees and ten Minutes West nine Chains & fifty Links to said Hackinsack River, Then returning to said Stake the Place of Beginning, and from thence runs South thirty Degrees and fifty Minutes West nine Chains and five Links along the Edge of the Upland to a Stake, Thence North fifty four Degrees and ten Minutes West twelve Chains to said Hackinsack River, Then up along said River 'til it meets the first mentioned Line.

The Fourth (being a Lot in the Town mark'd on the Map No. 158)

Begins at a Stake (which Stake is the Easterly Corner of a Town Lot in Dirck Teunise's Patent mark'd on the Map No. 163), and from said Stake runs South forty eight Degrees West two Chains and eighty seven Links to a Street, Then South forty two Degrees East ninety eight Links along said Street to a Stake, Thence North forty eight Degrees East two Chains and eighty seven Links to a Stake, Thence North forty two Degrees West ninety eight Links to the Place of Beginning.

The Fifth (being an Out-Garden Plot near the Town mark'd on the Map No. 115)

Begins at a Stake by a Street (which Stake is the Northerly Corner of an Out-Garden Plot in Hans Dedrick's Patent mark'd on the Map No. 114) and from said Stake runs South forty Degrees East six Chains and ninety Links to a Stake, Thence North forty eight Degrees East One Chain and fifty two Links to a Stake, Thence North forty one Degrees and thirty Minutes West six Chains and ninety Links to said Street, Thence South forty eight Degrees West one Chain and twenty eight Links along said Street to the Place of Beginning.

The Patent of Philip Carteret to Pieter Jacobse dated the fifth Day of August One thousand Six hundred and seventy one for sundry Parcels of Land lying in and about the Town of Bergen.

Our Survey whereof shews and we adjudge them to be five Tracts.

The First whereof (being two Lots in the Town which adjoining together are included in one Survey mark'd on the Map No. 159)*

---

* *Lot No.* 159 consisted of three house lots and garden in the town = 2 acres. This, with the next lot, was owned by Peter Merselis in 1764. It afterwards got into the

* **Beginning** at a Stake (which Stake is the Easterly Corner of a *47
Town Lot in Anglebert Stienheysen's Patent mark'd on the Map No. 152)
and from said Stake runs South forty eight Degrees West one Chain and
forty four Links to a Stake, Thence South forty two Degrees East ninety
six Links to a Stake, Thence North forty eight Degrees East, one Chain
and forty four Links to a Stake, Thence South forty two Degrees East
two Chains and forty one Links to a Street, Then North forty eight Degrees East one Chain and forty six Links along said Street to another
Street, Then North forty two Degrees West four Chains and eighty Links
along said other Street to the Square, Thence South forty eight Degrees
West one Chain and forty six Links to a Stake, Thence South forty two
Degrees East One Chain and forty three Links to the Place of Beginning.

The Second (being an Out-Garden adjoining the Town mark'd on
the Map No. 105)

Begins at a Stake by a Street (which Stake is the Northerly
Corner of an Out-Garden in Hendrick Teunise's Patent mark'd on the
Map No. 106) and from said Stake runs South forty one Degrees East
six Chains and ninety Links to a Stake, Thence North forty eight De-
grees East, One Chain and fifty one Links to a Road, Then North forty
Degrees West six Chains and ninety Links along said Road to said
Street, Then South forty eight Degrees West one Chain and forty one
Links along said Street to the Place of Beginning.

The Third (being a Tract of Upland and Meadow mark'd on the
Map No. 85)

Begins at a Stake standing by the Middle Road (which Stake is
the Southerly Corner of a Lot in Fredrick Philipse's Patent mark'd on the
Map No. 86) and from said Stake runs North forty eight Degrees West
sixty one Chains and twenty Links to Hackinsack River, Then returning
to said Stake the Place of Beginning; And from thence runs South fifteen
Degrees West five Chains and seventy three Links along said Road to a
Stake, Thence North forty nine Degrees and forty Minutes West fifty
four Chains and sixty four Links to said Hackinsack River, Then up
along said River as it runs 'til it meets the first mentioned Line.

---

possession of Walter Clendenny, who died seized, Aug. 7, 1822. His executors sold
the end adjoining the square (where the store now is) to Jacob D. Van Winkle, Oct.
28, 1822; the E. end they sold to Rev. John Cornelison, and the middle to Peter Sip,
who sold to Cornelison.

Lot No. 105 was in the new maize land W. of the road = 11 acres. It was sold
by Clendenny's executors to John D. Van Winkle.

Lot No. 85, meadow joining said land = 16¼ acres, owned by Peter Merselis in
1764, and remained in his family till after 1840. *Vide Note to Lot* 11, *New Field Book*.

Lot No. 58 lay S. of the maize land E. of the road = 6 acres. This was also
owned by Merselis in 1764. Walter Clendenny married *Jannetje*, daughter of Merselis
Merselis, and his heirs owned the lot in 1840.

Lot No. 121 formerly belonged to Hans Diedricks, bounded S. by the creek between Andriesen and said meadow, E. by upland in common, W. by the bay, N. by
meadow in common

The Patent also included a lot at Pembrepock = 40 acres, bounded N. by Lourens
Andriesen, E. by the bay, S. by "John the Soldier"; the whole = 87 acres. *Vide
Note to Gilbertse's Patent*, p. 15.

The Fourth (mark'd on the Map No. 58)

Begins at a Stake (which Stake is the Southerly Corner of a Lot in Jan Lubertse's Patent mark'd on the Map No. 57) and from said Stake runs North forty nine Degrees and thirty Minutes West twenty Chains to a Stake by a Road, Thence South forty Degrees West three Chains and sixty Links along said Road to a Stake, Thence South forty nine Degrees and thirty Minutes East twenty nine Chains & forty Links to a Stake, Thence North thirty five Degrees East three Chains and eighty Links to the Place of Beginning.

*48   * **The Fifth** (being a Piece of Meadow mark'd on the Map No. 121)

Begins at the Mouth of a small Creek (which Creek empties into Hackinsack River and is the Division betwixt this Meadow, and the Meadow in Barent Christian's Patent mark'd on the Map No. 122) and from the Mouth of said Creek runs North eighty six Degrees and forty Minutes East nine Chains and eighty five Links along said Hackinsack River to the Mouth of a Ditch, Then South forty four Degrees East fifteen Chains and forty Links up along said Ditch to a Stake by the Edge of the Upland, Thence South twenty six Degrees and fifty Minutes West nine Chains and thirty eight Links along the Edge of the Upland to a Stake at the head of said Creek, Thence down said Creek as it runs to the Place of Beginning.

There is further granted to Peter Jacobse by this Patent, a Parcel of Land lying at Pembrepogh said to contain forty Acres; This Parcel or Piece of Land, We survey'd under the Original Patent for it; which was granted by Petrus Stuyvesant to Lubert Gilbertse fifth Day of December One thousand six hundred and fifty four, as mark'd on the Map No. 20.

The Patent of Philip Carteret to Nicholas Varlet & Balthazer Bayard dated the tenth Day of August, one thousand six hundred and seventy one, for sundry Parcels of Land lying in and about the Town of Bergen.

Our Survey whereof shews, and we adjudge them to be four Tracts.

The First whereof (being a Tract of Upland and Meadow mark'd on the Map No. 83)*

º Bayard was a brewer, a brother of Nicholas; came from Amsterdam; in October, 1664, married Maritje, daughter of Govert Lookerman; was a clerk in the Secretary's office from 1664 to 1660; appointed schepen in Bergen December 17, [1663, and March 17, 1664; represented Bergen in the first and second General Assembly in East Jersey in 1668. Shortly after this he returned to N. Y. He was appointed schepen in New Orange August 16, 1673; assistant alderman in 1686, '87, and alderman in 1691.

Lot No. 83 lay N. E. of Harman Smeeman, S. W. of Paulus Lendertsen, 100 rods along the road = 27 morgens 90 rods. The N. part of this lot was owned by Johannis Van Houten in 1764, and by him sold to Cornelius G. Van Rypen. *Vide Note to Coerten's 1st Patent*, p 25. The S. part belonged to Hans Van Rypen and passed from him to his son Garret, whose four daughters, viz., *Elizabeth*, wife of Daniel Van Rypen, *Hannah*, wife of John G. Van Horne, *Isabella*, wife of John Van Buskirk, and *Margaret*, wife of Cornelius Van Winkle, inherited the property.

Begins at a Stake standing by the Middle Road (which Stake is the Easterly Corner of a Lot in Hendrick Teunise's Patent mark'd on the Map No. 82) and from said Stake runs North sixty four Degrees and ten Minutes West fifty four Chains and sixty Links to Hackinsack River, Then returning to said Stake the Place of Beginning and from thence runs North twenty one Degrees East five Chains and fifty one Links along said Road, Then North twenty five Degrees East four Chains and eighty Links along said Road, Then North thirty five Degrees East Eight Chains and Sixty one Links along said Road to a Stake, Thence North fifty one Degrees and Ten Minutes West fifty Chains and ninety Links to said Hackinsack River, Then down said River as it runs to where it meets the first mentioned Line.

* **The Second** (being also a Tract of Upland and Meadow mark'd *49 on the Map No. 68)

Begins at a Stake standing by a Road (which Stake is the Southerly Corner of a Lot in Harman Edward's Patent mark'd on the Map No. 69) and from said Stake runs North fifty four Degrees and ten Minutes West eighty one Chains and forty nine Links to Hackinsack River, Then returning to said Stake the Place of Beginning and from thence runs South thirty three Degrees West seven Chains and thirty four Links along said Road, Then South thirty nine Degrees West two Chains and ninety Links along said Road to a Stake, Thence North fifty four Degrees and ten Minutes West thirty seven Chains and eight Links to a Stake at

---

Lot No. 68 included a meadow extending to the Kill van Kull = 8 1-6 morgens, and a wood lot lying S. W. of William de Backer, N. E. of Harman Smeeman, 38x150 rods = 9 morgens 572 rods. It was owned by Altje van Rypen, wife of Daniel Van Winkle in 1764, and after her death by her eldest son *Jeremiah*, who died seized May 3, 1837. *Vide Note to Teunise's Patent,* p 54.

Lot No. 160 lay N. E. of the "Plain," as Bergen Square was then called, W. of Lourens Andriesen, 15x12½ rods.

Lot No. 109 consisted of two out gardens, 15x5 rods; owned by Arent Toers in 1764. *Vide Note to Steenhuysen's Patent,* p 32. The whole=144 acres.

The patentees held as joint tenants. Varlet died before a division was made; whereupon Bayard took the land by right of survivorship. On Dec 11, 1686, he sold three of the lots in question, lying between Harman Edwards and Casper Steinmets, 50x150 rods, extending from the road to the meadow, with the meadow 38 rods N. W. to the Hackensack River; together with two house lots in the town to Tadeus Michielsen, who for some years remained in possession, and then sold to Jacob Luby, who died seized in 1697. He had one daughter Annetje, who married Mattheus Cornelise Van Nieuwkerck, Dec. 14, 1670, and had children: *Grietje*, who married Aelt Juriansen, July 7, 1695, *Jacomyntje*, *Jacob*, and *Geertruy*. To these, as the heirs of Jacob Luby, John De Forest and Susanna his wife, daughter of Nicholas Varlet, gave a deed for the same lots June, 10, 1699. From them Jan A. Sip obtained a deed for the same property, Oct. 25, 1699. By will dated March 14, 1699, Bayard gave all his lands to his children, *Ariantje, Anna Maria, Jacobus, Govert,* and *Judith.* They quit-claimed to Jan A Sip, April 30, 1713. *Vide Note to Van Vorst's Patent,* p 60.

Lot 160 yet remains in the family of Richard Sip, deceased.

Lot 109, it seems, was sold by Tuers to Newkirk, and in the partition of July 7, 1795, it fell to Hendrick, who left it to his two sons, and in the partition between them, July 24, 1835, it fell to Garret H. *Vide Note to Pieterse's Patent,* p 40.

the Edge of the Meadow, Thence North fifty two Degrees East three Chains and seventy Links along said Meadow Edge to a Stake, Thence North fifty four Degrees and ten Minutes West forty four Chains and seventy five Links to said Hackinsack River, Then up along said River 'til it meets the first mentioned Line.

The Third (being two Lots in the Town of Bergen which adjoining together are comprehended in one Survey mark'd on the Map No.160)

Begins at a Stake by a Street (which Stake is the Northerly Corner of a Town Lot in Dirck Teunise's Patent mark'd on the Map No. 163) and from said Stake runs North forty eight Degrees East two Chains and ninety three Links along said Street to another Street, Thence South forty two Degrees East two Chains and forty three Links along said other Street to a Stake, Thence South forty eight Degrees West two Chains and ninety three Links to a Stake, Thence North forty two Degrees West two Chains and forty three Links to the Place of Beginning.

The Fourth (being an Out Garden Plot near the Town mark'd on the Map No. 109)

Begins at a Stake standing by a Street (which Stake is the westerly Corner of an Out Garden Plot in Jacob Luby's first Patent mark'd on the Map No. 108) And from said Stake runs South forty Degrees East seven Chains to a Stake, Thence South forty four Degrees West three Chains and thirty five Links to a Stake, Thence North forty Degrees West eight Chains and fifty five Links to a Stake, Thence North thirty nine Degrees East Sixty five Links to a Stake, Thence South forty eight Degrees East one Chain and forty four Links to a Stake, Thence North forty eight Degrees East two Chains and fifty six Links along the Old Burying Ground and the Street to the Place of Beginning.

*50
* **The Patent** of Philip Carteret to Dow Harmense, dated the twelfth Day of May One thousand six hundred and sixty eight; For sundry Parcels of Land lying in and about the Town of Bergen.

Our Survey whereof shews, and we adjudge them to be five Tracts.

The First whereof (being a Tract of Upland and Meadow mark'd on the Map No. 79)*

---

* This patentee came from Friesland with his wife and four children and arrived here June, 1658, in the ship *Brownfish*.

Lot No. 79 was behind Christian Pietersen's land, 20 rods wide.

Lot No. 80 was N. E. of Christian Pietersen's land, S. W. of Caspar Steinmets, 28 rods wide, extending from the road to the river = 20 morgens.

Lot No. 65 was lot No. 15 in the original allotment; 19 rods wide, extending from the road to the river = 8¾ morgens. The heirs of Michael DeMott sold the upland to the Peytons, the N. half of which is now owned by Dr. Josiah Peyton.

Lot No. 161, in the town, 7 rods and half a foot by 12¼ rods.

Lot No. 93, an out garden, 8x26 rods.

It was in the survey of these lots in the new maize land, in Nov., 1660, by Jacques Cortelyou, sworn surveyor, preparatory to a grant, that the name of Bergen first appears. The patentee died seized, leaving two sons, *Harman* and *Teunis* To these two sons he left his property, by will dated March 25, 1678, recorded May 9, 1678.

DOW HARMENSE.

Begins at a Stake (which Stake is the Northerly Corner of a Lot in Gerrit Garritse's Patent mark'd on the Map No. 78) and from said Stake runs North sixty six Degrees and thirty Minutes West sixty two Chains and eighty four Links to Hackinsack River, Then returning to said Stake the Place of Beginning and from thence runs South fifty nine Degrees and fifteen minutes West four Chains and eighty seven Links to a Stake, Thence North sixty six Degrees and thirty Minutes West Sixty three Chains to said Hackinsack River, Then up along said River, 'til it meets the first mentioned Line.

The Second (being also a Tract of Upland and Meadow mark'd on the Map No. 80)

Begins at a Stake standing by the Middle Road (which Stake is the Easterly Corner of a Lot in Gerrit Gerritse's Patent mark'd on the Map No. 78) and from said Stake runs North sixty six Degrees and thirty Minutes West Seventy five Chains and twelve Links to Hackinsack River, Then returning to said Stake the Place of Beginning and from thence runs North twenty four Degrees East five Chains and twenty five Links along said Road to a Stake, Thence North sixty six Degrees and thirty Minutes West sixty eight Chains to said Hackinsack River, Then down along the said River, 'til it meets the first mentioned Line.

The Third (being also a Tract of Upland and Meadow mark'd on the Map No. 65)

Begins at a Stake by a Road (which Stake is the Southerly Corner of a Lot in Caspar Stymat's Second Patent mark'd on the Map No. 66) and from said Stake runs North fifty four Degrees and ten Minutes West seventy eight Chains to Hackinsack River, Then returning to said Stake the Place of Beginning and from thence runs South thirty nine Degrees West three Chains & fifty Six Links along said Road to a Stake, Thence North fifty four Degrees & ten Minutes West seventy seven Chains and ninety Links to said Hackinsack River, Then up along said River, 'til it meets the first mentioned Line.

* **The Fourth** (being a Lot in the Town of Bergen mark'd on the Map No. 161) *51

Begins at a Stake standing in the Corner of two Streets (which Stake bears South seventeen Degrees and forty five Minutes West one Chain and forty four Links from the Easterly Corner of the Widow Van Riper's House) And from said Stake runs South forty two Degrees East two Chains and thirty two Links along a Street to a Stake, Thence South forty eight Degrees West one Chain and forty six Links to a Stake, Thence North forty two Degrees West two chains and thirty two Links to another Street, Then North forty eight Degrees East one Chain and forty six Links along said other Street to the Place of Beginning.

Teunis (named in the deed Teunis Douwensen Tallman) sold the property in question to Mattys DeMott, Oct. 31, 1705. *Vide Note to Stoffelsen's Patent*, p. 6. Michael, the nephew of George, by will dated May 13, 1831, devised lots Nos. 79 and 80 to his son Garret, who left them to his only son Michael, who, dying in 1850, left them to his two children John H. and Josephine H. These sold to The Marion Building Company, incorporated Feb. 26, 1866.

Michael sold Lot 93 to Sip

𝕮𝖍𝖊 𝕱𝖎𝖋𝖙𝖍 (being an Out Garden Plot near the Town mark'd on the Map No. 93)

𝕭𝖊𝖌𝖎𝖓𝖘 at a Stake by a Street (which Stake is the Southerly Corner of an Out Garden Plot in Adrian Post's Patent mark'd on the Map No. 100) and from said Stake runs North forty eight Degrees West four Chains and ninety Links to a Stake, Thence South forty nine Degrees and thirty Minutes West One Chain and twenty two Links to a Stake, Thence South forty one Degrees and thirty Minutes East four Chains and eighty Links to said Street, Then North fifty Degrees East One Chain and seventy five Links along said Street to the Place of Beginning.

𝕮𝖍𝖊 𝕻𝖆𝖙𝖊𝖓𝖙 of Philip Carteret to John Berry dated the twentyeth Day of July One thousand six hundred and sixty nine for sundry Parcels of Land lying in and about the Town of Bergen.

𝕺𝖚𝖗 𝕾𝖚𝖗𝖛𝖊𝖞 whereof shews, and we adjudge them to be Three Tracts.

𝕮𝖍𝖊 𝕱𝖎𝖗𝖘𝖙 whereof (being a Lot in the Town of Bergen mark'd on the Map No. 162)*

° These lots were sold to Berry by Samuel Edsall, July 12, 1670.

Lot No. 162 was bounded N. W. by Balthazar Bayard's house, S. E. by the road, S. W. by Hans Diedrick's house.

Lot No. 125 lay between the road and Lourens Adriensen's land (formerly Bartholemew Lott), bounded N. E. by the woods, N. W. by the N. E. lane "that goeth into the woods."

Lot No. 70. The six upland lots lay in the "common field," bounded S. E. by the highway, 14x150 rods. The six meadow lots adjoined the N. W. end of the upland lots; were of the same width and extended to the river. Judging by the subdivision of the allotment to this Patent, nearly the whole of it was in the Newkirk family in 1764. Mathevis and Hendrick were sons of Gerrit. Mathevis, jr., and Jacob, were sons of Poulus. Gerrit and Poulus must have partitioned Lot 125 before their death. Garret taking the S. half, and Poulus the N. half. Mathevis and Hendrick partitioned the S. half, July 7, 1795; Mathevis taking the N. half and Hendrick the S. half. Mathevis gave his half to his son Garret H. by deed dated Aug. 1, 1810, who, by will dated April 7, 1832, proved Oct. 31, 1832, divided the same between his sons *Garret G.* and *Henry.* Garret received all N. of Newkirk Street and Henry all S. of that street. Garret still owns all W. of Palisade Ave., except a small piece on the W. end, which he sold to Maria, wife of Smith Garrabrant. All E. of Palisade Ave. he has sold in parcels to Blakely Wilson and others. Henry died Aug. 29, 1861.

Mathevis, jr., after his father Poulus, owned the N. half of Lot 125. He died seized, Nov. 12, 1818, and the same passed to his only son, *John M.*, who sold the same to Jones and others.

Henry's land within this Patent, and what his father bought of the Van Houten tract E. of the town, was inherited by his children, *James M., Henry H., Garret, John, Mary*, wife of George V. De Mott, and *Eliza*, wife of Francis P. Gautier.

In the partition between Mathevis and Hendrick *Lot* 70 was divided as follows: Mathevis took the N. half, which was afterwards partitioned between his sons. Hendrick took the S. half, which was partitioned between his sons, *Garret H.* and *George*, the former taking the E. half and the latter the W. half. *Vide Note to Pieterse's Patent*, p. 40.

Begins at a Stake (which Stake is the Easterly Corner of the Town) And from said Stake runs North forty two Degrees West One Chain and eighteen Links along a Street to a Stake, Thence South forty eight Degrees West two Chains and ninety one Links to a Stake, Thence South forty two Degrees East, One Chain and eighteen Links to another Street, Thence North forty eight Degrees East two Chains and ninety one Links along said other Street to the Place of Beginning.

* **The Second** (said in the Patent to be two Plantations and which adjoining together we have comprehended in one Survey mark'd on the Map No. 125)

Begins at a Stake (which Stake is the Southerly Corner of an Out- *52 Garden-Plot in Hans Dedricks Patent mark'd on the Map No. 114) And from said Stake runs South thirty five Degrees and fifty five Minutes East thirteen Chains and forty six Links to a Stake, Thence North fifty one Degrees and fifteen Minutes East twenty eight Chains and forty Links to a Stake, Thence North thirty eight Degrees and forty five Minutes West nineteen Chains and twenty eight Links to a Post of the Fence by the Road that leads from the Town to the English Neighbourhood (which said Post stands South Eleven Degrees and ten Minutes West three Chains and four Links from the Easterly Corner of a Lot in Caspar Stymats first Patent mark'd on the Map No. 34) And from said Post runs South thirty one Degrees West three Chains and ninety six Links along said Road, Then South forty one Degrees and thirty Minutes West seven Chains and fifteen Links along said Road to the Turn thereof, Then North seventy four Degrees and thirty Minutes West Ten Chains and twenty Links along said Road to a Stake, Then South nine Degrees East four Chains and ten Links to a Stake, Then South forty two Degrees West thirty eight Links to a Street, Then South forty two Degrees East three Chains and twenty Links along said Street to a Stake at the Corner of another Street, Then South forty eight Degrees West sixty Links along said other Street to a Stake, Thence South forty two Degrees and fifty Minutes East six Chains and ninety Links to a Stake, Thence South forty eight Degrees West five Chains and ninety six Links to the Place of Beginning.

The Third (said in the Patent to be six Lots of Wood Land and six Lots of Meadow joining, All which twelve Lots as adjoining together we have comprehended in one Survey mark'd on the Map No. 70)

Begins at a Stake standing by a Road (which Stake is the Southerly Corner of a Lot in Jan Lubertse's Patent mark'd on the Map No. 71) and from said Stake runs North fifty four Degrees and ten Minutes West seventy eight Chains, and eighty eight Links to Hackinsack River, Then returning to said Stake the Place of Beginning, and from thence runs South thirty six Degrees and twenty Minutes West two Chains and eighty one Links along said Road, Then South thirty three Degrees West twelve Chains and ninety four Links along said Road to a Stake, Thence North fifty four Degrees and ten Minutes West eighty one Chains and forty nine Links to said Hackinsack River, Then up along said River as it runs 'til it meets the first mentioned Line.

* **The Patent** of Philip Carteret to Tielman Van Vleck *53 dated the twenty fifth Day of March One thousand Six hundred and seventy, for sundry Parcels of Land near the Town of Bergen.

Our Survey whereof shews and we adjudge them to be two Tracts.

The First whereof (being a Tract of Upland and Meadow mark'd on the May No. 72)*

Begins at a Stake (which Stake is the Northerly Corner of a Lot in Jacob Luby's Patent marked on the Map No. 61) and from said Stake runs North sixty nine Degrees and ten Minutes West twenty six Chains and thirty six Links to a Stake at the Edge of the Meadow, Thence North thirty eight Degrees East three Chains and forty Links along said Meadow Edge to a Stake, Thence North sixty eight Degrees and forty Minutes West to Hackinsack River, Then returning to the first mentioned Stake the Place of Beginning and from thence runs South twenty eight Degrees and fifty Minutes West ten Chains to a Stake in the Turn of a Road (which Stake is the Northerly Corner of a Lot in Harman Edward's Patent mark'd on the Map, No. 143) and from said Stake runs South thirty six Degrees and twenty Minutes West four Chains and eighty Links along said Road to a Stake, Thence North fifty four Degrees and ten Minutes West thirty Chains to a Stake at the Edge of the Meadow, Thence South thirty six Degrees and twenty Minutes West five Chains and seventy four Links along the Meadow Edge to a Stake, Thence North fifty four Degrees and ten Minutes West forty eight Chains and eighty eight Links to said Hackinsack River, Then up along the same 'til it reaches the other Line, that strikes said River.

The Second (being an Out Garden Plot near the Town mark'd on the Map No. 129)

Begins at a Post (standing on the Northwest side of a Road which Post is the southerly Corner of the Church Yard and bears South nineteen Degrees and forty Minutes West one Chain and twenty two Links from the Southerly Corner of the Church) And from said Post runs North

---

* This patentee may justly be regarded as the founder of Bergen. He came originally from Bremen, studied under a Notary in Amsterdam, came to this country about 1658, and was admitted to practice the same year. *N. Y. Col. MSS.*, viii, 932. He was made the first schout, and president of the Court of Bergen, Sept. 5, 1661. *New Neth. Reg.*, 100.

Lot No. 72 extended from the road to the river, 48 chains x 40 rods=44 acres owned by Levinus Winne in 1764. This and Lot 72 were in his family after 1840.

Lot No. 129, bounded N. and W. by the common=¼ acre.

Lot No. 134 was half of his meadow, and was probably included in the 44 acres above described, as was also Lot No. 135, sold by him to Ide Van Vorst, March 25, 1668. The Patent mentions but two lots. Martin Winne sold to Peter Sip, April 13, 1814, a strip along the N. side of the Church lot (a little N. of Highland Ave.), and extending back from the road to the rear of the lot; bounded N. by John S. Winne =¼ acre. John S. Winne sold the N. half of this lot to John E. Smith, May 1, 1816=⅛ acre. *Vide Note to Lot* 363, p. 192. (John S. was the only son of Martin Winner by his wife Gertrude Sickles. John S. had a twin sister who died Sept. 23, 1806. She was born July 19, 1791. John died Feb., 1856, intestate, leaving one child, John. His daughter Eleanor P. married Richard Vreeland, and died before her father.) *Vide Note to Lubbertse's Patent*, p. 45.

sixty three Degrees and ten Minutes West one Chain and eighty six Links along the Church Yard to a Stake, Thence South forty Degrees West one Chain and seventy eight Links to a Stake, Thence South thirty Degrees West sixty seven Links to a Stake, Thence South sixty three Degrees and ten Minutes East two Chains and eighty two Links to a Stake by the said Road, Thence North fourteen Degrees and twenty Minutes East two Chains and forty six Links along said Road to the Place of Beginning.

Beside the foregoing Patent to Tielman Van Vleek; there has* *54 been been laid before us a certify'd Copy of a Transport or Deed of Conveyance from said Van Vleck to Ide Corneliese bearing Date the twenty fifth Day of May One thousand six hundred and sixty eight for a Lot of Upland with one half of the Meadow adjoining thereto and a House Lot in the Town of Bergen. Which three Lots of Land are in the said Transport express'd to be, "A certain Parcel of his the said Tielman's Land lying and being in and about Bergen specify'd by the Patent and Survey specifying the same." Which Patent tho' search'd for has not been found. But there has been produced to us the Patent of Philip Carteret dated the thirty first Day of May, One thousand six hundred sixty eight granting and confirming to said Corneliese the said Lot of Upland with one half of the Meadow adjoining thereto; And which in Conformity to said Patent we have run out for him (as the same are mark'd on our Map, The Upland No. 88; and have of the Meadow No. 135) Whence we conceive the other Half of the Meadow remains to be run out and ascertain'd; and we have accordingly run out the same.

Our Survey whereof shews and we adjudge it to be a Tract mark'd on the Map No. 134)

Beginning at a Stake standing by the Edge of the Upland (which Stake is the Northeasterly Corner of the Lot of Upland in Ide Corneliese's Patent mark'd on the Map No. 88) And from said Stake runs North forty four Degrees and twenty Minutes West fourteen Chains and fifty three Links to Bridge Creek, Then returning to said Stake the Place of Beginning and from thence runs South eighty two Degrees West nine Chains and fifteen Links along the edge of the Upland to a Stake, Thence South thirty five Degrees West one Chain and seventy seven Links along the Edge of said Upland to a Stake, Thence North forty four Degrees and twenty Minutes West eleven Chains and eighty seven Links to said Bridge Creek. Then up along the said Creek the several Courses thereof as it runs 'til it meets the first mentioned Line.

The first **Patent** of Philip Carteret to Hendrick Teunise dated the twelfth Day of May, One thousand six hundred and Sixty eight for sundry Parcels of Land lying in and about the Town of Bergen.

Our Survey whereof shews and we adjudge them to be four Tracts.

The First whereof (being a Tract of Upland and Meadow mark'd on the Map No. 82)*

---

* The original grant for these lots was dated Sept. 11, 1662.

Lot No. 82 was in the new maize land = 20 morgens. It seems to have been owned by Harman Smeeman in 1671. *Vide Note to Varlet and Bayard's Patent*, p. 48.

*55 * **Begins** at a Stake standing by the Middle Road (which Stake is the Southerly Corner of a Lot in Varlet and Bayard's Patent mark'd on the Map No. 83) And from said Stake runs North sixty four Degrees and

---

Lot No. 73 was a meadow behind Michiel Jansen's meadow, butting upon the woods, and parted by a creek from Jansen's meadow = 4¾ morgens. This lot was sold by the patentee to Fitje Hartman, April 26, 1688, for 425 guilders "light currency." In this deed the grantor is described as "Reverend Hendrick Teunisse," and yet makes his mark. It was owned by Michael Hartmanse Vreeland in 1764. *Vide Note to Claesen's Patent,* p. 12.

Lot No. 165 lay between Jans Swaen and Paulus Lendertsen, 7¼x12¼ rods.

Lot No. 106, between the same parties, 7x25 rods. The whole = 48 acres.

This land (except *Lot No.* 73) was bought of the patentee by Jacob Jacobsen Van Winckel, by whose will, dated Sept. 3, 1708, proved Oct. 16, 1732, the same was given to the children of his first wife, viz.: *Hendrick, Catherine,* and *Samuel.* Samuel quit-claimed to Hendrick Dec. 17, 1743, who remained owner of most of it in 1764. Hendrick, by will dated Nov. 29, 1766, proved April 20, 1769, gave to his son *Jacob* his house-lot, garden, and orchard, also a lot lying between Ide Sip and the lane leading to the Bergen Farms, also two lots, each 20 rods wide, extending from the road to the Hackensack River = 40 acres; also one quarter of the commons adjudged to him for the Patents of Teunise and Edwards, and one quarter belonging to the plantations formerly bought of Arent Laurens, Guert Coerten, and Nicholas Varlet. To *Daniel* he gave a lot between Casparus Prior and Cornelius Van Rypen, about 19x150 rods, also a piece of meadow on the river, also all his right in four plantations lying between the Mill and Kuyper's land, bought of Arent Laurens, Guert Coerten, and Nicholas Varlet; (this mill was on Bridge Creek, in the meadow W. of the Long Dock tunnel. This land afterwards was owned by the Merselis family); also one quarter of the commons adjudged to him for the Patents of Teunise and Edwards. To *Hendrick* he gave a house and lot in the town, on Academy street, E. of the square, and a garden opposite, also one quarter of the commons adjudged to him for the Patents of Teunise and Edwards. To *Joseph* he gave two lots called Rockland (also called the Clip, at the junction of the Bergen Woods road and Hackensack Turnpike); also a lot called Klein Suckie; also Goose Neck Meadow; also the commons adjudged to him for the Patent of Steenhuysen; also one quarter of the commons adjudged to him for the Patents of Teunise and Edwards; also one quarter of all other commons.

By *Daniel's* will, dated July 2, 1810, proved Sept. 9, 1845, he gave to his son *Jerrie* his homestead on the road leading to Bergen Point (between Duncan and Fair View Aves.); also a lot of meadow on the Hackensack; also a lot of upland and cedar swamp. To *Henry* he gave lot S. of Newark Ave. E. of Chestnut Ave. down to Mill Creek. *Vide New Field Book and Map B.*

Joseph, by will dated Sept. 4, 1807, proved Aug. 14, 1809, gave to his nephews, *John* and *Jacob,* the land where they then lived. Joseph, son of Abraham, received nine acres where the testator lived, the salt meadow near Mill Creek, and the cedar swamp bought of Casparus Prior. The rest of his property he devised to Daniel, Henry, and Abraham, sons of Jacob Van Winkle; Jerrie and Henry, children of his brother Daniel; Jacob, son of his brother Henry; Joseph, son of Abraham, and Joseph, son of George Shepherd, equally. *Vide Note to Lot* 319, p. 207.

Jerry Van Winkle, by will dated June 14, 1834, proved Sept. 4, 1837, gave to his three grandsons, Daniel G., John G., and Garret S., all his land. John G. received one-half of the wood lot called De Wildehousen, i.e. Indian Village, now in West Hoboken. *Vide Note to Varlet's and Bayard's Patent,* p. 48.

ten Minutes West fifty four Chains and sixty Links to Hackinsack River, Then returning to the said Stake the Place of Beginning and from thence runs South twenty six Degrees West seven Chains and sixty five Links along said Road to a Stake, Thence North sixty four Degrees and ten Minutes West sixty Chains and sixty Links to said Hackinsack River, Then up along said River as it runs 'til it meets the first mentioned Line.

The Second (being a piece of Meadow lying back of Communipan mark'd on the Map No. 73)

Begins at a Stake in a Heap of Stones standing by the Edge of the Upland (which Stake bears from the East Corner of a large Rock before Michael Vreelands Door North fifty three Degrees East two Chains and eighty four Links, and is distant forty Links on a Southeasterly Course from Derck Sycan's Creek) And from said Stake runs North twenty seven Degrees and fifteen Minutes East twenty four Chains and thirty four Links along the Edge of the Upland to a Stake standing by the Head of a small Creek, Thence South forty six Degrees and thirty Minutes East two Chains and seventy five Links to where said small Creek falls into Derck Sycan's Creek, Then down along said Sycan's Creek Southeasterly and Westerly as it runs 'til it comes within forty Links Distance of the Stake the Place of Beginning. Thence Northwesterly forty Links to said Stake.

The Third (being a Lot in the Town of Bergen mark'd on the Map No. 165)

Begins at a Stake standing by a Street (which Stake is the Easterly Corner of a Town Lot in Guert Gerritse's Patent mark'd on the Map No. 154) And from said Stake runs North forty eight Degrees East one Chain and forty four Links along said Street to a Stake, Thence North forty two Degrees West two Chains and forty one Links to a Stake, Thence South forty eight Degrees West one Chain and forty four Links to a Stake, Thence South forty two Degrees East two Chains and forty one Links to the Place of Beginning.

The Fourth (being an Out-Garden-Plot near the Town mark'd on the Map No. 106)

Begins at a Stake standing by a Street (which Stake is the northerly Corner of an Out Garden Plot in Guert Gerritse's Patent mark'd on the Map No. 107) And from said Stake runs South forty one Degrees East six Chains & ninety Links to a Stake, Thence North forty eight Degrees East one Chain & thirty three Links to a Stake, Thence North forty one Degrees West six Chains and ninety Links to said street, Then South forty eight Degrees West one Chain and thirty one Links along said street to the Place of Beginning.

*****The Patent** of Philip Carteret to Hans Dedrick dated the *56 twelfth Day of May One thousand six hundred and sixty eight for sundry Parcels of Land lying in and about the Town of Bergen.

Our Survey whereof shews and we adjudge them to be five Tracts.

The First whereof (being a Tract of Upland and Meadow mark'd on the Map No. 75)*

---

* This patentee has the honor of being the second person to "keep a hotel" in Bergen, being licensed Feb. 13, 1671. He was appointed lieutenant in the Bergen

Begins at a Stake standing by the Middle Road (which Stake is the easterly Corner of a Lot in Fredrick Philipse's Patent mark'd on the Map No. 74) and from said Stake runs North sixty eight Degrees and forty Minutes West to Hackensack River, Then returning to said Stake the Place of Beginning and from thence runs North four Degrees east two Chains and eighty eight Links along said Road to a Stake, Thence North sixty seven Degrees and twenty Minutes West to said Hackensack River, Then down along said River 'til it meets the first mentioned Line.

The Second (being also a Tract of Upland and Meadow mark'd on the Map No. 84)

Begins at a Stake standing by the Middle Road (which Stake is the Southerly Corner of a Lot in Peter Jacobse's Patent mark'd on the Map No. 85) And from said Stake runs North forty nine Degrees and forty Minutes West fifty four Chains and sixty four Links to Hackensack River, Then returning to said Stake the Place of Beginning; and from thence runs South twenty eight Degrees West three Chains and thirty two Links along said Road to a Stake, Thence North fifty one Degrees and ten Minutes West fifty four Chains and Seventy Links to said Hackensack River, Then up along said River 'til it meets the first mentioned Line.

The Third (being an Out Garden Plot near the Town mark'd on the Map No. 114)

Begins at a Stake by a Street (which Stake is the westerly Corner of an Out Garden Plot in the Jan Lubertse's Patent mark'd on the Map No. 115) And from said Stake runs South forty Degrees East six Chains and ninety Links to a Stake, Thence South forty eight Degrees West one Chains and fifty three Links to a Stake (being the westerly Corner and Place of Beginning of a Lot in John Berry's Patent mark'd on the Map No. 125 (and from said Stake runs North forty Degrees West six Chains

---

militia Sept. 4, 1673; was one of the patentees of Aquacknonck, May 28, 1679; died Sept. 30, 1698.

Lot No. 75, 16 rods wide, stretching N. W. and W. along the wagon way to the Kil Van Kol = 8 morgens.

Lot No. 84, 18 rods wide, stretching N. W. from the road to the river = 16 morgens 350 rods.

Lot No. 110 at an early date was owned by the Tuers family, and was owned by Arent in 1764. It was sold by that family to the church at Bergen, and now forms part of the burying ground.

Lot No. 114, between Jan Lubbertsen and the cart-way, 7x25 rods. This lot was in possession of his son *Wander* in 1714, and he must have died seized Aug. 13, 1732.

Lot No. 166, between Jan Lubbertsen and the Guardque (guardhouse?) 15x12¼ rods; owned by Abraham Diedricks in 1764. The whole = 54 acres.

The patentee died Sept. 30, 1698, and probably left this land to his son *Wander* who died intestate Aug, 13, 1732. His children *Johannis, Garret, Cornelius, Abraham, Antje*, wife of Johannis Vreeland, and *Margaret* Van Rypen, widow, sold to their brother *Daniel*, Feb. 17, 1764, a lot called "Smiths land"= 7 morgens, also a lot of meadow, also the Steenhuysen lot, and Lot 114. They partitioned in 1755. *Vide Note to Steenhuysen's Patent*, p. 32.

and ninety Links to a Stake at the Corner of said Street, Thence North forty eight Degrees East one Chain & fifty two Links along said Street to the Place of Beginning.

The Fourth (being two Out Garden Plots near the Town which adjoining together are comprehended in one Survey mark'd on the Map No. 110) *57

Begins at a Stake by a Road leading from the Town to Bergen Point (which Stake is the Westerly Corner of an Out Garden in Paulus Peterse's Patent mark'd on the Map No. 103) And from said Stake runs South fifty three Degrees and fifty Minutes East two Chains and thirty Links to a Stake, Thence North thirty nine Degrees East forty Links to a Stake, Thence South forty Degrees East eight Chains and fifty five Links to a Stake, Thence South forty four Degrees West three Chains to a Stake, Thence North forty Degrees West nine Chains and sixty Links to the said Road, Then North fourteen Degrees and twenty Minutes east two Chains and forty six Links along said Road to the Place of Beginning.

The Fifth (being two Lots in the Town of Bergen which adjoining together are comprehended in one Survey mark'd on the Map No. 166)

Begins at a Stake (which Stake is the Southerly Corner of a Town Lot in Jan Lubertse's Patent mark'd on the Map No. 158) And from said Stake runs South forty two Degrees East two Chains and thirty seven Links along said Street to another Street, Then North forty eight Degrees East two Chains and eighty Seven Links along said other Street to a Stake, Thence North forty two Degrees West two Chains and thirty seven Links to the Stake, Thence South forty eight Degrees west two Chains and eighty seven Links to the Place of Beginning.

The Patent of Petrus Stuyvesant to Dirck Teunise dated the fourteenth Day of September, One thousand six hundred & sixty two for sundry Parcels of Land lying in and about the Town of Bergen.

Our Survey whereof shews and we adjudge them to be two Tracts.

The First whereof (mark'd on the Map No. 76)*

Begins at a Stake by the Middle Road (which Stake is the Easterly Corner of a Lot in Hans Dedricks Patent mark'd on the Map No. 75) and from said Stake runs North sixty seven Degrees and twenty Minutes West twenty one Chains & eighty Links to a Stake, Thence North forty Degrees East ten Chains and fifty five Links to a Stake, Thence South sixty six Degrees and thirty Minutes East fifteen Chains and fifty five Links to said Road, Then South three Degrees West ten Chains and forty Links along said Road to the Place of Beginning.

*** The Second** (being a Lot in the Town of Bergen mark'd on the Map No. 163) *5͏͏

º *Vide Note to Gerrit Gerritsen's Patent*, p. 58. Lot 76 was owned by Hartman Van Wagenen after 1840. Lot 163 was probably sold by Johannis Van Wagenen to Joris De Mott shortly after 1764. *Vide Note to Stoffelsen's Patent*, p. 9. Michael De Mott sold it to Garret Benson, who sold to Abraham Speer, the present owner.

Begins at a Stake (which Stake stands North fifty seven Degrees East One Chain and fifty seven Links from a Stake standing nearly in the Middle of the Square; which last Stake bears North forty seven Degrees East six Chains and fifty three Links from the Easterly Corner of the Church) And from said first Stake the Place of Beginning runs South forty two Degrees East two Chains and forty three Links to a Stake, Thence North forty eight Degrees East one Chain and forty one Links to a Stake, Thence North forty two Degrees West two Chains and forty three Links to the Street, Then South forty eight Degrees West one Chain and forty one Links along said Street to the Place of Beginning.

It is to be Observ'd, there is an Out-Garden in this Dutch Patent (mark'd on our Map No. 94) which we have run out and survey'd for Guert Coerten under his first Patent from Philip Carteret dated twelfth of May One thousand six hundred and sixty eight, it appearing from the Description in both Patents to be the very same Garden. So that Coerten must have purchased it of Teunise and got it confirm'd to him in his said Patent from Carteret.

There is also a Lott of Upland and Meadow mentioned in this Dutch Patent (mark'd on our Map No. 91) Which we have run out & survey'd for Guert Coerten under his first Patent from Philip Carteret dated twelfth of May, One thousand six hundred and sixty eight, it appearing most probable from the Description in both Patents to be the same Lot. So, that (as well as the Out-Garden) Coerten must also have purchas'd this Lot of Upland and Meadow of Teunise and got it confirm'd in his said first Patent from Carteret. And this is the more probable, as we cou'd find no other Place that wou'd suit the Description given of this Lot, neither does Mr. Van Wagenen the present Owner and Possessor of this Dutch Patent claim, or know anything of such Lot.

The Patent of Philip Carteret to Gerrit Gerritse, dated the twelfth Day of May one thousand six hundred and sixty eight for sundry Parcels of Land lying in and about the Town of Bergen.

Our Survey whereof shews and we adjudge them to be four Tracts.

The First whereof (being a Tract of Upland and Meadow mark'd on the Map No. 77)*

° *Lot No.* 77, N. E. of Hans Diedrick's, on the half part of the creupel bosch, S. W. of Douwe Harmansen, 6¼ rods wide from the swamp to the creek; with the meadow = 28 morgens.

Lot No. 78, along the highway S. W. of Douwe Harmansen, N. E. of Derrick Teunisen, 20x70 rods = 2½ morgens.

Lot No. 167, between Samuel Edsall and Adrian Post, 7½x12½ rods.

Lot No. 98, an out-garden between Guert Coerten and Arian Laurensen, 8 rods wide, and goes to Fredrick Philipsen's land = 17 acres.

The Patentee was the ancestor of the Van Wagenen family, By his will, dated Oct 13, 1708, he gave all the land included in this Patent, and the preceding Patent to his eldest son *Johannis*. By the will of Johannis, dated July 54, 1752, proved Nov. 8, 1759, he gave all his lands in Bergen to his son Johannis, who was the owner in 1764. By his will, dated March 15, 1794, proved June 17, 1797, all his real estate passed to his son Jacob. By his will, dated June 25, 1835, proved Aug. 2, 1839, it

* **Begins** at a Stake (which Stake is the Westerly Corner of the *59 second Lot in this Patent next to be describ'd and mark'd on the Map No. 78 and said stake is also the Northerly Corner of a Lot in Dirck Teunise's Patent mark'd on the Map No. 76) and from said Stake runs North sixty six Degrees and thirty Minutes West to H ickinsack River, Then returning to said Stake the Place of Beginning; And from thence runs South forty Degrees West ten Chains and fifty five Links to a Stake, Thence North sixty seven Degrees and twenty Minutes West to said Hackinsack River, Then up along said River 'til it meets the first mentioned Line.

The Second (mark'd on the Map No. 78)

Begins at a Stake by the Middle Road (which Stake is the Easterly Corner of a Lot in Dirck Teunise's Patent mark'd on the Map No. 76) And from said Stake runs North fifteen Degrees East three Chains and eighty six Links along said Road to a Stake, Thence North sixty six Degrees and thirty Minutes West twelve Chains and twenty eight Links to a Stake, Thence South fifty nine Degrees and fifteen Minutes West four Chains and eighty seven Links to a Stake, Thence South sixty six Degrees and thirty Minutes East fifteen Chains and fifty five Links to the Place of Beginning.

The Third (being a Lot in the Town of Bergen mark'd on the Map No. 167)

Begins at a Stake by a Street (which Stake is the Northerly Corner of a Town Lot in Adrian Post's Patent mark'd on the Map No. 164) And from said Stake runs South forty two Degrees East two Chains and thirty two Links to a Stake, Thence North forty eight Degrees East one Chain and forty two Links to a Stake, Thence North forty two Degrees West two Chains and thirty two Links to said Street, Then South forty eight Degrees West one Chain and forty two Links along said Street to the Place of Beginning.

The Fourth (being an Out-Garden-Plot near the Town mark'd on the Map No. 98)

Begins at a Stake by a Road (which Stake is the Southerly Corner of an Out-Garden-Plot in Guert Coerten's first Patent mark'd on the Map No. 97) And from said Stake runs North thirty nine Degrees and twenty Minutes West four Chains and Eighty Links to a Stake, Thence South forty nine Degrees and thirty Minutes West one Chain and twenty Links to a Stake, Thence South thirty nine Degrees and twenty Minutes East four Chains and eighty Links to said Road, Then North fifty Degrees East one Chain and twenty Links along said Road to the Place of Beginning.

* **The Patent** of Philip Carteret to Ide Corneliese dated the *60 thirty first day of May One thousand six hundred and sixty eight, for a Piece of Upland and a Piece of Meadow lying to the Northward of the Town of Bergen.

---

went to his son, *Hartman* and grandchildren Cornelius, Jacob, and Christiana, children of his son *John*. Lot 167 now forms part of the homestead of Hartman.

Of Lot 77 Hartman sold all between West Side Ave. and the meadow to the United States Watch Company. A strip 100 feet in depth on the E. side of the Ave. he sold to Abel R. Corbin.

Our Survey whereof shews and we adjudge them to be two Tracts.

The First (being the Piece of Upland mark'd on the Map No. 88)*

Begins at a Stake standing by the Middle Road (which Stake is the easterly Corner of a Lot in Jacob Luby's Patent mark'd on the Map No. 87) And from said Stake runs North thirty four Degrees and fifteen Minutes East six Chains & eighty six Links along said Road to a Stake, Thence north four Degrees east three Chains to a Stake on the Top of the Hill, Thence north nine Degrees and thirty Minutes West sixteen Chains and thirty Links to a Stake, by the Edge of the Meadow, Thence South eighty two Degrees west nine Chains and fifteen Links along said Meadow Edge to a Stake, Thence South thirty five Degrees West five Chains & fifty five Links along said Meadow Edge, Then South forty one Degrees west five Chains and fifty Links along said Meadow Edge to a Stake, Thence South forty four Degrees and twenty Minutes East twenty Chains and sixty Links to the Place of Beginning.

The Second (being the Piece of Meadow mark'd on the Map No. 135)

Begins at a Stake (which Stake is the westerly Corner of the Lot of Upland last above describ'd) And from said Stake runs north forty four Degrees and twenty Minutes West thirteen Chains and sixty Links to Bridge Creek, Then returning to said Stake the Place of Beginning and from thence runs north forty one Degrees East five Chains and fifty Links along the Meadow Edge, Then North thirty five Degrees East three

---

* These lots were sold to the patentee by Tielman Van Vleck March 25, 1668. In the deed:

Lot No. 88 includes: 1st, a house lot lying W. beside Hendrick Jansen Van Ostrum, E. by Adrian Van Laer, 7¼x17¼ rods ; 2nd, a lot N. E. of Jacob Luby, with the meadow = 7¼ morgens.

Lot No. 135 included half of Van Vleck's meadow = 9 acres.

The patentee died seized, and this with his other lands passed to his eldest son *Cornelius*. Cornelius sold the land in question to his brother-in-law, Jan Adrianse Sip, Dec. 3, 1706.

By Sip's will dated, April 11, 1709, proved Oct. 22, 1734, his son Ide received all his real estate in Bergen. By Ide Sip's will, dated April 19, 1760, proved April 12, 1762, his son *Cornelius* received the homestead in the town, and *Garret* received the orchard on the opposite side of the street in severalty. These two sons then received all their father's other lands in common. They partitioned by mutual deeds of release, April 1, 1765. In this partition Cornelius received as follows :

The N. half of Lots 60 and 61, and half of the meadow at the W. end of said two lots. The N. half of Lots 88, 135 and 377 ; the N. E. half of Lot 141 ; the E. half of Lots 44 and 229 ; the S. half of Lots 68, 136 and 323 ; the S. W. half of Lot 118 ; the W. half of Lots 342 and 369 ; also the W. half of a lot in Fredrick Phillip's Patent, adjudged to Cornelius and Garret Sip, also the whole of the lot whereon his house then stood ; also Lots 285 and 256. His brother Garret received the remaining half of each of the lots divided. The deeds were executed in the presence of George Clinton, of New York, and are unrecorded. By his will, dated Sept. 22, 1775, Garret gave all his lands in Bergen to his son *Peter*, who gave all his lands to his sons *Garret* and *Richard*. Vide Note to *Philipsen's, Patent*, p 28.

Chains and seventy eight Links along said Meadow Edge to a Stake, Thence North forty four Degrees and twenty Minutes west eleven Chains and eighty seven Links to said Bridge Creek, Then down along the said Creek the several Courses thereof as it runs 'til it meets the first mentioned Line.

The Patent of Philip Carteret to Arent Laurense dated the tenth Day of October, One thousand six hundred and seventy for sundry Parcels of Land lying in and about the Town of Bergen.

Our Survey whereof shews & we adjudge them to be five Tracts.

* **The First** whereof (being a Tract of Upland and Meadow *61 mark'd on the Map No. 123)*

Begins at a Stake (which Stake is the Southerly Corner of a Lot in John Berry's Patent mark'd on the Map No. 125) And from said Stake

---

º This patentee was one of the commissioners to fortify Bergen in 1663. *New Neth. Reg.*, 153. He received from the Dutch Governor a grant for a piece of land near Bergen, May 29, 1664. *N. Y. Col. MSS.* x, part ii, 222.

Lot No. 123 was 82 rods wide, and "with the Bergh or Hill" = 14 morgens, 144 rods. Within this lot is the present "Mount Pleasant" or "Point of Rocks," as was also Prior's Mill. Abraham Prior owned part of this lot in 1764. *Vide Note to Lot* 335, p. 214. Jacob Prior died seized of at least a portion of it—will dated Dec. 25, 1824, proved March 15, 1825. His executors, Casparus Prior, John E. Post, and John J. Van Horne, conveyed the lot called the "Hill" to Merselis J. Merselis, April 25, 1827. The heirs of Sarah Vanderhoof gave a deed for the same lot to Merselis May 14, 1827. The executors conveyed a plot S. of the railroad to John S. Darcy, Jan. 14, 1833; he to Ashbel W. Corey, June 15, 1835; he to Charles F. Voorhis, May 14, 1837, who mortgaged to George Vreeland, Jan. 29, 1840. This mortgage was foreclosed and the property sold by Sheriff Newkirk to William Colgate, Oct 21, 1842; he in part to John C. Gilbert, Oct. 29, 1842.

Peter Sickles, Jacob Outwater, and George Newkirk, quit-claimed to Aaron Vanderbilt 14 acres, May 5, 1825. Vanderbilt died seized and intestate. George Newkirk and Joseph Budd were appointed administrators. They, in pursuance of an order of the court, dated June 15, 1835, sold 10 40-100 acres to John C. Gilbert, Sept. 8, 1835; also a plot to Henry Southmayd on the same day. Gilbert died seized (will dated Oct. 31, 1849, proved Jan. 17, 1855), and the part of lot is now owned by his son William S.

Lot No. 92 lay between Guert Coerten's plantation = 8 morgens. It was owned by Johannis Van Houten in 1764. *Vide Note to Lot* 25, *New Field Book*, and went to the Zabriskie family. *Vide Note to Lot* 4. *Map A., New Field Book*.

Lot No. 99 adjoined Christian Pieterse, was 8x20 rods.

Lot No. 112 extended from the highway to the creupel bosch; was owned by Arent Toers in 1764. *Vide Note to Steenhuysen's Patent*, p. 32.

Lot No. 113 lay between the houses of Adrian Post and Capt. Varlet, and was 5 x15 rods. The whole = 48 acres.

The patentee conveyed Lots 99 and 113 to Gerrit Gerritse March 17, 1688. *Vide Note to Gerritse's Patent*, p. 58, and *Note to Teunise's Patent*, p. 54. Lot 113 yet remains in the Van Wagenen family, being the lot whereon Hartman Van Wagenen now resides.

runs South thirty five Degrees and fifty five Minutes East, twenty seven Chains and fourteen Links to a Stake standing by the Side of a Creek, Then returning to said first Stake the Place of Beginning and from thence runs North fifty one Degrees and fifteen Minutes East eighteen Chains and fifty Links to a Stake, Thence South thirty eight Degrees and forty five Minutes East thirty nine Chains and seventy five Links to Horsimus Creek, Then down along said Horsimus Creek as it runs to the Mouth of the first mentioned Creek where it's said the Old Mill stood, Then up along the said first mentioned Creek (including an Island of Meadow) to where the first mentioned Line strikes the said first mentioned Creek.

The Second (mark'd on the Map No. 92)

Begins at a Stake (which Stake is the Northeasterly Corner of a Lot in Guert Coerten's first Patent mark'd on the Map No. 91) and from said Stake runs North forty five Degrees East twelve Chains and eighteen Links to a Stake (standing in the Road that leads from the Town to the English Neighbourhood); Thence North fifty Degrees West twenty Chains and eighty Links to a Stake by the Edge of the Meadow, Thence South forty two Degrees and thirty Minutes West five Chains along the Meadow Edge, Then South forty five Degrees and Ten Minutes West eight Chains and forty Links along said Meadow Edge to a Stake, Thence South forty three Degrees East twelve Chains to a Stake; Thence South sixty seven Degrees and thirty Minutes East nine Chains and twenty four Links to the Place of Beginning.

The Third (being an Out-Garden-Plot near the Town mark'd on the Map No. 99)

Begins at a Stake standing by a Road (which Stake is the Southerly Corner of an Out-Garden-Plot in Garret Garretse's Patent mark'd on the Map No. 98) And from said Stake runs North thirty nine Degrees and twenty Minutes West four Chains and eighty Links to a Stake, Thence South forty nine Degrees and thirty Minutes West, two Chains and twenty seven Links to a Stake by the Road, Thence South forty six Degrees and forty Minutes East five Chains and two Links along said Road to a Stake in the Turn of the Road, Thence North fifty Degrees East eighty Links along said Road to the Place of Beginning.

The Fourth (being four other Out-Garden-Plots which as lying and adjoining together we have comprehended in One Survey mark'd on the Map No. 112)

*62 * **Begins** at a Stake standing by the Road leading from the Town to Bergen Point (which Stake is the Westerly Corner of an Out-Garden-Plot in Harman Edward's Patent mark'd on the Map No. 111) and from said Stake runs South nineteen Degrees West five Chains and sixty Links along said Road to a Stake at the Turn of the Road to Comunipan, Thence South eight Degrees East seven Chains and twenty Links along said Comunipan Road to a Stake, Thence North forty four Degrees East eight Chains and seventy Links to a Stake, Thence North forty Degrees West eight Chains and six Links to the Place of Beginning.

The Fifth (being a Lot in the Town of Bergen mark'd on the Map No. 113)

Begins at a Stake by a Street (which Stake is the Southerly Corner of a Town Lot in Adrian Post's Patent mark'd on the Map No. 164)

And from said Stake runs South forty two Degrees East ninety seven Links along said Street to a Stake, Thence North forty eight Degrees East two Chains and eighty five Links to a Stake, Thence North forty two Degrees West ninety seven Links to a Stake. Thence South forty eight Degrees West two Chains and eighty five Links to the Place of Beginning.

The Patent of Petrus Stuyvesant to Nicholas Varlet dated the eighteenth Day of October One thousand six hundred and sixty three, for sundry Parcels of Land lying in and about the Town of Bergen.

Our Survey whereof shews and we adjudge them to be five Tracts.

The First whereof (mark'd on the Map No. 127)*

Begins at a Stake (which Stake is the easterly Corner of a Lot in John Berry's Patent mark'd on the Map No. 125) and from said Stake runs South thirty eight Degrees forty five Minutes East fifteen Chains to Horsimus Creek, Then returning to said Stake the Place of Beginning, And from thence runs North thirty two Degrees East fourteen Chains and fifty Links to a Stake, Thence South fifty Degrees East seventeen Chains to said Horsimus Creek, Then down along said Creek as it runs 'til it meets the first mentioned Line.

The Second (being a Piece of Meadow mark'd on the Map No. 126)

Begins at a Stake standing by the Edge of the Upland (which Stake is the southerly Corner of a Lot in Guert Coerten's Second Patent mark'd on the Map No. 124) and from said Stake runs South thirty eight Degrees and forty five Minutes * East twenty Chains and seventy five Links to Horsimus Creek, Then up along the said Creek as it runs to a Stake (which Stake is the southerly Corner of the last describ'd Lot mark'd on the Map No. 127) and from said last Stake runs along between the Meadow and Upland to the Place of Beginning.

*63

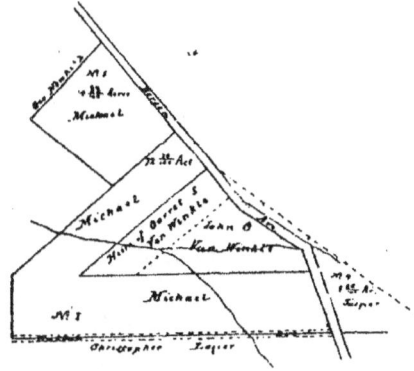

^a *Lot No.* 104 was owned by Arent Toers in 1764. *Vide Note to Steenhuysen's Patent*, p 32. His son *Nicholas* conveyed it to Michael Simmons July 3, 1797. Simmons reconveyed to Toers the next day.

Lot No. 128 was owned by Robert Leake in 1764. Leake was the King's Commissary-General in North America. He died on Friday, Dec. 31, 1773, at his seat in the Bowery, N. Y., in the 54th year of his age. In a notice of his death at the time, it was said:—" He was long a faithful Servant of the Crown ; a loving Husband ; tender Parent ; one of the best of Masters, and a Friend to all Tradesmen." He was buried in Trinity churchyard. His eldest son, *Robert William*, inherited his property. It does not appear that this heir was ever in America. By letters of attorney, dated July 7, 1774, he empowered John George Leake to sell his lands. His attorney sold this lot = 17¾ acres to Peter Stuyvesant, Aug. 18, 1784, who

The Third (being a Lot in the Town of Bergen mark'd on the Map No. 168)

Begins at a Stake by a Street (which Stake is the northerly Corner of a Town Lot in John Berry's Patent mark'd on the Map No. 162) and from said Stake runs North forty two Degrees West One Chain and nineteen Links along said Street to a Stake, Thence South forty eight Degrees West One Chain and forty five Links to a Stake, Thence South forty two Degrees East One Chain and nineteen Links to a Stake, Thence North forty eight Degrees East one Chain and forty five Links to the Place of Beginning.

The Fourth (being an Out Garden near the Town mark'd on the Map No. 104)

Begins at a Stake (standing South twenty five Degrees West one Chain and eighty Links from the westerly Corner of the Out Gardens in Arent Lawrense's Patent mark'd on the Map No. 112) and from said Stake runs south eighty two Degrees West seven Chains and ninety seven Links to a Stake, Thence North thirty Degrees East four Chains to a Stake, Thence South sixty nine Degrees and fifteen Minutes East six Chains and fifteen Links to the Place of Beginning.

The Fifth (mark'd on the Map No. 128)

Begins at a Stake (which Stake is the Place of Beginning of the last describ'd Lot or Out Garden mark'd on the Map No. 104) and from said Stake runs South eighty two Degrees West seven Chains and ninety seven Links to a Stake, Thence South eight Degrees East twenty one Chains and thirty four Links to a Stake, Thence North eighty two Degrees East seven Chains & ninety seven Links to a Stake, Thence North eight Degrees West twenty one Chains and thirty four Links to the Place of Beginning.

The Patent of Philip Carteret to Hendrick Van Ostrum, dated the tenth Day of November One thousand six hundred and seventy seven for a parcel of Upland & a parcel of Mea-

---

sold the W. half = 8 47-100 acres to Casparus Prior, Sept. 1, 1784. Of this half Prior died seized, and by will devised it to the children of his son *Nicholas*, viz.: *Hannah*, wife of David L. Van Horne, *Michael*, and *Jasper*. Among these it was partitioned by commissioners; report confirmed March Term, 1845. Prior's interest in this lot fell to Michael, who sold all that fell to him in the annexed sketch to Jacob M. Merselis. *Vide Note to Gerritse's Patent*, p 41.

The E. half of Lot 128 Stuyvesant, by will dated Nov. 20, 1821, proved Jan. 9, 1822, gave to his children *Peter* and *Mary* (wife of Peter Kip) who, with their mother Lenah, conveyed the same to Cornelius Van Horne; May 7, 1833, who conveyed to Moses B. Bramhall, March 31, 1851, who conveyed to Samuel Bostwick, April 1, 1851, two acres on the N. end. This portion Bostwick mapped (map filed July 7, 1861). *Vide Note to Lot* 389, p. 215.

Lot No. 127 was owned by several parties in 1764. *Vide New Field Book*.

Lot No. 168 was in doubtful ownership in 1764. *Vide Lot* 257, p 218. Garret Van Rypen sold it and Lot 257, Oct. 1, 1785, to Jacob Everson, who sold to Peter Sip, July 6, 1791, in exchange for the "Peach Orchard," which was afterwards owned by Dennison and then by Wm. Wright and Samuel Wescott. Lots 168 and 257 were owned by Richard Sip, son of Peter, at the time of his death in 1865.

dow lying eastward of the Town of Bergen. Which Upland & Meadow as adjoining together we have comprehended in one Survey, mark'd on the Map No. 131.*

Our Survey whereof shews and we adjudge it to be a Tract *65 **Beginning** at a Stake standing South fifty Degrees East one Chain from a Red Cedar Tree mark'd K. C. C. (which Tree is the Westerly Corner of Claas Jansen Van Purmerant's Patent mark'd on the Map No. 132) And from said Stake runs South fifty Degrees East forty four Chains to Horsimus Creek, Then returning to said Stake the Place of Beginning; And from thence runs South forty Degrees west fifteen Chains and fourteen Links to a Stake, Thence fifty Degrees East thirty nine Chains and seventy eight Links to said Horsimus Creek, Then up along the said Creek as it runs 'til it meets the first mentioned Line.

The Patent of Philip Carteret, to Claas Jansen Van Purmerant dated the thirty first Day of March One thousand six hundred and sixty eight for a Parcel of upland, and a Parcel of Meadow lying eastward of the Town of Bergen. Which Upland and Meadow as adjoining together we have comprehended in one Survey, mark'd on the Map No. 132.†

Our Survey whereof shews and we adjudge it to be a Tract **Beginning** at a Red Cedar Tree mark'd K C C and from thence runs South fifty Degrees East forty four Chains to Horsimus Creek, Then returning to said Tree the Place of Beginning and from thence runs North forty Degrees East eighteen Chains to a Stake, Thence South fifty Degrees East twenty four Chains and fifty three Links to a Stake by the Edge of the Meadow, thence South thirty five Degrees and fifteen Minutes West one Chain to a Stake, Thence South sixty three Degrees East two Chains and eighty Links, Then East six Chains and eighty Links along the Northerly Branch of Horsimus Creek, Then South twenty five Degrees East five Chains and forty four Links along said Branch, Then North eighty eight Degrees West five Chains and thirty Links along said Branch, Then South nineteen Degrees East three Chains and forty Links along said Branch to the Main Creek of Horsimus, Then down along said Creek as it runs the several Courses thereof 'til it comes to the first mentioned Line.

---

a This consisted of two lots: *Upland* 19x19 rods, extending from his meadow on the E. to a highway on the W = 22 acres; *Meadow* 19 chains long, 15 chains wide on the N. end and 11 chains on the S. end = 15 acres, lying between Hoboken and Harsimus. These two lots were sold by the patentee to Annetje, the widow of Claas Jansen Van Purmerent June 3, 1691. By her and her eldest son *Cornelius* it was sold to her son, *Hendricus Kuyper*, June 12, 1714. Kuyper sold this lot to John Dey. *Vide Note to Van Purmerent's Patent*, p 7.

† This tract was at one time owned by Jan Everson Carsebom; by him conveyed to Nicholas Varlet, and by him to the patentee. The upland is described as bounded E. by Hendrick Jansen Van Ostrum, W. by the Great Fall (*i.e.* the Showhank brook passing down the hill a little S. of Rommelt and Leicht's brewery), in size 60x120 rods = 20 morgens. The meadow thereto annexed extended from Harsimus Creek back to the hill = 22 acres. The patentee died seized and intestate, and his property was inherited by his eldest son, *Cornelius*, who sold to his brother Hendrick, June 12, 1714. *Vide Note to Van Purmerent's Patent*, p. 7.

The Patent of Petrus Stuyvesant to Jan Vinge, dated the fourth Day of June One thousand six hundred and sixty three for a Piece of Meadow lying easterly of the Town of Bergen.

Our Survey whereof shews, and we adjudge it to be a Tract (mark'd on the Map No. 143)*

Beginning at a Stake standing by the Edge of the Upland (which Stake is the westermost Corner of the Patent of Hoboken mark'd on the Map No. 2) and from said Stake runs Southwesterly along the Edge of the Upland to a Stake (which Stake is the easterly Corner of Claas Jansen Van Purmerant's Patent mark'd on the Map No. 132) and from said Stake runs South thirty five Degrees and fifteen Minutes West One Chain to a Stake, Then South sixty three Degrees East two Chains and eighty Links, Then East six Chains and eighty Links along the Northerly Branch of Horsimus Creek, Then South twenty five Degrees East two Chains & sixty four Links along said Branch to a Stake, Thence North sixty nine Degrees and ten Minutes East thirty four Chains and fifty two Links to Hoboken Creek, Then up along the said Creek the several Courses thereof as it runs to the Place of Beginning.

The Patent of Petrus Stuyvesant to Cornelius Ruyven, Paulus Lindertz, Allerd Anthony and Johannis Ver Bruggen, dated the twenty first Day of November One thousand six hundred and sixty three for a Meadow (of old call'd Jacob Slaughis Meadow) lying upon the West side of Hudson's River.

Our Survey whereof shews and we adjudge it to be a Tract (mark'd on the Map 145).†

---

* Vinge was an heir of Jan Jansen Damen; Schepen in 1655, '56, '61; admitted to the rights of a Great Burgher, April 14, 1657; was twice married, the last time to Wieshe Haytes, Feb. 15, 1682. He died without issue in 1691.

This lot belonged to the devisees of Sir Peter Warren in 1764. *Vide Lot No.* 213, p.219. 18 acres in the N.E. corner of this Patent were conveyed by Charles, Lord Southampton and Henry Seymour Conway to Coll McGregor, May 25, 1795, and by him to John Stevens, April 6, 1797. It consisted of meadow lying S.W. of Hoboken Creek, beginning on the N. side of Van Purmerent's land, then up along the great creek to the small creek under the hill = 9 morgens.

Sir Peter Warren married the eldest daughter of Stephen De Lancey, of New York, and it is probable that the above-named grantors were his executors.

† The Slaugh here named was the enterprising individual who attempted to take the life of Kieft. For this exploit he was shot and his head stuck on a post.

Van Ruyven was the old secretary under Stuyvesant, with whom he came here in 1647, being then a young bachelor. He married Hillegond, daughter of Domine Johannes Megapolensis, June 24, 1654; was engaged in the dry goods and general store business; was Alderman in N. Y. in 1665, '70, '72, '73.

Lindertz, known also as Leenders, Leendertzen, Van der Grist, Van den Grift, Van der Grift and Van die Grift, was one of the early settlers. He left Holland in command of the ship *Great Gerrit*, Dec. 25, 1646, and arrived at Manhattan May 11, 1647, with Stuyvesant, by whom he was appointed naval agent. He was one of the Select Men; a lieutenant in the Burgher corps of New Amsterdam in 1653; a schepen in 1653, '54; and burgomaster in 1657, '58, '61, '64. After the surrender he took the oath of allegiance to the English, and remained in the country until 1671, then

Beginning at a Heap of Stones by the Southerly End of said Meadow & near the River, And from thence runs North four Degrees West five Chains and ninety Links along the Edge of the Upland, Then North twelve Degrees East Ten Chains and twelve Links along said Upland, Then South sixty seven Degrees & thirty Minutes West four Chains and twelve Links along said Upland, Then North twenty eight Degrees and thirty Minutes East eight Chains, Then North forty four Degrees East two Chains and thirty Links along said Upland, Then North thirty nine Degrees and thirty Minutes East fifteen Chains along said Upland, Then North twenty seven Degrees East twelve Chains and sixty Links along said Upland, Then North seventy four Degrees East Eleven Chains and six Links along said Upland, Then North sixty two Degrees East sixteen Chains to said Hudson's River, Then down along said River as it runs to the Place of Beginning.

The Patent of Petrus Stuyvesant to Nicholas Varlet and Nicholas Bayard dated the tenth Day of December, One

---

returned to Europe, leaving his property in the hands of agents. He resided on the W. side of Broadway, near the present Trinity Church. He came near being a victim of the Indian raid on New Amsterdam in 1655. *Col. Hist. of N. Y.*, ii, 43; *Val. Hist. of N. Y.*, 61.

Anthony was a prosperous merchant in New Amsterdam; schepen in 1653; burgomaster from 1655 to 1661; schout from 1662 to 1665, and sheriff from 1666 to 1673. As an official he was unpopular, and among the lower classes went by the name of "the hangman." He died in 1685.

Ver Bruggen, sometimes called Van Brugh, came hither at an early date, and settled in Rensselaerswyck. He afterwards came to New Amsterdam; was a corporal in the Burgher corps in 1653; schepen in 1655, '56, '61; made a great burgher April 12, 1657; orphan master in 1663; burgomaster in 1673, '74, '75; captain of the militia, in New Orange, in 1637; member of the common council in 1683; alderman in 1677; took the oath of allegiance in 1664, and was assessed at 14,000 florins in 1674.

This patent was confirmed by Gov. Carteret, March 31, 1668. It included two pieces of meadow.

1st—Meadow, as well the salt as the reed meadow, about half a Dutch league N. of Wihaken, "Antiently known by the name of Jacob Slaugh's Meadow."

2d—Meadow, about a Dutch league further up, called by the name of Moertien Danidts valley, or meadow. In the corruption of this latter name may be found the present *Mordanis* meadow.

Anthony sold to Cornelius Van Borsum, June 28, 1678, his interest in the above tracts, "known by the names of Jacob Slaugh and Moertje Daniels.

A small part of this meadow was sold by John Somerindyke, executor of Richard Somerindyke, to Arthur McCarter, Aug. 1829. McCarter sold to Robert Annett, June 8, 1835; Annett to Michael Carling, Jan. 26, 1848; Carling to Henry A. W. Barclay and William R. Townsend 32 6-100 acres, and the right to the shore front, 2 52-100 acres; Barclay and Townsend to Dudley S. Gregory, Dec. 6, 1849; Gregory to Nathaniel Dole, March 1, 1864. The title to the meadow is in great obscurity. It seems to have passed, by descent, among non-residents. There is not any recorded paper title. The rapid increase in the value of this property will, without a doubt, soon bring about a legal settlement of the ownership, which has been an uncertainty for more than a century. *Vide Note to Lot No.* 219, p. 77.

thousand six hundred and sixty three. Confirm'd by Patent from Philip Carteret to said Varlet and Bayard, dated the thirtyeth Day of October One thousand six hundred and sixty seven for a certain Plantation or Parcel of Land and Meadow call'd Sekakus, lying in the Kill Van Cul.

Our Survey where.f shews and we adjudge it to be a Tract (mark'd on the Map No. 146).*

---

* *Secaucus*, Sikakes, an Indian word, signifying the *place where the snake hides*.

The wording of Carteret's Patent is as follows: "Doe hereby Give, Grant and Confirme unto Nicholas Ver Lett Esqr. of the Towne of Bergen and Nicholas Bayard of New Yorke a Sartain Plantation or P'rcel of Land lying and being in the Kill van Cole known in the Indian Language by the Name of Sickakus which was lawfully purchased from the Indians and Paid for as may appear by the Bill of Sale made by the Indyans the 30th day of January in the Year of Our Lord 1658, Stila Nova, Which said Parcell of Land together with all the Land and Meadows round about it and annexed Thereunto with the Creek and Creeks, Ponds, Poules, Swamps and Isletts as far as it Reaches to the Fine Land, Fishing, Fowling, Hunting, with all and Singular the Appurtenances" &c. "as of the Manner of East Greenwich in free and Common Socage, Yielding and Paying to the said Lord PrPrietors" &c "One half Penny of Lawfull Money of England for every Acre." "The said Plantation or Parcell of land is Esteemed and Valued according to the Survey and Agreement made to Contain, both of Upland and Meadow the Sum of two thousand Acres English Measure."

In 1674 the Indians raised a question as to the Dutch title to the Island. They contended that the deed to Stuyvesant included only "Espatingh and its dependencies." But the Dutch Council at Fort Willem Hendrick, having examined the deed and heard arguments, decided that the land was included in the sale. The Indians replied that they did not know this, and thought "they ought to have a present of an anker of rum." To extinguish their title this was given, *Col. Hist. of N. Y. ii*, 707, and the simple ones were satisfied. While in possession of the patentees Varlet died, and Samuel Edsall and Peter Stoutenburgh were appointed his administrators. They joined Bayard in selling the tract, April 24, 1676, to Edward Earle, Jr., of Maryland. Earl sold to Judge William Pinhorne, March 26, 1679, for £500, one undivided half of the tract, also one half of all the stock, "Christian and negro servants." The following schedule was annexed to the deed: "One dwelling house, containing two lower rooms and a lean-to below staires, and a loft above, Five tobacco houses, one hors, one mare and two Coults, eight oxen, ten Cows, one bull, foure yearlings, and seven Calves, between thirty and forty hoggs, foure negro men, five christian servants." Not long after this, Scott in his "Model of the government of East Jersey," calls the place "a brave plantation."

Pinhorne and Earle held in common until April 15, 1682, when a division was made. Earle took the upper, and Pinhorne the lower portion of the Island. On the E. boundary of Pinhorne's land was a creek, which took its name from the Judge and to this day is known as Pinhorne's Creek. On the S. end of the Island is a bluff, known at different times as "Slangen Bergh," and "Snake Hill." "Mount Pinhorne" was the high land, a little N. E. of Snake Hill. It was for some time questioned whether or not this tract was within the old township of Bergen. To settle this question, the Proprietors directed a survey, Oct. 30, 1686; which was made by George Keith, and it was found to be within the township. Pinhorne claimed that his deed included the swamp E. of the creek and resisted the claim of the Freeholders that it was Common Land. In 1694 he sued Caspar Steinmets in trespass for cutting timber in the

Beginning at the Mouth of Pinhorne's Creek (on the Northeasterly side of Hackinsack River) And thence runs up along said Pinhorne's Creek the several Courses thereof as it runs to a Creek or Ditch (which communicates or joins said Pinhorne's Creek with another Creek call'd Crom, a-Kill) Then along said Creek or Ditch as it runs to said Crom, a-Kill Creek, Then down along said Crom, a-Kill Creek the several Courses thereof as it runs to said Hackinsack River, Then down along the said Hackinsack River the several Courses thereof as it runs to the Mouth of said Pinhorne's Creek the Place of Beginning.

* **Besides** the several **Patented Tracts** foregoing   67

swamp, but I do not know that the case was ever brought to trial. On May 10, 1717, he executed a deed for his land to John Barclay, of Perth Amboy, in trust for the grantor and his wife, and after their death to his children. But having some misgivings about it he destroyed this deed. After his death his widow and children filed a bill in Chancery to prohibit the Freeholders of Bergen cutting timber in the swamp E. of the creek The trustees filed an answer. The result I do not know, but there can be no doubt that these pretentions were groundless, and the Field Book properly places the tract W. of the Creek.

By Pinhorne's will, dated May 10, 1719, proved April 12, 1720, he gave his lands to his wife for life; then to be divided between his grandson John Pinborne, Col. Edmund Kingsland, who married his daughter *Mary;* his daughter *Martha*, widow of Chief Justice Mompesson (she afterwards married Richard Warman), and *Elizabeth* who married Timothy Bagley, each one quarter. In the summer of 1729, Col. Kingsland advertised "Mount Pinhorne" for sale — "600 acres of timber, 200 acres of cleared land, 1000 acres of meadow, with a new house and barn, two orchards of about 1200 bearing apple trees." The heirs of Pinhorne sold part of this tract to Thomas Alsop, of Long Island, Dec. 15, 1730. In this purchase John Bard afterwards became interested. By Col. Kingsland's will, dated July 29, 1741, proved July 26, 1742, he left his interest in this tract to his children *William Edmund, Roger, Isaac, Edmund, Mary, Anna, Hester, Catharine,* and *Elizabeth*, wife of George Leslie. By will dated May 20, 1728 (1748?), proved Sept. 18, 1751, Leslie gave the property received from Kingsland to his children *George W., John, Edmund, James,* and *Margaret*.

Earle's will, dated May 16, 1709, proved May 3, 1717, gave his lands to his wife for her life, then to his son *Edward* for his life, then to his grandson Edward in fee. This grandson's will was dated Oct. 18, 1750, proved May 12, 1755. His children were *Edward, John, Philip, Anthebe, Robert, Elizabeth, Hester,* and *Mary*, wife of John Nelson. Among these children he divided up his lands, but in what proportion I cannot say. Edward (4th), by will dated Nov. 2, 1787, proved Jan. 25, 1788, gave to his sons *Richard* and *John* all his Secaucus lands. His children were *Richard, John, Edward, Cecelia,* wife of Rodman Fields, and *Mary*. The poor-house farm is on the S. part of the Pinhorne tract. Job Smith sold it to Albert A. Westervelt, 200 acres, March 15, 1820; Westervelt to Abel I. Smith, April 28, 1820; Abel to "The Trustees of the Freeholder's Inhabitants of the Township of Bergen," April 29, 1820. The trustees, &c., sold the same to the "Overseers of the Poor of the Township of Bergen," May 3, 1833, who sold to the Board of chosen Freeholders of Hudson County.

Andrew Tead et ux. owned a large tract at Secaucus. They sold to Robert Leake, of N. Y., 400 acres, March 27, 1762. Leake died seized, and his property was inherited by his eldest son *Robert William*, who empowered John George Leake, July 7, 1774, to sell. He sold this tract to John Stevens, March 10, 1795.

We found a **Tract** now in the possession of Captain Archibald Kennedy at Horsimus. The State of The Title to which (being neither Patent nor Grant) we found to be very intricate.

It appears, that, the States of Holland granted New Netherland to The West Indie Company of Amsterdam. That, the said West Indie Company by their Governors in New Netherland purchas'd from Time to Time large Tracts from the Indians, and patented out the same in severalty to Dutch Subjects. This Tract at Horsimus (in possession of Kennedy) appears to be a Part remaining unpatented of a Large Tract of Land, now the Township of Bergen, purchas'd of the Indians by Governor Petrus Stuyvesant for the Use of said West Indie Company.

It appears probable that this Tract at Horsimus was peculiarly reserv'd for said West Indie Company having been always call'd **The West Indie Company's Farm.**

It's presum'd, that, this Tract stood thus circumstanc'd at the Time of the Surrender of this Country by the Dutch in the Year One thousand six hundred and sixty four; And, that, it remain'd secured to the said West Indie Company by the first Article of that Surrender; And as it was in their Possession by their Tenant at the Time of granting the Charter of Bergen; We conceive, it did not pass, by that Charter, And therefore is no part of the Common Lands of the Township of Bergen.

Then as to the Bounds, We find, That, Horsimus is a Tract nearly circumscrib'd by a natural Boundary. But as there has been laid before us several Patents hereafter mentioned for sundry Parcels of Land lying within that Boundary, and which we have run out, and ascertain'd there; Thence we are of Opinion, That, (The West Indie Company's Farm or) The Tract now in Possession of Captain Kennedy is limited by that natural Boundary of Horsimus, **Excepting and reserving** those Lands granted by and mention'd in the said several Patents.

Our Survey therefore of the Land now in Possession of Captain Kennedy at Horsimus Shews, and we Adjudge it (under the Exception & Reservation after * mention'd) to be a Tract mark'd on the Map No. 169 *

*68

---

a After the purchase of Pauw's interest in Pavonia, this tract was held with great tenacity by the Dutch West India Company, and became known as their farm. By them it was regarded as the natural outlet for all the native commerce attracted to New Amsterdam from the vast country on this side of the Hudson. Its ownership was the main cause of Pauw's troubles, for the other directors were convinced that it gave him too much control of the Indian trade. Though for a long time diverted, commerce is returning to its first love, and old Ahasimus, with its surroundings, again becomes a depot for the great West and South of this country; and, as the natural terminus of the Pacific lines of railway, of the trade of the Orient. It originally included the whole of Ahasimus, but was reduced to about 383 acres by grants to Van Vorst and others. It was reserved to the Company by the first of the "Articles of Capitulation" in 1664: "We consent that the States General, or West India Company, shall freely injoy all farms and houses (except such as are in the forts)" etc. *O'Cal. N. N.,* ii, 532   But war between England and Holland having been declared Feb. 22, 1665, Gov. Nicolls, by proclamation in N. Y., June 15, 1665,

Beginning at the Mouth of Horsimus Creek on the Northwest side of Hudson's River or York Bay (which Creek seperates Horsimus from Comunipan and other Lands of Bergen) And thence running up along the said Creek the several Courses thereof as it runs to the Westerly End of a Ditch (that was formerly cut to answer the Purpose of a Fence from said Horsimus Creek to a small Creek that runs up out of the Bay or Cove betwixt Horsimus and Hoboken Creek) and then along said Ditch to the said small Creek, Then down along the said small Creek as it runs to the Mouth thereof in the said Cove betwixt Horsimus and Hoboken, Then down along said Cove to Hudson's River or York Bay, Then along said River or Bay as the same runs to the Place of Beginning. But specially excepting and reserving as included within the Limits and Survey above describ'd the sundry Parcels of Land following, to wit,

First. A House Lot mark'd on the Map No. 3, and a Tract of Upland and Meadow mark'd on the Map No. 6 both of which we have run out under the Patent of Philip Carteret to Ide Corneliese Van Vost dated the thirtieth Day of March One thousand six hundred and sixty eight.

"after the usual ringing of the City Hall bell three times," declared confiscated to the king the real and personal property of the Dutch W. I. Co., "in consequence of the Company's inflicting all sorts of injury on his Royal Majestie's subjects." From this time the Governors of N. Y. claimed the tract for the Duke of York, and it was known as the "Duke's Farm." By them leases were given. On March 1, 1667, Jacob Stoffelsen and wife received a lease to run from Jan. 1, 1667, for and during the life of the "longest liver." The wife survived Stoffelsen, and married Caspar Steinmets. He obtained a lease April 12, 1674, in right of his wife. Aug. 17, 1678, his wife being dead, he received a lease of the farm for life. Aug. 13, 1685, Gov. Dongan gave to John Palmer a lease for ninety-nine years of the reversion, "from the feast of St. Michael, the Archangel, next ensuing after the determination of the estate" of Steinmets. *Deeds (Albany),* vii, 170; *Col. Hist. of N. Y.,* iii, 411, Feb. 5, 1686, *John* and *Garret,* sons of Caspar Steinmets, bought the Palmer lease, and, after the death of their father, divided the farm; John taking the S. half, and Garret taking the N. half. Feb. 24, 1708. John conveyed his interest in the farm to his wife for her life, then to his nephew, Jacob Prior. After John's death, his widow married Peter Van Wooglem. They and Jacob Prior assigned to David Hennion, *alias* David Danielson, the remainder of the term under the Palmer lease. This was about 1715. In the meantime the freeholders of Bergen claimed the farm as common land under Carteret's grant of 1668. This the proprietors denied, and claimed it for themselves. Acting upon this claim they disposed of it, and the following is the history of the title as derived from them.

Robert West, one of the proprietors, by lease and release dated April 1 and 2, 1684, sold his interest in East Jersey to Thomas Cox. Cox sold to Sir Eugenius Cameron, of Lochiel, 13-40ths of his interest of 1-24th part, April 2 and 3, 1685. Sir Eugenius sold to Donald Cameron July 30, 1716. Donald Cameron sold to Evan Drummond, Nov. 17, 1721. Drummond sold one-half of said 13-40ths to James Alexander, July 17 and 18, 1723. Alexander reconveyed to Drummond 383 acres of unappropriated land, Feb. 22 and 23, 1724. On the 26th of the same month this amount of land was surveyed to Drummond by the Surveyor-General, "upon a tract of land formerly called the West India Company's Farm."

This survey was endorsed, with the approval of 16-20ths of the proprietors. The

Second. A House Lot mark'd on the Map No. 4, A Garden and Orchard Lot mark'd on the Map No. 7, And a Farm Lot mark'd on the Map No. 8, Which three Lots, we have run out under the Patent of Petrus Stuyvesant to Claas Jansen Van Purmerant, dated the thirty first Day of January, One thousand six hundred and sixty two.

Third. A Tract of Land call'd Paulus Hook mark'd on the Map No. 5, which we have run under the Patent of Philip Carteret to Abraham Isaacsen Plank, dated the twelfth Day of May One thousand Six hundred and Sixty eight.

Fourth. A Piece of Land mark'd on the Map No. 9, Which we have run out under the Patent of Petrus Stuyvesant to Jacob Stoffel-

---

money for the purchase and cost of location was furnished by Archibald Kennedy. Feb. 13, 1724, Drummond executed a declaration of trust that he held the land for the use and benefit of Kennedy. In 1725 Drummond filed a bill in Chancery against Danielson for that part of the farm held by him. Gov. Burnet made a decree in accordance with the prayer of the bill, Aug. 17, 1727. Sept. 18, 1727, Danielson acknowledged Kennedy as his landlord, and accepted from him a lease of the S. half of the farm until May 1, 1728. Oct. 10, 1727, Garret Steinmets, who was yet holding the N. half of the farm under the Palmer lease, surrendered to Kennedy, and accepted from him a lease for life at the rent of *one ear of Indian corn when demanded*, and a proper proportion of the Quit-rents reserved to the proprietors. Steinmets assigned his interest in this lease to Mattys De Mott Feb. 20, 1729.

On the expiration of Danielson's lease, Kennedy took possession of the S. half of the farm. The death of Garret Steinmets in 1733 gave Kennedy the possession of the N. half.

Drummond's will was dated Dec. 13, 1736. Andrew Johnson, his surviving executor, transferred the title to Kennedy, April 24, 1747. Thus his possession was complete, and his title as perfect as the proprietors could make it. He died June 14, 1763. By his will, his son Archibald, Earl of Casselis, received two-thirds of the property, and his daughter Catherine one-third. Catherine sold her interest in the farm to her brother, May 16, 1765, for £1333 6s. 8d.

From the time that Kennedy took possession of the farm, there was a continual strife between him and the freeholders of Bergen. Trespasses, ejectments, injunctions, indictments, verdicts, and decrees followed each other for nearly three-quarters of a century. Kennedy filed a bill for quiet possession Sept. 8, 1785. This was dismissed by Chancellor Paterson, March 6, 1793. The decree of dismissal was opened, and the cause reargued Feb. 11, 1794. A decree, dated Feb. 20, 1794, was made that the freeholders should bring a suit in ejectment in the Supreme Court, to be tried before a special jury from Somerset County, and the verdict certified to the Chancellor. Such suit was brought, and the jury rendered a verdict in favor of the freeholders, Feb. 27, 1800. Kennedy still held on, and a bill was filed asking the court to give effect to the verdict. A compromise was at last effected, and both parties sold to John B. Coles, of N. Y., Feb. 4, 1804.

Kennedy, Earl of Casselis, died Dec. 29, 1794, leaving two sons, *John* and *Robert*, who, by his will, dated Jan. 19, 1794, received all his lands in America. In 1803 they made Robert Watts, of N. Y., their attorney in fact, to sell their lands, and he executed the deed to Coles.

John B. Coles died seized, Jan. 2, 1827. His children were *Hannah, Eliza F., Isaac W., Benjamin U., John B.,* and *William F.*

WEST INDIA COMPANY'S FARM.   135

sen dated the seventh Day of May, One thousand six hundred and sixty four.

Fifth. A Piece of Meadow mark'd on the Map No. 10, Which we have run out under the Patent of Philip Carteret to Petrus Stuyvesant dated the thirty first Day of July, One thousand six hundred and sixty nine.

> * **We also** found a small Piece of Land lying southerly *69 from and near to the Town of Bergen, Which had been antiently, either by the Act, or the general Consent of the Freeholders, set apart for the Purpose of a Burying Ground.

Our Survey whereof shews and we adjudge it to be a Tract, mark'd on the Map No 170 *

Beginning at a Stake standing by a Street (which Stake is the Easterly Corner of an Out Garden Plot in Paulus Pieterse's Patent mark'd on the Map No. 103) And from said Stake runs South thirty nine Degrees West two Chains and two Links to a Stake, Then South forty eight Degrees East one Chain and forty four Links to a Stake, Then North forty eight Degrees East one Chain and seventy six Links, to the Corner of said Street, Then North forty two Degrees West One Chain and seventy five Links along said Street to the Place of Beginning.

> **We also** found another small Piece of Land lying Southwesterly from, and near to the Town of Bergen; Which it is said had been antiently appropriated either by the Act or general Consent of the Freeholders for the Incouragement of Mechanicks setling near the Town.

Our Survey whereof shews, and we adjudge it to be a Tract mark'd on the Map No 171 †

The Farm was mapped in 1804, map made by Joseph F. Mangin.

The tract not being Patent land, no common land was allotted to it. Yet by virtue of his claim to the Farm, it was feared Kennedy might succeed in getting a portion of the commons. He quit-claimed all his right thereto for £310, to Wm. Bayard, Hendrick Kuyper, Cornelius Van Vorst, Cornelius Garrabrants, Cornelius Brinkerhoff, Michael Vreelandt, George Vreelandt, Andries Segaerd, Jacob Van Wagenen, George Cadmus, Peter Buskirk, John Buskirk, Margaret Buskirk, Johannis Van Wagenen, Abraham Sickles, Garret Newkirk, and Daniel Diedricks.

In front of this Tract, lying under the water in Harsimus Cove, a part of which is now the Long Dock property, a tract = 53½ acres was surveyed by the proprietors to Elisha Boudinot, May 21, 1802. He sold to Nathaniel Budd Jan. 2, 1804, who sold to Willis Hall Oct. 1, 1835. On the same day Hall gave to Budd a consideration mortgage for $12,000. Hall sold to the N. J. Harbor Company (incorporated March 13, 1837) May 31, 1837. The mortgage was foreclosed, decree dated Oct. 18, 1840, execution dated Jan. 7, 1841, and Henry Newkirk, sheriff, sold to Mary Bell, Aug. 7, 1841. *Gough* vs. *Bell*, 2 Zab., 441.

* This lot is still used for the purpose of sepulture. It has, as a burying-ground, been enlarged by additional ground.

† The earliest record of private ownership shows this lot to be in the Winner family. How and when they obtained it I do not know. It lies in the S.W. corner of Glenwood and Bergen Aves. The S. half has descended to its present owner, John Winner, *Vide Note to Van Vleck's Patent*, p. 53. John Winner sold the N. half to Peter Stuyvesant, April 26, 1787, who occupied and kept tavern in an old house thereon. *Vide Note to Varlet's Patent*, p. 62. George Tise is the present owner.

Beginning at a Post in the Corner of a Fence (which Post is the Southerly Corner of the Parsonage House Lot mark'd on the Map No 174) and from said Post runs South twenty two Degrees West six Chains and eighty Links to a Stake, Then North sixty nine Degrees and fifteen Minutes West three Chains and sixty Links to a Stake, Thence North twenty six Degrees and thirty Minutes East six Chains and fifteen Links to a Stake, Thence South sixty seven Degrees and fifty Minutes East three Chains and twelve Links to the Place of Beginning.

*70 * **Haveing** thus discover'd and exhibited the **Limits** of the Township of Bergen, and of the **Appropriated Lands** therein contain'd, We were thereby enabled to discover, what Part of the said Township is **Common Land** to be divided according to the said Partition Act.

And out of which common lands so discover'd; We thought fit (agreeable to the direction of the said Partition Act) first to set apart a Tract (lying at Bergen Point adjoining to Kill Van Cul) which we think will be sufficient to defray the Charges of making a General Partition of the said Common Lands.

Our Survey of which said Tract for Charges shews and we do adjudge it to be a Tract mark'd on the Map No 172 *

Beginning at a White Oak Tree (standing on the Southeasterly Point of Upland, on the West Side of the Northeast Harbour, which White Oak Tree is mark'd with a Blaze and three Notches on each of its four Sides and bears from the West Corner of Cornelius Criuser Jun$^{r's}$ House on Staten Island North forty four Degrees and fifteen Minutes West; and from the Chimney of Mrs Gruesbeek's House North fifty two Degrees and thirty Minutes East) And from said White Oak Tree runs Northeasterly along Kill Van Cul to the Edge or Southwesterly Point of the Meadow, Then Northerly along betwixt the Upland and Meadow to a Stake (standing North two Degrees and fifty five Minutes West twenty seven Chains and twenty eight Links from said White Oak Tree), and from Said Stake runs North eighty five Degrees West forty six Chains and thirty seven Links to a Stake, Thence North fifty one Degrees

---

° This lot was sold by the Commissioners of the Bergen Commons to Hendricus Kuyper, the highest bidder, at public auction, Sept. 5, 1764, for £7300, "proclamation or lawful money of New Jersey." The deed to Kuyper was dated Sept. 10, 1764, and on the same day he endorsed on the deed a declaration, that he held the same in trust as follows: 2-18ths for Anthony White of New Brunswick; 1-18th for George Vreelandt; 1-18th for Michael Cornelise Vreelandt; 1-18th for Garret Newkirk; 1-18th for Thomas Brown; 1-18th for Joris Cadmus; 1-18th for Jacob Van Horne; 1-18th for Cornelius Van Vorst; 1-18th for Cornelius Garrabrants, Jr.; 1-18th for Claas Vreelandt; 1-18th for Jacob Van Wagenen, Jr.; all of Bergen; 1-18th for William Bayard; 1-18th for John Van Dalson, both of N. Y. City; 1-18th for John Mersereau, of Staten Island; and 1-18th for himself. These parties had furnished the purchase money in the above proportions.

The money received for the lot was more than enough to defray the expenses of the allotment, and the following is interesting as showing what became of the surplus. It seems to have been copied from original papers in the possession of Azariah Dunham about 1799. It was entitled:

West thirty Chains to New Ark Bay, Then down along said Bay to Kill Van Cul, Then Easterly along Kill Van Cul to the Place of Beginning, containing about three hundred and forty three Acres and a Half.

["Corporation of Bergen's Powers to the Trustees to appropriate surplus moneys to charges of Subdivision &c."]

"Know all men by these presents, that whereas, by an Act of the Legislature of the Colony of New Jersey, Entitled "an Act appointing Commissioners for finally settling & determining the several Rights, Titles and Claims to the Common Lands of the Township of Bergen, and for making a partition thereof in just and equitable proportions among those, who shall be adjudged by the said Commissioners to be entitled to the same." The Commissioners therein named and appointed were directed to set apart & sell so much of said Common Lands as they should think sufficient to defray the Charges of a general partition of the said Common Lands, and out of the moneys arising by such sale to detain in their hands the charges of the said general partition, and to pay the surplus (if any) to the Trustees of the Freeholders inhabitants of the said Township of Bergen, for the use of the Corporation.

And whereas, at a public meeting of the said Freeholders Inhabitants of said Township of Bergen, with the Trustees held at the Town of Bergen, on the second day of July last past, it was agreed and concluded, as well by the Trustees as the Freeholders Inhabitants of the said Township and Corporation of Bergen, that out of the surplus money arising by the sale of the Land aforesaid if sufficient for that purpose, the arrears of Quit Rents due from the Township to the General Proprietors of the Eastern Division of New Jersey, should be paid and discharged, and also, that out of the same if sufficient the Trustees should have all their reasonable demands against the said Township fully satisfied; and if any of the said surplus should then remain, it was also agreed and concluded that the same should be proportioned & divided among the said Freeholders and Inhabitants.

And whereas the Land so set apart hath, pursuant to the said Law, been lately sold, and produced a much greater sum of money than was expected, insomuch that after defraying the expense of the General Partition, discharging the Quit Rents to the General Proprietors, and the reasonable demands of the Trustees, a surplus will then remain sufficient (as it is conceived) to defray the whole charge that may accrue in making a Subdivision of the said Common Lands, if applied to that purpose.

And whereas, the charges attending the said Subdivision seem by the said law intended to be raised by selling a part of the Commons allotted to each respective Patent, which method, if pursued would be attended with length of time and many other inconveniences, troublesome to the Commissioners, and detrimental to the general interest of the Freeholders.

Therefore we the Subscribers, Freeholders Inhabitants of the Township & Corporation of Bergen, taking into Consideration the above matters, and finding that the law seems rather to permit than enjoin such sales to be made, do hereby appropriate such surplus money aforesaid, raised by the sale of the land aforesaid, set apart & sold for defraying the charge of the General Partition remaining after defraying the same, and the Quit Rents to the Proprietors, and the reasonable demands of the said Trustees, or so much of the said surplus as may be sufficient for that purpose, to be a fund for defraying the charge that may accrue on making all the subdivisions of the said Common Lands. And we do hereby authorize, impower, and order, Johannis Uriance, Hendricus Kuyper, and Helmigh Van Houte, or either of them (who we acknowledge to be Trustees) to pay unto, or otherwise suffer Charles Clinton, William Donaldson, Azariah Dunham, John Berrien, Abraham Clark jr, and

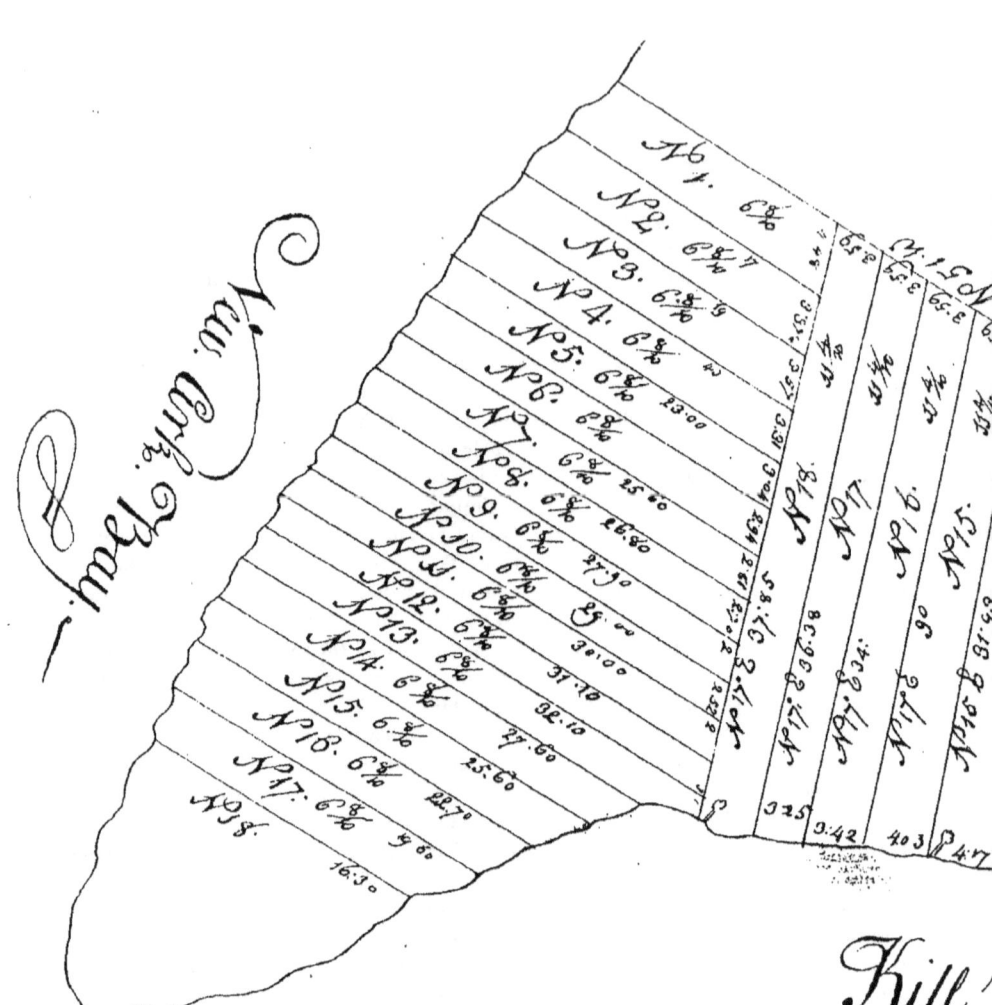

March 7, 1756.
Protracted pr scale of 4 Chains
to an Inch by
A: Dunham

Van Kull.

In the next Place we had Regard to the Right and Allotments due to the Church and Free School.

Jacob Spicer, or the major part of them (Commissioners in and by the law aforesaid named and appointed) to retain in their hands so much of the said surplus money, as will fully pay the whole charges of making the said Subdivisions of the said Common Lands, taking the said Commissioners receipts for each and every persons particular charge thereof, which receipts when produced shall be sufficient to discharge them, the said Trustees, and each of them, their, and each of their heirs, Executors and administrators of, and from so much of the said surplus money as the said receipt shall express to have been paid on account of the Subdivisions aforesaid. And we do hereby ratify & confirm whatsoever our said Trustees above named, any or either of them shall do in, and about the premises, pursuant to the power and directions above granted and prescribed, which shall be final and conclusive to us, and each of us our and each of our successors, heirs, executors and administrators, any act, matter, or thing whatsoever heretofore done by us any or either of us to the contrary hereof in any wise notwithstanding. And we, the said Johannis Uriance, Hendricus Kuyper, and Helmigh Van Houte, Trustees aforesaid and subscribers in quality of Freeholders, inhabitants & members of the said Township and corporation of Bergen, having an interest in the said surplus money, do, on our part hereby agree as follows:

Firstly, that so much of the said surplus money shall be applied to defray the charges of the said subdivisions of the said Common Lands as shall be sufficient for that purpose.

Secondly, that we will punctually conform to the power and directions above granted and prescribed by the other members of the Corporation aforesaid, and to each of them will account and pay their several respective proportions of all the said surplus money that shall remain in our hands (after our own reasonable demands and the charges of making the Subdivisions aforesaid) shall be thereout fully paid and discharged; if any part of the said surplus shall then so remain in our hands, not needed for the purposes aforesaid, and for the final ratification and true performance of these presents, We, the said Freeholders, Inhabitants, and Members of the Said Township and Corporation of Bergen (Trustees inclusive) have hereunto set our hands the Eleventh day of December, seventeen hundred and sixty-four.

Reynier V. Giese,	Gerrit Sip,	William Bayard,
Hendrick Van Winkle,	Edward Earle,	Daniel Diedericks,
George Vreelandt,	Henry Fielding,	Gerrit Van Reipen,
his	his	his
Jacob I. G. Van Wagene,	Levinis x Winne,	Matthewwis R Van Nukerk,
mark	mark	mark
Arent Toers,	Abraham Diedericks,	Hermanus Veeder,
Johannis Diedericks,	Cornelius Van Vorst,	Seil Marselis,
Hendrick Sigells,	Zacharias Sickels,	Philip Smith,
his	his	his
Jacobus x Van Boskerck,	Michael M Vreeland,	Johannis M. Wynner,
mark	mark	mark.
Joris Cadmus,	John Van Horn,	Mindert Garrabrants,
Andries Seagaerd,	Job Smith,	Pieter Merselis,
Johannis Vreelandt,	Hendrick Blinkerhof,	Cornelius Sip,
Johannis Van Wagenen,	Hartman Brinkerhoef,	Philip Earle,
his	his	marck
Garret G. N Newkirk,	Matthias x Evison,	Michael N Hartmanse Vreeland,
mark	mark	seyn
Abraham Sickels,	Cornelius Garrabrants,	Margrieta Van Boskerck,
Mattheus Newkirk,	John Van Houte,	Daniel Van Reypen,
	Jacobus Vanderhoef,	Cornelius Jurreyanse,
his		

JOHANNIS x JURREYANSE, HENDERICUS KUYPER, HELMIGH VAN HOUTE,
mark
Trustees.

We do not find, That, there is, or ever was more than one Church in this Township, nor that, this Church is incorporated by any Charter,

We, the Subscribers, do hereby certify that the above written and foregoing is a true copy of an Original instrument, now in our possession, signed by the Freeholders, Inhabitants of the Township of Bergen, and as their Act to us delivered in quality of their Trustees for the uses and purposes therein mentioned, and by us also agreed to and signed, and by virtue and in pursuance thereof, we do hereby suffer, authorize and impower Charles Clinton, William Donaldson, Azariah Dunham, John Berrien, Abraham Clark jr. and Jacob Spicer and the major part of them to retain in their hands (as a fund for the purposes hereinafter mentioned) the sum of four thousand three hundred twenty-two pounds ten shillings and three pence, being the surplus at present remaining of the money produced by the sale of the land set apart and sold for defraying the charges of making a General Petition of the Common Lands of the said Township, after the said charges and one thousand pounds more advanced to the said Trustees for paying the Quit Rents, due from the said Township to the General Proprietors of the Eastern Division of New Jersey were thence deducted, which s^d surplus so remaining and amounting to the sum of four thousand three hundred and twenty-two pounds ten shillings and three pence as aforesaid, We consent and agree shall by them the said Charles Clinton, William Donaldson, Azariah Dunham, John Berrien, Abraham Clark and Jacob Spicer (or the major part of them) be applied and deposited as follows : (that is to say)

Firstly, that after our own reasonable demands against the said Freeholders Inhabitants of the said Township of Bergen shall be adjusted between them and us so much of the surplus shall be applied to pay the same as shall be sufficient for that purpose.

Secondly, that so much more of the said surplus shall be applied to defray the charges of making subdivisions of the Common Lands of the said Township of Bergen as shall be sufficient for that purpose, and if then any part of the said surplus shall remain the said part so remaining shall be deposited in our hands for the use of the Corporation of Bergen, to be accounted for and paid to the members thereof in proportion to their several rights as we have already agreed to do, hereby giving and granting unto the said Charles Clinton, William Donaldson, Azariah Dunham, John Berrien, Abraham Clark, Jacob Spicer and the major part of them our full power and authority in and about the premises and ratifying and confirming whatsoever they, or the major part of them shall do agreeable to the power and directions above granted and prescribed.

In witness whereof we have hereunto set our hands the 18th day of December 1764.

JOHANNIS X JURYANSE,
his true mark
HENDERICUS KUYPEN,
HELMIGH VAN HOUTE."

The tract was divided into 37 lots ; 18 fronting on Newark Bay, and 18 on Kill Van Kull, besides one other lot for the use of a ferry to Staten Island. Kuyper's associates received from him a deed for a lot on the bay, a lot on the kill, and 1-18th of the ferry lot. These deeds were dated March 7, 1765, and to each was annexed an original map, made by Azariah Dunham, one of the Commissioners, showing the division of the tract. The map, which I have reproduced, was copied from the original annexed to the deed to Cornelius Van Vorst. Only two deeds, viz., to Joris Cadmus and George Vreeland, are on record.

*₇₁ but is a Religious Society maintain'd from the first Settlement of the Country * according to the Mode of the protestant Churches in the

KILL VAN KULL LOTS.

Nos. 1 and 2 were sold by Peter Ward, Sheriff, to James Bard Jan. 2, 1789, on an execution against Catherine Kuyper, administratrix of Henricus Kuyper, deceased. Edward Nichol sold the same to Charles Henry Lambert-Preudhomme Du Pont Jan. 14, 1800, who sold Lot No. 1 to Peter Van Buskirk Oct. 17, 1800, which he probably gave to his son-in-law, Cornelius Vreeland. Hartman Vreeland, David M. Demarest, Jasper Cadmus, and William Vreeland, conveyed to Peter Crary by two deeds, Dec. 24 and 25, 1747, several acres which lay within this lot, and possibly within Lot No. 2. The land hereabouts seems to have been mapped by R. M. Cary, surveyor, Dec. 10, 1847. Crary conveyed to Samuel D. Ingham and Matthew C. Jenkins a strip 300 feet on Kill Van Kull, by 272 feet deep, May 4, 1848; also another strip May 23, 1848. Hartman Vreeland et al. to Ingham and Jenkins over six acres east of the church lot Jan. 5, 1848. *Vide Note to Lot No.* 418, p. 155, and *Note to Lot No.* 5, p. 70. Ingham and Jenkins to William B. Reed and Philip Van Wart March 5, 1851, who partitioned March 1, 1852. Reed to Charles H. Winfield and Frederick F. Betts the S. E. corner May 25, 1855. Betts quit-claimed to Winfield Oct. 6, 1855; Winfield to Reed Aug. 6, 1856; Reed to Henry Paret April 30, 1857.

Lot No. 2 (?) seems to have been owned by Peter Van Buskirk, and by him given to his son-in-law, William Vreeland, who conveyed to James L. Simonson, May 27, 1826, the whole lot, except half an acre in the S. W. corner, which he conveyed to Cornelius Simonson June 13, 1836. James L. Simonson conveyed to the Reformed Church of Bergen Neck Nov. 5, 1829; the church to Geo. W. Bruen Oct. 12, 1836; Bruen to the church Aug. 6, 1840; the church to John Paret Oct. 24, 1853. Paret also purchased the half-acre owned by Cornelius Simonson. Retaining this half-acre and some additional ground, he sold the residue of the lot to Samuel C. White, the present owner. Paret died seized of the S. W. corner Oct. 8, 1866, leaving children, *Caroline, Mary E., William, Henry,* and *Thomas D.*

No. 3 was owned by Thomas Brown, and was inherited by his grandson, Andrew Gautier. Thomas B. Gautier sold it to David Leary Nov. 7, 1798, who sold to James Van Zyle May 1, 1804. Abraham Bedell sold it to Geo. W. Bruen Oct. 10, 1836 except ¼ acre in the S. W. corner sold to Wm. Stringham Dec. 27, 1831. *Vide Note to Andriesen's Patent,* p. 13.

No. 4 was deeded by Kuyper to Garret Newkirk. *Vide Note to Berry's Patent,* p. 51. By Newkirk's heirs, viz.: John Van Dalson, Matthew G., and Henry Newkirk, it was sold to James Van Buskirk Feb. 7, 1795. He, by will, dated Sept. 8, 1823, proved Dec. 27, 1823, gave it to his son Nicholas, who conveyed it to James Van Buskirk, by whom it was reconveyed to Nicholas March 17, 1849. Jacob Van Horn sold two acres off of the rear end of this lot to George McIntyre May 9, 1796. McIntyre's will, dated May 9, 1800, made his wife Dorcas his executrix. She sold all of her husband's lands at Bergen Point to Casparus or Jasper Zabriskie Jan. 1, 1802.

No. 5 was deeded by Kuyper to Joris Cadmus. He sold the W. half to Wilhelmus Vreeland. By will, dated Sept. 10, 1798, proved in Richmond Co., N. Y., Vreeland gave to his son Cornelius part of Lots Nos. 5 and 6 = 4 acres, who sold the same to Peter Vreeland July 17, 1818. On a partition of Cornelius' property, the whole of Lots Nos. 5 and 6 fell to his son Peter, who sold to Michael Zabriskie Aug. 8, 1833, who conveyed to Albert M. Zabriskie Feb. 19, 1834, who sold to Alexander M. Bruen May 25, 1835, who sold to George W. Bruen Oct. 10, 1835, who mortgaged to the

United Provinces from whence they have receiv'd their Ministers, and being now, and heretofore subject to, or a Part of the Classis of Amsterdam.

Vreeland heirs separately, May 2, 1836. By Henry Newkirk, Sheriff, the same was sold on foreclosure, decree dated Aug. 2, 1841, to Hartman Vreeland, David M. Demarest, William Vreeland, William Vreeland, jr., Jasper Cadmus et ux., and Elizabeth Cadmus, April 18, 1842. William Vreeland, jr., sold his interest to Hartman Vreeland and Jasper Cadmus, jr., Dec. 19, 1843. Peter Vreeland quit-claimed to its then owners Sept. 18, 1847, who sold to George W. Poillon Sept. 25, 1847, who sold to William P. Lee and James A. Williamson Sept. 1, 1860. *Vide Note to Lot* 418, p. 155.

No. 6 was deeded by Kuyper to Claas Vreeland, by whose will, dated July 23, 1801, proved May 21, 1803, it was given to his son Stephen, who sold it to Cornelius Vreeland July 29, 1806. *Vide Note to Lot No.* 5, p. 70.

No. 7 was deeded by Kuyper to Jacob Van Wagenen. Charles H. L Preudhomme du Pont sold it to John Butler April 12, 1804, excepting a strip = half an acre, which had been sold by him to Wm. Harrington, and by him to Martin Woods April 15, 1815. At one time the lot belonged to Richard Laurence. Woods sold to Jasper Zabriskie May 22, 1818. *Vide Note to Lot* 13, p. 70. Michael and Albert M. Zabriskie sold this and half of Lot 8 to George W. Bruen May 25, 1835.

No. 8 was deeded by Kuyper to Job Smith, and by him devised to his son John, who sold it to John Butler Oct. 26, 1793, who sold the W. half of it to Du Pont April 12, 1804, and the E. half to Jasper Zabriskie June 18, 1808. *Vide Note to Lot* 7, p. 70.

No. 9 was, with Lot No. 15, deeded by Kuyper to Anthony White. He died seized of Lots Nos. 9, 14, and 15, and Lots Nos. 1, 5, and 15 on Newark Bay. He left three children, *Johanna*, wife of John Bayard; *Euphemia*, wife of Wm. Paterson; and *Anthony W*. On partition of his estate, Aug. 27, 1798, *Lot* 9 on the Kill, and Lot 1 on the bay fell to Johanna; *Lots* 14 on the kill and 5 on the bay fell to Euphemia. Bayard et ux. sold *No* 9 to Peter Post Jan. 8, 1799, who sold to Du Pont Jan. 11, 1800, who sold to Elias Burger April 24, 1810, who sold to James R. Mullany, of the U. S. Navy, Jan. 14, 1824, who empowered his son *James R. M. Mullaney*, March 23, 1839, to sell. This attorney sold to Peter Vreeland and Michael Zabriskie May 7, 1839, that portion of the lot lying S. of Third Street. This deed is defective, because it was not executed by him as attorney. This defect was cured by the heirs giving a deed, Dec. 6, 1865. Vreeland sold his undivided half to Michael Zabriskie Sept. 9, 1840, who sold to his son *Albert M.* Oct. 25, 1841. He mapped it in 1841, and filed his map April 2, 1842. All of the lots have since been sold That part of the lot lying N. of Third Street, Elias Burger held at the time of his death, and by his will it passed to his daughter Maria. *Vide Note to Lot No.* 1, p. 70. Her trustees sold it to William Stringham, Feb. 2, 1847. Her children, who were of age, also gave deeds. Stringham sold in parcels to Winfield Stringham March 1, 1850; to Mary M., wife of William H. Wolvern; to James R. Stringham, to Sarah E. Earl, Jan. 2, 1862; and to John J. Van Buskirk. The kill end of the lot was divided on Zabriskie's map into two lots: one of them was conveyed by Albert M. to Michael Zabriskie Oct. 23, 1844, and by him to Rufus Story March 5, 1850. The other lot Albert M. conveyed to Daniel Lockwood Aug. 18, 1846; Lockwood to George W. Sands Aug. 12, 1848; Sands to John T. Mercereau Sept., 1848; Mercereau to William B. Reed Sept. 29, 1849; Reed to Rufus Story March 5, 1850.

No. 10 was deeded by Kuyper to Daniel Smith. He sold to Du Pont March 17,

The present Minister is the Reverend Mr. William Jackson. The Elders are now Messrs. Jacob Van Wagenen, Gerrit Newkirk, Zachariah

1795, who sold to John Henry Beaureaux Pusey de Nemours Jan. 9, 1800, who sold by Peter Samuel du Pont his attorney to Victor du Pont de Nemours May 11, 1802. This and the *Ferry Lot* lying E. comprise the land whereon the La Tourette House (then known as *Bon Sejours*, or *Good Stay*) now stands. Du Pont sold his interest in "Good Stay" to Raphael Duplanty Jan. 24, 1806, who sold to Charles Cottinal Feb. 7, 1807. By Cottinal's will, dated May, 1806, proved July 3, 1807, Anthony Girard was named executor with power to sell. He sold "Good Stay" at public auction to Elias Burger April 11, 1808. Burger, by will dated March 1, 1816, proved March 17, 1827, gave the same to his daughter *Maria*, wife of James R. Mullany. She died seized in 1830, leaving seven children, viz.: *Mary B., Jane A., James R., Elias B., Andrew J., John R. B.*, and *Erena Arietta*. By act of the Legislature, Jan. 20, 1843, Mary B., James R., and Elias B. were authorized to sell the property. They sold to David La Tourette April 30, 1845. On the same day the children executed another deed to La Tourette, who died seized (will, dated Feb. 3, 1862, proved Jan. 21, 1865), and his children now own what they have not sold.

No. 11 was deeded by Kuyper to George Vreeland. By his will, dated May 4, 1793, proved Aug. 14, 1795, he gave this lot and *No.* 2 on the Bay to his grandson George Vreeland, who sold *No.* 11 to James R. Mullany May 1, 1821, taking a consideration mortgage which was foreclosed and the lot sold by the sheriff to Albert M. Zabriskie May 26, 1837. Albert sold to Michael Zabriskie July 1, 1840, who sold to Jahiel Parmley Aug. 22, 1849, and Aug. 20, 1850; who sold to Edmund C. Bramhall Nov. 26, 1862. The deed of Aug. 20, 1850, was erroneous in description, but corrected by Zabriskie's executors Nov. 26, 1862.

No. 12 was deeded by Kuyper to Cornelius Garrabrants, who by will, dated April 7, 1814, proved July 30, 1814, gave the same to his daughters, *Jane*, wife of John Van Horne, and *Lenah*, wife of John G. Vreeland. *Vide Note to Lot No.* 417, p. 144. These devisees with their husbands by joint deed conveyed the same to Michael Zabriskie Aug. 13, 1822; who conveyed to his son, *Albert M.*, Aug. 31, 1840. Michael's wife, Jane, did not join in this deed, hence they executed another Oct. 22, 1844. Albert M. Zabriskie conveyed it to Andrew D. Mellick April 26, 1854; Mellick to George D. Phelps May 5, 1857. Henry B. Beaty, sheriff, on execution, sold Mellick's interest in the lot to Abigail Ayres March 26, 1859, and Phelps conveyed to Ayres June 28, 1860; Ayres to Charles A. Sherman July 2, 1860; Sherman to Andrew D. Mellick, jr., April 2, 1866.

No. 13 was known as the "Red House Lot." It was sold by Charity Stockholme to Peter Samuel Du Pont de Nemours April 11, 1800; who sold to John Xavier Bureaux Pusy May 11, 1802; who, by his attorney Peter Samuel Du Pont de Nemours, sold to Victor Du Pont de Nemours May 11, 1802; who sold to Jasper Zabriskie May 31, 1802. Zabriskie, by will without date, codicil dated Oct. 27, 1828, proved Nov. 15, 1828, gave it to his son *Michael* for life, then to his lawful issue "by any after marriage." On failure of such issue, then to the children of his grandson Albert M. Under this will it came to the children of Albert M. His son *Michael A.* sold one undivided eighth to Elizabeth D., wife of Andrew D. Mellick, Feb. 25, 1856. *David Zabriskie* sold one-eighth to his father, Albert M., Dec. 27, 1856. Samuel T. Brown, Hanson Carragan, and Jasper G. Cadmus, Commissioners, sold to Robert Mackie Dec. 13, 1858. This last deed does not seem to have been satisfactory, hence Albert M. Zabriskie, and his children, *Margaret Ann, Jane A., Gertrude L., Albert A.*, and *Samuel S.* (the last four infants), and Mellick deeded to Mackie. Mackie sold to

Sickles and Abraham Dedricks. The Deacons are now Mess.rs. Johannis Van Wagenen, George Cadmus, Abraham Prior, and Hendrick Kuyper.

Elizabeth D. Mellick, April 28, 1859, a strip about 36 feet wide off of the E. side of this lot, which she sold to Abigail Ayres July 2, 1860; who sold to Charles A. Sherman July 2, 1860; who sold to Andrew D. Mellick, jr., April 2, 1866. The following deeds were given by the Zabriskie children to Catherine, wife of Robert Mackie: Samuel S., April 18, 1836; Gertrude L., July 14, 1862; Jane A., July 7, 1860; Albert A., July 12, 1864.

The following brief record of the Zabriskie family will be interesting in this connection, and of assistance in tracing out titles. Albert Zabriskie m. Machtelt Van der Linden Dec. 17, 1676. His son *Joost* was b. 1687, d. July 30, 1756. *Albert*, the son of Joost (?), was b. 1730, m. Geertruy Westervelt, and d. Sept., 1785. He had ch. I. *Christiana*, b. Dec. 13, 1752; II. *Benjamin*, b. Dec. 31, 1754; III. *Joost*, b. March 8, 1757; IV. *Casparus* (or Jasper), b. Aug. 12, 1759; V. *Hendrickje*, b. Nov. 19, 1761; VI. *Antje*, b. Aug. 25, 1764; VII. *Ossiltje*, b. Dec. 27, 1766; VIII. *Rachel*, b. Dec. 28, 1768; IX. *Jan*, b. Nov. 19, 1770.

CASPARUS, m. 1st, Annetje Vreeland; 2d, Jane, dau. of Henry Kipp of New Barbadoes Neck, July 3, 1791; d. Oct. 19, 1828. By his first wife he had *Michael*, b. May 31, 1785, m. Jane, dau. Jan Ackerman, Sept. 6, 1807. By his 2d wife he had *Gertrude*, b. June 26, 1792, m. Hermanus Garretson, of Staten Island, Feb. 20, 1803, d. Feb. 27, 1822.

MICHAEL had ch. *Albert M.*, b. May 31, 1808, m. Ann M., dau. of Capt. David La Tourette, Oct. 9, 1828.

GERTRUDE had ch. I. *Jasper*, b. Dec. 11, 1809, d. April 5, 1813; II. *John*, b. July 7, 1811, d. Aug. 18, 1811; III. *Albert*, b. Feb. 22, 1813, d. Sept. 9, 1814; IV. *Jasper*, b. Nov. 10, 1816.

Françoise, the widow of Pusy, released to Elias Burger her right of dower in *Lots Nos.* 11, 13, 14, *and* 15 Sept. 1, 1812.

No. 14. *Vide Note to Lot No.* 9, p. 70. This lot and *Lot No.* 15 on the Kill and *Lots Nos.* 1 *and* 15 on the Bay were sold by John N. Cummings to Pusy Jan. 1, 1800, who by his attorney Samuel Du Pont sold to Victor Du Pont, who sold to Jasper Zabriskie. *Vide Note to Lot No.* 13, p. 70, and *Note to Lot No.* 413, p. 142. This lot formed part of the estate partitioned among Jasper Garretson's children. Alathea sold her allotment, plot A, of share 6, to Benjamin F. Woolsey June 17, 1870.

No. 15. *Vide Notes to Lots Nos.* 9 *and* 14, p. 70.

No. 16 was, with *Lot No.* 16 on the Bay, deeded by Kuyper to Cornelius Van Vorst.

No. 18 and Lot No. 18 on the Bay were owned by Michael and Abraham Van Tuyl. Michael joined "the Army of the King," in January, 1779, his property was confiscated, and his interest in these lots sold at public auction May 15, 1787. Cornelius Haring, agent for forfeited estates, gave to Andrew Van Tuyl and George Douglas, June 20, 1787, a deed for one-half of this lot, one-half of lot 18, on the Bay, and 1-36th of the Ferry lot. It seems that Michael had sold the Kill lot to Richard Varick Sept. 12, 1774, and Varick's devisees, Abraham and Richard Varick, sold the same to George McIntyre, May 1, 1790.

I give these dates as I find them. McIntyre died seized. By his will dated Sept. 19, 1800, he gave to his wife Dorcas one-third of his lands, and made her his executrix. In March term, 1801, the Court ordered the property sold. At auction Aug. 24, 1801, she sold to Casparus Zabriskie 8 24-100ths acres on rear of lot No. 18, and 2 acres on rear of Bay lot No. 4. She, with her second husband, Moses Allen, sold 15 5-100ths acres, including Lot No. 18. Elias Enyard sold one acre on the front of this lot to

And as the Minister, Elders, and Deacons form a Consistory and have the Care both of the Temporalities and Spiritual Government of the said

John M. Enyard April 4, 1823. It had been conveyed to him by Nicholas Enyard. Jacob A. Van Horne gave to David La Tourette a deed for it Jan. 19, 1833.

NEWARK BAY LOTS.

No. 1 was deeded by Kuyper to William Bayard. Anthony White died seized of it. *Vide Note to Kill Lots Nos.* 9 and 14. Françoise, widow of Jean Xavier Bureaux de Pusy, sold her interest in this and Bay lot No. 5 to Charles H. L. Preudhomme du Pont Feb. 10, 1807; who sold Lot No. 1 to Jacob Van Horne Jan. 21, 1811; who sold to Hermanus Garretson Feb. 17, 1819. James Simonson seems to have owned a part of this lot, and sold to Cornelius C. Van Buskirk, Jan. 12, 1820, one acre; who sold the same to Hermanus Garretson Oct. 2, 1820; who sold the whole lot to David La Tourette March 6, 1821.

No. 2. *Vide Note to Kill Lot No.* 11. George Vreeland sold it to Andrew Van Horne May 18, 1816. John G. Vreeland sold it to David La Tourette Oct. 9, 1820 (Andrew Van Horne gave La Tourette a deed for it March 4, 1831).

No. 4. The rear part of this lot was sold by Andrew Van Horne to David La Tourette, May 1, 1818.

No. 5. *Vide Note to Kill Lots Nos.* 9 and 14. Sold by John N. Cummings to John H. L. Bureaux De Pusy Jan. 1, 1800. *Vide Note to Bay Lot No.* 1. Andrew Van Horne, jr., sold a part of this lot to David La Tourette March 29, 1820.

Nos. 6 *and* 7, sold by Walter Clendenny to Cornelius Van Buskirk Oct. 18, 1809. Van Buskirk et al. sold the same in parcels to David La Tourette. (Deed for 13 6-10th acres, dated Jan. 5, 1822.)

No. 8 was deeded by Kuyper to Claas Vreeland. *Vide Note to Kill Lot No.* 6. It was sold by Nicholas Enyard to Cornelius C. Van Buskirk May 25, 1816.

No. 9 was deeded by Kuyper to Jorvis Cadmus. *Vide Note to Kill Lot No.* 5. Peter, William, and Zebulon La Rosa sold it to David La Tourette March 22, 1817. They owned it as early as 1795.

Lot 10. Nicholas Inyard sold 4 1-10th acres of this lot to David La Tourette Aug. 18, 1819.

No. 11. This was owned by Thomas Brown, probably deeded to him by Kuyper. In 1794 his widow was in possession. On her death it passed to her grandson Andrew Gautier, *Vide Note to Andriessen's Patent,* p. 13, who sold to Peter Post July 18, 1796; who sold to Du Pont Jan. 11, 1800. Cornelius C. Van Buskirk, sold 5 1-10th acres of this and lot 10 to James Simonson Jan. 12, 1820; who sold to David La Tourette March 13, 1821.

No. 12 was sold by Catherine Kuyper, widow and administratrix of Hendricus Kuyper, to Egbert Post Sept. 26, 1794, and by him to Henry Van Horne April 28, 1813.

No. 13. *Vide Note to Kill Lot No.* 1. John Van Dalson, a son-in-law of Hendrick Kuyper, *Vide Note to Van Purmerent's Patent,* p. 7, sold his interest in this lot to Egbert Post Sept. 26, 1794, who sold to Henry Van Horne April 28, 1813.

No. 14 was deeded by Kuyper to Daniel Smith, who sold to Egbert Post Sept. 26, 1794; who sold to Henry Van Horne April 28, 1813.

No. 15. *Vide Note to Kill Lot No.* 9.

No. 17. Sold in part by Ichabod Gruman to George McIntyre May 1, 1787, and in part to Moses Van Ame July 18, 1788. Ichabod and Hannah Gruman and John Holder united in another deed to Van Ame, July 19, 1788. George McIntyre owned it in 1790.

CHURCH LOTS.   145

Church as they and the People of the said Church declare to us referring for further Testimony of the Truth thereof to the Books and Records of the said Church.

We Do set off, adjudge and allot to them the said Minister and Elders and Deacons and their successors in Office forever, The sundry Tracts or Lots of Land hereafter describ'd being parcel of the said Common Lands, to be by them held and injoy'd for the Use of said Church and Congregation.

Our Survey of which sundry Tracts or Lots of Land, for said Church shews, and we do adjudge them to be four Tracts or Lots.

The First being that whereon the Church stands with the Burying Yard adjoining to it (mark'd on the Map No 173) *

Begins at a stake standing by the Northwest side of the Road leading from the Town to Bergen Point (which Stake is the Easterly Corner of an Out Garden Plot in Tielman Van Vleck's Patent mark'd on the Map No 129) and from the said Stake runs North nineteen Degrees and forty Minutes East two Chains and thirty three Links to a Stake standing at the Easterly Corner of the Church Yard. Thence North forty three Degrees and fifteen Minutes West One Chain to a Stake standing at the Northerly Corner of the Church Yard, Thence South forty Degrees and twenty Minutes West two Chains and seventy four links to a Stake, Thence South sixty three Degrees and ten Minutes East one Chain and eighty six Links to the Place of Beginning.

The Second being that whereon the Parsonage House now stands with the Garden and a small Piece of Pasture land adjoining thereto (mark'd on the Map No 174)†

Begins at a Stake standing by the Northwest side of the Road that leads from the Town to Bergen Point (which Stake is the Southerly Corner of an Out Garden Plot * in Tielman Van Vleck's Patent mark'd *72 on the Map No 129) and from said Stake runs South fourteen Degrees and twenty Minutes West six Chains and seventy five Links along said Road to a Post (which Post is the easterly Corner of the Piece of Land

---

No. 18. *Vide Note to Kill Lot No.* 18. Forty acres, including nearly all of lots 15, 16, 17, and 18, were conveyed to Jacob Rabineau by Cornelius Van Horne June 16, 1836.

FERRY LOT.

The interests of the different owners of this lot became consolidated in Charles Henry Lambert Preudhomme du Pont, in 1800. I will not attempt to trace the several transfers. At that time it lay E. of the road. He annexed it to Lot No. 10, by procuring a relocation of the road to the E. side of the Lot, Feb 17, 1801. *Vide Note to Kill Lot No.* 10. It is well to observe that the road as now in existence is entirely upon the Ferry lot, and that the road was opened to the water and there connected with the Ferry. For many years, however, its use to the water's edge has been abandoned.

º Yet owned by the Church.

† This lot extended along the W. side of the road to Bergen Point, from a point about 100 feet N. of Highland ave., S. to Glenwood ave. On this lot the Church

appropriated for Mechanicks mark'd on the Map No 171,) And from said Post runs North sixty seven Degrees and fifty Minutes West three Chains and twelve Links to a Stake, Thence South twenty six Degrees and thirty Minutes West six Chains and fifteen Links to a Stake, Thence North sixty nine Degrees and fifteen Minutes West One Chain and ninety Links to a Stake, Thence North thirty Degrees East thirteen Chains to a Stake (standing at the Westerly Corner of the said Out Garden Plot in Tielman Van Vleck's Patent mark'd on the Map No 129) and from said Stake runs South sixty three Degrees and ten Minutes East two Chains and eighty two Links to the Place of Beginning.

The Third is a Farm Lot lying Southerly of the Town of Bergen and back of Comunipan mark'd on the Map No 175)*

Beginning at a Stake standing by a Brook or Creek (which Stake is the Southerly Corner of Fytje Hartman's second Patent mark'd on the Map No 15) and from said Stake runs North forty nine Degrees and

---

now stands. A strip N. of Highland ave., about 100 hundred feet in width, was sold by the Church to Garret Sip, May 5, 1863. This is marked No. 1, in the accompanying diagram. No. 2 is still owed by the Church. No. 3 was sold to John

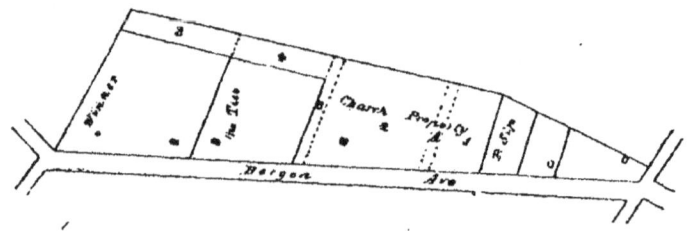

Blinner Nov. 25, 1863. No. 4 was sold to Isaac S. Taylor Jan. 7, 1868. A is Highland ave., and B. is Glenwood ave.

* Bergen Church was incorporated Dec. 20, 1771, by Act of the Legislature. On March 5, 1806, the Congregation determined to sell their lands, and the Consistory decided to sell this lot to the highest bidder. The E. part of the lot was sold to Jacob Prior April 30, 1806 (Elias Earl bought a piece of the lot, which Abraham Vreeland afterwards purchased). These sales were confirmed Jan. 28, 1814. Owing to an inaccuracy in the description, a new deed was given to Prior Dec. 5, 1809. His purchase was on the E. end of the lot = 30¾ acres and six perches. By will, dated Aug. 14, 1830, Prior gave this lot to his children *Nicholas* and *Gitty*, wife of Henry Allen. Allen et ux. sold their interest in the lot Oct. 2, 1833, and confirmed it by another deed July 16, 1850.

Nearly half of the lot remained in possession of the Church. The Consistory resolved, Sept. 21, 1835, to take the sense of the Congregation as to selling the lands of the Church. A paper was circulated for that purpose, and the result was 94 votes for the sale; 1 vote for the sale, "except the lands near where the church now is," and — votes for the sale, "except the old parsonage lot"; nays, none. An act was passed in 1837 empowering the Church to sell lands. The W. half of the lot = 31 80-100 acres, bounded N. E. by the heirs of Clendenny and David Vreeland, S. E. by Nicholas Prior, S. W. by John E. Post, N. W. by the old road, was sold to Stephen Garretson Feb. 11, 1839. The grantee being a deacon in the Church at the time, a question was raised as to his title. A confirmatory deed was executed May 31, 1851. Garretson sold to Luman Sherwood June 10, 1851, and he to Edwin J. Brown Sept. 27, 1852.

twenty Minutes West forty two Chains and eighty four Links to a Stake, Thence South thirty five Degrees West two Chains and sixty two Links to a Stake, Thence North fifty Degrees and ten Minutes West six Chains and seventy seven Links to a Stake, Then South forty three Degrees and thirty Minutes West thirteen Chains and eighty Links to a Stake, Thence South fifty Degrees East twenty five Chains and thirty four Links to a Stake (being the Northerly Corner of Dirck Classen's Patent mark'd on the Map No 17) and from said Stake runs South twenty seven Degrees and thirty Minutes East twenty three Chains and eighty six Links along said Dirck Classen's Line to a Stake by the Edge of the Meadow which is the easterly Corner of said Dirck Classin's Patent No 17, Then North twenty seven Degrees and fifteen Minutes East Eleven Chains and four Links along the Edge of the Meadow to a Stake standing by the Head of a small Creek, Thence South forty six Degrees and thirty Minutes East two Chains and seventy five Links to where said small Creek falls into Dirck Sycan's Creek, Then up along said Sycan's Creek Northeasterly as it runs to the Place of Beginning.

The Fourth is a Lot of timber'd Land mark'd on the Map No 176*

Beginning at a Stake (which Stake stands North thirty six Degrees and thirty Minutes East ninety four Chains and fifty Links from large Stone mark'd **A 1764** planted at a Corner of Wiehaken Commons) and from said * Stake runs North fifty two Degrees and thirty Minutes West *73 thirty eight Chains to a Stake, Thence North thirty six Degrees and thirty Minutes East three Chains and ninety five Links to a Stake, Thence South fifty two Degrees and thirty Minutes East thirty eight Chains to a Stake, Thence South thirty six Degrees and thirty Minutes West three Chains and ninety five Links to the Place of Beginning.

  And for the **Free School** of the said Town of Bergen We have set apart sundry Tracts or Lots of Land hereafter describ'd being also Parcel of the said Common Land.

  Our Survey of which sundry Tracts or Lots of Land for said Free School shews, and we do adjudge them to be three Tracts or Lots.

The First (being that House Lot in the Town whereon the School House now stands mark'd on the Map No 177) †

Begins at a Stake standing by a Street (which Stake is the Westerly Corner of a House Lot in Jan Lubertse's Patent mark'd on the Map No 158) and from said Stake runs North forty two Degrees West One Chain and forty five Links along said Street to the Square, Then North forty eight Degrees East one Chain and forty five Links to the easterly

---

 ° This lot was sold by the Church to Joseph Danielson May 9, 1838. It lies at New Durham.

 † This is the lot on which the old Columbia Academy stood, and on which the public School house now is, on the E. side of the Square. On this Lot a School House was erected in the earliest days of Bergen. It was standing in 1668, *Vide Note to Lubbertse's Patent*, p. 45, and used for church purposes until 1680. *Vide Long Isl. Hist. Soc.* i.

148   SCHOOL LOTS.

Corner of said Square, Then South forty two Degrees East one Chain and forty five Links to a Stake, Thence South forty eight Degrees West One Chain and forty five Links to the Place of Beginning.

The Second (being a Pasture Lot lying southwesterly from and near to the Town mark'd on the Map No 178) *

Begins at a Stake (which Stake is the Northwesterly Corner of a Lot in Nicholas Varlet's Patent mark'd on the Map No 128) and from said Stake runs South eight Degrees East twenty one Chains and seventy Links to a Stake (standing in the Northeasterly Line of the Tract in Nicholas Jansen the Baker's Patent mark'd on the Map No 12) And from said Stake runs North forty nine Degrees and forty five Minutes West fourteen Chains and sixty Links to a Stake standing at the Northerly Corner of the said Tract in Nicholas Jansen the Baker's Patent mark'd on the Map No 12) And from said Stake runs North forty one Degrees and forty five Minutes East three Chains and seventy two Links to a Stake, Thence North thirty Degrees East ten Chains and fifty five Links to the Place of Beginning.

*74   * **The Third** (being another Pasture Lot lying Northeasterly from and near to the Town mark'd on the Map No 179) †

º This was a small triangular lot lying in the S. angle formed by the junction of Bergen ave. and a short street through which the horse cars now pass from Bergen ave. to Monticello ave. It was divided into three lots by the Trustees of Columbia Academy, all fronting N. W. on Bergen ave. They sold *Lot No.* 1, June 6, 1810, to Garret Van Winkle, bounded N. W. by Bergen ave., E. by Casparus Prior, S. W. by *Lot No.* 2. This I take to be the N. part of the tract.

They also sold 12-100ths of an acre to Richard Van Rypen May 19, 1810, and 4 48-100 acres to Casparus Prior June 6, 1810, being Lot No. 2, bounded N. W. by the road, N. E. by Lot No. 1, S. E. by Jacob Van Wagenen and Prior, and S. W. by Brinkerhoff. They also sold to Prior 18-100ths of an acre N. W. of the road March 9, 1814. *Vide Map in Note to Varlet's Patent*, p. 62.

† This lot lies E. of Bergen ave., and extends from Magnolia ave. on the S.

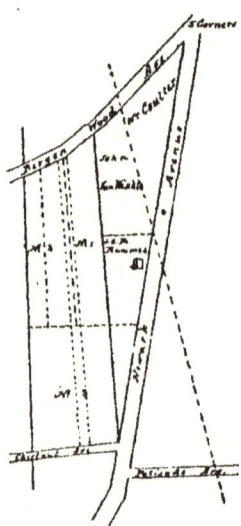

to about 100 feet N. of Prospect st. or Pavonia ave. The trustees of Columbia Academy divided it into three parcels. *No.* 1 they sold to Joseph Simonson. *No.* 2 they sold in two parcels, the N. half to Samuel Osborn, April 4, 1808; the S. half to Richard Stager, on the same date. These sales were confirmed by the Legislature. *Vide Laws of* 1814, p. 202.

Simonson sold to Garret J. Newkirk May 4, 1809. Newkirk died seized Aug. 22, 1818, leaving children, *Jacob, George, Sophia*, wife of James Provost, *Garret* and *Catherine*, wife of George Vreeland. These children inherited *Lot No.* 1. Jacob, George, and Sophia conveyed their interest to John Tise July 9, 1835. Garret conveyed to Tise Sept. 13, 1836. Catherine conveyed to Tise April 9, 1838. Tise was now owner of *No.* 1   He conveyed it to Richard Tise March 25, 1845. On execution against John Tise, Sheriff Van Winkle conveyed to Geo. Coghill July 18, 1846; who quit-claimed to Richard Tise Feb. 5, 1847; who conveyed to Jared W. Graves

Begins at a Stake standing by the Road that leads rom the Town to the English Neighbourhood (which Stake is the Northerly Corner of a Lot in John Berry's Patent mark'd on the Map No 125) and from said Stake runs North thirty one Degrees and thirty Minutes East six Chains and sixty two Links along said Road to a Stake, Thence South thirty eight Degrees and forty five Minutes East nineteen Chains and twenty eight Links to a Stake standing in the Northwesterly Line of a Lot in Nicholas Varlet's Patent, mark'd on the Map No 127) Thence South thirty two Degrees West six Chains and sixty two Links along said Varlet's Line to a Stake being the easterly Corner of the said Lot of John Berry mark'd on the Map No 125, Thence North thirty eight Degrees and forty five Minutes West nineteen Chains and twenty eight Links along the Line of said Berry to the Place of Beginning.

Feb. 5, 1847; who conveyed to Andrew L. Cadmus and Wm. G. Plummer Oct. 31, 1857. On foreclosure of a mortgage, Ogden, master, conveyed to Wm. G. Plummer, Andrew L. Cadmus, and Silas H. Jessup. The property was mapped in 1868. This part of *No.* 1 lies W. of Willow Court street. What lies E. of that street, and immediately S. of the Court House, John R. McPherson conveyed to the Board of Chosen Freeholders a short time ago, and it is now a part of the Court House property. Osborn conveyed his half of *No.* 2 to Jacob Newkirk May 16, 1809, and Stager conveyed his half to the same Newkirk June 29, 1809. Newkirk died seized Aug. 15, 1860, leaving children, *Jacob, Abraham, Sophia,* wife of Blakely Wilson, and *Effie,* wife of Daniel Van Winkle. It is now owned by Mrs. Graves (Hudson City Seminary), Thomas E. Bray, John W. Gaffney, St. Joseph's Church, *et al.* The Trustees sold *No.* 3 to Henry Van Winkle April 4, 1808. He died seized Dec. 13, 1848. By will he left all his lands to Peter Bently and Jacob Van Wagenen in trust for his two daughters, *Aletta,* wife of Dr. John M. Cornelison, and *Effie,* wife of William Thomas.

* **And** then we proceeded to a **Partition** of the Residue or the *75 said **Common Lands.** Alloting and ann exinga Share of the same to each Patent or Grant. And this Allotment is to them severally in the Order in which they are above arrang'd.*

To the Patent of Wiehaken granted by William Kieft to Maryn Adrianse dated the Eleventh Day of May One thousand six hundred and forty seven and confirm'd by Patent from Philip Carteret to said Maryn Adrianse dated the eighteenth Day of April One thousand six hundred and seventy.

We do **allot** that Parcel of Land which on the Map is mark'd No 201†

Our Survey whereof shews and we adjudge it to be a Tract

Beginning at a Heap of Stones (ten Links North from a Black Oak Tree mark'd on its North side W B which said Heap of Stones is the Northerly Corner of said Wiehaken Patent which on the Map is mark'd No 1) And from said Place of Beginning runs South thirty seven Degrees and a Half West thirty-seven Chains and sixty seven Links to another Heap of Stones being the Westerly Corner of said Wiehaken Patent, Thence North fifty two Degrees and thirty Minutes West nineteen Chains and seventy Links to a large Stone mark'd W B, Then North thirty three Degrees East thirty nine Chains to a Stake, Thence South fifty two Degrees and thirty Minutes East six Chains and thirty Links to a Stone planted and mark'd **A 1764**, Then North thirty six Degrees and thirty Minutes East twelve Chains and thirty Links to a Stake,

---

º In the allotment of the Common Lands the Commissioners had regard to the location of the Patents to which they were allotted. From and including the Weehawken Patent south along the river to and including Dirck Sycan's first Patent, the owners thereof received lands extending from the river back to what was known as the Bergen Line. The reason assigned for this was, that these persons could boat their fuel from their wood-lots to their homes. The district in which these lots, assigned to the shore owners lay, was known by the general name of Slonga. It lay between Weehawken and the northerly bounds of the county.

The owners of the patented lands south of the southerly bounds of Dirck Sycan's first Patent received their commons in that immediate vicinity—in Greenville and Bayonne; then known as Minkakwa, Pembrepogh, and Bergen Point.

The owners of patented lands on the Hill received their commons north of the patented lands, and between the westerly line of the shore lots and the easterly line of the Secaucus Commons. This district was known by the general name of Bergen Woods, but sometimes called the Bergen Lots.

The lands allotted to the patent of Secaucus were known by the name of the Secaucus Commons.

It is scarcely necessary to remind the reader that the private ownership of the lots hereinafter described, having been held in common up to that time, does not date beyond the Field Book.

† *Lots Nos.* 201, 202, 203, were confiscated as the property of William Bayard. *Vide Note to Hoboken Patent,* p 6. Haring, the agent for forfeited estates, caused the land embraced within these three lots to be surveyed and laid out into 19 lots. Careful search and extended inquiry have been made for this map, but without success.

Then North fifty two Degrees and thirty Minutes East forty three Chains and seventy five Links to a Red Oak Tree on the East side of a Brook (being the Northerly Corner of Jacob Luby's Patent mark'd on the Map No 144), Thence along the Line of said Luby's Patent South fifty nine Degrees West thirteen Chains and twenty one Links to the Line of said Wiehaken Patent, Then along said Wiehaken Patent North fifty two Degrees and thirty Minutes West to the Place of Beginning, Containing (an after Allowance for the Hill) about One hundred & thirty three Acres.

Nevertheless, I have been able, with proper assistance, to reproduce the map from the descriptions in the Haring deeds. I have no doubt of its accuracy as here inserted, reduced to one third of the size of the lots on the Field Map.

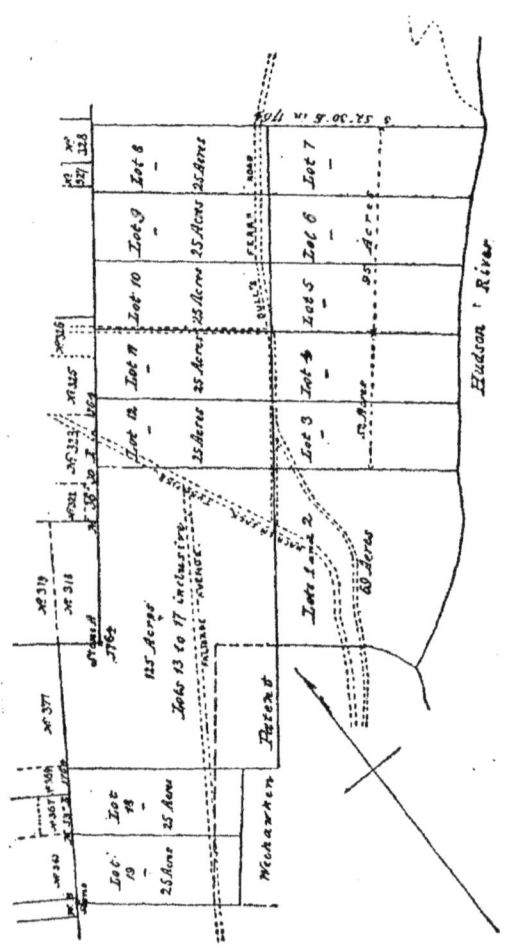

Lots Nos. 1 and 2=65 acres, Haring sold to Daniel Baldwin Dec. 1, 1784. This tract includes Kings Point, or "Highwood." Baldwin conveyed to Daniel Smith March 28, 1788, who conveyed it to his son Daniel Sept. 3, 1796; who conveyed to David Hennion July 25, 1815. Hennion gave to Smith a mortgage. Smith seems to have died about this time, and his heirs released to Charles Watts in February and March, 1819; who conveyed to Moses Isaacs Nov. 4, 1819. Smith assigned the Hennion mortgage to Philip Earle, who foreclosed and purchased the property at sheriff's sale June 3, 1822. The Hoboken Land Improvement Company conveyed to James G. King June 6, 1842, 14 4-10 acres, including the "Point." Mr. King purchased of Philip Earle's executors two acres near the gate house April 18, 1840. All of these two lots lying E. of the Bulls Ferry road is now owned by the heirs of James G. King.

Lots Nos. 3 and 4. The Commissioners of the loan office of Bergen County, *Vide Act of the Legislature, passed May* 26, 1786, sold these lots to Peter Zabriskie, executor of Jacob Zabriskie, March 4, 1791. Zabriskie conveyed them to James Van Horne March 12, 1792. They are now owned by the heirs of James G. King.

* To the Patent of Hobocken granted by Petrus Stuyve- *76
sant to Nicholas Varlet dated the fifth Day of February One
thousand six hundred and sixty three and confirm'd by
Patent from Philip Carteret to said Nicholas Varlet dated
the twelfth day of May One thousand six hundred and sixty
eight.

We do **allot** the three several Parcels of Land following.

Our Survey whereof shews, and we adjudge them to be three Tracts

The First whereof (mark'd on the Map No 233) lying on the Southeast side of the High Hill adjoining the said Patent of Hobocken

Begins at a Heap of Stones (being South fifty two Degrees and a Half East three Chains and forty Links from the Westermost Corner of Wiehaken Patent) and from said Place of Beginning runs South thirty three Degrees West twenty eight Chains on the Top of the Hill, Then South fifty seven Degrees East two Chains, Then South thirty three Degrees West thirty Chains to a Heap of Stones by a Dogwood Tree blaz'd, Then South fifty seven Degrees East one Chain, Then South thirty three Degrees West ten Chains, Then South fifty seven Degrees East two Chains, Then South thirty three Degrees West eleven Chains and thirty Links to a Heap of Stones in a Path that goes down the Hill towards Hobocken, Then North fifty seven Degrees West One Chain, Then South thirty three Degrees West nineteen Chains and twelve Links,

---

Lots Nos. 5, 6, 7, 8. Daniel Baldwin seems to have owned these lots. On an execution against him, Peter Ward, sheriff, sold them to Jonas Ward March 25, 1788. Elijah Gardner afterwards owned at least part of them—probably purchased from Ward. Matthias Ludlam seems to have owned a considerable part of these lots, which he conveyed to David Deas Oct. 7, 1789, in trust for James Deas (who had married Susanna, daughter of Ludlam), for life, then to his children. By will, dated April 18, 1812, proved May 30, 1812, James Deas gave all his lands to his wife for life, then to his children equally. These heirs conveyed to James Brown 26 42-100 acres July 31, 1852, and 19 acres to James G. King Jan. 10, 1853. This last tract seems to have been covered by a deed from Henry Ludlam to James Deas Aug. 8, 1796; also by a deed from Francis Myerhoff to James Hanna June 22, 1808. Mr. King also purchased from the Deas heirs, Nov. 26, 1849, the strip lying between the top of the hill and the river.

Lot No. 9. On an execution against Robert Neil, Peter Ward, sheriff, sold this lot to James Grier Jan. 1, 1790; who sold to Elijah Gardner March 26, 1801. He died seized.

Lot No. 10 was sold by Haring to Aaron Wyman, who conveyed to Elijah Gardner Feb. 24, 1787. Of this lot and several others Gardner died seized in June, 1807, leaving his property to his three sons, *James F., John* and *Thomas.* The last two released to James F. July 4, 1827; who died in 1852, leaving *Charles E., James, Robert, Elijah* and two daughters.

Lot No. 11 was sold by Haring to William Jackson May 10, 1784. Jackson died seized, and by will gave this lot and *Lot No.* 12 to his sons, *Henry* and *John F.* The latter conveyed his interest to Henry Dec. 23, 1815. He sold the two lots to John Zule May 1, 1819; who sold to William J. Cantello Nov. 29, 1827; who sold to Peter Kerrigan June 14, 1828; who conveyed to Cantello June 6, 1834; who conconveyed to Enoch Durar Oct. 22, 1844; who conveyed to the Hudson County Real Estate Company Feb 23, 1852. It was mapped in 1852; map filed March 15, 1855.

Then South fifteen Degrees West eight Chains and seventy Links, Then South fifty five Degrees West three Chains, Then South thirty five Degrees West six Chains to a large Heap of Stones near the top of the Hill, Then Southeasterly down the Hill to the Edge of the Meadow at the Westermost Corner of Hobocken Patent, Then running Northeasterly between the Salt Meadow and foot of the Hill along said Hobocken Patent 'til it comes to said Wiehaken Patent, Then North fifty two Degrees and thirty Minutes West along the Line of said Wiehaken Patent to the Place of Beginning, containing about fifty seven Acres of broken Land being the Face of the Hill.

The Second (mark'd on the Map No 203)

Begins at a Stake standing North thirty six Degrees and thirty Minutes East fourteen Chains and twenty five Links from a Stone planted and mark'd **A 1764** (which Stake is the Northerly Corner of a Parcel of Land mark'd on the Map No. 202 allotted to the small Patent of Jacob Luby) and from said Stake the Place of Beginning) * runs South fifty two Degrees and thirty Minutes East fifty two Chains and fifty Links to Hudson's River, Then returning to said Stake the Place of Beginning and from thence runs North thirty six Degrees and thirty Minutes East sixty two Chains and twenty-five Links to a Stake standing near two large Trees each mark'd D, Thence South fifty two Degrees and Thirty Minutes East fifty seven Chains and fifty Links to a Heap of Stones near Hudson's River, Then Southerly down said Hudson's River as the same runs till it meets the first mentioned Line in the Survey that runs to said River, containing (after an Allowance for the Hill) about three hundred and sixteen Acres.

*77

The Third (mark'd on the Map No 219) *

Durar reserved the S. corner of the plot which embraced not only *Lots Nos.* 11 and 12, but the N. E. corner of *Lot No.* 13, lying E. of the Hackensack turnpike. The tract now comprises that part of Union Hill lying E. of the Bergen line and S. of Paine or Union street.

Lot No. 12 was sold by Haring to William Jackson May 6, 1784. He conveyed to Robert Neil Oct. 23, 1784. It was owned by John Seely in 1789. Jonas Ward conveyed it to Henry Jackson Aug. 4, 1790. Jackson conveyed to John Stevens the N. W. corner, lying W. of the turnpike May 23, 1807, *Vide Note to Lot No.* 11, Lots Nos. 13, 14, 15, 16, 17, were sold in one body by Haring to John Stevens Aug. 25, 1784. Stevens conveyed to Henry Jackson the S. E. corner of the N. part of the tract (or *Lot No.* 13) lying E. of the turnpike May 23, 1807. It remained in the Stevens family until it was conveyed to the Hoboken Land Improvement Company, who yet own the most of it.

Lot No. 18 was sold by Haring to William Jackson May 6, 1784.

Lot No. 19 was sold by Haring to Cornelius Van Vorst March 21, 1785, *Vide Note to Van Purmerent's Patent*, p. 7. Van Vorst gave it by will to the heirs of his daughter Neeltje, wife of Henry Traphagen, who conveyed 21 acres to Hiram Gilbert and Cyrus S. Browning Oct. 19, 1835. Gilbert quit-claimed to Browning Oct. 19, 1835. John P. Lester owned it in 1840. J. P. Richardson owned the balance lying in the N. E. corner of the lot.

* Sold by Cornelius Haring, agent for Forfeited Estates, to Cornelius Huyler Aug. 25, 1784; *also*, a lot of salt meadow N. of Somerindyke in a square, 2 chs. 75 lks., bounded S. by Somerindyke, W. by Secaucus Commons, N. by meadow, now or late

Begins at a Stake standing by Hudson's River (being the Eastermost Corner of a Parcel of Land mark'd on the Map No 218 alloted to the Patent of Jan Vinge) and from said Stake runs North fifty two Degrees and thirty Minutes West twenty four Chains to a Stake in a large Heap of Stones near a Beach Tree mark'd (being the Northermost Corner of the said Lot of Common Land allotted to said Jan Vinge's Patent), Thence North thirty six Degrees and thirty Minutes East eighteen Chains and sixty three Links to a Stake in the Northeast End of a Swamp, Thence South fifty two Degrees and thirty Minutes East nineteen Chains and fifty Links to Mordaini's Meadow, Thence Southerly along betwixt the Meadow and Upland to Hudson's River, Thence Southerly along said Hudson's River as the same runs to the Place of Beginning, containing (after an Allowance for the Hill) about thirty seven acres.

*78

To the Patent granted by Philip Carteret to Ide Corneliese Van Vost dated the thirtieth Day of March One thousand six hundred and sixty eight for sundry Parcels of Land lying at Horsimus.

We do allot the two several Parcels of Land following,

Our Survey whereof shews and we adjudge them to be two Tracts

The First whereof (mark'd on the Map No 211) *

of Oliver De Lancy, E. by the river = 2 3-4 acres. *Vide Note to Van Ruyven's Patent,* p. 65; *also,* a lot of meadow bounded S. by Jacob Van Orden, W. by Secaucus Commons, N. by the property of the State, E. by the river = 4¼ acres; *also,* a piece of Mordanis Meadow, bounded E. by the river, W. by *Lot No.* 219, N. by a creek = 2 acres. Cornelius Huyler died seized, and his executors, Abraham and Peter Huyler, sold 4¼ acres, known as "Freemason's Island," to George De Mott Nov. 1, 1827, On the same day De Mott resold it to Abraham Huyler; who sold it to Jacob S. Platt Aug. 6, 1836. Of "Freemason's Island" Cornelius Huyler seems to have died seized, and it was then divided into lots and, I believe, distributed among his children. The 4¼ acre lot was part of it. In this last deed was included 22 72-100 acres including the dock at Bulls Ferry; also 5 45-100 acres of Mordanis Meadow next to Hardingbrooks. Platt conveyed to Abraham Mitchell, John De Groot, and Joseph J. Waldron, each an undivided third Aug. 6, 1836. Waldron conveyed his third to Charles Waldron; who conveyed to Mitchell Aug. 29, 1838.

* Van Vorst died seized Sept. 30, 1818. By his will he gave to his son John one-half of his property at Showhank and at Slonga, and to his grandson Cornelius the other half. These devisees partitioned by deed Oct. 26, 1821. John took 40 acres out of the E. part of the Slonga lot, and Cornelius received 27 18-100 acres. At the same time they also partitioned the property at Showhank, which included *Lots Nos.* 237, 238, and 239 (formerly of Kuyper). Cornelius received two lots; one of upland = 51 43-100 acres, the other of upland and meadow = 13 83-100 acres. John received two lots; one of upland = 51 43-100 acres, the other of upland and meadow (on which was the Showhank Mill) = 13 83-100 acres. This mill stood at the bottom of the ravine, a little N. of the Hoboken Road. It was destroyed by fire in 1835. Cornelius sold to John 33 83-100 acres at Showhank June 5, 1824.

Of the E. end of this lot John died seized Jan. 30, 1832. The Commissioners in partition sold to Dudley S. Gregory, Oct. 30, 1843, the Slonga lot. *Vide Note to Van Vorst's Patent,* p. 6. Cornelius had the W. part, and died seized Jan. 3, 1852, leaving children, *Elizabeth, Cornelius, Mary B.,* wife of Wm. P. Powers, *Sarah,* wife of Robert Sewell, *Anna G., Julia, Susan,* wife of Louis Dezarmauld. *William B., Antoinette,* wife of *Toler* Booraem, who yet own their father's part of the Slonga lot.

Begins at a Stake standing North thirty six Degrees and thirty Minutes East One hundred and fifty six Chains and twelve Links from a large Stone planted in a Corner of Wiehaken Commons mark'd A 1704 (which Stake is the Northermost Corner of a Lot of Common Land allotted to one of Claas Jansen * Van purmerant's Patents and mark'd on the Map No 210) and from said Stake runs South fifty two Degrees and thirty Minutes East sixty two Chains and forty Links to Hudson's River, Then returning to said Stake the Place of Beginning and from thence runs North thirty six Degrees and thirty Minutes East Eleven Chains and fourteen Links to a Stake standing fifteen Links Southwest from a Red Oak Tree mark'd L And from the last mentioned Stake runs South fifty two Degrees and thirty Minutes East sixty Chains to Hudson's River, Then Southerly along said River as the same runs 'til it meets the first Line that runs to said River, containing (after an Allowance for the Hill) about sixty six Acres.

The Second mark'd on the Map No 237 *

Begins at a Stake standing South thirty three Degrees West fifty eight Chains and sixty six Links from a large Stone mark'd W B planted at the Westermost Corner of Wiehaken Commons (and which Stake is the Westermost Corner of a Lot of Common Land mark'd on the Map No 236 allotted to Peter Jacobse's Patent) and from said Stake runs South thirty three Degrees West seventeen Chains and eighty three Links to a Stone planted, Thence South fifty seven Degrees East twenty eight Chains and ten Links to a Stake on the Top of the Hill in the Line of the Common Land allotted to the Patent of Hobocken, Then North thirty three Degrees East five Chains and fourteen Links, Then North fifty seven Degrees West two Chains, Then North thirty three degrees East ten Chains, Then North fifty seven Degrees West one Chain, Then north thirty three Degrees East two Chains and sixty nine Links to the Southerly Corner of the aforesaid Lot mark'd on the Map No 236, Then North fifty seven Degrees West twenty five Chains and ten Links to the Place of Beginning, containing about forty seven Acres.

> To the Patent granted by Petrus Stuyvesant to Claas Jansen Van Purmerant dated the thirty first Day of January One thousand six hundred and sixty two and confirm'd by Patent from Philip Carteret to said Van Purmerant dated the thirtieth Day of March One thousand six hundred and sixty eight, for sundry Parcels of Land lying at and near Horsimus.

We do **allott** a certain Parcel of Land (mark'd on the Map No. 240) †

---

* *Lot No.* 238 was also Van Vorst's. Cornelius took the N. half, and John the S. half of these two lots. Washington Village is, in part, on these tracts. *Vide Note to Lot No.* 211, p. 77.

† *Vide Note to Purmerent's Patent*, p. 7. Kuyper sold this Lot and Van Purmerent's Patent, Lot No. 132, to John Dey Jan. 1, 1780. I find also a deed of Helmig Van Houten to John Dey, dated May 20, 1784, for a part of Kuyper's Lot = 25 19-100 acres, bounded N. by Van Vorst and S. by grantee. This would seem to be the N. part of *Lot No.* 239. When and to whom Kuyper sold it I do not know, but Dey appears now to be the owner of *Lots Nos.* 132, 239, *and* 240. He sold in par-

Our Survey whereof shews and we adjudge it to be a Tract
* **Beginning** at a Stake by the Meadow Edge (which Stake is an *79
Easterly Corner of said Claas Jansen Van Purmerant's Patent mark'd on
the Map No 132) and from said Stake runs along the Line of Van Pur-
merant's Patent North fifty Degrees West twenty four Chains and fifty
three Links to the Northermost Corner thereof, Then continuing North
fifty Degrees West ten Chains to a Stone planted and mark'd HK,
Thence North thirty three Degrees East twenty one Chains and sixty six
Links to a Stake, Thence South fifty seven Degrees East twenty nine
Chains and fifty Links to the Commons alloted to the Patent of Hobock-
en mark'd on the Map No 233, Then along the same South fifteen
Degrees West two Chains, Then South fifty five Degrees West three
Chains, Then South thirty five Degrees West six Chains to a large Heap
of Stones near the Top of the Bank or Hill, Then running on a Course
South sixty three Degrees and forty Minutes East to the Meadow Edge,
Then Southwesterly along the Meadow Edge to the Place of Beginning,
containing about seventy two Acres.

> To the Patent of Philip Carteret to Abraham Isaacsen Plank
> dated the twelfth Day of May One thousand six hundred and
> sixty eight for a Neck of Land call'd Paulus Hook.

cels to different persons. Dey sold to Jacob P. Newkirk Nov. 24, 1783, 18 acres, and on Nov. 16, 1784, 5¼ acres adjoining. By Newkirk's will, dated Nov. 16, 1817, proved Aug. 26, 1818, he gave the above purchase to his son *John J.*, who sold 21 59-100 acres to Hiram Gilbert and Cyrus S. Browning. On a part of this the Beacon Race Course was afterwards erected. Gilbert sold his interest to Browning Oct. 19, 1835. Browning conveyed one-half of his interest to Alexander L. Botts April 5, 1838, and one-quarter of his interest to John Tonele, jr., Sept. 5, 1838, and the remaining quarter to Tonele Sept. 7, 1838. Botts conveyed one-quarter of his interest to Ebenezer Montague Nov. 28, 1838, and the remaining quarter to Montague Dec. 9, 1839. New-kirk held a mortgage on the property, which he foreclosed and the property was sold at sheriff's sale to Montague Aug. 31, 1840. Montague sold to Catherine Pasman April 22, 1842. By her will, dated Nov. 28, 1850, proved April 10, 1852, she gave it to her children, *John L.* and *Ellen*, wife of Ebenezer Montague. Previous to the sale under fore-closure, and on July 29, 1840, Tonele sold to John P. Lester, who sold to Edwin R. V. Wright all his interest Sept. 9, 1843. Wright released to Montague April 1, 1854, and Montague to Morrell, Vanderbeek, Mills, and Davy. Where the Pencil factory now is, Pasman conveyed to Abraham Collerd Dec. 5, 1850; Collerd to Marian B. and Isabell F. Laidlaw Oct. 24, 1865.

Dey sold to Jacob Newkirk three acres, one rod W. of the road leading to Show-hank Brook.

He sold to John H. Van Houten Sept. 2, 1785, part of *Lot No.* 240, but how much do not know.

He sold to Mathew P. Newkirk June 10, 1791, 20 acres.

Jacob Newkirk sold Jan. 22, 1816, to John Van Vorst, 44 acres and 2 roods at Showhank.

Dey conveyed to Cornelius Van Vorst, Feb. 1, 1790, 20 acres, extending from Kuy-per's bridge over Harsimus creek to a point one rod W. of Palisade ave. and bounded N. by Showhank brook. On May 1, 1792, Dey conveyed to Van Vorst three lots; one lying N. of Showhank brook, extending from Hoboken creek; the other two be-tween Showhank brook and John Stevens' line.

𝖂𝖊 do 𝖆𝖑𝖑𝖔𝖙𝖙 a certain Parcel of Land (mark'd on the Map No 238)*

𝕺𝖚𝖗 𝕾𝖚𝖗𝖛𝖊𝖞 whereof shews and we adjudge it to be a Tract

𝕭𝖊𝖌𝖎𝖓𝖓𝖎𝖓𝖌 at a Stone planted (standing South thirty three Degrees West seventy four Chains and ninety four Links from a large Stone mark'd W. B. planted in the West Corner of Wiehaken Commons) and from said Place of Beginning runs South thirty three Degrees West sixteen Chains and forty four Links to a Stone mark'd O (being the Northermost Corner of a Lot of Common Land allotted to the Patent of Hendrick Van Ostrum mark'd on the Map No 239) Thence South fifty seven Degrees East twenty seven Chains and ten Links to the Common Land allotted to the Patent of Hobocken mark'd on the Map No 233, Thence North thirty three Degrees East ten Chains and twenty eight Links, Then South fifty seven Degrees East One Chain, Then North thirty three Degrees East six Chains and sixteen Links to a Stake, Then North fifty seven Degrees West twenty eight Chains and ten Links to the Place of Beginning, containing about forty four Acres.

*80

* To the Patent of Petrus Stuyvesant to Jacob Stoffelsen dated the seventh Day of May One thousand six hundred and sixty four for a Piece of Land at Horsimus.

𝖂𝖊 do 𝖆𝖑𝖑𝖔𝖙𝖙 a certain Parcel of Land (mark'd on the Map No 247)†

𝕺𝖚𝖗 𝕾𝖚𝖗𝖛𝖊𝖞 whereof shews and we adjudge it to be a Tract

𝕭𝖊𝖌𝖎𝖓𝖓𝖎𝖓𝖌 at a Stake (standing North thirty three Degrees East Eighty nine Links from a large Stone mark'd W B planted at the Westermost Corner of Wiehaken Commons) and from said Stake runs South thirty three Degrees West two Chains and fifty nine Links to a Stake, Thence North fifty seven Degrees West thirty Chains, Then North thirty three Degrees East two Chains and fifty nine Links to a Stake, Thence South fifty seven Degrees East thirty Chains to the Place of Beginning, Containing about seven Acres.

To the Patent of Philip Carteret to Petrus Stuyvesant dated the thirty first day of July One thousand six hundred and sixty nine for a Piece of Meadow at Horsimus.

𝖂𝖊 do 𝖆𝖑𝖑𝖔𝖙𝖙 a certain Parcel of Land (mark'd on the Map No 217)

𝕺𝖚𝖗 𝕾𝖚𝖗𝖛𝖊𝖞 whereof shews and we adjudge it to be a Tract

𝕭𝖊𝖌𝖎𝖓𝖓𝖎𝖓𝖌 at a Stake standing by Hudson's River (being the Northeastermost Corner of a Lot of Common Land allotted to Englebert Steinheysen's Patent mark'd on the Map No 216) and from said Stake runs North fifty two Degrees and thirty Minutes West twenty four Chains and forty Links to a Stake, Thence North thirty six Degrees and

---

○ *Vide Note to Lot No.* 237, p. 78.

† This Lot and *Lot No.* 246 belonged to the De Motts. *Vide Note to Stoffelsen's Patent*, p. 9. Michael died seized May 27, 1832. He left these two lots to his sons *George* and *Garret;* George took the S. half, and Garret the N. half. It was entailed to their heirs male. George died in 186-, leaving sons, *George, James, Huyler, Henry, Thomas, Edward,* and *Henson,* who have since partitioned.

thirty Minutes East four Chains and forty seven Links to a Stake in a large Heap of Stones, Thence South fifty two Degrees and thirty Minutes East twenty four Chains and forty Links to said Hudson's River, Then along said River Southwesterly as the same runs to the Place of Beginning, containing (after an Allowance for the Hill) about nine Acres.

> * To the Patent of Philip Carteret to Claas Comptah alias Claas Petersen Cors dated the third Day of June, One thousand six hundred and seventy one for a Parcel of Upland and Meadow lying at Communipan.

*81

We do **allot** the two several Parcels of Land following

Our Survey whereof shews, and we adjudge them to be two Tracts

The First whereof (mark'd on the Map No 208)

Begins at a Stake (standing North thirty six Degrees and thirty Minutes East one hundred and twenty eight Chains and forty four Links from a large Stone mark'd **A, 1764,** planted at one of the Corners of Wiehaken Commons) and from said Stake runs South fifty two Degrees and thirty Minutes East forty seven Chains and seventy five Links to the Edge of Slaugh's Meadow, Then returning to said Stake, the Place of Beginning, and from thence runs North thirty six Degrees and thirty Minutes East sixteen Chains and fourteen Links to a Stake. Thence South fifty two Degrees and thirty Minutes East fifty seven Chains to said Slaugh's Meadow, Then down along the same betwixt the Upland and Meadow 'til it meets with the first Line that runs to said Meadow, containing (after an Allowance for the Hill) about eighty two Acres.

The Second (mark'd on the Map No 263)

Begins at a Stake (being the Southermost Corner of a Parcel of Common Land allotted to Fredrick Phillipse's Patent mark'd on the Map No 262) And from said Stake runs South thirty six Degrees West twenty three Chains and sixty two Links to a Stake, Thence South fifty Degrees West one Chain and eighty eight Links to a Stake, Thence North forty three Degrees and forty five Minutes West sixty eight Chains and twenty Links to a Stake by the side of Hackinsack River, Thence up along said River North sixty five Degrees and ten Minutes East five Chains and forty eight Links, Then North thirty one Degrees East ten Chains and thirty four Links to a Stake by said River, (being a Corner of a Lot of Meadow in Paulus Peterse's Patent mark'd on the Map No 120) Thence South fifty four Degrees and ten Minutes East eleven Chains and twenty Links to a Stake between the Meadow and Upland, Thence along the Edge of the Meadow North twenty two Degrees East eight Chains and seventy five Links to a Stake (being the Westerly Corner of the said Parcel of Common Land allotted to Fredrick Phillipse's * Patent) Thence along the line thereof South forty three Degrees and forty five Minutes East fifty six Chains and fifty Links to the Place of Beginning, containing about one hundred and fifty five Acres.

*82

> To the Patent of Philip Carteret to Nicholas Jansen Baker dated the twelfth Day of May one thousand six hundred and sixty eight for two Tracts of Land lying at Comunipan

We do **allot** the two several Parcels of Land following

Our Survey whereof shews and we adjudge them to be two Tracts

The First whereof mark'd on the Map No 206 *

*81 **Begins** at a Stake (being the Northerly Corner of a Lot of Common Land alloted to Fytje Hartman's Patent mark'd on the Map No 205 which Stake stands North thirty six Degrees and thirty Minutes East, One hundred and thirteen Chains and forty five Links from a large Stone mark'd **A 1764**, standing in one of the Corners of Wiehaken Commons) And from said Stake runs South fifty two Degrees and thirty Minutes East forty eight Chains to the Edge of Slaugh's Meadow, Then returning to said Stake the Place of Beginning; and from thence runs North thirty six Degrees and thirty Minutes East nine Chains and forty Links to a Stake, Thence South fifty two Degrees and thirty Minutes East forty seven Chains and fifty Links to said Slaugh's Meadow, Then down along the same betwixt the Upland and Meadow 'til it meets the aforesaid Line that runs to said Meadow, containing (after an Allowance for the Hill) about forty Acres.

The Second (mark'd on the Map No 259) †

Begins at a Stake (standing in the Line of Dirck Sycan's Patent mark'd on the Map No 18 which Stake is the easterly Corner of a Lot

---

° *Vide Note to De Backer's Patent*, p. 10. Adjudged to Cornelius Brinkerhoff, p. 131. Hendrick by will, dated Feb. 12, 1834, gave to his grandchildren, Henry, Cornelius, and John, the Lot in question, with *Subdivision No.* 305. John took the upper, Cornelius the middle, Henry the lower part of the two Lots.

† *Vide Note to De Backer's Patent*, p. 10, and *Lot No.* 206, p. 82. In the N. W. corner of this Lot Hendrick conveyed one acre to Daniel Van Clief Dec. 26, 1815. It was known as the Long Bridge Lot, and was left by Hendrick to his grandsons; Cornelius taking the N. part. He died seized June 13, 1850, and it was partitioned between his two children, *Cornelius* and *Eleanor C.*, as per annexed sketch, by Commissioners, whose report was confirmed by the Orphan's Court in Oct. Term, 1857. Eleanor C. conveyed her portions to Jeremiah W. Dwight, by her guardian, April 1, 1864 (she was then an infant). Her husband, Wm. H. Speer, and her guardian executed another deed to Dwight on same day. Cornelius conveyed his portions of this tract to Esther A., wife of Edmund C. Bramhall, July 6, 1860. The lot not having been properly partitioned between John, Cornelius, and Henry Brinkerhoff, their heirs released the above purchase to Mrs. Bramhall Nov. 24, 1865. The S. part of the Lot fell to Henry and John Brinkerhoff, who conveyed to David Gould and Abraham Morrell. These grantees mapped (map filed), and sold in lots. The Lot adjoins Woodlawn ave., in Greenville.

COMMON LANDS. 161

of Common Land alloted to said Dirck Sycan's Patent mark'd on the Map No 258) and from said Stake runs along said Sycan's Patent North forty two Degrees East twenty Chains and forty six Links to a Stake, Thence North forty three Degrees and forty five Minutes West thirty Chains and seventy five Links to a Stake, Thence South thirty six Degrees West seven Chains and sixty four Links to a Stake, Thence South fifty Degrees West twelve Chains and eighty seven Links to the Northermost Corner of the aforesaid Common Land alloted to Dirck Sycan's Patent, Then along * the Line of the same South forty three Degrees and forty five Minutes East thirty one Chains and seventy five Links to the Place of Beginning; containing about sixty two Acres. *83

To the first Patent of Philip Carteret to Fytje Hartman dated the twelfth Day of May one thousand six hundred and sixty eight for a Tract of Land lying at Communipan.

We do **allot** a certain Parcel of Land (mark'd on the Map No 205)

Our Survey whereof shews, and we adjudge it to be a Tract **Beginning** at a Stake (being the Northermost Corner of a Parcel of Common Land allotted to Dirck Claasen's Patent mark'd on the Map No 204, which said Stake stands North thirty six Degrees and thirty Minutes East eighty nine Chains from a large Stone mark'd **A 1764** planted in one of the Corners of Wiehaken Commons) and from said Stake runs South fifty two Degrees and thirty Minutes East forty seven Chains to a Stake in the Edge of Slaugh's Meadow where the same joins the Upland, Then returning to the first mentioned Stake the Place of Beginning and from thence runs North thirty six Degrees and thirty Minutes East twenty four Chains and forty five Links to a Stake, Thence South fifty two Degrees and thirty Minutes East forty eight Chains to the said Slaughs Meadow, Then along the same Southwesterly betwixt the Upland and Meadow to the aforesaid Stake in the Edge of the Meadow, Containing (after an Allowance for the Hill) about one hundred and four Acres.

To the Second Patent of Philip Carteret to Fytje Hartman dated the twelfth Day of May One thousand six hundred and sixty eight, for a Tract of Land lying behind Communipan

We do **allot** a certain Parcel of Land (mark'd on the Map No 260)

Our Survey whereof shews and we adjudge it to be a Tract **Beginning** at a Stake (standing in the Line of Dirck Sycan's Patent mark'd on the Map No 18 and which Stake is the Easterly Corner of a Parcell of Common Land allotted to the Patent of Nicholas Jansen Baker mark'd on the Map No 259) * And from said Stake runs *84 North forty two Degrees East fifteen Chains and twenty two Links to a large Cedar Stake (being the Northerly Corner of said Dirck Sycan's Patent mark'd on the Map No 18 and the westerly Corner of Dirck Claasen's Patent mark'd on the Map No 17;) and from said Cedar Stake runs North twenty eight Degrees East six Chains and ninety Links to a Stake, Thence North forty three Degrees and forty five Minutes West thirty one Chains and twenty eight Links to a Stake, Then South thirty six Degrees West twenty two Chains and eight Links to a Stake, Then South forty three Degrees and forty five Minutes East thirty Chains and seventy five Links to the Place of Beginning, containing about sixty nine Acres.

>To the first Patent of Philip Carteret to Dirck Claasen dated the twelfth Day of May One thousand six hundred & sixty eight for a Tract of Upland and Meadow call'd Kewan.

We do **allot** the two several Parcels of Land following

Our Survey whereof shews and we adjudge them to be two Tracts,

The First whereof (mark'd on the Map No 213)

Begins at a Stake (being the Northerly Corner of a Parcel of Common Land alloted to Dirck Sycan's Patent mark'd on the Map No 212 which said Stake stands North thirty six Degrees and thirty Minutes East One hundred & seventy eight Chains and sixty five Links from a large Stone mark'd **A 1764** planted in a Corner of Wiehaken Commons) and from said Stake runs South fifty two Degrees and thirty Minutes East fifty nine Chains to Hudson's River, Then returning to said Stake the Place of Beginning and from thence runs North thirty six Degrees and thirty Minutes East eight Chains and ninety three Links to a Stake, Thence South fifty two Degrees and thirty Minutes East fifty five Chains to said Hudson's River, Then down the same as it runs 'til it meets the first Line running thereto containing (after an Allowance for the Hill) about forty eight Acres.

The Second (mark'd on the Map No 261)

Begins at a Stake (being the Easterly Corner of a Lot of Common Land alloted to Fytje Hartman's Patent mark'd on the Map No 260 standing also in the Line of Dirck Claasen's Patent at Stony Point *85 mark'd on the * Map No 17) and from said Stake runs North twenty eight Degrees East thirty two Chains and thirty Links to a Stake being the Northerly Corner of said Dirck Claasen's Patent, Thence North fifty one Degrees and forty five Minutes West twenty five Chains and forty five Links to a Stake (being the Eastermost Corner of a Lot of Common Land allotted to Fredrick Philipse's Patent mark'd on the Map No 262) and from the last mentioned Stake runs South thirty six Degrees West twenty seven Chains and twenty eight Links to a Stake, Thence South forty three Degrees and forty five Minutes East thirty one Chains and twenty eight Links to the Place of Beginning, containing about Eighty two Acres.

>To the second Patent of Philip Carteret to Dirck Claasen dated the twelfth Day of May One thousand six hundred and sixty eight for a Tract of Land call'd Stony Point.

We do **allot** a certain Parcel of Land (mark'd on the Map No 204) *

º Adjudged to Michael Cornelisse Vreeland, p. 140. *Vide Note to Claesen's 2d Patent*, p. 12. Michael by will, dated Oct. 30, 1824, gave this, and his "bush lot" near Bergen Point (*Subdivision No.* 422) to his three sons, *John, Mindert,* and *Michael.* The S. part of *Lot No.* 205, *Subdivision No.* 301, also passed by this will to his three sons, 84 acres.

MICHAEL CORNELIESE VREELANDT.

Our Survey whereof shews and we adjudge it to be a Tract **Beginning** at a Stake (being the Northerly Corner of a Lot of Common Land allotted to Hobocken Patent mark'd on the Map No 203, which Stake stands North thirty six Degrees and thirty Minutes East seventy six Chains and fifty Links from a large Stone mark'd A 1764 standing in a Corner of Wiehaken Commons) And from said Stake runs South fifty two Degrees and thirty Minutes East fifty seven Chains and fifty Links to a Stake by Hudson's River near the Southerly Point of Slaugh's Meadow, Then returning to said Stake the Place of Beginning and from thence runs North thirty six Degrees and thirty Minutes East twelve Chains and fifty Links to a Stake, Then South fifty two Degrees and thirty Minutes East forty seven Chains to said Slaugh's Meadow,

*86

Mindert sold 11 41-100 acres to John W. Leavitt July 3, 1840. The three sons conveyed to Robert Pierce, Nov. 27, 1859, 26 acres, bounded N. W. by parties of the first part, N. E. by Stephen Vreeland, S. E. by Slaugh's Meadow and the river, S. W. by Mrs. Deas. Mindert and Michael sold to said Pierce 15 30-100 acres, bounded N. W. by their own wood lot, S. W. by John M. Vreeland, S. E. by grantee, N. E. by Stephen Vreeland.

John M. Vreeland sold to Michael Saunier and Joseph Danielson 7 64-100 acres Aug. 21, 1835, who sold the same to Robert Pierce Dec. 8, 1835. Pierce sold to James Brown, June 22, 1836, the three tracts last above described. Brown sold to John W. Leavitt, Jan. 30, 1841, 14 52-100 acres of his above purchase, bounded N. E. by Stephen Vreeland, N. W. by Mindert Vreeland, S. W. and S. E. by grantor. Leavitt gave to Brown a consideration mortgage which was foreclosed, and the 14 52-100 acres sold by Lorenzo Jaquins, sheriff, to John W. Leavitt, jr., July 1, 1848. Before this, however, John W. had sold the whole tract bought of Brown to Samuel Leavitt May 1, 1845. Samuel died seized and intestate, leaving a widow, Sophronia; children, *Theodosia* Hazen, *Elizabeth*, *Esther*, and *Julia*, and grandchildren, *Isabel Brinsmade*, and *Silence L. Brinsmade*, children of Thomas F. Brinsmade and *Silence Leavitt*. Theodosia Hazen was then dead without issue. The other heirs were minors. In May Term, 1849, the Orphan's Court appointed commissioners, who sold to John W. Leavitt, jr., Dec. 15, 1849, two lots, one = 14 41-100 acres, the other = 1 54-100 acres. John W. sold to Rodman M. Price May 28, 1850, = 26 91-100 acres, who sold to Francis Price May 10, 1851, = 52 acres. *Vide Note to Lot No.* 306, p. 129.

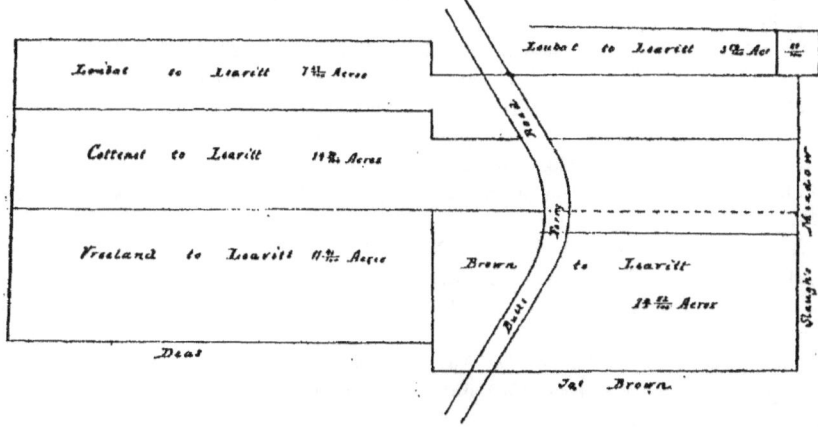

Then down along the same betwixt the Meadow and Upland to said Hudson's River, Then down along said River 'til it meets the first mentioned Line, Containing (after an Allowance for the Hill) about sixty four Acres.

To the first Patent of Philip Carteret to Dirck Sycan dated the twelfth Day of May, One thousand six hundred and sixty eight for a Tract of Upland and Meadow lying at Mingackqua

*86 * **We** do **allot** the three several Parcels of Land following **Our Survey** whereof shews and we adjudge them to be three Tracts,

The First whereof (mark'd on the Map No 212)*

Begins at a Stake (being the Northerly Corner of a Lot of Common Land allotted to Ide Cornelison Van Vost's Patent mark'd on the Map No 211,) Which Stake stands North thirty six Degrees and thirty Minutes East one hundred and sixty seven Chains and twenty six Links from a large Stone mark'd **A 1764** standing in a Corner of Wiehaken Commons) and from said Stake (the Place of Beginning) runs South fifty two Degrees and thirty Minutes East sixty Chains to Hudson's River, Then returning to said Stake the Place of Beginning; and from thence runs North thirty six Degrees and thirty Minutes East eleven Chains and thirty nine Links to a Stake, Thence South fifty two Degrees and thirty Minutes East fifty nine Chains to said Hudson's River, Then down the same as it runs 'til it meets the first mentioned Line containing (after an Allowance for the Hill) about sixty six Acres.

The Second (mark'd on the Map No 258)

Begins at a Gum Sapling (being the Westermost Corner of said Dirck Sycan's Patent mark'd on the Map No 18) and thence runing along the Line of the same North forty two Degrees East twenty four Chains and seventy Links to the Southermost Corner of a Lot of Common Land (allotted to Nicholas Jansen Baker's Patent) mark'd on the

---

° This and *Lots Nos.* 258 *and* 265 were adjudged to George Vreeland, p. 141. By his will, dated May 4, 1793, proved Aug. 14, 1795, he gave to his sons, *John* and *Garret, Lots Nos.* 212, 258, 265, 394, 417, *and* 427. The devisees partitioned Feb. 25, 1796.

Garret received by this partition the N. half of *Lot No.* 212 = 33 acres, and the whole of *Lot No.* 394. *Lot No.* 265 at Droyer's Point had been divided into lots, of which Garret took *No.* 3 = 3 acres, 1 rood, 9 perches; also, part of *No.* 2 = 5 acres, 3 roods, 28 perches. Garret, by will, gave these lands to his sons George and Richard, who partitioned Oct. 20, 1823. George sold the S. half of the N. half to Michael Saunier and Joseph Danielson June 18, 1832, who sold to William Cooper June 15, 1833.

George released his interest in *Lot No.* 394 to Richard, who sold it to Michael Vreeland. *Lot No.* 3, at Droyer's Point, they sold to Andrew D. Mellick and Thomas J. Jones, deed to be given in Nov., 1871; *Lot No.* 2, at Droyer's Point, now held by them in common.

John received the S. half of *Lot No.* 212; 3 acres, 2 roods, and 14 rods of *Lot No.* 235; part of *Lot No.* 2 at Droyer's Point = 4 acres, 3 roods, 7 rods; and the whole of *Lots Nos.* 417 *and* 427.

Map No 259, Thence along the Line thereof North forty three Degrees and forty five Minutes West thirty one Chains and seventy five Links to a Stake, Then South fifty Degrees West fourteen Chains and sixty six Links to the Line of Lawrens Andrieses Patent mark'd on the Map No 19, Thence along the Line thereof South twenty seven Degrees and thirty Minutes East thirty five Chains and eighty Links to the Place of Beginning, Containing about sixty four Acres.

The Third (mark'd on the Map No 265)

Begins at a Stake standing in a Swampy Creek (being the Northerly Corner of Lawrence Andriese's Patent mark'd on the Map No 19) and from said Stake runs North twenty seven Degrees and thirty Minutes West twenty four Chains and ninety Links to the Edge of the Meadow, Then along said Meadow Edge South twenty six Degrees and fifty Minutes West five Chains and seventy two Links, to a Stake (being the Southerly Corner of a Lot of Meadow in Peter Jacobse's Patent * mark'd on the Map No 121) Then South six Degrees East five Chains and ten Links, Then South forty Degrees and thirty Minutes East two Chains and fifty nine Links to a large Red Oak Tree mark'd standing near the Meadow Edge, Then South forty Degrees West twelve Chains and forty eight Links to a Stone near the Mouth of a Creek call'd the swampy Creek, Then up along said swampy Creek as the same runs to the Place of Beginning, containing about eighteen Acres of Upland and Meadow.

*87

To the Patent of William Kieft to Claas Carstensen Norman dated the twenty fifth Day of March, One thousand six hundred and forty seven, and confirm'd (with an Addition of Land) by Patent from Philip Carteret to Lawrens Andriese, dated the twenty sixth Day of March One thousand six hundred and sixty seven for a Parcel of land lying at Mingackqua,

We do **allot** a certain Parcel of Land (mark'd on the Map No 266)

Our Survey whereof shews and we adjudge it to be a Tract

Beginning at a Stake, (being the Southerly Corner of a Lot of Common Land allotted to Lubert Gilbertse's Patent) mark'd on the Map No 267, which Stake stands South thirty nine Degrees West sixty three Chains and ninety seven Links from a Stone mark'd B planted in the Westermost Corner of a Lot of Common Land (allotted to Barnt Christian's Patent) mark'd on the Map No 277; And from said Stake (the Place of Beginning) runs North fifty one Degrees West forty Chains to New Ark Bay, Then returning to the first mentioned Stake; and from thence runs South thirty nine Degrees West seventeen Chains and eighty eight Links to a Stake in the Line of a Tract of Land set apart for sale mark'd on the Map No 172, Thence along the Line thereof North eighty five Degrees West thirteen Chains and thirty seven Links to a Stake (being a Corner of said Land set apart for Sale), Then along the Line thereof North fifty one Degrees West thirty Chains to said New Ark Bay, Then along said Bay Northeasterly as the same runs 'til it meets the first mentioned Line containing about one hundred Acres.

To the Patent of Petrus Stuyvesant to Lubert Gilbertse dated the fifth Day of December, One thousand six hundred & fifty four for a Piece of Land lying at Mingackqua

*88   **We** do **allot** the two several Parcels of Land following

Our Survey whereof shews and we adjudge them to be two Tracts

The First whereof (mark'd on the Map No 278) *

Begins at New Ark Bay the Westermost Corner of said Lubert Gilbertse's Patent mark'd on the Map No 20; and from thence runs North sixty two Degrees and thirty Minutes East eighteen Chains and fifty six Links to the Northermost Corner of said Gilbertse's Patent (being in the Line of Lawrence Andrieses Patent mark'd on the Map No 19) Thence North twenty seven Degrees and thirty Minutes West thirteen Chains and eighty six Links to said New Ark Bay, Then down the same as it runs to the Place of Beginning containing about twelve Acres.

The Second (mark'd on the Map No 267) †

Begins at a Stake being the Southerly Corner of a Lot of Common Land (allotted to Severin Lawrense's Patent) mark'd on the Map No 268; which Stake stands south thirty nine Degrees West forty five Chains and seventy five Links from a Stone mark'd B standing in the Westermost Corner of a Lot of Common Land (allotted to Barnt Christian's Patent) mark'd on the Map No 277, and from said Stake runs North fifty one Degrees West forty Chains and twenty Links to New Ark Bay, Then returning to said Stake the Place of Beginning; and from thence runs South thirty nine Degrees West eighteen Chains and twenty two Links to a Stake being the easterly Corner of a Lot of Common Land (allotted to Lawrence Andriese's Patent) mark'd on the Map No 266 Then along the Line thereof North fifty one Degrees West forty Chains to said New Ark Bay, Then up along the same as it runs 'til it meets the first mentioned Line containing about seventy three Acres.

---

* This Lot was adjudged to Jacob Van Wagenen, p. 144. *Vide Note to Lubert Gilbertse's Patent*, p. 14.

† Adjudged 'to Jacob Van Wagenen, p. 144. He conveyed to his grandson, Cornelius Van Buskirk, a strip, 1 chain and 25 links wide = 5 acres, out of the S. E. side of the lot, Dec. 10, 1794. Van Buskirk sold the same to John G. Vreeland and Lenah ux. Jan. 1, 1798. Of the balance of the Lot Van Wagenen died seized. *Vide Note to Spier's Patent*, p. 15. His surviving executor conveyed a strip next N. of Van Buskirk's, 6 chains and 35 links wide, to James R. Mullany May 15, 1824; who died siezed, and his heirs conveyed to David La Tourette March 30, 1848. The surviving executor conveyed to David La Tourette, Feb. 5, 1824, a strip 3 chains and 5 links wide next N. of the Van Buskirk strip.

About 1824 all of Van Wagenen's lands were sold in parcels. Of *Lots Nos. 267 and 268* were sold to John Van Buskirk 8 34-100 acres May 1, 1824; 8 34-100 acres to James Van Buskirk May 1, 1824; 8 34-100 acres to William C. Vreeland May 1, 1824; 5 acres to Michael B. Terhune May 1, 1824; 13 acres to Michael Zabriskie Feb. 5, 1824; and 17 92-100 acres to Michael Zabriskie. These tracts have since been sold, and are now owned by Solon Humphreys, Jacob R. Schuyler, Henry Meigs, General Morris, Charles Morris, Nehemiah B. Lane, and Alpha Phillips. *Vide Note to Lot No. 417*, p. 144.

To the Patent of Philip Carteret to Severin Lawrens dated the twelfth Day of May One thousand six hundred and sixty eight for a Piece of Land at Mingackqua formerly granted by a Dutch Patent to Jan Corneliesen Buis

🕮𝖊 do 𝖆𝖑𝖑𝖔𝖙 the two several Parcels of Land following

𝕺𝖚𝖗 𝕾𝖚𝖗𝖛𝖊𝖞 whereof shews and we adjudge them to be two Tracts

* 𝕿𝖍𝖊 𝕱𝖎𝖗𝖘𝖙 whereof (mark'd on the Map No 279) * *89

𝕭𝖊𝖌𝖎𝖓𝖘 at New Ark Bay, at the westernmost Corner of Lubert Gilbertse's Patent mark'd on the Map No 20, and thence runs along the Line thereof South twenty seven Degrees and thirty Minutes East twenty chains and seventeen Links to the Northermost Corner of said Severin Lawrens's Patent mark'd on the Map No 31, Then along the Line thereof South sixty two Degrees and thirty Minutes West twelve Chains and twenty five Links to a Stake being the westermost Corner of said Severin Lawrense's Patent, Thence North twenty seven Degrees and thirty Minutes West to said New Ark Bay, Then up along said Bay as it runs to the Place of Beginning, Containing about twenty three Acres.

𝕿𝖍𝖊 𝕾𝖊𝖈𝖔𝖓𝖉 (mark'd on the Map No 268) †

𝕭𝖊𝖌𝖎𝖓𝖘 at the Southermost Corner of a Lot of Common Land (allotted to Hendrick Jansen Spier's Patent) mark'd on the Map No 269 which Stake stands South thirty nine Degrees West thirty seven Chains and Seventy three Links from a Stone mark'd B standing in the Westermost Corner of a Lot of Common Land (allotted to Barnt Christian's Patent) mark'd on the Map No 277 and from said Stake runs North fifty one Degrees West forty Chains to New Ark Bay, Then returning to said Stake the Place of Beginning; and from thence runs South thirty nine Degrees West eight Chains and two Links to a Stake being the Eastermost Corner of a Lot of Common Land (allotted to Lubert Gilbertse's Patent) mark'd on the Map No 267, Thence North fifty one Degrees West forty Chains and twenty Links to said New Ark Bay, Then up said Bay as the same runs 'til it meets the first mentioned Line containing about thirty two Acres.

To the Patent of Philip Carteret to Hendrick Jansen Spier dated the twelfth Day of May One thousand six hundred and sixty-eight for a Piece of Land lying at Mingackqua.

🕮𝖊 do 𝖆𝖑𝖑𝖔𝖙 the two several Parcels of Land following,

𝕺𝖚𝖗 𝕾𝖚𝖗𝖛𝖊𝖞 whereof shews, and we adjudge them to be two Tracts

𝕿𝖍𝖊 𝕱𝖎𝖗𝖘𝖙 whereof (mark'd on the Map No 280)‡

𝕭𝖊𝖌𝖎𝖓𝖘 at the Northermost Corner of said Hendrick Jansen Spier's Patent mark'd on the Map No 22, and from thence runs North twenty seven Degrees * and thirty Minutes West to New Ark Bay, then returning to the Place of Beginning and from thence runs South sixty two Degrees and thirty Minutes West sixteen Chains and forty-two Links to the Westerly Corner of said Hendrick Jansen Spier's Patent, Thence North *90

º Adjudged to Jacob Van Wagenen, p. 145.   *Vide Note to Spier's Patent,* p. 15.
† Adjudged to Jacob Van Wagenen, p. 145.   *Vide Note to Lot No.* 276, p. 88.
‡ Adjudged to Widow Spier et al. p., 145, *Vide Note to Spier's Patent,* p. 15.

twenty seven Degrees and thirty Minutes West to said New Ark Bay, Then up said Bay as the same runs 'til it meets the first mentioned Line containing about fifty Acres, binding Southerly upon the Patent to Dirck Sycan mark'd on the Map No 23.

The Second (mark'd on the Map No 269)*

Begins at a Corner of a Tract of Common Land allotted to Jansen's & Edsal's Patent at Constable's Hook) mark'd on the Map No 270; Which Corner is South thirty nine Degrees West thirty two Chains and nine Links from a Stone mark'd B standing in the westermost Corner of a Lot of Common Land (Allotted to Barn't Christian's Patent) mark'd on the Map No 277 and from said firs mention'd Corner runs North fifty one Degrees West forty one Chains to New Ark Bay, Then returning to said first mentioned Corner the Place of Beginning and from thence runs South thirty nine Degrees West five Chains and sixty four Links to a Stake (being the Easterly Corner of Lot No 268), Thence North fifty one Degrees West forty Chains to said New Ark Bay, Then up said Bay as the same runs 'til it meets the first mentioned Line, containing about twenty two Acres.

> To the Second Patent of Philip Carteret to Dirck Sycan dated the twelfth Day of May One thousand six hundred and sixty eight for two Parcels of Land lying at Pembrepogh.

We do **allot** a certain Parcel of Land mark'd on the Map No 271)

Our Survey whereof shews and we adjudge to be a Tract

Beginning at a Stake standing North thirty nine Degrees East fifty Links from a Stone mark'd B standing in the Westermost Corner of a Lot of Common Land (allotted to Barnt Christian's Patent) mark'd on the Map No 277 and from said Stake runs North fifty one Degrees West forty Chains to New Ark Bay, Then returning to said Stake the Place of Beginning and from thence runs North thirty nine Degrees East twenty Chains and sixty Links to a Stake, Thence North fifty one Degrees West forty one Chains & forty nine Links to said New Ark Bay, Then down said Bay as the same runs 'til it meets the first mentioned Line Containing about eighty four Acres.

*91

> * To the Patent of Philip Carteret to Thomas Davison dated the twenty second Day of December, One thousand six hundred and sixty nine for a Parcel of Land lying at Pembrepogh.

We do **allot** a certain Parcel of Land (mark'd on the Map No 272)

Our Survey whereof shews and we adjudge it to be a Tract

Beginning at a Stake, being the Easterly Corner of a Lot of Common Land (allotted to Dirck Sycan's Patent) mark'd on the Map No

---

* Adjudged to the Widow Spier, et al., p. 145, *Vide Note to Lot No.* 423, p. 147, and *Lot No.* 423, p. 147. It was probably sold to Vreeland by the heirs of Spier, *Vide Note to Spier's Patent*, p. 15.

271; Which Stake stands North thirty nine Degrees East twenty one Chains and twelve Links from a Stone mark'd B standing in the westermost Corner of a Lot of Common Land (allotted to Barnt Christian's Patent) mark'd on the Map No 277 And from said Stake runs North fifty one Degrees West forty one Chains and forty nine Links to New Ark Bay then returning to said Stake the Place of Beginning and from thence runs North thirty nine Degrees East ten Chains and three Links to a Stake, Thence North fifty one Degrees West forty two Chains and twenty Links to said New Ark Bay, Then down said Bay as the same runs 'til it meets the first mentioned Line, Containing about forty two Acres.

To the Patent of Philip Carteret to Thomas Davison, dated the twelfth Day of December One thousand six hundred & sixty nine for a Parcel of Land lying at Pembrepogh.

We do **allot** a certain Parcel of Land mark'd on the Map No 275)*

Our Survey whereof shews and we adjudge it to be a Tract, **Beginning** at a Stake, being the Eastermost Corner of a Lot of Comon Land (allotted to Peter Jansen Slaat's Patent) mark'd on the Map No 274; which Stake stands North thirty nine Degrees East fifty three Chains & forty five Links from a Stone mark'd B standing in the westermost Corner of a Lot of Comon Land (allotted to Barnt Christian's Patent) mark'd on the Map No 277; and from said Stake runs North fifty-one Degrees West forty two Chains & twenty Links to New Ark Bay, Then returning to the said Stake the Place of Beginning; And from thence runs North thirty nine Degrees East seven Chains & seventy Links to a Stake, Then North forty two Degrees West thirty nine Chains to New Ark Bay, Then down along said Bay 'til it meets the first mentioned Line, Containing about forty three Acres.

* To the Patent of Petrus Stuyvesant to Peter Jansen Slaat *92 dated the fifth Day of December One thousand six hundred & fifty four confirm'd by Patent from Philip Carteret to said Slaat dated the twelfth Day of May One thousand six hundred and sixty eight for a Parcel of Land lying at Pembrepogh

We do **allot** a certain Parcel of Land mark'd on the Map No 274 †

---

* This and *Lot No.* 274 were adjudged to George Cadmus, p. 149, *Vide Note to Slott's Patent*, p. 17. John Cadmus received from his father, Jasper, Jan. 20, 1820, 75 acres next S. of *Lot No.* 276, also 18 acres of meadow. He also bought from Rachel Vreeland five acres, April 26, 1831, and from Michael M. Vreeland, Feb. 7, 1832, Lot No. 2, on the Commissioners' Map of Cornelius Vreeland's estate. Of these tracts he died seized, in July, 1832, leaving his widow Elizabeth and children, *Rachel*, wife of Cornelius Van Buskirk, *Jasper, jr.*, *Elizabeth*, wife of Abraham Woods, *William*, *Richard*, and *Martha*, among whom his estate was partitioned by commissioners in 1844. By deeds, in 1859, Jasper and William conveyed their interest in the tract to Peter Bently, *et al.* The village of Bayonne was laid out on this lot.

† *Vide Note to Slott's Patent*, p. 17. Jasper sold to Jasper, jr., land and salt meadow = 75 acres, Jan. 21, 1820. Jasper, jr., by will, dated May 28, 1853, gave to his son *Jasper* the N. half of his farm and meadow, and of the upland adjoining the meadow of Stephen Terhune, and to his son *William* the S. half of his farm.

Our Survey whereof shews and we adjudge it to be a Tract **Beginning** at a Stake, being the Eastermost Corner of a Lot of Common Land (allotted to Hendrick Jansen Van Schalckwyck's Patent) mark'd on the Map No 273; which Stake stands North thirty nine Degrees East forty three Chains and twenty seven Links from a Stone mark'd B standing in the westermost Corner of a Lot of Common Land (allotted to Barnt Christian's Patent) mark'd on the Map No 277; And from said stake runs North fifty one Degrees West forty four Chains and forty Links to New Ark Bay, Then returning to said Stake the Place of Beginning and from thence runs North thirty nine Degrees East ten Chains and eighteen Links to a Stake, Then North fifty one Degrees West forty two Chains and twenty Links to said New Ark Bay, Then down said Bay as the same runs 'til it meets the first mention'd Line containing about forty three Acres.

To the Patent of Petrus Stuyvesant to Hendrick Jansen Van Schalckwyck dated the fifth Day of December One thousand six hundred and fifty four; confirm'd by Patent from Philip Carteret to Hessel Vygerse dated the thirtieth day of March one thousand six hundred and seventy five, for a Parcel of Land lying at Pembrepogh.

We do allot a certain Parcel of Land (mark'd on the Map No 273)*

Our Survey whereof shews and we adjudge it to be a Tract **Beginning** at a Stake, being the Eastermost Corner of a Lot of Common * Land (allotted to Thomas Davison's Patent) mark'd on the Map No 272; which Stake stands North thirty nine Degrees East thirty one Chains and fifteen Links from a Stone mark'd B standing in the Westermost Corner of a Lot of Common Land (allotted to Barnt Christian's Patent) mark'd on the Map No 277; and from said Stake runs North fifty one Degrees West forty two Chains and twenty Links to New Ark Bay, Then returning to said Stake the Place of Beginning; and from thence runs North thirty nine Degrees East twelve Chains and twelve Links to a Stake, Thence North fifty one Degrees West forty four Chains and forty Links to said New Ark Bay, Then down said Bay as the same runs 'til it meets the first mentioned Line; containing about fifty two Acres.

*93

---

* Adjudged to John Van Horne, p. 150. By his will, dated Sept. 22, 1786, proved Jan. 23, 1787, he gave this Lot to his sons *John* and *Garret*. Garret died seized, in common with John, April 17, 1809, leaving his property to his two sons, *John G.* and *Mindert*. These partitioned with their uncle John, he taking the S. half of the Lot. They took the N. half and partitioned April 14, 1838, Mindert taking the S. half, which he sold to Wm. Harriman in 1862, John G. taking the N. half, which he sold to Keeney and Halladay, who sold to Solon Humphreys. John's half passed to his sons, *John, Peter*, and *Garret*, who partitioned, running the lines N. E. and S. W. Peter took the W. end; John took the middle, and Garret's sons *John* and *Stephen* (he being then dead) took the E. end. Stephen died at sea (as is supposed) without issue, and his interest passed to his brother John and uncle John, who partitioned, running the line N. W. and S. E.; the uncle taking the S. part and the brother the N. part. *Vide Note to Lot No.* 304, p. 133.

To the Patent of Philip Carteret to Catharine formerly the Widow of Jacob Wallingen Van Horne, Then the Widow of Jacob Stoffelsen, dated the thirty first Day of March One thousand six hundred & sixty eight for a Parcel of Land lying at Pembrepogh.

We do **allot** a certain Parcel of Land mark'd on the Map No 276 *

Our Survey whereof shews and we adjudge it to be a Tract, **Beginning** at a Stake by New Ark Bay being the Westermost Corner of Catharine Stoffelsen's Patent mark'd on the Map No 29; and from thence runs along the Line thereof South twenty seven Degrees and thirty Minutes East thirty seven Chains and fifty one Links to a Stake (standing North twenty seven Degrees and thirty Minutes West seven Chains and seventy two Links from the Northermost Corner of Barnt Christian's Patent mark'd on the Map No 30) And from said last mentioned Stake runs South thirty nine Degrees West seven Chains & seventy two Links to a Stake in the Line of a Lot of Common Land (allotted to Thomas Davison's Patent) mark'd on the Map No 275; Thence along the said Line North forty two Degrees West thirty three Chains and fifty Links to said New Ark Bay, Then up said Bay as the same runs to the Place of Beginning; Containing about forty one Acres.

* To the Patent of Philip Carteret to Barnt Christian dated *94 the twenty sixth Day of March One thousand six hundred and sixty seven for a Piece of Land lying at Pembrepogh and a Piece Meadow at New Ark Bay

We do **allot** a certain Parcel of Land (marked on the Map No 277)

Our Survey whereof shews and we adjudge it to be a Tract **Beginning** at a Stone mark'd B being a Corner of a Lot of Common Land (allotted to Jansen & Edsal's Patent at Constables Hook) mark'd on the Map No 270; and from said Stone runs North thirty nine Degrees East sixty one Chains and fifteen Links to a Stake being the Eastermost Corner of a Lot of Common Land (allotted to Thomas Davison's Patent) mark'd on the Map No 275, Thence along the Line thereof North forty two Degrees West five Chains and fifty Links to the Southerly Corner of a Lot of Common Land (allotted to Catharine Stoffelsen's Patent) mark'd on the Map No 276, Then North thirty nine Degrees East seven Chains and seventy two Links to a Stake,. Thence South twenty seven Degrees and thirty Minutes East seven Chains and seventy two Links to the Northermost Corner of Barnt Christian's Patent marked on the Map No 30, Then along the Line thereof South twenty eight Degrees and thirty Minutes West fifty five Chains and twenty nine Links to the Westermost Corner thereof, Then South twenty seven Degrees and thirty Minutes East fifteen Chains and sixty five Links to a Stake, Then South twenty Degrees West two Chains and thirty Links to a Stake by the Meadow Edge, Then South forty Degrees West four Chains to a Stake, Thence North fifty one Degrees West twenty six Chains and sixty two Links to the Place of Beginning, Containing about sixty seven Acres.

▫ This Lot was adjudged to Jacob Van Horne, p. 150. *Vide Note to Stoffelsen's Patent*, p. 18.

To the Patent of Richard Nicolls to Nicholas Jansen and Saml Edsal dated the twenty sixth Day of October One thousand six hundred and sixty four for a Neck of Land call'd Nip Nixon lying at the Mouth of Kill Van Cul

We do **allot** a certain Parcel of Land (mark'd on the Map No 270)

Our Survey whereof shews and we adjudge it to be a Tract

*95 * **Beginning** at a Stake by the Meadow Edge being the Southermost Corner of a Lot of Common Land (allotted to Barnt Christian's Patent) mark'd on the Map No 277; and from said Stake runs North fifty one Degrees West twenty six Chains and sixty two Links to a Stone mark'd B being the Westermost corner of the said Lot of Common Land allotted to Barnt Christian's Patent, Thence North thirty nine Degrees East fifty Links to the Southermost Corner of a Lot of Common Land (allotted to Dirck Sycan's Patent) mark'd on the Map No 271; Then along the Line thereof North fifty one Degrees West forty Chains to New Ark Bay, Then down said Bay as the same runs thirty two Chains and sixty Links measured on a streight Line to the Northermost Corner of a Lot of Common Land (allotted to Hendrick Jansen Spier's Patent) mark'd on the Map No 269, Then along the Line thereof South fifty one Degrees East forty one Chains to a Stake (standing South thirty nine Degrees West thirty two Chains and nine Links from the said Stone mark'd B), Then South thirty nine Degrees West forty nine Chains and seventy six Links along the End of several Lots of Common Land to a Stake in the Line of the Lot of Common Land set apart for sale mark'd on the Map No 172; Then along said Line South eighty five Degrees East thirty three Chains to a Stake standing in the Edge of the Meadow, Then along said Meadow Edge Northeasterly to the Place of Beginning, containing about three hundred and five Acres.

To the Patent of Philip Carteret to Mark Noble and Samuel Moore dated the twentieth day of July one thousand six hundred and sixty nine for sundry Parcels of Land lying in and about the Town of Bergen

We do **allot** the two several Parcels of Land following

Our Survey whereof shews and we adjudge them to be two Tracts

The First whereof (mark'd on the Map No 227)

Begins at a Stake being the Easterly Corner of a Lot of Common Land (allotted to Dirck Garritse's Patent) mark'd on the Map No 226; and which Stake stands North thirty six Degrees and thirty Minutes East One hundred and nineteen Chains and fifteen Links from a large Stone mark'd **A 1764**, planted in a Corner of Wiehaken Commons; and
*96 from said Stake runs North thirty six * Degrees and thirty Minutes East fifteen Chains and twenty seven Links to a Stake, Thence North fifty two Degrees and thirty Minutes West thirty eight Chains to a Stake, Thence South thirty six Degrees and thirty Minutes West fifteen Chains and twenty seven Links to a Stake, Thence South fifty two Degrees and thirty Minutes East thirty eight Chains to the Place of Beginning; containing about fifty eight Acres.

The Second mark'd on the Map No 251)

Begins at a Stake, at the Eastermost Corner of a Lot of Common Land (allotted to Varlet and Bayard's Patent) mark'd on the Map No 250; which Stake stands North thirty three Degrees East twenty seven Chains and seventy Links from the Eastermost Corner of a Lot in Arent Lawrense's Patent mark'd on the Map No 92; And from Stake runs North fifty seven Degrees West eighty two Chains to Pinhorne's Creek then returning to said Stake the Place of Beginning and from thence runs North thirty three Degrees East fourteen Chains and thirty six Links to a Stake, Thence North fifty seven Degrees West seventy four Chains to said Pinhorne's Creek; Then Down said Creek as the same runs 'til it meets the first mentioned Line, Containing about one hundred & five acres of Land and Meadow.

> To the first Patent of Philip Carteret to Caspar Stymets dated the twelfth Day of May One thousand six hundred and sixty eight for two Parcels of Land and Meadow near the Town of Bergen

We do **allot** a certain Parcel of Land (mark'd on the Map No 225)*

Our Survey whereof shews and we adjudge it to be a Tract

Beginning at a Stake being the Eastermost Corner of a Lot of Common Land (allotted to the Church) mark'd on the Map No 176, which Stake stands North thirty six Degrees and thirty Minutes East ninety eight Chains and forty five Links from a large Stone mark'd **A 1764** planted in a Corner of Wiehaken Commons; and from said Stake runs North thirty six Degrees and thirty Minutes East nine Chains and fourteen Links to a Stake, Thence North fifty two Degrees and thirty Minutes West thirty eight Chains to a Stake, Thence South thirty six Degrees and thirty Minutes West nine Chains and fourteen Links to a Stake, Thence South fifty two Degrees & thirty Minutes East thirty eight Chains to the Place of Beginning, Containing about thirty four Acres.

> * To the Second Patent of Philip Carteret to Caspar Stymets dated the twelfth Day of May One thousand six hundred and sixty eight for sundry Parcels of Land in and about the Town of Bergen,

*97

We do **allot** a certain Parcel of Land mark'd on the Map No 223

ᵃ This lot was adjudged to Pieter Merselis, p. 161. It was inherited by Merselis Merselis. By his will, dated March 15, 1799, proved Dec. 5, 1800, he gave the S. W. half to his son *John*, who sold to Merselis Merselis Aug. 17, 1801, who sold to John and Jacob Merselis May 26, 1807, who sold to Henry Van Glahn June 12, 1807. John Merselis gave to John J. Van Horne a deed for this half May 21, 1839. The N. E. half went to John's sisters, Jannetje, wife of Walter Clendenny, and Anne, wife of Josiah Hornblower. This half seems to have been sold to William Dally and others. Dally sold to John Woolmington. I am not certain as to correctness of what is above said concerning the S. W. half. It seems by Douglass' Map to have been in Mrs. Parks, the daughter of John Merselis, in 1840. It is either on this half, or on the *Church Lot No. 176*, that Glahnville now is.

Our Survey whereof shews and we adjudge it to be a Tract

Beginning at a Stake being the eastermost Corner of a Lot of Common Land (allotted to Garret Garretse's Patent) mark'd on the Map No 222 which Stake stands North thirty six Degrees and thirty Minutes East sixty seven Chains and three Links from a large Stone mark'd A 1761 planted in a Corner of Wiehaken Commons and from said Stake runs North thirty six Degrees and thirty Minutes East twenty seven Chains and forty seven Links to a Stake, Thence North fifty two Degrees & thirty Minutes West thirty eight Chains to a Stake, Thence South thirty six Degrees and thirty Minutes West twenty seven Chains and forty seven Links to a Stake, Thence South fifty two Degrees and thirty Minutes East thirty eight Chains to the Place of Beginning, Containing about One hundred and four Acres.

> To the Patent of Philip Carteret to Adrian Post, dated the twelfth Day of May One thousand six hundred and sixty eight for sundry Parcels of Land lying in and about the Town of Bergen,

We do **allot** a certain Parcel of Land (mark'd on the Map No 264)

Our Survey whereof shews and we adjudge it to be a Tract

Beginning at a Stake standing in the Line of Laurence Andriesse's Patent mark'd on the Map No 19; which Stake is the Westermost Corner of a Lot of Common Land (allotted to Dirck Sycan's Patent) mark'd on the Map No 258; and from said Stake runs North twenty seven Degrees and thirty Minutes West fifty three Chains and fifty six Links to the Edge of the Meadow, Then North twenty six Degrees and fifty Minutes East three Chains and sixty six Links to a Stake (being the eastermost Corner of a Lot of Meadow in Peter Jacobse's Patent mark'd on the Map No 121,) Thence * North forty four Degrees West fifteen Chains and forty Links running most part of the Way along a Ditch to the Mouth of the same at the Hackinsack River, Then from the Mouth of said Ditch up along said River North sixty five Degrees and ten Minutes East seven Chains and fifty two Links to a Stake by the side of said River being the Westerly Corner of a Parcel of Common Land and Meadow (allotted to Claas Petersen Cors's Patent) mark'd on the Map No 263; Then along the Line thereof South forty three Degrees and forty five Minutes East sixty eight Chains and twenty Links to a Stake in the Line of a Lot of Common Land (allotted to Nicholas Jansen Baker's Patent) mark'd on the Map No 259; Thence South fifty Degrees West twenty five Chains and sixty Links to the Place of Beginning, Containing about One hundred and five acres.

*98

> To the first Patent of Philip Carteret to Guert Coerten dated the twelfth Day of May One thousand six hundred & sixty eight, for sundry Parcels of Land in & about the Town of Bergen,

We do **allot** a certain Parcel of Land (mark'd on the Map No 215)

Our Survey whereof shews and we adjudge it to be a Tract

Beginning at a Stake being the Northermost Corner of a Lot of Common Land (allotted to Hans Dederick's Patent) mark'd on the Map No 214 which Stake stands North thirty six Degrees and thirty Minutes East One hundred and ninety six Chains and fourteen Links from a large Stone mark'd **A. 1764** planted in a Corner of Wiehaken Commons; and from said Stake runs South fifty two Degrees and thirty Minutes East fifty five Chains to Hudson's River, Then returning to said Stake the Place of Beginning and from thence runs North thirty six Degrees and thirty Minutes East eleven Chains and forty eight Links to a Stake, Then South fifty two Degrees and thirty Minutes East fifty four Chains to said Hudson's River, Then down said River as it runs to the aforementioned Line running thereto Containing (after an Allowance for the Hill) about fifty nine Acres.

> * To the second Patent of Philip Carteret to Guert Coerten dated the twelfth Day of May One thousand six hundred and sixty eight for sundry Parcels of Land lying in & about the Town of Bergen

*99

We do **allot** a certain Parcel of Land (mark'd on the Map No 243)

Our Survey whereof shews and we adjudge it to be a Tract

Beginning at a Stake standing North thirty three Degrees East four Chains and fifteen Links from a Stone mark'd **IK**, being the westermost Corner of a Lot of Common Land (allotted to Claas Jansen Van purmerants Patent) mark'd on the Map No 240; and from said Stake runs North thirty three Degrees East twenty one Chains and fifty Links to a Stake being the Southermost Corner of a Lot of Common Land (allotted to Engleburt Steinheysen's Patent) mark'd on the Map No 244; And from the last mentioned Stake runs North fifty seven Degrees West twenty eight Chains and twenty Links to a Stake in the Road leading from the Town to the English Neighbourhood, Then along said Road South ten Degrees West eight Chains and sixty one Links to a Stake, Then South four Degrees East nine Chains and seventy five Links along said Road to a Stake, Thence South twenty six Degrees and forty Minutes East eight Chains and eighty one Links along said Road to a Stake, Thence South fifty Degrees East eleven Chains and thirty Links to the Place of Beginning, Containing about forty five Acres.

> To the Third Patent of Philip Carteret to Guert Coerten dated the twenty first Day of March One thousand six hundred & seventy for a Piece of Meadow lying Northerly of the Town

We do **allot** a certain Parcel of Land (mark'd on the Map No 235)

Our Survey whereof shews, & we adjudge it to be a Tract

Beginning at a Stake being the westermost Corner of a Lot of Common Land (allotted to Frederick Phillipse's Patent) mark'd on the Map No 234; which * Stake stands South thirty three Degrees West seven Chains and forty one Links from a Stone mark'd **WB** planted in the westermost Corner of Wiehaken Commons, and from said Stake runs South thirty three Degrees West nineteen Chains and forty two Links to

*100

a Stake, Thence South fifty seven Degrees East twenty three Chains and ten Links to a Stake on the Hill on the Line of a Slip of Common Land (allotted to Hobocken Patent) mark'd on the Map No 233; Then along the Line thereof North thirty three Degrees East nineteen Chains and forty two Links to a Stake. Thence North fifty seven Degrees West twenty three Chains and ten Links to the Place of Beginning, Containing about forty four Acres.

> To the Patent of Philip Carteret to Frederick Philipse dated the twelfth Day of May One thousand six hundred and sixty eight for sundry Parcels of Land lying in and about the Town of Bergen

We do allot the two several Parcels of Land following,

Our Survey whereof shews and we adjudge them to be two Tracts,

The First whereof (mark'd on the Map No 234) *

Begins at a large Stone mark'd **W B** planted in the Westermost Corner of Wiehaken Commons; and from said Stone runs South thirty three Degrees West seven Chains and forty one Links to a Stake, Thence South fifty seven Degrees East twenty three Chains and ten Links to a Stake, Thence North thirty three Degrees East five Chains and sixty one Links to a Stake, Thence North fifty seven Degrees West twenty three Chains and ten Links to the Place of Beginning; Containing about fifteen Acres.

The Second (mark'd on the Map No 262)

Begins at a Stake (standing in the Road that leads from the Town to Bergen Point, which Stake is South forty three Degrees and forty five Minutes East fifty Links from the Southerly Corner of a Lot in Guert Garretse's Patent (mark'd on the Map No 102) and from said Stake runs South thirty six Degrees West thirty three Chains and thirty eight Links to a Stake, Thence North forty three Degrees and forty five Minutes West fifty six Chains and fifty Links to a Stake by the Meadow Edge, Thence North thirty Degrees & fifty Minutes East nine Chains and fifty five Links along the Meadow Edge, Then North thirty Degrees east sixteen Chains and sixty Links along the said Meadow Edge to a Stake * (standing in the Southerly Line of said Lot of Guert Garretse mark'd on the Map No 102,) Thence South fifty four Degrees and ten Minutes east thirty five Chains along said Guert Garretse's Line, Then along the same South fifty Degrees and ten Minutes East twenty three Chains and sixty five Links to the Place of Beginning, Containing about One hundred and sixty eight Acres.

*101

> To the Patent of Philip Carteret to Anglebert Stienheysen dated the twenty second Day of July One thousand six hundred & seventy for sundry Parcels of Land lying in and about the Town of Bergen.

We do allot the two several Parcels of Land following

---

* This Lot was adjudged to Philip French, p. 171. *Vide Note to Philipse's Patent*, p. 28.

Our Survey whereof shews and we adjudge them to be two Tracts,

The First whereof (mark'd on the Map No 216)

Begins at a Stake (being the Northerly Corner of a Lot of Common Land allotted to the first Patent to Guert Coerten mark'd on the Map No 215 and said Stake stands North thirty six Degrees and thirty Minutes East two hundred and seven Chains and sixty two Links from a large Stone mark'd **A 1764** planted in a Corner of Wiehaken Commons) and from said Stake runs South fifty two Degrees and thirty Minutes East fifty four Chains to Hudson's River, Then returning to said Stake the Place of Beginning; and from thence runs North thirty six Degrees and thirty Minutes East nine Chains and forty six Links to a Stake, Thence South fifty two Degrees and thirty Minutes east fifty one Chains and eighty Links to said Hudsons River, Then down along the same as it runs 'til it meets the first mentioned Line, Containing after an Allowance for the Hill) about forty seven Acres.

The Second (mark'd on the Map No 244)

Begins at a Stake (being the Southerly Corner of a Lot of Common Land allotted to Dirck Tunisse's Patent mark'd on the Map No 245 and which Stake stands South thirty three Degrees West forty five Chains and fifty Links from a large Stone mark'd **W B** planted at the westerly Corner of Wiehaken Comons) And from said Stake runs North fifty seven Degrees West thirty Chains to a Stake, Thence South thirty three Degrees West forty One Chains & sixty nine Links to a Stake, Thence South forty five Degrees West twelve Chains & eighteen Links to a Stake, Thence south sixteen Degrees & five Minutes East five Chains & sixty eight Links to a Stake, Thence South fifty seven Degrees east twenty eight Chains & twenty Links to a Stake, Thence Northerly three Degrees east fifty seven Chains & forty two Links to the Place of Beginning, Containing about one hundred and seventy one Acres.

* To the Patent of Philip Carteret to Thomas Fredrick alias *102 De Cuyper dated the tenth Day of November One thousand six hundred & seventy seven for sundry Parcels of Land in and about the Town of Bergen,

We do **allot** the two several Parcels of Land following

Our Survey whereof shews and we adjudge them to be two Tracts,

The First whereof (mark'd on the Map No 232)*

Begins at a Stake (being the Easterly Corner of a Lot of Common Land allotted to Jacob Luby's Patent mark'd on the Map No. 231 and which Stake stands North thirty six Degrees and thirty Minutes East two hundred & sixteen Chains & sixteen Links from a large Stone

---

* This and *Lot No.* 284 were adjudged to Michael and George De Mott, p. 181. *Vide Note to Stoffelsen's Patent*, p. 9. This lot was divided between Michael and the heirs of George. Michael sold the north half to Joseph Danielson, after 1840, who died seized in 1860. The south half was sold, in 1867, by commissioners appointed to divide the De Mott property to J. and R. Gardner, who sold to the Rev. Wm. V. Mabon in 1869.

mark'd **A 1764** planted at a Corner of Wiehaken Commons) and from said Stake runs North fifty two Degrees and thirty Minutes West thirty eight Chains to a Stake, Thence North thirty six degrees and thirty Minutes East thirteen Chains and nine Links to a Stake, Thence South fifty two Degrees and thirty Minutes East thirty eight Chains to a Stake, Thence South thirty six Degrees and thirty Minutes West thirteen Chains and nine Links to the Place of Beginning, Containing about forty nine Acres.

The Second (being a small Lot in the Town of Bergen mark'd on the Map No 284)

Begins at a Stake (which Stake is the Southerly Corner of a Town Lot in Englebert Stienheysen's Patent mark'd on the Map No 152) And from said Stake runs South forty two Degrees East ninety six Links to a Stake, Thence South forty eight Degrees West One Chain and thirty eight Links to a Stake, Thence North forty two Degrees West ninety six Links to a Stake, Thence North forty eight Degrees East One Chain and thirty eight Links to the Place of Beginning, Containing about one eighth of an Acre.

To the Patent of Petrus Stuyvesant to Herman Edwards, dated the fourteenth Day of September One thousand six hundred and sixty two for sundry Parcels of Land lying in & about the Town of Bergen,

*103 * **We** do **allot** a certain Parcel of Land (mark'd on the Map No 249)

Our Survey whereof shews and we adjudge it to be a Tract **Beginning** at a Stake (standing North fifty two Degrees and thirty Minutes West six Chains and thirty Links from a large Stone mark'd **A 1764**, planted at a Corner of Wiehaken Commons and from said Stake runs North fifty two Degrees and thirty Minutes West thirty Chains to a Stake, Thence South thirty three Degrees west twenty four Chains and twenty Links to a Stake, Thence South fifty seven Degrees East thirty Chains to a Stake, Thence North thirty three Degrees East twenty one Chains and ninety-five Links to the Place of Beginning, Containing about sixty eight Acres.

To the Patent of Philip Carteret to Guert Garretse, dated the twenty second Day of July One thousand six hundred and seventy, For Sundry Parcels of Land lying in and about the Town of Bergen,

We do **allot** a certain Parcel of Land (mark'd on the Map No 221)

Our Survey whereof shews and we adjudge it to be a Tract

Beginning at a Stake (being the easterly Corner of a Lot of Common Land allotted to Hendrick Tunisse's Patent mark'd on the Map No 220; And which stake stands North thirty six Degrees and thirty Minutes East eighteen Chains and forty three Links from a large Stone mark'd **A 1764** planted at a Corner of Wiehaken Commons) and from said Stake runs North fifty two Degrees and thirty Minutes West thirty eight Chains to a Stake, Thence North thirty six Degrees and thirty Minutes East twenty nine Chains and eighty six Links to a Stake, Thence South fifty two Degrees and thirty Minutes East thirty eight Chains to a Stake, Thence South thirty six Degrees and thirty Minutes West twenty nine Chains and eighty six Links to the Place of Beginning, Containing about One hundred & thirteen Acres.

    * To the Patent of Petrus Stuyvesant to Paulus Pieterse dated *104 the seventh Day of March One thousand six hundred and sixty three and confirm'd to said Pieterse by Patent from Philip Carteret dated the twelfth Day of May One thousand six hundred and sixty eight, for sundry Parcels of Land lying in and about the Town of Bergen,

We do allot the three several Parcels of Land following

   Our Survey whereof shews and we adjudge them to be three Tracts

The First whereof (mark'd on the Map No 252)*

Begins at a Stake (standing at the easterly Corner of a Lot of Common Land allotted to the Patent of Noble and Moore mark'd on the Map No 251) and from said Stake runs North fifty seven Degrees West seventy four Chains to Pinhornes Creek, Then returning to said Stake the Place of Beginning; and from thence runs North thirty three Degrees East twelve Chains and thirty five Links to a Stake, Thence North fifty seven Degrees West fifty three Chains to said Pinhornes Creek, Then down along the said Creek as it runs 'til it meets the first mentioned Line, Containing about seventy four Acres.

The Second (mark'd on the Map No 253) †

Begins at a Stake (being the Northerly Corner of a Lot of Common Land allotted to Englebert Steinheysen's Patent, mark'd on the Map No 216; and which Stake stands North thirty six Degrees and thirty Minutes East two hundred and seventeen Chains and eight Links from a large Stone mark'd A 1764 planted at a Corner of Wiehaken Commons) And from said Stake runs South fifty two Degrees and thirty Minutes East twenty seven Chains and forty Links to a Stake, Thence North thirty six Degrees and thirty Minutes East five Chains and forty eight Links to a Stake, Thence North fifty two Degrees and thirty Minutes West twenty seven Chains and forty Links to a Stake, Thence South thirty six Degrees and thirty Minutes West five Chains and forty eight Links to the Place of Beginning, Containing about fifteen Acres.

---

  * This lot was adjudged to Garret Newkirk, p. 187, *Vide Note to Pieterse's Patent*, p. 40. In the partition between Mathevis and Hendrick, the former took the south half and the latter the north half. Hendrick gave his share to his two sons, *Garret H.*, who took the south half, and *George*, who took the north half. *Vide Note to Philipse's Patent*, p. 28.

  † This lot was adjudged to Garret Newkirk, p. 187. By his will it was given to his two sons, *Mathevis* and *Hendrick*, from whom it passed undivided to *Garret* and *Aaron*, sons of *Mathevis*, and *Garret H.* and *George*, sons of Hendrick. These four sold the east end to Abraham Huyler, the middle to Stephen Vreeland, and the west end to John George Leake, Dec. 1, 1812. Each purchaser took about one-third of the lot. *Vide Note to Lot No.* 400, p. 172. Leake died seized and intestate without lawful heirs, and, with other lands adjoining, it escheated to the State. *Vide O'Hanlin vs. Den. Spencer* 31 ; 1 *Zab.* 582.

The Third (mark'd on the Map No 281) *

Begins at a Stake (being the Southerly Corner of a Lot of Land in Peter * Jacobse's Patent mark'd on the Map No 58) and from said Stake runs North forty nine Degrees and thirty Minutes West twenty nine Chains and forty Links to a Stake, Thence South forty Degrees West four Chains and fifteen Links to a Stake, Thence South fifty Degrees and ten Minutes East thirty Chains and thirty Links to a Stake, Thence North thirty five Degrees East three Chains and seventy four Links to the Place of Beginning, Containing about Eleven Acres.

*105

> To the Patent of Philip Carteret to Dirck Garretse, dated the twelfth Day of May One thousand six hundred and sixty eight, for sundry Parcels of Land in & about the Town of Bergen,

We do **allot** a certain Parcel of Land (mark'd on the Map No 226)

Our Survey whereof shews and we adjudge it to be a Tract **Beginning** at a Stake (being the easterly Corner of a Lot of Common Land allotted to Casper Stymet's first Patent mark'd on the Map No 225; And which Stake stands North thirty six Degrees and thirty Minutes East One hundred and seven Chains and fifty nine Links from a large Stone mark'd **A 1764** planted at a Corner of Wiehaken Commons) And from said Stake runs North fifty two Degrees and thirty Minutes West thirty eight Chains to a Stake, Thence North thirty six Degrees and thirty Minutes East eleven Chains and fifty six Links to a Stake, Thence South fifty two Degrees and thirty Minutes East thirty eight Chains to a Stake, Thence South thirty six Degrees and thirty Minutes West, eleven Chains & fifty six Links to the Place of Beginning, containing about forty four Acres.

> To the Patent of Petrus Stuyvesant to Jacob Luby, dated the fourteenth Day of September One thousand six hundred and sixty two for sundry Parcels of Land lying in and about the Town of Bergen

We do **allot** a certain Parcel of Land (mark'd on the Map No 231)

Our Survey whereof shews, and we adjudge it to be a Tract * **Beginning** at a Stake (being the Easterly Corner of a Lot of Common Land allotted to Tielman Van Vleck's Patent marked on the Map No 230 and which Stake stands North thirty six Degrees and thirty Minutes East one hundred and ninety one Chains and fifty two Links from a large stone mark'd **A 1764** planted in a Corner of Wiehaken Commons) And from said Stake runs North fifty two Degrees and thirty

*106

---

* This lot was adjudged to Garret Newkirk, p. 187. It lies near the Catholic Cemetery, near the Hackensack river. It was partitioned by his two sons, *Mathevis* and *Hendrick*. Mathevis took the north half, which went to his sons *Garret* and *Aaron*. Hendrick took the south half, which went to his son *Garret H.*, who sold it to his brother *George* and brother-in-law *Hartman Van Wagenen*. George's interest went to his son *Abraham P.* He and Van Wagenen partitioned; he taking the south half, and Van Wagenen the north half.

Minutes West thirty eight Chains to a Stake, Thence North thirty six Degrees and thirty Minutes East twenty four Chains and sixty four Links to a Stake, Thence South fifty two Degrees and thirty Minutes East thirty eight Chains to a Stake, Thence South thirty six Degrees and thirty Minutes West twenty four Chains and sixty four Links to the Place of Beginning, Containing about ninety three Acres.

To the Patent of Philip Carteret to Jacob Luby dated the tenth Day of November one thousand six hundred and seventy seven, for sundry Parcels of Land lying at and near Wiehaken in the Township of Bergen

We do **allot** a certain Parcel of Land (mark'd on the Map No 202)

Our Survey whereof shews and we adjudge it to be a Tract

Beginning at a Stake (standing North thirty six Degrees and thirty Minutes East twelve Chains and thirty Links from a large Stone mark'd A 1764 planted at a Corner of Wiehaken Commons) And from said Stake runs South fifty two Degrees and thirty Minutes East forty three Chains and seventy five Links to a Red Oak Tree (on the East side of a Brook being the Northerly Corner of the two small Lotts in Jacob Luby's Patent mark'd on the Map No 144) And from said Tree runs South forty one Degrees and thirty Minutes East three Chains and fifty two Links along the Line of said Luby's Patent. then South twenty six Degrees East four Chains and twenty four Links along the Line of said Patent to Hudson's River, Then returning to said Stake the Place of Beginning; And from thence runs North thirty six Degrees and thirty Minutes East one Chain and ninety five Links to a Stake, Thence South fifty two Degrees and thirty Minutes East fifty two Chains and fifty Links to said Hudson's River; Then down along said River as it runs 'til it comes to the Easterly Corner of said Jacob Luby's Patent, Containing (after an Allowance for the Hill) about nine Acres.

* To the Patent of Philip Carteret to Jan Lubertse dated the twelfth day of May One thousand six hundred and sixty eight for sundry Parcels of Land lying in & about the Town of Bergen *107

We do **allot** the two several Parcels of Land following

Our Survey whereof shews and we adjudge them to be two Tracts

The First whereof (mark'd on the Map No 248)

Begins at a Stake (standing North thirty three Degrees East eighty nine Links from a large Stone mark'd W B being the westerly Corner of Wiehaken Commons) And from said Stake runs North fifty seven Degrees West thirty Chains to a Stake, Thence North thirty three Degrees East sixteen Chains & sixteen Links to a Stake, Thence South fifty seven Degrees East thirty Chains to a Stake, Thence South thirty three Degrees West sixteen Chains and sixteen Links to the Place of Beginning, Containing about forty eight Acres.

The Second mark'd on the Map No 282 *

---

* This Lot was adjudged to Arent Toers, p. 195. *Vide Note to Steenhuysen's Patent,* p. 32.

Begins at a Stake (by the Road that leads from the Town to the English Neighbourhood; which Stake is the Easterly Corner of a Lot in Englebert Steinheysen's Patent mark'd on the Map No 38) and from said Stake runs North seventy five Degrees and fifty Minutes West twenty eight Chains and ninety Links to a Stake by the Middle Road, Then North twenty Degrees and fifteen Minutes East Seven Chains and ninety Links along said Middle Road to a Stake, Thence South seventy five Degrees and fifty Minutes East twenty eight Chains and five Links to the first mentioned Road, Then South fourteeen Degrees and ten Minutes West seven Chains and eighty seven Links along said Road to the Place of Beginning, Containing about twenty two Acres.

To the Patent of Philip Carteret to Peter Jacobse dated the fifth Day of August One thousand six hundred and seventy one for sundry Parcels of Land lying in and about the Town of Bergen

*108

* **We** do **allot** a certain Parcel of Land (mark'd on the Map No 236)

Our Survey whereof shews and we adjudge it to be a Tract

Beginning at a Stake (standing South thirty three Degrees West twenty six Chains and eighty three Links from a large Stone mark'd W B in the Westermost Corner of Wiehaken Commons and which Stake is the Westerly Corner of a Lot of Common Land allotted to Guert Coerten's third Patent mark'd on the Map No 235) and from said Stake runs South thirty three Degrees West thirty Chains and twenty eight Links to a Stake, Thence South fifty seven Degrees East twenty five Chains and ten Links to a Stake, Thence North thirty three Degrees East twenty seven Chains and thirty one Links to a Stake, Thence North fifty seven Degrees West two Chains to a Stake, Thence North thirty three Degrees East two Chains and ninety seven Links to a Stake, Thence North fifty seven Degrees west twenty three Chains and ten Links to the Place of Beginning, Containing about seventy five Acres.

To the Patent of Philip Carteret to Nicholas Varlet & Balthazar Bayard dated the tenth Day of August One thousand six hundred and seventy one for sundry Parcels of Land lying in & about the Town of Bergen

We do **allot** the six several Parcels of Land following

Our Survey whereof shews, and we adjudge them to be six Tracts

The First whereof (mark'd on the Map No 250)

Begins at a Stake (being the Southerly Corner of a Lot of Common Land allotted to Noble & Moore's Patent mark'd on the Map No 251) And from said Stake runs North fifty seven Degrees West eighty two Chains to Pinhorne's Creek, Then returning to said Stake the Place of Beginning and runs South thirty three Degrees West twenty seven Chains and seventy Links to a Stake (being the Easterly Corner of a Lot in Arent Lawrense's Patent mark'd on the Map No 92) and from said Stake runs North fifty Degrees West twenty Chains and eighty Links to a Stake, Thence South forty two Degrees and thirty Minutes West five Chains,

Then South forty five Degrees and ten Minutes West eight Chains and forty Links to a Stake, Thence North forty three Degrees west twenty Chains and forty seven Links to Bridge Creek, Thence North forty two Degrees West forty eight Chains and thirty * eight Links to said Pin- *109
hornes Creek, Then up along said Creek the several Courses thereof as it runs 'til it meets the first mentioned Line, Containing about two hundred and fifty six acres.

The Second (being a Lot in the Town of Bergen Mark'd on the Map No 285)*

Begins at the Southerly Corner of said Lot (which Corner is North thirty four Degrees and thirty Minutes East one Chain and sixty Links from a Stake standing near the Middle of the Square, which Stake is North forty seven Degrees East six Chains and fifty three Links from the Easterly Corner of the Church) and from said Southerly Corner runs North forty two Degrees West two Chains and forty five Links to a Stake, Thence North forty eight Degrees East two Chains and Eighty Six Links to a Stake, Thence South forty two Degrees East two Chains and forty five Links to a Stake by a Street; Thence South forty Eight Degrees west two Chains and eighty six Links along said Street to the Place of Beginning, Containing about Half an Acre.

The Third (being another small Lot in the Town mark'd on the Map No 286) †

Begins at a Stake (being the easterly Corner of a Town Lot in said Varlet & Bayard's Patent mark'd on the Map No 160) and from said Stake runs South forty eight Degrees West two Chains and ninety one Links to a Stake, Thence South forty two Degrees East ninety eight Links to a Stake, Thence North forty eight Degrees East two Chains and ninety one Links to a Stake by said Street, Thence North forty two Degrees west ninety eight Links along said Street to the Place of Beginning, Containing about one Quarter of an Acre.

The Fourth (being a small Piece of Land lying easterly from and near the Town mark'd on the Map No 224)‡

Begins at a Stake by a Street (which is the Northerly Corner of an Out-Garden-Plot in Jan Lubertse's Patent mark'd on the Map No 115) and from said Stake runs North forty eight Degrees East three Chains and four Links along said Street to a Stake, Thence South forty two Degrees and fifty Minutes East six Chains and ninety Links to a Stake, Thence South forty eight Degrees West two Chains & ninety one Links

---

* This Lot was adjudged to Cornelius and Garret Sip, p. 201. *Vide Note to Van Vorst's Patent*, p. 60. It was sold Aug. 1, 1793, by Edo Merselis and Ariantje, his wife, Levinus Winne and Annatje, his wife, Thomas Vreeland and Jannetje, his wife, Jerry Van Winkle and Antje, his wife, Michael Vreeland and Peter Sip, heirs of Cornelius Sip. to the Reformed Church in Bergen. The church sold it in parcels—to Thomas Taylor April, 1863; to Charles J. Timson April, 1863; to Benjamin C. Taylor May and Aug., 1863; and to John W. Morton March 28, 1864.

† This Lot was adjudged to Cornelius and Garret Sip, p. 201. *Vide Note to Van Vorst's Patent*, p. 60. It yet remains in the Sip family, and is annexed to *Lot No.* 160, of which Richard Sip died seized April 10, 1865.

‡ This Lot was adjudged to Johannis Van Rypen, p. 201. *Vide Note to Coerten's Patent*, p. 25, and *Note to Noble and Moore's Patent*, p. 20.

to a Stake, Thence North forty one Degrees & thirty Minutes West six Chains and ninety Links to the Place of Beginning, Containing about two Acres.

The Fifth (being another small Piece of Land lying Northeasterly from & near the Town, Mark'd on the Map No 241) *

*110 ***Begins** at a Stake (being the Corner of a Well ninety three Links from the Northerly Corner of Garrit Sip's House) and from said Stake runs North forty two Degrees East three Chains and ninety six Links to a Stake at the Corner of Zachariah Sickle's Barn, Then North seventy four Degrees and thirty Minutes West two Chains and sixty five Links to a Stake, Thence South forty Degrees West two Chains and sixty four Links to a Stake by a Road or Street, Thence South forty two Degrees East two Chains and thirty two Links along said Road or Street to the Place of Beginning, Containing about three Quarters of an Acre.

The Sixth (being another small Piece of Land lying Northeasterly from & near the Town mark'd on the Map No 287) †

Begins at a Stake by a Street (being a Westerly Corner of a Lot in John Berry's Patent mark'd on the Map No 125) And from said Stake runs North forty two Degrees West three Chains and eighteen Links to a Corner of said Street, Then North forty two Degrees East two Chains and seventy Links along the Road leading from the Town to the English Neighbourhood to a Stake, Then South nine Degrees East four Chains and ten Links to a Stake, Thence South forty two Degrees West thirty eight Links to the Place of Beginning, Containing about a Quarter of an Acre.

> To the Patent of Philip Carteret to Dow Harmense dated the twelfth Day of May One thousand six hundred and sixty eight for sundry Parcels of Land lying in and about the Town of Bergen,

We do **allot** a certain Parcel of Land (mark'd on the Map No 246) ‡

Our Survey whereof shews, and we adjudge it to be a Tract

Beginning at a Stake (being the Southerly Corner of a Lot of Common Land allotted to Jacob Stoffelse's Patent mark'd on the Map No 247, And stands south thirty three Degrees West one Chain & seventy Links from a large Stone mark'd WB planted at the westerly Corner of Wiehaken Commons) and from said Stake runs South thirty three Degrees West thirty nine Chains and eighty three Links to a Stake, Thence North fifty

---

* This lot was adjudged to Zacharias Sickles, p. 201. It remained in that family until it was sold by Peter Sickles to Dr. Thomas B. Gautier, who sold to Andrew L. Cadmus May 20, 1835, who sold to Daniel Fanshaw May 2, 1836, who sold to Wiley.

† This lot was adjudged to Zacharias Sickles, p. 201, and is now owned by Maria, wife of Smith Garrabrant, and, with what was bought of the Newkirks, forms her homestead. *Vide Note to Berry's Patent*, p. 51. It was sold by Peter Sickles to Dr. Thomas B. Gautier, who sold the same to Andrew L. Cadmus May 20, 1835, who sold to Daniel Fanshaw May 2, 1836.

‡ This lot was adjudged to Michael and George De Mott, p. 201. *Vide Note to Harmensen's Patent*, p. 50.

seven Degrees West thirty Chains to a Stake, Thence North thirty three Degrees East thirty nine Chains and eighty three Links to a Stake, Thence South fifty seven Degrees East thirty Chains to the Place of Beginning, Containing about one hundred and twenty six Acres.

> *To the Patent of Philip Carteret to John Berry dated the twentieth Day of July One thousand six hundred and sixty nine for sundry Parcels of Land lying in and about the Town of Bergen

*111

We do **allot** that Parcel of Land which on the Map is mark'd No. 228)

Our Survey whereof shews, and we adjudge it to be a Tract **Beginning** at a Stake (being the Easterly Corner of a Lot of Common Land allotted to Noble & Moore's Patent mark'd on the Map No 227 and stands North thirty six Degrees and thirty Minutes East One hundred and thirty four Chains and forty two Links from a large Stone mark'd **A 1764** planted in a Corner of Wiehaken Commons) and from said Stake runs North fifty two Degrees and thirty Minutes West thirty eight Chains to a Stake, Thence North thirty six Degrees and thirty Minutes East thirty four Chains and forty three Links to a Stake, Thence South fifty two Degrees and thirty Minutes East thirty eight Chains to a Stake, Thence South thirty six Degrees and thirty Minutes West thirty four Chains and forty three Links to the Place of Beginning, Containing about one hundred and thirty Acres.

> To the Patent of Philip Carteret to Tielman Van Vleck dated the twenty fifth Day of March One thousand six hundred and seventy for sundry Parcels of Land near the Town of Bergen,

We do **allot** a certain Parcel of Land (mark'd on the Map No 230)

Our Survey whereof shews and we adjudge it to be a Tract **Beginning** at a Stake (being the Easterly Corner of a Lot of Common Land allotted to Ide Cornelise's Patent mark'd on the Map No 229 and stands North thirty six Degrees and thirty Minutes East One hundred and seventy seven Chains and seventy eight Links from a large Stone mark'd **A 1764** planted at a Corner of Wiehaken Commons) and from said Stake runs North fifty two Degrees and thirty Minutes West thirty eight Chains to a Stake, Thence North thirty six Degrees and thirty Minutes East thirteen Chains and seventy four Links to a Stake, Thence* South fifty two Degrees and thirty Minutes East thirty eight Chains to a Stake, Thence South thirty six Degrees and thirty Minutes West thirteen Chains and seventy four Links to the Place of Beginning, Containing about fifty two Acres.

*112

> To the Patent of Philip Carteret to Hendrick Tunise dated the twelfth Day of May One thousand six hundred and sixty eight for sundry Parcels of Land lying in & about the Town of Bergen.

We do **allot** the two several Parcels of Land following

24

Our Survey whereof shews and we adjudge them to be two Tracts

The First whereof mark'd on the Map No 220)

Begins at a large Stone mark'd **A 1764** planted at a Corner of Wiehaken Commons and from said Stone runs North fifty two Degrees & thirty Minutes West thirty eight Chains to a Stake, Thence North thirty six Degrees & thirty Minutes East eighteen Chains and forty three Links to a Stake, Thence South fifty two Degrees and thirty Minutes East thirty eight Chains to a Stake, Thence South thirty six Degrees and thirty Minutes West eighteen Chains and forty three Links to the Place of Beginning. Containing about seventy Acres.

The Second (being a Lot in the Town of Bergen mark'd on the Map No 255) *

Begins at a Stake standing by a Street (being the Southerly Corner of a Town Lot in Fredrick Philipse's Patent mark'd on the Map No 149) and from said Stake runs North forty eight Degrees East two Chains and eighty two Links to a Stake, Thence South forty two Degrees East ninety seven Links to a Stake, Thence South forty eight Degrees West One Chain and forty one Links to a Stake, Thence South forty two Degrees East two Chains and forty five Links to a Stake by another Street, Thence South forty eight Degrees West one Chain and forty one Links along said other Street to a Stake at the Corner, Thence North forty two Degrees West three Chains and forty two Links along the first mentioned Street to the Place of Beginning. Containing about Half an Acre.

*113

* To the Patent of Philip Carteret to Hans Dederick dated the twelfth Day of May One Thousand six hundred and sixty eight, for sundry Parcels of Land lying in and about the Town of Bergen.

We do allot a certain Parcel of Land (mark'd on the Map No 214)

Our Survey whereof shews and we adjudge it to be a Tract

Beginning at a Stake (being the Northerly Corner of a Lot of Common Land allotted to Dirck Claasen's Patent mark'd on the Map No 213 and stands North thirty six Degrees and thirty Minutes East One hundred and eighty seven Chains and fifty eight Links from a large Stone mark'd **A 1764** planted in a Corner of Wiehaken Commons) And from said Stake runs South fifty two Degrees & thirty Minutes East fifty five Chains to Hudson's River, Then returning to said Stake the Place of Beginning; And from thence runs North thirty six Degrees and thirty Minutes East eight Chains and fifty six Links to a Stake, Thence South fifty two Degrees and thirty Minutes East fifty five Chains to said Hudson's River, Then down along the same as it runs 'till it meets the first mentioned Line. Containing (after an Allowance for the Hill) about forty four Acres.

To the Patent of Petrus Stuyvesant to Dirck Tunise dated the fourteenth Day of September One thousand six hundred and sixty two for sundry Parcels of Land lying in & about the Town of Bergen.

---

* This Lot was adjudged to Hendrick Van Winkle, p. 207. *Vide Note to Teunise's Patent*, p. 54.

We do **allot** a certain Parcel of Land (mark'd on the Map No 245)*

Our Survey whereof shews & we adjudge it to be a Tract

Beginning at a Stake (being the Southerly Corner of a Lot of Common Land allotted to Dow Harmense's Patent mark'd on the Map No 246 and stands South thirty three Degrees West forty one Chains and fifty three Links from a large Stone planted at the westerly Corner of Wiehaken Commons mark'd **W B**) and from said Stake runs North fifty seven Degrees West thirty Chains to a Stake, Thence South thirty three Degrees West three Chains & ninety seven Links to a Stake, Thence South fifty seven Degrees East thirty Chains to a Stake, Thence North thirty three Degrees East three Chains and ninety seven Links to the Place of Beginning, Containing about twelve Acres.

> * To the Patent of Philip Carteret to Garret Garretse, *114 dated the twelfth Day of May One thousand six hundred & sixty eight for sundry Parcels of Land lying in & about the Town of Bergen,

We do **allot** a certain Parcel of Land (mark'd on the Map No 222)†

Our Survey whereof shews, and we adjudge it to be a Tract

Beginning at a Stake being the Easterly Corner of a Lot of Common Land allotted to Guert Garretse's Patent mark'd on the Map No 221 and stands North thirty six Degrees and thirty Minutes East forty eight Chains and twenty nine Links from a large Stone mark'd **A 1764** planted at a Corner of Wiehaken Commons) and from said Stake runs North fifty two Degrees and thirty Minutes West thirty Eight Chains to a Stake, Thence North thirty six Degrees and thirty Minutes East eighteen Chains and seventy four Links to a Stake, Thence South fifty two Degrees and thirty Minutes East thirty eight Chains to a Stake, Thence South thirty six Degrees and thirty Minutes West eighteen Chains and seventy four Links to the Place of Beginning, Containing about seventy One Acres.

> To the Patent of Philip Carteret to Ide Corneilise dated the thirty-first Day of May one thousand six hundred & sixty eight for a Piece of Upland and a Piece of Meadow lying to the Northward of the Town of Bergen.

We do **allot** the two several Parcels of Land following,

Our Survey whereof shews and we adjudge them to be two Tracts

The First whereof (mark'd on the Map No 229)‡

---

* This Lot was adjudged to Johannis Van Wagenen, p. 210. *Vide Note to Gerritse's Patent*, p. 58, and *Note to Lot No. 232*, p. 114.

† This Lot was adjudged to Johannis Van Wagenen, p. 211. *Vide Note to Gerritse's Patent*, p. 50. Jacob gave the north half to his son *Hartman*.

‡ This lot was adjudged to Cornelius and Garret Sip, p. 211. *Vide Note to Van Vorst's Patent*, p. 60. John and Robert E. Gardner now own about 18 acres west of the Dallytown road, bought of the Sips.

Begins at a Stake being the Easterly Corner of a Lot of Common Land allotted to John Berry's Patent mark'd on the Map No 228 and stands North thirty six Degrees and thirty Minutes East One hundred and sixty eight Chains and eighty five Links from a large Stone mark'd **A. 1764.** planted at a Corner of Wiehaken Commons) and from *115 said Stake runs North fifty two Degrees and thirty Minutes West * thirty eight Chains to a Stake, Thence North thirty six Degrees and thirty Minutes East eight Chains and ninety three Links to a Stake, Thence South fifty two Degrees and thirty Minutes East thirty eight Chains to a Stake Thence South thirty six Degrees and thirty Minutes West eight Chains and ninety three Links to the Place of Beginning. Containing about thirty four Acres.

The Second (being a Lot in the Town of Bergen mark'd on the Map No 256)*

Begins at a Stake by a Street being the Easterly Corner of a Lot of Common Land in the Town allotted to Varlet & Bayard's Patent mark'd on the Map No 285) and from said Stake runs North forty two Degrees West two Chains and forty five Links to a Stake, Thence North forty eight Degrees East One Chain and forty six Links to a Stake by another Street, Thence South forty two Degrees East two Chains and forty five Links along said other Street to a Stake at a Corner, Thence South forty eight Degrees West One Chain and forty six Links along said first mentioned Street to the Place of Beginning. Containing about one Quarter of an Acre.

To the Patent of Philip Carteret to Arent Lawrense dated the tenth Day of October One thousand six hundred and seventy for sundry Parcels of Land lying in and about the Town of Bergen

We do allot a certain Parcel of Land Southeasterly from, and near the Town (mark'd on the Map No 254)

Our Survey whereof shews and we adjudge it to be a Tract **Beginning** at a Stake (being the Southerly Corner of an Out Garden Plot in Hans Dedrick's Patent mark'd on the Map No 114) and from said stake runs South thirty five Degrees and fifty five Minutes East forty Chains and sixty Links to a Creek call'd Oyster Creek (that runs into Horsimus Creek and which said Oyster Creek is the Northerly Bounds of Claas Pietersen Cols' Patent mark'd on the Map No 11) Then returning to said Stake the Place of Beginning; and from thence runs South forty eight Degrees West four Chains and eighty six Links to a Stake, Thence South forty four degrees West twenty Chains to the Easterly Line of a Lot in Nicholas Varlet's Patent mark'd on the Map No 128, Then South eight Degrees East fourteen Chains and ninety four Links along said Varlet's Line to the Corner, Then South eighty two *116 Degrees West eight Chains and fifty seven Links along * Varlet's Southerly Line to the Northeasterly Line of Nicholas Jansen the Baker's Patent mark'd on the Map No 12; Then South forty nine Degrees and forty five Minutes East seventeen Chains along said Baker's Line to a Stake (being the westerly Corner of said Baker's Patent mark'd on

---

* This lot was adjudged to Cornelius and Garret Sip, p. 211. *Vide Note to Van Vorst's Patent*, p. 60.

COMMON LANDS.   189

the Map No 13) Thence North forty Degrees and fifteen Minutes East twenty six Chains and twenty five Links along the Line of said Bakers last mention'd Patent to the Northerly Corner thereof, Then South forty nine Degrees and forty five Minutes East seven Chains along the Northeasterly Line of said Bakers last mention'd Patent to a Stake by a small Creek, Then down the said small Creek 'til it empties into said Oyster Creek, Then down along said Oyster Creek the several Courses thereof as it runs til it meets the first mentioned Line. Containing about one hundred Acres.

To the Patent of Petrus Stuyvesant to Nicholas Varlet dated the eighteenth Day of October One thousand six hundred & sixty three for sundry Parcels of Land lying in and about the Town of Bergen.

We do **allot** the two several Parcels of Land following

Our Survey whereof shews and we adjudge them to be two Tracts,

The First whereof (mark'd on the Map No 242)

Begins at a Stake (being the Northerly Corner of Claas Jansen Vanpurmerants Patent mark'd on the Map No 132) And from said Stake runs South forty Degrees West eighteen Chains along said Van Purmerant's Line to a Stake at his westerly Corner, Thence South fifty Degrees East one Chain to the Northerly Corner of Hendrick Van Ostrums Patent mark'd on the Map No 131 Thence South forty Degrees west fifteen Chains and fourteen Links along said Van Ostrum's Line to his westerly Corner, Thence South fifty Degrees East eight Chains and one Link to the Northerly Corner of a Lot in Anglebert Steinheysen's Patent mark'd on the Map No 130, Thence South thirty two Degrees West twenty two Chains and thirty eight Links to the Easterly Corner of a Lot of Common Land allotted to the Free School mark'd on the Map No 179, Then North thirty eight Degrees & forty five Minutes West twenty Chains along the Line of said School Lot to the Road leading from the Town to the English Neighbourhood, Then North twelve Degrees & twenty Minutes East nine Chains along said Road, Then North fourteen Degrees and ten Minutes East nineteen Chains and twelve Links along said Road, Then North forty one Degrees East nine Chains and fifty Links along said Road, Then North forty four Degrees and thirty Minutes East seventeen Chains and Twelve Links * along said Road to a Stake, (being the Easterly Corner of a Lot in Anglebert Steinheysen's Patent mark'd on the Map No 89,) Thence North sixteen Degrees East four Chains & twenty two Links to a Stake, Thence South fifty Degrees East eleven Chains and thirty Links to a Stake, Thence South thirty three Degrees West four Chains and fifteen Links to a Stake, Thence South fifty Degrees East Ten Chains to the Place of Beginning, Containing about One hundred and twenty three Acres. *117

The Second (being a small Lot in the Town of Bergen mark'd on the Map No 257)

Begins at a Stake (being the westerly Corner of a Town Lot in said Nicholas Varlet's Patent mark'd on the Map No 168) and from said Stake runs South forty eight Degrees West One Chain and forty six Links to a Stake, Thence South forty two Degrees East One Chain and nineteen Links to a Stake, Thence North forty eight Degrees East One Chain and forty six Links to a Stake, Thence North forty two Degrees West One Chain and nineteen Links to the Place of Beginning, Containing about One Eighth of an Acre.

>To the Patent of Philip Carteret to Hendrick Van Ostrum dated the tenth Day of November One thousand six hundred and seventy seven, For a Parcel of Upland, and a Parcel of Meadow lying Eastward of the Town of Bergen.

We do allot the two several Parcels of Land following

Our Survey whereof shews and we adjudge them to be two Tracts

The First whereof (mark'd on the Map No 209)*

Begins at a Stake (being the Northerly Corner of a Lot of Common Land allotted to Claas Pietersen Cors's Patent mark'd on the Map No 208 and which Stake stands North thirty six Degrees & thirty Minutes East One hundred & forty four Chains & fifty-eight Links from a large Stone mark'd **A 1764** planted in a Corner of Wiehaken Commons) And from said Stake runs South fifty two Degrees and thirty Minutes East fifty seven Chains to the Edge of Slaugh's Meadow (which Meadow is mark'd on the Map 145) And then returning to said Stake the Place of Beginning & from thence runs North thirty six Degrees and thirty Minutes East two Chains & and fifty five Links to a Stake, Then South fifty two Degrees and thirty Minutes East fifty eight Chains to the Edge of said Slaugh's Meadow, Then along betwixt the said Meadow & Upland 'til it meets the first mentioned Line. Containing (after an Allowance for the Hill) about fourteen Acres.

*118 *** The Second** (mark'd on the Map No 239)

Begins at a Stake (standing South thirty three Degrees West one Chain & thirty eight Links from a large Stone mark'd **WB** planted in the Westermost Corner of Wiehaken Commons; And which Stake is the westerly Corner of a Lot of Common Land allotted Abraham Isaacsen Plank's Patent mark'd on the Map No 238) And from said Stake runs South fifty seven Degrees East twenty seven Chains and ten Links to a Stake, Thence South thirty three Degrees West eight Chains and eighty four Links to a Stake, Thence South fifteen Degrees West seven Chains and twenty Links to a Stake, Thence North fifty seven Degrees West twenty nine Chains and fifty Links to a Stake, Thence North thirty three Degrees East fourteen Chains and forty four Links to the Place of Beginning. Containing about thirty nine Acres.

>To the Patent of Philip Carteret to Claas Jansen Vanpurmerant, dated the thirty first Day of March One thousand six

---

° This lot was adjudged to Hendricus Kuyper, p. 208. *Vide Note to Lot No.* 240, p. 78. John Dey sold this and *Lot No.* 210 to Cornelius Garrabrants April 12, 1791. This conveyance recites a deed from Archibald Kennedy to Kuyper Oct. 10, 1767. Garrabrants devised these lots to his sons *Cornelius* and *Peter*. Peter died seized and intestate Dec. 24, 1825, and Cornelius Van Winkle and James Van Buskirk, administrators, sold his half, containing twenty-three acres, to Michael Carling June 3, 1828.

hundred and sixty eight for a Parcel of Upland and a Parcel of Meadow lying eastward of the Town of Bergen

We do **allot** a certain Parcel of Land (mark'd on the Map No 210)*

Our Survey whereof shews and we adjudge it to be a Tract,

Beginning at a Stake (standing North thirty six Degrees and thirty Minutes East One hundred and forty seven Chains and thirteen Links from a large Stone mark'd **A. 1764** planted in a Corner of Wiehaken Commons; and which Stake is the Northerly Corner of a Lot of Common Land allotted to Hendrick Van Ostrum's Patent mark'd on the Map No 209) And from said Stake runs South fifty two Degrees and thirty Minutes East fifty eight Chains to the Edge of Slaugh's Meadow, Then returning to said Stake the Place of Beginning and from thence runs North thirty six Degrees and thirty Minutes East eight Chains and ninety nine Links to a Stake, Thence South fifty two Degrees and thirty Minutes East sixty two Chains and forty Links to Hudson's River, Then down along said River to said Slaugh's Meadow, then along betwixt said Meadow and the Upland 'till it meets the first mentioned Line that comes to said Meadow, Containing (after an Allowance for the Hlil) about fifty one Acres.

> * To the Patent of Petrus Stuyvesant to Jan Vinge dated the fourth Day of June One thousand six hundred & sixty three for a Piece of Meadow lying Easterly of the Town of Bergen.

*119

We do **allot** a certain Parcel of Land (mark'd on the Map No 218)

Our Survey whereof shews and we adjudge it to be a Tract,

Beginning at a Stake (being the Northerly Corner of a Lot of Common Land allotted to Petrus Stuyvesant's Patent mark'd on the Map No 217) and from said Stake runs South fifty two Degrees and thirty Minutes East twenty four Chains and forty Links to Hudson's River, Then returning to said Stake the Place of Beginning; and from thence runs North thirty six Degrees and thirty Minutes East seven Chains and forty one Links to a Stake, Thence South fifty two Degrees and thirty Minutes East twenty Chains to said Hudson's River, Then down along said River as it runs 'til it meets the first mentioned Line, Containing (after an Allowance for the Hill) about fifteen Acres.

> To the Patent of Petrus Stuyvesant to Cornelis Van Ruyven, Paulus Lindertz, Alerd Anthony & Johannis Verbruggen, Dated the twenty first Day of November, One thousand six hundred & sixty three, For a Meadow (of old call'd Jacob Slaugh's Meadow) lying upon the West Side of Hudson's River.

We do **allot** a certain Parcel of Land (mark'd on the Map No 207)

---

o This lot was adjudged to Hendricus Kuyper, p. 218. *Vide Note to Lot* 209, p. 117. This lot was owned by Cornelius Huyler in 1804. *Vide Note to Lot No.* 219, p. 77.

Our Survey whereof shews and we adjudge it to be a Tract **Beginning** at a Stake (standing North thirty six Degrees & thirty Minutes East One hundred & twenty two Chains & eighty five Links from a large Stone mark'd **A. 1764** planted in a Corner of Wiehaken Commons and which Stake is the Northerly Corner of a Lot of Common Land allotted to Nicholas Jansen the Baker's Patent mark'd on the Map No 206) and from said Stake runs South fifty two Degrees and thirty Minutes East forty seven Chains and fifty Links to the Edge of said Slaugh's Meadow, Then returning to said Stake the Place of Beginning;

*120 And from thence runs North thirty * six Degrees & thirty Minutes East five Chains and fifty nine Links to a Stake, Thence South fifty two Degrees and thirty Minutes East forty seven Chains and seventy five Links to the Edge of said Slaugh's Meadow, Then along betwixt the Meadow and Upland 'til it meets the first mentioned Line that comes to said Meadow, Containing (after an Allowance for the Hill) about twenty four Acres.

To the Patent of Petrus Stuyvesant to Nicholas Varlet and Nicholas Bayard, Dated the tenth Day of December, One thousand six hundred and sixty three; confirm'd by Patent from Philip Carteret to said Varlet and Bayard; Dated the thirtieth Day of October One thousand six hundred and sixty seven, For a certain Plantation or Parcel of Land and Meadow called Sekakus, lying in the Kill Van Cull

We do **allot** a certain Parcel of Land (mark'd on the Map No 283),

Our Survey whereof shews and we adjudge it to be a Tract **Beginning** at a Stake standing by Pinhorne's Creek (being the most Northerly Corner of a Lot of Common Land allotted to Paulus Pieterse's Patent mark'd on the Map No 252) and from said Stake runs South fifty seven Degrees East fifty three Chains to a Stake (being the Easterly Corner of said Lot No 252) Thence North thirty three Degrees East seventy four Chains and thirty four Links to a Stake (being the Northerly Corner of a Lot of Common Land allotted to Herman Edwards's Patent mark'd on the Map No 249) Thence North fifty two Degrees and thirty Minutes West one Chain and seventy Links to a Stake (being the Westerly Corner of a Lot of Common Land allotted to Hendrick Tunise's Patent mark'd on the Map No 220) Thence North thirty six Degrees and thirty Minutes East two hundred and twenty nine Chains and twenty five Links to a Stake (being the Northerly Corner of a Lot of Common Land allotted to Thomas Fredrick alias De Cuyper's Patent mark'd on the Map No 232) Thence South fifty two Degrees and thirty Minutes East thirty eight Chains to a Stake (being the Easterly Corner of said Lott No 232) Thence South thirty six Degrees and thirty Minutes West six Chains and ten Links to a Stake (being the Northerly Corner of a Lot of Common Land allotted to Paulus Pieterse's Patent mark'd on the Map No 253) Thence South fifty two Degrees & thirty Minutes East twenty seven Chains and forty Links to a Stake (being the Easterly Corner of said Lot No 253)

*121 Thence North thirty six Degrees * and thirty Minutes East twenty five Chains and sixty three Links to a Stake (being the Northerly Corner of a Lot of Common Land allotted to Nicholas Varlet's Patent mark'd on the Map No 219) Thence South fifty two Degrees and Thirty Minutes East nineteen Chains and ninety Links to the Edge of Mordainis Meadow (being the Easterly Corner of said Lot No 219) Then Northerly along the Edge of said Mordainis Meadow where the same joins the Upland 'til it comes to bear South forty nine Degrees East from a Chesnut Tree (being the Place of Beginning of the General Bounds of the Township of Bergen) Then North forty nine Degrees West thirty five Links to said Chessnut Tree, Thence North forty nine Degrees West ninety seven Chains along the Line of the Northern Bounds of the Township to a Stake mark'd 𝕰 & 𝕭 standing by the side of the Eastermost Branch of a small Creek, Thence running down the said Creek, Northerly, Westerly and Southwesterly as the same runs 'till it comes into Hackinsack River, Then down along said Hackinsack River Southwesterly as it runs 'till it comes to the Mouth of a Creek call'd Crom a Kill, then up along said Crom a Kill the several Courses thereof as it runs to a Creek or Ditch (which communicates or joins said Crom a Kill with Pinhorne's Creek) Then along said Creek or Ditch as it runs to said Pinhorne's Creek, Then down along said Pinhornes Creek the several Courses thereof as it runs to the Place of Beginning, Containing about two thousand two hundred Acres.

*122

The **First Part** of the Field Book

Comprehending { The General Bounds of the Township The Location of the Several Patents & Grants and The **General Partition** of the **Common Lands**;

Ending upon this Page, The Commissioners with their Surveyor, have signed the same,

Geor: Clinton Surveyor	Char. Clinton Will. Donaldson Az. Dunham John Berrien Abra Clark Jun. Jacob Spicer

☞ * **As** the Commissioners have been necessarily led in the Course of this Work to make use of a great multiplicity of Figures, in order thereby to distinguish the very great variety of seperate Locations, They think it proper here for the sake of Distinction to observe;

First—That All patented and other appropriated Lands are (in the Field Books and Maps) distinguished by the Numbers 1—2—3 and so on regularly upwards to Number 179.

Second—That all Lots of **Common Land** as allotted to the respective Patents upon the General Partition are (in the Field Books & Maps) distinguished by the Numbers 201—202—203 and so on regularly upwards to Number 287.

Third—That all **Subdivisions** of **Common Land** are (in the Field Books and Maps) distinguished by the Numbers 301—302—303 & so on regularly upwards to Number 431.

Note—The Lots of Common Laid out to the Patents upon the General Partition are mark'd out and delineated on the schedules A & B by BLACK Lines, and the Subdivisions made of the said Lots are mark'd out & distinguish'd on both the said Schedules by PRICK'D Lines.

Part Second.

This is one of the FIELD-BOOKS

Of the Partition and Division of the Common Lands

Which have been allotted to each respective Patent or Grant within the Bounds & Limits of the Township of **Bergen**—Made in pursuance of a Law of the Province of New Jersey in America, pass'd in the fourth Year of the Reign of his present Majisty King George the third,—Entitled " An Act appointing Commissioners for finally setling and determining the several Rights, Titles and Claims to the Common Lands of the Township of Bergen and for making a Partition thereof in just & equitable Proportions among those who shall be adjudged by the said Commissioners to be Entitled to the same." The General Partition by the said Act directed having been compleated as the same is recorded in the First Part of this book. We Charles Clinton, William Donaldson, Azariah Dunham, John Berrien & Abraham Clark Junr., five of the Commissioners named in the said Act did make and subscribe a **Notice** in the words following, to wit;

" **To all** whom these Presents may concern and particularly to such
" as claim any Interest in the Common Lands of the Township of Bergen
" in the County of Bergen in the Province of New Jersey:

" **Whereas** by a late Law of the Colony of New Jersey entitled an
" Act appointing Commissioners for finally setling and determining the
" several Rights, Titles and Claims to the Common Lands of the Town-
" ship of Bergen and for making a Partition thereof in just & equitable
" Proportions among those who shall be adjudged by the said Commis-
" sioners to be entitled to the same. Certains Persons are therein named
" as Commissioners of whom we the Subscribers are the Major Part, And
" whereas such of the Commissioners as took upon them the Execution
" of said Law did meet in the said Township of Bergen pursuant to
" public Notice thereof given agreeable to the Directions of the said Law
" and did run out & ascertain as well the Bounds and Limits of the said
" Township of Bergen as the Bounds and Limits of each and every
" Patent and Grant contained within the Bounds and Limits of the said
" Township as came to the Knowledge of the Commissioners. And also
" allotted to each Patent & Grant so run out & ascertained such Propor-
" tions of the Common Lands within said Township as the said Commis-
" sioners judged Right, agreeable to the Directions of the said Law.
" Now Therefore towards compleating the Trust in the said Commis-
" sioners or the Major Part of them reposed, We the subscribers do hereby
" give public Notice That at Ten o'Clock in the Forenoon of Tuesday
" the sixteenth Day of October next at the House of Stephen Bourdet at
" Wiehaken in the said Township of Bergen We or a majority of the said

"Commissioners will meet to make a Partition and Division of the said Common Lands allotted to each respective Patent or Grant within the Bounds & Limits of the said Township of Bergen, to which a Share of the Common Lands have been allotted as aforesaid among all such Persons who may be adjudged to be interested therein. And We do hereby request all Persons concerned or claiming Interest in the Common Lands allotted to the said respective Patents or Grants to produce to us some or one of us their Titles and make out their Claims to the same by the time above prefixed, in order that we may be truly informed thereof and thereby be enabled to adjudge the same in the most just and equitable Manner,

"Given under our Hands the twenty first Day of July in the Year one thousand seven hundred and sixty four."

Sign'd { Char Clinton
Will: Donaldson
Az. Dunham
John Berrien
Abra: Clark Junr.

As by the same original Notice filed in the Office of the Clerk of the County of Bergen may appear—A true Copy of which said Notice was printed and published in two of the public News Papers commonly called the New York Gazette & Mercury, to wit, in the Gazette Numbers 294, 295, 296, 297, 298, 299, 300, 301, 302, 303, 304, & 305, and in the Mercury Numbers 665, 666, 667, 668, 669, 670, 671, 672, 673, 674, 675, & 676, as by the same News Papers refference being thereto had may appear. Copies of which said Notice were also affixed on the Court House in Hackinsack and the Church in Bergen.

And we the said five Commissioners having met pursuant to the said Notice and before ent'ring upon the Execution of the Business being joined by Jacob Spicer We the said six Commissioners with George Clinton one of our Surveyors (Jonathan Hampton the other Surveyor having been notified and not attending) did proceed to the Subdivision of the Common Lands which have been allotted to each respective Patent or Grant within the Bounds and Limits of the said Township of Bergen.

And here we think it needful to observe—That inasmuch as the Field Work or Surveys of the Subdivision which are to be recorded in this **Second Part** of the Field Book cannot be laid down and represented on the Schedule or Map of the General Partition without rendering (in many Respects) the whole Map unintelligible, We have therefore found it necessary to annex (to the Schedule of the General Partition) two other Schedules protracted from a larger Scale for the Purpose of the Subdivision. Which three Schedules together, do form and make up the **one whole map.** One of these Schedules of the Subdivision we have distinguished by the Title " **Schedule A,** " and the other by the Title

*125 " **Schedule B,** " And upon these * two Schedules we have laid down and represented the Surveys of the whole Subdivision.

And We think it further necessary in Regard to these two Schedules of the Subdivision to observe once for all—That as each and every of the

Lots of Common Land which have been allotted to the respective Patents upon the General Partition are represented on the Schedule or Map of the said General Partition, and are there respectively distinguished by a particular Number, So we have laid down each and every of these Lots in their Order upon the two Schedules of the Subdivision and have there distinguished them by the very same Numbers as they are respectively distinguished on the said Schedule or Map of the General Partition excepting a few small Lots of Common Land lying in and about the Town which may be seen in the Town Plot on the Map of the General Partition.

And these Things being premised We proceeded in the Business of the Subdivision and that in the Order following, to wit,

With Respect to the Lot of Common Land which has been allotted, To the Patent of Wiehaken granted by William Kieft to Maryn Adrianse, dated the eleventh Day of May one thousand six hundred and forty seven, and confirm'd by patent from Philip Carteret to said Maryn Adrianse dated the eighteenth Day of April one thousand six hundred and seventy, being that Lot of Common Land which in the Field Book & Map of the General Partition is distinguished by the Number 201.

William Bayard Esqr claimed the said Lot, and upon Examination of his Title we conceive him to be the true Proprietor And do therefore adjudge the said Allotment to belong to him.

With Respect to the three Lots of Common Land which have been allotted To the Patent of Hobocken granted by Petrus Stuyvesant to Nicholas Varlet dated the fifth Day of February one thousand six hundred and * sixty three, and *126 confirm'd by Patent from Philip Carteret to said Nicholas Varlet dated the twelfth Day of May One thousand six hundred & sixty eight, being these three Lots of Common Land, which in the Field Book & Map of the General Partition are distinguished by the Numbers 233, 203 & 219.

William Bayard Esqr claimed the said three Lots, and upon Examination of his Title, we conceive him to be the true Proprietor, And Do therefore adjudge the said three Allotments to belong to him.

With Respect to the two Lots of Common Land, which have been allotted To the Patent granted by Philip Carteret to Ide Corneliese Van Vost dated the thirtieth Day of March one thousand six hundred & sixty eight, being these two Lots of Common Land which in the Field Book & Map of the General Partition are distinguished by the Numbers 211 and 237

Cornelius Van Vost claimed the said two Lots, and no other Person or Persons claiming the same or a Subdivision thereof We upon Examination of his Title conceive him to be the true Proprietor, And Do therefore adjudge the said two Allotments to belong to him.

*127

With Respect to the Lot of Common Land which has been allotted To the Patent granted by Petrus Stuyvesant to Closs Jansen Vanpurmerant dated the thirty * first day of January One thousand six hundred and sixty two And confirmed by Patent from Philip Carteret to said Vanpurmerant dated the thirtieth Day of March one thousand six hundred & sixty eight, being that Lot of Common Land which on the Field Book and Map of the General Partition is distinguished by the Number 240.

Hendericus Kuyper Esq, claimed the said Lot, and no other Person or Persons claiming the same or a Subdivision thereof, We upon Examination of his Title conceive him to be the true Proprietor, And do therefore adjudge the said Allotment to belong to him.

With respect to the Lot of Common Land which has been allotted To the Patent of Philip Carteret to Abraham Isaacsen Plank dated the twelfth Day of May one thousand six hundred and sixty eight being that Lot of Common Land which in the Field Book & Map of the General Partition is distinguished by the Number 238.

Cornelius Van Vost claimed the said Lot, and no other Person or Persons claiming the same or a Subdivision thereof, We upon Examination of his Title conceive him to be the true Proprietor, And do therefore adjudge the said Allotment to belong to him.

*128

* With Respect to the Lot of Common Land which has been allotted to the Patent of Petrus Stuyvesant to Jacob Stoffelsen dated the seventh Day of May one thousand six hundred and sixty four, being that Lot of Common Land which in the Field Book & Map of the General Partition is distinguished by the Number 247.

Michael De Mott & George De Mott claimed the same Lot as Tenants in Common thereof, and upon Examination of their Titles We conceive them to be the true Proprietors And do therefore adjudge the said Allotment to belong to them the said Michael & George De Mott in equal moietys.

With Respect to the Lot of Common Land which has been allotted To the Patent of Philip Carteret to Petrus Stuyvesant dated the thirty first Day of July One thousand six hundred and sixty nine, being that Lot of Common Land which in the Field Book & Map of the General Partition is distinguished by the Number 217.

Petrus Stuyvesant claimed the said Lot and no other Person or Persons claiming the same or a Subdivision thereof We upon Examination of his Title conceive him to be the true Proprietor And Do therefore adjudge the said Allotment to belong to him.

* This is a Subdivision of the two Lots of Common Land which have been allotted To the Patent of Philip Carteret to Class Comptah alias Class Pietersen Cors dated the third Day of June one thousand six hundred and seventy one, being these two Lots of Common Land which in the Field Book and Map of the General Partition are distinguished by the Numbers 208 & 263

And upon Examination of the Titles of Myndert Garrabrants and Cornelius Garrabrants (no other Person claiming.)

We adjudge a certain Portion of said Allotment No 208 to belong to said Myndert Garrabrants.

Our Survey of which said Portion (as laid down on Subdivision Schedule A) shews, and we adjudge it to be a Tract mark'd No 306 *

Beginning at a Stake (standing North thirty six Degrees and thirty Minutes East one hundred and twenty eight Chains and forty four Links from a large Stone mark'd **A 1764** planted at one of the Corners of Wiehaken Commons) and from said Stake runs South fifty two Degrees and thirty Minutes East forty seven Chains and seventy five Links to the Edge of Slaugh's Meadow, Then returning to said Stake the Place of Beginning and from thence runs North thirty six Degrees and thirty Minutes East eight Chains and forty two Links to a Stake, Thence South fifty two Degrees and thirty Minutes East fifty two Chains and forty Links to said Slaugh's Meadow, Then down along betwixt the Meadow and Upland 'till it meets with the above mentioned Line that runs to said Meadow, Containing (after an Allowance for the Hill) about forty one Acres.

And we adjudge a certain Portion of said Allotment No 208 to belong to said Cornelius Garrabrants.

Our Survey of which said Portion (as laid down on Subdivision Schedule A) shews * and We adjudge it to be a Tract mark'd No 307 †

° Mindert Garrabrants died seized May 5, 1781. *Vide Note to Cos' Patent,* p 9. Mindert 4th sold a part of this Lot to Samuel T. Moore in 1834, who sold to Michael Saunier and Joseph Danielson three acres and seventy-five one-hundredths of an acre Aug. 25, 1835, who sold to Francis Price Aug. 20, 1836. Mindert sold thirty-two acres to Thomas Biggs Aug. 4, 1835, who sold to Justus E. Earle March 1, 1836, who sold to Francis Price. *Vide Note to Lot No.* 207, p 119. He also sold to Moore seven acres and seventy-five hundredths of an acre Oct. 6, 1835, who sold to Francis Price Aug. 8, 1836.

† Cornelius died seized, and the Lot passed by will to his son Cornelius, and from him to his sons *Cornelius* and *Peter*. *Vide Note to Cos' Patent,* p. 9. Cornelius took the S. half and died seized. It was sold by Jane, his daughter and widow of Cornelius Van Horne, to Comstock, who sold to Niles. Peter took the north half and died seized. His administrators sold twenty-three and eighty-five one-hundredths acres to Michael Carling June 3, 1828. *Vide* also a deed to Cornelius Garrabrants of the same date for two Lots, one lying north of Cornelius and one south.

Beginning at a Stake (being the Northermost Corner of the Tract No 306 adjudged to said Myndert Garrabrants last above described) and from said Stake runs South fifty two Degrees and thirty Minutes East fifty two Chains and forty Links to the Edge of Slaugh's Meadow; Then returning to said Stake the Place of Beginning and from thence runs North thirty six Degrees and thirty Minutes East seven Chains and seventy two Links to a Stake; Thence South fifty two Degrees and thirty Minutes East fifty seven Chains to said Slaugh's Meadow then down along betwixt the Upland and Meadow 'till it meets the first Line that runs to said Meadow Containing (after an Allowance for the Hill) about forty one Acres.

And we adjudge a certain Portion of said Allotment No 263 to belong to said Myndart Garrabrants.

Our Survey of which said Portion (as laid down on Subdivision Schedule B) shews, and we adjudge it to be a Tract mark'd No 407 *

Beginning at a Stake (being the Southermost Corner of a Lot of Common Land allotted to Frederick Philipse's Patent mark'd on the Map No 262) and from said Stake runs South thirty six Degrees West thirteen Chains and fifty Links to a Stake, Thence North forty three Degrees and forty five Minutes West sixty five Chains and thirty five Links to Hackinsack River; Then North thirty one Degrees East three Chains & forty one Links up along said River to a Stake (being a Corner of a Lot of Meadow in Paulus Pieterse's Patent mark'd on the Map No 120). Thence South fifty four Degrees and ten Minutes East Eleven Chains and twenty Links to a Stake between the Meadow and Upland; Thence along the Edge of the Meadow North twenty two Degrees East eight Chains and seventy five Links to a Stake (being the westerly Corner of said Lot of Common Land allotted to Frederick Philipse's Patent, Then along the Line thereof South forty three Degrees and forty five Minutes East fifty six Chains and fifty Links to the Place of Beginning. Containing about seventy seven Acres and a Half.

And we adjudge a certain Portion of said Allotment No 263 To belong to said Cornelius Garrabrants.

Our Survey of which said Portion (as laid down on Subdivision Schedule B) * shews, and we adjudge it to be a Tract mark'd No 408 †

*131

Beginning at a Stake (being the Southermost Corner of the Tract No 407 adjudged to said Myndert Garrabrants last above described) and

---

* This Lot lies in Greenville, S. of Myrtle avenue. Mindert died Sept. 20, 1814, leaving children, *Mindert, Catherine*, wife of Garret Van Horne, and *Hannah*, wife of Michael Vreeland. The two sisters bought out their brother July 3, 1815, and partitioned by deed Oct. 20, 1815, Michael taking the N. E. half, and Catherine the S. W. half. Catherine left it to her sons *John G.* and *Mindert*. They partitioned April 14, 1838. Mindert sold his share to Jacob Stolz, who sold to Bidwell.

† *Vide Note to Cos' Patent*, p. 12, and *Note to Lot No.* 307, p. 130. *Jane*, daughter of Cornelius Garrabrants and widow of Cornelius Van Horne, yet owns the part her father received. Peter died seized, and commissioners were appointed Jan. Term, 1837, who sold to Garret Vreeland 23 96-100 acres, who sold to Abraham Post July 5, 1837.

from said Stake runs South thirty six Degrees West ten Chains and twelve Links to a Stake, Thence South fifty Degrees West one Chain and eighty eight Links to a Stake, Thence North forty three Degrees and forty five Minutes West sixty eight Chains and twenty Links to a Stake by the Side of Hackinsack River, Then up along said River North sixty five Degrees and ten Minutes East five Chains and forty eight Links; Then North thirty one Degrees East six Chains and ninety three Links up along said River to a Stake (being the Westerly Corner of the Tract No 407 last above described) Thence South forty three Degrees and forty five Minutes East sixty five Chains and thirty five Links to the Place of Beginning, Containing about seventy seven Acres and a Half.

With Respect to the two Lots of Common Land which have been allotted to the Patent of Philip Carteret to Nicholas Jansen Baker, dated the twelfth Day of May One thousand six hundred and sixty eight, being these two Lots of Common Land which in the Field Book & Map of the General Partition are distinguished by the Numbers 206 & 259

Cornelius Jorsen Blinkerhof claimed the said two Lots and no other Person or Persons claiming the same or a Subdivision thereof We upon Examination of his Title conceive him to be the true Proprietor And do therefore adjudge the said two Allotments to belong to him.

* This is a Subdivision of the Lot of Common Land which has been allotted To the first Patent of Philip Carteret to Fytje Hartman dated the twelfth Day of May one thousand six hundred and sixty eight—being that Lot of Common Land which in the Field Book & Map of the General Partition is distinguished by the Number 205. *132

And upon Examination of the Titles of the several Persons claiming Parts and Shares thereof,

We do adjudge a certain Portion of said Allottment No 205 to belong to Michael Corneliese Vreelandt.

Our Survey of which said Portion (as laid down on Subdivision Schedule A) shews and We adjudge it to be a Tract mark'd No 301 *

Beginning at a Stake (being the westerly Corner of said Allotment No 205) and from said Stake runs South fifty two Degrees and thirty Minutes East forty seven Chains to Slaugh's Meadow, Then returning to said Stake the Place of Beginning and from thence runs North thirty six Degrees and thirty Minutes East three Chains and twelve Links to a Stake; Thence South fifty two Degrees and thirty Minutes East forty seven Chains to said Slaugh's Meadow; Then Southward along betwixt the Meadow and Upland 'til it meets the first mentioned Line running to said Meadow—Containg (after an Allowance for the Hill) about thirteen Acres and two Tenths.

* *Vide Note to Lot No. 204, p. 85.*

And we adjudge a certain Portion of said Allotment No 205 to belong to Michael Hartman Vreelandt.

Our Survey of which said Portion (as laid down on Subdivision Schedule A) shews and we adjudge it to be a Tract mark'd No 302 *

*133   * **Beginning** at a Stake (being the Northerly Corner of the Tract No 301 adjudged to Michael Corneliese Vreelandt last above describ'd) And from thence runs South fifty two Degrees and thirty Minutes East forty seven Chains to Slaugh's Meadow, Then returning to said Stake the Place of Beginning, and from thence runs North thirty six Degrees and thirty Minutes East three Chains and twelve Links to a Stake, Thence South fifty two Degrees & thirty Minutes East forty seven Chains to said Slaugh's Meadow; Then Southward along betwixt the Meadow and Upland 'til it meets the first mentioned Line running to said Meadow — Containing (after an Allowance for the Hill) about thirteen Acres & two Tenths

And we adjudge a certain Portition of said Allotment No 205 To belong to Johannis Vreelandt.

Our Survey of which said Portion (as laid down on Subdivision Schedule A) shews, and we adjudge it to be a Tract mark'd No 303 †

Beginning at a Stake being the Northerly Corner of the Tract No 302 adjudged to Michael Hartman Vreelandt last above describ'd) And from thence runs South fifty two Degrees and thirty Minutes East forty seven Chains to Slaugh's Meadow, Then returning to said Stake the

---

° Until the title comes to Stephen Vreeland. *Vide Note to Dirck Claesen's 1st Patent*, p. 12. Stephen sold the Lot to Michael Saunier and Joseph Danielson Oct. 7, 1835, who sold to Joseph Alphonse Loubat May 4, 1836, who sold to Francis Cottenet May 28, 1836, who sold to John W. Leavitt Feb. 28, 1841, the same lot, also eighty-eight one-hundredths of an acre. *Vide Note to Lot No. 204.*

† Vreeland died seized and intestate, and this lot passed by descent to his daughter Antje, wife of Johannis Van Wagenen. By his will, dated Nov. 24, 1792, and by her will, dated May 27, 1794, proved Sept. 1, 1794, they gave all their property to their two children, *Leah*, wife of David Lozier, and *Antje*, wife of Guilliam Outwater, for life equally, and then to the children of each. These devisees partitioned by mutual release Nov. 26, 1799; Lozier taking the north half, containing seven acres, one rood, and sixteen perches, and Outwater the south half. Leah Lozier died in 1809, leaving children, *Altje*, wife of Simon Campbell; *Jane*, wife of William A. Ackerman; and *Antje*, wife of Jacob H. Brinkerhoff. Antje Outwater died, leaving children, *Jacob G., John G., Matilda,* wife of Abraham Sickels, and *Altje*, wife of Michael G. Vreeland. Vreeland *et ux*. sold all their interest to Abraham Sickles Sept. 12, 1809. William A. Ackerman and wife sold their interest (one undivided third) in Lozier's half to Cornelius Bogert June 25, 1833. Bogert, Campbell, and Brinkerhoff sold the Lozier half to Michael Saunier June 17, 1835, who sold to Loubat Oct. 24, 1835. Jacob G. Outwater sold three and a-half acres (of the Outwater half) to Henry Drayton Dec. 30, 1835, who sold to Ebenezer Deas June 1, 1835 (deed unrecorded), who sold to Joseph Alphonse Loubat Oct. 7, 1835.

The partition between Lozier and Outwater was confirmed by the Orphan's Court Nov. 26, 1799. *Vide Note to Lot No. 399*, p. 140.

Place of Beginning and from thence runs North thirty six Degrees and thirty Minutes East three Chains and twelve Links to a Stake, Thence South fifty two Degrees and thirty Minutes East forty seven Chains to said Slaugh's Meadow, Then Southward along betwixt the Meadow and Upland 'till it meets the first mentioned Line running to said Meadow, Containing (after an Allowance for the Hill about thirteen Acres and two Tenths.

    And we adjudge a certain Portion of said Allotment No 205 To belong to John Van Horne

        Our Survey of which said Portion (as laid down on Subdivision Schedule A) shews and we adjudge it to be a Tract mark'd No 304 *

    Beginning at a Stake (being the Northerly Corner of the Tract No 303 adjudged to Johannis Vreelandt last above describ'd) and from said Stake runs South fifty two Degrees and thirty Minutes East forty seven Chains to Slaugh's Meadow, Then returning to said Stake the Place of Beginning; and from thence runs North thirty six Degrees and thirty Minutes East twelve Chains & forty Links to a Stake, Thence South fifty two Degrees * and thirty Minutes East forty eight Chains to said *134 Slaugh's Meadow, Then Southward along betwixt the Meadow and Upland 'til it meets the first mentioned Line running to said Meadow, Containing (after an Allowance for the Hill) about fifty two Acres & Eight Tenths.

    And we adjudge a certain Portion of said Allotment No 205 To belong to Cornelius Jorsen Blinkerhoof.

        Our Survey of which said Portion (as laid down on Subdivision Schedule A) shews and we adjudge it to be a Tract mark'd No 305 †

    Beginning at a Stake (being the Northerly Corner of the Tract No 304 adjudged to John Van Horne last above describ'd) And from said

---

    ° Van Horne devised this lot to his sons *John* and *Garret*. Garret died seized of an undivided half April 7, 1808. He devised it to his two sons, *John G.* and *Mindert*. They and the uncle partitioned Dec. 13, 1817. *Vide Note to Hartman's 1st Patent*, p. 11. John took the south half, and they the north half. Of their half, the part ying between the Bull's Ferry Road and the Bergen lots, they sold to William Spencer Inch; between the road and river, nine and a half acres, they sold to Michael Saunier June 10, 1836. By will, dated Aug. 12, 1343, John gave his interest in this lot to his son *John J.*, and his grandsons, John G. and Stephen C., sons of *Garret*. Stephen died at sea, July 15, 1842, intestate and without issue, and his interest passed to his uncle John J. and brother John G. *Vide Note to Lot No. 273*, p 92, and *Note to Lot No. 393*, p. 136. By his will, John divided up his property; the lot just below Myrtle avenue (i.e., his half of *Lot No. 393*), his part of *Lot No. 273*, and his part of *Lot No. 304*, to his son *John*, John G. and *Stephen C.*, children of his son *Garret*, and Agnes and Jane, children of his son *Peter*. John received the homestead on the shore, where he now lives.

    † For a history of this title until it gets into Henry, Cornelius, and John Brinkerhoff, *Vide Note to De Backer's Patent*, p. 10. These three partitioned, Henry taking the south third, Cornelius the next north, and John the upper.

Stake runs South fifty two Degrees and thirty Minutes East forty eight Chains to the Edge of Slaugh's Meadow, Then returning to said Stake the Place of Beginning; And from thence runs North thirty six Degrees and thirty Minutes East two Chains and sixty nine Links to a Stake (being the Northermost Corner of said Allotment No 205), Then South fifty two Degrees and thirty Minutes East forty eight Chains to said Slaugh's Meadow, Then Southward along betwixt the Meadow and Upland 'til it meets the first mentioned Line running to said Meadow, Containing (after an Allowance for the Hill) about Eleven Acres and Six Tenths.

This is a Subdivision of the Lot of Common Land which has been allotted To the Second Patent of Philip Carteret to Fytje Hartman dated the twelfth Day of May one thousand six hundred and sixty eight—being that Lot of Common Land which in the Field Book & Map of the General Partition is distinguished by the Number 260.

And upon Examination of the Titles of the several Persons claiming Parts & Shares thereof

*135   * **We** do adjudge a certain Portion of said Allotment No 260 To belong to Michael Hartman Vreelandt.

Our Survey of which said Portion (as laid down on Subdivision Schedule B) shews, and we adjudge it to be a Tract mark'd No 397 *

Beginning at a Stake (being the Northerly Corner of Allotment No 260) and from thence runs South forty three Degrees and forty five Minutes East twenty Chains and forty seven Links to a Stake; Thence South forty six Degrees and fifteen Minutes West five Chains and eighty three Links to a Stake, Thence North forty three Degrees and forty five Minutes West nineteen Chains and forty two Links to a Stake in the Road, Thence North thirty six Degrees East five Chains and ninety four Links to the Place of Beginning, Containing about Eleven Acres and a Half.

And we adjudge a certain Portion of said Allotment No 260 To belong to Michael Corneliese Vrelandt.

Our Survey of which said Portion (as laid down on Subdivision Schedule B) shews, and We adjudge it to be a Tract mark'd No 396 †

Beginning at a Stake (being the Easterly Corner of the Tract No 397 adjudged to Michael Hartman Vrelandt last above described) and from thence runs South forty six Degrees and fifteen Minutes West five Chains and sixty Links to a Stake, Thence South forty three Degrees and forty five Minutes East twelve Chains and sixty nine Links to a Stake, Thence North twenty eight Degrees East five Chains and ninety Links to a Stake (being the Eastermost Corner of said Allotment No 260) Thence North forty three Degrees and forty five Minutes West ten Chains and eighty one Links to the Place of Beginning, Containing about six Acres and six Tenths.

---

* Until the title comes to Stephen Vreeland. *Vide Note to Claesen's 1st Patent,* p. 12.
† *Vide Note to Lot No. 204,* p. 85.

And we adjudge a certain Portion of said Allotment No 260 To belong to George Vreelandt Esqr.

Our Survey of which said Portion (as laid down on Subdivision Schedule B) shews, and we adjudge it to be a Tract mark'd No 394 *

* **Beginning** at a Stake (being the westerly Corner of the Tract No *136 396 adjudged to Michael Corneliese Vreelandt last above described, and from said Stake runs South forty six Degrees and fifteen Minutes West three Chains and seventy three Links to a Stake, Thence South forty three Degrees and forty five Minutes East thirteen Chains and twenty two Links to a Stake, Thence North forty two Degrees East two Chains and eighty Links to a Stake, Thence North twenty eight Degrees East one Chain to a Stake, Thence North forty three Degrees and forty five Minutes West twelve Chains and sixty nine Links to the Place of Beginning, Containing about four Acres and nine Tenths.

And we adjudge a certain Portion of said Allotment No 260 To belong to Johannis Vreelandt.

Our Survey of which said Portion (as laid down on Subdivision Schedule B) shews, And we adjudge it to be a Tract mark'd No 395 †

Beginning at a Stake (being the westerly Corner of the Tract No 394 adjudged to George Vreelandt last above described) And from thence runs North forty three Degrees and forty five Minutes West eighteen Chains and eighty two Links to a Stake in the Road, Thence North thirty six Degrees East three Chains and fifty four Links to a Stake (being the westermost Corner of the Tract No 397 adjudged to Michael Hartman Vreelandt above described), Thence South forty three Degrees and forty five Minutes East nineteen Chains and forty two Links to a Stake, Thence South forty six Degrees and fifteen Minutes West three Chains and fifty Links to the Place of Beginning, Containing about six Acres and six Tenths.

And we adjudged a certain Portion of said allotment No 260 To belong to John Van Horne,

Our Survey of which said Portion (as laid down on Subdivision Schedule B) shews, and we adjudge it to be a Tract marked No 393 ‡

Beginning at a Stake in the Road (being the westerly Corner of the Tract No 395 adjudged to Johannis Vreelandt last above described) And from thence runs South forty three Degrees and forty five Minutes East

---

◦ *Vide Note to Lot No.* 212, p. 86. Richard Vreeland conveyed his share in this lot to Michael, son of Michael Vreeland of Stony Point, July 22, 1833. George conveyed to Sannier and Danielson.

† *Vide Note to Lot No.* 303, p. 133.

‡ *Vide Note to Lot No.* 273, p. 92. In the partition John took the northeast half and John G. and Mindert the southwest half. The Lot lay south of Myrtle ave. and east of the old road. John G. and Mindert sold to Jacob Stolz, who sold to Bidwell. John's half went to his three sons, John, Peter, and Garret. *Vide Note to Lot No.* 304, p. 133. John J. Van Horne sold four acres and eighty-six one-hundredths of an acre of this lot to Edmund C. Bramhall July 15, 1859.

(along the Lines of the Tracts No 395 & No 394 adjudged to Johannis Vreelandt and George Vreelandt) thirty two Chains and four Links to a Stake, Thence South forty two Degrees West seven Chains and seventy nine Links to a Stake, Thence North forty three Degrees & forty five *137 Minutes West thirty one Chains and * twenty Links to a Stake in the Road, Thence North thirty six Degrees East seven Chains and ninety Links to the Place of Beginning, Containing about twenty four Acres & seven Tenths

And we adjudged a certain Portion of said Allotment No 260 To belong to Joseph Waldron,

Our Survey of which Said Portion (as laid down on Subdivision Schedule B) shews & We adjudge it to be a Tract mark'd No 392 *

Beginning at a Stake in the Road (being in the westerly Corner of the Tract No 393 adjudged to John Vanhorne last above described) and from said Stake runs South forty three Degrees and forty five Minutes East eleven Chains and six Links to a Stake, Thence South forty six Degrees and fifteen Minutes West four Chains and sixty two Links to a Stake, Thence North forty three Degrees and forty five Minutes West ten Chains & twenty seven Links to a Stake (being the westerly Corner of said Allotment No 260) Thence North thirty six Degrees East four Chains and seventy Links to the Place of Beginning, Containing about five Acres.

And we adjudge a certain Portion of said Allotment No 260 To belong to James Collard.

Our Survey of which said Portion (as laid down on Subdivision Schedule B) shews and we adjudge it to be a Tract mark'd No. 390†

Beginning at a Stake (being the Southerly Corner of the Tract No 393 adjudged to John Vanhorne above described) and from said Stake runs South forty two Degrees West four Chains and sixty three Links to a Stake (being the Southerly Corner of said Allotment No 260), Thence North forty three Degrees and forty five Minutes West ten Chains and thirty four Links to a Stake, Thence North forty six Degrees and fifteen Minutes East four Chains and sixty two Links to a Stake, Thence South forty three Degrees and forty five Minutes East ten Chains to the Place of Beginning, Containing about four Acres and nine Tenths.

*138   * And as to the remaining Part or Portion of said Allotment No 260 being the Proportion which we adjudge to one equal fourteenth Part of this Patent Michael Van Veghten deceased (son of Dirck Van Veghten and Jannitje Michielse) was the person we find last seized of said one fourteenth Part of the Patent

---

○ Waldron sold this lot to Cornelius Garrabrants May 23, 1769. *Vide Note to Cos' Patent*, p. 15. Cornelius and Peter partitioned, Cornelius taking the south half, which his daughter Jane, widow of Cornelius Van Horne, sold to —— Harrison. Peter took the north half, which he sold to Isaac Van Wart Nov. 6, 1819.

† Collerd by will, dated Nov. 27, 1790, proved Dec. 6, 1791, gave all his realty to his son *John*. John sold this lot to John E. Post April 1, 1810.

but it not appearing satisfactorily to us in whom the same is now vested We declare not to whom the said remaining Part or Portion of Common Land does now belong.

Our Survey of which said remaining Part or Portion (as laid down on Subdivision Schedule B) shews and we adjudged it to be a Tract mark'd No 391

Beginning at a Stake (being the Northerly Corner of the Tract No 390 adjudg'd to James Collard last above described) And from the said Stake runs South forty six Degrees and fifteen Minutes West four Chains and sixty two Links to a Stake, Thence North forty three Degrees and forty five Minutes West Ten Chains and fourteen Links to a Stake, Thence North forty six Degrees and fifteen Minutes East four Chains and sixty two Links to a Stake, Thence South forty three Degrees and forty five Minutes East ten Chains and fourteen Links to the Place of Beginning, Containing about four Acres and nine Tenths.

This is a Subdivision of the Lots of Common Land which have been allotted to the first Patent of Philip Carteret to Dirck Clossen dated the twelfth Day of May one thousand six hundred & sixty eight, being these two Lots of Common Land which in the Field Book & Map of the General Partition are distinguished by the Numbers 213 and 261.

And upon Examination of the Titles of Michaelse Hartman Vreelandt and Johannis Vreelandt.

* **We** adjudge a certain Portion of said Allotment No 213 to *139 belong to said Michielse Hartman Vreelandt.

Our Survey of which said Portion (as laid down on Subdivision Schedule A) shews and we adjudge it to be a Tract mark'd No 308 *

Beginning at a Stake (being the westerly Corner of said Allotment No 213) and from said Stake runs South fifty two Degrees and thirty Minutes East fifty nine Chains to Hudson's River, Thence returning to said Stake the Place of Beginning and from thence runs Northerly thirty six Degrees and thirty Minutes East four Chains and thirty eight Links to a Stake, Thence South fifty two Degrees and thirty Minutes East fifty seven Chains to said Hudson's River, Then down along said River 'til it meets the first mentioned Line Containing (after an Allowance for the Hill) about twenty four Acres.

And we adjudge a certain portion of said Allotment No 213 to belong to said Johannis Vreelandt.

Our Survey of which said Portion (as laid down on

ᵃ Until the title comes to Stephen Vreeland. *Vide Note to Dirck Claesen's* 1st *Patent,* p. 12. Stephen Vreeland to Abraham Bertholf, two acres and sixty-two one-hundredths of an acre, bounded, northeast by David Lozier, southeast by the river, southwest by Garret Vreeland, northwest by grantor, May 4, 1814. This included a small lot in the southeast corner of the tract. He sold the balance of the lot to William Cooper July 8, 1833. Bertholf sold to Jacob G. Dyckman Oct. 3, 1835, who sold to Cooper Oct. 6, 1835. The village of Guttenberg is partly on this lot.

Subdivision Schedule A) shews, and we adjudge it to be a Tract mark'd No 309 *

Beginning at a Stake (being the Northerly Corner of the Tract No 308 adjudged to Michaelse Hartman Vreelandt last above described) and from said Stake runs South fifty two Degrees and thirty Minutes East fifty seven Chains to Hudson's River, Then returning to said Stake the Place of Beginning and from thence runs North thirty six Degrees and thirty Minutes, East four Chains and fifty five Links to a Stake (being the Northermost Corner of said Allotment No 213), Thence South fifty two Degrees and thirty minutes East fifty five Chains to said Hudson's River, Then down along said River 'til it meets the first mentioned Line, Containing (after an Allowance for the Hill) about twenty four Acres.

And we adjudge a certain Portion of said Allotment No 261 to belong to said Michaelse Hartman Vreelandt.

Our Survey of which said Portion (as laid down on Subdivision Schedule B) shews and we adjudge it to be a Tract mark'd No 398 †

*140 * **Beginning** at a Stake in the Road (being the westermost Corner of said Allotment No 261) And from thence runs North thirty six Degrees East thirteen Chains and eighty five Links to a Stake in the Road; Thence South forty three Degrees and forty five Minutes East twenty eight Chains and seventy nine Links to a Stake, Thence South Twenty eight Degrees West fourteen Chains and fifty three Links to a Stake, Thence North forty three Degrees and forty five Minutes West thirty one Chains and twenty eight Links to the Place of Beginning, Containing about forty one Acres.

And we adjudge a certain Portion of said Allotment No 261 to belong to said Johannis Vreelandt.

Our Survey of which said Portion (as laid down on Subdivision Schedule B) shews, and we adjudge it to be a Tract mark'd No 399 ‡

---

* *Vide Note to Lot No.* 303, p. 133, and *Note to Lot No* 399, p. 140. Leah Lozier's share was afterwards owned by Cornelius C. Bogert, who sold the same, containing twelve acres, to William Cooper May 1, 1835. Outwater then owned the north half of the lot. The Outwater heirs sold three acres to Michael G. Vreeland Sept. 12, 1809, whose son Hartman sold it to Abraham Huyler, Dec. 31, 1827, who sold to Cooper Feb. 1, 1839. The whole lot is within the village of Guttenberg.

† *Vide Note to Dirck Claesen's 1st Patent*, p. 12. This lot and *Lot No*. 397, containing fifty-two and a half acres, were partitioned between Stephen and Michael, the former taking the south half, which was divided between his two sons, *Nicholas S.* and *Stephen B.* Michael took the north half, which was divided between his two sons, *Garret* and *Nicholas*, the former taking the north half and the latter the south half. Myrtle avenue lies on the line between *Lots Nos.* 397 and 398.

‡ *Vide Note to Lot No.* 303, p. 133. This lot was partitioned between Lozier and Outwater in 1794, Lozier taking the north half. Outwater the south half. The Newark and New York Railroad now passes through it. The heirs of Lozier, viz., his widow Leah and children, *Abby*, wife of Simon Campbell, *Jane*, wife of Wm. A. Ackerman, and *Anne*, wife of Jacob H. Brinkerhoff, sold his half to John E. Post

Beginning at a Stake (being the Northermost Corner of the Tract No 398 adjudged to Michielse Hartman Vreelandt last above described) And from thence runs North thirty six Degrees East thirteen Chains and forty three Links to a Stake (being the Northermost Corner of said Allotment No 261), Thence South fifty one Degrees and forty five Minutes East twenty five Chains and forty five Links to a Stake, Thence South twenty eight Degrees West seventeen Chains and seventy seven Links to a Stake, Thence North forty three Degrees and forty five Minutes West twenty eight Chains and seventy nine Links to the Place of Beginning, Containing about forty one Acres.

With respect to the Lot of Common Land which has been allotted To the second Patent of Philip Carteret to Derick Classen, dated the twelfth Day of May one thousand six hundred and sixty eight, being that Lot of Common Land which in the Field Book & Map of the General Partition is distinguished by the Number 204.

Michael Corneliese Vreelandt claimed the said Lot and upon Examination of his Title we conceive him to be the true Proprietor And do therefore adjudge the said Allotment to belong to him.

* With respect to three Lots of Common Land which have been allotted to the first Patent of Philip Carteret to Dirck Sycan dated the twelfth day of May One thousand six hundred and sixty eight, being these three Lots of Common Land, which in the Field Book and Map of the General Partition are distinguished by the Numbers 212, 258 and 265. *141

George Vreelandt Esqr claimed the said three Lots, and upon Examination of his Title we conceive him to be the true Proprietor, And do therefore adjudge the said three Allotments To belong to him.

This is a Subdivision of the Lot of Common Land which has been allotted to the Patent of William Kieft to Class Carstensen Normand, dated the twenty fifth Day of March one thousand six hundred and forty seven and confirmed (with an Addition of Land) by Patent from Philip Carteret to Lawrence Andriese dated the twenty sixth Day of March one thousand six hundred and sixty seven, being that Lot of Common Land which in the Field Book and Map of the General Partition is distinguished by the Number 266.

And upon Examination of the Titles of the several Persons claiming Parts and Shares thereof,

* **We** do adjudge a certain Portion of said Allotment No 266 to belong to Thomas Brown. *142

April 2, 1817, bounded north by the church lot, east by John Vreeland, south by heirs of Outwater, west by old road. The heirs of Outwater sold their interest to Michael G. Vreeland Sept. 12, 1809. By several deeds from the heirs of Outwater and Lozier, in 1852, all of their interest in this lot vested in Edmund C. Bramhall. Five acres were sold by Abraham Sickles to Jacob Prior June 15, 1813.

Our Survey of which said Portion (as laid down on Subdivision Schedule B) shews and we adjudge it to be a Tract mark'd No 413 *

Beginning at a Stake by New Ark Bay (being the northwestermost Corner of the Lot of Common Land at bergen Point No 172 sold for defraying the Expences of the General Partition) and from said Stake runs South fifty one Degrees East thirty Chains (along the Line of said Lot No 172 to a Stake being a Corner of said Lot No 172, Thence South eighty five Degrees East thirteen Chains and thirty seven Links (along the Line of said Lot No 172) to a Stake, Thence North thirty nine Degrees East twenty six Links to a Stake, Thence North fifty one Degrees West forty Chains and eighty three Links to a Stake by New Ark Bay; Thence down along the said Bay to the Place of Beginning, Containing about twenty seven Acres and seven Tenths.

And we adjudge a certain Portion of said Allotment No 266 to belong to Lawrence Brown, the only Son of Thomas Brown by his former Wife Anna.

Our Survey of which said Portion (as laid down on Subdivision Schedule B) shews, and we adjudge it to be a Tract mark'd No 414 †

Beginning at a Stake (being the Eastermost Corner of the Tract No 413 adjudged to Thomas Brown last above described) And from said Stake runs North fifty one Degrees West forty Chains and eighty three Links to a Stake by New Ark Bay. Then returning to said Stake the Place of Beginning And from thence runs North thirty nine Degrees East five Chains and ninety eight Links to a Stake; Thence North fifty one Degrees West forty Chains and fifty six Links to a Stake by New Ark Bay, Then down along said Bay 'till it meets the first mentioned Line, Containing about twenty four Acres and seven Tenths.

*143

* **And we** adjudge a certain Portion of said Allotment No 266 To belong to Fytje the wife of Andries Seegaerd

Our Survey of which said Portion (as laid down on Subdivision Schedule B) shews, and we adjudge it to be a Tract mark'd No 415 †

---

* Andrew Gautier and Thomas Gautier sold this and *Lots Nos.* 414 *and* 415 to Jasper Zabriskie April 12, 1798. Jacob Zabriskie conveyed the same to Hermanus Garretson Sept. 14, 1820, who conveyed it Jasper Zabriskie April 2, 1823. Zabriskie by will, without date, codicil dated Oct. 27, 1828, gave to his son Michael the "Red House" and lot at Bergen Point, containing about twelve acres; also seventeen acres between Mullany and Peter Vreeland, and to his grandson, Albert M., about fifty acres north of Benjamin Zabriskie. *Vide Note to Lot No.* 419, p. 155. To his grandson, Jasper Garretson, the remainder of his lands, including a lot at Bergen Point for life, then to the issue of his body. *Vide Note to Andriesen's Patent*, p. 13. This latter devise included the easterly portion of *Lots Nos.* 413, 414, 415. Garretson held possession until his death, Sept. 1. 1861. He left the following children as heirs of this property, viz., *Hartman, John H. K., Alathea W., Percival, Mary Ann*, and *Martha*, all minors. Guardians were appointed and the property partitioned by commissioners, report confirmed Oct. Term, 1861. *Vide Note to Lot No.* 14, p. 70.

† *Vide Note to Lot No.* 413, p. 142.

Beginning at a Stake (being the Eastermost Corner of the Tract No 414 adjudged to Lawrence Brown last above described) And from said Stake runs North fifty one Degrees West forty Chains and fifty six Links to a Stake by New Ark Bay, Then returning to said Stake the Place of Beginning and from thence runs North thirty nine Degrees East five Chains and eight Links to a Stake, Thence North fifty one Degrees West six Chains to a Stake, Thence North thirty nine Degrees East one Chain to a Stake, Thence North fifty one Degrees West thirty four Chains and twenty six Links to a Stake by New Ark Bay, Thence down along said Bay 'till it meets the first mentioned Line, Containing about twenty four Acres and seven Tenths.

And we adjudge a certain Portion of said Allotment No 266 to belong to Cornelius Jorsen Blinkerhoof

Our Survey of which said Portion (as laid down on Subdivision Schedule B) shews, and we adjudge it to be a Tract mark'd No 416 *

Beginning at a Stake (being the Eastermost Corner of the Tract No 415 adjudged to Fytje Seegaerd last above described) And from said Stake runs North thirty nine Degrees East two Chains to a Stake, Thence North fifty one Degrees West six Chains to a Stake. Thence South thirty nine Degrees West two Chains to a Stake, Thence South fifty one Degrees East six Chains to the Place of Beginning, Containing about One Acre & two Tenths.

And we adjudge a certain Portion of said Allotment No 266 To belong to George Vreelandt Esqr.

* **Our Survey** of which said Portion (as laid down on *144 Subdivision Schedule B) shews, and we adjudge it to be a Tract mark'd No 417 †

Beginning at a Stake (being the Eastermost Corner of the Tract No 416 adjudged to Cornelius Jorsen Blinkerhoof last above described) And from said Stake runs North fifty one Degrees West six Chains to a Stake, Thence South thirty nine Degrees West one Chain to a Stake, Thence North fifty one Degrees West thirty four Chains and twenty six Links to a Stake by New Ark Bay, Then returning to said Stake the Place of Beginning and from thence runs North thirty nine Degrees East four Chains and fifty six Links to a Stake (being the Eastermost Corner of said Allotment No 266,) Thence North fifty one Degrees West forty Chains to a Stake by New Ark Bay, Then down along said Bay 'till it meets the above mention'd Line that runs to said Bay, Containing about twenty one Acres and seven Tenths.

---

* *Vide Note to De Backer's Patent*, p. 10

† *Vide Note to Lot No.* 212, p. 86. On the partition this and lot 427 fell to John. He died seized, and Henry Newkirk *et al.* were appointed commissioners to sell his lands. They sold this lot to David La Tourette April 19, 1847; who conveyed part of it to Ellen, wife of Solon Humphreys, March 28, 1863, and part of it, with the adjoining lot (being part of *Lot No.* 267 sold to John G. Vreeland by Cornelius Van Buskirk). *Vide Note to Lot No.* 267, p. 88. Abraham B. Warner and Martin R. Cook now own part of *Lots Nos.* 414 *and* 415.

With respect to the two Lots of Common Land which have been allotted to the Patent of Petrus Stuyvesant to Lubert Gilbertse dated the fifth Day of December One thousand six hundred and fifty four, being these two Lots of Common Land which in the Field Book & Map of the General Partition are distinguished by the Numbers 278 & 267.

Jacob Van Wagenen claimed the said two Lots and no other Person or Persons claiming the same or a Subdivision thereof We upon Examination of his Title conceive him to be the true Proprietor and do therefor adjudge the said two Allotments to belong to him.

*145

* With respect to the two Lots of Common Land allotted to the Patent of Philip Carteret to Severin Lawrence dated the twelfth Day of May One thousand six hundred and sixty eight, being these two Lots of Common Land which in the Field Book & Map of the General Partition are distinguished by the Numbers 279 and 268.

Jacob Van Wagenen claimed the said two Lots and upon Examination of his Title we conceive him to be the true Proprietor and do therefor adjudge the said two Allotments to belong to him.

With respect to the two Lots of Common Land which have been allotted To the Patent of Philip Carteret to Hendrick Jansen Spier dated the twelfth Day of May one thousand six hundred and sixty eight, being these two Lots of Common Land which in the Field Book & Map of the General Partition are distinguished by the numbers 280 & 269.

Upon Examination of the Titles of the several Persons claiming being the Descendents of the Patentee, **We** do adjudge the said two Allotments to Catalintje Spier Widow for her Use during her natural Life; and in Trust for the Purposes mentioned and directed in the last Will and Testament of her Husband Barendt Spier dated the eighth Day of April one thousand seven hundred and forty two duly proved and recorded in the Prerogative Office at Perth Amboy.

*146

* **This** is a Subdivision of the Lot of Common Land which has been allotted To the second Patent of Philip Carteret to Derick Sycan dated the twelfth Day of May one thousand six hundred and sixty eight, being that Lot of Common Land which in the Field Book & Map of the General Partition is distinguished by the Number 271.

And upon Examination of the Titles of the several Persons claiming Parts and Shares thereof,

We do adjudge a certain Portion of said Allotment No 271 To belong to Michael Corneliese Vreelandt.

Our Survey of which said Portion (as laid down on

Subdivision Schedule B) shews, and we adjudge it to be a Tract mark'd No 422 *

Beginning at a Stake (being the Southermost Corner of said Allotment No 271) and from said Stake runs North fifty one Degrees West forty Chains to a Stake by New Ark Bay, Then returning to said Stake the Place of Beginning, And from thence runs North thirty nine Degrees East ten Chains and thirty one Links to a Stake, Thence North fifty one Degrees West fòrty Chains to a Stake by New Ark Bay, Then down along said Bay 'til it meets the first mentioned Line, Containing about forty one Acres.

And we adjudge a certain Portion of said Allotment No 271 to Jannitje Widow of Daniel Van Winkle during her Life, and after her Decease to her Daughter Antje now the Wife of Henry Fielding agreable to the Tenor of said Daniel Van Winkle's last Will and Testament, dated the third Day of June one thousand seven hundred and fifty one,

* **Our Survey** of which said Portion (as laid down on *147 Subdivision Schedule B) shews, and we adjudge it to be a Tract mark'd No 423 *

---

* *Vide Note to Sycan's 2d Patent*, p. 15. On partition between George and John Vreeland, John took the south half of this lot, and George the north half (the same then containing sixty acres). The partition was not formal. George died seized of part, devising the same to his children. His heirs divided the same into three parts, each containing ten acres and sixty-six one-hundredths of an acre; the north third was conveyed to Jacob Van Horne (†); the middle third to Thomas McDonald June 15, 1832; the southerly third to John Carragan. McDonald conveyed part of his third to Sebastian Jaclard July 17, 1854. Jaclard died seized, and his executors conveyed to Adele Buchanan Oct. 19, 1858. She died seized and the lot was inherited by her infant children, and by order in chancery was sold to Edward A. Willard.

† *Vide Note to Sycan's 2d Patent*, p. 15. Jan. 29, 1820, John Vreeland conveyed to Ann, Cornelia, Maria, Isabella, and Eliza, children of his daughter *Jannetje*, wife of Stephen Vreeland, 19 acres out of this lot and *Lot No.* 424, and eight acres out of *Lot No.* 269. He conveyed seven acres of *Lot No.* 269 to Cornelia Van Winkle Jan. 6, 1820. He also conveyed to her 23 acres of *Lots Nos.* 423 *and* 424. He also conveyed to his daughter Jane, wife of Aaron Newkirk, Jan. 29, 1820, seven acres out of *Lot No.* 269, and nineteen acres out of *Lots Nos.* 423 *and* 424. Jane Newkirk left her surviving her husband and *Cornelia*, wife of Daniel Vreeland, *Catherine*, wife of Cornelius Vreeland, and *Catelina*, wife of Cornelius Van Rypen. Catelina died before her father, leaving one child, *Jane*, who married Garrabrant Ryerson. The two daughters and granddaughter took Jane Newkirk's share in common. Aaron Newkirk gave his life estate to his two daughters by separate deeds July 1, 1832, who seem to have taken as by partition the land described in these deeds. Cornelia took the north part, and quit-claimed the south part to Catherine April 22, 1857, who sold to William Frost Aug. 16, 1859, who sold to Sidney L. Carragan June 8, 1863.

Abraham Van Buskirk owned about 3 acres in this tract adjoining the Plank road. He died in 1849, leaving *Jane*, wife of Henry Osborn, *Abraham* and *Cornelius* (*Peter* died before his father) who partitioned by deed Dec 15, 1849. Cornelius sold his share to Sidney L. Carragan Nov. 7, 1861. Garrabrant Ryerson *et ux.* sold half an acre to Thomas C. Crips June 1, 1838, near the present Station House. Crips sold to Jasper Cadmus Sept. 15, 1838, who sold to Elizabeth Cadmus Oct. 29, 1838.

Beginning at a Stake (being the Eastermost Corner of the Tract No 422 adjudged to Michael Corneliese Vreelandt last above described) And from said Stake runs North fifty one Degrees West forty Chains to a Stake by New Ark Bay, Then returning to said Stake the Place of Beginning; And from thence runs North thirty nine Degrees East ten Chains and thirty one Links to a Stake, Thence North fifty one Degrees West forty one Chains and forty nine Links to a Stake by New Ark Bay, Then down along said Bay 'till it meets the first mentioned Line, Containing about forty one Acres.

This is a Subdivision of the Lot of Common Land which has been allotted to the Patent of Philip Carteret to Thomas Davison, dated the twenty second Day of December one thousand six hundred and sixty nine, being that Lot of Common Land which in the Field Book and Map of the General Partition is distinguished by the Number 272.

And upon Examination of the Titles of sundry Persons claiming parts and Shares thereof

We adjudge a certain Portion of said Allotment No 272 to belong to Michael Corneliese Vreelandt

Our Survey of which said Portion (as laid down on Subdivision Schedule B) shews and we adjudge it to be a Tract mark'd No 425 *

*148 * **Beginning** at a Stake (being the Eastermost Corner of said Allotment No 272) And from said Stake runs North fifty one Degrees West forty two Chains and twenty Links to a Stake by New Ark Bay, Then returning to said Stake the Place of Beginning, and from thence runs South thirty nine Degrees West five Chains and one Link to a Stake, Thence North fifty one Degrees West forty one Chains and eighty four Links to a Stake by New Ark Bay, Then up along said Bay 'till it meets the first mentioned Line containing about twenty one Acres.

And we adjudge a certain Portion of said Allotment No 272 to Jannitje Widow of Daniel Van Winkle during her Life, and at her Decease to her daughter Antje now the Wife of Henry Fielding agreable to the Tenor of said Daniel Van Winkle's last Will and Testament dated the third Day of June one thousand seven hundred and fifty one.

Our Survey of which said Portion as laid down on Subdivision Schedule B) shews, and we adjudge it to be a Tract mark'd No 424 †

Beginning at a Stake (being the Southermost Corner of the Tract No 425 adjudg'd to Michael Corneliese Vreelandt last above described) and from said Stake runs North fifty one Degrees West forty one Chains and eighty four Links to a Stake by New Ark Bay, Then returning to said Stake the Place of Beginning, and from thence runs South thirty nine Degrees West five Chains and two Links to a Stake (being the

---

* *Vide Note to Sycan's 2d Patent*, p. 15. Michael Vreeland sold this lot to Egbert Post July 9, 1787. By will, dated Feb. 11, 1822, proved May 8, 1822, Post gave this lot to his grandson Garret Wauters.

† *Vide Note to Lot No.* 423, p. 147.

Southerly Corner of said Allotment No 272) Thence North fifty one Degrees West forty one Chains and forty nine Links to a Stake by New Ark Bay, Then up along said Bay 'till it meets the first mentioned Line, Containing about twenty one Acres.

*149 * With Respect to the Lot of Common Land which has been allotted to the Patent of Philip Carteret to Thomas Davison dated the twelfth Day of December One thousand six hundred and sixty nine, being that Lot of Common Land which in the Field Book and Map of the General Partition is distinguished by the Number 275.

George Cadmus claimed the said Lot and upon Examination of his Title we conceive him to be the true Proprietor thereof, and do therefore adjudge the said Allotment to belong to him.

With Respect to the Lot of Common Land which has been allotted to the Patent of Petrus Stuyvesant to Peter Jansen Slaat dated the fifth Day of December One thousand six hundred and fifty four, confirm'd by Patent from Philip Carteret to said Slaat dated the twelfth Day of May one thousand six hundred and sixty eight, being that Lot of Common Land which in the Field Book and Map of the General Partition is distinguished by the Number 274.

George Cadmus claimed the said Lot and upon Examination of his Title, we conceive him to be the true Proprietor thereof and do therefore adjudge the said Allotment to belong to him.

*150 * With respect to the Lot of Common Land which has been allotted to the Patent of Petrus Stuyvesant to Hendrick Jansen Van Schalckwyck dated the fifth Day of December one thousand six hundred & fifty four, confirmed by Patent from Philip Carteret to Hessel Vygerse dated the thirteenth Day of March one thousand six hundred and seventy five; being that Lot of Common Land which in the Field Book & Map of the General Partition is distinguished by the Number 273.

John Van Horne claimed the said Lot and upon Examination of his Title We conceive him to be the true Proprietor thereof and do therefore adjudge the said Allotment to belong to him.

With respect to the Lot of Common Land which has been allotted to the Patent of Philip Carteret To Catharine formerly the Widow of Jacob Wallingen Van Horne, then the Widow of Jacob Stoffelsen dated the thirty first Day of March one thousand six hundred and sixty eight, being that Lot of Common Land which in the Field Book & Map of the General Partition is distinguished by the Number 276.

Jacob Van Horne claimed the said Lot, and no other Person or Persons claiming the same, or a Subdivision thereof We upon Examination of his Title, conceive him to be the true Proprietor and do therefore adjudge the said Allotment to belong to him.

*151 * **This** is a Subdivision of the Lot of Common Land which has been allotted to the Patent of Philip Carteret To

Barnt Christian, dated the twenty sixth day of March one thousand six hundred and sixty seven, being that Lot of Common Land which in the Field Book and Map of the General Partition is distinguished by the Number 277.

And upon Examination of the Titles of the several Persons claiming Parts and Shares thereof,

We do adjudge a certain Portion of said Allotment No 277 To belong to Fytje the wife of Andries Seegaerd.

Our Survey of which said Portion (as laid down on Subdivision Schedule B.) shews and we adjudge it to be a Tract mark'd No 426 *

Beginning at a Stone mark'd B (being the westermost Corner of said Allotment No 277) and from said Stone runs North thirty nine Degrees East four Chains and twelve Links to a Stake, Thence South fifty one Degrees East thirteen Chains and seventeen Links to a Stake, Thence South twenty eight Degrees & thirty Minutes West four Chains and eighteen Links to a Stake, Thence North fifty one Degrees West thirteen Chains and ninety five Links to the Place of Beginning, Containing about five Acres and a Half.

And we do adjudge a certain Portion of said Allotment No 277 To belong to George Vreelandt Esqr

*152

* **Our Survey** of which said Portion (as laid down on Subdivision Schedule B) shews, and We adjudge it to be a Tract mark'd No 427 †

Beginning at a Stake (being the Northerly Corner of the Tract No 426 adjudg'd to Fytje the wife of Andries Seegaerd last above described and from said Stake runs North thirty nine Degrees East four Chains and ninety four Links to a Stake, Thence South fifty one Degrees East twelve Chains and fifteen Links to a Stake, Thence South twenty eight Degrees and thirty Minutes West five Chains and two Links to a Stake; Thence North fifty one Degrees West thirteen Chains and seventeen Links to the Place of Beginning, Containing about six Acres and two Tenths.

And we adjudge a certain Portion of said Allotment No 277 To belong to Lawrence Brown the only Son of Thomas Brown by his former Wife Anna.

Our Survey of which said Portion (as laid down on Subdivision Schedule B) shews, and we adjudge it to be a Tract mark'd No 428 ‡

Beginning at a Stake (being the Northermost Corner of the Tract No 427 adjudged to George Vreelandt Esqr last above described) and from said Stake runs North thirty nine Degrees East five Chains and

---

◦ *Vide Note to Andriesen's Patent*, p. 13.

† *Vide Note to Lot No.* 212, p. 86.

‡ *Vide Note to Andriesen's Patent*, p. 13. Lawrence died seized, intestate and without issue. Shortly after the allotment, Peter Cole was in possession of this lot. He sold it to Cornelius Van Buskirk March 27, 1797 (deed unrecorded). *Vide Note to Stoffelsen's Patent*, p. 18.

thirty seven Links to a Stake, Thence South fifty one Degrees East eleven Chains and twenty four Links to a Stake standing in the Line of Barnt Christian's Patent, Thence South twenty eight Degrees and thirty Minutes West five Chains and forty nine Links to a Stake, Then North fifty one Degrees West twelve Chains and fifteen Links to the Place of Beginning, Containing about six Acres and two Tenths.

And we adjudge a certain Portion of said Allotment No 277 to belong to Thomas Brown.

* **Our Survey** of which said Portion (as laid down on Subdivision Schedule B) shews and we adjudge it to be a Tract mark'd No 429 *   *153

Beginning at a Stake (being the northermost Corner of the Tract No 428 adjudged to his son Lawrence Brown last above described) and from said Stake runs North thirty nine Degrees East five Chains and sixteen Links to a Stake, Thence South fifty one Degrees East ten Chains and thirty one Links to a Stake standing in the Line of Barnt Christian's Patent, Thence South twenty eight Degrees and thirty Minutes West five Chains and twenty two Links to a Stake, Thence North fifty one Degrees West eleven Chains and twenty four Links to the Place of Beginning, Containing about five Acres & a Half.

And we adjudge the two following Portions of said Allotment No 277 To belong to Jacob Vanhorne,

Our Survey of the first whereof (as laid down on Subdivision Schedule B) shews and we adjudge it to be a Tract mark'd No 430 †

Beginning at a Stake (being the northermost Corner of the Tract No 429 adjudged to Thomas Brown last above described) And from said Stake runs North thirty nine Degrees East forty one Chains and fifty six Links to a Stake (being the easternmost Corner of the Allotment of Common Land No 275) Thence North forty two Degrees west five Chains and fifty Links to a Stake (being the Southermost Corner of the Allotment of Common Land No 276) Thence North thirty nine Degrees East seven Chains and seventy two Links to a Stake (standing in the Line of Catharine Stoffelson's Patent) Thence South twenty seven Degrees and thirty Minutes East seven Chains and seventy two Links to a Stake (being the Northermost Corner of Barnt Christian's Patent) Thence (along the Line of said Barnt Christian's Patent) South twenty eight Degrees and thirty Minutes West forty seven Chains and ninety Links to a Stake (being the Easternmost Corner of the Tract No 429 adjudged To Thomas Brown last above described) Thence North fifty one Degrees West ten Chains and thirty one Links to the Place of Beginning.

* **Our Survey** of the other or second of said two Portions (as laid down on Subdivision Schedule B) shews and we adjudge it to be a Tract No 431 †   *154

○ Brown devised his lands in New Jersey as stated in *Note to Andriesen's Patent* p. 13. This lot was sold to Cornelius Van Buskirk May 13, 1797.

† *Vide Note to Stoffelsen's Patent*, p. 18.

JACOB VAN BUSKIRK.

Beginning at a Stake (being the Southermost Corner of the Tract No 426 adjudged to Fytje the Wife of Andries Seegaerd above described) and from said Stake runs North twenty eight Degrees and thirty Minutes East twelve Chains and fifty Links to a Stake (being the westermost Corner of Barnt Christian's Patent) Thence South twenty seven Degrees and thirty Minutes East fifteen Chains and sixty five Links to a Stake by the Meadow Edge, Thence South twenty Degrees West two Chains and thirty Links, Thence South forty Degrees West four Chains to a Stake, Thence North fifty one Degrees West twelve Chains and sixty seven Links to the Place of Beginning the said two Portions, Containing about forty three Acres and six Tenths.

153

This is a **Subdivision** of the Lot of Common Land which has been allotted to the Patent of Richard Nicolls to Nicholas Jansen and Samuel Edsall dated the twenty sixth Day of October, one thousand six hundred and sixty four, being that Lot of Common Land which in the Field Book & Map of the General Partition is distinguished by the Number 270.

And Upon Examination of the Titles of the several Persons Claiming Parts and Shares thereof,

We do adjudge a certain Portion of said Allotment No 270, To belong to Jacobus Van Buskirk.

Our Survey of which said Portion (as laid down on Subdivision Schedule B) shews and we adjudge it to be a Tract mark'd No 418 *

º *Vide Note to Jansen and Edsall's Patent,* p. 19. Van Buskirk by will gave four acres out of this lot to his son *Peter.* The residue he directed to be divided into four parts, and lots cast for a division between his sons *Peter* and *John.* They divided by deed March 25, 1767. Peter took the southwest half, and John the northeast half.

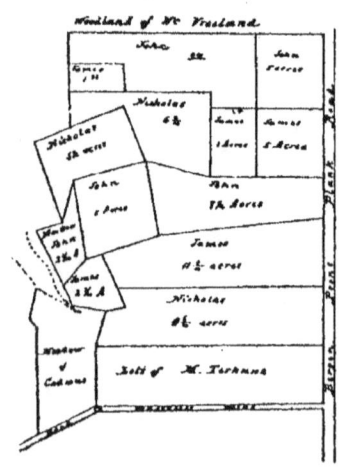

154

John left his interest in the tract to his son *Jacobus,* who by will, dated Sept. 8, 1823, gave all his realty to his sons, *John, Nicholas,* and *James.* They partitioned, as per diagram (in part). The map of their partition is on file. Peter by will, dated April 1, 1816, proved Aug. 7, 1819, gave eighty acres of upland and fifty acres of meadow to the children of his daughter *Rachel,* wife of William Vreeland. These were *William, Peter, Cornelius, Elizabeth,* wife of John Cadmus, and *Margaret,* wife of Jaspar Cadmus, jr. These, with their father, sold to George W. Bruen, May 2, 1836, what they received under their grandfather's will. Bruen gave five several mortgages to these five heirs May 2, 1836. Peter assigned his mortgage to Hartman Vreeland and David M. Demarest May 11, 1840. It was foreclosed, and the property sold by Sheriff Newkirk to Vreeland and Demarest, Wm. Vreeland, Wm. Vreeland, jr., Jaspar Cadmus and wife, and Elizabeth Cadmus, June 21, 1842. Wm. Vreeland, jr., sold his one-fifth to Vreeland and Demarest Dec. 19, 1843. They

* **Beginning** at a Stake standing in the Edge of the Salt Meadows *155
(being the northeasterly Corner of the Lot of Common Land at Bergen
Point No 172 sold for defraying the Expences of the General Partition) and
from said Stake runs along the Line of said Lot No 172 North eighty five
Degrees West thirty three Chains to a Stake (being the westerly Corner
of said Allotment No 270) Thence North thirty nine Degrees East sixty
five Chains and fifteen Links to a Stake (standing South thirty nine Degrees West sixteen Chains and seventy Links from a Stone mark'd B
standing in the westermost Corner of the Allotment of Common Land No
277,) And from said Stake runs South fifty one Degrees East twenty two
Chains and eighty Links to a Stake by the Meadow Edge, Thence along
Southerly betwixt the Meadow and Upland to the Place of Beginning,
Containing about one hundred and thirty six Acres and three Tenths.

And we adjudge a certain Portion of said Allotment No 270
to Margaret Widow of Andries Van Buskirk for her Use during
her natural Life, and in Trust for the Purposes & Uses mentioned
in the last Will and Testament of her Husband the said Andries
Van Buskirk dated the twenty fourth Day of May one thousand
seven hundred and sixty two

Our Survey of which said Portion (as laid down on
Subdivision Schedule B) shews, and we adjudge it to be a
Tract mark'd No 419 *

Beginning at a Stone mark'd B (standing in the westermost Corner of the Allotment of Common Land No 277) and from said Stone runs
North thirty nine Degrees East fifty Links to a Stake, Thence North fifty

---

sold, Jan. 7, 1848, to Mary, wife of Eburn H. Coutant, one hundred and sixty acres,
one rood, and sixteen perches, excepting a few parcels. Coutant sold part of his purchase to Roswell Graves by three deeds Jan. 10 and 13, 1853.   *Vide Note to Kill Van
Kull Lot No. 5, p. 70.*   II. Vreeland, Demarest, Wm. Vreeland, Jasper Cadmus and
wife, and Elizabeth Cadmus conveyed part of the tract to Samuel D. Ingham and
Mathew C. Jenkins Jan. 5, 1848. Jenkins by will, dated Nov. 23, 1854, proved May
24, 1855, empowered his executors to sell. They conveyed part of the tract to William
B. Reed May 13, 1857; Reed to Nathan R. Mosher May 2, 1860.   *Vide Note to Kill
Van Kull Lot No. 1, p. 70.*

º *Vide Note to Jansen and Edsall's Patent,* p. 19.   Helmus Vreeland, surviving
executor, sold one hundred and twenty-one acres and three-quarters of an acre on the
north side of this tract to Michael Vreeland May 10, 1784 (unrecorded).   Vreeland
sold fifty acres to Benjamin Zabriskie June 10, 1784, and fifty acres on same date to
Jasper Zabriskie.   The land sold to Benjamin lay on the south side of the tract, and
the lot of Jasper lay adjoining on the north.   Benjamin died seized, will dated Oct.
5, 1831, proved Feb. 29, 1832.   His executors sold to John Cadmus April 10, 1832,
whose administrators, under order of the court, sold to Jasper Cadmus, jr., May 1,
1833, who resold to Jasper on the same day, who by will, dated April 25, 1843, proved
Oct. 10, 1845, gave it to the children of his grandson Andrew, who is now residing
upon it.   Jasper died seized.   By will (without date), codicil dated Oct. 27, 1828,
he gave this lot to his grandson Albert M. (son of Michael) in tail. This devisee sold to
Joseph B. Close Jan. 20, 1854, and on same day was appointed special guardian for his
children.   The executors sold three and a half acres to Henry Vreeland Feb. 12,
1832.

one Degrees West forty Chains to New Ark Bay, Then returning to said Stone mark'd B the Place of Beginning, and from thence runs South thirty nine Degrees West eleven Chains and four Links to a Stake, Thence South fifty one Degrees East twenty three Chains and twenty Links to a Stake by the Meadow Edge, Thence South forty six Degrees West five Chains and sixty eight Links to a Stake, Thence North fifty one Degrees West twenty two Chains and eighty Links to a Stake (being the northerly Corner of the Tract No 418 adjudged to Jacobus Van Buskirk last above described (Thence South thirty nine Degrees West fifteen Chains and thirty nine Links to a Stake (being the Easterly Corner of the Allotment of Common Land No 269) Thence along the Line of said Allotment No 269 North fifty one Degrees west forty one Chains to said New Ark Bay, Then up along the said Bay Northerly 'till it meets the above mentioned Line that runs to said Bay, Containing about One hundred & forty three Acres.

*156   * **And we** adjudge a certain Portion of said Allotment No 270 To belong to Jacob Van Horne.

Our Survey of which said Portion (as laid down on Subdivision Schedule B) shews and we adjudge it to be a Tract mark'd No 420 *

Beginning at a Stake (standing South thirty Degrees west four Chains from a Stone mark'd B standing in the westerly Corner of the Allotment of Common Land No 277) And from said Stake runs South fifty one Degrees East eleven Chains and thirty seven Links to a Stake, Thence North thirty nine Degrees East four Chains to a Stake, Thence South fifty one Degrees East fifteen Chains and twenty five Links to a Stake by the Meadow Edge, Then returning to the first mentioned Stake the Place of Beginning; And from thence runs South thirty nine Degrees west seven Chains & four Links to a Stake (being a Corner of the Tract No 419 adjudged to Widow Van Buskirk last above described) Thence along the Line of said Tract No 419 South fifty one Degrees East twenty three Chains and twenty Links to a Stake by the Meadow Edge, Then Northeasterly along between the Meadow and Upland 'til it meets the above mention'd Line that runs to said Meadow, Containing about twenty one Acres & two Tenths.

And we adjudge a certain Portion of said Allotment No 270 To belong to George Cadmus.

Our Survey of which said Portion (as laid down on Subdivision Schedule B) shews, and we adjudge it to be a Tract mark'd No 421 †

Beginning at a Stone mark'd B (standing in the westerly Corner of the Allotment of Common Land No 277) And from said Stone runs South thirty nine Degrees West four Chains to a Stake (being the Place of Beginning of the Tract No 420 adjudged to Jacob Van Horne last above

---

o *Vide Note to Stoffelsen's Patent*, p. 18.

† *Vide Note to Slott's Patent*, p. 17. Jasper conveyed to his son eighteen acres of salt meadow near Constable's Hook Jan. 21, 1820. By will, dated April 25, 1843, proved Oct. 20, 1844, he gave to his grandson Jasper the remainder of this lot. *Vide Note to Lot No.* 275, p. 91.

described) Thence South fifty one Degrees East eleven Chains & thirty seven Links to a Stake, Thence North thirty nine Degrees East four Chains to a Stake, Thence North fifty one Degrees west eleven Chains and thirty seven Links to the Place of Beginning, Containing about four Acres and a Half.

* **This** is a **Subdivision** of the two Lots of Common Land which have been allotted To the Patent of Philip Carteret to Mark Noble and Samuel Moore dated the twentieth Day of July one thousand six hundred and sixty nine, being these two Lots of Common Land which in the Field Book and Map of the General Partition are distinguished by the Numbers 227 and 251. *157

And upon Examination of the Titles of the several Persons claiming Parts and Shares thereof

We do adjudge a certain Portion of said Allotment No 227 To belong to Peter Petersen Esqr

Our Survey of which said Portion (as laid down on Subdivision Schedule A) shews and we adjudge it to be a Tract mark'd on the map No 334

Beginning at a Stake (being the Southerly Corner of said Allotment No 227) And from thence runs North thirty six Degrees and thirty Minutes East seven Chains and thirty eight Links to a Stake, Thence North fifty two Degrees & thirty Minutes West thirty eight Chains to a Stake, Thence South thirty six Degrees & thirty Minutes West seven Chains and thirty eight Links to a Stake, Thence South fifty two Degrees and thirty Minutes East thirty eight Chains to the Place of Beginning, containing about twenty eight Acres.

And we adjudge a certain Portion of said Allotment No 227 To belong to Zachariah Sickels.

Our Survey of which said Portion (as laid down on Subdivision Schedule A) shews and we adjudge it to be a Tract mark'd No 335

* **Beginning** at a Stake (being the easternmost Corner of the Tract No 334 adjudg'd to Peter Peterson Esqr last above described) And from thence runs North thirty six Degrees and thirty Minutes East seven Chains and eighty nine Links to a Stake (being the Easternmost Corner of said Allotment No 227) Thence North fifty two Degrees and thirty Minutes west thirty eight Chains to a Stake, Thence South thirty six Degrees and thirty Minutes west seven Chains and eighty nine Links to a Stake, Thence South fifty-two Degrees and thirty Minutes east thirty eight Chains to the Place of Beginning Containing about thirty Acres. *158

And we adjudge a certain Portion of said Allotment No 251 To belong to Cornelius Blinkerhoof.

Our Survey of which said Portion (as laid down on Subdivision Schedule A) shews, and we adjudge it to be a Tract mark'd No 379 *

---

* Brinkerhoff sold eight and three-quarters acres of this lot to Cornelius and Garret Sip May 28, 1769. This must have been on the east end. Nicholas and

Beginning at a Stake (being the Southermost Corner of said Allotment No 251) And from thence runs North thirty three Degrees East four Chains and seventy eight Links to a Stake, Thence North fifty seven Degrees west fifty five Chains and thirty seven Links to a Stake in the Meadow, Thence South thirty three Degrees West four Chains and seventy eight Links to a Stake, Thence South fifty seven Degrees East fifty five Chains and thirty seven Links to the Place of Beginning Containing about twenty five Acres.

And we adjudge a certain Portion of said Allotment No 251 To belong to John, Jacobus, Peter, Garret and Mary Vanderhoofs in equal Shares as Tenants in Common.

Our Survey of which said Portion (as laid down on Subdivision Schedule A) shews, and we adjudge it to be a Tract mark'd No 380 *

Beginning at a Stake (being the Eastermost Corner of the Tract No 379 adjudg'd to Cornelius Blinkerhoof last above described) And from thence runs North thirty three Degrees East four Chains & seventy nine Links to a Stake, Thence North fifty seven Degrees west fifty five Chains & thirty seven Links to a Stake in the Meadow, Thence South thirty three Degrees West four Chains & senty nine Links to a Stake, Thence South fifty seven Degrees East fifty five Chains & thirty seven Links to the Place of Beginning, Containing about twenty five Acres.

* **And we** adjudge a certain Portion of said Allotment No 251 To belong to Heirs or Assigns of Joseph Hawkin's deceased.

Our Survey of which said Portion (as laid down on Subdivision Schedule A) shews and we adjudge it to be a Tract mark'd No 381

Beginning at a Stake (being the Eastermost Corner of the Tract No 380 adjudged to the Vanderhoof's last above described) And from thence runs North thirty three Degrees East four Chains and seventy nine Links to a Stake (being the Eastermost Corner of said Allotment No 251) Thence North fifty seven Degrees west fourteen Chains and sixty five Links to a Stake, Thence South thirty three Degrees west four Chains and seventy nine Links to a Stake, Thence South fifty seven Degrees East fourteen Chains & sixty five Links to the Place of Beginning, containing about seven Acres.

Garret Vreeland and John Zabriskie conveyed eight acres to Nicholas T. Winner May 3, 1830; he to Albert Aeschmann Nov. 19, 1840; he to Adolphus Willemer Oct. 6, 1843; he to John A. Aeschmann Oct. 22, 1847; he to Peter J. Murtha June 30, 1854. Murtha mortgaged to Samuel Guillaume June 30, 1854, who assigned to Claudius C. Becket July 10, 1855. The mortgage was foreclosed, and the property sold by Sheriff Beaty to Becket May 23, 1857; he to Guillaume same day; he to Teuner April 9, 1859; he to Misch April 25, 1860; he to Leonard G. Klinck July 25, 1860; he to Conrad C. Spengeman April 9, 1861; he to Henry Schneider Aug. 8, 1865; he to Charles Hespe Nov. 7, 1868.

^o Garret Vanderhoof was one of the family. By his will, dated July 31, 1797, proved Sept. 20, 1797, he gave his lands equally to his four daughters, *Maritje*, wife of Jacob Outwater, *Eve*, wife of Peter Sickles, *Ariantje*, wife of Aaron Vanderbilt, *Sarah*, wife of George Newkirk. The mother of these children was Sarah, daughter of Abraham Prior. These parties sold to Casparus Prior four acres and fifty-four one-hundredths of an acre.

And we adjudge a certain Portion of said Allotment No 251 To belong to Daniel Smith.

Our Survey of which said Portion (as laid down on Subdivision Schedule A) shews and we adjudge it to be a Tract mark'd No 382

Beginning at a Stake (being the westermost Corner of the Tract No 381 adjudged to the Heirs or Assigns of Hawkins last above described) And from thence runs North thirty three Degrees East four Chains and seventy nine Links to a Stake, Thence North fifty seven Degrees west sixteen Chains and seventy four Links to a Stake, Thence South thirty three Degrees west four Chains and seventy nine Links to a Stake, Thence South fifty seven Degrees East sixteen Chains and seventy four Links to the Place of Beginning, containing about seven Acres and a Half.

* **And we** adjudge a certain Portion of said Allotment No *160 251 To belong to Job Smith.

Our Survey of which said Portion (as laid down on Subdivision Schedule A) shews, and we adjudge it to be a Tract mark'd No 383

Beginning at a Stake (being the westermost Corner of the Tract No 382 adjudged to Daniel Smith last above described) And from thence runs North thirty three Degrees East four Chains and seventy nine Links to a Stake, Thence North fifty seven Degrees west twenty three Chains and ninety eight Links to a Stake, Thence South thirty three Degrees west four Chains and seventy nine Links to a Stake, Thence South fifty seven Degrees East twenty three Chains and ninety eight Links to the Place of Beginning, Containing about Ten Acres and a Half.

And we adjudge a certain Portion of said Allotment No 251 To belong to Peter Peterson Esqr.

Our Survey of which said Portion (as laid down on Subdivision Schedule A) shews, and we adjudge it to be a Tract mark'd No 384

Beginning at a Stake (being the northermost Corner of the Tract No 383 adjudged to Job Smith last above described) And from thence runs North fifty seven Degrees west eighteen Chains and sixty three Links To Pinhorne's Creek, Then returning to said Stake the Place of Beginning; And from thence runs South thirty three Degrees West fourteen Chains and thirty six Links to a Stake, Thence North fifty seven Degrees west twenty six Chains and sixty three Links to said Pinhorne's Creek, Then up along the said Creek as the same runs 'till it meets the first mentioned Line, containing about thirty Acres.

* With respect to the Lot of Common Land which has *161 been allotted To the first Patent of Philip Carteret to Caspar Stymets dated the twelfth Day of May One thousand six hundred and sixty eight; being that Lot of Common Land which in the Field Book and Map of the General Partition is distinguished by the Number 225.

Peter Marseilis claimed the said Lot, and no other Person or Persons claiming the same or a Subdivision thereof We upon Examination of his Title conceive him to be the True Proprietor And do therefore adjudge the said Allotment to belong to him.

This is a **subdivision** of the Lot of Common Land which has been allotted to the second Patent of Philip Carteret to Caspar Stymets dated the twelfth Day of May one thousand six hundred & sixty eight, being that Lot of Common Land which in the Field Book and Map of the General Partition is distinguished by the Number 223

And upon Examination of the Titles of the several Persons claiming Parts and Shares thereof,

We do adjudge a certain Portion of said Allotment No 223 To belong to Thomas Brown

*162   * **Our Survey** of which said Portion (as laid down on Subdivision Schedule A) shews, and we adjudge it to be a Tract mark'd 327 *

Beginning at a Stake (being the Southermost Corner of said Allotment No 223) And from thence runs North thirty six Degrees and thirty Minutes East three Chains and forty eight Links to a Stake, Thence North fifty two Degrees and thirty Minutes West thirty eight Chains to a Stake, Thence South thirty six Degrees and thirty Minutes West three Chains and forty eight Links to a Stake, Thence South fifty two Degrees and thirty Minutes East thirty eight Chains to the Place of Beginning, Containing thirteen Acres and One Tenth.

And we adjudge a certain Portion of said Allotment No 223 To belong to Jacob Vanderhoof

Our Survey of which said Portion (as laid down on Subdivision Schedule A) shews, and we adjudge it to be a Tract mark'd No 328 †

Beginning at a Stake (being the easternmost Corner of the Tract No 327 adjudged to Thomas Brown last above described) And from thence runs North thirty six Degrees and thirty Minutes East six Chains and forty five Links to a Stake, Thence North fifty two Degrees and thirty Minutes West thirty eight Chains to a Stake, Thence South thirty six Degrees and thirty Minutes west six Chains and forty five Links to a Stake, Thence South fifty two Degrees and thirty Minutes East thirty eight Chains to the Place of Beginning, containing about twenty four Acres and four Tenths.

And we adjudge a certain Portion of said Allotment No 223 To belong to Michael De Mott and George De Mott, in equal Moities.

---

* *Vide Note to Andriesen's Patent*, p. 13. Elizabeth, Thomas B., and Samuel T. Gautier sold this lot to Cornelius Doremus June 20, 1826.

† Garret Van Vorst seems to have owned the greater part, if not the whole, of this lot. He conveyed to Cornelius Van Vorst Aug. 2, 1826, who sold four acres in the north corner to Walter Weldon Aug. 11, 1836.

Our Survey of which said Portion (as laid down on Subdivision Schedule A) shews, and we adjudge it to be a Tract mark'd No 329 *

Beginning at a Stake (being the Easternmost Corner of the Tract No 328 adjudged to Jacob Vanderhoof last above described) And from thence runs North thirty six Degrees and thirty Minutes East six Chains and fifty eight Links to a Stake, Thence North fifty two Degrees and thirty Minutes West thirty eight Chains to a Stake, Thence South thirty six Degrees and thirty Minutes West six Chains and fifty eight Links to a Stake, Thence South fifty two Degrees and thirty Minutes East thirty eight Chains to the Place of Beginning. Containing about twenty five Acres.

And we adjudge a certain Portion of said Allotment No 223 To belong to Johannis Van Houte

Our Survey of which said Portion as laid down on Subdivision Schedule A) shews, and we adjudge it to be a Tract mark'd No 330 †

Beginning at a Stake (being the easternmost Corner of the Tract No 329 adjudged to the De Motts last above described) And from thence runs North thirty six Degrees and thirty Minutes East Ten Chains and ninety six Links To a Stake (being the easternmost Corner of said Allotment No 223) Thence North fifty two Degrees and thirty Minutes West thirty eight Chains to a Stake, Thence South thirty six Degrees and thirty Minutes West ten Chains and ninety six Links to a Stake, Thence South fifty two Degrees and thirty Minutes East thirty eight Chains to the Place of Beginning, containing about forty one Acres and a Half.

* **This** is a **subdivision** of the Lot of Common Land which has been allotted To the Patent of Philip Carteret To Adrian Post dated the twelfth Day of May one thousand six hundred & sixty eight, being that Lot of Common Land which in the Field Book & Map of the General Partition is distinguished by the Number 264.

And upon Examination of the Titles of the several Persons claiming Parts & Shares thereof,

We do adjudge a certain Portion of said Allotment No 264 To belong to Michael De Mott and George De Mott, in equal Moieties

Our Survey of which said Portion (as laid down on

---

* *Vide Note to Stoffelsen's Patent,* p. 9. This lot was known as the "Indian Spring Lot." Michael De Mott died seized and intestate. It was then divided into nine lots. Geo. De Mott and John M. Cornelison, administrators, sold two lots, containing seven acres, to James G. King Oct. 1, 1836, and two acres to John Morgan Oct. 1, 1836. John and Robert Gardner now own part of it, also the heirs of Job Seeley.

† The southeast corner of this lot seems to have gone to Van Houten's son-in-law, Jacob Zabriskie, who sold to James Brown in 1846, who gave the same to the Reformed Church, known as the Grove Church. Three acres of the lot was sold to Joseph Danielson by John Van Houten June 24, 1835, and Danielson seems to have bought all except the above church lot.

Subdivision Schedule B) shews, and we adjudge it to be a Tract mark'd No 409 *

Beginning at a Stake (being the easternmost Corner of said Allotment No 264.) And from said Stake runs South fifty Degrees West five Chains and sixty one Links to a Stake, Thence North forty three Degrees and forty five Minutes West forty one Chains and eighty seven Links to a Stake, Thence North fifty Degrees East five Chains and sixty one Links to a Stake, Thence South forty three Degrees and forty five Minutes East forty one Chains and eighty seven Links to the Place of Beginning, Containing about twenty three Acres and a Half.

*165

* **And we** adjudge a certain Portion of said Allotment No 264 To belong to Jacob Van Wagenen

Our Survey of which said Portion (as laid down on Subdivision Schedule B) shews, and we adjudge it to be a Tract mark'd No 412 †

Beginning at a Stake (being the northermost Corner of the Tract No 409 adjudg'd to the De Motts last above described) And from thence runs South fifty Degrees West thirteen Chains and fifty four Links to a Stake, Thence North twenty seven Degrees and thirty Minutes West Ten Chains and seventy five Links to a Stake in the Edge of the Meadow, Thence North twenty six Degrees and fifty Minutes East three Chains and sixty six Links to a Stake (being the easternmost Corner of a Lot of Meadow No 121 in Peter Jacobse's Patent) Thence along the Line of said Meadow North forty four Degrees West fifteen Chains and forty Links to the Mouth of a Ditch emptying into Hackinsack River,' Then up along said River North sixty five Degrees and ten Minutes east seven Chains and fifty two Links to a Stake, Thence South forty three Degrees and forty five Minutes East twenty six Chains and thirty three Links to the Place of Beginning, Containing about twenty four Acres and two Tenths.

And we do adjudge a certain Portion of said Allotment No 264 To belong to Johannis Van Wagenen

Our Survey of which said Portion (as laid down on Subdivision Schedule B) shews, and we adjudge it to be a Tract mark'd No 410 ‡

Beginning at a Stake (being the Southermost Corner of said Allotment No 264) And from thence runs North fifty Degrees East three Chains & two Links to a Stake, Thence North forty three Degrees and

---

° *Vide Note to Stoffelsen's Patent*, p. 9. Michael De Mott by will, dated May 10, 1831, proved May 19, 1834, gave to his sons, *George* and *Garret*, for life, then to their male issue, a lot of salt meadow near Brown's Ferry. To Garret he gave the " Long Bridge," *Lot No.* 409; also, a lot east of the Academy in Bergen ; also, ten acres north of Nicholas Tuers, and called the " bush land " ; also, the Brown's Ferry lot ; also, a lot back of the church ground.

† *Vide Note to Spier's Patent*, p. 15.

‡ *Vide Note to Gerritse's Patent*, p. 58. At an early day it passed to the Vreeland family. In the partition between Garret and John, this lot fell to John, who gave it to his nephew, Col. Jacob Vreeland, who conveyed it to Peter Rowe Jun. 29, 1841, in whom and his son *Norman L.* the most of it yet remains.

forty five Minutes West four Chains & one Link to a Stake, Thence South fifty Degrees West one Chain and ninety eight Links to a Stake, Thence South twenty seven Degrees and thirty Minutes East four Chains and seven Links to the Place of Beginning, Containing about One Acre.

And we do adjudge a certain Portion of said Allotment *166 No 264 To belong to Cornelius Gerritse alias Van Riper.

Our Survey of which said Portion (as laid down on Subdivision Schedule B) shews, and we adjudge it to be a Tract mark'd No 411 *

Beginning at a Stake (being the easternmost Corner of the Tract No 410 adjudged to Johannis Van Wagenen last above described); And from thence runs North fifty Degrees East sixteen Chains and ninety seven Links to a Stake, (being the Southermost Corner of the Tract No 409 adjudged to Michael & George De Motts above described). Thence North forty three Degrees and forty five Minutes West forty one Chains and eighty seven Links to a Stake, Thence South fifty Degrees west seven Chains and ninety three Links to a Stake, Thence South twenty seven Degrees and thirty Minutes East thirty eight Chains and seventy four Links to a Stake, Thence North fifty Degrees east one Chain and ninety eight Links to a Stake, Thence South forty three Degrees and forty five Minutes east four Chains and one Link to the Place of Beginning, containing about fifty seven Acres and three Tenths.

This is a **subdivision** of the Lot of Common Land which has been allotted To the first Patent of Philip Carteret To Guert Coerten dated the twelfth Day of May one thousand six hundred and sixty eight, being that Lot of Common Land which in the Field Book & Map of the General Partition is distinguished by the Number 215

And upon Examination of the Titles of the several Persons claiming Parts and Shares thereof

We do adjudge a certain Portion of said Allotment No 215 To belong to Cornelius Gerritse alias Van Riper.

---

* Van Rypen died Jan. 17, 1771.- By his will, dated Aug. 29, 1767, proved May 4, 1772, he gave to his son *Garret* a lot of salt meadow north of the Bergen Mills, and to his son *Daniel* all the remainder of his lands. Garret by will, dated Feb. 11, 1795, proved Oct. 12, 1795, gave all his realty to his brother Daniel. The lot in question was known as the "Long Bridge Lot." Daniel sold the north half of this lot to his son *Cornelius*, and the south half to his son *Richard* June 10, 1816. The north half is still owned by *Cornelius C.*, the son of Cornelius, Daniel's grantee, except ten acres taken from the south side, given by Cornelius to his son *Garret*, from whose heirs Selah Hill bought it. It is now owned by Samuel C. Nelson. Richard died seized, and by will, dated June 12, 1851, proved Aug. 5, 1851, named as executors Cornelius C. Van Rypen and John R. Romaine. He gave his property equally to his children, *Michael, Hannah*, wife of Abraham Vreeland; *Elizabeth, Effie, Daniel R., Catherine*, wife of Albert Zabriskie; *Cornelius R., Jane*, wife of Egbert Wauters; *George*, and *Aletta*, wife of John S. Tuttle. The property was partitioned by commissioners March 9, 1853. Part of the south half is yet owned by the heirs of Richard. It extended down to Waverly avenue in Greenville. *Vide Note to Coerten's first Patent*, p. 25.

*167   ***Our Survey** of which said Portion (as laid down on Subdivision Schedule A) shews, and we adjudge it to be a Tract mark'd No 314 *

Beginning at a Stake (being the westerly Corner of said Allotment No 215) And from thence runs South fifty two Degrees and thirty Minutes East fifty five Chains to Hudson's River, Then returning to said Stake the Place of Beginning and from thence runs North thirty six Degrees and thirty Minutes east five Chains and seventy four Links to a Stake, Thence South fifty two Degrees and thirty Minutes east fifty four Chains and fifty Links to said Hudson's River, Then down along said River as it runs 'till it comes to the first mentioned Line running to said River, containing (after an Allowance for the Hill) about twenty nine Acres and an Half.

And we adjudge a certain Portion of said Allotment No 215 To belong to Garrit Gerritse alias Van Riper.

Our Survey of which said Portion (as laid down on Subdivision Schedule A) shews, and we adjudge it to be a Tract mark'd No 315 †

Beginning at a Stake (being the Northermost Corner of the Tract No 314 adjudged to Cornelius Gerritse last above described) And from thence runs South fifty two Degrees and thirty Minutes East fifty four Chains and fifty Links to Hudson's River, Then returning to said Stake the Place of Beginning And from thence runs North thirty six Degrees and thirty Minutes east five Chains and seventy four Links to a Stake (being the Northermost Corner of said Allotment No 215) Thence South fifty two Degrees and thirty Minutes East fifty four Chains to said Hudson's River, Then down along said River as it runs 'till it comes to the first mentioned Line running to said River, Containing after an Allowance for the Hill about twenty nine Acres and an Half.

*168   * **This** is a **subdivision** of the Lot of Common Land which has been allotted To the second Patent of Philip Carteret To Guert Coerten dated the twelfth Day of May one thousand six hundred and sixty eight being that Lot of Com-

---

* *Vide Note to Lot No.* 411, p. 166. Van Rypen gave this to his sons *Derrick* and *Cornelius*; Derrick taking the south side, and Cornelius the north side, the most of which was given by deed to his son *Cornelius C.* This is the lot on which the Refugees had their Block House, which Gen. Wayne attempted to capture during the Revolutionary War. Daniel, Cornelius, and Richard Van Rypen sold to John Brower ten acres on the east end of the lot Dec. 20, 1799. Of this Matthias McDonald died seized, and it was partitioned among his children Sept. 21, 1837 (or 9). They sold at various times to John Meeks, the present owner *Vide Note to Lot No.* 315, p. 167.

† *Vide Lot No.* 411, p. 166. The rear part of the lot descended to Van Rypen's son *George*, who sold the same to William Day. who sold the west part of his purchase to Thomas Minack May 12, 1849, and to Michael Bull. Van Rypen sold eight acres to John Brower on the east end of the lot April 20, 1800. This, with (probably) *Lot No.* 316, William Day seems to have sold to George Suckley Sept. 19, 1832. Rutzen Suckley sold to John Meeks, the present owner, Sept. 1, 1851. This place was known as "Castle Hill," and the deed to Meeks covers fifty acres. *Vide Note to Lot No.* 316, p. 176.

mon Land which in the Field Book & Map of the General Partition is distinguished by the Number 243.

And upon Examination of the Titles of the several Persons claiming Parts & Shares thereof

𝕎𝕖 do adjudge a certain Portion of said Allotment No 243 To belong to Altje the Wife of Daniel Van Winkle

𝕆𝕦𝕣 𝕊𝕦𝕣𝕧𝕖𝕪 of which said Portion (as laid down on Subdivision Schedule A) shews, and we adjudge it to be a Tract mark'd No 354

𝔹𝕖𝕘𝕚𝕟𝕟𝕚𝕟𝕘 at a Stake being the Southermost Corner of said Allotment No 243) and from thence runs North thirty three Degrees East three Chains & twelve Links to a Stake, Thence North fifty Degrees west eleven Chains and thirty Links to a Stake, Thence South thirty three Degrees west three Chains and twelve Links to a Stake, Thence South fifty Degrees east eleven Chains and thirty Links to the Place of Beginning, containing about three Acres and an Half.

As to the remaining Part or Portion of said Allotment No 243 We find the Right to the same vested in the Freeholders of the Corporation of Bergen, But not being able to ascertain who these Freeholders were by Name We do not declare To whom the said remaining Part or Portion does particularly belong

* 𝕆𝕦𝕣 𝕊𝕦𝕣𝕧𝕖𝕪 of which remaining Part or Portion (as laid down on Subdivision Schedule A) shews, and we adjudge it to be a Tract mark'd No 355 * *169

𝔹𝕖𝕘𝕚𝕟𝕟𝕚𝕟𝕘 at a Stake (being the eastermost Corner of the Tract No 354 adjudged to Altje Van Winkle last above described) And from thence runs North thirty three Degrees East eighteen Chains and thirty eight Links to a Stake, (being the eastermost Corner of said Allotment No 243) Thence North fifty seven Degrees West twenty eight Chains and twenty Links to a Stake in the Road, Thence along said Road South ten Degrees west eighty Chains and sixty one Links to a Stake, Thence South four Degrees east nine Chains and seventy five Links to a Stake, Thence South twenty six Degrees and forty Minutes east eight Chains and eighty one Links to a Stake, Thence North thirty three Degrees east three Chains and twelve Links to a Stake, Thence South fifty Degrees east eleven Chains and thirty Links to the Place of Beginning, containing about forty one Acres & a Half.

𝕋𝕙𝕚𝕤 is a 𝕤𝕦𝕓𝕕𝕚𝕧𝕚𝕤𝕚𝕠𝕟 of the Lot of Common Land which has been allotted To the third Patent of Philip Carteret to Guert Coerten dated the twenty first Day of March one thousand six hundred & seventy being that Lot of Common Land which in the Field Book and Map of the General Partition is distinguished by the Number 235.

And upon Examination of the Titles of the several Persons claiming Parts & Shares thereof

𝕎𝕖 do adjudge a certain Portion of said Allotment No 235 To

---

* *Vide New Field Book* and *Map A.*

belong to Johannis Gerritse alias Urianse alias Van Riper alias **Beletje's Hans.**

*170   *** Our Survey** of which said Portion (as laid down on Subdivision Schedule A) shews, and we adjudge it to be a Tract mark'd No 345 *

Beginning at a Stake (being the Northermost Corner of said Allotment No 235) And from thence runs South thirty three Degrees west nine Chains & seventy one Links to a Stake, Thence South fifty seven Degrees East twenty three Chains and ten Links to a Stake, Thence North thirty three Degrees East nine Chains & seventy one Links to a Stake (being the Easternmost Corner of said Allotment No 235) Thence North fifty seven Degrees west twenty three Chains and ten Links To the Place of Beginning, containing about twenty two Acres.

And we adjudge a certain Portion of said Allotment No 235 To belong to Altje the Wife of Daniel Van Winkle

Our Survey of which said Portion (as laid down on Subdivision Schedule A) shews and we adjudge it to be a Tract mark'd No 347 †

Beginning at a Stake (being the westermost Corner of said Allotment No 235) And from thence runs North thirty three Degrees East four Chains and sixty five Links to a Stake, Thence South fifty seven Degrees east twenty three Chains and ten Links to a Stake, Thence South thirty three Degrees west four Chains and sixty five Links to a Stake Thence North fifty seven Degrees west twenty three Chains and ten Links to the Place of Beginning, containing about Ten Acres and an Half.

As to the remaining Part or Portion of said Allotment No 235 **We** find the Right to be last vested in Altje Urianse the daughter of Urian Thomasse, But we not being able to find in whom the same now vests **We** do not declare To whom the said remaining Part or Portion does belong.

*171   *** Our Survey** of which remaining Part or Portion (as laid down on Subdivision Schedule A) shews, and we adjudge it to be a Tract mark'd No 346

Beginning at a Stake (being the northwest Corner of the Tract No 347 adjudged to Altje the Wife of Daniel Van Winkle last above described) and from thence runs North thirty three Degrees east five Chains & six Links to a Stake, Thence South fifty seven Degrees east twenty three Chains and ten Links to a Stake, Thence South thirty three Degrees west five Chains and six Links to a Stake, Thence North fifty seven Degrees west twenty three Chains and ten Links to the Place of Beginning, containing about eleven Acres and an Half.

---

* This was *Johannis,* son of Gerrit Jurianse and Beelitje Dircks, and to distinguish him from every other Johannis Van Rypen then existing hereabouts, was known as Beelitje's Hans. *Vide Note to Gerritse's Patent,* p. 38. His property went to his only son *Garret* ("Long Gat"). *Vide Note to Noble and Moore's Patent,* p. 20.

† *Altje Van Winkle,* the wife of Daniel, was a daughter of Garret Jurianse, or Van Rypen. She had children *Juriaen* (called Jurry or Jerry), *Catreintje,* and *Hendrick* (known as Henry D.). *Vide Note to Teunisse's Patent,* p. 54. Jerry and Henry D. sold this lot to Hiram Gilbert and Cyrus S. Browning July 27, 1835.

This is a **Subdivision** of the two Lots of Common Land which have been allotted To the Patent of Philip Carteret to Henderick Philipse dated the twelfth Day of May One thousand six hundred and sixty eight, being these two Lots of Common Land which in the Field Book & Map of the General Partition are distinguished by the numbers 234 & 262

And upon Examination of the Titles of the several Persons claiming Parts & Shares thereof

We do adjudge the said Allotment No 234 (as the same is described, butted and bounded in the Field Book of the General Partion) To belong to Philip French Esqr.

* **And we** do adjudge a certain Portion of said Allotment No *172 262 To belong to Garret Newkirk.

Our Survey of which said Portion (as laid down on Subdivision Schedule B) shews, and we adjudge it to be a Tract mark'd No 400 *

Beginning at a Stake (being the eastermost Corner of said Allotment No 262) And from thence runs South thirty six Degrees west twelve Chains & three Links to a Stake in the Road, Thence North fifty Degrees and ten Minutes West fifty seven Chains and twenty Links to a Stake in the Edge of the Meadow, Thence North thirty Degrees east ten Chains and sixty six Links to a Stake, Thence South fifty four Degrees and ten Minutes East thirty five Chains to a Stake, Thence South fifty Degrees and ten Minutes east twenty three Chains and sixty five Links to the Place of Beginning, containing about sixty six Acres and an Half.

And we adjudge a certain Portion of said Allotment No 262 To belong to Peter Merselies

Our Survey of which said Portion (as laid down on Subdivision Schedule B) shews, and we adjudge it to be a Tract mark'd No 401 †

---

* *Vide Note to Pieterse's Patent,* p. 40. Garret died April 23, 1785, and by will gave his lands to his two sons *Matthew* and *Hendrick.* Cornelius, a brother of Garret, died intestate Sept. 10, 1781, a bachelor, and his property was inherited by his nephews Matthew and Hendrick. What and where this was I do not know, but he received some by his mother's will, dated Sept. 30, 1731, proved May 7, 1764. Matthew and Hendrick partitioned by deed July 7, 1795. Hendrick died July 8, 1795. By will, dated July 7, 1795, proved Sept. 28, 1811, he gave all his realty to his sons, *Garret* and *George.* Hartman Van Wagenen, who married their sister *Catherina,* quit-claimed March 4, 1814. They partitioned by deed July 24, 1825 (?). Garret died Aug. 28, 1832. By will without date, proved Oct. 31, 1832, he divided his lands between his sons *Henry* and *Garret.* To Henry he gave seven acres out of the homestead; also, a lot known as "Mason's Land," containing fourteen acres; also, a lot known as the "Arch Bridge Lot," containing two acres and a half; also his "Brown's Ferry Lot," containing ten acres; also, a wood lot called "Clausen Klip," containing three acres. To Garret he gave the homestead, less the seven acres, containing sixteen acres, and two acres of the "Arch Bridge Lot." The balance of his lands he gave to them jointly.

† *Vide Note to Lot No.* 349, p. 196. Walter Clendenny, it seems, became the owner

Beginning at a Stake (being the Southermost Corner of the Tract No 400 adjudged to Garrit Newkirk last above described) And from thence runs South thirty six Degrees west seven Chains and sixty seven Links to a Stake in the Road, Thence North fifty Degrees and ten Minutes West fifty six Chains and fifty two Links to a Stake in the Edge of the Meadow, Thence North thirty Degrees east seven Chains and seventy four Links to a Stake, Thence South fifty Degrees and ten Minutes East fifty seven Chains and twenty Links to the Place of Beginning, containing about forty three Acres and four Tenths.

  And we adjudge a certain Portion of said Allotment No 262 To belong to Cornelius Sip and Garrit Sip in equal Moieties.

*173   * **Our Survey** of which said Portion (as laid down on Subdivision Schedule B) shews, and we adjudge it to be a Tract mark'd No 402 *

Beginning at a Stake (being the Southermost Corner of the Tract No 401 adjudged To Peter Marselies last above described) And from thence runs South thirty six Degrees west four Chains and thirty four Links to a Stake in the Road, Thence North forty six Degrees and thirty seven Minutes west four Chains to a Stake Thence South thirty six Degrees west two Chains and fifty Links to a Stake, Thence North forty six Degrees and thirty seven Minutes west twenty one Chains and eight Links to a Stake, Thence North thirty nine Degrees & fifty Minutes East five Chains and thirty one Links to a Stake, Thence South fifty Degrees and Ten Minutes East twenty four Chains and fifty two Links to the Place of Beginning, Containing about thirteen Acres and Six Tenths.

  And we adjudge a certain Portion of said Allotment No 262 To belong to Harman Veder.

---

of this lot, as also of *Lots Nos.* 402, 403, 406, and died seized Aug. 7, 182?. The Legislature, *vide Session Laws of* 1836, p. 168, appointed trustees to dispose of his realty. Dr. John M. Cornelison and Cornelius Van Winkle conveyed to Nathan Dale Ellingwood sixty acres and four one-hundredths of an acre July 29, 1836; Ellingwood to Conrad W. Faber one undivided half Aug. 4, 1836; to Delia A. Sistare one undivided fourth Aug. 9, 1836, and to Edward Stainer one undivided fourth Jan. 12, 1837. Sistare quit-claimed to Ellingwood one undivided fourth June 6, 1840. (She married Maurice Hillyer April 22, 1841, and died Oct. 11, 1866, leaving six children.) Stainer to Peter Charles Pfeffel one undivided fourth July 9, 1840; Pfeffel to William Branker one undivided fourth Feb. 20, 1841. Ellingwood gave to the trustees a mortgage July 29, 1836. They assigned it to Nicholas Prior and Cornelius Brinkerhoff Dec. 27, 1836, who foreclosed, and Henry Newkirk, sheriff, sold to complainants, June 28, 1843, the whole property except one quarter which had been released from the mortgage. They sold to Ellingwood three-fourths July 1, 1843, Ellingwood to Prior and Brinkerhoff Oct. 7, 1843, who conveyed to Abraham Vreeland Oct. 3, 1844. Branker to Vreeland one undivided fourth in 1844. Leah Ann Brinkerhoff, one of Clendenny's heirs, quit-claimed to Vreeland Oct 5, 1844 Vreeland to Isaac B. and Delos E. Culver thirty-three acres and three hundred and fourteen one-thousandths of an acre. These grantees mapped their purchase, and the place is now known as West Bergen. Vreeland died seized of the east end of the tract, and it is now owned by his heirs. The tract lies just north of Myrtle avenue, and extends from the old Bergen Road to the Hackensack river.

 * *Vide Note to Van Vorst's Patent*, p. 74, and *Note to Lot No.* 401, p. 172.

Our Survey of which said Portion (as laid down on Subdivision Schedule B) shews, and we adjudge it to be a Tract mark'd No 403 *

Beginning at a Stake in the Road (being the Southermost Corner of Tract No 402 adjudged to Cornelius and Garrit Sip last above described) And from thence runs South thirty six Degrees west two Chains and fifty Links to a Stake in the Road; Thence North forty six Degrees and thirty seven Minutes west four Chains to a Stake, Thence North thirty six Degrees east two Chains and fifty Links to a Stake, Thence South forty six Degrees and thirty seven Minutes East four Chains to the Place of Beginning, Containing about nine Tenths of an Acre.

And we adjudge a certain Portion of said Allotment No 262 To belong to Abraham Dedericks.

* **Our Survey** of which said Portion (as laid down on *174 Subdivision Schedule B) shews, and we adjudge it to be a Tract mark'd No 404 †

Beginning at a Stake (being the Southermost Corner of the Tract No 403 adjudged to Harman Veder last above described) And from thence runs South thirty six Degrees west four Chains and eighty four Links to a Stake, Thence North forty three Degrees and forty five Minutes west three Chains and five Links to a Stake, Thence South thirty six Degrees west two Chains to a Stake, Thence North forty three Degrees and forty five Minutes west twenty two Chains and sixty six Links to a Stake, Thence North thirty nine Degrees and fifty Minutes east five Chains & fifty two Links to a Stake Thence South forty six Degrees and thirty seven Minutes east twenty five Chains and eight Links to the Place of Beginning, Containing about fifteen Acres.

And we adjudge a certain Portion of said allotment No 262 To belong to Abraham Sickles

Our Survey of which said Portion (as laid down on Subdivision Schedule B) shews, and we adjudge it to be a Tract mark'd No 405 ‡

Beginning at a Stake in the Road (being the Southermost Corner of the said Allotment No 262) And from thence runs North thirty six Degrees East two Chains to a Stake in the Road (being a Corner of the Tract No 404 adjudged to Abraham Dedericks last above described) thence North forty three Degrees and forty five Minutes west three Chains and five Links to a Stake, Thence South thirty six Degrees west two Chains to a Stake, Thence South forty three Degrees and forty five Minutes east three Chains and five Links to the Place of Beginning, containing about six Tenths of an Acre.

---

^a *Vide Note to Lot No.* 401, p. 172.

† Diedricks died Feb. 6, 1799. By will, dated May 29, 1790, proved March 9, 1799, he gave all his realty to his son *John*. From him it passed to his two daughters *Aegie*, wife of John Zabriskie, and *Geertje*, wife of John Van Winkle. Van Winkle and wife sold one undivided half to John Zabriskie April 12, 1831.

‡ By will, dated Jan. 18, 1804, proved May 28, 1804, Sickles gave all his lands to his daughter *Effie*, wife of Daniel Diedricks. *Vide Note to Lot No.* 317, p. 176.

*175   ***And we** adjudge a certain Portion of said Allotment No 262 To belong to Cornelius Dedericks.

Our Survey of which said Portion (as laid down on Subdivision Schedule B) shews, And we adjudge it to be a Tract mark'd No 406 *

Beginning at a Stake (being the westermost Corner of the Tract No 404 adjudged to Abraham Dedericks above described) And from thence runs North thirty nine Degrees and fifty Minutes east ten Chains and eighty three Links to a Stake (standing in the Line of the Tract No 401 adjudged to Peter Marselies above described) thence North fifty Degrees and ten Minutes west thirty two Chains to a Stake in the Edge of the Meadow, Thence south thirty Degrees & fifty Minutes west seven Chains and sixty eight Links to a Stake, Thence South forty three Degrees and forty five Minutes East thirty Chains and seventy nine Links to the Place of Beginning, containing about twenty eight Acres.

This is a **Subdivision** of the two Lots of Common Land which have been allotted to the Patent of Philip Carteret to Angleburt Steenhuysen dated the twenty second Day of July one thousand six hundred & seventy, being these two Lots of Common Land which in the Field Book and Map of the General Partition are distinguished by the Numbers 216 & 244.

And upon Examination of the Titles of the several Persons claiming Parts & Shares thereof

We do adjudge a certain Portion of said Allotment No 216 To belong to Hendrick Sickles

*176   ***Our Survey** of which said Portion (as laid down on Subdivision Schedule A) shews, and we adjudge it to be a Tract mark'd No 316 †

Beginning at a Stake (being the westermost Corner of said Allotment No 216) And from thence runs South fifty two Degrees and thirty Minutes East fifty four Chains to Hudson's River, Then returning to said Stake the Place of Beginning and from thence runs North thirty six Degrees and thirty Minutes East four Chains and twenty one Links to a

---

* Diedricks died Dec. 6, 1775. By will, dated Nov. 29, 1775, proved March 25, 1784, he gave to his granddaughter *Antje*, daughter of John Winne, and Aeltje Diedricks his dwelling house and garden. To *Daniel*, son of his brother Jacob, *Antje*, *Jannetje*, and *Martin*, children of John Winne, the residue of his lands. Antje married Daniel Van Winkle, and Jannetje married Garret Van Rypen. *Vide Note to Lot No.* 401, p. 172.

† This lot was near the Block House. Sickles died Jan. 20, 1777. By will dated June 22, 1776, proved May 12, 1783, he gave all his realty to his sons, *Derrick* and *John*. John sold to Jacob Brower fourteen acres on the front, bounded north by Daniel Diedricks, east by the river, south by Garret Van Rypen, and west by the grantor, April 29, 1786. *Vide Note to Steenhuysen's Patent*, p. 32. Sickles sold a little over three acres to John McDonald Sept. 20, 1815, who sold to George Suckley Feb. 2, 1839. I think Suckley owned the whole lot in 1840. John Meeks now owns it. *Vide Notes to Lots Nos.* 314 and 315, p. 167.

Stake, Thence South fifty two Degrees and thirty Minutes East fifty two Chains to said Hudson's River, Thence down along said River as it runs 'till it meets the first mentioned Line, Containing after an Allowance for the Hill about twenty one Acres.

And we adjudge a certain Portion of said Allotment No 216 To belong to Daniel Dedericks

Our Survey of which said Portion (as laid down on Subdivision Schedule A) shews, and we adjudged it to be a Tract mark'd No 317 *

Beginning at a Stake (being the northermost Corner of the Tract No 216 adjudged to Hendrick Sickles last above described) And from thence runs South fifty two Degrees and thirty Minutes east fifty two Chains to Hudson's River; Then returning to said Stake the Place of Beginning; And from thence runs North thirty six Degrees and thirty Minutes East five Chains and twenty five Links to a Stake (being the northermost Corner of said Allotment No 216), Thence South fifty two Degrees and thirty Minutes east fifty one Chains and eighty Links to said Hudson's River, Then down along said River as it runs 'til it meets the first mentioned Line, Containing after an Allowance for the Hill about twenty six Acres.

* **And we** adjudge a certain Portion of said Allotment No 244 *177 To belong to Johannis Van Wagenen

Our Survey of which said Portion (as laid down on Subdivision Schedule A) shews, and we adjudge it to be a Tract mark'd No 362.†

Beginning at a Stake (being the eastermost Corner of said Allotment No 244) and from thence runs South thirty three Degrees west nineteen Chains and thirty Links to a Stake, Thence North fifty seven Degrees west thirty Chains to a Stake, Thence North thirty three Degrees east nineteen Chains and thirty Links to a Stake (being the northermost Corner of said allotment No 244) Thence South fifty seven Degrees east thirty Chains to the Place of Beginning, Containing about fifty seven Acres and nine Tenths.

And we adjudge a certain Portion of said allotment No 244 To belong to Hendrick Van Winkle

Our Survey of which said Portion (as laid down on Subdivision Schedule A) shews, and we adjudge it to be a Tract mark'd No 361. ‡

º Diedricks died seized May 24, 1795. His daughter *Jannetje* married Stephen Simonson, and *Aegie* married Jacobus Collerd. Collerd died Aug. 11, 1791. His son Abraham inherited his mother's share of the lot, and died March 15, 1831, leaving two sons, *Jacob* and *Abraham*. Between these and the wife of Simonson, the lot was partitioned July 11, 1832; she receiving the south half of the lot, and they the north half. *Vide Note to Lot No.* 358, p. 179.

† *Vide Note to Gerritse's Patent*, p. 58, and *Note to Lot No.* 222, p. 114.

‡ *Vide Note to Teunise's Patent*, p. 54. By will, dated Dec. 29, 1766, proved April 20, 1769, Hendrick Van Winkle gave to his son *Joseph*, among other property, the commons allotted to him for the patent of Englebert Steenhuysen. Joseph sold forty

Beginning at a Stake (being the Southermost Corner of the Tract No 362 adjudged to Johannis Van Wagenen last above described) And from thence runs South thirty three Degrees west fourteen Chains and ninety Links to a Stake, Thence North fifty seven Degrees west thirty Chains to a Stake, Thence North thirty three Degrees east fourteen Chains and ninety Links to a Stake, Thence South fifty seven Degrees East thirty Chains to the Place of Beginning, Containing about forty four Acres and seven Tenths.

*178   **And we** adjudge a certain Portion of said Allotment No 244 To belong to Hendrick Sickles.

Our Survey of which said Portion (as laid down on Subdivision Schedule A) shews, and we adjudge it to be a Tract mark'd No 360.

Beginning at a Stake (being the Southermost Corner of the Tract No 361 adjudged to Hendrick Van Winkle last above described) And from thence runs South thirty three Degrees west six Chains and twenty Links to a Stake, Thence North fifty seven Degrees west thirty Chains to a Stake, Thence North thirty three Degrees east six Chains and twenty Links to a Stake, Thence South fifty seven Degrees east thirty Chains to the Place of Beginning, Containing about eighteen Acres and six Tenths.

And we adjudge a certain Portion of said Allotment No 244 To belong to Arent Toers.

Our Survey of which said Portion (as laid down on Subdivision Schedule A) shews, and we adjudge it to be a Tract mark'd No 359 *

Beginning at a Stake (being the southermost Corner of the Tract No 360 adjudged to Hendrick Sickles last above described) And from thence runs South thirty three Degrees west four Chains and seventy Links to a Stake Thence North fifty seven Degrees west thirty Chains and sixty Links to a Stake, Thence North forty five Degrees east three Chains and fifty three Links to a Stake, Thence North thirty three Degrees east one Chain and twenty nine Links to a Stake, Thence South fifty seven Degrees east thirty Chains to the Place of Beginning, Containing about fourteen Acres and one Tenth.

*179   **And we** adjudge a certain Portion of said Allotment No 244 To belong to Abraham Sickles.

---

acres and fifty-eight one-hundredths of an acre of the lot to Jacob Newkirk April 1, 1816. Newkirk by will, dated April 16, 1817, proved Aug. 26, 1818, gave the same to his son *Garret*, who died intestate Aug. 22, 1818, leaving five children. *Vide Note to School Lot No.* 179, p. 74. James Provost and wife sold one undivided fifth to her brothers, Jacob, George, and Garret, June 26, 1838. George Vreeland and wife sold one undivided fifth to Jacob and Garret March 12, 1849. George sold his interest in the lot to Jacob and Garret Sept. 1, 1849. Jacob and Garret agreed to sell the same to William Hexamer Dec. 24, 1852, and Hexamer assigned his interest in the agreement to the "West Hoboken Land Association No 2" April 25, 1853. Rachel (widow of Garret Newkirk deceased) and Jacob and Garret Newkirk deeded the same to said Association July 16, 1853. It was then laid out into lots, many of which were sold. The Newkirks, holding a mortgage on the lands, foreclosed it, and John M. Francis, sheriff, sold the same to Jacob and Garret Newkirk Dec. 22, 1860. The lot lies in the northerly part of Jersey City and is known as "Centre Hill."

o *Vide Note to Steenhuys n's Patent,* p. 32.

Our Survey of which said Portion (as laid down on Subdivision Schedule A) shews and we adjudge it to be a Tract mark'd No 358.*

Beginning at a Stake (being the southermost Corner of the Tract No 359 adjudged to Arent Toers last above described) And from thence runs South thirty three Degrees west three Chains and twelve Links to a Stake, Thence North fifty seven Degrees west thirty one Chains and twenty five Links to a Stake, Thence North forty five Degrees East three Chains and thirty six Links to a Stake, Thence South fifty seven Degrees east thirty Chains and sixty Links to the Place of Beginning, Containing about nine Acres and two Tenths.

And we adjudge a certain Portion of said Allotment No 244 To belong to Michael De Mott & George De Mott in equal Moieties.

Our Survey of which said Portion (as laid down on Subdivision Schedule A) shews and we adjudge it to be a Tract mark'd No 357 †

Beginning at a Stake (being the westermost Corner of the Tract No 358 adjudged to Abraham Sickles last above described) And from thence runs South forty five Degrees west one Chain and ninety three Links to a Stake, Thence South fifty seven Degrees east five Chains and forty eight Links to a Stake, Thence North thirty three Degrees east one Chain and seventy Links to a Stake. Thence North fifty seven Degrees west five Chains to the Place of Beginning, containing about six Tenths of an Acre.

* **As** To the remaining Part or Portion of said Allotment No *180 244 being the Proportion which we adjudge To the Proprietor or Proprietors of the Patented Lot No 130, sundry Persons (as Freeholders and Inhabitants of the Town of Bergen) claimed the same but the Allegations upon which they founded their Claims not appearing satisfactory to us **we** declare not to whom the said remaining Part or Portion does now belong.

Our Survey of which said remaining Part or Portion (as laid down on Subdivision Schedule A) shews and we adjudge it to be a Tract mark'd No 356

Beginning at a Stake (being the Southermost Corner of said Allotment No 244) And from thence runs North fifty seven Degrees west twenty eight Chains and twenty Links to a Stake (being a Corner of said Allotment No 244) Thence North sixteen Degrees and five Minutes west five Chains and sixty eight Links to a Stake, Thence North forty five Degrees east three Chains and thirty six Links to a Stake, Thence South fifty seven Degrees east five Chains and forty eight Links to a Stake, Thence North thirty three Degrees east one Chain and seventy five Links to a Stake, Thence South fifty seven Degrees east twenty six Chains and twenty five Links to a Stake, Thence South thirty three Degrees west

---

o Sickles died Feb. 16, 1804. By will, dated Jan. 18, 1804, proved May 28, 1804, he gave all his realty to his daughter *Effie*, wife of Daniel Diedricks. He died April 8, 1822. *Vide Note to Lot No.* 317, p. 176.

† *Vide Note to Stoffelsen's Patent*, p. 9.

nine Chains and twenty Links to the Place of Beginning, containing about twenty five Acres and nine Tenths.

With respect to the two Lots of Common Land which have been allotted To the Patent of Philip Carteret to Thomas Frederick alias De Cuyper dated the tenth Day of November One thousand six hundred and seventy seven, being these two Lots of Common Land which in the Field Book & Map of the General Partition are distinguished by the Numbers 232 & 284

*181   * Michael De Mott and George De Mott claimed the said two Lots as Tenants in Common tnereof, and upon Examination of their Titles we conceive them to be the true Proprietors.

And do therefore adjudge the said Allotments to belong to them the said Michael De Mott and George De Mott in equal Moieties.

This is a **Subdivision** of the Lot of Common Land which has been allotted To the Patent of Petruis Stuyvesant to Harman Edwards, dated the fourteenth Day of September One thousand six hundred and sixty two, being that Lot of Common Land which in the Field Book and Map of the General Partition is distinguished by the Number 249.

And upon Examination of the Titles of the several Persons claiming Parts & Shares thereof.

We do adjudge a certain Portion of said Allotment No 249 To belong to Hendrick Van Winkle.

Our Survey of which said Portion (as laid down on Subdivision Schedule A) shews, and we adjudge it to be a Tract mark'd No 371.*

Beginning, at a Stake (being the eastermost Corner of said Allotment No 249) And from thence runs South thirty three Degrees west seventeen Chains & forty-five Links to a Stake Thence North fifty seven Degrees west thirty Chains to a Stake, Thence North Thirty three Degrees east nineteen Chains and seventy Links to a Stake, (being the Northermost Corner of said Allotment No 249) Thence South fifty two Degrees & thirty Minutes east thirty Chains to the Place of Beginning, Containing about fifty four Acres and six Tenths.

*182   ***And we** adjudge a certain Portion of said Allotment No 249 To belong to Cornelius Sip & Garret Sip in equal Moieties.

---

* *Vide Note to Teunisse's Patent*, p. 54. Van Winkle sold to Cornelius Sip, July 30, 1774, twenty-three acres and a half, bounded, southeast by the road leading to Bergen Farms, southwest by Garret Sip, northwest by a small creek, and north by Cornelius Newkirk (deed unrecorded). Joseph Van Winkle sold to Matthias and Jacob Newkirk, Jan. 20, 1775, ten and a half acres, then bounded east by William Bayard, south by Garret Sip, west by grantor, and north by Hendrick Van Winkle. These grantees partitioned. Jacob died seized of the southwest half, and it was partitioned between his son *John J.*, and the heirs of his son *Garret*; the former taking the northwest half, and the latter the southwest half. John M. Newkirk sold the northwest half to John Speer June 16, 1835.

Our Survey ot which Said Portion (as laid down on Subdivision Schedule A) shews and we adjudge it to be a Tract mark'd No 369.*

Beginning at a Stake (being the southermost Corner ot the Tract No 371 adjudged to Hendrick Van Winkle last above described) And from thence runs South thirty three Degrees west four Chains and fifty Links to a Stake (being the Southermost Corner of said Allotment No 249) Thence North fifty seven Degrees west twenty six Chains and eight Links to a Stake Thence North thirty three Degrees East four Chains and fifty Links to a Stake, Thence South fifty seven Degrees east twenty six Chains and eight Links to the Place of Beginning, containing about eleven Acres and eight Tenths.

And we adjudge a certain Portion of said Allotment No 249 To belong to Arent Toers.

Our Survey of which said Portion (as laid down on Subdivision Schedule A) shews, and we adjudge it to be a Tract mark'd No 370 †

Beginning at a Stake (being the westermost Corner of said Allotment No 249) and from thence runs. North thirty three Degrees east four Chains and fifty Links to a Stake, Thence South fifty seven Degrees east three Chains and ninety two Links to a Stake; Thence South thirty three Degrees west four Chains and fifty Links to a Stake, Thence North fifty seven Degrees west three Chains and ninety two Links to the Place of Beginning, containing about One Acre and six Tenths.

* **This** is a **Subdivision** of the Lot of Common Land *183 which has been allotted To the Patent of Philip Carteret to Guert Garritse, dated the twenty second Day of July one thousand six hundred and seventy, being that Lot of Common Land which in the Field Book and Map of the General Partition is distinguished by the Number 221.

And upon Examination of the Titles of the several Persons claiming Parts and Shares thereof

We do adjudge a certain Portion of said Allotment No 221 To belong to Johannis Van Houta

Our Survey of which said Portion (as laid down on Subdivision Schedule A) shews, and we adjudge it to be a Tract mark'd No 320

Beginning at a Stake (being the southermost Corner of said Allotment No 221) And from thence runs North fifty two Degrees & thirty Minutes west one Chain and seventy six Links to a Stake; Thence North thirty six Degrees and thirty Minutes east five Chains and sixty seven Links to a Stake; Thence South fifty two Degrees and thirty Minutes east One Chain and seventy six Links to a Stake; Thence South thirty six Degrees and thirty Minutes west five Chains and sixty seven Links to the Place of Beginning, containing about One Acre.

---

* *Vide Note to Van Vorst's Patent,* p. 60.
† *Vide Note to Steenhuysen's Patent,* p 32.

*184

And we do adjudge a certain Portion of said Allotment No 221 To belong to Abraham Sickles.

Our Survey of which said Portion (as laid down on Subdivision Schedule A) shews and we adjudged, it to be a Tract mark'd No 321 *

Beginning at a Stake (being the westermost Corner of the Tract No 320 adjudged To Johannis Van Houte last above described) And from thence runs North fifty two Degrees and thirty Minutes west thirteen Chains and forty four Links to a Stake, Thence North thirty six Degrees and thirty Minutes east five Chains and sixty seven Links to a Stake, Thence South fifty two Degrees and thirty Minutes east thirteen Chains and forty four Links to a Stake, Thence South thirty six Degrees and thirty Minutes west five Chains and sixty seven Links to the Place of Beginning, Containing about seven Acres & five Tenths.

And we adjudge a certain Portion of said Allotment No 221 To belong to Garrit Newkirk.

Our Survey of which said Portion (as laid down on Subdivision Schedule A) shews, and we adjudge it to be a Tract mark'd No 322.†

Beginning at a Stake (being the westermost Corner of the Tract No 321 adjudged to Abraham Sickles last above described) And from thence runs North fifty two Degrees and thirty Minutes west twenty two Chains and eighty Links to a Stake (being the westermost Corner of said Allotment No 221), Thence North thirty six Degrees and thirty Minutes east five Chains and sixty seven Links to a Stake; Thence South fifty two Degrees and thirty Minutes east twenty two Chains and eighty Links to a Stake; Thence South thirty six Degrees and thirty Minutes West five Chains and sixty seven Links to the Place of Beginning, containing about twelve Acres and nine Tenths.

*185

* **And we** adjudge a certain Portion of said Allotment No 221 To belong to Johannis Dederick.

Our Survey of which said Portion (as laid down on Subdivision Schedule A) shews, and we adjudge it to be a Tract mark'd No 324

Beginning at a Stake (being the Northermost Corner of the Tract No 322 adjudged To Garrit Newkirk last above described) And from thence runs North thirty six Degrees and thirty Minutes east ten Chains and forty Links to a Stake; Thence South fifty two Degrees and thirty Minutes east twenty one Chains and fifty Links to a Stake; Thence South thirty six Degrees and thirty Minutes west Ten Chains and forty Links to a Stake; Thence North fifty two Degrees and thirty Minutes west twenty one Chains and fifty Links to the Place of Beginning Containing about twenty two Acres and three Tenths.

---

* *Vide Note to Lot No.* 358, p. 179.
† *Vide Note to Pieterse's Patent*, p. 40. In the partition between his sons *Mathern* and *Hendrick*, the former took the northwest half, and the latter the southeast half. *Vide Note to Lot No.* 400, p. 172.

And we adjudge a certain Portion of said Allotment No 221 To belong to Cornelius Sip & Garrit Sip in equal Moieties.

Our Survey of which said Portion (as laid down on Subdivision Schedule A) shews, and we adjudge it to be a Tract mark'd No 323 *

Beginning at a Stake (being the easternmost Corner of the Tract No 324 adjudged to Johannis Dedericks last above described) and from thence runs South fifty two Degrees and thirty Minutes east sixteen Chains and fifty Links to a Stake; Thence South thirty six Degrees and thirty Minutes west Ten Chains and forty Links to a Stake; Thence North fifty two Degrees and thirty Minutes west sixteen Chains and fifty Links to a Stake, Thence North thirty six Degrees and thirty Minutes East ten Chains and forty Links to the Place of Beginning, containing about seventeen Acres.

* **And we** adjudge a certain Portion of said Allotment No 221 *186 To belong to Johannis Garritse, alias Urianse, alias Van Riper, alias **Beletje's Hans**.

Our Survey of which said Portion (as laid down on Subdivision Schedule A) shews, and we adjudge it to be a Tract mark'd No 325 †

Beginning at a Stake (being the easternmost Corner of the Tract No 323 adjudged To Cornelius and Garrit Sip last above described) And from thence runs North thirty six Degrees and thirty Minutes east eight Chains & twenty six Links to a Stake; Thence North fifty two Degrees and thirty Minutes west thirty eight Chains to a Stake; Thence South thirty six Degrees and thirty Minutes west eight Chains and twenty six Links to a Stake; Thence South fifty two Degrees and thirty Minutes east thirty eight Chains to the Place of Beginning, containing about thirty one Acres and three Tenths.

As To the remaining Portion of said Allotment No 221 being the Proportion of the Common Land which we adjudge to the Proprietor of the westerly Part of the patented Lot No 102, Guert Gerritse the original Patentee was the Person we find last seized of the westerly Part of said patented Lot No 102; and it not appearing to us in whom the same is now vested; **we** declare not to whom the said remaining Portion of Common Land does now belong.

Our Survey of which said remaining Portion (as laid down on Subdivision Schedule A) shews and we adjudge it to be a Tract mark'd No 326 ‡

Beginning at a Stake (being the Easternmost Corner of said Allotment No 221) And from thence runs South thirty six Degrees and thirty Minutes west five Chains and fifty three Links to a Stake; Thence North fifty two Degrees & thirty Minutes west thirty eight Chains to a Stake; Thence North thirty six Degrees & thirty Minutes east five Chains &

---

a *Vide Note to Van Vorst's Patent*, p. 60.

† *Vide Note to Lot No 345*, p. 170, *and Note to Noble and Moore's Patent*, p. 20.

‡ This lot was owned by Garret Van Vorst, who died April 2, 1834. It is now owned by his son *Cornelius*.

fifty three Links to a Stake (being the northermost Corner of said Allotment No 221) Thence South fifty two Degrees & thirty Minutes east thirty eight Chains to the Place of Beginning, containing about twenty one Acres.

*187   * With Respect to three Lots of Common Land, which have been allotted To the Patent of Petrus Stuyvesant to Paulus Pieterse dated the seventh Day of March one thousand six hundred & sixty three and confirmed to said Pieterse by Patent from Philip Carteret dated the twelfth Day of May one thousand six hundred and sixty eight, being these three Lots of Common Land which in the Field Book & Map of the General Partition are distinguished by the Numbers 252, 253 & 281

Garret Newkirk claimed the said three Lots, and no other Person or Persons claiming the same or a Subdivision thereof **we** upon Examination of his Title conceive him to be the true Proprietor; and do therefore adjudge the said three Allotments to belong to him.

This is a **subdivision** of the Lot of Common Land which has been allotted To the Patent of Philip Carteret to Dirck Garritse dated the twelfth Day of May One thousand six hundred & sixty eight—being that Lot of Common Land which in the Field Book & Map of the General Partition is distinguished by the Number 226.

And upon Examination of the Titles of the several Persons claiming Parts & Shares thereof **We** do adjudge a certain Portion of said Allotment No 226 To belong to Michael De Mott & George De Mott in equal Moieties.

*188   * **Our Survey** of which said Portion (as laid down on Subdivision Schedule A) shews, and we adjudge it to be a Tract mark'd No 331 *

Beginning at a Stake (being the southermost Corner of said Allotment No 226) And from thence runs North fifty two Degrees and thirty Minutes west three Chains and fifty Links to a Stake, Thence North thirty six Degrees and thirty Minutes east One Chain and forty three Links to a Stake; Thence South fifty two Degrees and thirty Minutes east three Chains and fifty Links to a Stake, Thence South thirty six Degrees and thirty Minutes west one Chain and forty three Links to the Place of Beginning, containing about Half an Acre.

And we do adjudge a certain Portion of said Allotment No 226 To belong to Daniel Van Riper.

Our Survey of which said Portion (as laid down on Subdivision Schedule A) shews, and we adjudge it to be a Tract mark'd No 332 †

---

* *Vide Note to Stoffelsen's Patent*, p. 9. It was in the De Mott heirs after 1840. It is now owned by Joseph Masters.

† *Vide Note to Lot No.* 411, p. 166. Van Rypen gave this lot to his sons *Cornelius* and *Richard*. The interest of Cornelius was given to his sons, *Daniel* and *Cornelius C.*, the latter in trust for the heirs of Garret Van Rypen. It is owned in whole or in part by John Gardner.

Beginning at a Stake (being the easternmost Corner of a Tract No 331) adjudged to the Demotts last above described) And from thence runs North thirty six Degrees and thirty Minutes east four Chains and forty Links to a Stake; Thence North fifty two Degrees and thirty Minutes west thirty eight Chains to a Stake; Thence South thirty six Degrees and thirty Minutes west five Chains and eighty three Links to a Stake (being the westermost Corner of said Allotment No 226) Thence South fifty two Degrees and thirty Minutes East thirty four Chains and fifty Links to a Stake, Thence North thirty six Degrees and thirty Minutes East one Chain and forty three Links to a Stake; Thence South fifty two Degrees and thirty Minutes east three Chains and fifty Links to the Place of Beginning, containing about twenty one Acres & seven Tenths.

* **And we** adjudge a certain Portion of said Allotment No 226 *189
To belong to Sarah Prior, Widow of Caspar Prior for her Use during her natural Life, and at her decease To Nicholas Prior agreable to the last Will & Testament of said Caspar Prior his Father dated the twenty second Day of November One thousand seven hundred and fifty three

Our Survey of which said Portion (as laid down on Subdivision Schedule A) shews and we adjudge it to be a Tract mark'd No 333 *

Beginning at a Stake (being the Easternmost Corner of the Tract No 332 adjudged to Daniel Van Riper last above described) And from thence runs North thirty six Degrees and thirty Minutes east five Chains and seventy three Links to a Stake (being the easternmost Corner of said Allotment No 226) Thence North fifty two Degrees and thirty Minutes west thirty eight Chains to a Stake (being the northermost Corner of said Allotment No 226) Thence South thirty six Degrees and thirty Minutes west five Chains and seventy three Links to a Stake, Thence South fifty two Degrees and thirty Minutes east thirty eight Chains to the Place of Beginning, Containing about twenty one Acres & eight Tenths.

This is a subdivision of the Lot of Common Land which has been allotted To the Patent of Petrus Stuyvesant to Jacob Luby dated the fourteenth Day of September one thousand six hundred and sixty two, being that Lot of Common Land which in the Field Book & Map of the General Partition is distinguished by the Number 231.

And upon Examination of the Titles of the several Persons claiming Parts & Shares thereof,

* **We** do adjudge a certain Portion of said Allotment No 231 *190
To belong to Cornelius Sip & Garret Sip in equal Moieties.

Our Survey of which said Portion (as laid down on Subdivision Schedule A) shews, and we adjudge it to be a Tract mark'd No 342 †

Beginning at a Stake (being the southermost Corner of said Allotment No 231) And from thence runs North thirty six Degrees and thirty

---

* This lot remained in the Prior family until after 1840. *Vide Note to Gerritse's Patent*, p. 41.

† *Vide Note to Van Vorst's Patent*, p. 60. It was sold by Sip to Daniel Earle. It is now owned by Doeg, Earle, and Harriman in severalty.

Minutes east four Chains and eighty four Links to a Stake, Thence North fifty two Degrees & thirty Minutes West nineteen Chains to a Stake, Thence South thirty six Degrees & thirty Minutes west four Chains and eighty four Links to a Stake, Thence South fifty two Degrees and thirty Minutes east nineteen Chains to the Place of Beginning, containing about nine Acres.

And we adjudge a certain Portion of said Allotment No 231 To belong to Arent Toers.

Our Survey of which said Portion (as laid down on Subdivision Schedule A) shews, and we adjudge it to be a Tract mark'd No 343 *

Beginning at a Stake (being the easternmost Corner of said Tract mark'd No 342 adjudged to Cornelius and Garrit Sip last above described) And from thence runs North thirty six Degrees and thirty Minutes east eleven Chains and eighty two Links to a Stake, Thence North fifty two Degrees and thirty Minutes west thirty eight Chains to a Stake, Thence South thirty six Degrees and thirty Minutes west sixteen Chains and sixty six Links to a Stake (being the westermost Corner of said Allotment No 231) Thence South fifty two Degrees & thirty Minutes east nineteen Chains to a Stake, Thence North thirty six Degrees and thirty Minutes east four Chains and eighty four Links to a Stake, Thence South fifty two Degrees and thirty Minutes east nineteen Chains to the Place of Beginning, containing about fifty four Acres.

*191

* **And we** adjudge a certain Portion of said Allotment No 231 To belong to Johannis Van Houta.

Our Survey of which said Portion (as laid down on Subdivision Schedule A) shews, and we adjudge it to be a Tract mark'd No 344 †

Beginning at a Stake (being the easternmost Corner of the Tract No 343 adjudged To Arent Toers last above described) And from thence runs North thirty six Degrees and thirty Minutes east seven Chains and ninety eight Links to a Stake (being the easternmost Corner of said Allotment No 231) Thence North fifty two Degrees and thirty Minutes west thirty eight Chains to a Stake (being the northermost Corner of said Allotment No 231) Thence South thirty six Degrees and thirty minutes west seven Chains and ninety eight Links To a Stake, Thence South fifty two Degrees and thirty Minutes east thirty eight Chains to the Place of Beginning, containing about thirty Acres.

---

* *Vide Note to Steenhuysen's Patent*, p. 32. John S. Winner seems to have owned the southwest corner of this lot and sold the same to Thomas McDonald. It included all south of the north line of lot No. 342 extended west. The balance of the lot remained in the Tuers family until quite recently. The executors of Nicholas sold the west part to Thomas McDonald, the east part to Mrs. Wetherby, the present owners.

† Abraham Van Houten sold one-half of this lot to John George Leake March 10, 1807, who probably sold to Jesse Van Gelder. John Van Houten sold five acres out of the southeast corner of this lot to Abraham Huyler Aug. 10, 1815, who sold to McDonald, the present owner. John Van Houten sold seven acres and eighty-nine one-hundredths of an acre on the southwest side of the lot to Jesse Van Gelder Aug. 1, 1835.

With respect to the Lot of Common Land which has been allotted To the Patent of Philip Carteret to Jacob Luby dated the Tenth Day of November One thousand six hundred and seventy seven, being that Lot of Common Land which in the Field Book & Map of the General Partition is distinguished by the Number 202.

William Bayard Esqr. claimed the said Lot and upon Examination of this Title we conceive him to be the true Proprietor thereof And do therefore adjudge the said Allotment to belong to him.

* **This** is a **subdivision** of the two Lots of Common Land which have been allotted To the Patent of Philip Carteret to Jan Lubertse dated the twelfth Day of May one thousand six hundred & sixty eight, being these two Lots of Common Land which in the Field Book & Map of the General Partition are distinguished by the Numbers 248 & 282. *192

And upon Examination of the Titles of the several Persons claiming Parts & Shares thereof

We do adjudge a certain Portion of said Allotment No 248 To belong to Levinus Winne

Our Survey of which said Portion (as laid down on Subdivision Schedule A) shews, and we adjudge it to be a Tract mark'd No 363 *

Beginning at a Stake (being the Southermost Corner of the said Allotment No 248) And from thence runs North thirty three Degrees east nine Chains and seventy five Links to a Stake, Thence North fifty seven Degrees west twenty five Chains and ninety nine Links to a Stake, Thence South thirty three Degrees west nine Chains and seventy five Links to a Stake, Thence South fifty seven Degrees east twenty five

---

* Levinus Winne released to Johannis Winne May 27, 1773.

1st. The southerly half of a lot of meadow, bounded, south by the Newkirks, west by Hackensack river, north by said Levinus, and east by said Levinus and Johannis

2d. A lot between the middle road and meadow lying north of the Newkirks;

3d. The south half of a lot near the church of Bergen;

4th. The south half of *Lot No. 363.*

By will, dated Jan. 8, 1802, proved July 9, 1802, he gave all his lands to his wife for life; then to his son *Martin* a lot adjoining the Burying Ground, *vide Note to Van Vleck's Patent*, p. 53; to *Ide* or Edo his homestead farm in Bergen for life, then to his heirs. The residue of his lands he gave to Martin and Ide equally. Martin was to have the north half of a lot at Pannepack in Bergen Woods. Martin sold to Cornelius Van Vorst ten acres out of this lot April 14, 1814; and to Garret G. Van Vorst, jr., April 14, 1814 the part lying west of the old road, containing three acres. These two sons partitioned by deed May 7, 1804 (unrecorded). By will, dated April 23, 1796, proved Sept. 3, 1800, Johannis gave to his son *Martin* all his lands in the township except ten acres in Bergen Woods given to his daughter *Antje*, wife of Daniel Van Winkle.

Edo Winne, April 28, 1807, deeded all his property to his father-in-law, Nicholas Tuers, and Christopher Van Rypen in trust, to be divided among his children. *Vide Note to Lubbertse's Patent*, p. 45.

Chains and ninety nine Links to the Place of Beginning, Containing about twenty five Acres and four Tenths.

*193   **And we** adjudge a certain Portion of said Allotment No 248 To belong to Abraham Dedericks.

Our Survey of which said Portion (as laid down on Subdivision Schedule A) shews, and we adjudge it to be a Tract mark'd No 364 *

Beginning at a Stake (being the westermost Corner of the Tract No 363 adjudged to Levinus Winne last above described) And from thence runs North fifty seven Degrees west four Chains and one Link to a Stake (being the westermost Corner of said Allotment No 248) Thence North thirty three Degrees east one Chain and sixty eight Links to a Stake, Thence South fifty seven Degrees east four Chains and one Link to a Stake, Thence South thirty three Degrees west one Chain and sixty eight Links to the Place of Beginning Containing about six Tenths of an Acre.

And we adjudge a certain Portion of said Allotment No 248 To belong to Cornelius Dedericks

Our Survey of which said Portion (as laid down on Subdivision Schedule A) shews, and we adjudge it to be a Tract mark'd No 365 †

Beginning at a Stake (being the eastermost Corner of the Tract No 364 adjudged to Abraham Dedericks last above described) And from thence runs North fifty seven Degrees west four Chains and one Link to a Stake, Thence North thirty three Degrees east one Chain and sixty eight Links to a Stake, Thence South fifty seven Degrees east four Chains and one Link to a Stake, Thence South thirty three Degrees west one Chain and sixty eight Links to the Place of Beginning, Containing about six Tenths of an Acre.

*194   **And we** adjudge a certain Portion of said Allotment No 248 To belong to Arent Toers.

Our Survey of which said Portion (as laid down on Subdivision Schedule A) shews, and we adjudge it to be a Tract mark'd No 366 ‡

Beginning at a Stake (being the eastermost Corner of the Tract No 365 adjudged to Cornelius Dedericks last above described) And from thence runs North fifty seven Degrees west four Chains and one Link to a Stake, Thence North thirty three Degrees east twelve Chains and eighty Links to a Stake (being the northermost Corner of said Allotment No 248), Thence South fifty seven Degrees east four Chains and one Link to a Stake, Thence South thirty three Degrees west twelve Chains and eighty Links to the Place of Beginning containing about five Acres and two Tenths.

---

* Diedricks died Feb. 6, 1799. His children were *Johannis*, *Effie*, married John Zabriskie, and *Gertrude*, married John Van Winkle. Zabriskie had one daughter, *Ann*, married John R. Romaine.

† *Vide Note to Lot No.* 406, p. 175.

‡ *Vide Note to Steenhuysen's Patent*, p. 32.

And we adjudge a certain Portion of said Allotment No 248 To belong to Andries Prior.

Our Survey of which said Portion (as laid down on Subdivision Schedule A) shews, and we adjudge it to be a Tract mark'd No 367*

Beginning at a Stake (being the easternmost Corner of the Tract No 363 adjudged to Levinus Winne above described) And from thence runs North thirty three Degrees east six Chains and forty one Links to a Stake (being the easternmost Corner of said Allotment No 248) Thence North fifty seven Degrees west four Chains and sixty eight Links to a Stake, Thence South thirty three Degrees west six Chains and forty one Links to a Stake, Thence South fifty seven Degrees east four Chains and sixty eight Links to the Place of Beginning, Containing about three Acres.

* **And we** adjudge a certain Portion of said Allotment No 248 To belong to Gysber Van blairkum. *195

Our Survey of which said Portion (as laid down on Subdivision Schedule A) shews, and we adjudge it to be a Tract mark'd No 386

Beginning at a Stake (being the westernmost Corner of the Tract No 367 adjudged to Andries Prior last above described) And from thence runs North thirty three Degrees east six Chains and forty one Links to a Stake, Thence North fifty seven Degrees west twenty one Chains and thirty one Links to a Stake, Thence South thirty three Degrees west six Chains and forty one Links to a Stake, Thence South fifty seven Degrees east twenty one Chains and thirty one Links to the Place of Beginning, containing about thirteen Acres and two Tenths.

And we adjudge the said Allotment No 282 (as the same is described butted and bounded in the Field Book of the General Partition) To belong to said Arent Toers.

This is a **subdivision** of the Lot of Common Land which has been Allotted to the Patent of Philip Carteret To Peter Jacobse dated the fifth Day of August one thousand six hundred and seventy one, being that Lot of Common Land; which in the Field Book & Map of the General Partition is distinguished by the Number 236.

And upon Examination of the titles of the several Persons claiming Parts & Shares thereof

* **We** do adjudge a certain Portion of said Allotment No 236 *196 To belong to Jacob Van Wagenen

Our Survey of which said Portion (as laid down on Subdivision Schedule A) shews, and we adjudge it to be a Tract mark'd No 348 †

---

o Prior by will, dated May 12, 1788, unproved (by agreement among his children, viz., *Casparus, Hartman, Abraham*, and *Ariantje*, wife of Adam Rapp, dated April 10, 1792), gave all his realty to his sons Casparus and Abraham; Casparus took the northeast half of this lot, and Abraham the southeast half. Casparus died March 30, 1828, and Abraham died Sept. 18, 1830.

† *Vide Note to Gerritse's Patent*, p. 58.

Beginning at a Stake (being the northerly Corner of said Allotment No 236) And from thence runs South thirty three Degrees west seven Chains and sixty eight Links to a Stake, Thence South fifty seven Degrees East twenty five Chains and ten Links to a Stake, Thence North thirty three Degrees East four Chains and seventy one Links to a Stake, Thence North fifty seven Degrees west two Chains to a Stake; Thence North thirty three Degrees east two Chains and ninety seven Links to a Stake; Thence North fifty seven Degrees west twenty three Chains and ten Links to the Place of Beginning, Containing about eighteen Acres & four Tenths.

And we adjudge a certain Portion of said Allotment No 236 To belong to Peter Marselies

Our Survey of which said Portion (as laid down on Subdivision Schedule A) shews, & we adjudge it to be a Tract mark'd No 349 *

Beginning at a Stake (being the Westerly Corner of the Tract No 348 adjudg'd to Jacob Van Wagenen last above described) And from thence runs South thirty three Degrees west twenty two Chains and sixty Links to a Stake (being the westermost Corner of the said Allotment No 236) Thence South fifty seven Degrees east twenty five Chains and ten Links to a Stake (being the Southermost Corner of said Allotment No 236) Thence North thirty three Degrees east twenty two Chains & sixty Links to a Stake, Thence North fifty seven Degrees west twenty five Chains and ten Links to the Place of Beginning, containing about fifty six Acres & Six Tenths.

*197

* **This is a subdivision** of the six Lots of Common Land which have been Allotted to the Patent of Philip Carteret to Nicholas Varlet & Balthazar Bayard dated the Tenth Day of August one thousand six hundred & seventy one, being these six Lots of Common Land which in the Field Book & Map of the General Partition are distinguished by the Numbers 250, 285, 286, 224, 241 and 287.

---

* This lot was in the *Vlakje Creupel bosh*, now West Hoboken. Merselis died seized April 1, 1770. It was inherited by his son Merselis, by whose will, dated March 15, 1799, proved Dec. 5, 1800, it was divided among his children. *John* received the northeast half; *Jane*, wife of Walter Clendenny, and *Anne*, wife of Josiah Hornblower, each received one-quarter. *Vide Note to Lot No. 11, New Field Book*. John sold his half to Eleanor, wife of Michael Simmons, Feb. 13, 1802. Simmons and wife sold to his father, William Simmons, May 11, 1811. William died seized and intestate in 1828, leaving a widow and children, *Peter, David B., John A.* (who died about 1834), *William, Jane*, wife of Peter R. Huntington; *Sophia*, wife of Lewis Peak (she died in 1838); *Sarah Ann*, wife of Uriah H. Peak; and *Adelia*, wife of Nicholas S. Ludlam. William was a bachelor, and by will, dated Nov. 21, 1831, proved Dec. 10, 1832 (Liber 69 of Wills, N. Y. 547), gave his property to his mother. The other children, by deeds in February and March, 1836, sold to John Syms; who sold to George B. Inness in 1836, and to Cyrus S. Browning Dec. 27, 1837; Syms bought it again under foreclosure sale. He died seized of at least a part —will dated Nov. 14, 1868, proved Dec. 21, 1868. Jacob D. Van Winkle bought Clendenny's interest in this tract.

And upon Examination of the Titles of the several Persons claiming Parts and Shares thereof,

We do adjudge a certain Portion of said Allotment No 250 To belong to Johannis Van Houta

Our Survey of which said Portion (as laid down on Subdivision Schedule A) shews, and we adjudge it to be a Tract mark'd No 372 *

Beginning at a Stake (being the Southermost Corner of said Allotment No 250) And from thence runs North thirty three Degrees east eight Chains and seventy one Links to a Stake, Thence North fifty seven Degrees west thirty two Chains & twenty five Links to a Stake, Thence South forty four Degrees and five Minutes west eleven Chains and ninety Links to a Stake; Thence North forty two Degrees west fifty six Chains & seventy Links to Pinhornes Creek, Thence returning To the first mentioned Stake the Place of Beginning and from thence runs North fifty Degrees west twenty Chains and eighty Links to a Stake in the Edge of the Meadow, Thence South forty two Degrees and thirty Minutes west five Chains to a Stake, Thence South forty five Degrees and Ten Minutes west eight Chains and forty Links to a Stake, Thence North forty three Degrees west twenty Chains and forty seven Links to Bridge Creek; Then North forty two Degrees west forty eight Chains and thirty eight Links along a Ditch to said Pinhornes Creek, Then up along said Creek as it runs 'till it meets the above mentioned Line running to said Creek, containing about sixty three Acres and a Half.

* **And we** adjudge a certain Portion of said Allotment No 250 *198 To belong to Arent Toers.

Our Survey of which said Portion (as laid down on Subdivision Schedule A) shews, and we adjudge it to be a Tract mark'd No 378 †

Beginning at a Stake (being the easternmost Corner of said Allotment No 250) And from thence runs South thirty three Degrees west two Chains to a Stake, Thence North fifty seven Degrees west nine Chains to a Stake, Thence North thirty three Degrees east two Chains to a Stake, Thence South fifty seven Degrees east nine Chains to the Place of Beginning, Containing about one Acre and eight Tenths.

And we adjudge a certain Portion of said Allotment No 250 To belong to Cornelius Sip & Garrit Sip in equal Moieties.

Our Survey of which said Portion (as laid down on Subdivision Schedule A) shews, and we adjudge it to be a Tract mark'd No 377 ‡

Beginning at a Stake (being the Southermost Corner of the Tract No 378 adjudged to Arent Toers last above described) And from thence

---

* The front part of this lot, containing four acres, was sold by John Van Houte to Jacob Prior (his son-in-law), Jan. 7, 1806. He had previously released the rear part to his brother Helmigh. He sold twelve acres of it, adjoining the rear of the four acres sold to Jacob Prior, to his daughter *Sarah*, wife of Jacob Prior, Jan. 8, 1806.

† *Vide Note to Steenhuysen's Patent*, p. 32. It belonged to Tuers' heirs in 1840.

‡ *Vide Note to Van Vorst's Patent*, p. 60.

runs South thirty three Degrees west three Chains and nineteen Links to a Stake, Thence North fifty seven Degrees west eighty four Chains and eighty six Links to Pinhornes Creek; then returning to the first mentioned Stake the Place of Beginning and from thence runs North fifty seven Degrees west nine Chains to a Stake; Thence North thirty three Degrees east two Chains to a Stake; Thence North fifty seven Degrees west seventy three Chains to a Stake by Pinhornes Creek (being the Northermost Corner of said Allotment No 250) Thence down along said Pinhornes Creek as it runs 'till it meets the above mentioned Line running to said Creek, Containing about forty one Acres and a Half.

*199

* And we adjudge a certain Portion of said Allotment No 250 To belong to Johannis Gerritse alias Urianse alias Van Riper alias Beletje's Hans.

Our Survey of which said Portion (as laid down on Subdivision Schedule A) shews, and we adjudge it to be a Tract mark'd No 373 *

Beginning at a Stake (being the eastermost Corner of the Tract No 372 adjudg'd to Johannis Van Houta above described) And from thence runs North thirty three Degrees East eight Chains and seventy Links to a Stake; thence North fifty seven Degrees west forty three Chains and seventy five Links to a Stake; Thence South thirty three Degrees west eighteen Chains to a Stake, Thence South forty-two Degrees east nine Chains and thirty Links to a Stake, Thence North forty four Degrees and five Minutes east eleven Chains and ninety Links to a Stake Thence South fifty seven Degrees east thirty two Chains and twenty five Links to the Place of Beginning, Containing about forty nine Acres.

And we adjudge a certain Portion of said Allotment No 250 To belong to Cornelius Gerritse alias Van Riper.

Our Survey of which said Portion (as laid down on Subdivision Schedule A) shews, and we adjudge it to be a Tract mark'd No 374 †

Beginning at a Stake (being the westermost Corner of the Tract No 373 adjudged to Johannis Gerritse last above described) And from thence runs North forty two Degrees west forty seven Chains and forty Links to Pinhorne's Creek, Then returning to said Stake the Place of Beginning and from thence runs North thirty three Degrees East sixteen Chains and thirteen Links to a Stake; Thence North fifty seven Degrees west forty five Chains to said Pinhornes Creek; Then down along said Creek as it runs 'till it comes to the first mentioned Line running to said Creek, Containing about forty Six Acres.

*200

* And we adjudge a certain Portion of said Allotment No 250 To belong to Gerrit Gerritse alias Van Riper.

Our Survey of which said Portion (as laid down on Subdivision Schedule A) shews, and we adjudge it to be a Tract mark'd No 375 ‡

---

* *Vide Note to Coerten's first Patent*, p. 25.

† *Vide Note to Lot No.* 411, p. 166.

‡ Van Rypen died Aug. 30, 1795. Belicah Van Horne, Nicholas Tuers, and Jannetje, his wife; John Merselis, and Altje, his wife, released to Daniel Van Rypen all

Beginning at a Stake (being the easternmost Corner of the said Tract No 374 adjudged to Cornelius Garritse last above described) And from thence runs North fifty seven Degrees west forty five Chains to Pinhornes Creek, Then returning to said Stake the Place of Beginning; and from thence runs North thirty three Degrees east six Chains and ninety seven Links to a Stake; Thence North fifty seven Degrees west forty one Chains and eleven Links to said Pinhornes Creek; Then down along said Creek as it runs 'till it comes to the first mentioned Line running to said Creek containing about thirty Acres.

And we adjudge a certain Portion of said Allotment No 250 To belong to Altje the Wife of Daniel Van Winkle.

Our Survey of which said Portion (as laid down on Subdivision Schedule A) shews, and we adjudge it to be a Tract mark'd No 376 *

Beginning at a Stake (being the easternmost Corner of the Tract No 373 adjudged to Johannis Garritse above described) and from thence runs North thirty three Degrees east five Chains and ten Links to a Stake; Thence North fifty seven Degrees west forty three Chains and seventy five Links to a Stake, Thence South thirty three Degrees west five Chains and ten Links to a Stake, Thence South fifty seven Degrees east forty three Chains and seventy five Links to the Place of Beginning, containing about twenty two Acres and a Quarter.

And we adjudge the said two Allotments No 285 & 286 (as the same two Allotments are respectively described butted and bounded in the Field Book of the General Partition) To belong to said Cornelius Sip and Garrit Sip in equal Moyeties. *201

And we adjudge the said Allotment No 224 (as the same is described butted and bounded in the Field Book of the General Partition) To belong to said Johannis Garritse alias Urianse, alias Van Riper alias Beletje's Hans.

And we adjudge the said two Allotments No 241 and 287 (as the same two Allotments are respectively described, butted and bounded in the Field Book of the General Partition) To belong to Zachariah Sickles.

With respect to the Lot of Common Land which has been allotted To the Patent of Philip Carteret to Dow Harmense dated the twelfth Day of May One thousand six

---

of their interest in the property of Garret. *Vide Note to Lot No.* 315, p. 167, *and Lot No.* 411, p. 166. These three were sisters, daughters of Cornelius, brother of Garret Van Rypen.

º Altje Van Winkle was a Van Rypen and inherited with her brothers, Cornelius and Garret. John Sickles owned the east third of this lot, and conveyed the same to Stephen and Daniel Simonson April 1, 1815. Daniel released to Stephen Dec. 25, 1818; he to Abraham Collerd May 24, 1819. Collerd died seized and intestate, leaving his widow, Ann, and children, *Jacob, John,* and *Abraham.* John died when about six years old. Jacob married, but died without issue. Ann, the widow of Abraham; Maria, the widow of Jacob; and Abraham Collerd, conveyed to James Montgomery Sept. 26, 1851.

hundred and sixty eight, being that Lot of Common Land which in the Field Book & Map of the General Partition is distinguished by the Number 246.

Michael De Mott & George De Mott claimed the said Lot as Tenants in Common thereof; and upon Examination of their Titles **we** conceive them To be the true Proprietors; And do therefore adjudge the said Allotment To belong to them the said Michael and George De Mott in equal Moieties.

*202

* **This** is a **subdivision** of the Lot of Common Land which has been Allotted to the Patent of Philip Carteret to John Berry dated the twentyeth Day of July, one thousand six hundred and sixty nine, being that Lot of Common Land which in the Field Book and Map of the General Partition is distinguished by the Number 228.

And upon Examination of the Titles of the several Persons claiming Parts and Shares thereof,

We do adjudge a certain Portion of said Allotment No 228 To belong to Johannis Van Houta.

Our Survey of which said Portion (as laid down on Subdivision Schedule A) shews and we adjudge it to be a Tract mark'd No 336

Beginning at a Stake (being the southermost Corner of said Allotment No 228) And from thence runs North thirty six Degrees and thirty Minutes east three Chains and fifty eight Links to a Stake, Thence North fifty two Degrees and thirty Minutes west nineteen Chains to a Stake, Thence South thirty six Degrees and thirty Minutes west three Chains and fifty eight Links to a Stake, Thence South fifty two Degrees and thirty Minutes east nineteen Chains to the Place of Beginning, containing about six Acres.

*203

* **And we** adjudge a certain Portion of said Allotment No 228 To belong to Mathevis Newkirk & Henry Newkirk in equal Moieties.

Our Survey of which said Portion (as laid down on Subdivision Schedule A) shews, and we adjudge it to be a Tract mark'd No 337 *

Beginning at a Stake (being the easternmost Corner of the Tract No 336 adjudged To Johannis Van Houta last above described) And from thence runs North thirty six Degrees and thirty Minutes East fourteen Chains and fifty three Links to a Stake, Thence North fifty two Degrees and thirty Minutes west thirty eight Chains to a Stake, Thence South thirty six Degrees and thirty Minutes west eighteen Chains and eleven Links to a Stake (being the westermost Corner of said Allotment No 228) Thence South fifty two Degrees and thirty Minutes East nine-

---

* This lot was partitioned between Mathevis and Hendrick. Hendrick took the southerly half, and by will, dated July 7, 1795, proved Sept. 28, 1811, gave all his lands to his sons, *Garret* and *George*, equally. The village of West New York is on this lot. *Vide Note to Berry's Patent*, p. 51.

teen Chains To a Stake; Thence North thirty six Degrees and thirty Minutes east three Chains and fifty eight Links to a Stake, Thence South fifty two Degrees and thirty Minutes east nineteen Chains to the Place of Beginning, Containing about sixty two Acres.

And we adjudge a certain portion of said Allotment No 228 To belong to Mathevis Newkirk Jun_r.

Our Survey of which said Portion (as laid down on Subdivision Schedule A) shews, and we adjudge it to be a Tract mark'd No 338 *

Beginning at a Stake (being the easternmost Corner of the Tract No 337 adjudged to Mathevis & Henry Newkirk last above described) And from thence runs North thirty six Degrees and thirty Minutes east eight Chains and sixteen Links to a Stake, Thence North fifty two Degrees and thirty Minutes west thirty eight Chains to a Stake, Thence South thirty six Degrees and thirty Minutes West eight Chains and sixteen Links to a Stake; Thence South fifty two Degrees and thirty Minutes East thirty eight Chains to the Place of Beginning, containing about thirty one Acres.

* **And we** adjudge a certain Portion of said Allotment No 228 *204 To belong to Jacob Newkirk.

Our Survey of which said Portion (as laid down on Subdivision Schedule A) shews, and we adjudge it to be a Tract mark'd No 339 †

Beginning at a Stake (being the easternmost Corner of the Tract No 338 adjudged to Mathevis Newkirk Junr last above described) And from thence runs North thirty six Degrees and thirty Minutes east eight Chains and sixteen Links to a Stake (being the easternmost Corner of said Allotment No 228), Thence North fifty two Degrees and thirty Minutes west thirty eight Chains to a Stake (being the northermost Corner of said Allotment No 228) Thence South thirty six Degrees and thirty Minutes west eight Chains and sixteen Links to a Stake, Thence South fifty two Degrees and thirty Minutes east thirty eight Chains to the Place of Beginning containing about thirty one Acres.

---

* Newkirk sold the easterly half of this lot to Johannis Van Houten April 24, 1773, now owned by Danielson. Newkirk sold about one quarter of this lot to Johannis Van Wagenen April 24, 1773, and one quarter of Lot No. 339, containing, in all, fifteen and one-quarter acres. *Vide Note to Gerritse's Patent,* p. 58. It remained in the Van Wagenen family until sold to Louis Becker in 1853. John M., son of Mathevis, jr., sold fifteen acres and eighty-five one-hundredths of an acre to Joseph Danielson July 7, 1835, bounded northwest by Michael Fisher, northeast by Garret Newkirk, southeast by Jacob Van Wagenen, and southwest by Garret and Henry Newkirk. *Vide Note to Berry's Patent,* p. 51.

† Newkirk sold the easterly end of this lot to Jacob Van Wagenen; the balance he left to his two sons; *Garret,* who took the easterly part, and died seized Aug. 22, 1818, leaving *Jacob, George, Garret, Sophia,* wife of James Provost, and *Catherine,* wife of George Vreeland; and *John J.,* who took the westerly part, and died seized Aug. 15, 1860. The easterly part is now owned by John and Robert E. Gardner. Part of the westerly half was bought and mapped out, and is now known as "Frogtown." *Vide Note to Lot No.* 338, p. 203.

This is a **subdivision** of the Lot of Common Land which has been allotted To the Patent of Philip Carteret to Tielman Van Vleck dated the twenty fifth Day of March one thousand six hundred and seventy, being that Lot of Common Land which in the Field Book & Map of the General Partition is distinguished by the Number 230.

And upon Examination of the Titles of the several Persons claiming Parts & Shares thereof,

We do adjudge a certain Portion of said Allotment No 230 To belong to Levinus Winne.

*205   * **Our Survey** of which said Portion (as laid down on Subdivision Schedule A) shews, and we adjudge it to be a Tract mark'd No 340 *

Beginning at a Stake (being the Southermost Corner of said Allotment No 230) And from thence runs North thirty six Degrees and thirty Minutes east ten Chains and twenty four Links to a Stake, Thence North fifty two Degrees and thirty Minutes west Ten Chains to a Stake, Thence North thirty six Degrees and thirty Minutes east three Chains and fifty Links to a Stake, Thence North fifty two Degrees and thirty Minutes west eight Chains to a Stake (being the northermost Corner of said Allotment No 230) Thence South thirty six Degrees and thirty Minutes west thirteen Chains and seventy four Links to a Stake, Thence South fifty two Degrees and thirty Minutes East thirty eight Chains to the Place of Beginning, containing about forty eight Acres.

And we adjudge a certain Portion of said Allotment No 230 To belong to Isaac Van Vleck.

Our Survey of which said Portion as laid down on Subdivision Schedule A) shews and we adjudge it to be a Tract mark'd No 341 †

Beginning at a Stake (being the easternmost Corner of the Tract No 340 adjudged to Levinus Winne last above described) And from thence runs North thirty six Degrees thirty Minutes East three Chains and fifty Links to a Stake (being the easternmost Corner of said Allotment No 230) Thence North fifty two Degrees and thirty Minutes west ten Chains to a Stake, Thence South thirty six Degrees and thirty Minutes west three Chains and fifty Links to a Stake, Thence South fifty two De-

---

* *Vide Note to Lot No.* 363, p. 192. John S. Winne sold the westerly part of this lot to William Danielson, and the balance to Westerfield. In 1840, the latter family owned the whole of it, and yet own part of it. Danielson sold his purchase, containing twelve acres and ninety-five one-hundredths of an acre, to Henry Westerfield April 1, 1834. Elizabeth Westerfield sold the easterly part to William Cooper March 3. 1834, excepting three-quarters of an acre sold by John Rapp to Henry Rapp May 14, 1819. The village of Guttenberg is on this part of the lot, and the lots between it and the river. On Aug. 11, 1821, the executors of Thaddeus Goodyear sold to Jasper B. Westervelt sixteen acres, which I take to lie within this lot. Jasper conveyed it to Benjamin C. Westervelt (Westerfield ?) Feb. 5, 1823. This was the southerly part of the lot.

† Richard Earle owned this lot, and sold it to Esther Tysen, the present owner.

grees and thirty Minutes east ten Chains to the Place of Beginning, containing about three Acres and one Half.

This is a **subdivision** of the two Lots of Common *206 Land which have been allotted To the Patent of Philip Carteret to Hendrick Teunisse dated the twelfth Day of May one thousand six hundred and sixty eight, being these two Lots of Common Land which in the Field Book and Map of the General Partition are distinguished by the Numbers 220 and 255.

And upon Examination of the Titles of the several Persons claiming Parts & shares thereof,

We do adjudge a certain Portion of said Allotment No 220 To belong to Michael Hartman Vreelandt.

Our Survey of which said Portion (as laid down on Subdivision Schedule A) shews, and we adjudge it to be a Tract mark'd No 318 *

Beginning at a large Stone (mark'd A 1764 planted in a Corner of Wiehaken Commons) And from thence runs North thirty six Degrees & thirty Minutes east eighteen Chains and forty three Links to a Stake, Thence North fifty two Degrees and thirty Minutes West seven Chains and thirty Links to a Stake, Thence South thirty three Degrees west eighteen Chains and forty six Links to a Stake, Thence South fifty two Degrees and thirty Minutes east six Chains and thirty Links to the Place of Beginning, containing about twelve Acres & a Half.

* **And we** adjudge a certain Portion of said Allotment No *207 220 To belong to Hendrick Van Winkle.

Our Survey of which said Portion (as laid down on Subdivision Schedule A) shews, and we adjudge it to be a Tract mark'd No 319 †

Beginning at a Stake (being the westermost Corner of the Tract No 318 adjudg'd to Michael Hartman Vreelandt last above described) And from thence runs North thirty three Degrees east eighteen Chains and forty six Links to a Stake, Thence North fifty two Degrees and thirty Minutes west thirty Chains and seventy Links to a Stake (being the northermost Corner of said Allotment No 220) Thence South thirty six Degrees and thirty Minutes West eighteen Chains & forty three Links to a Stake (being the westermost Corner of said Allotment No 220) Thence South fifty two Degrees and thirty Minutes east thirty one Chains and seventy Links to the Place of Beginning, containing about fifty seven Acres & a Half.

---

* *Vide Note to Lot No.* 308, p. 139.

† *Vide Note to Teunisse's Patent,* p. 54. Joseph Van Winkle's nephews, John and Jacob, conveyed to Frederick Grosclaude and Edward Dubois six acres and forty one-hundredths of an acre Dec. 8, 1840. His nephew, Abraham, died intestate Nov. 4, 1823, seized of about six acres, which his heirs conveyed to Peter Perine June 4, 1824; he to Mary Jones March 16, 1827; she to Grosclaude Sept. 22, 1841; and he to Dubois April 1, 1853. Joseph's nephew, Daniel, received a portion, which was afterwards owned by his eldest son, *Cornelius,* who conveyed six acres to Grosclaude and Dubois Aug. 29, 1840, who partitioned May 18, 1843.

And we adjudge the said Allotment No 255 (as the same Allotment is described butted and bounded in the Field Book of the General Partition) To belong to the said Hendrick Van Winkle.

*208

  This is a **subdivision** of the Lot of Common Land which hath been allotted To the Patent of Philip Carteret to Hans Dedericks dated the twelfth Day of May one thousand six hundred and sixty eight, being that Lot of Common Land which in the Field Book and Map of the General Partition is distinguished by the Number 214.

And upon Examination of the Titles of the several Persons claiming Parts & Shares thereof,

We do adjudge a certain Portion of said Allotment No 114 To belong to Arent Toers.

Our Survey of which said Portion (as laid down on Subdivision Schedule A) shews, and we adjudge it to be a Tract mark'd No 311*

Beginning at a Stake (being the westernmost Corner of said Allotment No 214) And from thence runs North thirty six Degrees and thirty Minutes east two Chains and eighty two Links to a Stake, Thence South fifty two Degrees and thirty Minutes East eight Chains and eighty eight Links to a Stake, Thence South thirty six Degrees and thirty Minutes west two Chains and eighty two Links to a Stake, Thence North fifty two Degrees and thirty Minutes west eight Chains and eighty eight Links to the Place of Beginning, Containing about two Acres and a Half.

*209

  And we adjudge a certain Portion of said Allotment No 214 To belong to Johannis Dedericks.

Our Survey of which said Portion (as laid down on Subdivision Schedule A) shews, and we adjudge it to be a Tract mark'd No 312†

Beginning at a Stake (being the northernmost Corner of the Tract No 311 adjudged To Arent Toers last above described And from thence runs North thirty six Degrees and thirty Minutes east five Chains and seventy four Links to a Stake (being the northernmost Corner of said Allotment No 214, Thence South fifty two Degrees and thirty Minutes east eight Chains and eighty eight Links to a Stake, Thence South thirty six Degrees and thirty Minutes West five Chains and seventy four Links to a Stake, Thence North fifty two Degrees and thirty Minutes West eight Chains and eighty eight Links to the Place of Beginning, Containing about five Acres.

And we adjudge a certain Portion of said Allotment No 214 To belong to Cornelius Dedericks.

Our Survey of which said Portion (as laid down on

---

* *Vide Note to Steenhuysen's Patent*, p. 32.

† John Outwater sold to Thomas Prosser Feb. 1, 1837, two and one-quarter acres, which I take to be part of this lot.

Subdivision Schedule A) shews, and we adjudge it to be a Tract mark'd No 310 *

Beginning at a Stake (being the Southermost Corner of the Tract No 311 adjudged to Arent Toers above described) And from thence runs South fifty two Degrees and thirty Minutes east forty six Chains and twelve Links to Hudson's River, Then returning to the said first mentioned Stake the Place of Beginning and from thence runs North thirty six Degrees and thirty Minutes east four Chains and nine Links to a Stake, Thence South fifty two Degrees and thirty Minutes east forty six Chains and twelve Links to said Hudson's River, Then down along said River as it runs 'till it comes to the first mentioned Line running to said River, Containing after an Allowance for the Hill about seventeen Acres and a Half.

* **And we** adjudge a certain Portion of said Allotment No 214 *210 To belong to Abraham Dedericks.

Our Survey of which said Portion (as laid down on Subdivision Schedule A) shews, and we adjudge it to be a Tract mark'd No 313 †

Beginning at a Stake (being the northermost Corner of the Tract No 310 adjudged to Cornelius Dedericks last above described) And from thence runs South fifty two Degrees and thirty Minutes east forty six Chains & twelve Links to Hudson's River, Then returning to said first mentioned Stake the Place of Beginning; and from thence runs North thirty six Degrees and thirty Minutes east four Chains and forty seven Links to a Stake, Thence South fifty two Degrees and thirty Minutes east forty six Chains and twelve Links to said Hudson's River, Then down along said River as it runs 'till it comes to the first mentioned Line running to said River, Containing after an Allowance for the Hill about nineteen Acres.

With respect to the Lot of Common Land which has been allotted to the Patent of Petrus Stuyvesant to Derick Teunise dated the fourteenth Day of September one thousand six hundred and sixty two, being that Lot of Common Land which in the Field Book and Map of the General Partition is distinguished by the Number 245.

Johannis Van Wagenen claimed the said Lot and no other

---

* Diedricks died Dec. 6, 1775. His grandson, Martin Winne, sold twelve acres out of this tract (southerly side) to Conrad Rapp April 30, 1814. It extended from Lot No. 311 to the river, one chain and forty links in width. Rapp reconveyed to Winne Oct. 13, 1815, who conveyed to John Rapp March 26, 1816. *Vide Note to Lot No.* 406, p. 175. Diedrick's granddaughter, Ann, widow of Daniel Van Winkle, conveyed part of it to her sons, *Cornelius* and *Jacob*, May 8, 1835. Martin Winne sold to Ann Brower Feb. 26, 1823, nine acres, which I think lies in this lot.

† Diedricks had one son, *Johannis*, who received his property, and sold to Jonathan Youmans, May 29, 1800, the easterly end of this lot, bounded, southeast by the river, southwest by Martin Winne, northwest by grantor, northeast by John Brouwer. *Vide Note to Lot No.* 404, p. 174. Youmans sold to George Suckley July 1, 1813. Suckley sold to George C. De Kay March 1, 1836, who died seized, and his widow, Janet, sold the same to John Meeks March 7, 1850. Nathan Dane Ellingwood sold to George C. De Kay July 5, 1836, nine acres on the easterly side of this lot, extending from the river to the rear of the lot.

Person or Persons claiming the same, or a Subdivision thereof; **we** upon Examination of his Title conceive him to be the true Proprietor and do therefore adjudge the said Allotment to belong to him.

*211
    * With respect to the Lot of Common Land which hath been allotted To the Patent of Philip Carteret to Garrit Geritse dated the twelfth Day of May one thousand six hundred & sixty eight, being that Lot of Common Land which in the Field Book and Map of the General Partition is distinguished by the Number 222.

Johannis Van Wagenen claimed the said Lot & no other Person or Persons claiming the same or a Subdivision thereof, **we** upon Examination of his Title conceive him to be the true Proprietor And do therefore adjudge the said Allotment To belong to him.

    With respect to the two Lots of Common Land which have been allotted To the Patent of Philip Carteret to Ide Corneliese dated the thirty first Day of May one thousand six hundred and sixty eight, being these two Lots of Common Land which in the Field Book and Map of the General Partition are distinguished by the Numbers 229 and 256.

Cornelius Sip & Garrit Sip claimed the said two Lots as Tenants in Common thereof And no other Person or Persons claiming the same or a Subdivision thereof **we** upon Examination of their Titles conceive them to be the true Proprietors And do therefore adjudge the said two Allotments to belong to them.

*212
    * **This** is a **subdivision** of the Lot of Common Land which has been allotted To the Patent of Philip Carteret To Arent Lawrense, dated the Tenth Day of October one thousand six hundred and seventy, being that Lot of Common Land which in the Field Book & Map of the General Partition is distinguished by the Number 254.

    And upon Examination of the Titles of the several Persons claiming, Parts & Shares thereof,

We do adjudge a certain Portion of said Allotment No 254, To belong to Arent Toers.

    Our Survey of which said Portion (as laid down on Subdivision Schedule B) shews, and we adjudge it to be a Tract mark'd No 387 *

Beginning at a Stake (being the Southerly Corner of an Out-Garden Lot in Guert Gerritse's Patent mark'd on the Map No 107) And from said Stake runs South forty eight Degrees east two Chains and twenty five Links to a Stake, Thence South nine Degrees West two Chains to a Stake, Thence South twenty eight Degrees and twenty Minutes West twenty Chains and eighty two Links to a Stake, Thence south eighty two Degrees west four Chains and thirty seven Links to a Stake in the Line of a Lot of Land in Nicholas Varlet's Patent mark'd on the Map No 128, Thence along said Line North eight Degrees West eight Chains and five Links to a Stake, Thence North forty four Degrees east twenty Chains to the Place of Beginning, Containing about thirteen Acres & Six Tenths.

---

    * *Vide Note to Steenhuysen's Patent,* p. 32

* **And we** adjudge a certain Portion of said Allotment No 254 *213
To belong to Johannis Van Houta.

Our Survey of which said Portion (as laid down on Subdivision Schedule B) shews, and we adjudge it to be a Tract mark'd No 386 *

Beginning at a Stake (being the northermost Corner of said Allotment No 254) And from said Stake runs South forty eight Degrees west four Chains and eighty six Links to a Stake (being the Beginning Corner of the Lot last described adjudged to Arent Toers mark'd No 387) Thence South forty eight Degrees east two Chains and twenty five Links to a Stake, Thence South nine Degrees west two Chains to a Stake, Thence South twenty eight Degrees and twenty Minutes west eighteen Chains and five Links to a Stake, Thence South forty nine Degrees & forty five Minutes east ten Chains and eighty six Links to a Stake on the Side of the Hill, Thence North forty Degrees & fifteen Minutes east nineteen Chains and ninety Links to a Stake (standing in the Line of a Lot of Land in Arent Lawrence's Patent mark'd on the Map No 123) Thence North thirty five Degrees and fifty five Minutes west seventeen Chains and sixty eight Links to the Place of Beginning, Containing (after an Allowance for the Hill) about twenty six Acres & a Half.

And we adjudge a certain Portion of said Allotment No 254 To belong to Abraham Prior.

Our Survey of which said Portion (as laid down on Subdivision Schedule B) shews, and we adjudge it to be a Tract mark'd No 385 †

* **Beginning** at a Stake by a small Creek called Oyster Creek *214 (which Stake is the easternmost Corner of said Allotment No 254) And from said Stake runs North thirty five Degrees and fifty five Minutes west

---

* Van Houten's son, *Helmagh*, sold to Daniel Van Rypen, Jan 8, 1786, twelve acres out of this lot, near "Mill Rock," bounded, northwest by Nicholas Tuers, northeast by John Van Houten, southeast and southwest by Abraham Prior. From this description it seems that the lot must have been divided between Van Houten's two sons, *Helmagh*, who took the southwest half, and *John*, who took the northeast half. At least, part of John's half afterwards got into the Newkirk family. *Vide Note to Berry's Patent*, p. 51.

† By his will, dated June, 1799, proved Dec. 30, 1800, Prior gave to his daughter *Sarah*, wife of Garret Vanderhoof, *vide Note to Lot No.* 380, p. 158, all his realty except a house and lot, which he gave to his granddaughter Ariantje, wife of Aaron Vanderbilt. This lot she sold to Casparus Prior May 1, 1807. Vanderhoof and Sara Prior had children, *Maritje*, born July 3, 1769, married Jacob Outwater Sept. 30, 1797; *Eva*, born April 25, 1771, married Peter Sickles Oct. 8, 1791; *Hendrick*, born June 18, 1774, died Sept. 3, 1777; *Ariantje*, born Oct. 23, 1778, married Aaron Vanderbilt; *Sarah*, born Sept. 9, 1782, married George Newkirk Feb. 9, 1805. By will, dated July 31, 1797, proved Sept. 20, 1797, Vanderhoof gave all his realty to his wife for life, then to his children above named. May 5, 1825, these heirs sold to Casparus Prior four acres and fifty four one-hundredths of an acre out of the easterly corner of this lot, bounded southwest by meadow of Rev. John Cornelison and Henry Brinkerhoff, southeast by the creek, northeast and northwest by Jacob Prior. Casparus Prior died seized of this lot, and in the partition of his property, it fell to his grandson Michael. *Vide Note to Varlet's Patent*, p. 62, and *Note to Laurense's Patent*, p. 60.

twenty two Chains and ninety two Links to a Stake (being the eastermost Corner of Lot No 386 adjudged To Johannis Van Houta last above described) Thence South forty Degrees and fifteen Minutes west nineteen Chains and ninety Links to a Stake, Thence North forty nine Degrees and forty five Minutes west ten Chains and eighty six Links to a Stake, Thence South twenty eight Degrees and twenty Minutes west four Chains & seven Links to a Stake, Thence South forty nine Degrees & forty five Minutes east thirteen Chains and eight Links to a Stake, (in the Line of Nicholas Jansen the Baker's Patent mark'd on the Map No 13) Thence along said Baker's Line North forty Degrees and fifteen Minutes East thirteen Chains and twenty Links to a Stake in the Meadow (being the Northerly Corner of said Baker's Patent) Thence South forty nine Degrees and forty five Minutes east seven Chains along the northeasterly Line of said Baker's Patent to a Stake by a small Creek, Then down the said small Creek 'till it empties into said Oyster Creek, Then down along said Oyster Creek the several Courses thereof as it runs to the Place of Beginning, containing after an Allowance for the Hill about twenty two Acres and an half.

And we adjudge a certain Portion of said Allotment No 254 To belong to Johannis Van Wagenen.

Our Survey of which said Portion (as laid down on Subdivision Schedule B) shews and we adjudge it to be a Tract mark'd No 388 *

Beginning at a Stake (being the Southwestermost Corner of Lot No 387 adjudged To Arent Toers above described) And from said Stake runs South eight Degrees east six Chains and eighty nine Links to a Stake (being the Southeastermost Corner of a Lot of Land in Nicholas Varlet's Patent mark'd on the Map No 128) Thence North eighty two Degrees east three Chains and fifty six Links to a Stake, Thence North eight Degrees west five Chains & seventy nine Links to a Stake, Thence North twenty eight Degrees and twenty Minutes east one Chain and thirty Links to a Stake, Thence South eighty two Degrees west four Chains & thirty seven Links to the Place of Beginning, containing about two Acres and an Half.

*215 " * **As** to the remaining Part or Portion of said Allotment No 254 **we** find the Right to the same vested in the Freeholders of the Town of Bergen, but not being able to ascertain who those Freeholders were by Name we do not declare to whom the said remaining Part or Portion does particularly belong.

Our Survey of which said remaining Part or Portion (as laid down on Subdivision Schedule B) shews, and we adjudge it to be a Tract mark'd No 389 †

º *Vide Note to Gerritse's Patent*, p. 58.

† In a deed from Peter Stuyvesant to Casparus Prior, Aug. 18, 1784, it appears that Johannis Van Wagenen at that time was the owner of this lot. *Vide Lot No.* 34, *New Field Book*. He by will, dated March 15, 1794, proved June 17, 1797, gave all his lands to his son *Jacob*, who by will, dated June 25, 1835, proved Aug. 2, 1839, gave his lands to his son *Hartman*, who sold thirteen acres and sixty-one one-hundredths of an acre of this lot to Emily, wife of Moses B. Bramhall, March 1, 1850. Bramhall, with Jacob M. Merselis, mapped this lot and land adjoining, and filed the

Beginning at a Stake (being the Southeasternmost Corner of Lot No 388 adjudged To Johannis Van Wagenen last above described) And from said Stake runs South eighty two Degrees west twelve Chains and thirteen Links to a Stake (being the westernmost Corner of said Allotment No 254) Thence South forty nine Degrees and forty five Minutes east seventeen Chains to the Southermost Corner of said Allotment No 254, Thence North forty Degrees and fifteen Minutes east thirteen Chains and five Links to a Stake (being the Southermost Corner of Lot No 385 adjudged to Abraham Prior above described) Thence North forty nine Degrees and forty five Minutes west thirteen Chains and eight Links to a Stake, Thence South eight Degrees east five Chains and seventy nine Links to the Place of Beginning, containing about fifteen Acres.

This is a **subdivision** of the two Lots of Common Land which has been allotted To the Patent of Petrus Stuyvesant to Nicholas Varlet dated the eighteenth Day of October one thousand six hundred & sixty three, being these two Lots of Common Land which in the field book & Map of the General Partition are distinguished by the Numbers 242 & 257

* And upon Examination of the Titles of the several *216 Persons claiming Parts & Shares thereof

We do adjudge a certain Portion of said Allotment No 242 To belong to Garrit Garritse alias Van Riper

Our Survey of which said Portion (as laid down on Subdivision Schedule A) shews and we adjudge it to be a Tract mark'd No 353 *

Beginning at a Stake (being the easternmost Corner of said Allotment No 242) And from thence runs South forty Degrees west Ten Chains and thirty Links to a Stake, Thence North fifty Degrees west twenty one Chains to a Stake, Thence North forty four Degrees and thirty Minutes east ten Chains and forty nine Links to a stake, Thence North sixteen Degrees east four Chains and twenty two Links to a Stake, Thence South fifty Degrees east eleven Chains and thirty Links to a Stake, Thence South thirty three Degrees west four Chains and fifteen Links to a Stake, Thence South fifty Degrees east Ten Chains to the Place of Beginning, containing about twenty five Acres and an Half.

And we adjudge a certain Portion of said Allotment No 242 To belong to Robert Leake Esqr.

Our Survey of which said Portion (as laid down on Subdivision Schedule A) shews & we adjudge it to be a Tract mark'd No 352 †

Map Nov. 10, 1851. *Vide Note to Varlet's Patent*, p. 62. The north part of this lot, containing about five acres, belonged to Cornelius and Garret Sip. *Vide Lot No. 33, New Field Book*. Jacob Everson conveyed to Cornelius Sip six acres lying in the north side of this lot, bounded, southwest and northwest by the road from Communipaw to Bergen, northeast by Abraham Prior, southeast by Brinkerhoff's meadow, southwest by Van Wagenen. This description probably includes *Lot No. 33 on New Field Map C*.

º *Vide Note to Lot No.* 375, p. 200.

† Leake sold this lot to Robert Sickles and Cornelius Sip, who partitioned May 1, 1769; Sickles taking the northerly half, and Sip the southerly half. *Vide Note to Varlet's Patent*, p. 62.

Beginning at a Stake (being the Southermost Corner of the Tract No 353 adjudged to Garrit Garritse last above described) And from thence runs South forty Degrees west seven Chains and seventy Links to a Stake, Thence South fifty Degrees east One Chain to a Stake, Thence South forty Degrees west seven Chains & fourteen Links to a Stake, Thence North fifty Degrees west twelve Chains & sixty seven Links to a Stake, Thence North forty Degrees east two Chains & fifty four Links to a Stake, Thence North fifty Degrees west eight Chains & eighty two Links to a Stake, Thence North forty one Degrees east five Chains & seventy five Links to a Stake, Thence North forty four Degrees & thirty Minutes east six Chains & sixty three Links to a Stake, Thence South fifty Degrees east twenty one Chains to the Place of Beginning, containing about twenty nine Acres & seven Tenths.

*217 * **And we** adjudge a certain Portion of said Allotment No 242, To belong to Arent Toers.

Our Survey of which-said Portion (as laid down on Subdivision Schedule A) shews, and we adjudge it to be a Tract mark'd No 351 *

Beginning at a Stake (being the westermost Corner of the Tract No 352 adjudged to Robert Leake last above described) And from thence runs South forty one Degrees west two Chains and sixty Links to a Stake, Thence South fifty Degrees east eight Chains and thirty five Links to a Stake, Thence North forty Degrees east two Chains and fifty four Links to a Stake, Thence North fifty Degrees west eight Chains and eighty two Links to the Place of Beginning containing about two Acres and one Tenth

As to the remaining Part or Portion of said Allotment No 242 **we** find the Right to the same vested in the Freeholders of the Town of Bergen, But not being able to ascertain who those Freeholders were by Name we do not declare to whom the said remaining Part or Portion does particularly belong.

Our Survey of which remaining Part or Portion (as laid down on Subdivision Schedule A) shews and we adjudge it to be a Tract mark'd No 350

Beginning at a Stake (being the westermost Corner of the Tract No 351 adjudged to Arent Toers last above described) And from thence runs South fifty Degrees east twenty one Chains & two Links to a Stake, Thence South forty Degrees west eight Chains to a Stake, Thence South fifty degrees east eight Chains & one Link to a Stake, Thence South thirty two Degrees west twenty two Chains & thirty eight Links to a Stake (being the Southermost Corner of said Allotment No 242), Thence North thirty eight Degrees & forty five Minutes west twenty Chains to a Stake, Thence North twelve Degrees & twenty Minutes east nine Chains to a Stake, Thence North fourteen Degrees & ten Minutes East nineteen Chains to a Stake, Thence North forty one Degrees east one Chain & fifteen Links to the Place of Beginning, containing about fifty nine Acres & seven Tenths.

*218 * **As** to the Allotment No 257 being the Proportion of Common Land which we adjudged to the Proprietor of the Patented House Lot No 168; It not appearing satisfactory to us who the

---

* *Vide Note to Steenhuysen's Patent*, p. 32.

Proprietor of said House Lot is we do not declare to whom the said Allotment of Common Land does belong.

With respect to the two Lots of Common Land which have been allotted to the Patent of Philip Carteret to Hendrick Van Ostrum, dated the Tenth Day of November, one thousand six hundred and seventy seven, being these two Lots of Common Land which in the Field Book and Map of the General Partition are distinguished by the Numbers 209 & 239

Hendricus Kuyper Esqr. claimed the said two Lots and no other Person or Persons claiming the same or a Subdivision thereof we upon Examination of his Title conceive him to be the true Proprietor; And do therefore adjudge the said Allotment to belong to him.

* With respect to the Lot of Common Land which has *219 been allotted to the Patent of Philip Carteret to Claas Jansen Vanpurmerant, dated the thirty first Day of March one thousand six hundred and sixty eight, being that Lot of Common Land which in the Field Book and Map of the General Partition is distinguished by the Number 210

Hendricus Kuyper Esqr. claimed the said Lot and no other Person or Persons claiming the same or a Subdivision thereof we upon Examination of his Title conceive him to be the true Proprietor; And do therefore adjudge the said Allotment to belong to him.

With respect to the Lot of Common Land which has been allotted to the Patent of Petrus Stuyvesant to Jan Vinge, dated the fourth Day of June, one thousand six hundred and sixty three, being that Lot of Common Land which in the Field Book and Map of the General Partition is distinguished by the Number 218

Oliver De Lancey Esqr. claimed said Lot as Attorney for, and in Behalf of the Devisees of Sir Peter Warren deceased And upon Examination of the Title (no other Person or Persons claiming the same or a Subdivision thereof) we do adjudge the said Allotment To belong to the Devisees of said Sir Peter Warren agreable to his last Will & Testament bearing date the twenty sixth Day of July one thousand seven hundred and fifty two.

* With respect to the Lot of Common Land which has *220 been allotted to the Patent of Petrus Stuyvesant to Cornelius Van Ruyven, Paulus Lendertz, Alard Anthony and Johannis Ver Brugen dated the twenty first Day of November one thousand six hundred and sixty three, being that Lot of Common Land which in the Field Book & Map of the General Partition is distinguished by the Number 207.

We understand that a great Number of Persons claim Interest in the said Allotment as Tenants in Common thereof, But as few or no Title Papers have been laid before us we cannot judge who the true Proprietors are; And therefore decline proceeding to any Subdivision thereof.

*221 * With respect To the Lot of Common Land which has been allotted To the Patent of Petrus Stuyvesant to Nicholas Varlet and Nicholas Bayard dated the tenth Day of December, one thousand six hundred and sixty three, confirm'd by Patent from Philip Carteret to said Varlet & Bayard dated the thirtieth Day of October, one thousand six hundred and sixty seven, being that Lot of Common Land which in the Field Book & Map of the General Partition is distinguished by the Number 283.

William Bayard Esqr. claimed the said Lot as the sole Proprietor, at the same Time a great Number of other Persons claim'd the same as Tenants in Common thereof, And after a long Deliberation and the most mature Attention as well to the Nature of the various Claims as the Opinion of sundry Council deliver'd on the Subject **we** find the Mater upon the whole to be so intricate, obscure & doubtful that we are not able to obtain such Clearness & Unanimity as is necessary to enable us to pronounce upon the Mater being equally divided in Opinion, And therefore **we** do not declare to whom or among whom the said Allotment of Common Land does belong.

Given under our Hands at Bergen this 1st Day of March 1765.

Jacob Spicer

Char Clinton

Wm: Donaldson

Az: Dunham

John Berrien

Abra Clark Junr

...inton, Surveyor

Index to Field Book.

No of the original Patent		Survey of the Original Patent	Commons allotted to each Patent	Subdivision & to whom adjudged
1	Maryn Adrianse............	4	65	111
2	Nicholas Varlet.............	5	66	112
3	Ide Cornelieson Van Vorst......	6	67	112
4	Claas Jansen Van Purmerant.....	6	78	113
5	Abraham Isaacsen Plank........	7	68	114
6	Jacob Stoffelsen	7	69	114
7	Petrus Stuyvesant............	8	69	115
8	Claas Comptah alias Claas Pieterse Cors.........	8	70	115
9	Nicholas Jansen Backer.........	8	71	117
10	Fytie Hartmans 1st Patent	9	72	118
11	Fytie Hartmans 2d Patent......	9	72	121
12	Derrick Claasen 1st Patent	10	73	126
13	Derrick Claasen 2d Patent......	10	74	128
14	Dirck Sycan 1st Patent.........	11	74	128
15	Lawrens Adriesen.............	11	75	129
16	Lubert Gilbertse..............	12	76	132
17	Severin Lourens	12	77	132
18	Hendrick Jansen Spier.........	12	78	133
19	Dirck Sycan's 2d Patent........	13	78	133
20	Thomas Davison's 1st Patent....	13	79	135
21	Thomas Davison's 2d Patent....	14	79	136
22	Pieter Janse Slagt............	14	80	137
23	Hendrick Janse Van Schalkwyck..	15	80	137
24	Catherine Stoffelsen	15	81	138
25	Barent Christianse.............	16	81	138
26	Nicholas Jansen & Samuel Edsal..	16	82	142
27	Mark Noble & Samuel Moore....	17	83	145
28	Casper Stymets 1st Patent......	18	84	149
29	Casper Stymets 2d Patent.......	19	84	150
30	Adrian Post..................	20	85	152
31	Guert Coerten's 1st Patent......	22	85	155
32	Guert Coerten's 2d do	24	86	156
33	Guert Coerten's 3d do	25	87	158
34	Fredrick Phillips.............	25	87	160
35	Engelbert Steinhuysen..........	29	88	164
36	Thomas Fredrick alias De Cuyper.	31	89	169
37	Herman Edward..............	32	89	170
38	Guert Gerritse................	34	90	172
39	Powles Pieterse	36	90	176
40	Dirck Gerritse................	37	91	177
41	Jacob Luby's 1st Patent	38	92	179
42	Jacob Luby's 2d do	40	92	181
43	Jan Lubertse	41	93	182

No of the original Patent		Survey of the Original Patent	Commons allotted to each Patent	Subdivision & to whom adjudged
44	Petrus Jacobse................	42	94	186
45	Nicholas Varlet & Balthazar Bayard....................	48	94	187
46	Dow Harmense................	50	96	193
47	John Berry...	51	96	196
48	Tielman Van Vleck...........	53	97	198
49	Hendrick Teunisse...........	54	97	200
50	Hans Diedericks.............	56	98	202
51	Dirk Teunisse................	57	59	206
52	Gerrit Gerritse..............	58	100	207
53	Ide Cornelisse...............	60	100	208
54	Arent Lawrence..............	60	101	209
55	Nicholas Varlet..............	62	102	214
56	Hendrick Van Ostrum.........	63	103	218
57	Claas Jansen Van Purmerant.....	64	104	219
58	Jan Vinge...................	64	105	219
59	Van Ruyven, Linderick Anthony & Van Bruggen, Slaugh's meadow.	65	105	219
60	Nicholas Varlet & Nicholas Bayard	66	106	221

The Field Book consists of three parts.

First part Contains the Survey of the Original Grants or Patents from Page 4 to 64.

Second part Contains the Allotment and Survey of the Common Lands to each Grant from Page 65 to 107.

Third part Contains the Subdivisions and Judgment of the several Rights and Shares, 108 to 221.

The several Pages above mentioned are the Pages of the **Field Book.**

INDEX TO FIELD BOOK.

A List of all the **Patented Lands** within the Township of **Bergen** The Bounds and Limits whereof have been run out and ascertained by the **Commissioners** appointed for **Dividing** the **Common Lands** within the said Township.

Number of the Patents.	NAMES of the PATENTEES.	Situation of the PATENTED LANDS.	The Numbers in Figures Whereby, the Tract or Tracts contain'd in each respective PATENT, are distinguished & marked on the MAP of the TOWNSHIP.	Page on the Field Book where the Survey of each Patent begins.
1	Maryn Adriaense	Wiehaken	No 1	5
2	Nicholas Varlet	Hoebocken	No 2	6
3	Ide Cornelison Van Vost	Horsimus	No 3, 6	6
4	Claas Jansen Vanpurmerant	Do	No 4, 7, 8, 133	7
5	Abraham Isacsen Plank	Paulus Hook	No 5	8
6	Jacob Stoffelsen	Horsimus	No 9	9
7	Petrus Stuyvesant	Do	No 10	9
8	Claas Comptah, alias Claas Peterson Cors.	Communipan	No 11	9
9	Nicholas Jansen Baker	Do	No 12, 13	10
10	Fytje Hartman's 1st Patent	Do	No 14	11
11	Fytje Hartman's 2d Patent	Do	No 15	11
12	Dirck Claasen's 1st Patent	Kewan	No 16	12
13	Dirck Claesen's 2d Patent	Stony Point	No 17	12
14	Dirck Sycan's 1st Patent	Mingackque	No 18	13
15	Lawrence Andriesen	Do	No 19	13
16	Lubert Gilbertse	Do	No 20	14
17	Severen Laurence	Do	No 21	14
18	Hendrick Jansen Spier	Do	No 22	15

Number of the Patents.	NAMES of the PATENTEES.	Situation of the PATENTED LANDS.	The Numbers in Figures Whereby the Tract or Tracts contain'd in each respective PATENT, are distinguished & marked on the MAP of the TOWNSHIP	Page on the Field Book where the Survey of each Patent begins.
19	Dirck Sycan's 2d Patent	Pembrepogh	No 23, 24	15
20	Thomas Davisson's 1st Patent	Do	No 25	16
21	Thomas Davisson's 2d Do	Do	No 26	16
22	Peter Jansen Slaat	Do	No 27	17
23	Hendrick Jansen Van Schalckwyck	Do	No 28	17
24	Catharine Stoffelsen	Do	No 29	18
25	Barent Christian	Do	No 30, 122	18
26	Nicholas Jansen & Samuel Edsal	Nip Nixon Neck	No 31	19
27	Mark Noble & Samuel Moore	In and about the Town of Bergen	No 59, 32, 33, 39, 64	19
28	Caspar Stymat's 1st Patent	About the Town	No 34, 137	21
29	Casper Stymet's 2d Do	In & about the Town	No 81, 66, 101, 116, 95	21
30	Adnan Post	Do	No 35, 55, 117, 164, 100	23
31	Guert Coerten's 1st Patent	Do	No 36, 48, 54, 91, 94, 97, 147	25
32	Guert Coerten's 2d Do	Do	No 124, 148, 96	27
33	Guert Coerten's 3d Do	About the Town	No 139	28
34	Fredrick Philipse	In & about the Town	No 37, 74, 63, 60, 47, 53, 86, 142, 149, 150, 151, 41	28
35	Englebert Stienheysen	Do	No 38, 40, 89, 90, 138, 152, 130	32
36	Thomas Fredrick alias De Cuyper	About the Town	No 62, 45, 141, 42	34
37	Harman Edward	In & about the Town	No 43, 50, 69, 153, 111, 118	36
38	Guert Gerritse	Do	No 44, 51, 102, 136, 107, 154	38
39	Paulus Pieterse	Do	No 46, 52, 120, 155, 103	40
40	Dirck Gerritse	Do	No 49, 67, 156	41

INDEX TO FIELD BOOK. 269

41	Jacob Luby's 1st Patent	Do	No 56, 140, 61, 87, 108, 157 42
42	Jacob Luby's 2d Do	Near Wiehaken	No 144 44
43	Jan Lubertse	In & about the Town	No 71, 57, 119, 158, 115 45
44	Peter Jacobse	Do	No 159, 105, 85, 58, 121 46
45	Nicholas Varlet & Balthazar Bayard	Do	No 83, 68, 160, 109 48
46	Dow Harmense	Do	No 79, 80, 65, 161, 93 50
47	John Berry	Do	No 162, 125, 70 51
48	Tielman Van Vleck	Do	No 72, 129, 134 53
49	Hendrick Teunise	Do	No 82, 73, 165, 106 54
50	Hans Dedricks	Do	No 75, 84, 114, 110, 166 56
51	Dirck Teunise	Do	No 76, 163 57
52	Gerrit Gerritse	Do	No 77, 78, 167, 98 58
53	Ide Corneliese	About the Town	No 88, 135 60
54	Arent Laurense	In & about the Town	No 123, 92, 99, 112, 113 60
55	Nicholas Varlet	Do	No 127, 126, 168, 104, 128 62
56	Hendrick Van Ostrum	About the Town	No 131 63
57	Claas Jansen Van Purmerant	Do	No 132 64
58	Jan Vinge	Do	No 143 64
59	Van Ruyven, Lindertz, Anthony, Ver Brugen	Slaughs Meadow	No 145 65
60	Nicholas Varlet & Nicholas Bayard	Sekakus	No 146 66

A List in numerical Order of all the particular **Tracts** or **Lots** contained in the respective Patents within the Township of **Bergen**.

Number of Each Tract or Lot mark'd on said Map	In whose Patent contain'd	Numr. of the Patent in which contained	Page in the Field Book where the Survey of each particular Tract begins
1	Maryn Adrianse	1	5
2	Nicholas Varlet	2	6
3	Ide Cornelieson Van Vost	3	6
4	Claas Jansen Van Purmerant	4	7
5	Abraham Isaacsen Plank	5	8
6	Ide Cornelison Van Vost	3	6
7	Claas Jansen Van Purmerant	4	7
8	Claas Jansen Van Purmerant	4	8
9	Jacob Stoffelsen	6	9
10	Petrus Stuyvesant	7	9
11	Claas Comptah alias Claas Pieterson Cors	8	9
12	Nicholas Jansen Baker	9	10
13	Nicholas Jansen Baker	9	10
14	Fytje Hartman	10	11
15	Fytje Hartman	11	11
16	Dirck Claasen	12	12
17	Dirck Claasen	13	12
18	Dirck Sycan	14	13
19	Lawrens Andrieson	15	13
20	Gilbert Lubertse	16	14
21	Severin Laurens	17	14
22	Hendrick Jansen Spier	18	15
23	Dirck Sycan	19	15
24	Dirck Sycan	19	16
25	Thomas Davison	20	16
26	Thomas Davison	21	16
27	Peter Jansen Slaat	22	17
28	Hendrick Jansen Van Schalkwyck	23	17
29	Catharine Stoffelsen	24	18
30	Barnt Christian	25	18
31	Nicholas Jansen & Samuel Edsal	26	19
32	Mark Noble & Samuel Moore	27	20
33	Mark Noble & Samuel Moore	27	20
34	Caspar Stymets	28	21
35	Adrian Post	30	23
36	Guert Coerten	31	25
37	Fredrick Philipse	34	28
38	Englebert Steinhuysen	35	32
39	Mark Noble & Samuel Moore	27	20
40	Englebert Steinhuysen	35	32

INDEX TO FIELD BOOK. 271

Number of Each Tract or Lot mark'd on said Map	In whose Patent contain'd	Numr. of the Patent in which contained	Page in the Field Book where the survey of each particular Tract begins
41	Fredrick Philipse.................	34	31
42	Thomas Fredrick alias De Cuyper.........	36	35
43	Harman Edward................	37	36
44	Guert Gerritse.................	38	38
45	Thomas Fredrick alias De Cuyper.........	36	35
46	Paulus Pieterse.................	39	40
47	Fredrick Philipse.................	34	30
48	Guert Coerten.................	31	25
49	Dirck Garretse.................	40	41
50	Harman Edward................	37	36
51	Guert Garritse.................	38	38
52	Paulus Pieterse.................	39	40
53	Fredrick Philipse.................	34	30
54	Guert Coerten.................	31	25
55	Adrian Post...................	30	24
56	Jacob Luby...................	41	42
57	Jan Lubertse..................	43	45
58	Pieter Jacobse.................	44	47
59	Mark Noble & Samuel Moore...........	27	20
60	Fredrick Philipse.................	34	29
61	Jacob Luby...................	41	43
62	Thomas Fredrick alias De Cuyper........	36	34
63	Fredrick Philipse.................	34	29
64	Mark Noble & Samuel Moore...........	27	20
65	Dow Harmense.................	46	50
66	Casper Stymets.................	29	22
67	Dirck Garretse.................	40	42
68	Nicholas Varlet & Balthazar Bayard......	45	49
69	Herman Edward................	37	36
70	John Berry...................	47	52
71	Jan Lubertse..................	43	45
72	Tielman Van Vleck...............	48	53
73	Hendrick Tunisse................	49	55
74	Fredrick Philipse.................	34	29
75	Hans Dederick.................	50	56
76	Dirck Tunisse.................	51	57
77	Garret Garretse.................	52	58
78	Garret Garretse.................	52	59
79	Dow Harmense.................	46	50
80	Dow Harmense.................	46	50
81	Casper Stymets.................	29	22
82	Hendrick Tunise................	49	54
83	Nicholas Varlet & Balthazar Bayard......	45	48
84	Hans Dederick.................	50	56
85	Peter Jacobse.................	44	47
86	Fredrick Philipse.................	34	30

Number of Each Tract or Lot mark'd on said Map	In whose Patent contain'd	Numr. of the Patent in which contained	Page in the Field Book where the survey of each particular tract begins
87	Jacob Luby	41	43
88	Ide Cornelise	53	60
89	Englebert Steinheysen	35	32
90	Englebert Steinheysen	35	33
91	Guert Coerten	31	26
92	Arent Lawrense	54	61
93	Dow Harmense	46	51
94	Guert Coerten	31	26
95	Casper Stymets	29	23
96	Guert Coerten	32	28
97	Guert Coerten	31	26
98	Garret Garretse	52	59
99	Arent Lawrense	54	61
100	Adrian Post	30	24
101	Caspar Stymets	29	22
102	Guert Garretse	38	38
103	Paulus Pieterse	39	41
104	Nicholas Varlet	55	63
105	Peter Jacobse	44	47
106	Hendrick Tunise	49	55
107	Guert Garretse	38	39
108	Jacob Luby	41	43
109	Nicholas Varlet & Balthazar Bayard	45	49
110	Hans Dederick	50	57
111	Herman Edward	37	37
112	Arent Lawrence	54	61
113	Arent Lawrence	54	62
114	Hans Dedrick	50	56
115	Jan Lubertse	43	46
116	Casper Stymets	29	23
117	Adrian Post	30	24
118	Herman Edward	37	37
119	Jan Lubertse	43	46
120	Paulus Pieterse	39	40
121	Peter Jacobse	44	48
122	Barnt Christian	25	19
123	Arent Lawrense	54	60
124	Guert Coerten	32	27
125	John Berry	47	52
126	Nicholas Varlet	55	62
127	Nicholas Varlet	55	62
128	Nicholas Varlet	55	63
129	Tielman Van Vleck	48	53
130	Englebert Steinhuysen	35	34
131	Hendrick Van Ostrum	56	63
132	Claas Jansen Van Purmerant	57	64

INDEX TO FIELD BOOK.

Number of Each Tract or Lot mark'd on said Map	In whose Patent contain'd	Numr. of the Patent in which contained	Page in the Field Book where the survey of each particular Tract begins
133	Claas Jansen Van Purmerant.............	4	8
134	Tielman Van Vleck........	48	54
135	Ide Cornelise.........................	53	60
136	Guert Garretse	38	39
137	Caspar Stymets....	28	21
138	Englebert Steinhuysen	35	33
139	Guert Coerten...................	33	28
140	Jacob Luby.	41	43
141	Thomas Fredrick alias De Cuyper	36	35
142	Fredrick Philipse	34	30
143	Jan Vinge	58	64
144	Jacob Luby	42	44
145	Van Ruyven, Lindertz Anthony & Van Bruggen	59	65
146	Nicholas Varlet & Nicholas Bayard	60	66
147	Guert Coerten.	31	27
148	Guert Coerten.	32	27
149	Fredrick Philipse.	34	31
150	Fredrick Philipse.......	34	31
151	Fredrick Philipse....	34	31
152	Englebert Steinheysen	35	34
153	Herman Edward.	37	37
154	Guert Garretse.	38	39
155	Paulus Pieterse	39	41
156	Dirck Garretse	40	42
157	Jacob Luby.....	41	44
158	Jan Lubertse	43	46
159	Peter Jacobse	44	46
160	Nicholas Varlet & Balthazar Bayard	45	49
161	Dow Harmense......................	46	51
162	John Berry	47	51
163	Dirck Tunise	51	58
164	Adrian Post.	30	24
165	Hendrick Tunisse	49	55
166	Hans Dederick	50	57
167	Garret Garretse	52	59
168	Nicholas Varlet....	55	63

Beside the foregoing **Patents,** and before making **Division** of the **Common Lands** The Commissioners run out and ascertain'd the Bounds & Limits of the following **Tracts** or **Lots** of Land viz :

Numr. of Each Tract as mark'd on the Map		Page in the Field Book where the Surveys of these Tracts are recorded.
169	Being a Tract of Land & Meadow at Horsimus, in the Possession of Capt. Archibald Kennedy	67
170	Being a small Piece of Land lying south^{ly} from, and near the Town anciently appropriated for the Purpose of a Burying Ground	69
171	Being another small Piece of Land lying southwesterly from, and near the Town, anciently appropriated as a Settlement for Mechanicks	69
172	Being a Tract at Bergen Point, set apart by the Commissioners for Sale for defraying the Charges of the General Partition	70
173, 174, 175, 176	Being four Lots of Land, Allotted to the Use of the Church of Bergen	71–73
177, 178, 179	Being three Lots of Land, Allotted to the Use of the Free School at Bergen	73–74

Tracts or Lots of Common Land allotted to the respective Patents. Viz^t.		N.B. The Lots of Common Lands begin with No 201
Patent	Number of each Tract or Lot of common Land as mark'd on the Map	Page in the Field Book where the Survey of the respective Lots of Common Land begins.
1	Allotted .... No 201	75
2	do 233, 203, 219	76, 76, 77
3	do 211, 237	77, 78
4	do 240	78
5	do 238	79
6	do 247	80
7	do 217	80
8	do 208, 263	81, 81
9	do 206, 259	82, 82
10	do 205	83
11	do 260	83
12	do 213, 261	84, 84
13	do 204	85
14	do 212, 258, 265	86, 86, 86
15	do 266	87
16	do 278, 267	88, 88
17	do 279, 268	89, 89
18	do 280, 269	89, 90
19	do 271	90
20	do 272	91
21	do 275	91
22	do 274	92
23	do 273	92
24	do 276	93
25	do 277	94
26	do 270	95
27	do 227, 251	95, 96
28	do 225	96
29	do 223	97
30	do 264	97
31	do 215	98
32	do 243	99
33	do 235	99
34	do 234, 262	100, 100
35	do 216, 244	101, 101
36	do 232, 284	102, 102
37	do 249	103
38	do 221	103
39	do 252, 253, 281	104, 104, 104
40	do 226	105
41	do 231	106
42	do 202	106
43	do 248, 282	107, 107
44	do 236	108

Patent		Number of each Tract or Lot of common Land as mark'd on the Map.	Page in the Field Book where the Survey of the respective Lots of Common Land begin.
45	Allotted	250, 285, 286, 224, 241, 287	108, 109, 109, 109, 110, 110
46	do	246	110
47	do	228	111
48	do	230	111
49	do	220, 255	112, 112
50	do	214	113
51	do	245	113
52	do	222	114
53	do	229, 256	114, 115
54	do	254	115
55	do	242, 257	116, 117
56	do	209, 239	117, 118
57	do	210	118
58	do	218	119
59	do	207	119
60	do	283	120

INDEX TO FIELD BOOK.

A List in numerical Order of all the particular Tracts or Lots of Common Lands As allotted to the respective Patents.

Numr. of each Tract or Lot of Common Land.		Numr. of the Patent to which Allotted.	Numr. of each Tract or Lot of Common Land.		Numr. of the Patent to which Allotted.
No 201	Allotted to....	1	No 245	Allotted to....	51
202	do	42	246	do	46
203	do	2	247	do	6
204	do	13	248	do	43
205	do	10	249	do	37
206	do	9	250	do	45
207	do	59	251	do	27
208	do	8	252	do.	39
209	do	56	253	do	39
210	do	57	254	do	54
211	do	3	255	do	49
212	do	14	256	do	53
213	do	12	257	do	55
214	do	50	258	do	14
215	do	31	259	do	9
216	do	35	260	do	11
217	do	7	261	do	12
218	do	58	262	do	34
219	do	2	263	do	8
220	do	49	264	do	30
221	do	38	265	do	14
222	do	52	266	do	15
223	do	29	267	do	16
224	do	45	268	do	17
225	do	28	269	do	18
226	do	40	270	do	26
227	do	27	271	do	19
228	do	47	272	do	20
229	do	53	273	do	23
230	do	48	274	do	22
231	do	41	275	do	21
232	do	36	276	do	24
233	do	2	277	do	25
234	do	34	278	do	16
235	do	33	279	do	17
236	do	44	280	do	18
237	do	3	281	do	39
238	do	5	282	do	45
239	do	56	283	do	60
240	do	4	284	do	36
241	do	45	285	do	45
242	do	55	286	do	45
243	do	32	287	do	45
244	do	35			

An **Index** to the Field Book of the **Subdivisions** of the **Common Lands** of the Township of **Bergen**.

Number of each Patent.	NAMES of the PATENTEES.	The Numbers whereby the Lots of Common Land which have been allotted To the respective Patents Upon the General Partitions are distinguished.	The Numbers whereby The Subdivided Portions of the Common Lands are distinguished.	The Page in the Field Book where the Survey or Field Work of each Subdivided Portion of Common Land is recorded.	The Names of the Persons to whom the respective Allotments of the Common Lands are adjudg'd.
No 1	Maryn Adrianse,	201			William Bayard Esqr.
2	Nicholas Varlet	233, 203, 219			William Bayard Esqr.
3	Ide Corneliese Van Vost	211, 237			Cornelius Van Vost
4	Claas Jansen Vanpurmerant	240			Hendricus Kuyper Esqr.
5	Abraham Isaacsen Plank	238			Cornelius Van Vost
6	Jacob Stoffelsen	247			Michael & George De Mott
7	Petrus Stuyvesant	217			Petrus Stuyvesant
			306	129	Myndert Garrabrants
8	Claas Pietersen Cors.	208	307	130	Cornelius Garrabrants
		263	407	130	Myndert Garrabrants
			408	131	Cornelius Garrabrants
9	Nicholas Jansen Baker	206, 259	301		Cornelius Jorsen Blinkerhoof
			302	132	Michael Corneliese Vreelandt
			303	133	Michael Hartman Vreelandt
10	Feytie Hartman's 1st	205	304	133	Johannis Vreelandt
				133	John Van Horne
			305	134	Cornelius Jorsen Blinkerhoof

INDEX TO FIELD BOOK. 279

11 Feytie Hartman's 2d	260	135 Michael Hartman Vreelandt	397
		135 Michael Cornelise Vreelandt	396
		136 George Vreelandt Esqr.	394
		136 Johannis Vreelandt	395
		136 John Van Horne	393
		137 Joseph Waldron	392
		137 James Collard	390
		138 Not declared	391
12 Derick Classen's 1st	213	139 Michael Hartman Vreelandt	308
		139 Johannis Vreelandt	309
		140 Michael Hartman Vreelandt	398
		140 Johannis Vreelandt	399
13 Derick Classen's 2d	204	Michael Corneliese Vreelandt	
14 Derick Sycan's 1st	212, 258, 265	George Vreelandt Esqr.	
15 Lawrence Andriese	266	142 Thomas Brown	413
		142 Lawrence Brown	414
		143 Feytje Seegaerd	415
		143 Cornelius Jorsen Blinkerhoof	416
		144 George Vreelandt Esqr.	417
16 Lubert Gilbertse	278, 267	Jacob Van Wagenen	
17 Severin Lawrence	279, 268	Jacob Van Wagenen	
18 Hendrick Jansen Spier	280, 269	Widow Spier &c	
19 Derick Sycan's 2d	271	146 Michael Cor: Vreelandt	422
		147 Antje Fielding	423
20 Thomas Davison	272	148 Michael Cor: Vreelandt	425
		Antje Fielding	424
21 Thomas Davison	275	George Cadmus	
22 Peter Jansen Slaat	274	George Cadmus	
23 Hendrick Jansen Van Schalckwyck	273	John Van Horne	
24 Catharine Stoffelsen	276	Jacob Van Horne	

280   INDEX TO FIELD BOOK.

Number of each Patent.	NAMES of the PATENTEES.	The Numbers whereby the Lots of Common Land which have been allotted To the respective Patents Upon the General Partition are distinguished.	The Numbers where by The Subdivided Portions of the Common Lands are distinguished.	The Page in the Field Book where the Survey or Field Work of each Subdivided Portion of Common Land is recorded.	The Names of the Persons to whom the respective Allotments of the Common Lands are adjudg'd.
25	Barnt Christian	277	......	426	151 Feytje Seegaerd
			......	427	152 George Vreelandt Esqr.
			......	428	152 Lawrence Brown
			......	429	153 Thomas Brown
			......	430	153 Jacob Van Horne
			......	431	154 Jacob Van Horne
26	Nicholas Jansen & Saml Edsal	270	......	418	155 Jacobus Van Buskirk
			......	419	155 Widow Van Buskirk &c
			......	420	156 Jacob Van Horne
			......	421	156 George Cadmus
27	Mark Noble & Samuel Moore	227	......	334	157 Peter Pietersen Esqr.
			......	335	158 Zachariah Sickles
			......	379	158 Cornelius Blinkerhoff
			251	380	158 Vanderhoof's
			......	381	159 Joseph Hawkins
			......	382	159 Daniel Smith
			......	383	160 Job Smith
			......	384	160 Peter Pietersen Esqr.
28	Caspar Stymet's 1st	225	......	......	Peter Marselis
29	Caspar Stymet's 2d	223	......	327	162 Thomas Brown
			......	328	162 Jacob Vanderhoof
			......	329	163 Michael & George De Mott
			......	330	163 Johannis Van Houta

INDEX TO FIELD BOOK. 281

#	Name	Page refs	No.	Entry	Page
30	Adrian Post	264	164	Michael & George Demott	409
			165	Jacob Van Wagenen	412
			165	Johannis Van Wagenen	410
			166	Cornelius Gerritse al: Van Riper	411
			167	Cornelius Gerritse al: Van Riper	314
31	Guert Coerten's 1st	215	167	Garret Garritse al: Van Riper	315
			168	Altje Van Winkle	354
32	Guert Coerten's 2d	243	169	Not declar'd	355
			170	Beletje's Hans al: Van Riper	345
33	Guert Coerten's 3d	235	170	Altje Van Winkle	347
			171	Not declar'd	346
				Philip French Esqr.	
			172	Garret Newkirk	400
34	Fredrick Philipse	234	172	Peter Marselis	401
			173	Cornelius & Garret Sip	402
			173	Herman Veder	403
		262	174	Abraham Dederick	404
			174	Abraham Sickles	405
			175	Cornelius Dederick	406
			176	Hendrick Sickles	316
		216	176	Daniel Dederick	317
			177	Johannis Van Wagenen	362
35	Englebert Steinhuysen	244	177	Hendrick Van Winkle	361
			178	Hendrick Sickles	360
			178	Arent Toers	359
			179	Abraham Sickles	358
			179	Michael & George Demott	357
			180	Not declar'd	356
36	Thom: Fredrick al: De Cuyper	232, 284		Michael & George Demott	

INDEX TO FIELD BOOK.

Number of each Patent.	NAMES of the PATENTEES.	The Numbers whereby the Lots of Common Land which have been allotted To the respective Patents Upon the General Partition are distinguished.	The Numbers whereby The Subdivided Portions of the Common Lands are distinguished.	The Page in the Field Book where the Survey or Field Work of each Subdivided Portion of Common Land is recorded.	The Names of the Persons to whom the respective Allotments of the Common Lands are adjudg'd.
37	Harman Edwards	249		371	181 Hendrick Van Winkle
				369	182 Cornelius & Garret Sip
				370	182 Arent Toers
				320	183 Johannis Van Houta
				321	184 Abraham Sickles
				322	184 Garrit Newkirk
38	Guert Gerritse	221		324	185 Johannis Dedericks
				323	185 Cornelius & Garret Sip
				325	186 Beletje's Hans al: Van Riper
				326	186 Not declar'd
39	Paulus Pieterse	252. 253. 281		327	187 Garrit Newkirk
				331	188 Michael & George De Mott
40	Dirck Gerritse	226		332	188 Daniel Van Riper
				333	189 Widow Van Riper &c
				342	190 Cornelius & Garrit Sip
41	Jacob Luby	231		343	190 Arent Toers
				344	191 Johannis Van Houta
42	Jacob Luby	202			William Bayard Esqr

INDEX TO FIELD BOOK.

43 Jan Lubertse	...248	...363	192 Levinus Winne
		...364	193 Abraham Dederick
		...365	193 Cornelius Dederick
		...366	194 Arent Toers
		...367	194 Andries Prior
	...282	...368	195 Gysbert Van Blairkum
			Arent Toers
44 Peter Jacobse	...236	...348	196 Jacob Van Wagenen
		...349	196 Peter Marselis
		...372	197 Johannis Van Houta
		...378	198 Arent Toers
		...377	198 Cornelius & Garret Sip
		...373	199 Beletje's Hans al: Van Rip
		...374	199 Cornelius Gerritse al: Van Riper
	...250	...375	200 Garret Garretse al: Van Riper
		...376	200 Altje Van Winkle
45 Nicholas Varlet, and Balthazar Bayard	...285, 286		Cornelius & Garret Sip
	...224		Beletje's Hans al: Van Riper
	...241, 287		Zacharia Sickles
46 Dow Harmanse	...246	...336	202 Michael & George Demott
			Johannis Van Houta
47 John Berry	...228	...337	203 Mathevis & Henry Newkirk
		...338	203 Mathevis Newkirk Junr.
		...339	204 Jacob Newkirk
48 Tielman Van Vleck	...230	...340	205 Levinus Winne
		...341	205 Isaac Van Vleck
	...220	...318	206 Michael Hartman Vreelandt
49 Hendrick Teunise	...255	...319	207 Hendrick Van Winkle
			Hendrick Van Winkle

Number of each Patent.	NAMES of the PATENTEES.	The Numbers whereby the Lots of Common Land which have been allotted To the respective Patents Upon the General Partitions are distinguished.	The Numbers whereby The Subdivided Portions of the Common Lands are distinguished.	The Page in the Field Book where the Survey or Field Work of each Subdivided Portion of Common Land is recorded.	The Names of the Persons to whom the respective Allotments of the Common Lands are adjudg'd.
50	Hans Dedericks	214	311	208	Arent Toers
			312	209	Johannis Dederick
			310	209	Cornelius Dederick
			313	210	Abraham Dederick
51	Derick Teunisse	245			Johannis Van Wagenen
52	Garrit Gerritse	222			Johannis Van Wagenen
53	Ide Corneliese	229, 256			Cornelius & Garret Sip
54	Arent Lawrense	254	387	212	Arent Toers
			386	213	Johannis Van Houta
			385	214	Abraham Prior
			388	214	Johannis Van Wagenen
			389	215	Not declar'd
			353	216	Garrit Gerritse al: Van Riper
			352	216	Robert Leake Esq$_r$.
55	Nicholas Varlet	242	351	217	Arent Toers
			350	217	Not declar'd
56	Hendrick Van Ostrum	257			Not declar'd
57	Claas Jansen Vanpurmerant	209, 239			Hendericus Kuyper Esqr.
58	Jan Vinge	210			Hendericus Kuyper Esqr.
59	Van Ruyven et al.	218			Devisees of Sir Peter Warren
		207			Not declar'd
60	N: Varlet & N: Bayard	283			Not declar'd

CHAPTER V.

SECAUCUS COMMONS.

The preceding Field Book disposes of all the Land in the old Township of Bergen, and settles the ownership of nearly all the Common Lands except the Tract allotted to the Patent of Secaucus. This was not subdivided by the first commission and the reason therefor probably lay in the fact that many of the owners were non-residents who had, by inheritance, become owners of considerable parts of this Patent, which were undivided. This confusion of ownership practically prevented an allotment, until finally the political troubles between England and the Colonies intervened. As soon as peace was re-established efforts were made to obtain a subdivision of the allotment. But for several reasons further legislation was necessary to secure this object. Thereupon the Legislature of New Jersey enacted as follows:

CHAP. XLVIII.

A Supplementary ACT *to an Act, intitled, An Act appointing Commissioners for finally settling and determining the several Rights, Titles and Claims to the Common Lands of the Township of Bergen, and for making Partition thereof in just and equitable Proportions among those who shall be adjudged by the said Commissioners to be entitled to the same.*

WHEREAS an Act of the Legislature of *New Jersey* was passed in the Year One Thousand Seven Hundred and Sixty-three, intitled, *An* Act *appointing Commissioners for finally settling and determining the several Rights, Titles and Claims to the Common Lands of the Township of Bergen, and for making Partition thereof in just and equitable Proportions among those who shall be adjudged by the said Commissioners to be entitled to the same,* by which said Act *Jacob Spicer, Charles Clinton, William Donaldson, Azariah Dunham, John Berrien, Samuel Willis* and *Abraham Clark,* jun. Esquires, and the Majority of them, and the Survivors and Survivor of them, and the Majority of such Survivors, were appointed Commissioners for making Partition of the Common Lands of the Township of *Bergen* aforesaid, according to the Directions of the said Act: And whereas the said Commissioners, or the Majority of them, in or about the Year One Thousand Seven Hundred and Sixty-four, proceeded to execute the said Trust, and having first surveyed the Outlines of the said Township and the several Patents, and allotted them their respective Proportions of the common Land, made the Subdivisions thereof, and located to each and every Proprietor his and their respective Shares, according as the said Commissioners judged agreeably to Right, except in the single Instance herein particularly provided for: And whereas in making the Subdivisions aforesaid, a Patent was produced to them, called the Patent of *Secaucus,* dated the tenth Day of *December* in the Year of Our Lord One Thousand Six Hundred and Sixty-three, granted by *Peter Stuyvesant,* the then Dutch Governor, to *Nicholas Varlet* and *Nicholas Bayard,* and confirmed to the said *Varlet and Bayard* by Governor *Philip Carteret* on the Thirteenth Day of *October,* in the Year of our Lord One Thousand Six Hundred and

Sixty-seven, to which Patent the Commissioners set apart a certain Lot of Land, called the common Lands allotted to the Patent of *Secaucus*, in the Corporation of *Bergen*, and which said Lot is distinguished by the said Commissioners' Field-Books and Maps of the General Division by the Number Two Hundred and Eighty-three; Duplicates of both which said Books and Maps are said to be filed as of Record in the Secretary's Office in *Perth Amboy*, and in the Clerk's Office in the County of *Bergen*: AND WHEREAS a great Number of Persons did put in their Claims for the said Common Lands, in considering of which Claims many Difficulties occurred, and the Commissioners then present being equally divided in Opinion, were prevented from finally determining to whom the said Lot of Land did belong, as appears by the Record thereof made by the said Commissioners in their said Books: AND WHEREAS all of the said Commissioners appointed by the said Act, except two, are since deceased: AND WHEREAS many Difficulties and Inconveniencies have arisen in and about the Execution of the said Act, in the determining the Claims to the Lands allotted to the Patent of *Secaucus*, so that a total Obstruction is put to the Commissioners' further proceeding;

Sect. 1. BE IT THEREFORE ENACTED *by the Council and General Assembly of this State, and it is hereby Enacted by the Authority of the same,* That *Abraham Clark, Azariah Dunham, Silas Condict, John Carle,* and *Daniel Marsh,* Esquires, shall be, and are hereby appointed Commissioners for settling and finally determining in whom the Right or Rights of the said common Lands allotted to the Patent of *Secaucus* is or are vested; and if it shall appear to the said Commissioners, or the major Part of them, that a Division or Subdivision of the said common Lands is necessary, then the said Commissioners shall proceed to make Division thereof, and shall cause two Field-Books and Maps to be made, specifying the Bounds of each and every Lot, and to whom allotted, which said Maps and Field-Books shall be signed by the said Commissioners, or the major Part of them, and their Surveyor or Surveyors: And if the Commissioners shall be of Opinion that the Right of the said common Land is vested in one Person, they shall certify the same under their Hands; and one of the Field-Books and one Map of the Allottment with its Subdivisions, if such Subdivision is found necessary, or Certificate, shall be filed of Record in the Secretary's Office; and one other Field-Book, Map or Certificate, shall be filed in the Clerk's Office of the County of *Bergen,* to be kept and remain as Evidence, and shall be, and are hereby made conclusive Evidence of the Transactions of said Commissioners, and such Opinion of the said Commissioners shall be deemed good and valid in Law to establish the Right and Title of the Proprietor or Proprietors of the said common Lands.

2. *And be it further Enacted by the Authority aforesaid,* That the Commissioners hereby appointed, before they enter on the Execution of any Part of the Trust reposed in them by this Act, shall severally take an Oath, and qualify in the same Manner and Form as the Commissioners named in the above recited Act were required to do; and thereafter they, and their Surveyors and Chain-Bearers, shall be vested with the same Powers and Privileges respecting the said Lot of common Land allotted to the said Patent of *Secaucus,* and be entitled to the same Reward for their Services, and subject to the same Restrictions and Regulations, as the Commissioners appointed by the above recited Act, their Surveyors and Chain-Bearers were respectively entitled and subject

to, and the whole Expence which shall or may accrue by the Execution of this Act shall be paid and defrayed out of the Surplus or remaining Money appertaining to the Proprietors of the common Lands of the Corporation of the Township of *Bergen*, provided the same, or a sufficient Part thereof for defraying the Expence of the said Subdivision, can be obtained by the said Commissioners upon Demand of the Persons who were Trustees of the Freeholders of the Township of *Bergen*, at the Time the other Parts of the Commons of *Bergen* were divided, or of their Executors or administrators, to which Trustees at that Time the Surplus aforesaid is said to have been paid by their Commissioners; and in case the said Commissioners, upon their entering upon the Execution of the Business to which by this Act they are appointed, shall not be able to obtain from said Trustees or their Representatives upon Demand the Whole, or so much of the Money appertaining to the Proprietors of the common Land of *Bergen*, which was paid to the said Trustees by the former Commissioners, as in their Opinion will be sufficient to defray the Expence attending the Business to which by this Act, they are appointed; that then, and in such Case, the said Commissioners, or the major Part of them shall be, and they hereby are authorized, directed and empowered, to set apart so much of the common Land allotted to the Patent of *Secaucus*, as in their Opinion will be sufficient to complete the Settlement and Division of the said Commons; and the said Commissioners herein named, and the major Part of them, shall be, and they hereby are invested with all the Powers granted to the Commissioners named in and by the before recited Act for granting, conveying and assuring, the Land they may set apart as aforesaid; and any Sale or Sales by them to be made of such Land shall be good and valid, and entitle the Purchaser or Purchasers to an absolute Estate in Fee-Simple for the same, in which said Sale or Sales the said Commissioners shall be Governed by the same Rules, and in all Things conduct themselves in the same Manner, as the Commissioners named and appointed in the before recited Act were directed to govern and conduct themselves.

3. AND, to the End that the Trustees of the Freeholders and Inhabitants of *Bergen*, or their Executors or Administrators, may not on any Pretence whatever withhold any Part of the Money deposited in their Hands which remained of the Sale of Lands made by the Commissioners named and appointed in and by the before recited Act, after defraying thereout the Expence of the Division and Subdivision of said Commons, as far as they proceeded therein, together with other Disbursements made thereout by said Commissioners upon Request of the Trustees and Freeholders of said Township, *Be it Enacted by the Authority aforesaid*, That the said Trustees of the Freeholders of the Township of *Bergen*, in whose Hands the aforesaid Money was deposited, their Executors and Administrators respectively, shall be liable and account for all the Surplus Money deposited in their, or either of their Hands, which remained unexpended at the Time of closing the Field-Books by the Commissioners named and appointed in and by the before recited Act, which was raised by the Sale of a Tract of Land, Part of the common Lands of *Bergen* which was made by said Commissioners pursuant to said recited Act, which Money, deposited as aforesaid, the said Trustees of *Bergen*, their Executors and Administrators, are hereby required and enjoyned to pay to the Commissioners herein named, or the major Part of them, upon their demanding the same.

4. *And be it further Enacted by the Authority aforesaid*, That in Case any Money received by the Commissioners herein appointed, either of the Trustees of *Bergen*, or by the Sale of Lands pursuant to the Direction of this Act, may remain unexpended by said Commissioners in the due Execution of the Business for which they are appointed, the said Commissioners shall deposit so much of the said Money as they may find belongs to the Township of *Bergen*, in the Hands of the said Trustees of said Township, and the Remainder in the Hands of some Freeholder who they shall judge to be intitled to a Share of said common Lands, with an Account of the Part thereof each Person interested in said Commons is entitled to, taking a Receipt for the Money so deposited, with an Account of the Division to be made of the same, which Receipts shall discharge the said Commissioners, their Executors and Administrators, and the Person receiving the same shall be answerable therefor to the several Persons entitled thereto.

5. *And be it further Enacted by the Authority aforesaid*, That, for the more easy and ready acquiring Possession of such common Lands as shall be allotted and adjudged by Virtue of this Act, it shall and may be lawful for the said Commissioners, or the Majority of them, or the Survivors or Survivor of them, to issue a Precept under their hands and Seals, directed to the Sheriff of *Bergen* County, commanding him to cause full and actual Possession to be delivered to such Person or Persons to whom such common Lands shall be allotted as aforesaid, which said Sheriff is hereby required to execute said Precept, and if the Sheriff shall find it necessary, he may raise the *Posse Comitatus*, and exercise the same Power and Authority with which by Law he is invested in the Execution of a Writ of Possession in an Action of Ejectment. *Provided always*, That Nothing contained in this Act shall be deemed, construed, or understood to effect or destroy any Claim, Right or Title of the General Proprietors of the Eastern Division of this State to the Premises, or to any Part thereof, and saving also to this State all its Rights therein as if this Act had not passed. *Provided also*, That the Commissioners herein appointed shall meet and enter upon the Execution of this Act, as soon as they conveniently can after the passing thereof, having previously given one Month's Notice in the *New York* Gazette of the Time and Place of such their intended Meeting.

Passed at New-Brunswick, August 26, 1784.

Thus empowered, the new Commission proceeded with the work of subdividing the Secaucus Commons. The following is a copy of their Field-Book and Map, showing the result of their work. They were filed as directed in the Act, but strange to say, no evidence appears on them of their having been filed in the office of the Secretary of State. As to how they came to be filed in the Hudson County Clerk's office the reader is referred to what was said on *page* 24. There is no doubt that this work is marked with the same care and accuracy which are so characteristic of the work of the first Commissioners.

BERGEN

COMMON LANDS.

FILED IN THE OFFICE OF THE CLERK OF HUDSON COUNTY, MARCH 15, 1853.

R. GILCHRIST,
Clerk.

*THIS IS ONE OF THE FIELD BOOKS

Of the Partition and Division of Common Land allotted to the Patent of Secaucus in the Township of Bergen, made in pursuance of a Law of the State of New Jersey passed at New Brunswick the Twenty sixth Day of August in the Year of our Lord, One Thousand seven Hundred and Eighty four, Intitled

" A Supplementary Act to an Act intitled, an Act appointing Commissioners for finally settling and Determining the several Rights, Titles and Claims, to the Common Lands of the Township of Bergen and for making partition thereof in Just and Equitable proportions among those who shall be adjudged by the said Commissioners to be intitled to the same "

The Commissioners named and appointed in and by the said Act taking upon them the Execution of the trust thereby reposed three of them (to wit) Azariah Dunham Silas Condit and Daniel Marsh, were duly sworn as followeth

New Survey ss :

Be it Remembered that on the fifteenth day of December in the Year of our Lord One Thousand * seven Hundred and Eighty four Personally *2 appeared before me John Cleves Symms Esq[r.] one of the Justices of the Supreme Court of the State of New Jersey, Azariah Dunham Silas Condit and Daniel Marsh Esquires three of the Commissioners appointed in and by an Act passed at New Brunswick the 26th day of August 1784 intitled, an Act appointing Commissioners for Finally Settling and Determining the several rights and claims to the Common Lands in the Township of Bergen and for making partition thereof in Just and Equitable proportions among those who shall be adjudged by the said Commissioners to be intitled to the same, Passed in the fourth Year of George the third; and severally took the Oath required in and by the said recited Acts.

Taken and sworn at Solitude the day   Az: Dunham
and Year first aforesaid before me   Silas Condit
    John Cleves Symms   Daniel Marsh

The other two of the said Commmissioners (to wit) Abraham Clark and John Carle were duly sworn as follows.

New Jersey ss.

Abraham Clark and John Carle Esquires two of the Commissioners named and appointed in and by an Act of the Legislature of New Jersey intitled * A Supplementary Act intitled an Act appointing Commissioners *3 for Finally Settling and Determining the several Rights Titles and Claims to the Common Lands of the Township of Bergen, and for making partition thereof in Just and Equitable proportions among those who shall be adjudged by the said Commissioners to be intitled to the same passed the twenty sixth day of August last; Personally appeared before me Isaac Smith Esqr. second Justice of the Supreme Court, and being severally sworn on the Holy Evangelists of Almighty God did depose that they would respectively execute and perform the trust and services required of them severally by the before recited Act fairly and impartially according to the directions thereof and the best of their Skill and Judgment

Sworn before me this 22d day of December 1784
Isaac Smith

Albra: Clark
John Carle

as by the aforementioned Original despositions filed in the Office of the clerk of the County of Bergen may appear.

The said Azariah Dunham Silas Condit and Daniel Marsh being severally sworn as aforesaid did make and publish in the New York Gazet-
*4 teer from the 21st day of December 1784 to the 21st day * of January 1785 a Notification in the words following (there being no New York Paper by the name of Gazette published in New York at that time)

Notice is hereby given to all persons concerned, that the Commissioners appointed to and by an Act intitled a Supplementary Act to an Act intitled an Act appointing Commissioners for finally Settling and Determining the several Rights, Titles and Claims, to the Common Lands of the Township of Bergen, and for making partition thereof in Just and Equitable proportions among those who shall be adjudged by the said Commissioners to be intitled to the same (passed the 26th day of August 1784) Will meet on Monday the 24th day of January next at the House of Sylvanus Lawrence at Hobucken in the said Township of Bergen for the purpose of Settling and Finally determining in whom the Right or Rights to the Common Lands allotted to the Patent of Secaucus is or are Vested agreeable to the directions of the said Act.

December 20th 1784

Azariah Dunham
Silas Condit
Dan'l Marsh

We the Commissioners named in said Act having met Pursuant to the above Notification did appoint Thomas Clark to be Surveyor, who thereupon took the following Oath

*5 *Bergen County *ss.*

Thomas Clark of the County of Essex appointed Surveyor for Dividing the Common Lands allotted to the Patent of Secaucus by the Commissioners named and appointed by an Act intitled " A Supplementary Act to an Act intitled an Act appointing Commissioners for finally Settling and Determining the several Rights Titles and Claims to the Common Lands of the Township of Bergen and for making partition thereof in Just and Equitable proportion among those who shall be adjudged by the said Commissioners to be intitled to the same" being duly sworn deposeth that he will well and Truly execute and perform the trust and services required of him as Surveyor by the above said Act fairly and impartially

according to the Directions he may receive from the Commissioners named in said Act, to the best of his Skill and Judgment
Sworn the 25th day of Thoˢ Clark
January 1785 Before me
John Benson
One of the Judges of the Court of Common Pleas in said County.

As by the deposition filed in the Clerks Office of the County of Bergen may appear

* 𝔚𝔢 then caused an actual Survey to be taken of the Commons *6 after which we proceeded to consider the Claim put in by the Agent of Forfeited Estates for the County of Bergen, to all the Common Lands allotted to the Patent of Secaucus as formerly claimed and forfeited to the State by William Bayard, the said William Bayard having claimed the same as Heir at Law to Nicholas Bayard one of the Original Patentees of Secaucus and survivor to Nicholas Varlet the other Patentee;* which Patented Premises after the Decease of the said Nicholas Varlet was with all the appurtenances thereunto belonging, Granted and Conveyed by the Administrators of said Varlet and Nicholas Bayard, to Edward Earle by Deed dated the twenty fourth day of April in the Year One Thousand six hundred and seventy six Pursuant to Written Articles entered into by the said administrators and Nicholas Bayard on the one part, and Edward Earle on the other part dated the sixteenth day of October in the year One Thousand Six Hundred and seventy three, wherein the said administrators and Bayard agree to sell and convey to said Earle the Island Secaucus with Meadows &c according to the Patent, with such further Right and Interest as the same Island hath been possessed by the said Administrators and said Bayard

* 𝔚𝔥𝔦𝔠𝔥 Claim with the writings and Evidence produced for and *7 against the same being fully Considered, 𝔚𝔢 do adjudge that all the Right to the Commons belonging to the Patent of Secaucus passed with the Island of Secaucus by the grant from the administrators of Nicholas Varlet and from Nicholas Bayard to Edward Earle.

And whereas divers Persons Claimed a Right in the Commons of Secaucus under the said Edward Earle and fearing such Claimers had not exhibited all their Papers in support of their Rights we judging it proper to give a further time to produce the same did on the 26th day of February 1785 adjourn all further proceedings until the first Monday in April following and thereupon Published in the New York Gazetteer Weekly, for four weeks the following Advertisement.

The Subscribers Commissioners appointed by Law for adjusting and finally settling the Titles of the Claimants to the Common Lands Allotted to the Patent of Secaucus in the Township of Bergen having same time attended for the Purpose of their Appointment and being desirous of giving all Claimants sufficient time to produce their Claims hereby give *8 Notice that they have * adjourned until the first Monday in April next to meet at this place, at which time they will be ready to receive any further Claims and Evidences to support the same; Claims not produced at the above said time will necessarily be Excluded.

Hobucken February 26th 1785   Silas Condit
                       Abraham Clark   John Carle
                       Azariah Dunham   Daniel Marsh.

⁰ As to the claim of William Bayard, vid'e Field Book, p. 221.

Having met agreably to the foregoing Notice we proceeded first in making a Valuation of the several parts of the said Commons in Order to Divide the same according to Value after which we set apart a Certain parcel thereof to be sold towards defraying the expenses of the Division. The Lot set apart to be sold is marked A on the Map, and is twenty two chains in width extending across the Common Land from the Eastermost Bounds of the Commons to Pinhornes Creek between Parallel Lines running North fifty eight Degrees and thirty minutes West. The Southermost of which Lines is the Southermost Bounds of the said Common Land, the said Lot so set apart Contains by Estimation about One Hundred and Twenty Acres

*9   * **We** then proceeded to the Examination of the Titles of the several Persons Claiming parts and shares of the said Common Land, allotted to Secaucus, and upon the Examination thereof

We adjudge a Certain Portion or share of said Lands to belong to Daniel Smith

Our Survey of which said Portion as laid down on the Map shews, and **we** adjudge it to be a Tract of Land Marked No 1 *

Beginning at a Stake standing the south side of a run of water in a Gully, by the edge of the water Being the Eastermost Corner of the lot set apart for sale, standing also in the line of the Bergen Lots formerly subdivided and from said Stake runs North fifty eight degrees and thirty minutes west fifty five chains and fifty links to Pinhorns Creek, then returning to said stake the Place of Beginning and from thence running North thirty one degrees and thirty minutes east five chains and forty links to a stake in the line of the Bergen Lots, thence north fifty eight degrees and thirty minutes west fifty five chains and fifty links to said Pinhorns Creek, thence down said Creek as it runs to meet the first line running to the same containing about thirty acres.

*10   * **And we adjudge** a Certain Portion or share of said Common Lands to belong to Edmund William Kingsland of New Barbadoes Neck

Our Survey of which said Portion as laid down on the Map, shews, and **we** Adjudge it to be a Tract of Land Marked No 2 †

Beginning at the Eastermost Corner of the Last mentioned Lot No 1, from thence Running along the Line of said Lot north fifty eight degrees and thirty minutes west fifty five chains and fifty links to Pinhorns Creek, then returning to the place of Beginning from thence Running along the Bergen Lots North thirty one degrees and thirty minutes

---

* Daniel Smith left this lot to his son Daniel, who conveyed it to David Hennion July 25, 1815. Charles Watts owned part of it in 1819, and Garret Newkirk part of it in 1839.

† The interest of Kingsland in Secaucus came through his marriage with *Mary*, daughter of Judge Pinhorne. *Vide Note to Secaucus Patent*, p. 66. He conveyed this lot to Garret J. Van Rypen and Levinus Winne May 23, 1788. George Hillyer conveyed it to Samuel Fanshaw Aug. 28, 1839.

east eleven chains and ten links to a stake, thence north fifty eight degrees and thirty minutes west fifty eight chains to Pinhorns Creek, thence down said Creek as it runs till it meets the first line running to the same containing about sixty two Acres and a half Acre.

And we adjudge a Certain Portion or share of said Common Lands to belong to Mary Moore Widow of Austin Moore Esqr. deceased.

Our Survey of which said Portion as laid down on the Map, shews, and **we** adjudge it to be a Tract of Land marked No 3.*

*Beginning at a stake being the Easternmost Corner of the last mentioned Lot No 2 from thence running along the line thereof north fifty eight degrees and thirty minutes west fifty eight chains to Pinhorns Creek, then returning to the place of Beginning and from thence running along the Bergen Lots north thirty one degrees and thirty minutes east twenty eight chains and ninety nine links to a stake, thence north fifty eight degrees and thirty minutes west seventy one chains and fifty links to Pinhorns Creek, thence down said Creek as it runs, till it meets the first line running to the same, Containing about One Hundred and Eighty four Acres. *11

And we adjudge a Certain Portion or share of said Common Lands to belong to John Bard of the City of New York Doctor of Physick,

Our Survey of which said portion as laid down on the Map, shews, and **we** adjudge it to be a Tract of Land marked No 4.†

Beginning at a stake being the Easternmost Corner of the last mentioned Lot No 3 from thence running * along the line thereof north fifty eight degrees and thirty minutes west seventy one chains and fifty links to Pinhorns Creek, then returning to the place of Beginning and from thence running north thirty one degrees and thirty minutes east five chains and sixty eight links to a stake being the Northerly Corner of a lot of Common Land Allotted to Herman Edwards Patent Marked on the Map of the General Division of the Commons of Bergen No 249, thence *12

° The widow Moore, and her son William Augustin Moore, conveyed this tract Nov. 6, 1633, in parcels, as follows: To Nicholas Vreeland, forty-five acres; to Jacob Van Wagenen, forty acres; to Helmigh Van Houten, fifty acres; to Jasper Prior, twenty-five acres; and to Jacob Newkirk, twenty-five acres. These strips extended northwest and southeast from the line of the "Bergen Lots" to Pinhorne Creek, and were in order, beginning on the northerly bounds of the tract. Van Houten died seized. *Vide Note to Lot No. 4, New Field Book.* Part of his purchase was partitioned April 6, 1831, among the children of his grandson Helmigh, viz., *Garret, Catherine*, wife of John Vreeland, Junr, *Eliza*, wife of Jacob Greenlief, and *Rachel*, wife of Garret Newkirk.

† Bard conveyed this lot to Jacobus Van Buskirk July 29, 1739. *Vide Note to Jansen and Edsall's Patent*, p. 19. Part of this lot, containing fifty-four acres and six-tenths of an acre, he had bought in 1831 from Thomas Alsop; Alsop bought from the heirs of Pinhorne Dec. 15, 1730. It was a strip from the northerly side of Pinhorne's farm.

north fifty four degrees west one chain and seventy links to a stake being the westerly Corner of a Lot of Common Land Allotted to Hendrick Teunison's Patent marked on the Map of the General Division of the Commons No 220, thence north thirty five degrees east seven chains and eighty two links to a stake, thence north fifty eight degrees and thirty minutes west forty nine chains and forty five links to a Cedar Tree marked for a Corner in the Cedar Swamp, thence north thirty one degrees and thirty minutes east twenty six chains and sixty three links to Pinhorns Creek, thence down the said Creek as it runs till it meets with the first line running to the same, Containing about One Hundred and fifty four Acres.

*13   * **And we adjudge** a Certain Portion or share of said Common Lands to belong to Evert Banker of New York, Merchant.

Our Survey of which said Portion as laid down on the Map, shews, and **we** adjudge it to be a Tract of Land marked No 5 *

Beginning at a stake being the Eastermost Corner of the last mentioned Lot No 4 from thence running north fifty eight degrees and thirty minutes west forty nine chains and forty five links to a Cedar Tree Marked in the Cedar Swamp being a Corner of the last mentioned Lot, thence north thirty one degrees and thirty minutes East twenty six chains and sixty three links to Pinhorns Creek, then returning to the place of Beginning and from thence running along the line of the Bergen Lots north thirty five degrees east thirty three chains and fifty four links to a stake, thence north fifty eight degrees and thirty minutes West twenty six chains and sixty links to a stake by Cromkill on the North side of the mouth of Pinhorn's Ditch, thence along said Ditch northwest twelve chains to said Pinhorns Creek, then down the same as it runs till it meets with the last mentioned line that runs to said Creek, Containing about One Hundred and sixty five Acres.

*14   * **And we adjudge** a Certain Portion or share of said Common Land to belong to Edmond Kingsland.

Our Survey of which said portion as laid down on the Map, shews, and **we** adjudge it to be a Tract of Land Marked No 6.†

Beginning at a stake being the Eastermost Corner of the last mentioned Lot No 5, from thence running along the line thereof North fifty eight degrees and thirty minutes west twenty six chains and sixty links to a stake by the Cromkill on the north side of the mouth of Pinhorn's Ditch, then returning to the place of Beginning, from thence running along the line of the Bergen Lots north thirty five degrees east eight chains and forty two links to a stake, thence north fifty eight degrees and thirty minutes west twenty six chains and sixty three links to said Crom-

---

* Banker conveyed this lot to John E. Earle June 7, 1792. Earle conveyed the southwesterly part of it to Peter Sip June 25, 1800, and thirteen acres and eleven one-hundredths of an acre of it to Peter Wilson April 20, 1804. Jasper Cadmus sold one hundred and thirty acres and eleven one-hundredths of an acre to John Sturge, jr., Sept. 17, 1833 (July 30, 1829?), who conveyed to his son John Oct. 22, 1835.

† Kingsland conveyed this lot to Deborah, wife of James Outwater, Nov. 7, 1785.

kill, thence up said Kill as it runs till it meets with the first line from the Beginning that runs to the same Containing about Twenty two Acres and three Tenths of an Acre.

    And we adjudge a certain Portion or share of said Common Lands to belong to George Leislie.

    Our Survey of which said portion as laid down on the Map, shews, and **we** adjudge it to be a Tract of Land marked No 7.*

* Beginning at a Stake being the Eastermost Corner of the last mentioned Lot No 6, from thence Running North Fifty eight Degrees and Thirty Minutes West Twenty six Chains and sixty three Links to the Cromkill, then returning to the place of Beginning and from thence running along the line of the Bergen Lots North Thirty five Degrees East seven Chains and sixty seven links to a Stake, thence North Fifty eight Degrees and thirty minutes West Twenty seven Chains and seventy links to said Cromkill, Thence up said kill as it runs, till it meets with the first line from the Beginning that runs to the same, Containing about Twenty Acres and seven tenths of an Acre. *15

    And we adjudge a Certain Portion or Share of said Common Lands to belong to Josiah Hornblower Esqr. of Essex County.

    Our Survey of which said Portion as laid down on the Map, shews, and **we** adjudge it to be a Tract of Land Marked No 8.†

Beginning at a Stake being the Eastermost Corner of the last mentioned Lot No 7, from thence running North Fifty eight Degrees and thirty minutes West Twenty seven Chains and seventy links to the * Cromkill, then returning to the place of Beginning and from thence Running along the line of the Bergen Lots North Thirty five Degrees East seven Chains and twenty one Links to a stake, thence North Fifty eight Degrees and thirty minutes West Thirty one Chains to Cromkill, thence up said kill as it runs till it meets with the first line running from the Beginning to said kill, Containing about twenty Acres and seven tenths of an Acre. *16

    And we adjudge a Certain Portion or Share of said Common Lands to belong to William Earle late deceased, Garret Hopper and John Earle equally among them as Tenants in Common, the said William Earle's part thereof to be held and possessed by his Children in such proportion that each son have twice or double the share of each Daughter agreeably to a late Law directing the descent of Real Estate.

    ° Leslie's interest in Secaucus came through his marriage with Colonel Kingsland's daughter. He conveyed this lot to Helmigh Van Houten Aug. 13, 1785. *Vide Note to Lot No. 3, of Secaucus Commons, p. 11.*

    † Hornblower's interest in Secaucus came through his marriage with *Elizabeth*, daughter of William Kingsland. He conveyed this lot to Helmigh Van Houten Oct. 15, 1785. *Vide Note to Lot No. 3, of Secaucus Commons, p. 11.*

Our Survey of which said Portion as laid down on the the Map, shews, and **we** adjudge it to be a Tract of Land Marked No 9.*

Beginning at a Stake, being the Eastermost Corner of the last mentioned Lot No 8 from thence running North Fifty eight Degrees and thirty minutes West three Chains and forty two links to a stake, thence North six Degrees and fifteen minutes East * fourteen Chains and forty nine links to a Stake, thence South Fifty eight Degrees and thirty minutes East Ten Chains and thirty six links to a stake, in the line of the Bergen Lots, thence along said line South Thirty five Degrees West thirteen Chains and ten links to the place of Beginning, Containing about Nine Acres.

*17

And we adjudge a certain Portion or share of said Common Lands to belong to Job Smith of Secaucus.

Our Survey of which said Portion as laid down on the Map, shews, and **we** adjudge it to be a Tract of Land Marked No 10 †

Beginning at a Stake standing in the line of Lot No 8 adjudged to Josiah Hornblower at Three Chains and fifty two links from the Eastermost Corner of said Lot which stake is a Corner of the last mentioned Lot No 9, and from thence running North Fifty eight Degrees and thirty minutes West Twenty seven chains and fifty eight links to the Cromkill, then returning to the place of Beginning, and from thence running North six Degrees and fifteen minutes East Five Chains and twenty links to a stake standing in the line of Lot No 9, thence North Fifty eight * Degrees and thirty minutes West twenty seven Chains and five links to said Cromkill, thence up the said Kill as it runs till it meets with the first line from the Beginning running to the said Kill Containing about Twelve Acres and eight tenths of an Acre.

*18

And we adjudge a Certain Portion or Share of said Common Lands to belong to and among all the Children of Philip Smith late of Secaucus, deceased (which he left at the time of his decease) to be held and possessed by said Children in such proportion that each son have twice or double the share of each Daughter agreeably to a late Law directing the descents of Real Estates.

Our Survey of which said Portion as laid down on the Map, shews, and **we** adjudge it to be a Tract of Land Marked No 11

Beginning at a Stake being the Northeastermost Corner of the last mentioned Lot No 10 standing in the line of Lot No 9 and from said stake running North Fifty eight Degrees and thirty minutes West Twenty seven Chains and fifty eight links to the Cromkill, then returning to the place of Beginning and from thence running North six Degrees and

---

* Abraham Lozier and Mary, his wife, conveyed one-third of this lot to Cornelius Doremus Nov. —, 1796.

† Smith by will devised this lot to Cornelia, widow of John Smith, who conveyed it to Morris Ackerman Aug. 4, 1812.

fifteen minutes East six Chains and forty one * Links to the Stake standing in the line of Lot No 9, thence North fifty eight Degrees and thirty minutes West Twenty six Chains and thirty two links to said Cromkill, thence up said Kill as it runs till it meets with the first line from the beginning that runs to the same, Containing about Fifteen Acres and seven tenths of an Acre.

*19

      And we adjudge a Certain Portion or Share of said Common Lands to belong to Antlebe Earle

           Our Survey of which said Portion as laid down on the Map, shews, and **we** adjudge it to be a Tract of Land Marked No 12 *

Beginning at a stake being the Northeastermost Corner of the last mentioned Lot No 11 standing in the line of Lot No 9 and from said Stake running North Fifty eight Degrees and Thirty minutes West Twenty six Chains and thirty two links to the Cromkill, then returning to the place of Beginning and from thence running North six Degrees and fifteen minutes East four Chains and Eighty five links to a stake standing in the line of Lot No 5, thence North Fifty eight Degrees and Thirty minutes West twenty three Chains and sixty eight links to said Cromkill where the same makes a short bend, thence up said kill as it runs till it meets with the first line from the Beginning that runs to the same, Containing about Eleven Acres.

      *** And we adjudge** a Certain Portion or Share of said Common Lands to belong to the Heirs or Devisees of Joseph Hawkens formerly of New York deceased or such as may Legally Claim the same under him as we adjudge the right and Title to the said Portion of Commons was Vested in said Hawkens at the time of his decease but we know not who is or are now entitled thereto under him.

*20

           Our Survey of which said Portion as laid down on the Map, shews, and **we** adjudge it to be a Tract of Land Marked No 13 †

Beginning at a Stake being the North East Corner of the last mentioned Lot No 12 standing in the line of Lot No 15 and from said Stake running North Fifty Eight Degrees and thirty minutes West Twenty three Chains and sixty Eight links to the Cromkill where the same makes a short bend, then returning to the place of Beginning, and from thence running North six Degrees and fifteen minutes East five Chains and thirty seven Links to a stake, thence North Thirty two Degrees and forty five minutes East Eight Chains and ten links to a stake in the Road, thence North Fifty eight Degrees and Thirty minutes West thirty Chains and forty links to said Cromkill, thence up said Kill as it runs till it meets

---

   * Antlebe Earle's interest in Secaucus (at least in part), came through two deeds from Edward Earle, grandson of the original Earle, dated Sept. 20, 1755, and May 10, 1757. *Vide Note to Secaucus Patent,* p. 66.

   † William Hawkins, of Kinderhook, conveyed this lot to Enoch Smith, Dec. 12, 1792.

*21 with the first line from * the Beginning that runs to the same, Containing about Thirty eight Acres.

And we adjudge the Right and Title to a Certain Portion or Share of said Common Lands was Legally Vested in John Kingsland immediately after the decease of his Father Edmond Kingsland by Vertue of the last will and Testament of the said Edmond Bearing date the twenty ninth day of July in the year One Thousand seven hundred and forty one; But as no Person appeared to Claim said Portion or Share, we do not determine to whom the same doth now belong.

Our survey of which said Portion as laid down on the Map, sheweth, and **we** adjudge it to be a Tract of Land Marked No 14.

Beginning at a Stake standing in the Road being the Eastermost Corner of the last mentioned Lot No 13 and from thence Running North Fifty eight Degrees and Thirty minutes West Thirty Chains and forty links to the Cromkill, then returning to the place of Beginning, and from thence running North Thirty two Degrees and forty five minutes East *22 Thirteen Chains and twenty eight links * to a Stake, thence North Fifty eight Degrees and thirty minutes West Thirty Chains and Eighty links to said Cromkill, thence up said Kill as it runs till it meets with the first line running to the same from the Beginning, Containing about Forty one Acres.

And we adjudge a Certain Portion or Share of said Common Lands to belong to the Heirs or Devisees of James Sacket deceased; as We adjudge the Right and Title to said Portion of Commons was Legally Vested in said James Sacket at the time of his decease.

Our Survey of which said Portion as laid down on the Map, shews, and **we** adjudge it to be a Tract of Land Marked No 15.*

Beginning at a Stake planted in the line of the Bergen Lots, being the Eastermost Corner of Lot No 9 adjudged to Garret Hopper, John Earle and the Heirs of William Earle deceased, and from thence Running North Fifty eight Degrees and Thirty minutes West Ten chains and Thirty six links to a Stake being the Northermost Corner of Lot No 9, thence North six degrees and fifteen minutes East seven Chains *23 and thirty five links to a stake, thence North Thirty two * Degrees and forty five minutes East seventy four links to a stake in the Road standing in the line of Lot No 13, thence South Fifty eight Degrees and thirty minutes East thirteen Chains and Eighty eight links to a Stake in the line of the Bergen Lots, thence along said line South Thirty five degrees West seven Chains and forty one links to the place of beginning, Containing about Nine Acres and one tenth of an Acre.

---

* This lot was conveyed by William Sackett to Enoch Smith Nov. 3, 1787, and by John G. Leake to Cornelius Doremus, of Slotterdam, April 4, 1790. Sacket's interest in Secaucus arose by a deed from Joseph Sacket to him, July 21, 1762, for one-eighteenth of twenty acres he had bought of Edward Earle July 20, 1762.

And we adjudge a Certain Portion or Share of said Common Lands to belong to the Heirs or Devisees of William Sacket deceased; as We adjudge the Right and Title to said Portion of Commons was Legally Vested in said William Sacket at the time of his decease.

Our Survey of which said Portion as laid down on the Map, shews, and **we** adjudge it to be a Tract of Land Marked No 16 *

Beginning at a Stake planted in the line of the Bergen Lots being the Eastermost Corner of the last mentioned Lot No 15 and from thence Running North Fifty eight Degrees and thirty minutes West thirteen Chains and eighty eight links to a stake in the Road being the Northermost Corner of Lot No 15, thence North thirty two Degrees and * Forty five Minutes East six Chains and fifty links to a stake in the road, thence south Fifty eight Degrees and thirty minutes East, fourteen Chains and seventeen links to a stake in the line of the Bergen Lots, thence along said line South thirty five Degrees West six Chains and fifty one Links to the place of Beginning, Containing about Nine Acres and one tenth of an Acre. *24

And we adjudge a certain Portion or Share of Said Common Lands to belong to the Heirs or Devisees of John Sacket deceased; as We adjudge the Right and Title to said Portion of Commons was Legally Vested in said John Sacket at the time of his decease.

Our Survey of which said Portion as laid down on the Map, shews, and **we** adjudge it to be a Tract of Land Marked No 17.

Beginning at a stake planted in the Line of the Bergen Lots, being the Eastermost Corner of the last mentioned Lot No 16, and from thence Running North Fifty eight Degrees and Thirty minutes West Fourteen Chains and seventeen links to a stake in the road, thence North Thirty two Degrees and forty five minutes East six Chains and thirty seven links to a stake in the Road; thence south Fifty eight * Degrees and Thirty minutes East Fourteen Chains and Thirty eight links to a stake in the line of the Bergen Lots, thence along said line south Thirty five Degrees West six Chains and Thirty Eight links to the place of beginning; Containing about nine Acres and one tenth of an Acre. *25

And we adjudge a Certain Portion or Share of said Common Lands to belong to the Heirs or Devisees of Samuel Sacket deceased; as We adjudge the Right and Title to said Portion of Commons was Legally Vested in said Samuel Sacket at the time of his decease

Our Survey of which said Portion as laid down on the Map, shews the same in two Lots and **we** adjudge them to be the Two Tracts of Land Marked No 18 and No 23 †

---

* Sacket conveyed this lot to Enoch Smith Nov. 3, 1787.

† *Lot* 18. These two lots were sold by Samuel and Augustus Sacket to Paul Saunier June 3, 1780. *Lot No.* 18 forms part of the present Macpelah Cemetery, and

The first of which said Lots No 18 Begins at a Stake standing in the line of the Bergen Lots Being the Eastermost Corner of the last mentioned Lot Marked No 17 and from thence running North Fifty eight Degrees and thirty minutes West Fourteen Chains and thirty eight links to a stake in the road, thence North Thirty two Degrees and forty five *26 minutes East six * Chains and twenty six links to another stake in the Road, thence South Fifty eight Degrees and thirty minutes East Fourteen Chains and seventy links to a stake in the line of the Bergen Lots, thence along said line South thirty five Degrees West six Chains and Twenty seven links to the place of Beginning; Containing about Nine Acres and One tenth of an Acre.

The other of which said Lots Marked No 23 begins at a stake planted for a Corner in the line of the Bergen Lots, the said Stake being the Eastermost of a Lot or Portion of said Common Land hereinafter mentioned and adjudged to belong to Doctor Joseph Sacket, and from said Stake to the place of Beginning Running North Fifty eight Degrees and Thirty minutes West Fifty two Chains to the Cromkill, thence returning to the place of Beginning and from thence running along the Hills in the line of the Bergen Lots North Thirty five Degrees East, six

---

was a part of the "Frenchman's Garden." Concerning this garden I have met with the following poetic and somewhat sonorous accounts.

"In a wild and romantic situation on Bergen Creek, nearly opposite the City of New York, thirty acres of land were purchased for a garden and fruitery by the unfortunate Louis XVI., who as proprietor became a naturalized citizen, by act of the Legislature." *Warden's History of the United States*, ii., 53. This statement of Warden seems to have been based on a notice relating to this garden in the *New Jersey Journal*, June 27, 1787, in which it is said, "Part of this space is at present enclosing with a stone wall, and a universal collection of exotic, as well as domestic plants, trees and flowers are already begun to be introduced to this elegant spot, which in time must rival if not excel the most celebrated gardens of Europe. The situation is naturally wild and romantic, between two considerable rivers, in view of the main ocean, the city of New York, the heights of Staten Island, and a vast extent of distant mountains on the western side of the landscape." As "tall oaks from little acorns grow," so these exaggerated statements had their origin in the following simple fact. On March 3, 1786, André Michaux, in his petition to the Legislature of this State, set forth that the king of France had commissioned him as his Botanist to travel through the United States, that he had power to import from France any tree plant or vegetable that might be wanting in this country, that he wished to establish near Bergen a Botanical Garden of about thirty acres, to experiment in agriculture and gardening, and which he intended to stock with French and American plants, as also plants from all over the world. The Legislature granted his petition, and permitted him *as an alien* to hold not exceeding two hundred acres of land in this State.

He came to this country fortified with a flattering letter of introduction, dated at Vienna, Sept. 3, 1785, from the Marquis de La Fayette to Washington. *Correspondence of the American Revolution*, iv., 116. He was attached to the *Jardin des Plants* in Paris. He brought with him the gardener, Paul Saunier, who took the title to the ground bought for the garden. The place was stocked with many plants and trees, among which was the Lombard poplar. From this garden this once celebrated tree was spread abroad through the country and pronounced an exotic of priceless value. —*Old New York*, 23.

Chains and fifty four links on a Horizontal or level line to a stake planted for a Corner, thence North Fifty eight Degrees and thirty minutes West, Fifty three Chains to said Cromkill, then up said Kill as it Runs till it meets with the first line running to the same from the beginning; Containing about Thirty two Acres.

*27 **And we adjudge** a Certain Portion or share of said Common Lands to belong to the Heirs of Catharine De Hart deceased late Widow of Doctor Matthias De Hart deceased, as We adjudge the Right and Title to said Portion of Commons was Legally Vested in the said Catharine De Hart at the time of her decease

Our Survey of which said Portion as laid down on the Map, shews, and we adjudge it to be a Tract of Land Marked No 19 *

Beginning at a Stake standing in the line of the Bergen Lots, being the Eastermost Corner of the Lot No 18 adjudged to the Heirs or Devisees of Samuel Sacket deceased and from thence running North Fifty eight Degrees and thirty minutes West Fourteen Chains and seventy links to a stake in the Road, thence North Thirty two Degrees and forty five minutes East, one Chain and Thirty eight links to a stake being the Eastermost Corner of a Lot Marked No 14 laid out to the Right of John Kingsland, thence along the line of said Lot North Fifty eight Degrees and thirty minutes West, Thirty Chains and Eighty links to the Cromkill, then returning to the place of Beginning and from thence running along the line of the Bergen Lots North Thirty five Degrees East seven Chains * and Eighty eight links to a Stake, thence North Fifty eight *28 Degrees and thirty minutes West, Forty five Chains and forty links to said Cromkill then up the said Kill as it runs till it meets with the above mentioned line running to the same; Containing about Thirty one Acres.

And we adjudge a Certain Portion or Share of said Common Lands to belong to Colonel Nicholas Fish of New York

Our Survey of which said Portion as laid down on the Map, shews, and we adjudge it to be a Tract of Land Marked No 20

Beginning at a Stake in the line of the Bergen Lots, being a Corner of the last mentioned Lot No 19 and from thence running North Fifty eight Degrees and thirty minutes West Forty five Chains and forty links to the Cromkill, then returning to the place of Beginning, and from thence running along the Hills in the Line of the Bergen Lots, North Thirty five Degrees East, six Chains and thirty nine Links on a Horizontal or level line to a Stake, thence North Fifty eight Degrees and thirty minutes West Fifty three Chains and twenty links to the said Cromkill, thence up the said Kill as it runs till it meets with the above mentioned line * running to the same from the Beginning Containing about Twenty Nine *29 Acres.

---

* Catherine De Hart was a Kingsland. Job Hedden conveyed this lot to Enoch Smith April 11, 1788, and by Enoch Earle (who seems to have been an heir of Smith) to Robert Greenlief Aug. 16, 1803.

And we adjudge a Certain Portion or Share of said Common Lands to belong to the Heirs or Devisees of William Dobbs deceased; as we adjudge the Right and Title to said Portion of Commons was Legally Vested in the said William Dobbs at the time of his decease.

Our Survey of which said Portion as laid down on the Map, shews, and **we** adjudge it to be a Tract of Land Marked No 21 *

Beginning at a Stake Planted in the Line of the Bergen Lots, being the Eastermost Corner of the last mentioned Lot No 20 and from thence running along the line of the same North Fifty eight Degrees and thirty minutes West, Fifty three Chains and twenty links to the Cromkill, then returning to the place of Beginning, and from thence Running on the Hills in the line of the Bergen Lots North Thirty five Degrees East Five Chains and Eleven links on a Horizontal or level line to a stake, thence North Fifty eight Degrees and thirty minutes West, Fifty one Chains and fifty links to said Cromkill, thence up the said Kill as it runs *30 * till it meets with the aforementioned line running to the same from the Beginning, Containing about Twenty five Acres.

And we adjudge a Certain Portion or Share of said Common Lands to belong to Joseph Sacket Doctor of Physick

Our Survey of which said Portion as laid down the Map, shews, and **we** adjudge it to be a Tract of Land Marked No 22.†

Beginning at a Stake planted for a Corner in the line of the Bergen Lots, being the Eastermost Corner of the last mentioned Lot No 21, and from thence running along the Line of the same, North Fifty eight Degrees and thirty minutes West Fifty one Chains and fifty links to the Cromkill, then returning to the place of Beginning and from thence running on the Hills in the line of the Bergen Lots, North Thirty five Degrees East Three Chains and Eighty three Links on a Horizontal or level line to a stake being a Corner of a Lot hereinbefore adjudged to the Heirs or Devisees of Samuel Sacket deceased and Marked No 23 and from thence Running North Fifty eight Degrees and Thirty minutes *31 West Fifty two Chains to said Cromkill, * thence up the said Kill as it runs till it meets with the aforementioned line running to the same from the Beginning, Containing about Nineteen Acres.

And we adjudge the Right and Title to a Certain Portion or Share of said Common Lands was Legally Vested in Isaac Kingsland immediately after the decease of his Father Edmond

---

* Edward Earle, jr., conveyed to William Dobbs, June 10, 1763, one-third of his interest in twenty acres which he and Joseph Sackett, M.D., bought of Edward Earle July 20, 1762. On same day he conveyed one-third to Jonathan Fish, who conveyed to Dobbs Dec. 10, 1763. This accounts for Dobbs' interest in the Commons. This lot seems to have been owned by Joseph Van Winkle, as his executors, Jerry, Henry, and Abraham Van Winkle, conveyed it to Cornelius Smith May 24, 1810.

† This lot was conveyed by Nathaniel Wade to Enoch Smith Sept. 8, 1789, and by Henry Earle (probably an heir of Smith) to Nathaniel Earle July 20, 1792.

Kingsland by Virtue of the last Will and Testament of the said Edmon bearing date the Twenty ninth day of July, in the Year One Thousand Seven Hundred and forty one, But as no Person appeared to Claim said Portion or share we do not determine to whom the same doth now belong.

Our Survey of which said Portion as laid down on the Map, shews, and **we** adjudge it to be a Tract of Land Marked No 24

Beginning at a Stake planted in the line of the Bergen Lots, being the Eastermost Corner of a Lot hereinbefore adjudged to the Heirs or Devisees of Samuel Sacket deceased and marked No 23 and from said Beginning running North Fifty eight Degrees and thirty minutes West Fifty three Chains to the Cromkill, then returning to the place of Beginning and from thence Running on the * Hills in the line of the Bergen Lots North Thirty Five Degrees East Six Chains and three links in a Horizontal or level line, to a stake thence North Fifty eight Degrees and thirty minutes West Fifty two Chains to said Cromkill then up the said Kill as it runs till it meets with the above mentioned line, running to the same from the Beginning; Containing about Thirty Acres.

And we adjudge the Right and Title to a Certain Portion or Share of said Common Lands was Legally Vested in Hester Emot deceased Widow of William Emot immediately after the decease of her Father Edmond Kingsland by Virtue of the last Will and Testament of the said Edmon Kingsland bearing date the twenty ninth day of July in the Year One Thousand seven Hundred and forty one, But as no Person appeared to Claim said Portion or Share **we** do not determine to whom the same doth now belong.

Our Survey of which said Portion as laid down on the Map, shews, and **we** adjudge it to be a Tract of Land Marked No 25 *

Beginning at a Stake planted for a Corner in the line of the Bergen Lots, being the Eastermost * Corner of the last mentioned Lot No 24 and from said Stake Running North Fifty eight Degrees and Thirty minutes West Fifty two Chains to the Cromkill then returning to the place of Beginning and from thence running on the Hills in the line of the Bergen Lots, North Thirty five Degrees East, seven Chains and sixty six links on a Horizontal or level line to a Stake, thence North Fifty eight Degrees and thirty minutes West Fifty two Chains to said Cromkill, thence up the said Kill as it Runs till it meets with the above mentioned Line running to the same from the Beginning; Containing about Thirty Eight Acres.

And we adjudge a Certain Portion or Share of said Common Lands to belong to Hartman Brinkerhoof and Hendrick Brinkerhoof equally between them as Tenants in Common

---

* This lot was conveyed by John Brinkerhoff to John J. Williams June 6, 1799. It is quite probable that this may refer to lot 26.

Our Survey of which said Portion as laid down on the Map shews and **we** adjudge it to be a Tract of Land Marked No 26

Beginning at a Stake standing in the Line of the Bergen Lots, Being the Easternmost Corner of the last mentioned Lot Marked No 25 and from thence running North Fifty eight Degrees and Thirty minutes West Fifty two Chains to the Cromkill * then returning to the place of Beginning and from thence Running on the Hills in the Line of the Bergen Lots, North Thirty five Degrees East seven Chains and thirteen links on a Horizontal or level line to a Stake, thence North Fifty eight Degrees and thirty minutes West Fifty six Chains and fifty links to said Cromkill, thence up the said Kill as it runs till it meets with the above mentioned line running to the same from the Beginning, Containing about Thirty six Acres.

*34

And we adjudge a Certain Portion or Share of said Common Lands to belong to Edward Earle of Newark in the County of Essex in Right of his Father deceased.

Our Survey of which said Portion as laid down on the Map, shews, and **we** adjudge it to be a Tract of Land Marked No 27 *

Beginning at a Stake planted in the Line of the Bergen Lots, being the Easternmost Corner of the last mentioned Lot marked No 26 and from thence Running North Fifty eight Degrees and thirty Minutes West Fifty six Chains and fifty Links to the Cromkill, then returning to the place of Beginning and from thence running on the Hills in the Line of the Bergen Lots, North Thirty five Degrees * East Twenty one Chains and thirty seven Links on a Horizontal or level line to a Stake, thence North fifty eight Degrees and thirty Minutes West about Fifty two Chains to a Cove putting out of Hackensack River, thence Westerly along said Cove on the South side thereof untill it comes to the Mouth of the said Cromkill, thence up the said Kill as it Runs 'till it meets with the above mentioned Line running to the same from the Beginning, Containing about One Hundred and fourteen Acres.

*35

And we adjudge a Certain Portion or Share of said Common Lands to belong to Philip Earle of Secaucus.

Our Survey of which said Portion as laid down on said Map, shews, and **we** adjudge it to be a Tract of Land Marked No 28 †

Beginning at a Stake planted for a Corner in the Line of the Bergen Lots, Being the Easternmost Corner of the last mentioned Lot Marked No 27 and from thence Running North Fifty eight Degrees and thirty minutes West about Fifty two Chains to a Cove putting out of Hackensack River, then returning to the place of Beginning and from thence running

---

* Part of this lot was sold by Nathaniel Earle to John J. Williams April 17, 1786. Edward Earle conveyed (part of it) to Daniel Earle April 10, 1796.

† This lot was conveyed by Caspar Bogert, sheriff, to Casparus Cadmus Aug. 18, 1810. It is now owned by his son *Richard*.

along the line of the Bergen Lots * North Thirty five Degrees East Forty *36 five Chains & Twenty four links to a stake planted in the Line of a Lot of Common Land allotted in the Division of the Bergen Commons to Thomas Fredrick alias De Cuyper's Patent Marked on the Map of that Division No 232 which last mentioned Stake standeth five Chains and seventy three links from the Northermost Corner of the said Lot of Common Land, thence from said Stake Running North Fifty eight Degrees and thirty minutes West about Eighty Chains to Hackensack River, thence down said River as it runs to the above said Cove thence up said Cove on a direct line to the North Corner of the last mentioned Lot laid out to Edward Earle and No 27, thence along the Line of the same South Fifty eight Degrees and thirty minutes East about Fifty two Chains to the place of Beginning, Containing about Three Hundred Acres.

    And we adjudge a Certain Portion or Share of said Common Lands, to belong to Garret Van Gesen, Isaac Van Gesen and George Van Gesen equally among them as Tenants in Common.

        Our Survey of which said Portion as laid down on the Map, shews, and **we** adjudge it to be a Tract of Land Marked No 29*

* Beginning at a Stake planted for a Corner in the Line of a Lot of *37 Common Land allotted in the Division of the Bergen Commons to Thomas Fredrick alias De Cuyper's Patent marked on the Map of that Division No 232 the said Stake is the Eastermost Corner of the above mentioned Lot laid out to Philip Earle No 28 and from said Stake running North Fifty eight Degrees and thirty minutes west about Eighty Chains to Hackensack River, then returning to the place of Beginning and from thence running North Thirty five Degrees East five Chains and seventy three links to the Northermost Corner of the above said Lot allotted to the Patent of Thomas Fredrick alias De Cuyper, thence along the line thereof South Fifty four Degrees East Twenty six Chains and Thirty eight links to a Stake, thence North Thirty one Degrees and thirty minutes East Forty Chains and fifty links to the line of the Northermost bounds of the Township of Bergen, thence along said Line North Fifty Degrees and thirty minutes West Twenty six Chains and fifty five links to a Stake which standeth in a Course directly North Thirty one Degrees and thirty minutes East from the North Corner of the above said Lot allotted to the Patent of Thomas Fredrick alias De Cuyper, thence south thirty one Degrees and thirty minutes West Eight Chains and sixty links to a Stake, thence North Fifty eight Degrees and thirty minutes * West Sixty four *38 Chains and fifty links to the Creek that surrounds the Neck, thence down said Creek and Hackensack River, 'till it meets with the first line in this Survey Running to said River, Containing about Three Hundred and Fifty seven Acres.

    And we adjudge a Certain Portion or Share of said Common Lands to belong to the Heirs or Devisees of the Revd John Oglevie Deceased as we adjudge the Right and Title to said Portion of Commons was legally vested in the said John Oglevie at the time of his decease.

---

* Isaac Van Giesen died seized of an undivided third of this lot, leaving children, *Harriet*, wife of Elias Earle, *Thomas* and *Rynier I.*, who conveyed it to David Day June 14, 1809.

Our Survey of which said Portion as laid down on the Map, shews, and **we** adjudge it to be a Tract of Land Marked No 30 *

*39 Beginning at a Stake planted in the line of the Northermost bounds of the Township of Bergen being a Corner of the last mentioned Lot laid out to Garret, Isaac and George Van Gesen and marked No 29 which said Stake standeth in a Course directly North thirty one Degrees and Thirty minutes East from the Northermost Corner of a Lot of Land allotted in the Division of the Bergen Commons to the Patent of Thomas Fredrick alias De Cuyper and Numbered 232 and from said Beginning, Running south thirty one * Degrees and thirty minutes West Eight Chains and sixty links to a Stake Being another Corner of the said Van Gesens Lot, thence North Fifty eight Degrees and thirty minutes West, Sixty four Chains and fifty links to the Creek surrounding the Neck, thence up said Creek as the same Runs North Easterly, Easterly and South Easterly 'till it comes to the Line of the Northermost Bounds of the Township of Bergen, thence along said line south Fifty Degrees and thirty minutes East, to the place of Beginning, Containing about One Hundred and Thirty nine Acres.

And we adjudge a Certain Portion or Share of said Common Lands to belong to the Heirs or Devisees of Robert Leake late of New York deceased or to such as may Legally Claim the same under him as **we** adjudge the Right and Title to said Portion of Commons was Legally Vested in the said Robert Leake at the time of his Decease

Our Survey of which said Portion as laid down on the Map, shews, and **we** adjudge it to be a Tract of Land Marked No 31 †

*40 * Beginning at a Stake standing in the line of Northermost bounds of the Township of Bergen being the Eastermost Corner of a Lot of Land laid out to Garret, Isaac and George Van Gesons Numbered 29 and from said Stake running South Thirty one Degrees and thirty minutes West Forty Chains and Fifty links to a Lot laid out in the Division of the Commons of Bergen and Numbered in said Division 232, thence along the line thereof South Fifty four Degrees East Eleven Chains and sixty two links to the Eastermost Corner of said Lot, thence South Thirty five Degrees West, six Chains and ten links to a Stake being the Northerly Corner of a Lot of Land formerly laid out and Numbered 253,

---

* Ogilvie's widow, Margaret, George Ogilvie, and Mary, wife of Barent Ogilvie, devisees of Rev. John Ogilvie, D.D., conveyed this lot to Richard and John Earle July 1, 1786. Ogilvie was Assistant Minister of Trinity Church, New York, and died on Saturday, Nov. 26, 1774 He was stricken with apoplexy, Nov. 18th, while in the pulpit, having just given out his text, Ps. xcii. 15. Robert Grunti owned the lot in 1793.

† Leake's interest in Secaucus probably came through a deed to him from Andrew Teed, dated March 7, 1762. *Vide Note to Varlet's Patent*, p. 62. A tract which seems to answer to this lot was sold by John George Leake to Aaron Devoe, by two deeds dated July 7, 1789, and Nov. 15, 1794. Leake also conveyed to John Stevens, March 10, 1795, four hundred and twenty five acres in the Secaucus Commons, but where this tract lies I have not ascertained.

thence along the line thereof South Fifty four Degrees East Twenty seven Chains and forty links to a Stake being the Easterly Corner of said Lot No 253, thence North Thirty five Degrees East Twenty four Chains and Eighty five Links to a Stake in a Swamp being the Northermost Corner of a Lot of Land formerly laid out and Numbered 219, thence South Fifty four Degrees East Nineteen Chains and ninety Links to Mordainis Meadow, thence along the edge of said Meadow, where the same joins the upland till it comes to bear South Fifty Degrees and thirty minutes East from a Chesnut Tree standing upon a point of a narrow ridge of Land projecting towards the meadow which * Tree is the Place of Beginning of the General Bounds of the Township of Bergen, thence North Fifty Degrees and thirty minutes West Thirty five links to said Chesnut Tree, thence Continuing the same Course along the Line of the Northern Bounds of the Township of Bergen until it comes to the first mentioned Stake, the place of Beginning, Containing about One Hundred and Eighty nine Acres. *41

Having gone through the Division of the Common Land allotted to the Patent of Secaucus we think it proper as a greater Certainty to the Courses mentioned in the several surveys to give this information that the Magnetical Course with which all the lines are laid down and Run Varies from the true Course Three Degrees and forty minutes to the left Hand, so that a Meridian line North would be North Three Degrees and forty minutes East as the Magnet now Points.

That since the time the Common Land of Bergen was Divided we find a Variation of the Compass of one Degree and Thirty minutes which will account for the Difference of the Courses now given along the former Lines from what the surveys of the former Division mention.

* We think it proper also to remark that an attraction of the Needle is found more or less in every part of the Commons of Secaucus except on the Meadow at a distance from the upland which will render Lines run by the Compass on the upland very uncertain. Our lines are mostly run by Courses taken on the Meadow and Parallels thereto made on the upland. *42

In Witness that this is one of the Field Books of the Division of the Common Lands allotted to the Patent of Secaucus made pursuant to a Law of the State of New Jersey hereinbefore recited, We together with the Surveyor have hereunto set our Hands this fifteenth day of June in the Year of our Lord One Thousand seven Hundred and Eighty five.

      Abraham Clark ⎫
      Az. Dunham   ⎬ *Commissrs*
      Silas Condit
      John Earle
      Dan. Marsh ⎭

Thos. Clark
  Surveyor.

CHAPTER VI.

NEW FIELD BOOK.

It is with great pleasure that I submit to the public what I have named the NEW FIELD BOOK, and the MAPS accompanying the same. They are six years younger than the old Field Book, and yet, I do not doubt, have been for years wholly unknown. Controversies concerning certain lands lying in the vicinity of Newark avenue between Mill Creek and the old Bergen road seem to have arisen, and the parties in the dispute submitted all questions of title and boundary to the award of Johannis Demarest, Albert Zabrowsky, of Hackensack, and John Haring of "Orange Town." The submission I have not seen; the Survey and Maps (containing the award) were found in the possession of Dr John M. Cornelison. They are originals, in a good state of preservation, exact copies of which are here inserted. It may, I think, be taken for granted that they are the only ones in existence, and are now for the first time given to the inspection of the curious. They came to the present owner among the papers of Henry D. Van Winkle, owner of a portion of the land therein referred to. They throw much light on the title to the lands between the Five Corners and Mill Creek, and to *Lots Nos.* 355 and 389, the owners of which the Commissioners of Common Lands did not declare.

It is a matter of some curiosity to know how this Book and these Maps came into the possession of the Van Winkle family. In a deed, dated Dec. 20, 1774, given by the Van Idersteins (descendants of Tades Michielse) for some of the land included in the NEW FIELD BOOK, there is a reference to the same, and it is spoken of as "lodged in the hands of the Town Clerk." There is no mark upon either Book or Maps to show that they ever were filed. This recital, I presume, is conclusive that but one copy was made, and that it was considered public property. It is probable that Daniel Van Winkle, or some one of the family, was Town-clerk, and so came to the possession of the Book and Maps.

To All Christian People to whom these Presents shall come Greeting:

Whereas there is a Reference to us John Demarest, Albert Sabriskea and John Haring, by a certain written Instrument or Articles of Agreement, bearing Date the ninth Day of April last, of certain Controversies and Disputes between certain Freeholders and Inhabitants of the Corporation of Bergen in the County of Bergen and Province of New Jersey, touching and concerning the Rights and Titles to, and Division of certain Lands and Meadows lying in the Corporation of Bergen aforesaid, as by the said Written Instrument or Articles of Agreement doth more at large Appear, Reference being thereunto had, We therefore the Arbitrators named and appointed as aforesaid, having examined the Titles and heard the Proofs and Alligations of the Parties, **Do** in pursuance of the said Written Instrument or Articles of Agreement and Power thereby given us, Award, Order and Adjudge as followeth.

With respect to a certain Tract of Land laid down on Map A, Beginning at the Northerly Corner of a Tract of Land belonging to Altic Van Winkel and from thence Running South fifty four Degrees and forty seven Minutes East Eleven Chains and thirty three Links to Hendrick Kuypers Line, Thence along said Kuypers Line North thirty four Degrees East twenty six Chains and eighty nine Links to the Southermost Corner of a certain Tract of Land belonging to Abraham Sickels, Thence North fifty seven Degrees and fifty Minutes West twenty six Chains and twenty five Links to the Eastermost Corner of a small Lot of Land belonging to Michael and George Demoet, Thence South thirty two Degrees West one Chain and seventy five Links to the Southermost Corner of said small Lot, Thence North fifty eight Degrees and thirty Minutes West to the Kings High Road, Then along the several Courses of said Road until it comes to the aforesaid Tract of the above Named Altie Van Winkel, Thence North thirty three Degrees East two Chains and seventeen Links to the place of Beginning Containing about sixty three Acres.

We Adjudge that Certain Part or Portion (of the before mentioned Tract of Land) marked No 1 on Map A aforesaid, to belong to Abraham Sickels The said Part or Portion, Beginning at a Stake being the Eastermost Corner of the above said Tract of Land, and from thence Running North fifty seven Degrees and fifty minutes West twenty six Chains and twenty five Links to the Eastermost Corner of the aforesaid small Lot of Land belonging to Michael and George Demoet, Thence South thirty two Degrees West two Chains and thirteen Links, to a Stake, Thence South fifty seven Degrees and fifty Minutes East to said Kuypers Line, Thence along said Kuypers Line two Chains and thirteen Links to the Place of Beginning Containing five Acres, two Roods and fourteen Perches.*

We adjudge that Certain Part or Portion (of the before mentioned Tract of Land,) marked No 2 on Map A aforesaid to belong to Michael and George Demoet, The said Part or Portion No 2 Beginning at a Stake being the Southermost Corner of Portion No 1 aforesaid, and from thence Running South thirty four Degrees West four Chains and sixteen Links

---

* *Vide Note to Lot No.* 317, p. 176, and *Lot No.* 358, p. 179.

to a Stake in the before described Kuypers Line, and from thence Runs North fifty seven Degrees and fifty Minutes West to the said Kings Road, Thence along said Road to a Stake in the Line of the aforesaid small Lot belonging to Michael and George Demoet, Thence along said small Lot to Portion No 1, Thence to the Westermost Corner of said Portion No 1, and thence to the Place of Beginning Containing twelve Acres three Roods and twelve Perches.*

We Adjudge that certain Part or Portion (of the before mentioned Tract of Land,) marked No 3 on Map A aforesaid, to belong to Douwe Tallma The said Part or Portion No 3 Beginning at a Stake being the Southermost Corner of Portion No 2 aforesaid, and from Thence Running South thirty four Degrees West four Chains and five Links to a Stake in the before mentioned Kuypers Line, Thence North fifty seven Degrees and fifty Minutes West to the aforesaid Kings Road Thence Northerly along said Road to the Southwest Corner of Portion Number 2 aforesaid, thence along said Portion No 2 to the Place of Beginning, Containing eleven Acres eighteen Perches.†

We Adjudge that Certain Part or Portion (of the before mentioned tract of Land) marked No 4 on Map A to be the full Proportion and Dividend for the Purchase Money paid by Geurt Coerten, The said Part or Portion Beginning at a Stake being the Southermost Corner of Portion No 3 aforesaid, and from thence Runs South thirty four Degrees West four Chains and fifty three Links to a Stake in the before mentioned Kuypers Line, thence North fifty seven Degrees and fifty Minutes West to the aforesaid Kings Road, thence Northerly along said Road to the Southwest Corner of the aforesaid Portion No 3 thence along said Portion No 3 to the Place of Beginning, Containing eleven Acres, two Roods and five Perches.‡

We Adjudge that Certain Part or Portion (of the before mentioned Tract of Land) marked No 5 on Map A to be in part of the Proportion and Dividend for the Purchase Money paid by Jurian Thomason, The said Part or Portion Beginning at a Stake being the Southermost Corner of Portion No. 4 aforesaid, and from thence Runs South thirty four Degrees

---

* *Vide Note to Stoffelsen's Patent*, p. 9. Michael De Mott sold this lot to Albert and John V. H. Zabriskie April 10, 1841. John quit-claimed to Albert Oct. 24, 1844. Albert sold this with other lands to Edmund C. Bramhall April 1, 1865. This and *Lot No.* 3 were united in the De Motts. *Vide Note to Harmensen's Patent*, p. 50. It is probable that the above sales took only the south portion of *Lot No.* 2. He sold to Ann Collerd May 5, 1840, and to James Kerrigan Dec. 24, 1840.

† *Vide Note to Harmensen's Patent*, p. 50.

‡ This lot belonged to the Van Rypens. *Vide Note to Coerten's first Patent*, p. 25. Daniel Van Rypen sold seven acres of it to Helmigh Van Houten, who, by will dated Oct. 18, 1803, proved Dec. 3, 1803, gave the front half of it to his two daughters, *Catherine*, wife of Jacob Zabriskie, and *Effie*, wife of Myndert Garrabrants (afterward wife of Richard Lyon). His grandson Helmagh, gave to them a deed for the same Nov. 24, 1818. Lyon and Zabriskie partitioned (†) Nov 24, 1818. Catherine had two sons, *John V. H.*, and Albert Zabriskie. John released to Albert his interest in the three and a half acres Oct. 24, 1844, who sold to Edmund C. Bramhall April 1, 1865. *Vide Note to Lot No.* 2.

West two Chains and thirty seven Links to a Stake in the before mentioned Kuypers Line, thence North fifty seven Degrees and fifty minutes West to the aforesaid Kings Road, thence Northerly along said Road to the Southwest Corner of the aforesaid Portion No 4, thence along said Portion No 4 to the Place of Beginning, Containing three Acres two Rood and twenty Perches.

We Adjudge that certain Part or Portion (of the before mentioned Tract of Land) marked No 6 on Map A. to be the full Proportion and Dividend for the Purchase Money paid by Frederick Thomase, The said Part or Portion Beginning at a Stake being the Southermost Corner of Portion No 5 aforesaid, and from thence Runs South thirty four Degrees West three Chains and fifty five Links to a Stake in the before mentioned Kuypers Line, thence North fifty seven Degrees and fifty minutes West to the aforesaid Kings Road, thence Northerly along said Road to the Southwest Corner of the aforesaid Portion No 5 thence along said Portion No 5 to the Place of Beginning, Containing seven Acres two Rood and twenty Perches.

We Adjudge that certain Part or Portion (of the before mentioned Tract of Land) marked No 7 on Map A. to be the full Portion and Dividend for the Purchase Money paid by Adrian Post, the said Part or Portion Beginning at a Stake being the Southermost Corner of Portion No 6 afores'd and from thence Runs South thirty four Degrees West three Chains and five Links to a Stake in the before mentioned Kuypers Line, thence North fifty seven Degrees and fifty Minutes West to the aforesaid Kings Road thence Northerly along said Road to the Southwest Corner of the aforesaid Portion No 6 thence along said Portion No 6 to the Place of Beginning, Containing five Acres two Rood and thirty Perches.

We Adjudge that certain Part or Portion (of the before mentioned Tract of Land) marked No 8 on Map A. to be the full Portion and Dividend Purchased by Belitie Dirks from Hendrick Ostrum, the said Part or Portion Beginning at a Stake being the Southermost Corner of Portion No 7 aforesaid, and from thence Runs South thirty four Degrees West two Chains and eighty two Links to a Stake in the Eastermost Corner of the before mentioned Tract of the before named Altie Van Winkel, thence North fifty four Degrees and forty seven Minutes West to a Stake being the Northermost Corner of said Altie Van Winkel's Tract, thence South thirty three Degrees West to the aforesaid Kings Road, thence Northerly along said Road to the Southwest Corner of the aforesaid Portion No 7 thence along said Portion No 7 to the Place of Beginning, Containing our Acres and twelve Perches.

With respect to a Certain Tract of Land and Meadows laid down on Map B. Beginning at a Stake being the Southerly Corner of a Lot in John Berry's Patent and from thence Runs South thirty five Degrees and fifty five Minutes East ten Chains and forty Links to a Rock, thence North seventy two Degrees East six Chains and fifty Links to a Stake thence South fourteen Degrees and thirty five Minutes East five Chains and ten Links to a Stake, thence South sixty nine Degrees twenty Minutes West ten Chains and sixty seven Links to a Stake, thence South forty seven Degrees East three Chains and six Links, thence North forty two Degrees and thirty minutes East two Chains and seventy Links, thence

We the Subscribers do certify that this Map, is the
Map meant and intended by the name of Map B. in
Our Award mentioned and described. Witness Our
Hands the Ninth Day of July Anno Domini 1770 ☒

John Haring
Johannes demarest
Albert Zabrowsky

B. -

Nº 13. Patent Nº 130

Nº 14.

Nº 16.

Nº 17. Patent Nº 127

Nº 18.

Nº 19. Patent Nº 124

Nº 20.

Nº 22.

Nº 23. Patent Nº 123

Nº 21.

Nº 24.

E
S

This Map is and drawn by a Scale of Five Chains to one Inch, By Me John Harling Surveyor performed July the 7th day 1770

South fifty four Degrees and fifteen Minutes East one Chain and fifty Links, thence South seventy three Degrees and twenty Minutes East five Chains and ninety Links to the edge of the Meadows, thence the several Courses between said Meadows and Upland 'till it comes to where a certain Run of Water (commonly known or called by the Dutch Name of Oude Boomse Val)* empties into Horsimus Creek, thence along the said Creek Northerly and Easterly 'till it comes to the Meadows of the before mentioned Kuyper, thence North fifty Degrees and five Minutes West thirty nine Chains and forty three Links to the Westermost Corner of said Kuypers Land, thence North thirty nine Degrees and thirty Minutes East seven Chains and eight Links to a Stake, thence North fifty one Degrees and forty minutes West twenty two Chains and forty Links to the Kings Road, thence Southerly along the said Road 'till it comes to the School-Lot, thence South thirty eight Degrees and forty five Minutes East twenty Chains and fifty Links to the Eastermost Corner of the said School-Lot, thence South twenty nine Degrees West five Chains and thirty Links to the Southermost Corner of said School-Lot, thence South fifty one Degrees and thirty Minutes West nine Chains and ninety three Links to a Stake, thence South fifty Degrees and fifteen Minutes West eighteen Chains and thirty seven Links to the Place of Beginning Containing about one hundred and seventy nine Acres

We Adjudge that Certain Part or Portion (of the last mentioned Tract) marked No 9 on Map B. to be the full Portion and Dividend for the Purchase Money paid by Laurence Arentse, the said part or portion Beginning at a Stake being the Northermost Corner of said Last mentioned Tract, from thence South fifty one Degrees and forty Minutes East twenty two Chains and forty Links to a stake in said Kuypers Line, thence South thirty nine Degrees and thirty Minutes West two Chains and thirty Links to a Stake in said Kuypers Line, thence North fifty one Degrees and forty Minutes West to the said Kings Road, thence along said Road 'till it comes to the place of Beginning, Containing about four Acres two Rood and eighteen Perches.

We Adjudge that certain Part or Portion (of the last mentioned Tract) marked No 10 on Map B. to belong to Arent Toers. the said part or Portion Beginning at a Stake being the Southermost Corner of No 9 aforesaid, and from thence Runs South thirty nine Degrees and thirty Minutes West four Chains and seventy eight Links to the aforesaid Westermost Corner of Kuypers Land, thence North fifty Degrees and five Minutes West to the aforesaid Kings Road, thence Northerly along said

---

* This creek (if such it could be called) took its rise in a spring near the Beacon Race Course, and draining the surface between that point and the brow of the hill, passed down on the north side of Newark Avenue to the Mill Creek. It took its name from the old Tree yet standing on the top of the hill south of Prospect Avenue, known among the old people as the " oude boom" or old Tree. The bridge in Newark Avenue which spanned Mill Creek before it was filled in, was known as the "oude boom bridge." As a stream the " val " long since became insignificant. As the table lands above were improved and drainage attended to, the soil refused its tribute to the old creek, until finally, in the year of grace 1871, having nothing left but its mighty name, of which the present generation had not heard, and which they could not understand, it hid away in the sewer which is here constructed in Newark Avenue.

Road to the Southwest Corner of Portion No 9 aforesaid, from thence along said Portion No 9 to the Place of Beginning, Containing about nine Acres one Rood.

We Adjudge that certain Part or Portion (of the last mentioned Tract) marked No 11 on Map B. to belong to Merseles Merselese, the said Part or Portion Beginning at the Distance of two Chains from the Kings Road at a Stake, said Stake being a little to the Southeast of a Spring (which is laid out for the common Use of the Town) and in the Southwest side of the aforesaid Portion No 10 and from thence Runs South fifty Degrees and five minutes East to Horsimus Creek, then Running Southwesterly along said Creek to a Stake, which Stake (at Right-Angles) from the first Line of this said Portion No 11 is six Chains and fifty six Links, thence North fifty Degrees and five Minutes West to the aforesaid Kings Road, then Northerly along said Road five Chains and fifty Links, and from thence on a Straight Line to the place of Beginning, Containing about thirty five Acres one Rood.*

_{* Merselis must have bought lots 12 and 15 shortly after this allotment, but from whom I have not learned. The northwest corner of *Lot No.* 15, separated from the lot by Newark Avenue was sold by him to William Coulter April 22, 1797. By Merselis' will, dated March 15, 1799, proved Dec. 5, 1800, he gave to his son *John*, the southwest half of a lot in Bergen Woods, and three acres between the Paulus Hook and Hoboken roads; also the land where the mill stood (on Bridge Creek); to *Jacob* and *Peter*, he gave land in Harrington township in Bergen County; to *Jannetje*, wife of Walter Clendenny, he gave one quarter of the wood lot, and one quarter of the Vlackie creupel bosch; and to *Anne*, wife of Josiah Hornblower, he gave the platty creupel bosch, between said two roads. Clendenny sold three acres to Peter Stuyvesant May 12, 1802. Part of the Hornblower tract, with what he aded by purchase, was inherited by his daughter, wife of Thomas B. Gautier, and was partitioned among his children, April 25, 1848, as per annexed sketch.}

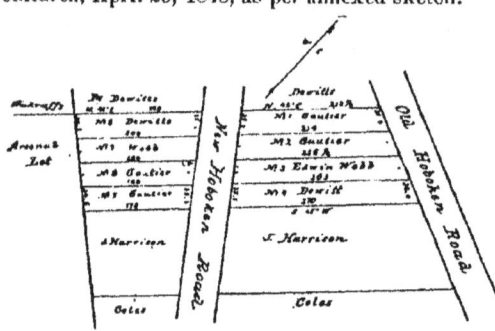

John Merselis sold to Cornelius Merselis, Sept. 2, 1799, the east half of the *Lutchie* (*Lot No.* 11?), bounded northeast by Tuers and Stuyvesant, east by Stevens southwest by Hoboken road, northwest by grantor. Two acres of this Cornelius sold to William Coulter, Oct. 10, 1801, and the balance to Michael Simmons, March 24, 1802, and July 4, 1802. The west half of the *Lutchie* John Merselis sold to his daughter *Altje* May 21, 1801. She afterwards married James Parks. This half lay between lot 10 and the Hoboken road. She deeded it to Altje, wife of John Merselis June 14, 1805. Coulter bought of Merselis Merselis, Aug. 4, 1807, a tract on top of the hill. Coulter sold it to Walter Clendenny, Sept. 21. 1807, who sold to John B. Coles, eighteen and one-half acres, Oct. 7, 1811. Peter Stuyvesant sold fifty and sixty-four one-hundredths acres to Philip Williams, Aug. 11, 1807, who sold to John B. Coles Oct. 1, 1807. John Merselis sold to John Heavenor May 27, 1719, three acres between the two roads, which, on execution, was afterwards sold to William Coulter.

We Adjudge that certain Part or Portion (of the last mentioned Tract) marked No 12 on Map B. to be the full Portion and Dividend for the Purchase Money Paid by Johannes Steymets, the said Part or Portion Beginning at the Westermost Corner of the above described Portion No 11, from thence Runs South fifty Degrees five Minutes East 'till it comes to a Line which Runs from the Eastermost Corner of the aforesaid School-Lot (on a Course North forty Degrees East) thence South forty Degrees West five Chains twenty five Links to a Stake, thence North fifty Degrees and five Minutes West to the aforesaid Kings Road, and then Northerly along said Road to the place of Beginning, Containing about thirteen Acres one Rood and thirty eight Perches.

We Adjudge that certain Part or Portion (of the last mentioned Tract) marked No 13 on Map B to be the full Portion and Dividend for the Purchase Money Paid by Adrian Peterson, the said Part or Portion Beginning at the Eastermost Corner of the last above described Portion No 12 thence Runs South forty Degrees West five Chains twenty five Links to a Stake, thence South fifty Degrees five Minutes East to Horsimus Creek, thence Easterly along said Creek to the Southermost Corner of the before described Portion No 11, thence along the said Portion No 11 to the place of Beginning, Containing ten Acres two Rood and twenty four Perches.

We Adjudge that certain Part or Portion (of the last mentioned Tract) marked No 14 on Map B. to be the full Portion and Dividend for the Purchase Money Paid by Derick Gerritse, the said Part or Portion Begining at the Westermost Corner of the before described Portion No 13, from thence South forty Degrees West five Chains twenty one Links to a Stake, thence South fifty Degrees and five Minutes East to Horsimus Creek, thence along said Creek 'till it comes to the afore described Portion No 13, and from thence on a direct Line to the Place of Beginning, Containing eight Acres one Rood *

We Adjudge that certain Part or Portion (of the last mentioned Tract) marked No 15 on Map B. to be the full Portion and Dividend for the Purchase Money Paid by Harme Eduards, the said Part or Portion Begining at a Stake being the Southermost Corner of the before described Portion No 12, thence Running South forty Degrees West five Chains and forty four Links to a Stake, thence North fifty Degrees and five Minutes West to the aforesaid Kings-Road, thence Northerly along said Road to the Westermost Corner of said Portion No 12, and from thence on a Direct Line to the place of Begining, Containing about thirteen Acres one Rood and thirty eight Perches

We Adjudge that certain Part or Portion (of the last mentioned Tract) marked No 16 on Map B. to Peter H. Peterse, the said Part or Portion Begining at the Westermost Corner of the before described Por-

---

* The half of this lot next to lot-13, Daniel Van Rypen sold to Jasper Prior Aug. 12, 1788. On the same day he sold to the same Prior the other half. Prior sold to Nathaniel Budd, who sold to John B. Coles March 27, 1806, who sold five acres, beginning at the southwest corner of lot 13, to the United States June 23, 1812. The United States sold it at public auction to John Halliard in April, 1871. This was known as the Arsenal property.

tion No 14, thence Running South forty Degrees West five Chains and seventy Links to a Stake, thence South forty nine Degrees East to Horsimus Creek, thence Northerly along said Creek to the Southermost Corner of the aforesaid Portion No 14, and from thence on a direct Line to the place of Begining Containing about nine Acres three Roods *

We Adjudge that certain Part or Portion (of the last mentioned Tract) marked No 17 on Map B. to be the full Portion and Dividend for the Purchase Money paid by Jacob Jacobse Van Winkel, said Part or Portion Begining at a Stake being the Westermost Corner of the before described Portion No 16 and from thence Runs South forty Degrees West forty four Links, thence South twenty nine Degrees West fifty one Links to a Stake, thence South forty nine Degrees East to Horsimus Creek, thence Northerly along the said Creek 'till it comes to the Southermost Corner of said Portion No 16, and from thence on a direct Line to the place of Begining, Containing about one Acre and two Roods.

We Adjudge that Certain Part or Portion (of the last mentioned Tract) marked No 18 on Map B. to be the full Portion and Dividend for the Purchase Money paid by Hendrick Teunese, said Part or Portion Begining at a Stake being the Westermost Corner of the above described Portion No 17 and from thence Running South twenty nine Degrees West four Chains and seventy Links to a Stake, thence South thirty nine Degrees East to Horsimus Creek, thence the several Courses of said Creek 'till it strikes the Southermost Corner of said Portion No 17, and from thence on a Direct Line to the place of Beginning, Containing about nine Acres, two Rood and seventeen Perches †

We Adjudge that Certain Part or Portion (of the last mentioned Tract) marked No 19 on Map B. to belong to Garret Newkerk said Part or Portion Begining at the Westermost Corner of the above described Portion No 18, and from thence Runing South fifty one Degrees and thirty Minutes West three Chains and Sixty six Links to a Stake, thence South thirty nine Degrees East to the edge of the Meadows, thence Northerly along said Meadow to the Southermost Corner of said Portion No 18, and from thence in a direct Line to the place of Begining, Containing about six Acres and twenty eight Perches.

---

* Thomas Gautier sold to Patrick Jackson, April 4, 1800, a lot bounded north by Lot No. 14; south by Daniel Van Winkle; west by a one rod road. This sale I take to include this lot. Henry Jackson owned ten acres bounded northwest by Newark Avenue, and adjoined Henry D. Van Winkle, the Arsenal property, and John B. Coles. It was sold for United States taxes, May 14, 1817, by Nathan Price, Collector, to Reuben D. Tucker, and Evan Evans, under an Act passed Jan. 9, 1815, and deed given Sept. 13, 1819. Benj. McGuinness sold the same to Henry D. Van Winkle, May 2, 1820. I take this to be *Lot No.* 16. Van Winkle afterwards gave up his purchase owing to some defect in the tax sale. *Vide Note to Lot No.* 201, p. 75. Henry Jackson sold it to John Ackland, May 1, 1834, who sold it to Gerard W. Morris May 23, 1838.

† Cornelius and Richard Van Rypen sold eight eight-tenths acres of this lot to John Burnet June 10, 1805. It was bounded E. by John Stevens, S. E. by Jacob Everson, S. W. by Cornelius Van Vorst, and N. W. by Peter Stuyvesant. Burnet sold to John Haynes Feb. 28, 1811.

We Adjudge that Certain Part or Portion (of the last mentioned Tract) marked No 20 on Map B. to be the full Portion and Dividend for the Purchase Money paid by Mattheus Corneliuse, said Part or Portion marked No 20 Begining at a Stake being the Westermost Corner of the before described Portion No 19, and from thence Running South fifty one Degrees and thirty Minutes West to a Stake, thence South thirty nine Degrees East to the Edge of the Meadows, thence Northerly along said Meadow to the Southermost Corner of said Portion No 19, and from thence in a direct Line to the place of Beginniug, Containing six Acres two Roods and seventeen Perches.

N. B. The above described Portion No 20 is in Breadth (being the Length of the first Line above described) three Chains and sixty Links.

We Adjudge that Certain Part or Portion (of the last mentioned Tract) marked No 21 on Map B. to belong to Cornelius Van Vourst, said Part or Portion Begining at the Northerly Corner of Pryer's Meadow, from thence Running South seventy five Degrees and fifty Minutes West to a Stake in the Road, thence South fourteen Degrees and thirty five Minutes East five Chains and ten Links to a Stake, thence South sixty nine Degrees and twenty Minutes West two Chains and sixty seven Links to a Stake, thence South forty seven Degrees East three Chains and six Links, thence North forty two Degrees and thirty Minutes East two Chains and seventy Links, thence South fifty four Degrees and fifteen Minutes East one Chain and fifty Links, thence South seventy three Degrees and twenty Minutes East five Chains and ninety Links to the edge of the Meadow, thence the several Courses between Up Land and Meadows to the place of Begining, Containing about eleven Acres and three Rood *

We Adjudge that certain Part or Portion (of the last mentioned Tract) marked No 22 on Map B. to belong to Johannes Dedrix and Daniel Dedrix, said Part or Portion Begining at the Westermost Corner of the before described Portion No 20 and from thence Runs South fifty one Degrees and fifty Minutes West three Chains and sixty two Links to a Stake, thence South thirty nine Degrees East 'till it comes to the before described Portion No 21 thence along said Portion No 21 'till it comes to the edge of the Meadow, thence along the edge of the Meadows to the Southermost Corner of said Portion No 20 and from thence in a direct Line to the place of Beginning, Containing about seven Acres †

We Adjudge that certain Part or Portion (of the last mentioned Tract) marked No 23 on Map B. to belong to John Van Blarkum, said Part or Portion Begining at the Westermost Corner of the above described Portion No 22 and from thence Runing about South fifty Degrees and sixteen Minutes West five Chains and fifty eight Links to a Stake, thence South thirty nine Degrees East 'till it comes to the Line of the before described Portion No 21, thence along said Line to the Southermost Corner of Portion No 22 aforesaid, and from thence on a direct Line to the place of Begining, Containing about nine Acres and eighteen Perches ‡

---

* Van Vorst sold this lot to Jacob Prior, April 20, 1787.

† Johannis Diedricks owned about 2¼ acres, lying on the W. end of this lot. This he sold to Daniel Diedricks, Dec. 27, 1771.

‡ *Vide Note to Lubbertse's Patent, p.* 45. Van Blarcom, it is probable, sold it to Cornelius Van Vorst; as he was the owner in 1774, as appears in a recital in the deed mentioned in the Note to the *Lot No.* 24.

We Adjudge that certain Part or Portion (of the last mentioned Tract) marked No 24 on Map B. to be the full Portion and Dividend for for the Purchase Money Paid by Thauda Michealson, said Part or Portion Begining at a Stake being the Westermost Corner of the above described Portion No 23, thence Running about South sixteen Degrees West eleven Chains and ninety four Links to a Stake being the Westermost Corner of the said last mentioned Tract, thence South thirty five Degrees and fifty five Minutes East ten Chains and forty Links to a Rock, thence North seventy two Degrees East six Chains and fifty Links to a Stake, being the Northwesterly Corner of the before described Portion No 21, thence along said Portion No 21, to the Southermost Corner of Portion No 23 aforesaid, and from thence with a direct Course to the place of Beginning, Containing about fifteen Acres one Rood and thirty two Perches *

We Adjudge that certain Part or Portion (of the last mentioned Tract) marked No 25 on Map B. to be the full Portion and Dividend for the Purchase Money Paid by Helmich Roelefse, said Part or Portion Begining at a Stake being the Westermost Corner of the before described Portion No 15, and from thence Running Southerly along the said Road to the Northermost Corner of the aforesaid School-Lot, thence South thirty eight Degrees and forty five minutes East nine Chains and seventy two Links to a Stake, thence North forty Degrees East to said Portion No 15, and from thence in a direct Course to the place of Begining, Containing about two Acres two Roods.†

We Adjudge that certain Part or Portion (of the last mentioned Tract) marked No 26 on Map B. to belong to Arent Toers, said Part or Portion Begining at a Stake being the Southermost Corner of the above described Portion No 25, and from thence Runs South thirty eight Degrees and forty five minutes East four Chains and fifteen Links to a Stake,

---

* Michielse's heirs, viz., Tadeus Johannis, Teunis, and Tadens Van Iderstein of New Barbadoes, sold this lot to Abraham Prior, Dec. 20, 1774.

† This lot was the south part of *Subdivision No.* 350, adjoining the School Lot. The arbitrators declare that it was a dividend for the money paid by Helmigh Roelofse (Van Houten), but do not adjudge to whom it belonged in 1770. Henry La Tourette Cole owned it in 1791. Peter Cole sold it to Joseph Simonson, May 11, 1797 ; who sold it to John Van Winkle, June 1, 1809 ; who sold it to John Priestly Peters, June 23, 1837 ; Peters sold it to Mortimer A. F. Harrison, April 19, 1841. This deed is lost and the record omits words of inheritance. It has since been sold in parcels to several persons. In 1870, Benj. Sisson bought the reversion of Peter's heir and brought an ejectment suit against the present occupants. The suit is now pending. The lot lies between the Court House property and Bergen Avenue. As to the Van Houten family, I have gathered the following : Helmigh Roelofse married Jannetje Pieterse, Sept. 1676. The "Van Houten" was afterwards added as a family name. *Houte* or *Houten*, means wooden; from *Hout*, wood. Roelofse had ten children among whom was *Johannis*, born Oct. 28, 1696, married Helena, daughter of Johannis Vreeland, and died Dec. 18, 1768. This is the Van Houten named in the Field Book. He left one son, *Johannis*, baptized June 17, 1735, married (1st) Altje, daughter of Hendrick Sickles, (2nd) Rachel De Maree, and died Oct. 31, 1807, leaving *Johannis, Sara, Helmig, Catrintje* and *Aegie*. Catrintje married Jacob Zabriskie, Dec. 12, 1801, and had two sons, *Albert* and *John H.*

thence North forty Degrees East to the aforesaid Portion No 15 thence along said Portion No 15 to the Easternmost Corner of said Portion No 25, and from thence in a direct Course to the place of Begining, Containing about one Acre and two Roods.*

We Adjudge all the remaining part of the last mentioned Tract, being the Portions marked No 27, No 28, No 29, No 30, No 31, and No 32 on Map B. to be with the before described Portion No 5, the full Proportion and Dividend for the Purchase Money paid by Jurian Thomason, the said Portions marked No 27, No 28, No 29, No 30, No 31, and No 32 Begining at the Southermost Corner of the above described Portion No 26 and from thence Runs South thirty eight Degrees and forty five minutes East to the Easternmost Corner of the School-Lot, thence North forty Degrees East to the Southermost Corner of said Portion No 15, thence North fifty Degrees and five minutes West to the Easternmost Corner of said Portion No 26, thence in a direct Course to the place of Begining, Containing about three Acres †

We Award and Order that the Owner or Owners for the Time being of the before described Portions No 12, No 13, No 14, No 15, No 16, No 17, No 18, No 19, No 20, No 22, No 23, No 25, No 26, No 27, No 28, No 29, No 30, No 31, No 32, shall have the Liberty and Privilidge of Passing and Repassing to and from his, her, or their respective Portion or Portions, as often and at such Times as the said Owner or Owners shall think fit, such Owner or Owners confineing him, her, or themselves in such Passing and Repassing to the Lane or Passage hereafter particularly described, to wit: Begining at the Road at the Northermost Corner of the aforesaid School-Lot, and Running from thence along the Northeasterly side of said School-Lot to the Easternmost Corner of said School-Lot, thence North forty Degrees East about eleven Chains and sixty Links, thence Returning to the said Easternmost Corner of the said School-Lot and Running along the Southeasterly side of said School-Lot and Lands belonging to the Newkerks 'till it comes into the aforesaid Portion No 23, the said Lane or Passage being in Breadth twenty five Links.

And with respect to a certain Tract of Land Begining at a Stake be-

---

o This lot was inherited by Nicholas, the son of Arent, and by him sold to Joseph Simonson (deed unrecorded). Simonson sold to Henry Speer the east end of the lot (now in part owned by Marcus Beach and Thomas E. Bray), and the west end (north of Newark Avenue) to Benjamin Thorp, who sold to Patrick Jackson, Jan. 21, 1802. The lot sold to Jackson was triangular, being thirty-two feet on its base, or east side, and eighty feet on Newark Avenue. The west end of the lot lying south of Newark Avenue, Simonson sold to John C. F. Rummel, Dec. 15, 1826, Rummel died seized, Jan. 13, 1840. Garret Sip et al. were appointed Commissioner, and sold his lands in parcels to John W. and Joseph H. Rummel, John Tice, Abel I. Smith, James Harrison and J. Dickinson Miller, at public auction, March 27, 1840. Harrison bought out some of the other purchasers, and sold to the Board of Chosen Freeholders the plot where the Court House and Jail now stand, April 7, 1841.

† The Thomasen here named was the ancestor of the Van Rypen family. Daniel Van Rypen et al., sold to John L. Cole one acre and thirty one-hundredths of an acre, bounded northeast by the road, southeast by Daniel Van Winkle, southwest by the school-lot, northwest by Simonson, Aug 10, 1803.

ing the Southeast Corner of a Lot of Land belonging to Johannes Van Wagenen, and from thence Runs South eighty one Degrees West thirteen Chains and seven Links to a Stake, thence South forty nine Degrees and fifty minutes East eighteen Chains and eighty Links, thence North thirty nine Degrees and forty Minutes East thirteen Chains and fifty six Links to a Stake, thence North forty one Degrees and forty five Minutes West fourteen Chains and twenty one Links to a Stake, thence South eight Degrees and ten minutes East five Chains and fifty Links to the place of Begining, Containing eighteen Acres one Rood. Note this last described Tract of Land is laid down on Map C.

We adjudge that Certain Part or Portion (of the last described Tract) marked No 33 on Map C. to belong to Cornelius Sip and Garret Sip, said Part or Portion Begining at the above said Southeast Corner of the aforesaid Johannes Van Wagenen's Land, and from thence Runs South thirty six Degrees and forty five Minutes East 'till it strikes the outward Boundary Line of the said Tract, thence North thirty nine Degrees and forty Minutes East five Chains and eighty Links being the Eastermost Corner of said Tract, thence North forty one Degrees and forty five Minutes West fourteen Chains and twelve Links to a Stake, Thence on a direct Course to the place of Begining, Containing about five Acres one Rood.*

And We Adjudge that Certain Part or Portion (of the last described Tract) marked No 34 on Map C. to be the full Portion and Dividend for the Purchase Money paid by Garret Garretse, said Part or Portion Begining at a Stake being the Southeast Corner of the before mentioned Johannis Van Wagenen's Land, and from thence Runs South eighty one Degrees West thirteen Chains and seven Links to a Stake being the Westermost Corner of said Tract, thence South forty nine Degrees and fifty minutes East eighteen Chains and eighty Links to the Southermost Corner of the said last described Tract, thence North thirty nine Degrees and forty minutes East seven Chains and seventy six Links to a Stake being the Southermost of the before described Portion No 33 and from thence in a direct Course to the place of Begining, Containing about thirteen Acres.†

Alway's Provided, and it is our Intent, Meaning and Order, that if it shall be made Appear that neither the aforesaid Douwe Tallma, nor his Father Harme Douwse Tallma is or were the legal Heir at Law of Douwe Harmse, that then our Judgment of and concerning the before described Portion marked No 3 on Map A. shall be Void and Reversed, any thing herein before to the Contrary hereof in any wise notwithstanding.‡

---

* This lot was afterwards owned by Jacob Everson, it is said, through exchange of Lots No. 168 and 257 in the town. Vide Note to Varlet's Patent, p. 62. Everson conveyed to Cornelius Sip, July 7, 1791.

† Garret Garretse named in the above description was the ancestor of the Van Wagenen family. Vide Note to Lot No. 389, p. 215.

‡ The expenses incurred in completing the foregoing work were borne by the individuals to whom portions of the land in controversy were adjudged. John Haring, one of the arbitrators, was a surveyor, and probably executed the survey. The following receipts, signed by the arbitrators, will give the reader an idea as to the manner in which the expenses were paid:

In Witness whereof We hereunto set our Hands and Seals this ninth Day of July in the tenth Year of the Reign of our Sovereign Lord George the Third, King of Great Britain &c. and in the Year of our Lord one thousand seven hundred and seventy.

Sealed and Delivered in   Johannis Demarest   [L.S.]
  the presence of   Albert Zabrowsky   [L.S.]
   Harmanies Veeder   John Haring   [L.S.]
   Rob.t Morris

"Receved the 10 day of July the sum of three pound & nine pens for the cost of the devision of said plantations for Lott No 2 being the full portion or devadent of said Lott for the cost and also Two pound Eleven shillings & six pens in full for the portion No 3 the full Cost of said portion we have Receved this of machiel De mott & Joris de mott in full for the above said perportion of said plantition and devisions I say Receved per me."

"Receved of Hendrick Sickels the 10 day of July the sum of one pound thirteen shillings & six pens being the full portion for the Lott No 6 for the cost of the Devision of said Lott out of the platation for the Division I say receved by us."

"Receved of Daniel Dederick the 10 day of July the sum of three pounds & nine pens for the cost of the devision of the Lott No 22 being the full portion for said Lott for the Devision of said Lot We say Receved per me."

CHAPTER VII.

NEW BARBADOES NECK.

HAVING passed in review the title of many tracts in the old Township of Bergen, it will not be out of place, though not as a part of the Field Book, to take a glance at that portion of "New Barbadoes Neck" now comprising the townships of Harrison and Kearney. This neck was known among the Indians by the name of *Mighgecticock*. It was estimated to contain five thousand three hundred and eight acres of upland and ten thousand acres of meadow. On the 4th of July, 1668, Captain William Sandford, of the Island of Barbadoes, purchased this tract from the Proprietors, on condition that he should settle thereon six or eight families or more within three years, and pay, in lieu of the half penny per acre quit rent, the yearly sum of £20 sterling, on every 25th of March; the first payment to be made March 25th, 1670. On the 20th of July, 1668, he purchased the claim of the Indians to the same tract; beginning at the mouth of the Hackensack and Pissawack Rivers, then "to goe up Northward into the Countrey about seaven Miles till it comes to a certain Brook or Spring now called Sandford's Spring." The consideration paid was: "170 fathoms of Black Wampam, 200 fathoms White Wampem, 19 Match Coates, 16 Guns, 60 double hands of powder. 10 pairs of Breetches, 60 Knives, 67 Barrs of Lead, One Anker of Brandy, three half Fats of Beer, Eleven Blankets, 30 Axes, 20 howes, and two Cookes of dozens."* This deed was signed by Tantaqua, Tamack, Anaren, Hanyaham, H. Gosque, and Ws Kenarenawack, who represented the Indian claimants.

Sanford's purchase seems to have been made in the interest of Major Nathaniel Kingsland, of the Parish of ChristChurch in the Island of Barbadoes. On June 1, 1671, Kingsland conveyed to Sandford one-third of the whole tract, measuring from the junction of the rivers northward, for £200. Kingsland having extinguished the Indians' title, now took measures to perfect his own.

On the 26th of March, 1673, Peter Watson and Ralph Wyatt, residents in England, for a consideration of £200 and "one Indian arrow" yearly, purchased of Berkley and Carteret that portion of the same tract which lies between a point opposite Newark and

---

* This last item is supposed to be a clerical error. It should probably read "two coats of duffels." *Proc. N. J. Hist. Soc.*, vii, 6. Duffels was a coarse kind of cloth. Sandford's Spring was afterwards known as Boiling Spring, now Rutherford Park, on the line of the Erie Railway.

the Brook opposite Espatin, and immediately conveyed the same to William Sandford in trust for Nathaniel Kingsland. This purchase extinguished the quit rent. It was confirmed by another deed dated May 21, 1673.

On the recapture of the country by the Dutch they seized upon Kingsland's interest in this tract, and on Oct. 1, 1673, ordered it to be sold. It was sold at public auction and a deed given, of which the following is a copy:

" Anthony Colve General of New Netherland, High Mightnesses the Lords States General of United Netherlands and his Serene Highness the Lord Prince of Orange:

All those who shall see these presents or hear the same read Greeting: Know ye: Whereas within this Province of New Netherland on the passing over thereof, there is found a certain plantation which belonged to Major Nathaniel Kingslant residing on the Island Barbadoes in the Carribees, which plantation with other lands and effects belonging to Subjects of the King of England etc. by a late Acte of confiscation under date of 20th Septr. last past by virtue of the war is declared confiscated and forfeited; and therefore in consequence of such confiscation has been seized and taken possession of for the behoofe of the Government; and the same plantation and its appurtenances on the 28th of October last exposed to sale at public vendue and sold to Jacob Melyn of Elizabeth town at Arthur Coll, who hath afterwards assigned and conveyed his right to the inhabitants of the town of New Work at Arthur Coll aforesaid, whereby certain obligations and covenants under date the 25th of October and the 25th Instant have agreed the effectual payment of the purchase money according to the conditions at the aforesaid Vendue stipulated and the purchase made by the aforesaid Jacob Melyn on the day of the date aforesaid, so it is, that I by Virtue of my commission in quality aforesaid have sold granted conveyed and ceded and do sell grant convey and cede hereby unto John Ogden, Jasper Crane, Jacob Melyn, Samuel Hopkins, John Ward, Abm. Pierson Senior and Stephen Freeman for and to the behoof of themselves and the rest to the Inhabitants of the town of New Work aforesaid, and to their successors heirs and descendants the aforesaid plantation heretofore belonging to Nathaniel Kingsland, being the just two third parts of a Neck of land lying at Arthur Coll between the Rivers Pessayack and Hackingsack beginning from the point of land opposite the town of New Work in Pessayack and running from thence on a Northwest line to a fall or run of Water opposite Espatin, with all the valleys on both sides and all the other appurtenances according to the respective ground briefs and patents in date 4th July 1668 thereof being and the purchases and conveyances from the Indians relating thereto; of which neck of land the aforesaid Nathaniel Kingsland on the 1st of July 1671 hath sold, transferred and conveyed unto William Santford residing at Arthur Coll aforesaid one just third part therof as more fully appears by the conveyance thereof being; which one just third part of the said Neck conveyed to the said William Sandford in manner aforesaid is reserved and remains to his behoof and is excluded from this conveyance it being the remaining two third parts of the aforesaid Neck of land with the valleys and other appurtenances thereof together with the houses, barns, fences and other buildings of the aforesaid Nathaniel

Kingsland thereon standing, which is hereby granted and conveyed unto the aforesaid [same parties] as well for themselves as the other Chosen Patentees for and to the behoof of the remaining Inhabitants of the town of New Work aforesaid. Therefore hereby to the behoof aforesaid, desisting from henceforth forever from all ownership, right, title or pretence to the aforesaid plantation, and the appurtenances thereof as aforesaid, Promising moreover to keep, fulfil and perform this conveyance firm binding and irrevocable and free from all incumbrances under obligations according to law thereto standing.

In witness whereof I have herewith with my own hand placed my usual signature. Done at Fort William Hendrick in New Netherland the 29th Nov. 1673.

A. COLVE.

By order of the Noble Lord Governor General of New Netherland.
N. BAYARD, Secry." *

' ○ *N. Y. Col. MSS.*, xxiii, 433.

The following acknowledgment shews that the title passed from Melyn to Marins, and from Marins as follows :

"Before me Nicolas Bayard appointed Secretary in the service of the Right Honorable the Governor General and Council in New Netherland, appeared John Catlin, as well for himself as attorney for Edward Ball, John Baldwin and Nathaniel Wheeler all inhabitants of the town of New Worcke at Arthur Col, who in the presence of the undernamed Councillors acknowledged and declared to be well and duly indebted unto Peter Jacobse Marins,* merchant here in the City New Orange, his heirs or descendants in a clear or net sum of Forty three pounds Sterling, six shillings and eight pence, the pound being computed at forty guilders, Wampum value, each arising from and on account of a like amount accepted by the abovenamed Pieter Jacobse Marins for account of said Appearers to be paid into the hands of Nicolas Bayard Vendue Master in part payment of the purchase money of the plantation heretofore belonging to Nathaniel Kingsland, purchased by Jacob Melyn at auction.

Which aforesaid sum of £43. 6. 8. Sterling, the pound computed at forty guilders Wampum value, they the Appearers, undertake or promise to pay or cause to be paid to the above named Peter Jacobse Marins, or his lawful order, after the lapse of three years after the date hereof, in good clean winter wheat and pork and peas all recovered at current prices here within this City of New Orange, to be delivered free of costs and charges, together with the interest at ten per cent per annum, commencing at the date hereof and continuing until the full and effectual payment of the Sum aforesaid.

For the greater security of the above named Peter Jacobse Marins and the full payment of the abovenamed sum, they, the appearers, place and pledge as a special Mortgage and bond, their the appearers plantation being a part of Kingsland's plantation bought at auction by Jacob

---

* *Marins* was a merchant in New York, living on the south side of Pearl street. He carried on an extensive business with Boston and other ports, and amassed a considerable fortune. He was invested with the rights of a small burgher April 14, 1657, chosen Alderman in New York for several years, and lived to an old age.

Melyn, situate at Achter Col, next the plantation of Wm Santford, in order to obtain and levy therefrom and thereon the abovementioned Sum free of costs and charges, in default of payment and further generally their persons and property moveable immoveable, subjecting the same to all Courts and Judges. In testimony of the truth, this is signed by the Appearers and the underwritten gentlemen in Fort William Hendrick this 23d March Anno 1674.

                            JOHN CATTLIN
                            To my knowledge
C. V. Ruyven.   N. BAYARD, Secretary.
Corn'* Steinwyck."

On the restoration of the country to the English, Kingsland came again into the possession of his plantation. By his will, dated March 14, 1685, he gave one-third of his lands in New Jersey—about three thousand four hundred and two acres—to his nephew, Isaac Kingsland, the other two-thirds to his children, *John, Nathaniel, Isabella*, wife of Henry Harding; *Caroline*, wife of John Barrow, jr.; *Mary*, wife of William Walley; and *Esther*, wife of Henry Applethwaite. By Isaac Kingsland's will, dated Jan 1, 1697-8, *Edmund*, his eldest son, received one-third of his plantation—about eleven hundred and thirty four acres. A part of this tract was sold by Edmund Kingsland to Arent Schuyler April 20, 1710, for £330. By will, dated July 29, 1741, proved July 26, 1742, Kingsland gave to his son *William* three hundred acres next adjoining Schuyler; also one-third of the meadow and one-third of the cedar swamp. His son, *Edmund Roger*, received the remainder of his realty. This latter devise was burdened with the payment of certain legacies, and in case they were not paid within one year, then the property devised to *Edmund R.* should go to his son *Isaac*, with the same burdens. The devisee refused to accept, and on Sept. 10, 1743, Isaac accepted the devise, and, by his will dated March 5, 1776, proved Aug. 23, 1783, gave to his son *Abraham* one-half of all his lands, and divided the remainder among his other children, *Isaac, Joseph, Charles, Aaron, Sarah*, and *Rachel*.

John Kingsland, by will dated Aug. 18, 1763, proved Aug. 10, 1768, gave the north half of his lands to his son *Richard*. The other half was divided among his children, *Elizabeth, Hester*, wife of Peter Butler; *Edmund*, and grandson John, son of *Isaac*.

Sandford settled at East Newark, where, in a short time, must have been erected a number of buildings. In 1680 his place was known as "*Santfort*, an English village opposite *Milfort*," now Newark.—*Long Island Hist. Soc.*, i, 266. He left all of his property to his wife Sarah. By her will, dated June 8, 1708, proved June 25, 1719, she gave to her daughter *Catharine*, wife of Johannis Van Imburgh, three hundred acres of woodland and one hundred acres of meadow; and to *Elizabeth*, wife of James

Davis, three hundred acres of land. To her son, *William*, she gave the farm of three hundred acres, with the meadow, for life, then to his son *William* in fee. He also received the residue of her lands. By will, dated Feb. 24, 1732, proved April 16, 1733, William Sandford, 2d, gave to his son *Richard* one-half of the Cedar Swamp, and the other half to his daughters, *Frances, Jennie*, and *Anne*.

By will, dated Feb. 22, 1749, proved April 7, 1750, William Sandford, 3d, gave to his only son, *William*, all his lands, consisting of three hundred acres, and one hundred and fifty acres of meadow. This was the farm mentioned in his grandmother's will, and in all probability lay where East Newark now is.

Peregrine Sandford (son of William, 2d), by will dated Nov. 6, 1740, proved June 14, 1750, gave his lands to his children, *Enoch, William, Jane, Aghie*, and *Elizabeth*.

A part of the Sandford tract, which I take to be the farm and meadow named in Sarah Sandford's will, was purchased by Col. Peter Schuyler, and thenceforth called Petersborough. By his will, dated March 21, 1761, proved May 28, 1762, Schuyler gave it to his only child *Catharine*, wife of Archibald Kennedy, Earl of Casselis. Kennedy and wife conveyed to James Duane, June 13, 1765, the farm on New Barbadoes Neck (Petersborough); also two tracts near Secaucus, between the line of the Bergen lots and Pinhorne's Creek and Cromkill, also Col. Schuyler's interest in the commons (?) in trust for themselves. Duane reconveyed to them and to the survivor June 15, 1765. The earl outlived his wife, and, by will dated Jan. 19, 1794, left his property in America to his sons, *John* and *Robert*. I do not know how the interest of John passed to Robert, but in 1803 he sold the tract where East Newark now is, to William Halsey. It was then a part of what was known as "Kennedy's Farm." In 1804, the name was changed to "Lodi." Halsey laid out a part of his purchase into ninety building plots, of at least one acre each.

Arent Schuyler, by will dated Dec. 17, 1724, proved July 6, 1732, gave his lands on New Barbadoes Neck to his son *John*, who left them to his son *Arent*, from whom they have descended to his grandchildren, Arent, Jacob R., etc.

CHAPTER VIII.

LIST OF MARRIAGES, BIRTHS, AND DEATHS, TAKEN FROM THE RECORD OF THE REFORMED CHURCH IN BERGEN.

MARRIAGES.

MALE.	FEMALE.	MARRIAGE DATE.
Ackerman Abraham	Aeltje Van Lone	May 13, 1683
Ackerman Garret	Maria Shepherd	April 25, 1813
Ackerman Garret H	Hannah Van Houten	July 29, 1819
Ackerman Jacob	Gitty Cubberly	April 10, 1819
Ackerman Jacob	Eunice Sturge	Sept. 1, 1822
Ackerman John C	Leah Lozier	April 19, 1808
Ackerman Koobes	Betje Belser	Nov. 27, 1782
Ackerman Levinus	Geertje Egberts	Aug. 3, 1679
Albertse Aert	Catharine Vreeland	June 26, 1692
Albertse Frans	Annetje Gysbertse	Nov. 12, 1683
Allen Moses	Dorcas Hubbins, *widow* of Geo. McIntyre	Oct. 12, 1810
Anderson Andrew	Jannetje Cadmus	May 23, 1801
Anderson John	Jane Evertson	April 14, 1805
Archer Joseph	Jane Earle	Jan. 6, 1806
Armington Abel	Sophia Fraser, *widow* of Sam'l Clark	May 26, 1816
Arselse Joseph	Elysabet Walings	May 6, 1678
Avery William	Mary Day	June 30, 1799
Aymar Peter	Ann Hunt	March 5, 1797
Aymar Peter	Elizabeth Van Antwerp	Aug. 11, 1802
Baker Samuel	Eliza Ann Farr	Feb. 29, 1823
Baldwin Jacobus Jansen	Peterje Claes	Dec. 12, 1696
Bandt Johannis Jansen	Willemyntje	June 27, 1797
Banker Obed	Catharine Anderson	April 4, 1824
Barentsen Dirck	Elysabet Gerrits	April 11, 1704
Bartholomew Louis	Margaret Post, *widow* of Gifford Bryant	July 1, 1826
Baten Peter	Helena Catharine Coops	Dec. 27, 1795
Beadle Joseph	Martha Trail	April 6, 1811
Bedell John	Mary Smith	May 10, 1800
Beekman Christopher	Maria Hunt	July 6, 1799
Belton Thomas	Margaret Gentleman, *widow* of James Bay	Aug. 25, 1805
Benson Robert	Charlotte Boyd	May 4, 1822
Berdolf Lourens	Hester Van Blercom	Aug. 24, 1707
Betts John	Mary Perry	June 9, 1822

MARRIAGE RECORD.

MALE.	FEMALE.	MARRIAGE DATE.
Bishop Seth	Ann, *widow* of John Millard	Oct. 5, 1809
Borton Jan	Hillegond Jacobs	Sept. 8, 1690
Boyd Thomas	Eleanor Coulter	Aug. 7, 1796
Boyd William	Leah Zabriskie	Sept. 27, 1827
Braambush David	Rachel Van Horne	March 26, 1795
Brewer David	Catharine Cadmus	June 22, 1824
Brinkerhoff Cornelis Hendricksen	Aagtje Hartmans Vreeland	May 24, 1708
Brinkerhoff Hartman	Claesje Van Houten	Oct. 20, 1744
Brinkerhoff Hartman	Elizabeth Van Houten	Oct. 21, 1797
Brinkerhoff Hartman	Eleanor Clendenny	Nov. 6, 1802
Brinkerhoff Hendrick	Leah Van Wagenen	June 19, 1779
Brinkerhoff Henry	Jane Van Horn	Jan. 18, 1827
Britain Abraham	Gitty Van Clief	Dec. 22, 1825
Britain Cornelius	Sarah Prior	Jan. 2, 1802
Britain Isaac	Mary Welsh	June 13, 1815
Bronson Jacob	Leah Slot	March 28, 1730
Brouwer Uldrick	Maria Van der Vorst	Oct. 8, 1738
Brower James	Ann Rapp	June 25, 1804
Brower Peter	Catherine Post	April 10, 1796
Bush David	Eliza Simmons	Feb. 20, 1819
Bush Jesse	Mary Barber	Oct. 12, 1812
Butts William W	Mary Earle	July 6, 1816
Buys Arien Pieterse	Tryntje Hendrickse Oosteroom	Sept. 30, 1672
Cadmus Andries Hendricksen	Grietje Claesen Kuyper	Oct. 22, 1725
Cadmus George	Elizabeth Vreeland	Nov. 14, 1812
Cadmus James	Maria De Mott	Feb. 28, 1828
Cadmus Jasper	Margaret Vreeland	Dec. 17, 1817
Cadmus John	Elizabeth Vreeland	Dec. 3, 1814
Cadmus Michael	Ann Sickles	June 9, 1827
Car John	Charlotte Hunt	Feb. 13, 1802
Carhart Isaac	Elizabeth Bowers	Dec. 1, 1806
Carlock George	Elizabeth Lozier	Aug. 8, 1801
Carlock Matthias	Ruth Ludlow	Oct. 7, 1797
Carlton John	Margaret Cozine	Jan. 23, 1812
Cassedy Quintilian	Sarah Vincent	April 10, 1814
Christianse Evertse	Lydia Meeker, *widow* of Geo. Abbot	March 31, 1816
Churchill John	Rosanna B. Lyon	Nov. 9, 1819
Claesen Andries	Pryntje Michielsen	March 25, 1668
Claesen Cornelis	Aeltje Teunise	Dec. 20, 1681
Claesen Gerbrand	Maritje Claas	Aug. 25, 1674
Claesen Jan	Tryntje Straatmaker	Oct. 8, 1694
Clark Moses A	Sarah Lee	Aug. 7, 1824
Clark William	Sarah Bridgart	June 6, 1820
Clendenny Merselis	Clara Brinkerhoff	Nov. 3, 1803
Clerke Charles	Susan Thorp	Nov. 6, 1798
Clintock Matthew	Gertrude Van der Beek	Dec. 23, 1809
Clugston John	Rachel Watson	April —, 1824

MARRIAGE RECORD.

MALE.	FEMALE.	MARRIAGE DATE.
Coddington John	Camilla Skinner	Aug 31, 1819
Cole Cornelius	Eleanor Speer	April 5, 1817
Collerd Abraham	Ann Vreeland	March 14, 1813
Collerd Jacobus	Aegie Diedricks	Nov. 29, 1789
Collerd Johannis	Geertje Prior	Dec. 19, 1782
Collerd John T.	Gertrude Collerd	May 14, 1814
Comyn Dirck Cornelise	Rachel Andriese	Oct. 21, 1707
Conkling John,	Julia Bond	Nov. 30, 1803
Conkling Josiah	Patty Earle	Jan. 22, 1822
Conkling Matthew	Sally Budd	Nov. 30, 1803
Cook Daniel	Phebe Tucker	Oct. 18, 1807
Corle Edward	Peggy Dezer, *widow* of John Compton	April 12, 1798
Cornelise Hendrick	Neeltje Cornelis	June 9, 1669
Cornelison Abraham	Catharine Du Bois	Feb 13, 1795
Cornelison John M.	Aletta Van Winkle	May 22, 1826
Cornelison Nathaniel	Hannah Van Blarcom	Dec. 26, 1804
Cowenhoven Peter	Elsie Lee	March 23, 1805
Coyeman Hendrick	Maritje Gerbrands	May 5, 1738
Cozine Abraham B.	Hannah Vreeland	Jan. 12, 1826
Crane Moses	Phebe Hunt	Jan. 1, 1803
Cubberly Jacob	Mary Prior	Jan. 4, 1806
Curtenius Fred'k Wm	Elizabeth Fowler	Feb. 15, 1826
Day John	Lucretia Westervelt	Dec. 15, 1798
Day Thomas	Mary Deser	July 20, 1802
Day Willem	Annatje Jacobse	April 14, 1691
De Green Christopher	Eliza Stilwell	May 31, 1819
De Groot Peter	Eleanor Brower, *widow* of John Mersereau	Oct 24, 1801
De Mott Garret	Margareth Mandeville	Jan. 16, 1813
De Mott George	Jane Vreeland	Oct. 1, 1808
De Mott George	Ellen Ann Smith	Jan. 18, 1827
De Mott Hendrick	Jannetje Van Wagenen	Oct. 30, 1740
De Mott Henry	Clara Brinkerhoff	Jan. 25, 1806
De Mott Jacob	Fitje Van Houten	Oct. 11, 1747
De Mott Mattys	Margrietje Blinckerhof	May 6, 1705
De Witt Gasharie	Christiana Hornblower	Nov. 13, 1819
De Wolff Haybrecht	Maria Bear	Sept. 23, 1798
Decker Abraham	Jane Ayres	July 29, 1815
Decker Benjamin	Jane Metsger	June 3, 1816
Denniston John	Rachel Van der Beek	April 30, 1818
Denniston Lucas	Cyntje Evertson	Oct. 8, 1807
Dezer Nathaniel	Clara Earle	Nov. 12, 1799
Diedricks Cornelius	Antje Roos	June 7, 1735
Diedricks Garret	Jannetje Van Nieuwkercke	April 21, 1733
Diedricks Jacob	Jannetje Van Winckel	Nov. 26, 1738
Diedricks Johannis	Geesje Van Winckel	May 2, 1724
Diedricks Johannis	Hester Vreeland	April 14, 1739
Diedricks Johannis	Antje Van Wagenen	Dec. 17, 1768
Diedricks Wander	Aeltje Gerrits	Nov. 27, 1693
Dixon Alexander	Abby Gregory	Jan. 2, 1802

MALE.	FEMALE.	MARRIAGE DATE.
Dixon Jonathan	Hannah Burnet	Dec. 13, 1794
Dixon Walter	Elizabeth Cole	Dec. 26, 1803
Dodd Joseph jr	Nancy Clark	June 5, 1813
Dorenius Cornelis Cornelisse	Rachel Pieterse,	Aug. 12, 1710
Dorstan John	Widow Jones	Aug. 6, 1794
Douwesen Paulus	Fitje Hendricks, widow	May 3, 1702
Druyts Levinus	Grietje Jans	June 1, 1665
Earle Cornelius	Hannah Nagle	July 28, 1804
Earle Daniel	Charlotte Nicolls	Oct. 21, 1800
Earle David	Polly De Gray	Aug. 24, 1800
Earle Edward jr	Elsje Vreeland	Feb. 13, 1688
Earle Edward	Johanna Day	Feb. 13, 1800
Earle Enoch	Mary Van Horne	July 29, 1804
Earle John W	Elizabeth Earle	April 4, 1809
Earle Justus	Ann Matilda Stagg	Oct. 5, 1822
Earle Morris	Peggy Metsger	Nov. 17, 1804
Earle Nathaniel	Geertje Duryee, widow of Jacob Post	April 6, 1829
Earle Peter	Letta Van Houten	July 28, 1816
Earle Peter	Susan Ackerman	July 4, 1823
Earle Philip I	Margaret Shepherd	Jan. 13, 1823
Earle Philip R	Adriana Van Rypen	March 6, 1812
Earle Rynier	Leah Earle, widow of James Van Horne	Feb. 24, 1805
Earle Rynier II	Mary Lee	Nov. 24, 1810
Earle William	Charity Earle	March 10, 1804
Edsal Johannis	Charity Smith	May 3, 1691
Edwards John	Mary Armstrong, widow of Henry Young	July 26, 1811
Emerson James	Ann J. Wier	Sept. 5, 1822
Everse Johannis	Scytje Speer	Aug. 20, 1744
Everse Johannis	Sally Griffin	Dec. 21, 1782
Evertson Abraham	Elizabeth Harrison	May 6, 1797
Evertson John	Hannah Van Houten	Feb. 3, 1818
Evertson John	Sarah Smith	Oct. 19, 1822
Fidler Thomas	Louise Holden	Jan. 10, 1799
Folkner Abraham	Mary M. Waling	June 20, 1827
Ford William	Catherine Sanford	March 17, 1808
Fransen Tomas	Neeltje Pieters	Sept. 29, 1706
Fredricksen Andries	—	April 11, 1704
Gardner James	Mary Earle	Dec. 30, 1807
Garrabrants James	Sarah Williamson widow of Vincent Hudson	April 19, 1815
Garrabrants Myndert	Aegie Van Houten	Nov. 13, 1800
Garrabrants Peter	Catharine Van Boskercke	Feb. 1, 1800
Garrabrants Peter	Jane Clendenny	Dec. 14, 1805
Garrabrants Peter	Ann Van Winkle	Feb. 15, 1814
Garrabrants Peter N	Caroline Gardner, widow of John Winans	Dec. 25, 1823
Garretson John	Catharine Ann Riker	Feb. 15, 1825
Garretson Nicholas	Elizabeth Durant	May 25, 1823

MALE.	FEMALE	MARRIAGE DATE.
Garretson Stephen	Hetty Fairchild	Feb. 16, 1824
Gautier Thomas B.	Elizabeth Hornblower	Oct. 15, 1816
Gerbrantse Claas	Maritje Jurianse	April 11, 1704
Gerbrantse Herpert	Hillegond Merselis	May 29, 1707
Gerbrantse Myndert	Treintje Jacobse Van Winckel	May 7, 1715
Gerbrantse Pieter	Chrystintje Jurianse	Aug. 1, 1698
Gerritse Johannis	Anna Walingse	Oct. 6, 1690
Gerritse Gerrit jr.	Kiesje Pieters	May 11, 1681
Gerritse Pieter	Constantia Van der Swalin	June 25, 1688
Gerritsen Cornelius	Aeltje van Winckel	June 29, 1728
Gerritsen Hendrick	Margrietje Straatmaker	April 3, 1701
Gerritsen Johannis	Catelyntje Helmigse	Nov. 4, 1703
Gilchrist Robert	Frances Vasher	Oct. —, 1812
Gilleland Thomas T.	Elizabeth Halenbeck	April 9, 1802
Guines Patrick	Ann Bagtmens, *widow*	Feb. 3, 1796
Golden Valentine	Rachel Van Houten	Oct. 16, 1825
Goodman John K.	Frances A. Stewart	Dec. 15, 1822
Goodwin Daniel	Mary S. Pray	Aug. 24, 1812
Gough Edward	Eliza Fairchild	July 10, 1829
Graham John	Catharine Ann Gray	July 20, 1817
Gray James	Eleanor Meadow	March 26, 1822
Greenlief Evert	Jane Danielson	June 4, 1827
Greenlief John	Rachel Sickles	Dec. 27, 1801
Greenlief Pieter	Mary Halenbeck	Dec. 25, 1804
Hadley James	Esther Day	June 24, 1797
Haff Uriah	Mary Garrabrants	Aug. 1, 1818
Halenbeck Joseph	Eleanor Earle	Feb. 7, 1802
Harrison Hiram	Mary Farrel	Jan. 21, 1829
Harsin Wassel	Susan Stagg	June 10, 1815
Hartmanse Claas	Elsje Pieters	Aug. 19, 1699
Hartmanse David	Annetje Straatmaker	March 29, 1692
Hartnet John	Ann Day	Aug. 10, 1822
Hebbe Jan	Annetje Cornelis	March 5, 1693
Helmigse Dirck	Metje Gerrebrantse	Sept. 9, 1711
Helmigse Peter	Claretje Post	April 8, 1703
Helmigse Roelof	Aagtje Cornelis Vreelant	April 21, 1701
Helmigse Roelof	Syntje Sickels	Dec. 15, 1711
Helmigsen Cornelis	Aagtje Johannissen Vreelandt	April 19, 1711
Hendrickse Hans	Treintje Pieters	July 31, 1683
Hendrickse Jan	Magliteltje Roelofse	July 22, 1683
Hendrickse Jan	Neeltje Janse Buys	June 23, 1684
Hendrickse Tomas	Susanna Lewn	May 20, 1683
Hennion David	Catlyntje Evertse	Dec. 21, 1782
Hennion Isaac	Margrietje Van Vorst	———, 1726
Hoagland Aaron	Esther Van Houten	Oct. 12, 1794
Hollinge Hendrick Tennissen	Styntje Jans	June 30, 1700
Holmes James	Catharine Van Winkle	Oct. 6, 1827
Hoof Frederick	Helen Vincent	April 24, 1819

MARRIAGE RECORD.

MALE.	FEMALE.	MARRIAGE DATE.
Hoppe Hendrick	Maritje Toers	March 14, 1680
Hoppe Mattys Adolphus	Anna Pieterse	April 15, 1683
Hornblower Josiah jr.	Hannah Town	Oct. 15, 1812
Howell Henry	Eliza Greenlief	Jan. 23, 1826
Huntley Nehemiah	Phebe Pollard	May 21, 1805
Ido Robert	Annetje Roome	Sept. 24, 1739
Ingles John	Mary Day	Nov. 26, 1808
Jackson Patrick	Mary Wright	Feb. 10, 1802
Jacobse Bartel	Eleanor Douglas	April 14, 1695
Jacobusse Thomas	Saertje Toers	Jan. 13, 1771
Janse Johannis	Anna Mary Van Giesen	March 21, 1686
Janse Pieter	Elysabet ———	June 22, 1685
Jansen Rutger	Annetje Gerrits	April 10, 1699
Jeffreys Edward	Mary Tamsen	———, 1720
Johnson Elias H.	Joanna H. Durant	March 10, 1821
Jones Joseph	Rebecca Clarke	Jan. 13, 1825
Joost Hendrick	Grietje Jacobs	May 23, 1665
Josi Pieter	Cornelia Daniels	April 6, 1686
Jurianse Aelt	Gerritje Mattheuse	July 7, 1695
Jurianse Gerrit	Beelitje Dircks (Van Noyer)	June 6, 1693
Jurianse Johannis	Sarah Kuyper	Dec. 2, 1740
Jurianse Johannis (wid'er)	Margretje Van Winkle	Sept. 5, 1742
Jurianse Tomas	Jannetje Straatmaker	June 2, 1691
Juriansen Harman	Maritje Fredrickse	June 20, 1709
Juriansen Jan	Neeltje Gerbrands	April 7, 1702
Kealy Edward	Susan Sturge	Dec. 24, 1808
Kingsland William	Leah Brown	May 20, 1813
Kip Peter	Mary Stuyvesant	Feb. 27, 1802
Kittleman Valentine	Janse Taylor, widow of Jonas Tompkins	Oct. 3, 1805
Lamb Samuel	Jane Clendenny	Jan. 26, 1812
Lamberson Garret	Phebe Ann Scharit	Jan. 1, 1825
Lane James B	Sarah Van Buskirk	Oct. 1, 1828
Lawson Samuel	Jane La Tourette	Oct. 9, 1824
Layman William	Maria Shepherd	March 17, 1824
Lee James	Margaret Cooper	May 8, 1813
Lee William	Rachel Eaton	Oct. 22, 1808
Lee William	Sarah La Tourette	Aug. 5, 1815
Lewis Jotham	Catharine Van Ziel	Dec. 30, 1804
Lisk John	Catreintje Huysman	June 20, 1767
Littlefield Daniel jr.	Melvina Morris	Oct. 24, 1824
Lubbers Roelof	Weseleena Steinmets	March 25, 1688
Lubbertse Lubbert	Hilletje Poulose	March 14, 1680
Lubi Jacob	Gerritje Cornelis	Sept. 4, 1672
Ludlow James	Nancy Lee	July 14, 1810
Ludlow Henry	Rachel Wright	Dec. 15, 1810
Ludlow Hugh	Elizabeth Sturge	Dec. 10, 1808

MALE.	FEMALE.	MARRIAGE DATE.
Lyon Henry	Ann Eliza Marsh	Jan. 6, 1818
Lyon Richard	Aegie Van Houten	Feb. 13, 1811
Machelsen Sjárel	Catrina Tomas	March 26, 1678
Mandeville Henry	Ann Outwater	April 23, 1817
Marselis Pieter (?)	Maritje Andriese	————, 1730
Marselisse Ide	Ariantje Sip	April 11, 1754
Marsh William	Phebe Heathorne	Oct. 9, 1824
Martin Merrit	Hannah Wauters	Aug. 4, 1829
Mattheuse Jacob	Sara Cornelis	May 15, 1707
Maybee Jasper	Catharine Edsall	Jan. 2, 1802
McCrindell Thomas	Elizabeth R. Cornelison	June 12, 1827
McCubberry Robert	Charity Prior, *widow* of Wm. Coulter	Oct. 30, 1825
McDonald Isaac	Ann Taylor	Dec. 25, 1824
McDonald Matthias	Hannah Brinkerhoff	Sept. 23, 1809
McElroy ———	Mary Ann Trim	May 16, 1822
McKey William	Mary Jenkins	Dec. 31, 1803
McLoughlin John	Phebe Britain	Dec. 25, 1828
McNeil Jacobus	Antje Lisk	May 15, 1768
McTavlan Robert	Eliza Coulter	April 8, 1818
Mead Peter T	Leah Mandeville	July 3, 1813
Mecolen Benjamin	Hannah Van Vorst	July 25, 1812
Meeker Hiram L	Mariah F. Randall	April 26, 1819
Meeker Samuel C	Maria Chadwick	Dec. 3, 1818
Merselis Jacob	Sally Merselis	Sept. 13, 1828
Merselis Merselis	Gertrude Prior	July 26, 1800
Merselis Peter	Jane De Mott	May 28, 1822
Mersereau John	Esther, *widow* of Christopher Garretson	Aug. 3, 1794
Mersereau John	Ann Waldron	Sept. 26, 1818
Mesier Peter D	Mary Van Wyck	Nov. 1, 1800
Meyers Andries	Vrouwtje Van de Vorst	Nov. 1, 1671
Meyers Johannis	Annetje Van de Vorst	June 12, 1677
Michielse Johannis	Neeltje Femens	July 23, 1670
Michielse Tades	Anna Steinmets	Sept. 21, 1679
Miet John	Annetje Baldwin	April 28, 1793
Mindell Conrad	Margaret Baker	Sept. 4, 1793
Mix Marvin P	Ann Maine	Jan. 10, 1815
Moore Abraham	Maria Van Gelder	Jan. 25, 1794
Moore James	Sally Moore	Sept. 17, 1796
Moore Samuel	Margaret Moore	Sept. 10, 1803
Moore Thomas	Elizabeth Lee	July 29, 1803
Morehouse Chauncey	Ann T. Crane	Feb. 16, 1822
Mulford David	Phebe Vincent	Feb. 6, 1808
Myers Garret	Jane Bogert	Dec. 18, 1799
Neesje Johannis	Antje Gerritsen Van Wagenen	Oct. 9, 1710
Negles Caleb	Julian Crane	April 24, 1817
Newkirk Aaron	Jannetje Vreeland	Nov. —, 1791
Newkirk Garret	Rachel Shepherd	Feb. 22, 1806
Newkirk Garret	Rachel Van Houten	Oct. 25, 1828

MALE.	FEMALE.	MARRIAGE DATE.
Newkirk George	Sally Van Derhoof	Feb. 9, 1805
Newkirk Henry	Eliza Provost	July 23, 1818
Newkirk John	Maritje Newkirk	Feb. 1, 1806
Nicoll Robert	Sarah V. D. Mesier	April 14, 1812
Nieuwkerck Jacob	Fitje Hennion	Feb. 13, 1769
O'Donoghue Cornelius	Mary Ann Willey, *widow* of Parkman Townsend	July 28, 1819
O'Reily John S.	Isabella Chambers	July 13, 1819
Opdyke Sibi	Maritje Adrianse Sip	Oct. 13, 1678
Osborn Samuel	Maria Shepherd	Dec. 1, 1804
Outwater Garret	Maria Van Winkle	Dec. 25, 1822
Outwater Jacob	Maritje Van Derhoof	Sept. 30, 1797
Outwater John	Eleanor Prior	Jan. 25, 1800
Palmer Peregrine	Susanna Wright	Aug. 20, 1817
Paulmier Stephen	Caroline Halsey	Dec. 7, 1824
Pelor George	Euphemia Deas, *widow* of Thos. Reed	May 13, 1805
Pieterse Andries	Johannis Steinmets	May 13, 1688
Pieterse Hessel	Lysbet Claes	June 24, 1690
Pieterse Merselis	Peterje Van de Voorst	May 12, 1681
Pieterse Pieter	Dirckje Egberts	Nov. 18, 1683
Pieterse Pieter	Treintje Hans Jacobse	Oct. 3, 1687
Pest Abraham	Effie Metsger	Jan. 27, 1798
Post Abraham	Jane Anderson	Nov. 27, 1819
Post Adrian	Catrintje Gerrits	April 17, 1677
Post Adrian	Elysabet Merselis	April 21, 1701
Post Egbert	Saertje Stuyvesant	Nov. 9, 1765
Post Frans	Maritje Cobus	April 22, 1690
Post Gerrit	Lea Straet	Dec. 25, 1704
Post Jacob	Elizabeth Maybee	April 5, 1797
Post Jacob	Keziah Duryee	May 20, 1817
Post Johannis	Elizabet Helmigse Van Houte	———, 1713
Post John E.	Abby Prior	May 9, 1794
Post Peter	Catelyntje Beekman	Nov. 17, 1710
Post Peter	Jannetje Diedricks	Feb. 7, 1795
Poulusen Dirck	Fitje Hartmans Vreeland	Aug. 19, 1699
Poulusen Martin	Margrietje Westervelt	March 25, 1694
Prier Casparus	Sarah Andriesen	March 13, 1714
Prier Teunis Janse	Catelyntje Tomase	Oct. 6, 1684
Prine Abraham	Peggy Coulter	Dec. 27, 1796
Prine Daniel	Helena Evertse	July 25, 1791
Prine Peter	Rachel Van Winkle	Feb. 11, 1819
Prior Abraham	Ann Waldron	Dec. 20, 1796
Prior Andries	Geertruy Sickles	Oct. 8, 1750
Prior Asa	Sarah H. Lyon	Sept. 12, 1820
Prior Nicholas	Martha Cadmas	Dec. 18, 1817
Prior Nicholas	Eleanor Garrabrants	Sept. 20, 1827
Prior Nicholas C.	Hannah Vreeland	Dec. 30, 1818
Pryer Abraham	Maritje Sickels	Dec 18, 1746

MARRIAGE RECORD.

MALE.	FEMALE.	MARRIAGE DATE.
Pryer Johannis	Geertje Siggelse	June 14, 1745
Puker William	Christiana Renny	Nov. 16, 1800
Randolph Absalom F.	Hannah Budd	Nov. 21, 1812
Randolph Lewis F.	Mary Meyer	May 26, 1824
Rapp Andrew	Catherine Britain	Oct. 2, 1823
Rapp John	Mary Van Clief	Dec. 16, 1813
Reddenhaus Abel	Catrina Janse Van Burger	July 26, 1696
Remsey Mungo	Adriana Veder, *widow* of Cor's Hennion	Feb. 8, 1803
Rodgers Joseph	Eliza O'Brien	July 26, 1811
Roelofse Cornelius	Magdaleena Van Giesen	Nov. 14, 1677
Roelofse Helmigh	Jannetje Pieterse	Sept. 3, 1676
Roelofse Tadeus	Treintje Claes	Jan. 8, 1678
Rosman Thomas	Ann Hennion	July 12, 1820
Ryder John	Clara Steinmets	Feb. 19, 1804
Ryerson Samuel C	Rachel Compton	June 15, 1805
Salter Paul	Elizabeth Cubberly	June 14, 1812
Scott William	Ann Lyon	April 2, 1799
Seaman Isaac	Sarah Crane	Jan. 30, 1819
Seaman James G.	Mary Cronk	June 29, 1822
Seaman Stephen	Jane Mills	June 3, 1819
Seely John	Keziah Van Ziel	June 23, 1800
Seely William	Ann Sickles	Aug. 8, 1802
Shay John	Dolly McWilliams	Feb. 20, 1819
Shieffer Nicholas	Lucretia Sisco	Oct. 16, 1825
Shepherd Abraham	Mary Earle	Sept. 12, 1812
Shepherd Joseph	Fanny Tuers	June 6, 1813
Shepherd Samuel	Ann Smith	Dec. 29, 1793
Shepherd Thomas	Rachel Banta	June 29, 1824
Sickles Abraham	Aegie Blinkerhoff	April 1, 1739
Sickles Abraham	Catherine Outwater	Dec. 8, 1798
Sickles Hendrick	Jenneke Stuyvesant	Feb. 1, 1767
Sickles Peter	Eva Van Derhoof	Oct. 8, 1791
Sickles Robert	Antje Winne	Oct. 8, 1749
Sickles Willem	Elysabet Kuyper	Aug. 10, 1732
Sickles Zacharias	Ariantje Hartmanse Vreeland	Nov. 7, 1719
Simmons Michael	Rachel Van Wart	Oct. 17, 1829
Simmons Stephen	Eliza Smith, *widow* of Asa Leonard	May 30, 1807
Simse James	Maritje Janse Daame, *widow* of Jan Remse	Sept. 10, 1697
Sip Arie	Grietje Helmigsen	———, 1711
Sip Garret	Margaret Newkirk	Nov. 10, 1811
Sip Henricus	Annette Bayard	Nov. 22, 1691
Sip Ide	Antje Van Wagenen	May 23, 1725
Sip Jan Ariantse	Johanna Van de Voorst	April 22, 1684
Sip Peter	Elizabeth Vreeland	Nov. 1, 1789
Slingerland George H.	Eliza Simonson	Feb. 19, 1825
Slot Jan	——— Andries	April 2, 1700
Smeeman Harman	Annetje Daniels	Dec. 9, 1668
Smith Abel	Jane Lozier	Oct. 6, 1802

43

MARRIAGE RECORD.

MALE.	FEMALE.	MARRIAGE DATE.
Smith Beekman	Elizabeth Sickles	June 1, 1803
Smith Cornelius	Peggy Shepherd	Oct. 21, 1797
Smith James	Rachel Huyler	Jan. 28, 1809
Smith John F	Altje Van Rypen	March 27, 1811
Smith Philip	Jane Ackerman	March 27, 1802
Speer John	Mary Hennion	July 30, 1803
Speer John G	Hannah Riker	Feb. 12, 1829
Speer William	Keziah Stagg	June 5, 1796
Spier Albertus	Orseltje Westervelt	June 5, 1744
Spier Barent Hendrickse	Catalyntje Hendricks	Aug. 6, 1698
Spier Johannis	Meya Franse	Aug. 12, 1679
Spier Johannis	Geertruy Roome	April 29, 1739
Stagg Abraham	Rachel Town	Feb. 1, 1800
Steinmets Casparus	Margrietje Hendricksen	Aug. 5, 1727
Steinmets Caspar	Treintje Jacobs	March 15, 1671
Steinmets Christophel	Joannetje Gerrits	Oct. 6, 1684
Steinmets Christophel	Sarah Van Neste	————, 1699
Steinmets Gerrit	Vrouwtje Claes	March 11, 1684
Steinmets Gerrit	Catrina Gerrits, *widow* of Adrian Post	July 31, 1691
Steinmets Johannis	Annetje Jacobse Van Winckel	Nov. 30, 1676
Stelting Roelof	Jacomyntje ————	Nov. 24, 1672
Stephens Nehemiah	Mary Beeman	June 25, 1808
Stillwell Ezekiel	Polly Carl, *widow* of Toby Smith	Nov. 18, 1798
Straatmaker Dirck	Treintje Buys	Nov. 27, 1698
Straatmaker Jan	Neeltje Buys, *widow* of Jacob Vygerse	Jan. 27, 1707
Straatmaker Jan Dirckse	Geesje Gerrits	Jan. 14, 1665
Stuyvesant Petrus	Pryntje Preyer	Oct. 27, 1733
Sutphen John	Jane Spader	June 17, 1814
Swartwout Roelof	Fransyntje Andries	Nov. 22, 1691
Sweet Antonio	Jannetje Cobus	May 8, 1693
Swiney John	Rachel Compton	June 15, 1805
Syckelse Hendrick	Maritje Lubbertse	Dec. 27, 1678
Tades Michiel	Treintje Jacobs	June 8, 1667
Tallman Anthony	Catherine Coulter	Oct. 21, 1829
Taylor Oliver	Margaret Van Horne	Feb. 20, 1811
Terhune Stephen	Eliza Vreeland	June 1, 1815
Terhune Stephen	Jane Terhune	June 9, 1821
Thomas Arie	Eliza Hill	Sept. 28, 1801
Thompson Nathaniel	Catherine Maseker	Dec. 29, 1798
Thorp Garrett	Helen Bond	Oct. 3, 1804
Tise Martin	Nancy Van Rypen	Dec. 24, 1829
Toers Abraham	Eleanor Van Winkle	Jan. 29, 1809
Toers Arent	Annetje Spier	July 19, 1730
Toers Claes Arentse	Jacomyntje Van Neste	July 8, 1684
Toers Lourens Arentse	Fransyntje Tomas	Aug. 15, 1672
Toers Nicholas	Jannetje Van Rypen	May 11, 1766
Tomase Arien	Maritje Cobusje	June 21, 1686
Tomase Johannis	Maritje Van Deusen, *widow* of Tymen Van Valen	Dec. 24, 1705

MALE.	FEMALE.	MARRIAGE DATE.
Tomase Frederick	Catherina Hoppe	Oct. 13, 1672
Tomase Tomas	Sara Van Dueselten	Sep. 17, 1701
Tompkins Abraham	Elizabeth Budd	May 12, 1805
Traphagen Henry	Neeltje Van Vorst	Jan. 25, 1803
Travis Simeon	Eliza Tompkins	Oct. 17, 1813
Tuers Aaron	Effie Van Winkle	Nov. 30, 1826
Tuers Abraham A.	Sarah Vanderbilt	Jan. 1, 1827
Vail Aaron	Elizabeth Gellard, *wid.* of Peter Robertson,	April 18, 1813
Van Antwerp William	Mary Clendenny	Jan. 13, 1821
Van Barkelow Hartmansen,	Maria Cortelyou	April 1, 1697
Van Blarcom Gysbert Jansen	Magdaleena La Komba	Jan. 16, 1706
Van Blarcom Johannis Janse	Metje Jans	July 16, 1693
Van Borckelaer Evert Evertson	Hillegond Jacobse	June 7, 1707
Van Boskerck Abraham	Elizabeth Cole	May 1, 1805
Van Boskerck Cornelius	Peggy Van Horne	Dec. 24, 1800
Van Boskerck James Jr.	Jane Garrabrants	Dec. 20, 1821
Van Boskerck John	Isabella Van Rypen	Nov. 20, 1814
Van Boskerck Lourens	Fitje Cornelise Vreeland	Sept. 18, 1709
Van Boskerck Nicholas	Jane Cadmus	Dec. 15, 1814
Van Buren Beekman	Ann Ackerman	Dec. 4, 1819
Van Buren Sylvester	Ann Amanda Vander Poel, *widow* of James Wrangle.	Jan. 1, 1801
Van Clief Daniel	Altje Diedricks	June 24, 1797
Van Clief Jacob	Maria Post	Dec. 25, 1823
Van Clief John	Ann Brown, *widow* of James Welsh	Aug. 13, 1809
Van Clift Gideon	Mary Harris	Oct. 24, 1802
Van Dalson Abraham	Sophia Cole	Dec. 1, 1814
Van Dalson Henry Jr.	Mary Ann Lyon	Oct. 19, 1818
Van Dalson John	Elsje Carlock, *widow* of Tunis Quinn	Nov. 16, 1800
Van den Bos Hendrick Janse	Maria Boas	Oct. 17, 1685
Van der Beek Abraham A.,	Elizabeth Cole	Feb. 11, 1817
Van der Bilt Jan Aertsen	Magdaleentje Hanse	Dec. 10, 1681
Van Derhoof Henry	Naomi Day	May 6, 1797
Van Derhoof Johannis	Maria Bertsie	April 22, 1738
Van der Heyden Wm. Anthony	Henrietta W. E. Van Holten	Aug. 16, 1800
Van der Koeren Hendrick,	Eva Jacoben Slot	———, 1723
Van der Linda Roelof	Susanna Hendrickse	Oct. 2, 1682
Van Giesen Abraham	Fitje Andriese	Oct. 4, 1691
Van Giesen Bastiaen	Aeltje Hendrickse	June 25, 1688
Van Giesen Isaac	Cornelia ———	Aug. 10, 1690
Van Giesen Jacob	Busje Pluvier	June 1, 1693
Van Giesen Jacob	Hillegont Claesen Kuyper	Sept. 26, 1708
Van Giesen Johannis	Aeltje Schopmoes	July 13, 1687
Van Giesen Rynier	Hendrickje Janse Buys	Oct. 17, 1699

MALE.	FEMALE.	MARRIAGE DATE.
Van Giesen Rynier	Catreintje Merselis	April 17, 1737
Van Hooren Rutgert	Neeltje Diedricks, *widow* of Jan Van Der- linden	April 25, 1697
Van Hooren Barent Ba- rentsen	———— Pieters	Feb. 23, 1712
Van Horne Andrew	Hannah Osborn	April 10, 1802
Van Horne Burger	Anna Boskerck	Feb. 12, 1801
Van Horne Cornelius	Sally Clendenny	Nov. 16, 1799
Van Horne Cornelius	Jane Garrabrants	Jan. 21, 1810
Van Horne Garret	Margaret T. Gautier	Jan. 5, 1812
Van Horne Henry	Catherine Vreeland	Dec. 17, 1809
Van Horne Jacob	Catherine Boskerck	Feb. 18, 1826
Van Horne John	Mary Prior	Dec. 27, 1805
Van Horne John G.	Hannah Van Rypen	Dec. 19, 1812
Van Horne Myndert	Mary Sickles	Oct. 12, 1816
Van Horne Peter	Mary Jerolamon	Oct. 4, 1824
Van Houten Helmigh	Catherine Van Rypen	Dec. 7, 1799
Van Houten Johannis	Annatje Collerd	Dec. 19, 1782
Van Houten John Jr.	Sally Mandeville	Dec. 20, 1821
Van Houten Joseph	Catherine Garretson	Sept. 20, 1801
Van Houten Michael	Altje Van Horne	Dec. 15, 1793
Van Houten Peter	Ann Winne	Feb. 26, 1815
Van Nieuwkercke Garrit Mattheusen	Catreintje Kuyper	Sept. 5, 1730
Van Nieuwkercke Mat- theus Corneliese	Anna Lubi	Dec. 14, 1670
Van Nieuwkercke Poulus,	Helena Spier	June 18, 1728
Van Pelt Tunis	Ann Vreeland	Sept. 21, 1826
Van Rypen Christopher	Gertrude Van Houten	Dec. 27, 1802
Van Rypen Cornelius	Altje Van Horne, *widow* of Michael Van Houten	May 31, 1807
Van Rypen Cornelius	Catherine Newkirk	Nov. 7, 1813
Van Rypen Cornelius R.	Mary Sickles	Sept. 15, 1827
Van Rypen Daniel	Elizabeth Van Rypen	Sept. 19, 1811
Van Rypen Daniel	Jannetje Winne	Nov. 19, 1785
Van Rypen Daniel	Jane Post	Sept. 7, 1826
Van Rypen Derrick	Jenneke Vreeland	Oct. —, 1792
Van Rypen Garret	Jane Hennion	Aug. 9, 1805
Van Rypen Garret	Elizabeth Simonson	Jan. 14, 1815
Van Rypen Garret C.	Hannah Evans	May 28, 1817
Van Rypen Garret C.	Eliza Van Wart	April 28, 1819
Van Rypen George	Clara Vreeland	July 23, 1814
Van Rypen Gerrit	Catreintje Van Rypen	March 2, 1799
Van Rypen Jerry	Aegie Diedricks, *widow* of Jacob Collerd	Sept. 13, 1807
Van Rypen Jurrie	Neeltje Van Hoorn	Dec. 18, 1790
Van Rypen Michael	Celia Cadmus	Dec. 21, 1816
Van Rypen Peter	Maria Vreeland	Dec. 13, 1828
Van Rypen Richard	Margaret Cadmus	Oct. 15, 1825
Van Steenwyck Peter Cor- nelise	Hendrickje Arentse	July 31, 1670

MALE.	FEMALE.	MARRIAGE DATE.
Van Tuyl Abraham	Metje Vreeland.	Dec. 8, 1738
Van Tuyl Michael	Saertje Hoeper	Aug. 3, 1766
Van Tuyl Michael	Sophia Cubberly.	Dec. 9, 1797
Van Voorst Cornelis	Fitje Gerrits	April 6, 1685
Van Voorst Cornelis	Claesie De Mott.	——, 1726
Van Vorst Garret	Cynthia Hennion	Dec. 25, 1810
Van Vorst Jacob.	Styntje Evertson	Jan. 21, 1809
Van Wagenen Cornelius	Catrina Sickles	Oct. 7, 1742
Van Wagenen Gerrit	Margrietje Van Winckel	March 22, 1746
Van Wagenen Gerrit Harmansen	Antje Sip	Oct 3, 1713
Van Wagenen Hartman	Catherine Newkirk	Aug. 16, 1812
Van Wagenen Helmigh	Maritje Blinckerhof.	Sept. 26, 1736
Van Wagenen Jacob.	Jannetje Van Houten	Oct. 7, 1742
Van Wagenen Jacob Gerritsen	Leah Gerrits	May 2, 1719
Van Wagenen Johannis	Aeltje Vreeland	Oct. 17, 1748
Van Wagenen Johannis	Neeltje Van Wagenen	Nov. 8, 1750
Van Wart Isaac	Sarah Van der Beek	June 15, 1816
Van Winckel Daniel	Rachel Straatmaker	May 15, 1707
Van Winckel Daniel	Jannetje Cornelise Vreeland	Sept. 3, 1709
Van Winckel Hendrick	Catreintje Waldron	May —, 1726
Van Winckel Henry	Catharine Van Wagenen	Jan. 10, 1801
Van Winckel Jacob Jacobse	Aeltje Daniels	Dec. 15, 1675
Van Winckel Jacob Jacobse	Grietje Hendricks Hollinge	March 26, 1695
Van Winckel Jacob Jacobsen Jr.	Fitje Poulus	March 26, 1703
Van Winckel Jacob Symonsen	Jacomyntje Mattheuse	April 21, 1701
Van Winckel Johannis Walingse	Hillegont Sippe	Sept. 30, 1710
Van Winckel Joseph	Janneke Vreeland, *widow* of Henry Newkirk	May 26, 1798
Van Winckel Symon Jacobse	Annetje Adrianse Sip	Dec. 15, 1675
Van Winckel Symon Jacobsen	Jannetje Alger	May 27, 1710
Van Winckel Waling Jacobse	Catherina Michielse	March 15, 1671
Van Winkle Abraham	Helen Evertson, *widow* of Daniel Perrine	Sept. 8, 1818
Van Winkle Cornelius	Margaret Van Rypen	Aug. 16, 1807
Van Winkle Garret	Cornelia Vreeland	Oct. 3, 1801
Van Winkle Jacob A.	Sally Cadmus	Feb. 7, 1808
Van Winkle Jacob D.	Ann Vreeland	Dec. 31, 1812
Van Winkle John G.	Ann Van Winkle	April 6, 1826
Van Winkle Joseph	Ann Cubberly	Nov. 23, 1805
Van Winkle Peter	Hannah Van Rypen	May 20, 1820
Van Winkle Walter	Phebe Tuers	May 21, 1807

MARRIAGE RECORD.

MALE.	FEMALE.	MARRIAGE DATE.
Van Woeglin Arie	Selytje Preyer	March 25, 1715
Vaveira Louis	Maria Machado	March 22, 1812
Vermeule Adriaen	Cathelyntje Hendrickse	July 1, 1708
Vreeland Abraham	Margrietje Jacobse Van Winckel	Oct. 28, 1699
Vreeland Abraham	Hannah Van Rypen	Nov. 30, 1816
Vreeland Claas	Catleintje Sip	Nov. 13, 1757
Vreeland Claas Hartmanse	Annetje Harmensen	May 24, 1697
Vreeland Cornelis Michielse	Metje Dirckse Braecke	May 12, 1681
Vreeland Cornelius C.	Catherine Outwater	Dec. 23, 1825
Vreeland Cornelius M.	Catherine Newkirk	Nov. 28, 1822
Vreeland Daniel	Cornelia Newkirk	Jan. 23, 1813
Vreeland Dirck Hartmanse	Margrietje Diedricks Banta	Oct. 20, 1702
Vreeland Elias Johannisen	Maritje Van Hooren	May 11, 1723
Vreeland Enoch J.	Sophia Ackerman	Jan. 23, 1828
Vreeland Enoch Michielse	Dirckje Meyers	June 20, 1670
Vreeland Enoch Michielse	Grietje Wessels	Aug. 23, 1691
Vreeland Enoch Michielse	Aagtje Van Hooren	Jan. 13, 1705
Vreeland Garret	Jane Winne	July 21, 1814
Vreeland Garret	Mary Smith	May 15, 1824
Vreeland Garret J.	Jane Vreeland	Dec. 19, 1822
Vreeland George	Catherine Newkirk	June 17, 1809
Vreeland Hartman	Maritje Gerbrant	Nov. 20, 1739
Vreeland Hartman	Eliza B. Gautier	Dec. 17, 1808
Vreeland Henry	Margaret Vreeland	Dec. 24, 1825
Vreeland Jacob	Catharine Brinkerhoff	Jan. 24, 1801
Vreeland Johannis	Helena Gerbrantse	June 21, 1778
Vreeland Johannis Johannisen	Antje Diedricks	————, 1726
Vreeland Johannis Michielse	Claesje Dirckse Braecke	May 14, 1682
Vreeland John	Polly Westervelt	July 30, 1796
Vreeland John	Hester Cadmus	March 17, 1804
Vreeland John	Rachel Mandeville	Nov. 19, 1818
Vreeland John G.	Catharine Van Houten	Feb. 1, 1817
Vreeland Michael	Maritje Toers	Nov. 27, 1691
Vreeland Michael	Geertje Sickles	Sept. 16, 1781
Vreeland Michael	Rachel De Groot	Feb. 13, 1796
Vreeland Michael	Annetje Garrabrants	Nov. 5, 1789
Vreeland Michael	Jane Van Derhoof	May 11, 1799
Vreeland Michael	Altje Outwater	Nov. 29, 1801
Vreeland Michael Hartmanse	Elysabet Gerrits	May 30, 1719
Vreeland Mindert	Catharine Cadmus	Jan. 18, 1823
Vreeland Nicholas	Hannah Winne	March 15, 1814
Vreeland Peter	Ann Vreeland	March 16, 1816
Vreeland Richard	Margaret De Mott	Dec. 9, 1815
Vreeland Stephen	Janneke Vreeland	Dec. 16, 1797
Vreeland Stephen	Altje Van Winkle, *widow* of John Mandeville	Nov. 29, 1828

MARRIAGE RECORD.

MALE.	FEMALE.	MARRIAGE DATE.
Vreeland Stephen	Elizabeth Van Rypen	Oct. 14, 1817
Vreeland William	Cornelia Vreeland	Jan. 30, 1814
Vreeland William	Catharine Sickles, *widow* of Leonard Johnson	Oct. 2, 1822
Wade Matthias	Eliza Ludlow	Sept. 28, 1822
Waldron Joseph	Antje Diedricks	Dec. 3, 1757
Waldron Joseph	Jemima Chambers	Dec. 27, 1807
Waldron Joseph	Sarah Van Derbeek, *widow* of Isaac Van Wart	Jan. 15, 1826
Wannamaker Abraham	Maria Wannamaker	April 5, 1817
Wannamaker Richard	Eliza Seely	June 10, 1820
Ward Alvah	Fanny Haff	July 4, 1818
Ward Peter	Maria Colfax	April 9, 1802
Warner Jacob	Hannah L. Farrington	Dec. 7, 1823
Wauters Garret	Cornelia Vreeland	Jan. 29, 1825
Webb, Dr. Edwin	Anna E. Hornblower	April 27, 1829
Welsh Alexander	Eliza G. Lynch	April 15, 1816
Welsh Archer G.	Margaret Stager	Dec. 25, 1823
Welsh Benjamin F.	Elizabeth Rapp	Jan. 3, 1810
Welsh Benjamin F.	Isabella Lewis	Feb. 26, 1820
Welsh Daniel	Catharine Van Winkle	Feb. 13, 1815
Welsh John	Leentje Steinmets	June 25, 1797
Welsh John	Gertrude Rapp	Aug. 7, 1811
West William	Hannah M. Tunis	Dec. 21, 1818
Westervelt Peter	Claesie Van Wagenen	Oct. 30, 1796
Westervelt William	Catherine Decker	Sept. 14, 1800
Wilbur Benjamin	Winckie Vreeland	April 15, 1797
Wilbur William	Eliza Osborn	Dec. 20, 1827
Williams John	Rebecca Smith	July 26, 1795
Willis Barney	Eliza Bryant	Nov. 21, 1813
Wilmarth William M.	Margaret Lyon	Feb. 10, 1818
Wilson John Alexander	Eliza Rose	July 22, 1818
Winne Edo	Aeltje Toers	Nov. 6, 1790
Winne Johannis	Aeltje Diedricks	Dec. 10, 1758
Winne John	Maria Mandeville	Dec. 11, 1790
Winne John S.	Mary Smith	Sept. 5, 1816
Winne Levinus	Annetje Sip	Oct. 8, 1749
Winne Martin	Rachel Van Winkle	April 1, 1797
Wood Abraham	Roeta. Clendenny	Oct. 12, 1783
Woods Walter	Sarah Post	March 6, 1818
Woods William	Mary Waldron	Feb. 28, 1820
Wright Daniel T.	Mary Field	May 11, 1806
Youmans Jeremiah	Letitia Oldis, *widow* of Lawrence Van Orden	Nov. 8, 1801
Zabriskie Albert	Machtelt Van de Linden	Dec. 17, 1676
Zabriskie Albert	Catharine Van Rypen	Nov. 7, 1822
Zabriskie Jacob	Catharine Van Houten	Dec. 12, 1801

MALE.	FEMALE.	MARRIAGE DATE.
Zabriskie Jacob	Catherine, *widow* of Helmigh Van Houten,	Jan. 3, 1829
Zabriskie John	Aegie Diedricks	June 11, 1805
Zabriskie John H.	Ann Winne	April 11, 1820

FEMALE.	MALE.	
Ackerman Ann	Beekman Van Buren	Dec. 4, 1819
Ackerman Jane	Philip Smith	March 27, 1822
Ackerman Sophia	Enoch J. Vreeland	Jan. 23, 1828
Ackerman Susan	Peter Earle	July 4, 1823
Alger Jannetje	Symon Jacobsen Van Winckel	May 27, 1710
Anderson Catherine	Obed Banker	April 4, 1824
Anderson Jane	Abraham Post	Nov. 27, 1819
Andries ———	Jan Slot	April 2, 1700
Andries Fransyntje	Roelof Swartwout	Nov. 22, 1691
Andriese Maritje	Pieter Marselis (?)	———, 1730
Andriese Rachel	Dirck Cornelise Comyn	Oct. 21, 1707
Andriesen Sarah	Casparus Prier	March 13, 1814
Arentje Hendrickje	Peter Cornelise Van Steenwyck	July 30, 1670
Armstrong Mary, *widow* of Henry Young	John Edwards	July 26, 1811
Ayres Jane	Abraham Decker	July 29, 1815
Bagtmens Ann, *widow*	Patrick Grimes	Feb. 3, 1796
Baker Margaret	Conrad Mindell	Sept. 4, 1793
Baldwin Annatje	John Miet	April 28, 1793
Banta Margrietje Diedricks	Dirck Hartmanse Vreeland	Oct. 20, 1702
Banta Rachel	Thomas Shepherd	June 29, 1824
Barber Mary	Jesse Bush	Oct. 12, 1812
Bayard Annetje	Henricus Sip	Nov. 22, 1691
Bear Maria	Haybrecht De Wolf	Sept. 23, 1798
Beekman Catelyntje	Peter Post	Nov. 17, 1710
Beeman Mary	Nehemiah Stephens	June 25, 1808
Belser Betje	Koobes Ackerman	Nov. 27, 1782
Bertse Maria	Johannis Vanderhoof	April 22, 1738
Blinkerhof Aegie	Abraham Sickles	April 1, 1739
Blinkerhof Margrietje	Mattys De Mott	May 6, 1705
Boas Maria	Hendrick Janse Van den Bos	Oct. 17, 1685
Bogert Jane	Garret Meyers	Dec. 18, 1799
Bond Helen	Garret Thorp	Oct. 3, 1804
Bond Julia	John Conkling	Nov. 30, 1803
Boskerck Anna	Burger Van Horne	Feb. 12, 1801
Boskerck Catherine	Jacob Van Horne	Feb. 18, 1826
Bowers Elizabeth	Isaac Carhart	Dec. 1, 1806
Boyd Charlotte	Robert Benson	May 4, 1822
Braecke Claesje Dirckse	Johannis Michielse Vreeland	May 14, 1682
Braecke Metje Dirckse	Cornelis Michielse Vreeland	May 12, 1681
Bridgart Sarah	William Clark	June 6, 1820
Brinkerhoff Catherine	Jacob Vreeland	Jan. 24, 1802
Brinkerhoff Clara	Merselis Clendenny	Nov. 3, 1803

MARRIAGE RECORD.

FEMALE.	MALE.	MARRIAGE DATE.
Brinkerhoff Clara	Henry De Mott	Jan. 25, 1806
Brinkerhoff Hannah	Matthias McDonald	Sept. 23, 1809
Brinkerhoff Maritje	Helmigh Van Wagenen	Sept. 26, 1736
Britain Catherine	Andrew Rapp	Oct. 2, 1823
Britain Phebe	John McLoughlin	Dec. 25, 1828
Brower Eleanor, *widow* of John Mersereau	Peter De Groot	Oct. 24, 1801
Brown Ann, *widow* of James Welsh	John Van Clief	Aug. 13, 1809
Brown Leah	William Kingsland	May 20, 1813
Budd Elizabeth	Abraham Tompkins	May 12, 1805
Budd Hannah	Absalom F. Randolph	Nov. 21, 1812
Budd Sally	Matthew Conkling	Nov. 30, 1803
Burnet Hannah	Jonathan Dixon	Dec. 13, 1794
Buys Hendrickje Janse	Rynier Van Giesen	Oct. 17, 1699
Buys Neeltje, *widow* of Jacob Vygerse	Jan Straatmaker	Jan. 27, 1707
Buys Neeltje Janse	Jan Hendrickse	June 23, 1684
Buys Treintje	Dirck Straatmaker	Nov. 27, 1698
Cadmus Catherine	David Brewer	June 22, 1824
Cadmus Catherine	Mindert Vreeland	Jan. 18, 1823
Cadmus Celia	Michael Van Rypen	Dec. 21, 1816
Cadmus Hester	John Vreeland	March 17, 1804
Cadmus Jane	Nicholas Van Buskirk	Dec. 15, 1814
Cadmus Jannetje	Andrew Anderson	May 23, 1801
Cadmus Margaret	Richard Van Rypen	Oct. 15, 1825
Cadmus Martha	Nicholas Prior	Dec. 18, 1817
Cadmus Sally	Jacob A. Van Winkle	Feb. 7, 1808
Carl Polly, *widow* of Toby Smith	Ezekiel Stillwell	Nov. 18, 1798
Carlock Elsje, *widow* of Tunis Quinn	John Van Dalson	Nov. 16, 1800
Chadwick Maria	Samuel C. Meeker	Dec. 3, 1818
Chambers Isabella	John S. O'Reily	July 13, 1819
Chambers Jemima	Joseph Waldron	Dec. 27, 1807
Claas Maritje	Gerbrand Claesen	Aug. 25, 1674
Claes Lysbet	Hessel Pieterse	June 24, 1690
Claes Pieterje	Jacobus Jansen Baldwin	Dec. 12, 1696
Claes Treintje	Tadeus Roelofse	Jan. 8, 1678
Claes Vrouwtje	Gerrit Steinmets	March 11, 1684
Clarke Nancy	Joseph Dodd, jr.	June 5, 1813
Clarke Rebecca	Joseph Jones	Jan. 13, 1825
Clendenny Eleanor	Hartman Brinkerhoff	Nov. 6, 1802
Clendenny Jane	Peter Garrabrants	Dec. 14, 1805
Clendenny Jane	Samuel Lamb	Jan. 26, 1812
Clendenny Mary	William Van Antwerp	Jan. 13, 1821
Clendenny Roeta	Abraham Wood	Oct. 12, 1783
Clendenny Sally	Cornelius Van Horne	Nov. 16, 1799
Cobus Jannetje	Antonio Sweet	May 8, 1693

FEMALE.	MALE.	MARRIAGE DATE.
Cobus Maritje	Frans Post	April 22, 1690
Cobusje Maritje	Arien Tomase	June 21, 1686
Cole Elizabeth	Walter Dixon	Dec. 26, 1803
Cole Elizabeth	Abraham Van Boskerck	May 1, 1805
Cole Elizabeth	Abraham A. Van der Beek	Feb. 11, 1817
Cole Sophia	Abraham Van Dalson	Dec. 1, 1814
Colfax Maria	Peter Ward	April 9, 1802
Collerd Annatje	Johannis Van Houten	Dec. 19, 1782
Collerd Gertrude	John T. Collerd	May 14, 1814
Compton Rachel	Samuel C. Ryerson	June 15, 1805
Cooper Margaret	James Lee	May 8, 1813
Coops Helena Catherine	Peter Baten	Dec. 27, 1795
Cornelis Annetje	Jan Hebbe	March 5, 1693
Cornelis Gerritje	Jacob Lubi	Sept. 4, 1672
Cornelis Neeltje	Hendrick Cornelise	June 9, 1669
Cornelis Sara	Jacob Mattheuse	May 15, 1707
Cornelison Elizabeth R.	Thomas McCrindell	June 12, 1827
Coulter Catherine	Anthony Tallman	Oct. 21, 1829
Coulter Eleanor	Thomas Boyd	Aug. 7, 1796
Coulter Eliza	Robert McFarlan	April 8, 1818
Coulter Peggy	Abraham Prine	Dec. 27, 1796
Cozine Margaret	John Carlton	Jan. 23, 1812
Crane Ann T.	Chauncey Morehouse	Feb. 16, 1822
Crane Julian	Caleb Negles	April 24, 1817
Crane Sarah	Isaac Seaman	Jan. 30, 1819
Cronk Mary	James G. Seaman	June 29, 1822
Cubberly Ann	Joseph Van Winkle	Nov. 23, 1805
Cubberly Elizabeth	Paul Salter	June 14, 1812
Cubberly Gitty	Jacob Ackerman	April 10, 1819
Cubberly Sophia	Michael Van Tuyl	Dec. 9, 1797
Daame Maritje Janse, *widow* of Jan Remse	James Simse	Sept. 10, 1697
Daniels Aeltje	Jacob Jacobse Van Winckel	Dec. 15, 1675
Daniels Annetje	Harman Smeeman	Dec. 9, 1668
Daniels Cornelia	Pieter Josi	April 6, 1686
Danielson Jane	Evert Greenlief	June 4, 1827
Day Ann	John Hartnet	Aug. 10, 1822
Day Esther	James Hadley	June 24, 1797
Day Johanna	Edward Earle	Feb. 13, 1800
Day Mary	William Avery	June 30, 1799
Day Mary	John Ingles	Nov. 26, 1808
Day Naomi	Henry Van Derhoof	May 6, 1797
Deas Euphemia, *widow* of Thomas Reed	George Pelor	May 13, 1805
De Gray Polly	David Earle	Aug. 24, 1800
De Groot Rachel	Michael Vreeland	Feb. 13, 1796
De Mott Claesie	Cornelis Van Vorst	———, 1726
De Mott Jane	Peter Merselis	May 28, 1822
De Mott Margaret	Richard Vreeland	Dec. 9, 1815

MARRIAGE RECORD. 347

FEMALE.	MALE.	MARRIAGE DATE.
De Mott Maria	James Cadmus	Feb. 28, 1828
Decker Catherine	William Westervelt	Sept. 14, 1800
Dezer Mary	Thomas Day	July 20, 1802
Dezer Peggy, *widow* of		
John Compton	Edward Corle	April 12, 1798
Diedricks Aegie	John Zabriskie	June 11, 1805
Diedricks Aegie, *widow* of		
Jacob Collerd	Jerry Van Rypen	Sept. 13, 1807
Diedricks Aegie	Jacobus Collerd	Nov. 29, 1829
Diedricks Aeltje	Johannis Winne	Dec. 10, 1758
Diedricks Altje	Daniel Van Clief	June 24, 1797
Diedricks Antje	Johannis Johannisen Vreeland	————, 1726
Diedricks Antje	Joseph Waldron	Dec. 3, 1757
Diedricks Jannetje	Peter Post	Feb. 7, 1795
Diedricks Neeltje, *widow* of		
Jan Van der Linden	Rutgert Van Hooren	April 25, 1697
Dircks (Van Noyer) Beelitje	Gerrit Jurianse	June 6, 1693
Douglas Eleanor	Bartel Jacobse	April 14, 1695
Du Bois Catharine	Abraham Cornelison	Feb. 13, 1795
Durant Elizabeth	Nicholas Garretson	May 25, 1823
Durant Johanna H.	Elias H. Johnson	March 10, 1821
Duryee Geertje, *widow* of		
Jacob Post	Nathaniel Earle	April 6, 1829
Duryee Keziah	Jacob Post	May 20, 1817
Earle Charity	William Earle	March 10, 1804
Earle Clara	Nathaniel Dezer	Nov. 12, 1799
Earle Elizabeth	John W. Earle	April 4, 1809
Earle Eleanor	Joseph Halenbeck	Feb. 7, 1802
Earle Jane	Joseph Archer	Jan. 6, 1806
Earle Leah, *widow* of James		
Van Horne	Rynier Earle	Feb. 24, 1805
Earle Mary	James Gardner	Dec. 30, 1807
Earle Mary	Abraham Shepherd	Sept. 12, 1812
Earle Mary	William W. Butts	July 6, 1816
Earle Patty	Josiah Conkling	Jan. 22, 1822
Eaton Rachel	William Lee	Oct. 22, 1808
Edsall Catharine	Jasper Maybee	Jan. 2, 1802
Egberts Dirckje	Pieter Pieterse	Nov. 18, 1683
Egberts Geertje	Levinus Ackerman	Aug. 3, 1679
Evans Hannah	Garret C. Van Rypen	May 28, 1817
Evertse Catlyntje	David Hennion	Dec. 21, 1782
Evertse Helena	Daniel Prine	July 25, 1791
Evertse Helena, *widow* of		
Daniel Prine	Abraham Van Winkle	Sept. 8, 1818
Evertson Cyntje	Lucas Denniston	Oct. 8, 1807
Evertson Jane	John Anderson	April 14, 1805
Evertson Styntje	Jacob Van Vorst	Jan. 21, 1809

FEMALE.	MALE.	MARRIAGE DATE.
Fairchild Eliza	Edward Gough	July 10, 1829
Fairchild Hetty	Stephen Garretson	Feb. 16, 1824
Farr Eliza Ann	Samuel Baker	Feb. 29, 1823
Farrell Mary	Hiram Harrison	Jan. 21, 1829
Farrington Hannah L.	Jacob Warner	Dec. 7, 1823
Femens Neeltje	Johannis Michielse	July 23, 1670
Field Mary	Daniel T. Wright	May 11, 1806
Fowler Elizabeth	Frederick William Curtenius	Feb. 15, 1826
Franse Meya	Johannis Spier	Aug. 12, 1679
Fraser Sophia, *widow* of Samuel Clark	Abel Armington	May 26, 1816
Fredrickse Maritje	Harman Juriansen	June 20, 1709
Gardner Caroline, *widow* of John Winans	Peter N. Garrabrants	Dec. 25, 1823
Garrabrants Annetje	Michael Vreeland	Nov. 5, 1789
Garrabrants Eleanor	Nicholas Prior	Sept. 20, 1827
Garrabrants Jane	James Van Buskirk, jr.	Dec. 20, 1821
Garrabrants Jane	Cornelius Van Horne	Jan. 21, 1810
Garrabrants Mary	Uriah Haff	Aug. 1, 1818
Garretson Catherine	Joseph Van Houten	Sept. 20, 1801
Garretson Esther, *wid.* of Christopher	John Mersereau	Aug. 3, 1794
Gautier Eliza B	Hartman Vreeland	Dec. 17, 1808
Gautier Margaret T	Garret Van Horne	Jan. 5, 1812
Gellard Elizabeth, *widow* of Peter Robertson	Aaron Vail	April 18, 1813
Gentleman Margaret, *wid.* of James Bay	Thomas Belton	Aug. 25, 1805
Gerbrands Maritje	Hendrick Coyeman	May 5, 1738
Gerbrands Neeltje	Jan Juriansen	April 7, 1702
Gerbrant Maritje	Hartman Vreeland	Nov. 20, 1739
Gerbrantse Helena	Johannis Vreeland	June 21, 1778
Gerbrantse Metje	Dirck Helmigse	Sept. 9, 1711
Gerrits Aeltje	Wander Diedricks	Nov. 27, 1693
Gerrits Annetje	Rutger Jansen	April 10, 1699
Gerrits Catrintje	Adrian Post	April 17, 1677
Gerrits Catrintje, *widow* of Adrian Post	Gerrit Steinmets	July 31, 1691
Gerrits Elysabet	Dirck Barentsen	April 11, 1704
Gerrits Elysabet	Michael Hartmanse Vreeland	May 30, 1719
Gerrits Fitje	Cornelis Van Vorst	April 6, 1685
Gerrits Jannetje	Christophel Steinmets	Oct. 6, 1684
Gerrits Leah	Jacob Gerritsen Van Wagenen	May 2, 1719
Gray Catharine Ann	John Graham	July 20, 1817
Greenlief Eliza	Henry Howell	Jan. 23, 1826
Gregory Abby	Alexander Dixon	Jan. 2, 1802
Griffin Sally	Johannis Everse	Dec. 21, 1782
Gysbertse Annetje	Frans Albertse	Nov. 12, 1683

MARRIAGE RECORD. 349

FEMALE.	MALE	MARRIAGE DATE.
Haff Fanny	Alvah Ward	July 4, 1818
Halenbeck Elizabeth	Thomas T. Gilleland	April 9, 1802
Halenbeck Mary	Pieter Greenlief	Dec. 25, 1804
Halsey Caroline	Stephen Paulmier	Dec. 7, 1824
Hanse Magdaleentje	Jan Aertsen Van der Bilt	Dec. 10, 1681
Harmensen Annetje	Claas Hartmanse Vreeland	May 24, 1697
Harris Mary	Gideon Van Clift	Oct. 24, 1802
Harrison Elizabeth	Abraham Evertson	May 6, 1797
Heathorne Phebe	William Marsh	Oct. 9, 1824
Helmigse Catelyntje	Johannis Gerritsen	Nov. 4, 1703
Helmigsen Grietje	Arie Sip	———, 1711
Hendricks Catalyntje	Barent Hendrickse Spier	Aug. 6, 1698
Hendricks Fitje, *widow*	Paulus Douwesen	May 3, 1702
Hendrickse Aeltje	Bastiaen Van Giesen	June 25, 1688
Hendrickse Cathelyntje	Adriaen Vermeule	July 1, 1708
Hendricksen Margrietje	Casparus Steinmets	Aug. 5, 1727
Hennion Ann	Thomas Rosman	July 12, 1820
Hennion Cynthia	Garret Van Vorst	Dec. 25, 1810
Hennion Fitje	Jacob Nieuwkerck	Feb. 13, 1769
Hennion Jane	Garret Van Rypen	Aug. 9, 1805
Hennion Mary	John Speer	July 30, 1803
Hill Eliza	Arie Thomas	Sept. 28, 1801
Hoeper Saertje	Michael Van Tuyl	Aug. 3, 1766
Holden Louise	Thomas Fidler	Jan. 10, 1799
Hollinge Grietje Hendricks	Jacob Jacobse Van Winckel	March 26, 1695
Hoppe Catherina	Frederick Tomase	Oct. 13, 1672
Hornblower Anna E	Edwin Webb, M. D	April 27, 1829
Hornblower Christiana	Gasharie De Witt	Nov. 13, 1819
Hornblower Elizabeth	Thomas B. Gautier	Oct. 15, 1816
Hubbins Dorcas, *widow* of George McIntyre	Moses Allen	Oct. 12, 1810
Hunt Ann	Peter Aymar	March 5, 1797
Hunt Charlotte	John Car	Feb. 13, 1802
Hunt Maria	Christopher Beekman	July 6, 1799
Hunt Phebe	Moses Crane	Jan. 1, 1803
Huyler Rachel	James Smith	Jan. 28, 1809
Huysman Catreintje	John Lisk	June 20, 1767
Jacobs Grietje	Hendrick Joost	May 23, 1665
Jacobs Hillegond	Jan Borton	Sept. 8, 1690
Jacobs Treintje	Caspar Steinmets	March 15, 1671
Jacobs Treintje	Michael Tades	June 8, 1667
Jacobse Annatje	Willem Day	April 14, 1691
Jacobse Hillegond	Evert Evertsen Van Borekelaer	June 7, 1707
Jacobse Treintje Hans	Pieter Pieterse	Oct. 3, 1687
Jans Grietje	Levinus Druyts	June 1, 1665
Jans Metje	Johannis Janse Van Blarcom	July 16, 1693
Jans Styntje	Hendrick Teunissen Hollinge	June 30, 1700
Jenkins Mary	William McKey	Dec. 31, 1803
Jerolamon Mary	Peter Van Horne	Oct. 4, 1824

FEMALE.	MALE.	MARRIAGE DATE
Jones, *widow*	John Dorstan	Aug. 6, 1794
Jurianse Chrystintje	Pieter Gerbrantse	Aug. 1, 1698
Jurianse Maritje	Claas Gerbrantse	April 11, 1704
Kuyper Catreintje	Garret Mattheusen Van Nieuwkerck	Sept. 5, 1730
Kuyper Elysabet	Willem Sickles	Aug. 10, 1732
Kuyper Grietje Claesen	Andries Hendricksen Cadmus	Oct. 22, 1725
Kuyper Sarah	Johannis Juriansen	Dec. 2, 1740
La Komba Magdaleena	Gysbert Jansen Van Blarcom	Jan. 16, 1706
La Tourette Jane	Samuel Lawson	Oct. 9, 1824
La Tourette Sarah	William Lee	Aug. 5, 1815
Lee Elizabeth	Thomas Moore	July 29, 1803
Lee Elsie	Peter Cowenhoven	March 23, 1805
Lee Mary	Rynier H. Earle	Nov. 24, 1810
Lee Nancy	James Ludlow	July 14, 1810
Lee Sarah	Moses A. Clark	Aug. 7, 1824
Lewis Isabella	Benjamin F. Welsh	Feb. 26, 1820
Lewn Susanna	Tomas Hendrickse	May 20, 1683
Lisk Antje	Jacobus McNeil	May 15, 1768
Lozier Elizabeth	George Carlock	Aug. 8, 1801
Lozier Jane	Abel Smith	Oct. 6, 1802
Lozier Leah	John C. Ackerman	April 19, 1808
Lubbertse Maritje	Hendrick Syckelse	Dec. 27, 1678
Lubi Anna	Mattheus Cornelise Van Nieuwkercke	Dec. 14, 1670
Ludlow Eliza	Matthias Wade	Sept. 28, 1822
Ludlow Ruth	Matthias Carlock	Oct. 7, 1797
Lynch Eliza G	Alexander Welsh	April 15, 1816
Lyon Ann	William Scott	April 2, 1799
Lyon Margaret	William M. Wilmarth	Feb. 10, 1818
Lyon Mary Ann	Henry Van Dalson, jr	Oct. 19, 1818
Lyon Rosanna B	John Churchill	Nov. 9, 1819
Lyon Sarah H	Asa Prior	Sept. 12, 1820
Machado Maria	Louis Vaveira	March 22, 1812
Maine Ann	Marvin P. Mix	Jan. 10, 1815
Mandeville Leah	Peter T. Mead	July 3, 1813
Mandeville Margaret	Garret De Mott	Jan. 16, 1813
Mandeville Rachel	John Vreeland	Nov. 19, 1818
Mandeville Sally	John Van Houten, jr	Dec. 20, 1821
Maseker Catherine	Nathaniel Thompson	Dec 29, 1798
Maybee Elizabeth	Jacob Post	April 5, 1797
Marsh Ann Eliza	Henry Lyon	Jan. 6, 1818
Mattheuse Gerritje	Aelt Jurianse	July 7, 1695
McWilliams Dolly	John Shay	Feb. 20, 1819
Meadow Eleanor	James Gray	March 26, 1822
Meeker Lydia, *widow* of		
George Abbot	Evertse Christianse	March 31, 1816
Merselis Catreintje	Rynier Van Giesen	April 17, 1737
Merselis Elysabet	Adrian Post	April 21, 1701
Merselis Hillegond	Herpert Gerbrantse	May 29, 1707

MARRIAGE RECORD. 351

FEMALE.	MALE.	MARRIAGE DATE.
Merselis Sally	Jacob Merselis	Sept. 13, 1828
Mesier Sarah V. D.	Robert Nicoll	April 14, 1812
Metsger Jane	Benjamin Decker	June 3, 1816
Metsger Peggy	Morris Earle	Nov. 17, 1804
Meyer Mary	Lewis F. Randolph	May 26, 1824
Meyers Dirckje	Enoch Michielse Vreeland	June 20, 1670
Michielse Catherina	Waling Jacobse Van Winckel	March 15, 1671
Michielse Pryntje	Andries Claesen	March 25, 1668
Millard Ann, *widow* of John	Seth Bishop	Oct. 5, 1809
Mills Jane	Stephen Seaman	June 3, 1819
Moore Margaret	Samuel Moore	Sept. 10, 1803
Moore Sally	James Moore	Sept. 17, 1796
Morris Melvina	Daniel Littlefield, jr	Oct. 24, 1824
Nagle Hannah E.	Cornelius Earle	July 28, 1804
Newkirk Catherine	George Vreeland	June 17, 1809
Newkirk Catherine	Hartman Van Wagenen	Aug. 16, 1812
Newkirk Catherine	Cornelius Van Rypen	Nov. 7, 1813
Newkirk Catherine	Cornelius M. Vreeland	Nov. 28, 1822
Newkirk Cornelia	Daniel Vreeland	Jan. 23, 1813
Newkirk Maritje	John Newkirk	Feb. 1, 1806
Nicolls Charlotte	Daniel Earle	Oct. 21, 1800
O'Brien Eliza	Joseph Rogers	July 26, 1811
Oldis Letitia, *widow* of Lawrence Van Orden	Jeremiah Youmans	Nov. 8, 1801
Oosteroom Tryntje Hendrickse	Ariaen Pieterse Buys	Sept. 30, 1672
Osborn Eliza	William Wilbur	Dec. 20, 1827
Osborn Hannah	Andrew Van Horne	April 10, 1802
Outwater Altje	Michael Vreeland	Nov. 29, 1801
Outwater Ann	Henry Mandeville	April 23, 1817
Outwater Catherine	Abraham Sickles	Dec. 8, 1798
Outwater Catherine	Cornelius C. Vreeland	Dec. 23, 1825
Perry Mary	John Betts	June 9, 1822
Pieters ———	Barent Barentsen Van Hooren	Feb. 23, 1712
Pieters Elsje	Claas Hartmanse	Aug. 19, 1699
Pieters Kiesje	Gerrit Gerritse, jr	May 11, 1681
Pieters Neeltje	Tomas Frausen	Sept. 29, 1706
Pieters Treintje	Hans Hendrickse	July 31, 1683
Pieterse Anna	Mattys Adolphus Hoppe	April 15, 1683
Pieterse Jannetje	Helmigh Roelofse	Sept. 3, 1676
Pieterse Rachel	Cornelis Cornelise Doremus	Aug. 12, 1710
Pluvier Busje	Jacob Van Giesen	June 1, 1693
Post Catherine	Peter Brower	April 10, 1796
Post Claretje	Peter Helmigse	April 8, 1703
Post Margaret, *widow* of Gifford Bryant	Louis Bartholomew	July 1, 1826

FEMALE.	MALE.	MARRIAGE DATE.
Post Jane	Daniel Van Rypen	Sept. 7, 1826
Post Maria	Jacob Van Clief	Dec. 25, 1823
Post Sarah	Walter Woods	March 6, 1818
Poulus Fitje	Jacob Jacobsen Van Winckel, jr	March 26, 1703
Pouluse Hilletje	Lubbert Lubbertse	March 14, 1680
Pray Mary S	Daniel Goodwin	Aug. 24, 1812
Preyer Pryntje	Petrus Stuyvesant	Oct. 27, 1733
Preyer Selytje	Arie Van Woeglin	March 25, 1715
Prior Abby	John E. Post	May 9, 1794
Prior Charity, *widow* of William Coulter	Robert McCubberry	Oct. 30, 1825
Prior Eleanor	John Outwater	Jan 25, 1800
Prior Geertje	Johannis Collerd	Dec. 19, 1782
Prior Gertrude	Merselis Merselis	July 26, 1800
Prior Mary	John Van Horne	Dec. 27, 1805
Prior Mary	Jacob Cubberly	Jan. 4, 1806
Prior Sarah	Cornelius Britain	Jan. 2, 1802
Provost Eliza	Henry Newkirk	July 23, 1818
Randall Maria F	Hiram L. Meeker	April 26, 1819
Rapp Ann	James Brower	June 25, 1804
Rapp Elizabeth	Benjamin F. Welsh	Jan. 3, 1810
Rapp Gertrude	John Welsh	Aug. 7, 1811
Renny Christiana	William Puker	Nov. 16, 1800
Riker Catharine Ann	John Garretson	Feb. 15, 1825
Riker Hannah	John G. Speer	Feb. 12, 1829
Roelofse Magliteltje	Jan Hendrickse	July 22, 1683
Roome Annetje	Robert Ido	Sept. 24, 1739
Roome Geertruy	Johannis Spier	April 29, 1739
Roos Antje	Cornelius Diedricks	June 7, 1735
Rose Eliza	John Alexander Wilson	July 22, 1818
Sanford Catherine	William Ford	March 17, 1808
Scharit Phebe Ann	Garret Lamberson	Jan. 1, 1825
Seely Eliza	Richard Wannamaker	June 10, 1820
Shepherd Margaret	Philip I. Earle	Jan. 13, 1823
Shepherd Maria	Samuel Osborn	Dec. 1, 1804
Shepherd Maria	Garret Ackerman	April 25, 1813
Shepherd Maria	William Layman	March 17, 1824
Shepherd Peggy	Cornelius Smith	Oct. 21, 1797
Shepherd Rachel	Garret Newkirk	Feb. 22, 1806
Sickles Ann	Michael Gadmus	June 9, 1827
Sickles Ann	William Seely	Aug. 8, 1802
Sickles Catharine, *widow* of Leonard Johnson	William Vreeland	Oct. 2, 1822
Sickles Catrina	Cornelius Van Wagenen	Oct. 7, 1742
Sickles Elizabeth	Beekman Smith	June 1, 1803
Sickles Geertje	Michael Vreeland	Sept. 16, 1781
Sickles Geertruy	Andries Prior	Oct. 8, 1750
Sickles Maritje	Abraham Pryer	Dec. 18, 1746

MARRIAGE RECORD.

FEMALE.	MALE.	MARRIAGE DATE.
Sickles Mary	Mindert Van Horne	Oct. 12, 1816
Sickles Mary	Cornelius Van Rypen	Sept. 15, 1827
Sickles Rachel	John Greenlief	Dec. 27, 1801
Sickles Syntje	Roelof Helmigse	Dec. 15, 1711
Siggelse Geertje	Johannis Pryer	June 14, 1745
Simonson Eliza	David Bush	Feb. 20, 1819
Simonson Eliza	George H. Slingerland	Feb. 19, 1825
Simonson Elizabeth	Garret Van Rypen	Jan. 14, 1815
Sip Annetje	Levinus Winne	Oct. 8, 1749
Sip Annetje Adrianse	Symon Jacobse Van Winckel	Dec. 15, 1675
Sip Antje	Gerrit Harmansen Van Wagenen	Oct. 3, 1713
Sip Ariantje	Ide Marselisse	April 11, 1754
Sip Catreintje	Claas Vreeland	Nov. 13, 1757
Sip Maritje Adrianse	Sibi Opdyke	Oct. 13, 1678
Sippe Hillegont	Johannis Walingse Van Winckel	Sept. 30, 1710
Sisco Lucretia	Nicholas Shiffer	Oct. 16, 1825
Skinner Camilla	John Coddington	Aug. 31, 1819
Slot Eva Jacobsen	Hendrick Van der Koeren	——— 1723
Slot Leah	Jacob Bronson	March 28, 1730
Smith Ann	Samuel Shepherd	Dec. 29, 1793
Smith Charity	Johannis Edsal	May 3, 1691
Smith Eliza, *widow* of Asa Leonard.	Stephen Simmons	May 30, 1807
Smith Ellen Ann	George De Mott	Jan. 18, 1827
Smith Mary	John Bedell	May 10, 1800
Smith Mary	John S. Winne	Sept. 5, 1816
Smith Mary	Garret Vreeland	May 15, 1824
Smith Rebecca	John Williams	July 26, 1795
Smith Sarah	John Evertson	Oct. 19, 1822
Spader Jane	John Sutphen	June 17, 1814
Speer Eleanor	Cornelius Cole	April 5, 1817
Speer Scytje	Johannis Everse	Aug. 20, 1744
Spier Annetje	Arent Toers	July 19, 1730
Spier Helena	Poulus Van Nieuwkercke	June 18, 1728
Stager Margaret	Archer G. Welsh	Dec. 25, 1823
Stagg Ann Matilda	Justus Earle	Oct. 5, 1822
Stagg Keziah	William Speer	June 5, 1796
Stagg Susan	Wassel Harsin	June 10, 1815
Steinmets Anna	Tades Michielse	Sept. 21, 1679
Steinmets Clara	John Rider	Feb. 19, 1804
Steinmets Johanna	Andries Pieterse	May 13, 1688
Steinmets Leentje	John Welsh	June 25, 1797
Steinmets Weseleena	Roelof Lubbers	March 25, 1688
Stewart Frances A	John K. Goodman	Dec. 15, 1822
Stilwell Eliza	Christopher De Green	May 31, 1819
Straatmaker Annetje	David Hartmanse	March 29, 1692
Straatmaker Jannetje	Tomas Jurianse	June 2, 1691
Straatmaker Margrietje	Hendrick Gerritsen	April 3, 1701
Straatmaker Rachel	Daniel Van Winckel	May 15, 1707
Straatmaker Tryntje	Jan Claesen	Oct. 8, 1694

FEMALE.	MALE.	MARRIAGE DATE.
Straet Lea	Gerret Post	Dec. 25, 1704
Sturge Elizabeth	Hugh Ludlow	Dec. 10, 1808
Sturge Eunice	Jacob Ackerman	Sept. 1, 1822
Sturge Susan	Edward Kealy	Dec. 24, 1808
Stuyvesant Jenneke	Hendrick Sickles	Feb. 1, 1767
Stuyvesant Mary	Peter Kip	Feb. 27, 1802
Stuyvesant Saertje	Egbert Post	Nov. 9, 1765
Tamsen Mary	Edward Jeffreys	———— 1720
Taylor Ann	Isaac McDonald	Dec. 25, 1824
Taylor Janse, *widow* of Jonas Tomkins	Valentine Kittleman	Oct. 3, 1805
Terhune Jane	Stephen Terhune	June 9, 1821
Teunise Aeltje	Cornelis Claesen	Dec. 20, 1681
Thorp Susan	Charles Clerke	Nov. 6, 1798
Toers Aeltje	Edo Winne	Nov. 6, 1790
Toers Maritje	Hendrick Hoppe	March 14, 1680
Toers Maritje	Michael Vreeland	Nov. 27, 1691
Toers Saertje	Tomas Jacobusse	Jan. 13, 1771
Tomas Catrina	Sjarel Machelsen	March 26, 1678
Tomas Fransyntje	Laurens Arentse Toers	Aug. 15, 1672
Tomase Catelyntje	Teunis Janse Prier	Oct. 6, 1684
Tomkins Eliza	Simeon Travis	Oct. 17, 1813
Town Hannah	Josiah Hornblower, jr	Oct. 15, 1812
Town Rachel	Abraham Stagg	Feb. 1, 1800
Trail Martha	Joseph Beadle	April 6, 1811
Trim Mary Ann	———— McElroy	May 16, 1822
Tucker Phebe	Daniel Cook	Oct. 18, 1807
Tuers Fanny	Joseph Shepherd	June 6, 1813
Tuers Phebe	Walter Van Winkle	May 21, 1807
Tunis Hannah M	William West	Dec. 21, 1818
Van Antwerp Elizabeth	Peter Aymar	Aug. 11, 1802
Van Blarcom Hannah	Nathaniel Cornelison	Dec. 26, 1804
Van Blercom Hester	Lourens Berdolf	Aug. 24, 1707
Van Boskercke Catharine,	Peter Garrabrants	Feb. 11, 1800
Van Burger Catrina Janse,	Abel Reddenhaus	July 26 1696
Van Buskirk Sarah	James B. Lane	Oct. 1, 1828
Van Clief Gitty	Abraham Britain	Dec. 22, 1825
Van Clief Mary	John Rapp	Dec. 16, 1813
Van de Vorst Annetje	Johannis Meyers	June 12, 1677
Van de Vorst Johanna	Jan Ariantje Sip	April 22, 1684
Van de Vorst Peterje	Merselis Pieterse	May 12, 1681
Van de Vorst Vrouwtje	Andries Meyers	Nov. 1, 1671
Van der Beek Gertrude	Matthew Clintock	Dec. 23, 1809
Van der Beek Rachel	John Denniston	April 30, 1813
Van der Beek Sarah, *widow* of Isaac Van Wart	Joseph Waldron	Jan. 15, 1826

MARRIAGE RECORD.

FEMALE.	MALE.	MARRIAGE DATE.
Van der Bilt Sarah	Abraham A. Tuers	Jan. 1, 1827
Van der Linden Machtelt,	Albert Zabriskie	Dec. 17, 1676
Van der Poel Ann Amanda, widow of James Wrangle,	Sylvester Van Buren	Jan. 1, 1801
Van der Swalin Constantia,	Pieter Gerritse	June 25, 1688
Van der Vorst Maria	Uldrick Brouwer	Oct. 8, 1738
Van Derhoof Eva	Peter Sickels	Oct. 8, 1791
Van Derhoof Jane	Michael Vreeland	May 11, 1790
Van Derhoof Maritje	Jacob Outwater	Sept. 30, 1797
Van Derhoof Sally	George Newkirk	Feb. 9, 1805
Van Deusen Maritje, wid. of Tymen Van Valen	Johannis Tomase	Dec. 24, 1705
Van Duesclten Sarah	Tomas Tomase	Sept. 17, 1701
Van Gelder Mariah	Abraham Moore	Jan. 25, 1794
Van Giesen Anna Mary	Johannis Janse	March 21, 1686
Van Giesen Magdaleena	Cornelis Roelofse	Nov. 14, 1677
Van Holton Henrietta W. E.,	Wm. Anthony Van der Heyden	Aug. 16, 1800
Van Hooren Aagtje	Enoch Michielse Vreeland	Jan. 13, 1705
Van Hooren Maritje	Elias Johannisen Vreeland	May 11, 1723
Van Hoorn Neeltje	Jurrie Van Rypen	Dec. 18, 1790
Van Horne Altje	Michael Van Houten	Dec. 15, 1793
Van Horne Altje, widow of Michael Van Houten	Cornelius Van Rypen	May 31, 1807
Van Horne Jane	Henry Brinkerhoff	Jan. 18, 1827
Van Horne Margaret	Oliver Taylor	Feb. 20, 1811
Van Horne Mary	Enoch Earle	July 29, 1804
Van Horne Peggy	Cornelius Van Buskirk	Dec. 24, 1800
Van Horne Rachel	David Braambush	March 26, 1795
Van Houte Elysabet Helmigse	Johannis Post	———, 1713
Van Houten Aegie	Myndert Garrabrants	Nov. 13, 1800
Van Houten Aegie	Richard Lyon	Feb. 13, 1811
Van Houten Catharine	Jacob Zabriskie	Dec. 12, 1801
Van Houten Catharine	John G. Vreeland	Feb. 1, 1817
Van Houten Catherine, widow of Helmigh	Jacob Zabriskie	Jan. 3, 1829
Van Houten Claesje	Hartman Brinkerhoff	Oct. 21, 1744
Van Houten Elizabeth	Hartman Brinkerhoff	Oct. 21, 1797
Van Houten Esther	Aaron Hoagland	Oct. 12, 1794
Van Houten Fitje	Jacob De Mott	Oct. 11, 1747
Van Houten Gertrude	Christopher Van Rypen	Dec. 27, 1802
Van Houten Hannah	Garret H. Ackerman	July 29, 1819
Van Houten Hannah	John Evertson	Oct. 19, 1822
Van Houten Jannetje	Jacob Van Wagenen	Feb. 3, 1818
Van Houten Letta	Peter Earle	July 28, 1816
Van Houten Rachel	Valentine Golden	Oct. 16, 1825
Van Houten Rachel	Garret Newkirk	Oct. 25, 1828
Van Lone Aeltje	Abraham Ackerman	May 13, 1683
Van Neste Sarah	Christophel Steinmets	——— —, 1699
Van Neste Jacomyntje	Claes Arentse Toers	July 8, 1684

MARRIAGE RECORD.

FEMALE.	MALE.	MARRIAGE DATE.
Van Nieuwkercke Jannetje	Garret Diedricks	April 21, 1733
Van Rypen Adriana	Philip R. Earle	March 6, 1812
Van Rypen Altje	John E. Smith	March 27, 1811
Van Rypen Catharine	Albert Zabriskie	Nov. 7, 1822
Van Rypen Catherine	Helmigh Van Houten	Dec. 7, 1799
Van Rypen Catreintje	Gerrit Van Rypen	March 2, 1799
Van Rypen Elizabeth	Daniel Van Rypen	Sept. 19, 1811
Van Rypen Elizabeth	Stephen Vreeland	Oct. 14, 1817
Van Rypen Hannah	John G. Van Horne	Dec. 19, 1812
Van Rypen Hannah	Abraham Vreeland	Nov. 30, 1816
Van Rypen Hannah	Peter Van Winkle	May 20, 1820
Van Rypen Isabella	John Van Buskirk	Nov. 20, 1814
Van Rypen Jannetje	Nicholas Toers	May 11, 1766
Van Rypen Margaret	Cornelius Van Winkle	Aug. 16, 1807
Van Rypen Nancy	Martin Tise	Dec. 24, 1829
Van Vorst Hannah	Benjamin Mecolen	July 25, 1812
Van Vorst Margrietje	Isaac Hennion	——, 1726
Van Vorst Neeltje	Henry Traphagen	Jan. 25, 1803
Van Wagenen Antje	Ide Sip	May 23, 1725
Van Wagenen Antje	Johannis Diedricks	Dec. 17, 1768
Van Wagenen Antje Gerritsen	Johannis Neesje	Oct. 9, 1710
Van Wagenen Catharine	Henry Van Winckel	Jan 10, 1801
Van Wagenen Claesie	Peter Westervelt	Oct. 30, 1796
Van Wagenen Jannetje	Hendrick De Mott	Oct. 30, 1740
Van Wagenen Leah	Hendrick Brinkerhoff	June 19, 1779
Van Wagenen Neeltje	Johannis Van Wagenen	Nov. 8, 1750
Van Wart Eliza	Garret C. Van Rypen	April 28, 1819
Van Wart Rachel	Michael Simmons	Oct. 17, 1829
Van Winckel Aeltje	Cornelius Gerritsen	June 29, 1728
Van Winckel Annetje Jacobse	Johannis Steinmets	Nov. 30, 1676
Van Winckel Geesje	Johannis Diedricks	May 2, 1724
Van Winckel Margrietje	Gerrit Van Wagenen	March 22, 1746
Van Winckel Margrietje Jacobse	Abraham Vreeland	Oct. 28, 1699
Van Winckel Trientje Jacobse	Myndert Gerbrantse	May 7, 1715
Van Winkle Aletta	John M. Cornelisen	May 22, 1826
Van Winkle Altje, *widow* of John Mandeville	Stephen Vreeland	Nov. 29, 1828
Van Winkle Ann	Peter Garrabrants	Feb. 15, 1814
Van Winkle Ann	John G. Van Winkle	April 6, 1826
Van Winkle Catharine	Daniel Welsh	Feb. 13, 1815
Van Winkle Catharine	James Holmes	Oct. 6, 1827
Van Winkle Effie	Aaron Tuers	Nov. 30, 1826
Van Winkle Eleanor	Abraham Toers	Jan. 29, 1809
Van Winkle Jannetje	Jacob Diedricks	Nov. 26, 1738
Van Winkle Margrietje	Johannis Jurianse, *widower*	Sept. 5, 1742
Van Winkle Maria	Garret Outwater	Dec. 25, 1822

MARRIAGE RECORD. 357

FEMALE	MALE	MARRIAGE DATE
Van Winkle Rachel	Martin Winne	April 1, 1797
Van Winkle Rachel	Peter Prine	Feb. 11, 1819
Van Wyck Mary	Peter D. Mesier	Nov. 1, 1800
Van Ziel Catharine	Jotham Lewis	Dec. 30, 1804
Van Ziel Keziah	John Seely	June 23, 1800
Vasher Frances	Robert Gilchrist	Oct. —, 1812
Veder Adriana, *widow of* Cornelius Hennion	Mungo Remsey	Feb. 8, 1803
Vincent Helen	Frederick Hoof	April 24, 1819
Vincent Phebe	David Mulford	Feb. 6, 1808
Vincent Sarah	Quintilian Cassedy	April 10, 1814
Vreeland Aagtje Cornelis	Roelof Helmigse	April 21, 1701
Vreeland Aagtje Hartmans	Cornelis Hendricksen Brinkerhoff	May 24, 1708
Vreeland Aagtje Johannissen	Cornelis Helmigsen	April 19, 1711
Vreeland Aeltje	Johannis Van Wagenen	Oct. 17, 1748
Vreeland Ann	Jacob D. Van Winkle	Dec. 31, 1812
Vreeland Ann	Abraham Collerd	March 14, 1813
Vreeland Ann	Peter Vreeland	March 16, 1816
Vreeland Ann	Tunis Van Pelt	Sept. 21, 1826
Vreeland Ariantje Hartmanse	Zacharias Sickles	Nov. 7, 1719
Vreeland Catharine	Aert Albertse	June 26, 1692
Vreeland Catherine	Henry Van Horne	Dec. 17, 1809
Vreeland Clara	George Van Rypen	July 23, 1814
Vreeland Cornelia	Garret Van Winkle	Oct. 3, 1801
Vreeland Cornelia	William Vreeland	Jan. 30, 1814
Vreeland Cornelia	Garret Wauters	Jan. 29, 1825
Vreeland Eliza	Stephen Terhune	June 1, 1815
Vreeland Elizabeth	Peter Sip	Nov. 1, 1789
Vreeland Elizabeth	George Cadmus	Nov. 14, 1812
Vreeland Elizabeth	John Cadmus	Dec. 3, 1814
Vreeland Elsje	Edward Earle, jr	Feb. 13, 1688
Vreeland Fitje Cornelise	Lourens Van Boskerck	Sept. 18, 1709
Vreeland Fitje Hartmans	Dirck Poulusen	Aug. 19, 1699
Vreeland Hannah	Nicholas C. Prior	Dec. 30, 1818
Vreeland Hannah	Abraham B. Cozine	Jan. 12, 1826
Vreeland Hester	Johannis Diedricks	April 14, 1739
Vreeland Jane	George De Mott	Oct. 1, 1808
Vreeland Jane	Garret J. Vreeland	Dec. 19, 1822
Vreeland Janneke	Stephen Vreeland	Dec. 16, 1797
Vreeland Jannetje	Aaron Newkirk	Nov. —, 1791
Vreeland Jannetje Cornelise	Daniel Van Winckel	Sept. 3, 1709
Vreeland Jenneke	Derrick Van Rypen	Oct. —, 1792
Vreeland Jenneke, *widow of* Henry Newkirk	Joseph Van Winckel	May 26, 1798
Vreeland Margaret	Jasper Cadmus	Dec. 17, 1817
Vreeland Margaret	Henry Vreeland	Dec. 24, 1825
Vreeland Maria	Peter Van Rypen	Dec. 13, 1828

MARRIAGE RECORD.

FEMALE.	MALE.	MARRIAGE DATE.
Vreeland Metje	Abraham Van Tuyl	Dec. 8, 1738
Waldron Ann	Abraham Prior	Dec. 20, 1796
Waldron Ann	John Mersereau	Sept. 26, 1818
Waldron Catreintje	Hendrick Van Winckel	May —, 1726
Waldron Mary	William Woods	Feb. 28, 1820
Waling Mary M	Abraham Folkner	June 20, 1827
Walings Elysabet	Joseph Arselse	May 6, 1678
Walingse Anna	Johannis Gerritse	Oct. 6, 1690
Wannamaker Maria	Abraham Wannamaker	April 5, 1817
Watson Rachel	John Clugston	April —, 1824
Wauters Hannah	Merrit Martin	Aug. 4, 1829
Welsh Mary	Isaac Britain	June 13, 1815
Wessels Grietje	Enoch Michielse Vreeland	Aug. 23, 1691
Westervelt Lucretia	John Day	Dec. 15, 1798
Westervelt Margrietje	Martin Poulusen	March 25, 1694
Westervelt Polly	John Vreeland	July 30, 1796
Westervelt Orseltje	Albertus Spier	June 5, 1744
Wier Ann J	James Emerson	Sept. 5, 1822
Wiley Mary Ann, *widow* of Parkman Townsend	Cornelius O'Donoghue	July 28, 1819
Williamson Sarah, *widow* of Vincent Hudson	James Garrabrants	April 19, 1815
Winne Ann	Peter Van Houten	Feb. 26, 1815
Winne Ann	John H. Zabriskie	April 11, 1820
Winne Antje	Robert Sickles	Oct. 8, 1749
Winne Hannah	Nicholas Vreeland	March 15, 1814
Winne Jane	Garret Vreeland	July 21, 1814
Winne Jannetje	Daniel Van Rypen	Nov. 19, 1785
Wright Mary	Patrick Jackson	Feb. 10, 1802
Wright Rachel	Henry Ludlow	Dec. 15, 1810
Wright Susanna	Peregrine Palmer	Aug. 20, 1817
Zabriskie Leah	William Boyd	Sept. 27, 1827

BIRTHS.

FATHER.	MOTHER.	CHILD.	DATE OF BIRTH.
Aarsen Matthew	Sophia Van Vorst	Johannis	July 28, 1744
Ackerman Abraham	Aeltje Van Laer	Adrian	March 26, 1695
Ackerman Garret	Maria Shepherd	John	June 1, 1814
Ackerman Garret	Maria Shepherd	Catharine V, W	Feb. 24, 1817
Ackerman Garret	Maria Shepherd	Gitty K	Dec. 14, 1819
Ackerman Garret	Maria Shepherd	George	Sep. 19, 1821
Ackerman Garret	Maria Shepherd	Jacob	Dec. 22, 1824
Ackerman Garret H	Hannah Van Houten	Rebecca Ann	July 3, 1820
Ackerman Garret H	Hannah Van Houten	Elizabeth	Sept. 5, 1822
Ackerman Garret H	Hannah Van Houten	Edward	Aug. 9, 1824
Ackerman Hendrick	Rebecca Halenbeck	Johannis	Sept. 10, 1780

BIRTH RECORD.

FATHER.	MOTHER.	CHILD.	DATE OF BIRTH.
Ackerman Hendrick	Rebecca Halenbeck	Edward	May 2, 1783
Ackerman Hendrick	Rebecca Halenbeck	Mary	Jan. 12, 1794
Ackerman Jacob	Gitty Cubberly	John	March 30, 1820
Ackerman Jacob	Gitty Cubberly	Thomas	Oct. 24, 1821
Ackerman Jacob	Gitty Cubberly	Mary	July 21, 1823
Ackerman Jacob	Gitty Cubberly	Peter	April 30, 1825
Ackerman John	Antje Dempsey	John	Nov. 20, 1778
Ackerman Lourens	Geertje Egberts	Jannetje (bap)	April 18, 1682
Ackerman Morris	Cornelia Smith	Lena	Oct. 12, 1806
Ackerman Morris	Cornelia Smith	John	March 17, 1808
Allen Samuel	Maria Shepherd	Allen D	June 29, 1821
Anderson Andrew	Jannetje Cadmus	Jane	April 6, 1802
Anderson Andrew	Jannetje Cadmus	George	Dec. 7, 1803
Anderson Andrew	Jannetje Cadmus	Mary	Jan. 1, 1806
Anderson Andrew	Jannetje Cadmus	Catherine	Sept. 21, 1807
Anderson Andrew	Jannetje Cadmus	John	March 30, 1810
Anderson Andrew	Jannetje Cadmus	Joanna Elizabeth	July 25, 1812
Anderson Andrew	Jannetje Cadmus	William	Aug. 14, 1814
Anderson Andrew	Jannetje Cadmus	Effie	Sept. 13, 1818
Anderson Andrew	Sally Van Rypen	Jane	May 6, 1807
Anderson John	Jannetje Evertson	Catherine	March 29, 1809
Anderson John	Jannetje Evertson	Elizabeth	Nov. 10, 1811
Anderson John	Jannetje Evertson	Christina	} Jan. 17, 1814
Anderson John	Jannetje Evertson	Rachel V. R	
Anderson William	Sarah Van Rypen	Mary	Aug. 24, 1802
Anderson William	Sarah Van Rypen	John	Dec. 25, 1803
Anderson William	Sarah Van Rypen	Mary	July 29, 1805
Anderson William	Sarah Van Rypen	Thomas	Sept. 9, 1809
Anderson William	Sarah Van Rypen	Elizabeth V	Sept. 18, 1811
Anderson William	Sarah Van Rypen	Ann D	Sept. 13, 1814
Anderson William	Sarah Van Rypen	Catherine	March 3, 1817
Anderson William	Sarah Van Rypen	Catherine	April 22, 1820
Andriesen Lourens	Jannetje Jans	Pieter (bap)	Jan. 1, 1666
Banta Arie	Leena Westervelt	Aegie	April 2, 1786
Banta Gerrit	Neeltje Gerbrantse	Cornelis	Aug. 8, 1766
Banta Hendrick	Margrietje Diedricks	Hendrick	Nov. 21, 1785
Banta Wiert	Leah De Groot	Pieter	Feb. 16, 1766
Barentse Cornelis	Cornelia Hendrickse	Barent (bap)	April 17, 1677
Barley Samuel	Mary Woods	Ruth Ann	Dec. 9, 1819
Barr David	Maria Meyers	Jane	Jan. 10, 1805
Barr David	Maria Meyers	David	Aug. 19, 1808
Bertholf Guilliam	Mareteintje Hendricks	Hendrick (bap)	April 6, 1686
Bertings Jan	Hillegont Jacobs	Annetje (bap)	March 26, 1695
Blinkerhoff Cornelis	Aagtje Vreeland	Maritje	Feb. 27, 1709
Blinkerhoff Cornelis	Aagtje Vreeland	Claesje	Dec. 31, 1710
Blinkerhoff Cornelis	Aagtje Vreeland	Hendrick	Dec. 13, 1713
Blinkerhoff Cornelis	Aagtje Vreeland	Aegie	March 23, 1715
Blinkerhoff Cornelis	Janneke Kip	Hendrick	Dec. 31, 1770
Blinkerhoff Hendrick	Leah Van Wagenen	Hartman	April 15, 1781

BIRTH RECORD.

FATHER.	MOTHER.	CHILD.	DATE OF BIRTH.
Blinkerhoff Hendrick	Leah Van Wagenen	Catleyntje	July 13, 1784
Blinkerhoff Hendrick	Leah Van Wagenen	Claesje	April 8, 1788
Blinkerhoff John	Sally Smith	Sara	Feb. 17, 1787
Bly Yorgwells	Roos Gilbert	Abigail	Oct. 8, 1775
Bokee Abraham	Janneke Jacobse	Janneke (bap)	April 2, 1688
Bokee Abraham	Janneke Jacobse	Jacob (bap)	April 22, 1690
Bosch Michael	Antje Smith	Jannetje	June 19, 1798
Bougert Jan Cornelise	Angemitje Streickers	Jacob (bap)	June 23, 1679
Bougert Jan Cornelise	Angemitje Streickers	Rachel (bap)	April 18, 1682
Boyd Thomas	Nellie Coulter	Andrew	Nov. 30, 1798
Boyd Thomas	Nellie Coulter	John	Jan. 10, 1810
Braembush David	Rachel Van Horne	Catrina	Sept. 29, 1795
Braman John	Ann Agnes Beauman	Eliza L	June 14, 1815
Brinkerhoff Hartman	Neeltje Clendenny	Hendrick	Aug. 28, 1803
Brinkerhoff Hartman	Neeltje Clendenny	Walter C	Aug. 8, 1805
Brinkerhoff Hartman	Neeltje Clendenny	Cornelius	Aug. 26, 1806
Brinkerhoff Hartman	Neeltje Clendenny	John V. W	Sept. 27, 1812
Brinkerhoff Hartman	Neeltje Clendenny	Janet M	Feb. 27, 1816
Brinkerhoff Hartman	Neeltje Clendenny	Leah Ann	April 29, 1819
Brisday Berney	Polly Berdet	Louise	June 20, 1772
Britain Cornelius	Sally Prior	Abraham	March 12, 1803
Britain Cornelius	Sally Prior	Catherine	Nov. 25, 1804
Britain Cornelius	Sally Prior	Phebe	July 21, 1807
Britain Cornelius	Sally Prior	Phebe	July 21, 1809
Britain Cornelius	Sally Prior	Mary	March 27, 1811
Britain Cornelius	Sally Prior	Eleanor P	March 21, 1813
Britain Cornelius	Sally Prior	Cornelius	Feb. 13, 1815
Britain Cornelius	Sally Prior	Andrew	Nov. 5, 1816
Britain Cornelius	Sally Prior	Nathaniel	Oct. 9, 1818
Brooks Richard	Sarah Brooks	Yardes	April 27, 1777
Brouwer Jacob	Lea Slop	Johannis	Feb. 6, 1731
Brouwer Jacob	Lea Slop	Coobis	Sept. 30, 1735
Brouwer Jacob	Lea Slop	Hester	Sept. 6, 1739
Brouwer Uldrick	Hester Du Bois	Abraham	March 9, 1701
Brouwer Uldrick	Hester Du Bois	Isaac	Jan. 30, 1703
Brouwer Uldrick	Hester Du Bois	Jacob	Sept. 11, 1705
Brower Jacobus	Jannetje Van Saen	Jannetje	Dec. 30, 1770
Brower Jacobus	Jannetje Van Saen	Jacobus	Aug. 7, 1783
Brower Johannis	Catrina Waldron	Jacob	April 13, 1762
Brower Johannis	Catrina Waldron	Joseph	Sept. 16, 1763
Brower Johannis	Catrina Waldron	Leah	Dec. 25, 1765
Brower Uldrick	Maria Van de Vorst	Johannis	June 19, 1739
Brower Uldrick	Maria Van de Vorst	Abraham	July 26, 1743
Brower Uldrick	Maria Van de Vorst	Thomas	Feb. 3, 1746
Browning William	Mary Ann Garretson	Elizabeth Ann	Oct. 28, 1821
Browning William	Mary Ann Garretson	Mary	Oct. 26, 1822
Browning William	Mary Ann Garretson	William G	March 26, 1825
Bush David	Eliza Simmons	Elizabeth Jane	April 20, 1820
Bush David	Eliza Simmons	Garret	Jan. 12, 1823
Bush David	Eliza Simmons	Eleanor Maria	Dec. 10, 1824

BIRTH RECORD.

FATHER.	MOTHER.	CHILD.	DATE OF BIRTH.
Buys Arien Pieterse	Treintje Hendrickse (Oostrum)	Gertruyt (bap)	Jan. 15, 1678
Buys Arien Pieterse	Treintje Hendrickse (Oostrum)	Pieter (bap)	Dec. 12, 1679
Buys Arien Pieterse	Treintje Hendrickse (Oostrum)	Geertruyt	April 24, 1682
Buys Arien Pieterse	Treintje Hendrickse (Oostrum)	Hendrick (bap)	April 2, 1684
Buys Arien Pieterse	Treintje Hendrickse (Oostrum)	Jacob (bap)	Oct. 11, 1686
Buys Arien Pieterse	Treintje Hendrickse (Oostrum)	Johannis (bap)	April 2, 1689
Buys John	Annatje Merselis	Daniel	June 10, 1775
Cadmus Casparus	Catlyntje Dod	Saertje	
Cadmus Casparus	Catlyntje Dod	Joris	Dec. 4, 1789
Cadmus Casparus	Catlyntje Dod	John	Feb. 21, 1792
Cadmus Casparus	Catlyntje Dod	Casparus	Jan. 10, 1794
Cadmus Casparus	Catlyntje Dod	Jenneke	Dec. 22, 1795
Cadmus Casparus	Catlyntje Dod	Seelitje	Oct. 24, 1797
Cadmus Casparus	Catlyntje Dod	Martha	Dec. 7, 1799
Cadmus Casparus	Catlyntje Dod	Michael	Oct. 27, 1801
Cadmus Casparus	Catlyntje Dod	Richard	Nov. 22, 1803
Cadmus Casparus	Catlyntje Dod	Catherine	Jan. 15, 1806
Cadmus Casparus	Catlyntje Dod	Andrew	March 14, 180
Cadmus Casparus	Catlyntje Dod	Eleanor	May 21, 1810
Cadmus Dirck	Jannetje Van Hooren	Neeltje	June 23, 1736
Cadmus Dirck	Jannetje Van Hooren	Catharina	May 27, 1738
Cadmus Dirck	Jannetje Van Hooren	Andries	Oct. 28, 1733
Cadmus George	Elizabeth Vreeland	Jasper	Oct. 30, 1813
Cadmus John	Elizabeth Vreeland	Rachel	Sept. 6, 1816
Cadmus John	Elizabeth Vreeland	Catherine	Nov. 28, 1818
Cadmus John	Elizabeth Vreeland	Jasper	Oct. 30, 1821
Cadmus John	Elizabeth Vreeland	Elizabeth	Dec. 8, 1823
Cadmus Joris	Jannetje Vreeland	Jenneke	June 17, 1753
Cadmus Joris	Jannetje Vreeland	Jannetje	Jan 7, 1758
Cadmus Joris	Jannetje Vreeland	Jannetje	March 17, 1759
Cadmus Joris	Jannetje Vreeland	Joris	Oct. 10, 1761
Cadmus Joris	Jannetje Vreeland	Metje	Dec. 22, 1764
Cadmus Joris	Jenneke Preyer	Dirck	March 16, 1769
Cadmus Joris	Jenneke Preyer	Casparus	Aug. 16, 1770
Cadmus Joris	Aegie Fielding	Jannetje	Feb. —, 1780
Cadmus Joris	Aegie Fielding	Aegie	Jan. —, 1784
Cadmus Joris	Aegie Fielding	Margrietje	Sept. 14, 1795
Cadmus Joris	Aegie Fielding	Henry	Aug. 19, 1796
Cadmus Peter	Blandina Kip	Elisabet	March 3, 1776
———— ————	Keetje Caelden	Margrietje Van Winkle	May 2, 1779
Cain James	Maritje Van Tuyl	Sarah	March 3, 1797
Caljer Jacobus	Geertje Diedricks	Jacobus	Oct. 9, 1765

FATHER.	MOTHER.	CHILD.	DATE OF BIRTH.
Car David	Antje Westervelt	Polly	Feb. 10, 1799
Cassedy Samuel	Eliza H. Strachan	William S	June 8, 1819
Cassedy Samuel	Eliza H. Strachan	Caroline	Jan. 2, 1822
Cavalier Johannis	Catlyntje ——	Margrietje	Sept. 24, 1733
Ceunnel Christian	Dirckje Verveule	Sara	July 17, 1767
Ceunnel Christian	Dirckje Verveule	Elisabet	Oct. 13, 1770
Christianse Barrent	Claesje Dircks	Jannetje	May 25, 1627
Claesen Andries	Pryntje Michielse	Sarah	Sept. 16, 1691
Claesen Cornelis	Aeltje Teunise Bougert	Claas	April 2, 1689
Claesen Cornelis	Aeltje Teunise Bougert	Hillegont	June 6, 1700
Claesen Gerbrand	Maritje Claes	Herpert	Nov. 12, 1679
Claesen Gerbrand	Maritje Claes	Cornelis	Jan. 24, 1689
Claesen Gerbrand	Maritje Claes	Meyndert	June 12, 1691
Claesen Gerbrand	Maritje Claes	Gertrude	April 16, 1696
Claesen Hendrick	Jannetje ——	Catrina	——, 1710
Claesen Hendrick	Jannetje ——	Annetje	April 13, 1712
Claesen Jan	Treintje Straatmaker	Giesje	March 26, 1695
Claesen Jan	Treintje Straatmaker	Claas	Nov. 30, 1696
Claesen Jan	Treintje Straatmaker	Annetje	June 30, 1698
Clendenny Merselis	Elizabeth Herring	Walter	June 11, 1805
Clendenny Merselis	Elizabeth Herring	Abraham	Jan. 4, 1807
Clendenny Merselis	Clara Brinkerhoff	Hartman B	May 28, 1810
Clendenny Merselis	Clara Brinkerhoff	John B	Oct. 23, 1811
Clendenny Merselis	Elizabeth Van Horne	John V. H	Dec. 22, 1818
Clendenny Walter	Jenneke Merselis	Merselis	Nov. 24, 1778
Clendenny Walter	Jenneke Merselis	Neltje	July 9, 1781
Clendenny Walter	Jenneke Merselis	Jannetje	March 4, 1787
Clendenny Walter	Jenneke Merselis	Elizabeth	June 24, 1789
Clendenny Walter	Jenneke Merselis	Nancy	Jan 27, 1792
Clendenny Walter jr.	Osseltje Duryee	Sally	Nov. 10, 1793
Clendenny Walter jr.	Osseltje Duryee	Jane	Nov. 7, 1796
Clendenny Walter jr.	Osseltje Duryee	Rebecca	Feb. 11, 1801
Clendenny Walter jr.	Osseltje Duryee	Walter	Jan. 16, 1803
Clendenny Walter jr.	Osseltje Duryee	James P. M	Aug. 3, 1805
Cocks Robert	Mary Lee	Mary Jane	Jan. 1, 1807
Cole John	Dosie Fulwood	Sophia	Aug. 19, 1793
Cole John	Dosie Fulwood	Susanna	Sept. 8, 1795
Cole John	Dosie Fulwood	Charlotte	Sept. 1, 1803
Cole John	Dosie Fulwood	Esther P	April 24, 1806
Collerd Abraham	Ann Vreeland	Jacob	Jan. 30, 1820
Collerd Abraham	Ann Vreeland	Abraham	June 25, 1822
Collerd Jacobus	Aegie Diedricks	Abraham	Oct. 17, 1790
Collerd Jacobus	Aegie Diedricks	Jacobus	June 20, 1793
Collerd Jacobus	Aegie Diedricks	Geertje	Nov. 11, 1795
Collerd Johannis	Geertruy Prior	Johannis	Sept. 9, 1783
Collerd Johannis	Geertruy Prior	Jacobus	Dec. 19, 1785
Collerd Johannis	Geertruy Prior	Geertruy	June 15, 1788
Collerd Johannis	Geertruy Prior	Hendrick	Oct. 23, 1790
Collerd Jurrie	Polly Tolder	Annatje	March 21, 1776
Cornelise Mattheus	Anna Lubi	Grietje (bap)	July 23, 1673

BIRTH RECORD.

FATHER.	MOTHER.	CHILD.	DATE OF BIRTH.
Cornelise Mattheus	Anna Lubi	Jacomyntje (bap)	April 2, 1678
Cornelise Mattheus	Anna Lubi	Cornelis (bap)	March 11, 1680
Cornelise Mattheus	Anna Lubi	Jacob (bap)	Nov. 21, 1682
Cornelise Mattheus	Catrina Poulus	Jannetje	July 8, 1687
Cornelise Mattheus	Catrina Poulus	Treintje	Dec. 17, 1688
Cornelise Mattheus	Catrina Poulus	Jan	April 22, 1690
Cornelise Mattheus	Catrina Poulus	Jannetje (bap)	March 17, 1692
Cornelise Mattheus	Catrina Poulus	Pieter	Aug. 26, 1694
Cornelise Mattheus	Catrina Poulus	Gerrit	Nov. 18, 1696
Cornelise Mattheus	Catrina Poulus	Poulus	Aug. 21, 1699
Cornelise Mattheus	Catrina Poulus	Cornelis	Sept. 3, 1703
Cornelise Pieter	Hendrickje Aerts	Cornelis	April 18, 1676
Cornelise Pieter	Hendrickje Aerts	Arent (bap)	Oct. 7, 1678
Cornelise Pieter	Hendrickje Aerts	Andries (bap)	Aug. 21, 1681
Cornelise Pieter	Hendrickje Aerts	Andries (bap)	June 30, 1684
Cornelison Rev. John	Catherine Mesier	John	Feb. 24, 1794
Cornelison Rev. John	Catherine Mesier	Mary M	July 31, 1797
Cornelison Rev. John	Catherine Mesier	John M	April 29, 1802
Cornelison Rev. John	Catherine Mesier	Elizabeth	Aug. 6, 1804
Cornelison Rev. John	Catherine Mesier	William Henry	April 23, 1807
Cornelison Rev. John	Catherine Mesier	Helen Amelia	Jan. 8, 1811
Cornelison Michael	Rachel Bearmore	Elizabeth	Feb. 6, 1794
Coulter Andrew	Isabella Gamble	William	Sept. 8, 1820
Coulter William	Geertje Prior	Mary	Nov. 11, 1795
Coulter William	Geertje Prior	Andrew	May 19, 1798
Coulter William	Geertje Prior	Catherine	Sept. 21, 1800
Coulter William	Geertje Prior	Elizabeth	Jan. 16, 1802
Coulter William	Geertje Prior	Harriet	May 10, 1804
Coulter William	Geertje Prior	Catherine	Dec. 1, 1806
Coulter William	Geertje Prior	William Henry	Feb. 20, 1809
Coulter William	Geertje Prior	Walter	June 4, 1811
Coulter William	Geertje Prior	Jacob	April 4, 1813
Coulter William	Geertje Prior	Julia Ann	Aug. 27, 1814
Coulter William	Geertje Prior	Jacob	Jan. 11, 1817
Coulter William	Geertje Prior	Mary	Jan. 11, 1817
Coulter William	Geertje Prior	Charity	April 21, 1819
Craig Andrew	Catherine Ferguson	Mary Elizabeth	Nov. 14, 1814
Craig Andrew	Catherine Ferguson	Helen	July 9, 1816
Creeven Tomas	Jannetje ———	Anna (bap)	April 14, 1691
Crum Henry	Mary Mesler	Elizabeth	July 31, 1801
Crystyn Jan	Helena Been	Margrietje (bap)	April 14, 1691
Cubberly Jacob	Polly Prior	Thomas	Nov. 6, 1806
Cubberly Jacob	Polly Prior	Catherine	Dec. 19, 1807
Cubberly Jacob	Polly Prior	Ann	Feb. 11, 1810
Cubberly Jacob	Polly Prior	Thomas	Feb. 11, 1812
Cubberly Jacob	Polly Prior	Mary M	Dec. 24, 1813
Cubberly Jacob	Polly Prior	Eleanor	May 28, 1816
Cubberly Jacob	Polly Prior	Jasper	Aug. 13, 1818
Cubberly Jacob	Polly Prior	Eliza	Jan. 22, 1822
Cubberly Thomas	Mary Mersereau	Ann	Nov. 14, 1780

FATHER.	MOTHER.	CHILD.	DATE OF BIRTH.
Cubberly Thomas	Mary Mersereau	Sophia	Nov. 10, 1782
Cubberly Thomas	Mary Mersereau	Thomas	March 7, 1794
Cubberly Thomas	Mary Mersereau	Gitty	March 12, 1798
Curtenius Peter	Mary Lozier	John	April 1, 1801
Cuzzy Joseph	Mary Wannamaker	William	June 23, 1812
Day Barnabas	Mary Burdet	Davit	June 5, 1767
Day Willem	Annetje Jacobs	Hester (bap)	June 2, 1691
Day Willem	Annetje Jacobs	Jacob	May 11, 1695
Day Willem	Annetje Jacobs	Johannis	Nov. 3, 1697
Day Willem	Annetje Jacobs	Johannis	Sept. 26, 1699
Day Willem	Annetje Jacobs	Hendrick	Feb. 20, 1704
Day Willem	Annetje Jacobs	Jenneke	Sept. 17, 1706
Day William	Margaret Herring	Phebe	July 30, 1806
De Grau Abel	Maayke Van Eiderstyn	Casparus	Oct. 15, 1758
De Grau Abel	Maayke Van Eiderstyn	Johannis	April 30, 1762
De Grau Abel	Maayke Van Eiderstyn	Cornelis	June 9, 1770
De Groot ————	Berber Caspers	Metje (bap)	June 24, 1678
De Groot Pieter	Hester Brouwer	Leya	June —, 1759
De Maree Davit, Jr.	Rachel Lerson	Susanna (bap)	April 7, 1679
De Maree Davit, Jr.	Rachel Lerson	Rachel (bap)	June 21, 1680
De Maree Jan	Jacobmyntje Douwen	Lea (bap)	April 18, 1682
De Maree Samuel	Mary Davison	Davit (bap)	Oct. 3, 1681
De Maree Smit François,	Catelyntje Cortens	Pryntje (bap)	April 6, 1686
De Mott Garret	Margaret Mandeville	Elizabeth	March 14, 1814
De Mott Garret	Margaret Mandeville	Michael	June 15, 1816
De Mott Garret	Margaret Mandeville	Mary M	March 3, 1820
De Mott Garret	Margaret Mandeville	Margaret Elizabeth	Sept. 23, 1824
De Mott George	Jane Vreeland	Maria M	Aug. 11, 1816
De Mott George	Jane Vreeland	Garret	Jan. 7, 1820
De Mott George	Jane Vreeland	George	April 27, 1822
De Mott Hendrick	Claesje Brinkerhoff	Lea	Nov. 23, 1806
De Mott Hendrick	Claesje Brinkerhoff	Michael	March 31, 1809
De Mott Hendrick	Claesje Brinkerhoff	Henry B	Dec. 1, 1813
De Mott Mattys	Margrietje Blinkerhoff	Michael	Aug. 7, 1708
De Mott Mattys	Margrietje Blinkerhoff	Antje	Dec. 24, 1711
De Mott Mattys	Margrietje Blinkerhoff	Johannis	Aug. 7, 1716
De Mott Mattys	Margrietje Blinkerhoff	Joris	Nov. 3, 1718
De Mott Mattys	Margrietje Blinkerhoff	Jacob	Feb. 22, 1720
De Mott Mattys	Margrietje Blinkerhoff	Maritje	April 15, 1723
De Mott Michael	Maritje Mandeville	Joris	June 1, 1787
De Mott Michael	Maritje Mandeville	Garret	Nov. 4, 1789
De Mott Michael	Maritje Mandeville	Johannis	July 8, 1792
De Mott Michael	Maritje Mandeville	Margrietje	March 27, 1795
De Mott Michael	Maritje Mandeville	Jannetje	Dec. 31, 1797
De Mott Michael	Maritje Mandeville	Maria	April 23, 1802
De Mott Michael	Maritje Mandeville	Cathelina	May 6, 1807
De Vael Ned	Nancy ————	Emma	———, 1786
De Vouw Nicola	Mary Esi	Susanna (bap)	Oct. 11, 1680
De Witt Gasherie	Christiana Hornblower	Anna Maria	Aug. 29, 1820

BIRTH RECORD.

FATHER.	MOTHER.	CHILD.	DATE OF BIRTH.
De Witt Gasherie	Christiana Hornblower	Gasherie	June 10, 1822
Denniston Lucas	Cynthia Evertson	Elizabeth	July 21, 1813
Denniston Lucas	Cynthia Evertson	James	} May 25, 1818
Denniston Lucas	Cynthia Evertson	Isaac	
Denniston Lucas	Cynthia Evertson	Hannah Maria	May 14, 1821
Denniston Lucas	Cynthia Evertson	Elizabeth Jane	Feb. 6, 1825
Dewing Michael	Ruth Cabwin	Jared	Sept. 29, 1790
Dey John	Femmetje Crein	Benjamin	Sept. 22, 1788
Dey John	Femmetje Crein	Peter	Oct. 2, 1790
Diedricks Abraham	Geertruy Bow	Antje	Sept. 11, 1740
Diedricks Abraham	Geertruy Bow	Johannis	April 9, 1743
Diedricks Abraham	Geertruy Bow	Aeltje	March 20, 1747
Diedricks Abraham	Geertruy Bow	Margrietje	April 1, 1751
Diedricks Cornelis	Antje Roos	Aeltje (bap)	Sept. 28, 1735
Diedricks Daniel	Aegie Sickles	Jannetje	June 16, 1769
Diedricks Daniel	Aegie Sickles	Aegie	Jan. 9, 1772
Diedricks Daniel	Aegie Sickles	Antje	Nov. 15, 1779
Diedricks Jacob	Jannetje Van Winkle	Jannetje	Nov. 16, 1745
Diedricks Jacob	Fitje Verveel	Geertruy	May 1, 1769
Diedricks Jacob	Fitje Verveel	Daniel	Dec. 20, 1770
Diedricks Jacob	Fitje Verveel	Aeltje	May 28, 1775
Diedricks Johannis	Geertruy Van Winkle	Antje	March 19, 1733
Diedricks Johannis	Hester Vreeland	Margrietje	April 7, 1741
Diedricks Johannis	Hester Vreeland	Maritje	March 26, 1743
Diedricks Johannis	Hester Vreeland	Lea	Oct. 30, 1745
Diedricks Johannis	Hester Vreeland	Aeltje	June 2, 1753
Diedricks Johannis	Antje Van Wagenen	Aegie	Nov. 23, 1769
Diedricks Johannis	Antje Van Wagenen	Aegie	Dec. 21, 1774
Diedricks Johannis	Antje Van Wagenen	Geertje	July 1, 1778
Diedricks Wander	Aeltje Gerrits	Annetje	Oct. 7, 1695
Diedricks Wander	Aeltje Gerrits	Gerrit	July 22, 1697
Diedricks Wander	Aeltje Gerrits	(daughter)	Oct. 27, 1700
Diedricks Wander	Aeltje Gerrits	(son)	Dec 8, 1702
Diedricks Wander	Aeltje Gerrits	Margrietje	Oct. 7, 1705
Diedricks Wander	Aeltje Gerrits	Jacob (bap)	Dec. 3, 1708
Dietivet Abraham	Jannetje Bokee	Ragel (bap)	April 6, 1686
Dietivet Abraham	Jannetje Bokee	Magdelena (bap)	Oct. 1, 1688
Dod James	Maritje Van Schyver	Thomas	Aug. 28, 1783
Dod James	Maritje Van Schyver	Johannis	Feb. 14, 1788
Dod James	Maritje Van Schyver	Hendrick	Feb. 22, 1790
Doele Rutgert	Elysabet Doele	Andries (bap)	Nov. 4, 1666
Doremus Cornelis	Jannetje Joas	Jannetje (bap)	June 2, 1691
Doremus William	Geertruy Van Houten	Sally	Feb. 3, 1805
Dreyts Lourens	Grietje Jans	Catryn (bap)	March 10, 1667
Duryea John	Frances Demarest	James	Dec. 3, 1813
Duryea John	Frances Demarest	Maria D	Oct. 23, 1816
Duryea John	Frances Demarest	Jane	May 7, 1820
Duryea John	Frances Demarest	Sarah	Nov. 17, 1821
Duryee John	Annatje ———	Geesje	June 5, 1797

BIRTH RECORD.

FATHER.	MOTHER.	CHILD.	DATE OF BIRTH.
Earle Anthilbe	Elizabet Edsall	Edward	Dec. 23, 1778
Earle Billi	Catreintje Bos	Elsje	June 22, 1769
Earle Cornelius	Elizabeth Duncan	Maritje	Aug. 9, 1771
Earle Daniel	Maritje Williams	Saertje	Feb. 26, 1771
Earle Edward jr	Elsje Vreeland	Edward (bap)	April 22, 1690
Earle Edward jr	Elsje Vreeland	(son)	May 28, 1692
Earle Edward jr	Elsje Vreeland	Hannah	March 26, 1695
Earle Edward jr	Elsje Vreeland	Maanedirck	Oct. 6, 1696
Earle Edward jr	Elsje Vreeland	Johannis	Sept. 8, 1698
Earle Edward jr	Elsje Vreeland	(son)	May 1, 1703
Earle Edward jr	Elsje Vreeland	(daughter)	Oct. —, 1704
Earle Enoch	Phebe Smith	Morris	Aug. 29, 1793
Earle Hendrick	——	Hendrick	July 17, 1784
Earle Nathaniel	Polly ——	Neeltje	Feb. —, 1773
Earle Philip R	Adriana Van Rypen	Elizabeth Ann	Dec. 12, 1812
Earle Philip R	Adriana Van Rypen	Thomas D	Feb. 8, 1814
Earle Philip R	Adriana Van Rypen	John	Jan. 20, 1817
Earle Philip R	Adriana Van Rypen	Mary B	Oct. 26, 1817
Earle Philip R	Adriana Van Rypen	Alexander	July 26, 1819
Earle Philip R	Adriana Van Rypen	Aletta Jane	Dec. 9, 1821
Edsall Samuel	Jenneke Edsall	Joanna (bap)	Sept. 4, 1667
Edsall Samuel	Jenneke Edsall	Sara (bap)	Oct. 9, 1673
Edsall Samuel	Jenneke Edsall	Benjamin (bap)	Oct. 22, 1674
Edsall Samuel	Jenneke Edsall	Rutje (bap)	April 2, 1687
Ellen Tamml	Elisabet Pouelse	Rachel	March 3, 1766
Epke Hendrick	Maritje Lubbertse	Angemitje (bap)	April 18, 1682
Epke Hendrick	Maritje Lubbertse	Roelof (bap)	Aug. 25, 1683
Eth Benjamin	Peggy Brower	Keetje	March 1, 1786
Everse Barent	Jennie McDonald	Barent	March 12, 1783
Everse Barent	Jennie McDonald	Jacob	Sept. 5, 1784
Everse Barent	Jennie McDonald	Barent	March 12, 1786
Everse Barent	Jennie McDonald	Jenneke	Dec. 18, 1788
Everse Johannis	Fitje Spier	Johannis	June 2, 1745
Everse Johannis	Fitje Spier	Barent	May 30, 1747
Everse Johannis	Fitje Spier	Jacob	Dec. 16, 1749
Everse Johannis	Fitje Spier	Catlyntje	March 11, 1760
Everse Johannis	Styntje Eiderstein	Elisabet	Oct. 9, 1777
Everse Johannis	Styntje Eiderstein	Johannis	Oct. 14, 1780
Everse Mattheus	Helena Spier	Maritje	March 27, 1755
Everse Mattheus	Helena Spier	Catlyntje	May 12, 1758
Everse Mattheus	Helena Spier	Barent	Dec. —, 1760
Everse Mattheus	Helena Spier	Leena	Aug. 29, 1763
Everse Mattheus	Helena Spier	Leah	July 5, 1768
Evertse Evert	Hillegont Jacobse	Evert	Feb. 12, 1708
Evertse Jacob	Catreintje Smith	Jannetje	March 20, 1782
Evertse Jacob	Catreintje Smith	Fitje	April 17, 1787
Evertse Jacob	Catreintje Smith	Catreintje	March 28, 1792
Evertse Johannis	Sara Griffins	Styntje	Jan. 4, 1784
Evertse Johannis	Sara Griffins	Fitje	April 13, 1785
Evertse Johannis	Sara Griffins	Johannis	Feb. 18, 1788

BIRTH RECORD.

FATHER.	MOTHER.	CHILD.	DATE OF BIRTH.
Fielding Hendrick	Aagtje Van Winckel	Catreina	June 24, 1759
Fielding Hendrick	Aagtje Van Winckel	Aegie	Oct. 19, 1761
Fielding Hendrick	Aagtje Van Winckel	Margrietje	Aug. 29, 1763
Fielding Henry	Martha Dunn	Daniel	June 23, 1821
Fransen Jan	Fitje Vreeland	Elias	Dec. —, 1694
Fransen Thomas	Treintje Jans Breested	Maritje (bap)	June 14, 1691
Fransen Thomas	Treintje Jans Breested	Jan	Oct. —, 1694
Fransen Thomas	Treintje Jans Breested	(son)	Oct. 26, 1696
Fransen Thomas	Treintje Jans Breested	(dau., 8th ch.)	Oct. 9, 1705
Fredricksen Andries	Neeltje Dircks	Maritje	March 21, 1704
Fredricksen Thomas	Maritje Ariaens	Jannetje	July 8, 1668
Gardner Harmans	Maria Retan	Leah	April 14, 1777
Garrabrants Cornelius	Jannetje Kip	Pieter	Sept. 12, 1779
Garrabrants Jacob	Keetje Earle	Myndert	Oct. 11, 1783
Garrabrants James	Sarah Williamson	Albert W	June 2, 1816
Garrabrants Myndert	Elizabeth ——	Treintje	May 29, 1773
Garrabrants Myndert	Aegie Van Houten	Myndert	Sept. 29, 1801
Garrabrants Myndert	Aegie Van Houten	John	July 1, 1804
Garrabrants Myndert	Rachel Jerolamon	Effie V. H	March 7, 1822
Garrabrants Peter	Catrina Van Buskirk	Cornelius	Feb. 8, 1802
Garrabrants Peter	Catrina Van Buskirk	Jannetje	June 26, 1803
Garrabrants Peter	Jannetje Clendenny	Eleanor	Oct. 25, 1807
Garrabrants Peter	Jannetje Clendenny	Cornelius	Sept. 24, 1810
Garrabrants Peter	Ann Van Winkle	Catherine V. B	Sept. 19, 1814
Garrabrants Peter	Ann Van Winkle	Abraham	May 3, 1819
Gautier Andrew	Hannah Turner	Hannah	Oct. 20, 1800
Gautier Samuel T. E.	Hannah Augusta Stagg	Samuel Ten Eyck	April 13, 1823
Gautier Thomas B	Elizabeth Hornblower	Josiah H	Nov. 12, 1818
Gerbrands Cornelius	Jannetje Prier	Maritje	Nov. 9, 1717
Gerbrands Cornelius	Jannetje Prier	Catherina	Oct. 13, 1721
Gerbrands Cornelius	Jannetje Prier	Gerrebrand	Sept. 10, 1723
Gerbrands Cornelius	Jannetje Prier	Teunis	April 8, 1728
Gerbrands Cornelius	Jannetje Prier	Cornelis	Oct. 27, 1728
Gerbrands Cornelius	Jannetje Prier	Neeltje	June 6, 1733
Gerbrantse Claas	Maritje Jurians	Gerbrants	Jan. 7, 1705
Gerbrantse Cornelius	Jannetje Van Hooren	Helena	Dec. 11, 1757
Gerbrantse Cornelius	Jannetje Van Hooren	Cornelius	—— ——
Gerbrantse Cornelius	Jannetje Van Hooren	Jannetje	—— ——
Gerbrantse Cornelius	Jannetje Van Hooren	Neeltje	Nov. 28, 1769
Gerbrantse Cornelius	Leena Van Hooren	Jannetje	March 5, 1788
Gerbrantse Gerbrand	Catreina Spier	Jannetje	March 1, 1760
Garbrantse Herpert	Hellegont Merselis	Maritje	May 12, 1708
Gerbrantse Myndert	Treintje Van Winckel	Maritje	March 9, 1715
Gerbrantse Myndert	Treintje Van Winckel	Jacob	Nov. 4, 1717
Gerbrantse Myndert	Treintje Van Winckel	Gerrebrand	Feb. 19, 1719
Gerbrantse Myndert	Treintje Van Winckel	Grietje	Feb. 19, 1721
Gerbrantse Myndert	Treintje Van Winckel	Metje	March 30, 1724
Gerbrantse Myndert	Treintje Van Winckel	Jannetje	April 3, 1726
Gerbrantse Myndert	Treintje Van Winckel	Myndert	Sept. 1, 1740

BIRTH RECORD.

FATHER.	MOTHER.	CHILD.	DATE OF BIRTH.
Gerritse Gerrit	Annetje Harmans	Hermanns (bap)	March 10, 1667
Gerritse Gerrit	Annetje Harmans	Hendrick (bap)	Oct. 25, 1675
Gerritse Gerrit	Annetje Harmans	Johannis	Jan. 11, 1678
Gerritse Gerrit jr	Neesje Pieters	Elysabet	March 3, 1682
Gerritse Gerrit jr	Neesje Pieters	Pieter	Oct. 4, 1684
Gerritse Gerrit jr	Neesje Pieters	Eva	April 14, 1687
Gerritse Gerrit jr	Neesje Pieters	Abraham (6th ch.)	Feb. 22, 1695
Gerritse Gerrit jr	Neesje Pieters	————	Oct. 14, 1699
Gerritse John	Metje Cadmus	Jannetje	March 25, 1782
Gerritsen Cornelius	Aeltje Van Winkle	Cornelius	May 26, 1740
Gerritsen Cornelius	Aeltje Van Winkle	Geurt	May 16, 1729
Gerritsen Juriaen	Margrietje Diedricks	Gerrit	Sept. 14, 1729
Gerritsen Juriaen	Margrietje Diedricks	————	Oct. 7, 1733
Gerritsen Juriaen	Margrietje Diedricks	Aeltje	March 4, 1735
Gerritsen Juriaen	Margrietje Diedricks	Beelitje	April 24, 1737
Gerritsen Juriaen	Margrietje Diedricks	Gerrit	April 6, 1739
Gilchrist Robert	Frances Vasher	Fanny	Sept. 25, 1817
Gilchrist Robert	Frances Vasher	Sarah	Aug. 22, 1819
Gould Lebbeus	Sarah Van Orden	Sarah	Aug. 20, 1818
Hanna James	Sarah Deas	James D.	July 29, 1812
Harding James J	Christiana Brown	Christiana Gertrude,	June 29, 1822
Harmansen Jan	Neeltje Jans	Aertje (bap)	April 14, 1691
Heathorne John	Margaret Kirk	Elizabeth S. K	May 7, 1810
Hedden James	Elizabeth Ball	Sarah Ann	Dec. 6, 1805
Helmigse Pieter	Claesje Post	Jannetje	Feb. 16, 1704
Helmigse Roelof	Aegtje Cornelise Vreeland	Helmigh	March 11, 1704
Helmigse Roelof	Aegtje Cornelise Vreeland	Aegtje	Oct. 18, 1708
Hendrickse Claas	Willemyntje Hendrickje Spier	Hendrick (bap)	June 25, 1688
Hendrickse Claas	Willemyntje Hendrickje Spier	Fransyntje (bap)	April 14, 1691
Hendricksen Jan	Annetje Preyer	Johannis (bap)	March 19, 1733
Hennion David	Catelyntje Everse	Maritje	March 13, 1783
Hennion David	Catelyntje Everse	Fitje	Dec. 23, 1785
Hennion David	Catelyntje Everse	Antje	Feb. 24, 1794
Hennion Gerrit	———— ————	Ide	April 3, 1736
Hesselse Pieter	Elysabet Gerrits	Maritje (bap)	Oct. 8, 1777
Hesselse Pieter	Elysabet Gerrits	Johannis (bap)	March 25, 1680
Hesselse Pieter	Elysabet Gerrits	Ragel	Sept. 14, 1682
Hesselse Pieter	Elysabet Gerrits	Ariantje (bap)	April 6, 1685
Hesselse Pieter	Elysabet Gerrits	Jannetje (bap)	Oct. 3, 1687
Hesselse Pieter	Elysabet Gerrits	Vrouwtje (bap)	Oct. 5, 1691
Hoppe Andries	Abigail Hoppe (Ackerman ?)	Hendrick	May 21, 1708
Hoppe Andries	Abigail Hoppe (Ackerman ?)	(daughter)	April 28, 1710
Hoppe Hendrick	Maritje Jans	Andries	Dec. 21, 1681

BIRTH RECORD.

FATHER.	MOTHER.	CHILD.	DATE OF BIRTH.
Hoppe Hendrick	Maritje Jans	Jan (bap)	June 26, 1682
Hoppe Hendrick	Maritje Jans	Willem (bap)	April 2, 1684
Hoppe Hendrick	Maritje Jans	Treintje (bap)	Oct. 5, 1685
Hoppe Mateys Adolf	Annetje Poulus	Andries (bap)	April 2, 1684
Hornblower Josiah	Annetje Merselis	Elizabeth	Dec. 23, 1793
Hornblower Josiah	Annetje Merselis	Christiana	Nov. 10, 1795
Hornblower Josiah	Annetje Merselis	Merselis Henry	Nov. 2, 1797
Hornblower Josiah	Annetje Merselis	James K	Sept. 11, 1806
Hornblower Josiah	Annetje Merselis	William J. V. H.	Oct. 22, 1809
Hornblower Josiah	Annetje Merselis	Jane	Oct. 3, 1811
Hornblower Josiah	Hannah Town	Anna Elizabeth	Aug. 21, 1813
Hornblower Josiah	Hannah Town	Josiah Henry	April —, 1817
Howard Thomas	Maria Moffat	Thomas H	Dec. 20, 1815
Howard Thomas	Maria Moffat	William H	Nov. 18, 1820
Howard William	Charity Greenlief	Jane	Aug. 17, 1795
Huysman Sjarel	Adriantje Dirckse	Mary (bap)	March 25, 1680
Huysman Sjarel	Adriantje Dirckse	Crystyn (bap)	June 26, 1682
Jackson Rev. William	Annetje Freelinghuysen, William		Aug. 14, 1758
Jackson Rev. William	Annetje Freelinghuysen, Theodorus		Dec. 26, 1760
Jackson Rev. William	Annetje Freelinghuysen, Hannah		Jan. 27, 1763
Jackson Rev. William	Annetje Freelinghuysen, Hendrick		Feb. 9, 1765
Jackson Rev. William	Annetje Freelinghuysen, Peterick		April 17, 1767
Jackson Rev. William	Annetje Freelinghuysen, Johannis		June 8, 1768
Jackson Rev. William	Annetje Freelinghuysen, Patrick		April 28, 1770
Jackson Rev. William	Annetje Freelinghuysen, Ferdinandus		Sept. 15, 1771
Jackson Rev. William	Annetje Freelinghuysen, Eva		Sept. 17, 1774
Jackson Rev. William	Annetje Freelinghuysen, Robert		Dec. 21, 1778
Jacobs Bartel	Eleanor Douglas	(son)	Aug. 27, 1695
Jacobs Bartel	Eleanor Douglas	Waling	July —, 1705
Janse Pieter	Maritje Jacobs	Jacob (bap)	Feb. 17, 1669
Janse Willem	Beelitje Tysen	Hendrick (bap)	April 17, 1677
Jansen Claes	Annetje Cornelis	Elysabet (bap)	March 10, 1667
Jansen Claes	Annetje Cornelis	Hendrick (bap)	April 22, 1676
Jansen Claes	Annetje Cornelis	Geertje	July 21, 1678
Jansen Claes	Annetje Cornelis	Jacob (bap)	Oct. 11, 1680
Jansen Claes	Annetje Cornelis	Hillegontje (bap)	Dec. 4, 1683
Jansen Isaac	Jannetje Boerum	Johannis	Aug. 7, 1775
Jorise Hendrick	Claesje Cornelis	Geertje	Feb. 20, 1679
Jorise Hendrick	Claesje Cornelis	Margrietje	June 13, 1681
Jurianse Alt	Gerritje Mattheus	Annetje	May 1, 1696
Jurianse Cornelis	Aeltje Van Winckel	Belia	Oct. 10, 1741
Jurianse Cornelis	Aeltje Van Winckel	Jannetje (bap)	April 16, 1745
Jurianse Cornelis	Aeltje Van Winckel	Aeltje	June 7, 1748
Jurianse Cornelis	Aeltje Van Winckel	Cornelius	Dec. 8, 1750
Jurianse Gerrit	Beelitje Dircks	Elysabet	May 14, 1694
Jurianse Gerrit	Beelitje Dircks	Lea	Sept. 11, 1697
Jurianse Gerrit	Beelitje Dircks	Juriaen	Aug. 15, 1699
Jurianse Gerrit	Beelitje Dircks	(son)	Dec. 4, 1701
Jurianse Gerrit	Beelitje Dircks	(son)	Jan. 17, 1704

BIRTH RECORD.

FATHER.	MOTHER.	CHILD.	DATE OF BIRTH.
Jurianse Gerrit	Beeltje Dircks	Aeltje	March 29, 1705
Jurianse Gerrit	Beeltje Dircks	Cornelis (bap)	Oct. 6, 1707
Jurianse Gerrit	Beeltje Dircks	Johannis	June 3, 1710
Jurianse Tomas	Jannetje Straatmaker	Gerrit (bap)	March 29, 1692
Jurianse Tomas	Jannetje Straatmaker	Juriaen (bap)	Oct. —, 1692
Karseboom Jan Dirckse,	Grietje Jasperse	Annetje (bap)	Oct. 19, 1667
Karseboom Jan Dirckse,	Grietje Jasperse	Annetje (bap)	Feb. 17, 1669
Karseboom Jan Dirckse,	Grietje Jasperse	Annetje (bap)	Oct. 9, 1673
Kells James	Elizabeth Pearson	Susanna	July 27, 1795
Kells James	Elizabeth Pearson	William F.	Dec. 15, 1799
Kells James	Elizabeth Pearson	James	March 3, 1802
Kells James	Elizabeth Pearson	John	April 23, 1805
Kells James	Elizabeth Pearson	Thomas	Sept. 30, 1808
Kells James	Elizabeth Pearson	Susanna	March 21, 1812
Kells James	Elizabeth Pearson	Phebe	April 8, 1815
Kelly John	Lea Diedricks	John	May 23, 1784
Ker David	Antje Westervelt	Cornelius	Aug. 26, 1802
Kip Peter	Polly Stuyvesant	Abraham	Sept. 8, 1802
Kool Pieter	Susanna La Tourette	Elizabet	Oct. 7, 1772
Kool Pieter	Susanna La Tourette	Isaac	July 4, 1774
Lasomba Anthoin	Styntje Jans	Catrina (bap)	April 6, 1686
Lasomba Anthoin	Styntje Jans	Magdaleena (bap)	April 2, 1688
Lewe Jacob	Elysabet Hendrickse	Jannetje (bap)	April 18, 1682
Lozier Nicholas	Maritje Kroese	Jacob	March 10, 1775
Lubbertse Jan	Maddaleentje Jans	Johannis (bap)	Nov. 3, 1667
Lubbertse Jan	Maddaleentje Jans	Willem (bap)	April 7, 1679
Lubbertse Jan	Maddaleentje Jans	Gysbert	May 21, 1682
Lubbertse Lubbert jr.	Hilletje Pouluse	Pieter (bap)	April 18, 1682
Lubbertse Lubbert jr.	Hilletje Pouluse	Aeltje (bap)	April 6, 1685
Lubbertse Tys	Treintje Jans	Annetje (bap)	Oct. 4, 1668
Lyon Richard	Sarah Hendricks	Moses	Feb. 25, 1802
Lyon Richard	Sarah Hendricks	John Joseph	Nov. 15, 1809
Lyon Richard	Aegie Van Houten	Mary H.	Feb. 24, 1812
Lyon Richard	Aegie Van Houten	David	March 26, 1814
Lyon Richard	Aegie Van Houten	Anson G.	Feb. 9, 1816
Macheleyn Sjarel	Catrina Tomas	Annetje (bap)	April 14, 1691
Macheleyn Sjarel	Catrina Tomas	Solomon	May 27, 1696
Macheleyn Sjarel	Elizabeth Mandeville	Frona Ann	Nov. 24, 1819
Mandeville John	Altje Van Winkle	Henry	Feb. 7, 1811
Mandeville John	Altje Van Winkle	John V. W.	March 31, 1813
Mandeville John	Altje Van Winkle	John	May 23, 1815
Marleen Sjarel	Catrina Tomas	Sara (bap)	April 18, 1682
Marleen Sjarel	Margrietje Martin	James	Feb. 12, 1760
McCubbery ——	Mary Boudell	Alexander	Nov. 8, 1821
McDaniel Thomas	Antje Van Scheyve	John	May 23, 1787
McDaniel Thomas	Antje Van Scheyve	Matthewes	Aug. 27, 1789
McDonald Randall	Ann Cameron	Adeline Margaretta,	April 29, 1815

BIRTH RECORD.

FATHER.	MOTHER.	CHILD.	DATE OF BIRTH.
McDonald Randall	Ann Cameron	Amelia Susan	Dec. 10, 1817
McDonald Richard	Margaret Cadmus	John	April 2, 1822
McDonald Thomas	Hannah Vreeland	Rachel	Sept. 8, 1816
Merrit Willem	Catrina Hendricks	Lena	May 13, 1696
Merselis Ide	Ariantje Sip	Pieter	May 24, 1759
Merselis John	Aeltje Van Rypen	Merselis	Jan. 8, 1776
Merselis John	Aeltje Van Rypen	Cornelius	Oct. 15, 1778
Merselis John	Aeltje Van Rypen	Aeltje	Dec. 29, 1780
Merselis John	Aeltje Van Rypen	Elisabet	Jan. 19, 1784
Merselis John	Catrina Tomas	Margaret	Feb. 23, 1809
Merselis Merselis	Elisabet Vliereboom	Johannis	Sept. 13, 1754
Merselis Merselis	Elisabet Vliereboom	Aeltje	March 19, 1759
Merselis Merselis	Elisabet Vliereboom	Pieter	Feb. 18, 1762
Merselis Merselis	Elisabet Vliereboom	Jacob	Dec. 29, 1764
Merselis Merselis	Elisabet Vliereboom	Aeltje	Dec. 16, 1769
Merselis Merselis	Elisabet Vliereboom	Annetje	Nov. 26, 1773
Merselis Merselis	Geertje Prior	John	Nov. 14, 1800
Merselis Merselis	Geertje Prior	Jacob	Dec. 25, 1801
Merselis Merselis	Geertje Prior	Elizabeth	Jan. 23, 1804
Merselis Merselis	Geertje Prior	Sarah	Feb. 20, 1807
Merselis Peter	Maritje Andries	Andries	May 31, 1732
Merselis Peter	Jannetje Duryee	Elisabet	Aug. 13, 1787
Merselis Peter C.	Jane De Mott	Mary M.	May 21, 1823
Merselissen Pieter	Jenneke Preyer	Pieter (bap)	April 11, 1723
Merselissen Pieter	Jenneke Preyer	Andries	Feb. 4, 1725
Merselissen Pieter	Jenneke Preyer	(9th ch.)	Oct. 15, 1732
Merselissen Pieter	Jenneke Preyer	Antje (bap)	March 4, 1735
Merselissen Pieter	Jenneke Preyer	Johanna	Jan. 17, 1737
Mersereau John T.	Ann Waldron	Joseph	March 4, 1821
Mersereau John T.	Ann Waldron	Stephen	Aug. 19, 1822
Mersereau John T.	Ann Waldron	Helen	Dec. 18, 1823
Metzger Johannis	Jannetje Fielding	Jacob	Feb. 15, 1775
Meyer John	Elizabet ——	Elizabet	Nov. 7, 1773
Michielse Tades	Annetje Steinmets	Michiel	Oct. 11, 1680
Michielse Tades	Annetje Steinmets	Jannetje	Oct. 12, 1682
Michielse Tades	Annetje Steinmets	Annetje	Aug. 6, 1684
Michielse Tades	Annetje Steinmets	Johannis (bap)	April 2, 1689
Miller John	Elizabet Bertholf	Wyburg	Oct. 28, 1776
Moore Abraham	Sarah Brinkerhoff	Sarah S.	June 29, 1808
Musker John	Elizabeth Post	John	Feb. 6, 1804
Neefie Gerrit	Eva Van Houten	Robert	Sept. 27, 1804
Newkirk Arent	Jannetje Vreeland	Catlyntje	Nov. 6, 1792
Newkirk Arent	Jannetje Vreeland	Kneelia	Oct. 2, 1794
Newkirk Arent	Jannetje Vreeland	Matthevis	May 22, 1799
Newkirk Arent	Jannetje Vreeland	Catherina	May 15, 1807
Newkirk Barent	Antje Toers	Arent	Sept. 1, 1768
Newkirk Barent	Antje Toers	Jannetje	Nov. 15, 1777
Newkirk Gerrit	Catrina Cuyper	Hendrick	April 4, 1741
Newkirk Gerrit	Polly Ackerman	Catlyntje	Oct. 10, 1788

FATHER.	MOTHER.	CHILD.	DATE OF BIRTH.
Newkirk Gerrit	Polly Ackerman	Margrietje	May 22, 1796
Newkirk Gerrit	Polly Ackerman	Sally	June 25, 1793
Newkirk Gerrit	Polly Ackerman	Sally	Dec. 18, 1796
Newkirk Gerrit	Polly Ackerman	Hendrick	Dec. —, 1799
Newkirk Gerrit	Polly Ackerman	Gerrit	Oct. 17, 1808
Newkirk Gerrit	Rachel Shepherd	Jacob	Nov. 26, 1807
Newkirk Gerrit	Rachel Shepherd	Matthew	July 4, 1811
Newkirk Gerrit	Rachel Shepherd	Sophia	Nov. 24, 1812
Newkirk Gerrit	Rachel Shepherd	Garret	March 18, 1815
Newkirk Gerrit	Rachel Shepherd	Catherine	March 14, 1817
Newkirk Hendrick	Jenneke Vreeland	Gerrit	Jan. 8, 1781
Newkirk Hendrick	Jenneke Vreeland	Joris	Nov. 28, 1783
Newkirk Hendrick	Jenneke Vreeland	Catreintje	Sept. 7, 1791
Newkirk Henry	Eliza Provost	James M.	June 27, 1819
Newkirk Jacob	Fitje Hennion	Maritje	July 18, 1770
Newkirk Jacob	Fitje Hennion	Poulus	April 15, 1776
Newkirk Jacob	Fitje Hennion	Jacob	April 28, 1778
Newkirk Jacob	Fitje Hennion	Maritje	July 13, 1782
Newkirk Jacob	Fitje Hennion	Johannis	Oct. 23, 1786
Newkirk John	Mary Newkirk	John	Oct. 20, 1810
Newkirk John	Mary Newkirk	Sophia	May 31, 1813
Newkirk John	Mary Newkirk	Matthew	June 20, 1816
Newkirk John J	Gertrude Collerd	Jacob	May 29, 1815
Newkirk John J	Gertrude Collerd	Abraham	Oct. 3, 1817
Newkirk John J	Gertrude Collerd	Garret	Aug. 29, 1821
Newkirk John J	Gertrude Collerd	Sophia	Sept. 25, 1823
Newkirk Joris	Sarah Van Derhoof	Jane	Dec. 6, 1805
Newkirk Joris	Sarah Van Derhoof	Henry	Dec. 19, 1808
Newkirk Joris	Sarah Van Derhoof	Garret	Sept. 28, 1812
Newkirk Joris	Sarah Van Derhoof	Jane Maria	Feb. 17, 1816
Newkirk Joris	Sarah Van Derhoof	Abraham P	Dec. 21, 1819
Newkirk Mattevis	Catlyntje Toers	Gerrit	April 9, 1766
Newkirk Mattevis	Catlyntje Toers	Arent	Oct. 22, 1768
Newkirk Mattevis	Geertje Kog	Johannis	May 18, 1781
Olcott John S	Sarah Batchelor	Mary	May 9, 1822
Olphertz Sjoert	Fitje Roels	Annetje (bap)	June 10, 1666
Oosterum Jan Hendrick	Morchteltje Roelof	Treintje	June 20, 1684
Osborn Samuel	Maria Shepherd	Elizabeth	Oct. 3, 1806
Osborn Samuel	Maria Shepherd	John	Sept. 20, 1808
Osborn Samuel	Maria Shepherd	Jacob	Jan. 31, 1813
Osborn Samuel	Maria Shepherd	Rachel Catherine	June 24, 1815
Osborn Samuel	Maria Shepherd	Anna D.	May 4, 1825
Outwater Garret	Ann Van Winkle	Jacob	April 9, 1824
Outwater Guilliam	Antje Vreeland	Johannis	Nov. 5, 1775
Outwater Guilliam	Antje Vreeland	Aeltje	Dec. 11, 1781
Outwater Jacob	Maritje Van Derhoof	Gerrit	July 22, 1801
Outwater Jacob	Maritje Van Derhoof	John	May 11, 1807
Outwater John	Neeltje Prior	Anne	Sept. 25, 1800
Outwater John	Neeltje Prior	Catherine	Oct. 20, 1806

BIRTH RECORD.

FATHER.	MOTHER.	CHILD.	DATE OF BIRTH.
Outwater John	Neeltje Prior	Gitty	July 4, 1810
Park James	Altje Merselis	John M	Dec. 24, 1810
Park James	Altje Merselis	Merselis M	Oct. 19, 1813
Peron Willem	Elisbet Sickels	Josias	July 21, 1695
Philipsen Robert	Geertruy Reddenhaus	Abram	Nov. 12, 1711
Pieterse Christian	Treintje Cornelis	Metje (bap)	Aug. 19, 1666
Pieterse Merselis	Pieterje Van Voorst	Elysabet (bap)	April 18, 1682
Pieterse Merselis	Pieterje Van Voorst	Hellegontje	Sept. 27, 1684
Pieterse Merselis	Pieterje Van Voorst	Annetje	March 25, 1695
Pieterse Merselis	Pieterje Van Voorst	Catrina	Nov. 18, 1696
Pieterse Merselis	Pieterje Van Voorst	Leena	Aug. 11, 1699
Pieterse Poulus	Treintje Moertins	Cristina (bap)	April 14, 1667
Pieterse Poulus	Treintje Moertins	Aeltje (bap)	June 23, 1679
Post Abraham	Ann Speer	John	Oct. 2, 1821
Post Adrian	Catrina Gerrits	Adrian	Jan. 24, 1678
Post Adrian	Catrina Gerrits	Gerrit (bap)	Jan. 1, 1680
Post Adrian	Catrina Gerrits	Claertje (bap)	Dec. 4, 1681
Post Adrian	Catrina Gerrits	Pieter (bap)	Oct. 2, 1688
Post Adrian	Catrina Gerrits	Johannis (bap)	June 10, 1690
Post Adrian	Raegel Sickels	Parcel Amelia	Dec. 16, 1780
Post Adrian	Raegel Sickels	Egbert	Nov. 15, 1787
Post Adrian	Raegel Sickels	Jenneke	Feb. 25, 1790
Post Adrian	Raegel Sickels	Hendrick	May 2, 1792
Post Adrian	Raegel Sickels	Sarah	June 21, 1798
Post Adrian	Raegel Sickels	Cornelius	July 1, 1802
Post Adrian	Raegel Sickels	Cornelius	Sept. 29, 1803
Post Egbert	Saertje Stuyvesant	Adrian	March 30, 1766
Post Egbert	Saertje Stuyvesant	Pryntje	June 23, 1769
Post Egbert	Saertje Stuyvesant	Pieter	Nov. 4, 1771
Post Egbert	Saertje Stuyvesant	Johannis	Dec. 18, 1773
Post Egbert	Saertje Stuyvesant	Cornelius	May 26, 1780
Post Egbert	Saertje Stuyvesant	Pryntje	July 13, 1784
Post Frans	Maritje Kobis	Adrian (bap)	March 29, 1692
Post Johannis	Catreintje Ritan	Saertje	July 3, 1765
Post John	Keziah Duryee	John	Oct. 30, 1819
Post John	Keziah Duryee	Jacob D	June 20, 1822
Post Peter	Jannetje Diedricks	Saertje	March 26, 1795
Post Peter	Jannetje Diedricks	Jacob	July 7, 1797
Post Peter	Jannetje Diedricks	Jane	May 31, 1801
Post Peter	Sarah Van Tuyl	Sarah	Nov. 11, 1796
Post Peter jr	Osseltje Duryee	Martha K	July 30, 1798
Poulise Pieter	Treintje Hans Jacobs	Treintje (bap)	Oct. 1, 1688
Poulise Pieter	Treintje Hans Jacobs	Geertje (bap)	June 2, 1691
Preeyh Thomas	Margrietje Preeyhs (?)	Jan (bap)	March 27, 1674
Preyer Abraham	Maritje Sickles	Ariaen (bap)	Sept. 28, 1747
Preyer Abraham	Maritje Sickles	Sara	Feb. 9, 1751
Preyer Andries	Johanna Steinmets	Feelitje (bap)	Feb. 24, 1694
Preyer Andries	Johanna Steinmets	Johannis (bap)	May 18, 1696
Preyer Andries	Johanna Steinmets	Jenneke, (5th ch)	Feb. 24, 1699

FATHER.	MOTHER.	CHILD.	DATE OF BIRTH.
Preyer Andries	Geertruy Sickles	Casparus	June 14, 1753
Preyer Andries	Geertruy Sickles	Zacharias	May 26, 1755
Preyer Andries	Geertruy Sickles	Johannis	Nov. 17, 1756
Preyer Andries	Geertruy Sickles	Hartman	Dec. 20, 1759
Preyer Andries	Geertruy Sickles	Abraham	Jan. 31, 1762
Preyer Andries	Geertruy Sickles	Ariaentje	Nov. 10, 1764
Preyer Casparus	Saertje Andriesen	Anna (bap)	———, 1715
Preyer Casparus	Saertje Andriesen	Pryutje	Oct. 22, 1717
Preyer Casparus	Saertje Andriesen	Johannis	June 26, 1722
Preyer Casparus	Saertje Andriesen	Casparus	———, 1724
Preyer Casparus	Saertje Andriesen	Nicholas	June —, 1726
Preyer Casparus	Saertje Andriesen	Abraham	Sept. 23, 1729
Preyer Casparus	Saertje Andriesen	Selytje	Sept. 20, 1731
Preyer Casper Cornelise, Neeltje Jans		Susanna (bap)	April 6, 1686
Preyer Cornelis	Hendrickje Jans	Cornelis (bap)	April 2, 1688
Preyer Johannis	Geertruy Sickles	Geertruy	July 11, 1748
Preyer Johannis	Geertruy Sickles	Hendrick	April 30, 1751
Prine Peter	Rachel Van Winkle	Daniel	Dec. 29, 1819
Prine Peter	Rachel Van Winkle	Abraham V. W.	July 12, 1821
Prine Peter	Rachel Van Winkle	Barney E.	Feb. 22, 1823
Prior Abraham	Antje Waldron	Andries	April 14, 1798
Prior Abraham	Antje Waldron	Anne	March 1, 1801
Prior Abraham	Antje Waldron	Joseph	Aug. 6, 1807
Prior Casparus	Catreintje Clendenny	Geertje	July 5, 1778
Prior Casparus	Catreintje Clendenny	Nelly	Feb. 1, 1780
Prior Casparus	Catreintje Clendenny	Saertje	Sept. 29, 1781
Prior Casparus	Catreintje Clendenny	Polly	May 10, 1784
Prior Casparus	Antje Van Wagenen	Nicholas	Jan. 13, 1798
Prior Hartman	Syntje Post	Andries	Nov. 16, 1787
Prior Jacob	Sally Idoo	Abigail	Jan. 24, 1774
Prior Jacob	Sally Idoo	Geertje	Nov. 10, 1779
Prior Jacob	Sally Idoo	Polly	May 17, 1783
Prior Jacob	Sarah Van Houten	Aeltje	Aug. 20, 1793
Prior Jacob	Sarah Van Houten	Nicholas	June 23, 1796
Prior Jacob	Sarah Van Houten	Aeltje	June 8, 1804
Prior Nicholas	Hester Banta	Casparus	Feb. 8, 1762
Prior Nicholas	Hester Banta	Jacob	Sept. 13, 1767
Prior Nicholas C.	Hannah Vreeland	Ann V. W.	July 18, 1820
Pryne Samuel	Jane Dickson	Eleanor	June 25, 1803
Ralemont Jacob	Pietertje Claes	Johannis	Sept. 19, 1697
Ralft Leery	Sara Buys	Sara	Sept. 25, 1776
Rapp Alam	Ariantje Prior	Geertruy	May 28, 1787
Rapp Adam	Ariantje Prior	Johannis	Dec. —, 1788
Rapp Adam	Ariantje Prior	Elizabeth	May 4, 1792
Rapp Adam	Ariantje Prior	Andrew	May 23, 1802
Rapp Andrew	Catherine Britain	Adam	July 30, 1824
Rapp John	Mary Van Clief	John Adam	Oct. 2, 1814
Rapp John	Mary Van Clief	Abraham	Nov. 12, 1816
Rapp John	Mary Van Clief	Daniel	Sept. 26, 1818

BIRTH RECORD.

FATHER.	MOTHER.	CHILD.	DATE OF BIRTH
Rapp John	Mary Van Clief	Gitty	June 3, 1820
Rapp John	Mary Van Clief	John	March 12, 1822
Rapp John	Mary Van Clief	Adam	May 8, 1824
Rappleye Barnardus	Deborah Gidney	Margrietje	Nov. 20, 1788
Rappleye Joris jr	Antje Van de Voort	Powel	June 12, 1789
Reddenhaus Abel	Catrina Jans (Lubberts)	Josiah	Jan. 15, 1698
Reddenhaus Abel	Catrina Jans (Lubberts)	Jannetje	Sept. 6, 1699
Reddenhaus Abel	Catrina Jans (Lubberts)	Geertruyt	March 3, 1701
Reddenhaus Abel	Catrina Jans (Lubberts)	Hendrick	Jan. 14, 1703
Reddenhaus Abel	Catrina Jans (Lubberts)	Hendricus	Oct. 5, 1705
Reddenhaus Abel	Catrina Jans (Lubberts)	Johannis	Feb. 7, 1708
Reddenhaus Abel	Catrina Jans (Lubberts)	Sofia	March 10, 1710
Reed Henry	Joanna Hugill	Henry	Oct. 6, 1802
Reed Henry	Joanna Hugill	Joanna	Oct. 6, 1802
Rendell William	Sarah Outwater	Susanna	Sept. 14, 1793
Riker Henry	Rachel Van Houten	John K	June 10, 1823
Roelofse Cornelis	Maddaleena Van Giesen	Grietje	Aug. 10, 1648
Roelofse Cornelis	Maddaleena Van Giesen	Roelof (bap)	Dec. 31, 1679
Roelofse Cornelis	Maddaleena Van Giesen	Rynier (bap)	Dec. 9, 1681
Roelofse Cornelis	Maddaleena Van Giesen	Hendrick	Nov. 8, 1683
Roelofse Cornelis	Maddaleena Van Giesen	Dirckje	Nov. 27, 1685
Roelofse Cornelis	Maddaleena Van Giesen	Johannis	Oct. 6, 1687
Roelofse Cornelis	Maddaleena Van Giesen	Cornelis (bap)	Oct. 22, 1690
Roelofse Helmigh	Jannetje Pieters	Roelof (bap)	June 11, 1677
Roelofse Helmigh	Jannetje Pieters	Pieter	Jan. 23, 1680
Roelofse Helmigh	Jannetje Pieters	Cornelis (bap)	March 21, 1682
Roelofse Helmigh	Jannetje Pieters	Catelyntje	Feb. 17, 1685
Roelofse Helmigh	Jannetje Pieters	Jacob	Oct. 11, 1687
Roelofse Helmigh	Jannetje Pieters	Dirck	Oct. 11, 1687
Roelofse Helmigh	Jannetje Pieters	Gerritje	Jan. 7, 1691
Roelofse Helmigh	Jannetje Pieters	Lysbet	Oct. 16, 1693
Roelofse Helmigh	Jannetje Pieters	Johannis	Oct. 28, 1696
Roelofse Helmigh	Jannetje Pieters	Jannetje	Nov. 2, 1699
Roelofse Tonis	Treintje Claes	Gerritje	Jan. 10, 1679
Roelofse Tonis	Treintje Claes	Roelof	Aug. 28, 1680
Roelofse Tonis	Treintje Claes	Annetje	Aug. 13, 1682
Roelofse Tonis	Treintje Claes	Jannetje (bap)	May 23, 1687
Roelofse Tonis	Treintje Claes	Vrouwtje (bap)	June 24, 1688
Roelofse Tonis	Treintje Claes	Johannis (bap)	Oct. —, 1690
Roos Gerrit	Judith Arentsen Toers	Johannis	May —, 1710
Roos Gerrit	Judith Arentsen Toers	Antje	— —, 1712
Roos Gerrit	Judith Arentsen Toers	Nicholas	Feb. —, 1714
Ross John	Agnes McKitrick	Ann	Oct. 28, 1799
Rycksen Hendrick	Fitje Jacobs	Dirck (bap)	July 8, 1688
Salter Paul	Elizabeth Cubberly	Thomas	May 21, 1813
Salter Paul	Elizabeth Cubberly	John	Aug. 24, 1815
Salter Paul	Elizabeth Cubberly	Mary	July 25, 1817
Salter Paul	Elizabeth Cubberly	Paul La Tourette	April 1, 1820
Salter Paul	Elizabeth Cubberly	Susan	Sept. 2, 1823

BIRTH RECORD.

FATHER.	MOTHER.	CHILD.	DATE OF BIRTH.
Seely William	Annetje Sickles	Eliza	June 1, 1803
Seely William	Annetje Sickles	Mary	Feb. 3, 1805
Shepherd George	Catrientje Van Winkle	Leah	Dec. 4, 1790
Shepherd George	Catreintje Van Winkle	Peggy	April 12, 1793
Shepherd George	Catreintje Van Winkle	Thomas	Jan. 28, 1796
Shepherd George	Catreintje Van Winkle	Jacob	Feb. 10, 1798
Shepherd George	Catreintje Van Winkle	Thomas	Aug. 18, 1800
Shepherd George	Catreintje Van Winkle	Margaret	Nov. 1, 1803
Shepherd George	Catreintje Van Winkle	Catharine	Sept. 29, 1805
Shepherd Joseph	Fanny Tuers	Catherine V. W.	Jan. 23, 1814
Shepherd Joseph	Fanny Tuers	Esther	Feb. 2, 1816
Shepherd Joseph	Fanny Tuers	Jacob V. W.	Aug. 15, 1818
Shepherd Joseph	Fanny Tuers	Garret N.	June 1, 1820
Shepherd Joseph	Fanny Tuers	Phebe V. W.	June 28, 1822
Shepherd Joseph	Fanny Tuers	Joseph	July 4, 1824
Shepherd Samuel	Annatje Smith	Peggy	Dec. 21, 1793
Shepherd Samuel	Annatje Smith	James	Sept. 6, 1797
Shipper Joris	Catreintje Van Winkle	Raegel	Sept. 4, 1784
Shipper Joris	Catrientje Van Winkle	Joseph	Sept. 20, 1786
Shipper Joris	Catreintje Van Winkle	Maria	Oct. 16, 1788
Sickles Abraham	Polly Van Waert	Abraham	June 28, 1776
Sickles Abraham	Polly Van Waert	Rachel	Feb. 24, 1779
Sickles Abraham	Polly Van Waert	Antje	Feb. 27, 1783
Sickles Abraham	Polly Van Waert	Elysabeth	March 15, 1785
Sickles Abraham	Polly Van Waert	Geertruy	Feb. 10, 1788
Sickles Abraham	Polly Van Waert	Polly	Aug. 6, 1796
Sickles Abraham	Polly Van Waert	Antje	May 10, 1802
Sickles Abraham	Polly Van Waert	Polly	Sept. 18, 1807
Sickles Abraham A.	Catherine Outwater	Aeltje	Dec. 12, 1810
Sickles Abraham A.	Catherine Outwater	Rachel	Oct. 9, 1817
Sickles Daniel	Antje Diedricks	Zacharias	June 25, 1769
Sickles Hendrick	Jenneke Stuyvesant	Rachel	May 1, 1770
Sickles Hendrick	Effie Bray	Anna Maria	Sept. 24, 1803
Sickles Henry	Abigail McCarthy	John Henry	July 28, 1818
Sickles Johannis	Sarah Waldron	Hendrick	July 21, 1771
Sickles Peter	Eva Van Derhoof	Hendrick	June 27, 1792
Sickles Peter	Eva Van Derhoof	Gerrit	March 26, 1807
Sickles Robert	Antje Winne	Martin	Aug. 13, 1750
Sickles Robert	Antje Winne	Ariantje	Aug. 31, 1758
Sickles Zacharias	Eleanor Toers	Frances	Oct. 17, 1785
Sickles Zacharias	Eleanor Toers	Raeggel	Sept. 13, 1787
Sickles Zacharias	Aeltje Toers	Johannis	Aug. 9, 1791
Sickles Zacharias	Aeltje Toers	Sarah	Jan. 30, 1795
Sickles Zacharias	Aeltje Toers	John Fred'k	Aug. 18, 1807
Siggles Abraham	Aagtje Blinkerhof	Aagtje	Feb. 20, 1740
Siggels Abraham	Martje Blinkerhof	Geertruy	May 8, 1744
Siggels Hendrick	Geertruy Fredricks	Robert	March 25, 1718
Siggels Hendrick	Geertruy Fredricks	Catrina	Aug. 26, 1720
Siggels Hendrick	Geertruy Fredricks	Geertruy	Oct. 26, 1722
Siggels Hendrick	Geertruy Fredricks	Fredrick	Dec. 21, 1725

BIRTH RECORD.

FATHER.	MOTHER.	CHILD.	DATE OF BIRTH.
Siggels Hendrick	Geertruy Fredricks	Johannis	Sept. 11, 1728
Siggels Hendrick	Sara Ackerman	Hendrick	Aug. 5, 1737
Siggels Hendrick	Sara Ackerman	Aeltje	Oct. 8, 1739
Siggels Johannis	Claesje Blinckerhof,	Aagtje	Dec. 26, 1727
Siggels Johannis	Claesje Blinckerhof	Aagtje	May 16, 1729
Siggels Johannis	Claesje Blinckerhof	(son)	July 5, 1733
Siggels Robert	Geertruyt Reddenhaus,	Zacharias (bap)	Nov. —, 1694
Siggels Robert	Geertruyt Reddenhaus,	Mary	April 14, 1697
Siggels Robert	Geertruyt Reddenhaus,	Geertruyt	Sept. 10, 1699
Siggels Robert	Geertruyt Reddenhaus,	Joanna	June 2, 1702
Siggels Robert	Geertruyt Reddenhaus,	Willem (9th ch., 5th son)	Oct. 26, 1704
Siggels Zacharias	Ariantje Hartmanse Vreeland	Geertruy	Feb. 14, 1729
Siggels Zacharias	Rachel Van Winckel	Daniel	Aug. 10, 1737
Siggels Zacharias	Rachel Van Winckel	Abraham	Aug. 25, 1754
Simmerman Henry	Margaret Merryendall	Anna Maria	July 21, 1819
Simmons John	Mary Ackerman	Henry	March 4, 1825
Simmons Michael	Nelly De Pew	Eliza	Nov. 21, 1800
Simonson Daniel	Elizabeth Williams	Phebe Ann	Sept. 18, 1818
Simonson Daniel	Elizabeth Williams	Stephen	Nov. 21, 1820
Simonson Daniel	Elizabeth Williams	John W	Nov. 7, 1822
Simonson Daniel	Elizabeth Williams	Jane D	Dec. 27, 1824
Simonson Joseph	Elizabeth Wynants	Jacob	Aug. 4, 1798
Simonson Joseph	Elizabeth Wynants	Elizabeth	Nov. 13, 1800
Simonson Joseph	Elizabeth Wynants	Isaac	Jan. 9, 1803
Simonson Joseph	Elizabeth Wynants	Joseph	Dec. 17, 1804
Simonson Joseph	Elizabeth Wynants	Joanna	Aug. 25, 1807
Simonson Stephen	Jannetje Diedricks	Elizabeth	Dec. 6, 1793
Simonson Stephen	Jannetje Diedricks	Antje	July 9, 1796
Simonson Stephen	Jannetje Diedricks	Jacob	Aug. 12, 1802
Simonson Stephen	Jannetje Diedricks	Aefie	July 4, 1805
Simonson Stephen	Jannetje Diedricks	Abraham	April 8, 1808
Sip Cornelius	Beelitje Vreeland	Antje	May 20, 1763
Sip Cornelius	Beelitje Vreeland	Ide	May 3, 1764
Sip Cornelius	Beelitje Vreeland	Ide	Jan. 14, 1771
Sip Ide	Antje Van Wagenen	Catelyntje	Aug. 5, 1731
Sip Ide	Antje Van Wagenen	Ariantje (bap)	June 2, 1733
Sip Ide	Antje Van Wagenen	Jannetje (bap)	Sept. 30, 1735
Sip Ide	Antje Van Wagenen	Gerrit (bap)	Aug. 21, 1740
Sip Garret	Margaret Newkirk	Jane	Oct. 6, 1812
Sip Garret	Margaret Newkirk	Maria	Feb. 26, 1814
Sip Garret	Margaret Newkirk	Peter	Nov. 10, 1815
Sip Gerrit	Jenneke Merselis	Antje	Sept. 6, 1764
Sip Gerrit	Jenneke Merselis	Pieter	Aug. 18, 1767
Sip Gerrit	Jenneke Merselis	Jenneke	March 12, 1770
Sip Jan Ariaensen	Joanna Van Vorst	Ide	Sept. 3, 1695
Sip Jan Ariaensen	Joanna Van Vorst	Johannis	May 10, 1698
Sip Jan Ariaensen	Joanna Van Vorst	Cornelis	Sept. 28, 1700
Sip Jan Ariaensen	Joanna Van Vorst	Abraham (bap)	April 11, 1704

FATHER.	MOTHER.	CHILD.	DATE OF BIRTH.
Sip Jan Ariaensen	Joanna Van Vorst	Hendrick	Sept. 30, 1706
Sip Jan Ariaensen	Joanna Van Vorst	Helena (11th ch.)	Nov. 7, 1708
Sip Peter	Elizabeth Vreeland	Maritje	Feb. 27, 1795
Sip Peter	Elizabeth Vreeland	Derrick	Aug. 31, 1800
Slot Pieter	Maritje Jacobs	Jan (bap)	Jan 1, 1666
Smit Morgen	Catje Tades	Cornelis (bap)	March 4, 1735
Smith Abel	Rachel Douwe	Catreintje	March 18, 1785
Smith Abel	Rachel Douwe	Sara	July 20, 1787
Smith Abel	Jans Lozier	Rachel	Dec. 19, 1806
Smith Baker	Elizabeth Sickles	Mary	Sept. 17, 1803
Smith Cornelius	Sara Bush	Jacobus	Feb. 2, 1793
Smith Cornelius	Sara Bush	Hillegont	Sept. 20, 1794
Smith Cornelius	Sara Bush	Jannetje	Oct. 20, 1796
Smith Cornelius	Peggy Hepburn	Maria	Oct. 9, 1798
Smith Cornelius	Peggy Hepburn	Sarah	Nov. 11, 1799
Smith Cornelius	Margaret Shepherd	Thomas	May 26, 1812
Smith Jacobus	Jannetje Bos	Catreina	Feb. 7, 1759
Smith Jacobus	Jannetje Bos	Antje	Nov. 13, 1760
Smith Jacobus	Jannetje Bos	Leya	Nov. 11, 1762
Smith Jacobus	Jannetje Bos	Cornelius	Nov. 9, 1765
Smith Job	Mary Earle	Catrina	Jan. 22, 1792
Smith John	Nancy De Maree	Nancy	Feb. 5, 1780
Smith John E	Altje Van Rypen	Ann D	July 25, 1814
Smith John E	Altje Van Rypen	Phebe H	Sept. 19, 1816
Smith Samuel	Ann Simonson	David	Feb. 14, 1817
Smith Samuel	Ann Simonson	Charles	May 14, 1819
Snyder Jacob	Maritje Van Blarcom	Sarah	Oct. 7, 1795
Solder Daniel	Jacemyntje Toers	Johannis	April 30, 1762
Solder Daniel	Jacomyntje Toers	Annatje	July 7, 1764
Solder Daniel	Jacomyntje Toers	Sara	Feb. 16, 1767
Solder Daniel	Jacomyntje Toers	Jacomyntje	July 13, 1770
Spier Abraham	Aagtje Sickles	Aagtje	March 23, 1755
Spier Albertus	Osseltje Westervelt	Catlyntje	May 13, 1745
Spier Albertus	Osseltje Westervelt	Johannis	Aug. 28, 1746
Spier Albertus	Osseltje Westervelt	Barent	March 4, 1750
Spier Barent	Catelyntje Jacobs	Jacob (bap)	Sept. 25, 1704
Spier Barent	Catelyntje Jacobs	Benjamin (bap)	July 28, 1706
Spier Benjamin	Maritje Spier	Barent	Feb. —, 1736
Spier Benjamin	Maritje Spier	Sara	Aug. 18, 1737
Spier Derrick	Rachel Kuyper	John	Sept. 16, 1808
Spier Derrick	Rachel Kuyper	Cooper Andrew	Sept. 9, 1810
Spier Hans	Treintje Pieters	Hendrick (bap)	Oct. 5, 1685
Spier Hans	Treintje Pieters	(daughter, bap)	Oct. 3, 1687
Spier Hans	Treintje Pieters	Johannis (bap)	Oct. —, 1690
Spier Johannis	Maritje Franse	Hendrick (bap)	June 13, 1681
Spier Johannis	Maritje Franse	Frans (bap)	April 2, 1683
Spier Johannis	Maritje Franse	Geertruyt (bap)	April 6, 1685
Spier Johannis	Maritje Franse	Maddaleen (bap)	April 11, 1687
Spier Johannis	Maritje Franse	Jannetje (bap)	April 2, 1689
Spier Johannis	Maritje Franse	Rachel (bap)	April 14, 1691

BIRTH RECORD. 379

FATHER.	MOTHER.	CHILD.	DATE OF BIRTH.
Spier Johannis	Gertruy Roome	Johannis	Feb. 11, 1746
Spier John	Maritje Hennion	Hendrick	May 18, 1804
Spier John	Maritje Hennion	David	Aug. 6, 1805
Spier John	Maritje Hennion	John	May 31, 1807
Spier John	Maritje Hennion	Garret	Sept. 22, 1809
Spier John	Maritje Hennion	Robert	June 15, 1816
Spier John	Maritje Hennion	Garret	Oct. 29, 1820
Spier Tomas Janse	Catrina Tomas	Maritje (bap)	April 6, 1686
Stager Richard	Elizabeth Kingsland	William M.	Dec. 25, 1815
Steinmets Casper	Jannetje Gerrits	Joanna (bap)	Dec. 29, 1667
Steinmets Christopher	Jannetje Gerrits	Casparus (bap)	Oct 11, 1686
Steinmets Christopher	Jannetje Gerrits	Annetje (bap)	Oct. 1, 1688
Steinmets Christopher	Jannetje Gerrits	——— (bap)	April 14, 1691
Steinmets Christopher	Jannetje Gerrits	Jannetje (bap)	Oct. —, 1692
Steinmets Gerrit	Vrouwtje Claes	Annetje	June 25, 1686
Steinmets Gerrit	Vrouwtje Claes	Annetje	Oct. 1, 1688
Steinmets Gerrit	Catrina Gerrits	Ariantje	March 15, 1695
Steinmets Gerrit	Catrina Gerrits	Casper	June 12, 1696
Steinmets Gerrit	Catrina Gerrits	Hermanus (bap)	May 10, 1698
Steinmets Gerrit	Catrina Gerrits	Helena (5th ch.)	Feb. 25, 1703
Steinmets Hermanus	Elsje ———	Antje	Jan. —, 1731
Stevenson Albert	Jesitje Ryniers	Antje (bap)	April 22, 1690
Straatmaker Jan	Geesje Gerrits	Janjnete (bap)	Dec. 26, 1666
Straatmaker Jan	Geesje Gerrits	Annetje (bay)	Feb. 17, 1669
Straatmaker Jan	Geesje Gerrits	Gerrit (bap)	Oct 2, 1676
Stuyvesant Casparus	Sara Cowenhoven	Pieter	Nov. 6, 1761
Stuyvesant Casparus	Sara Cowenhoven	Samuel	Oct. 8, 1766
Stuyvesant Casparus	Sara Cowenhoven	Johannis	April 22, 1770
Stuyvesant Casparus	Sara Cowenhoven	Saara	Nov. 15, 1773
Stuyvesant Casparus	Sara Cowenhoven	Ned	Dec. 12, 1778
Stuyvesant Petrus	Pryntje Preyer	Pieter (bap)	March 4, 1735
Stuyvesant Petrus	Pryntje Preyer	Kasper	March 1, 1736
Stuyvesant Petrus	Pryntje Preyer	Jenneke	Nov. 28, 1737
Stuyvesant Petrus	Pryntje Preyer	Pieter	Oct. 17, 1739
Stuyvesant Petrus	Pryntje Preyer	Sara	Nov. 1, 1741
Stuyvesant Petrus	Pryntje Preyer	Catrina	April 15, 1744
Stuyvesant Petrus	Pryntje Preyer	Johannis	Jan. 2, 1746
Stuyvesant Pieter	Lena De Mare	Pieter	Sept. 20, 1770
Stuyvesant Pieter	Lena De Mare	Maria	Nov. 22, 1780
Terheun Albert Alberts	Hendrickje Stevens	Rachel (bap)	April 22, 1690
Terx Tomas	Margrietje Terx	Willem (bap)	March 25, 1680
Toers Abraham	Frenkye Santfort	Cornelius	June 11, 1769
Toers Abraham	Eleanor Van Winkle	Ann	Dec. 1, 1809
Toers Abraham	Eleanor Van Winkle	Esther	Aug. 30, 1811
Toers Abraham	Eleanor Van Winkle	Walter	May 27, 1814
Toers Abraham	Eleanor Van Winkle	Joseph	Sept. 25, 1816
Toers Arent	Annetje Spier	Jacomyntje	April 2, 1731
Toers Arent	Annetje Spier	Jacomyntje (bap)	March 19, 1733
Toers Arent	Annetje Spier	Catelyntje	March 4, 1735

FATHER.	MOTHER.	CHILD.	DATE OF BIRTH.
Toers Arent	Annetje Spier	Nicholas	March 23, 1737
Toers Arent	Annetje Spier	Catreintje	Sept. 30, 1739
Toers Claas Arentse	Jacomyntje Van Neste	Annetje	June 27, 1685
Toers Claas Arentse	Jacomyntje Van Neste	Judith (bap)	April 11, 1687
Toers Claas Arentse	Jacomyntje Van Neste	(daughter)	Feb 4, 1694
Toers Claas Arentse	Jacomyntje Van Neste	Pietertje	Sep. 6, 1696
Toers Class Arentse	Jacomyntje Van Neste	Arent	June 10, 1699
Toers Claas Arentse	Jacomyntje Van Neste	Nicholas (7th ch.)	May 11, 1703
Toers Claas Arentse	Jacomyntje Van Neste	Joris	May 16, 1707
Toers Lourens Arentse	Fransyntje Tomas	Johannis (bap)	April 6, 1685
Toers Lourens Arentse	Fransyntje Tomas	Tomas (bap)	April 11, 1687
Toers Lourens Arentse	Fransyntje Tomas	Maritje (bap)	Sept. 30, 1869
Toers Lourens Arentse	Fransyntje Tomas	Ariaen (bap)	May 29, 1694
Toers Lourens Arentse	Fransyntje Tomas	(12th ch., 8th son)	Sept. 20, 1696
Toers Nicholas	Jannetje Van Rypen	Annetje	April 3, 1770
Toers Nicholas	Jannetje Van Rypen	Arent	Jan. 27, 1784
Toleman James	Phebe Garrison	Eliza G	March 26, 1824
Tomase Arien	Maritje Cobose	Maritje (bap)	April 2, 1688
Tomase Frederick	Catrina Hoppe	Andries (bap)	Jan. 1, 1679
Tomase Frederick	Catrina Hoppe	Cristina (bap)	Aug. 5, 1681
Tomase Frederick	Catrina Hoppe	Maritje (bap)	Nov. 11, 1684
Tomase Frederick	Catrina Hoppe	Dirck (bap)	April 14, 1691
Tomase Johannis	Maritje Van Deusen	Thomas	May 7, 1707
Tomase Johannis	Maritje Van Deusen	Abraham	Sept. 29, 1708
Tomase Johannis	Maritje Van Deusen	Arie	Dec. 17, 1711
Tomase Juriaen	Reykje Hermans	Aeltje (bap)	April 2, 1684
Tomase Juriaen	Reykje Hermans	Grietje	Oct. 5, 1691
Tomase Tomas	Saertje Duesler	Jannetje	Aug. 27, 1702
Tonise Hendrick	Grietje Saannels	Trintje (bap)	Aug. 15, 1667
Traphagen Henry	Neeltje Van Vorst	Anna V. H	Nov. 28, 1803
Traphagen Henry	Neeltje Van Vorst	Cornelius V.	Aug. 5, 1805
Traphagen Henry	Neeltje Van Vorst	Hannah Maria	Sept. 27, 1807
Traphagen Henry	Neeltje Van Vorst	Henry M.	June 8, 1809
Tysen Gerrit	Hannetje Harmans	Pieter (bap)	Nov. 3, 1667
Tysen Toniss	Gerritje Gerrits	Hendrickje	May 22, 1676
Van Benthuysen Pieter,	Margrietje Olpertz	Isaac	Oct 14, 1741
Van Buren Beekman	Ann Ackerman	Ann D.	Aug. 28, 1820
Van Buren Beekman	Ann Ackerman	John	Aug. 22, 1822
Van Buren Beekman	Ann Ackerman	Gitty K.	July 25, 1824
Van Buren Sylvester	Ann Doughty	William D.	Nov. 13, 1799
Van Buskirk Cornelius,	Beeltje Van Wagenen	Cornelis	Sept. 15, 1747
Van Buskirk Cornelius,	Maria Demarest	Esther	July 7, 1808
Van Buskirk Jacobus	Sara Vreeland	Antje	March 19, 1790
Van Buskirk Jacobus	Sara Vreeland	Jacobus	Oct. 21 1797
Van Buskirk Jeremiah,	Ann Garritse	Eliza Ann	Oct. 17, 1817
Van Buskirk John	Eleanor Banta	Jane	June 16, 1821
Van Buskirk Nicholas	Jane Cadmus	James	Sept. 10, 1815
Van Buskirk Nicholas	Jane Cadmus	Jasper	Oct. 17, 1817
Van Clief Daniel	Elizabeth Vanderbeek	Gertrude	June 29, 1812

BIRTH RECORD.

FATHER.	MOTHER.	CHILD.	DATE OF BIRTH.
Van Clief Daniel	Elizabeth Vanderbeek	Adrian V.	Jan. 5, 1816
Van Clief Daniel	Elizabeth Vanderbeek	Maria	Nov. 13, 1817
Van Clief Daniel	Elizabeth Vanderbeek	Helen	Nov. 29, 1819
Van Clief Daniel	Elizabeth Vanderbeek	John	March 27, 1823
Van Clief Daniel	Elizabeth Vanderbeek	Eliza	May 5, 1824
Van Clief Daniel	Aeltje Diedricks	Daniel	March 2, 1798
Van Clief John	Geertruy Diedricks	Fitje	May 19, 1793
Van Clief John	Geertruy Diedricks	Fitje	July 17, 1795
Van Clief John	Geertruy Diedricks	Mary	Dec. 4, 1797
Van Clief John	Geertruy Diedricks	Jacob	Aug. 25, 1800
Van Clief John	Geertruy Diedricks	John	July 9, 1802
Van Clief John	Geertruy Diedricks	Jane	May 1, 1805
Van Clief John	Geertruy Diedricks	Gitty	Sept. 18, 1806
Van Clief John	Geertruy Diedricks	Jane	Oct. 24, 1808
Van de Linden Roelof	Susannah Hendricks	Claesje (bap).	June 22, 1685
Van de Walin Hendrick	Grietje ———	Mary (bap.)	Nov. 3, 1667
Van der Beek Abraham	Hannah Terhune	Abraham	June 21, 1810
Van der Beek Abraham	Hannah Terhune	Stephen	July 27, 1812
Van der Bilt Aaron	Ariantje Van der Hoof	Beelitje	March 2, 1796
Van der Bilt Aaron	Ariantje Van der Hoof	Gerrit	Oct. 4. 1800
Van der Bilt Aaron	Ariantje Van der Hoof	Catherine	Jan. 3, 1811
Van der Bilt Aaron	Ariantje Van der Hoof	Maria	Oct. 6, 1812
Van der Bilt Aaron	Ariantje Van der Hoof	Elizabeth	Dec. 27, 1815
Van der Bilt Aaron	Ariantje Van der Hoof	Nancy	June 9, 1817
Van der Hoof Gerrit	Saertje Preyer	Maritje	July 3, 1769
Van der Hoof Gerrit	Saertje Preyer	Eva	April 25, 1771
Van der Hoof Gerrit	Saertje Preyer	Hendrick	June 18, 1774
Van der Hoof Gerrit	Saertje Preyer	Ariantje	Oct. 23, 1778
Van der Hoof Gerrit	Saertje Preyer	Sara	Sept. 9, 1782
Van der Hoof Hendrick	Eva Slot	Johannis (bap)	March 30, 1724
Van der Hoof Hendrick	Eva Slot	Maritje	June 30, 1732
Van der Hoof Hendrick	Eva Slot	Sara	May 19, 1741
Van der Hoof Petrus	Rachael Van Clerk	Hendrick	Oct. 22, 1770
Van der Veren Johannis	Doretea Jans	Hendrick	May 12, 1697
Van der Veren Johannis	Doretea Jans	Abraham	April 2, 1700
Van der Veren Johannis	Doretea Jans	Gerrit (9th ch., 7th son)	July 12, 1705
Van Galen Lourens	Trintje Vreeland	Joanna	Aug. 21, 1701
Van Galen Lourens	Trintje Vreeland	(son)	Oct. 12, 1703
Van Galen Lourens	Trintje Vreeland	(daughter)	Feb. 4, 1706
Van Galen Lourens	Trintje Vreeland	Maria	May 31, 1708
Van Galen Lourens	Trintje Vreeland	Catrina (bap)	April 3, 1711
Van Gelder Cobus	Sara Ackerman	Isaac	Oct. 1, 1778
Van Gelder Cobus	Sara Ackerman	John	Feb. 16, 1780
Van Gelder Cobus	Sara Ackerman	Samuel	March 23, 1784
Van Gelder Isaac	Elisabet Wekken	Isaac	June 15, 1774
Van Giesen Abraham	Fitje Andries	Rynier	Aug. 7, 1694
Van Giesen Abraham	Fitje Andries	(daughter)	Sept. 19, 1696
Van Giesen Abraham	Fitje Andries	Abraham (6th ch.)	Nov. 18, 1702
Van Giesen Bastian	Aeltje Hendricks	Hendrick (bap)	Oct. —, 1690

BIRTH RECORD.

FATHER.	MOTHER.	CHILD.	DATE OF BIRTH.
Van Giesen Bastian	Aeltje Hendricks	Rynier (bap)	Oct. —, 1692
Van Giesen Bastian	Aeltje Hendricks	Dirck (7th ch. 6th son)	Aug. 3, 1705
Van Giesen Isaac	Cornelia Hendricks	Rynier	Dec. 10, 1692
Van Giesen Isaac	Cornelia Hendricks	Rynier	March 5, 1694
Van Giesen Isaac	Cornelia Hendricks	Joris	Sept. 22, 1696
Van Giesen Isaac	Cornelia Hendricks	Dirckje	Aug. 15, 1699
Van Giesen Isaac	Cornelia Hendricks	Claesje	April 13, 1702
Van Giesen Isaac	Cornelia Hendricks	Rynier	Nov. 17, 1704
Van Giesen Rynier	Dirckje Cornelis	Abraham (bap)	Dec. 26, 1656
Van Hooren Jacob	Catreintje Stuyvesant	Raeggel	Oct. 25, 1775
Van Hooren Jacob	Catreintje Stuyvesant	Catreintje	June 21, 1780
Van Hooren Jan	Helena Sip	Jannetje	Feb. 25, 1736
Van Hooren Jan	Helena Sip	Johannis	Aug. 2, 1742
Van Hooren Johannis	Beeltje Van Rypen	Johannis	March 30, 1765
Van Hooren Johannis	Beeltje Van Rypen	Aeltje	Sept. 7, 1769
Van Hooren Johannis	Beeltje Van Rypen	Neeltje	Dec. 28, 1771
Van Hooren Johannis	Beeltje Van Rypen	Gerrit	June 28, 1774
Van Hooren John	Jannetje Garrabrants	John	June 23, 1785
Van Hooren John	Jannetje Garrabrants	Cornelius	Feb. 3, 1787
Van Hooren Rutgert	Neeltje Diedricks	Joris	Feb. 8, 1700
Van Hooren Rutgert	Neeltje Diedricks	Jan	Feb. 23, 1702
Van Hooren Rutgert	Neeltje Diedricks	Maritje	March 21, 1704
Van Hooren Rutgert	Neeltje Diedricks	Annetje	Feb. 6, 1707
Van Horne Cornelius	Sally Clendenny	Barent	March 11, 1800
Van Horne Cornelius	Jane Garrabrants	Cornelius G.	March 9, 1811
Van Horne Cornelius	Jane Garrabrants	John	April 18, 1813
Van Horne Cornelius	Jane Garrabrants	Helen	Nov. 1, 1815
Van Horne Cornelius	Jane Garrabrants	Cornelius	Oct. 14, 1820
Van Horne Cornelius	Jane Garrabrants	Belina	Dec. 14, 1822
Van Horne Garret	Margaret Gautier	Eliza	March 31, 1816
Van Horne Garret	Margaret Gautier	John	April 4, 1819
Van Horne Garret	Margaret Gautier	Stephen S.	Dec. 9, 1823
Van Horne Gerrit	Trintje Garrabrants	Myndert	July 21, 1795
Van Horne Henry	Catherine Vreeland	Gertrude	March 17, 1811
Van Horne Henry	Catherine Vreeland	Jacob	Sept. 18, 1813
Van Horne Jacob	Leah Earle	Jacobus	Dec. 15, 1793
Van Horne John	Jannetje Garrabrants	Gerrit	Sept. 11, 1790
Van Horne John	Jannetje Garrabrants	Peter	March 26, 1793
Van Horne John	Jannetje Garrabrants	Daniel	March 22, 1795
Van Horne John	Polly Preyer	Jane	June 10, 1810
Van Horne John	Polly Preyer	Jacob	June 8, 1814
Van Horne John	Polly Preyer	Sarah	Dec. 2, 1818
Van Horne John G.	Hannah Van Rypen	Catherine	July 15, 1814
Van Horne John G.	Hannah Van Rypen	Garret	April 20, 1820
Van Horne Myndert	Mary Sickles	Garret	Sept. 26, 1817
Van Horne Myndert	Mary Sickles	Mary	Feb. 10, 1822
Van Horne Peter	Ann Ross	Agnes	Nov. 3, 1818
Van Horne Peter	Ann Ross	Jane	Jan. 12, 1821
Van Horne Peter	Ann Ross	John	Jan. 23, 1823
	Van Houten Annetje	Matje (bap)	March 10, 1667

BIRTH RECORD. 383

FATHER.	MOTHER.	CHILD.	DATE OF BIRTH.
Van Houten Helmigh	Aagtje Vreeland	Jenneke	Nov. 13, 1756
Van Houten Helmigh	Aagtje Vreeland	Michael	March 9, 1761
Van Houten Helmigh	Aagtje Vreeland	Jenneke	Oct. 16, 1762
Van Houten Helmigh	Aagtje Vreeland	Michael	Dec. 17, 1768
Van Houten Helmigh	Catherine Van Rypen	Catherine	Sept. 20, 1800
Van Houten Helmigh	Catherine Van Rypen	John	Aug. 27, 1803
Van Houten Helmigh	Catherine Van Rypen	Gerrit	Sept 10, 1806
Van Houten Helmigh	Catherine Van Rypen	Elizabeth V. R.	July 23, 1811
Van Houten Helmigh	Catherine Van Rypen	John	April 29, 1814
Van Houten Helmigh	Catherine Van Rypen	Jane	Nov. 7, 1816
Van Houten Helmigh	Catherine Van Rypen	Helmigh	Jan. 12, 1821
Van Houten Johannis Helmigsen	Helena Johannise Vreeland	Johannis (bap)	June 17, 1735
Van Houten Johannis	Aeltje Sickles	Johannis	Jan. 22, 1763
Van Houten Johannis	Aeltje Sickles	Sara	Feb. 15, 1775
Van Houten Johannis	Rachel De Maree	Helmigh	Aug 1, 1779
Van Houten Johannis	Rachel De Maree	Catrintje	Nov. 14, 1781
Van Houten Johannis	Rachel De Maree	Aegie	Aug. 27, 1783
Van Houten John	Annatje Collerd	Geertje	Feb. 10, 1784
Van Houten John	Annatje Collerd	Johannis	Feb. 11, 1789
Van Houten John	Annatje Collerd	Aeltje	Jan. 9, 1791
Van Houten John	Annatje Collerd	Sara	June 25, 1795
Van Houten John	Annatje Collerd	Annatje	March 15, 1798
Van Houten John	Annatje Collerd	Johannis	Aug. 27, 1802
Van Houten John	Sarah Mandeville	Nicholas M	March 11, 1822
Van Houten John	Sarah Mandeville	John	April 13, 1825
Van Kleeck Baltus Barentse	Trintje Janse Buys	Pieter (bap)	Oct. 5, 1685
Van Kleeck Baltus Barentse	Trintje Janse Buys	Pieter (bap)	Oct. 1, 1688
Van Laer Adrian	Abigail Ver Planck	Abraham	Nov. 3, 1667
Van Naamen Evert	Wyntje Van Name	Elysabet (bap)	April 3, 1711
Van Nieuwkirk Gerret Mattheusen	Catrintje ———	Catrintje	Aug. 9, 1731
Van Nieuwkirk Paulus Mattheusen	Helena Spier	Catrina	May 10, 1729
Van Nieuwkirk Paulus Mattheusen	Helena Spier	Catelyntje (bap)	May 7, 1733
Van Nieuwkirk Paulus Mattheusen	Helena Spier	Barent (bap)	March 12, 1738
Van Nieuwkirk Paulus Mattheusen	Helena Spier	Jannetje	May 26, 1740
Van Ooglem Dirck Janse	Elysabet Cornelis	Beelitje	March 24, 1673
Van Reenan Gerrit	Eltje Everts	Evert (bap)	Oct. 7, 1678
Van Reenan Gerrit	Eltje Everts	Jan (bap)	April 2, 1683
Van Roon Rynier Josiasen	Constantine Van de Swalin	Josias (bap)	April 6, 1686

FATHER.	MOTHER.	CHILD.	DATE OF BIRTH.
Van Rypen Christopher,	Geertje Van Houten	Annatje	April 10, 1803
Van Rypen Christopher,	Geertje Van Houten	Nancy	July 23, 1804
Van Rypen Christopher,	Geertje Van Houten	Henry	Sept. 12, 1806
Van Rypen Christopher,	Geertje Van Houten	John	July 22, 1808
Van Rypen Christopher,	Geertje Van Houten	Alexander	Nov. 25, 1812
Van Rypen Christopher,	Geertje Van Houten	Elizabeth	Nov. 28, 1817
Van Rypen Christopher,	Geertje Van Houten	Gitty	Sept. 15, 1820
Van Rypen Christopher,	Geertje Van Houten	Jane	Dec. 8, 1823
Van Rypen Cornelis	Elisabet Vreeland	Daniel	March 7, 1788
Van Rypen Cornelius	Vrouwtje Gerritse	Gerrit	July 20, 1797
Van Rypen Cornelius	Vrouwtje Gerritse	Helena	Sept. 24, 1799
Van Rypen Cornelius	Vrouwtje Gerritse	Derrick	Sept. 10, 1801
Van Rypen Cornelius	Aeltje Van Horne	John	May 4, 1808
Van Rypen Cornelius	Aeltje Van Horne	Cornelius	April 8, 1813
Van Rypen Daniel	Elisabet Ter Heun	Catrintje	Dec. 2, 1762
Van Rypen Daniel	Elisabet Ter Heun	Cornelis	May 23, 1767
Van Rypen Daniel	Elizabeth Van Rypen	Elizabeth Ann	April 3, 1822
Van Rypen Derrick	Jenneke Vreeland	Michael	Nov. 8, 1793
Van Rypen Derrick	Jenneke Vreeland	Elizabeth	Nov. 22, 1795
Van Rypen Derrick	Jenneke Vreeland	Annatje	June 25, 1797
Van Rypen Derrick	Jenneke Vreeland	Aegie	Dec. 19, 1801
Van Rypen Derrick	Jenneke Vreeland	Daniel	Sept. 7, 1803
Van Rypen Derrick	Jenneke Vreeland	Cornelius	March 17, 1805
Van Rypen Derrick	Jenneke Vreeland	Catherine	Sept. 24, 1807
Van Rypen Derrick	Jenneke Vreeland	Jane	Dec. 27, 1809
Van Rypen Derrick	Jenneke Vreeland	George	Sept. 23, 1811
Van Rypen Derrick	Jenneke Vreeland	Helena	April 20, 1813
Van Rypen Derrick	Jenneke Vreeland	Letta	Oct. 16, 1819
Van Rypen Garret	Jannetje Winne	Johannis	May 10, 1789
Van Rypen Garret	Jannetje Diedricks	Jurrie	July 20, 1767
Van Rypen Garret	Eliza Van Wart	Fanny G.	Oct. 3, 1820
Van Rypen Garret	Eliza Van Wart	Henry G.	Aug. 4, 1823
Van Rypen Garret C.	Hannah Evans	Ann Elizabeth	Feb. 19, 1818
Van Rypen Garret C.	Hannah Evans	Benjamin E.	May 9, 1820
Van Rypen Garret C.	Hannah Evans	Harriet E.	March 29, 1822
Van Rypen Garret C.	Hannah Evans	Benjamin	June 23, 1824
Van Rypen Garret J.	Elizabeth Simonson	Eleanor V. H.	March 10, 1819
Van Rypen Gerrit	Catrintje Van Wagenen,	Margrietje	Oct. 10, 1775
Van Rypen Gerrit	Catrintje Van Wagenen,	Grietje	Dec. 31, 1780
Van Rypen Gerrit	Catrintje Van Wagenen,	Catlyntje	Nov. 29, 1782
Van Rypen Gerrit	Catrintje Van Wagenen,	Elisabet	July 13, 1785
Van Rypen Gerrit	Catrintje Van Wagenen,	Margrietje	Oct. 30, 1788
Van Rypen Gerrit	Leena Vreeland	Joris	June 3, 1787
Van Rypen Gerrit	Catrintje Van Rypen	Annatje	July 12, 1794
Van Rypen Michael	Celia Cadmus	Catherine	Sept. 22, 1817
Van Rypen Michael	Celia Cadmus	Richard	Sept. 25, 1818
Van Rypen Michael	Celia Cadmus	Jasper	Sept. 28, 1820
Van Rypen Michael	Celia Cadmus	Jane	Jan. 4, 1823
Van Rypen Michael	Celia Cadmus	Catherine	April 25, 1825
Van Vaert Benjamin	Mary Wilson	James W.	Dec. 8, 1809

BIRTH RECORD.

FATHER.	MOTHER.	CHILD.	DATE OF BIRTH.
Van Vaert Benjamin	Mary Wilson	Jacob	March 20, 1812
Van Vaert Benjamin	Mary Wilson	Benjamin Henry	March 3, 1814
Van Vorst Cornelis	Fitje Gerrits (Van Wagenen)	Ide	July 9, 1687
Van Vorst Cornelis	Fitje Gerrits (Van Wagenen)	Hillegont (bap)	April 14, 1691
Van Vorst Cornelis	Fitje Gerrits (Van Wagenen)	Annetje	Jan. 5, 1693
Van Vorst Cornelis	Fitje Gerrits (Van Wagenen)	Ide (5th ch.)	Dec. 24, 1695
Van Vorst Cornelis	Fitje Gerrits (Van Wagenen)	Johannis	May 7, 1697
Van Vorst Cornelis	Fitje Gerrits (Van Wagenen)	Hendrick	Jan. 29, 1699
Van Vorst Cornelis	Fitje Gerrits (Van Wagenen)	Cornelis	March 8, 1700
Van Vorst Cornelis	Fitje Gerrits (Van Wagenen)	Jacob	May 7, 1702
Van Vorst Cornelis	Fitje Gerrits (Van Wagenen)	Jenneke	March 8, 1704
Van Vorst Cornelis	Fitje Gerrits (Van Wagenen)	Maritje	May 22, 1706
Van Vorst Cornelius	Annatje Van Hoorn	Cornelius	Sept. 6, 1753
Van Vorst Cornelius	Annatje Van Hoorn	Johannis	March 3, 1761
Van Vorst Cornelius	Annatje Van Hoorn	Claesje	Aug. 31, 1765
Van Vorst Cornelius	Annatje Van Hoorn	Neeltje	Sept. 16, 1768
Van Vorst Cornelius	Hannah Gilbert	Cornelius	Aug. 6, 1794
Van Vorst Cornelius	Hannah Gilbert	Susan	Oct. 15, 1798
Van Vorst Cornelius	Hannah Gilbert	Anna	March 26, 1803
Van Vorst Cornelius	Sarah S. Brower	Elizabeth B	Nov. 3, 1817
Van Vorst Cornelius	Sarah S. Brower	Susan	Aug. 22, 1819
Van Vorst Cornelius	Sarah S. Brower	Cornelius	March 7, 1822
Van Vorst Garret	Cynthia Hennion	Elizabeth	Nov. 6, 1811
Van Vorst Garret	Cynthia Hennion	David	Feb. 20, 1823
Van Vorst Ide	Hilletje Jans	Joanna (bap)	April 16, 1666
Van Vorst Jacob	Christina Evertson	Sarah	Feb. 22, 1822
Van Vorst John	Sarah Vasher	Ann Eliza	June 2, 1817
Van Vorst John	Sarah Vasher	Cornelia	Nov. 15, 1818
Van Vorst John	Sarah Vasher	Sarah Frances	Sept. 12, 1820
Van Vorst John	Sarah Vasher	John	Sept 25, 1822
Van Wagenen Cornelius	Helena Bow	Annatje	Dec. 17, 1749
Van Wagenen Helmigh	Maritje Blinkerhoff	Aeffie	Aug. 9, 1737
Van Wagenen Helmigh	Maritje Blinkerhoff	Catlyntje	Dec. 25, 1738
Van Wagenen Helmigh	Maritje Blinkerhoff	Maritje	April 7, 1741
Van Wagenen Jacob	Jannetje Van Houten	Jacobus (bap)	March 8, 1736
Van Wagenen Jacob	Jannetje Van Houten	Catlyntje	July 23, 1744
Van Wagenen Jacob	Jannetje Van Houten	Helena	April 22, 1747
Van Wagenen Jacob	Aagtje Vreeland	Annatje	Dec. 31, 1757
Van Wagenen Jacob	Aegie Blinkerhof	Claesje	March 17, 1778
Van Wagenen Jacob	Aegie Blinkerhof	Catlyntje	Aug. 3, 1872

BIRTH RECORD.

FATHER.	MOTHER.	CHILD.	DATE OF BIRTH.
Van Wagenen Jacob	Aegie Blinkerhof	Johannis	July 27, 1785
Van Wagenen Jacob	Aegie Blinkerhof	Hartman	Nov. 15, 1790
Van Wagenen Jacob Gerritse	Lea Gerrits	Gerrit	May —, 1720
Van Wagenen Jacob Gerritse	Lea Gerrits	Neesje	Sept. 2, 1724
Van Wagenen Jacob Gerritse	Lea Gerrits	Johannis	March 11, 1727
Van Wagenen Jacob Gerritse	Lea Gerrits	Beelitje	March 11, 1727
Van Wagenen Johannis	Neesje Van Wagenen	Jacob	Oct. 7, 1751
Van Wagenen Johannis	Neesje Van Wagenen	Catlyntje	Jan. 4, 1754
Van Wagenen Johannis	Neesje Van Wagenen	Leya	Dec. 17, 1756
Van Wagenen Johannis	Neesje Van Wagenen	Antje	Sept. 25, 1761
Van Wagenen Johannis	Aeltje Vreeland	Lea	Dec. 4, 1759
Van Wagenen Johannis Gerritse	Catlyntje Helmigse	Aeltje	Sept. 6, 1705
Van Wagenen Johannis Gerritse	Catlyntje Helmigse	Helmigh	Feb. 18, 1708
Van Wagenen Johannis Gerritse	Catlyntje Helmigse	Gerrit	Oct. 7, 1710
Van Wagenen Johannis Gerritse	Catlyntje Helmigse	Jannetje (6th ch.)	Feb. 22, 1821
Van Winkle Abraham	Antje Clendenny	Walter	Oct. 4, 1785
Van Winkle Abraham	Antje Clendenny	Walter	March 26, 1787
Van Winkle Abraham	Antje Clendenny	Abraham	Feb. 18, 1789
Van Winkle Abraham	Antje Clendenny	Eleanor	Feb. 6, 1791
Van Winkle Abraham	Antje Clendenny	Rachel	July 22, 1793
Van Winkle Abraham	Antje Clendenny	Nancy	July 16, 1795
Van Winkle Abraham	Antje Clendenny	Catherine	Jan. 11, 1798
Van Winkle Abraham	Mary Gordon	Joseph	July 9, 1810
Van Winkle Abraham	Mary Gordon	Hannah	July 29, 1811
Van Winkle Abraham	Mary Gordon	William G.	Jan. 27, 1815
Van Winkle Cornelius,	Margrietje Van Rypen	Garret V. R.	Dec. 30, 1807
Van Winkle Cornelius,	Margrietje Van Rypen	Ann	Dec. 24, 1809
Van Winkle Cornelius,	Margrietje Van Rypen	John	July 3, 1812
Van Winkle Cornelius,	Margrietje Van Rypen	Daniel	April 19, 1817
Van Winkle Cornelius,	Margrietje Van Rypen	Cornelius	Dec. 25, 1819
Van Winkle Cornelius,	Margrietje Van Rypen	Catherine V. R	Jan. 22, 1823
Van Winkle Daniel	Jannetje Cornelise Vreeland	Metje	Dec. 31, 1710
Van Winkle Daniel	Jannetje Cornelise Vreeland	Aeltje	April 13, 1712
Van Winkle Daniel	Aeltje Juriaensen	Juriaen	Feb. 22, 1761
Van Winkle Daniel	Aeltje Juriaensen	Catrintje	Jan. 30, 1765
Van Winkle Daniel	Aeltje Juriaensen	Hendrick	Nov. 27, 1774
Van Winkle Daniel	Antje Winne	Cornelius	Aug. 6, 1783
Van Winkle Daniel	Antje Winne	Aeltje	April 11, 1786
Van Winkle Daniel	Antje Winne	Jacob	Oct. 28, 1788
Van Winkle Daniel	Antje Winne	Rachel	Jan. 25, 1791

BIRTH RECORD.

FATHER.	MOTHER.	CHILD.	DATE OF BIRTH.
Van Winkle Daniel	Antje Winne	Johannis	Jan. 10, 1795
Van Winkle Daniel	Antje Winne	Daniel	May 18, 1798
Van Winkle Garret	Cornelia Vreeland	Daniel	Feb. 26, 1802
Van Winkle Garret	Cornelia Vreeland	John	Nov. 25, 1804
Van Winkle Garret	Cornelia Vreeland	Garret	June 4, 1807
Van Winkle Garret	Cornelia Vreeland	Michael	Jan. 16, 1810
Van Winkle Garret	Cornelia Vreeland	Stephen	June 15, 1813
Van Winkle Hendrick	Catrintje Waldron	Daniel (bap)	March 4, 1735
Van Winkle Hendrick	Catrintje Waldron	Johannis	May 9, 1739
Van Winkle Hendrick	Catrintje Waldron	Joseph	June 4, 1740
Van Winkle Hendrick	Jannetje Brouwer	Catrina	Jan. 26, 1772
Van Winkle Hendrick	Sara Spier	Raegel	March 29, 1775
Van Winkle Hendrick	Sara Spier	Raegel	Feb. 13, 1777
Van Winkle Hendrick	Sara Spier	Johannis	Nov. 7, 1778
Van Winkle Hendrick	Sara Spier	Jacob	Feb. 20, 1789
Van Winkle Hendrick	Catelyntje Van Wagenen	Aeltje	March 21, 1805
Van Winkle Hendrick	Catelyntje Van Wagenen	Jacob	Sept. 27, 1806
Van Winkle Hendrick	Catelyntje Van Wagenen	Effie	Sept. 11, 1818
Van Winkle Jacob	Rachel Commegaer	Daniel	July 21, 1758
Van Winkle Jacob	Rachel Commegaer	Catrintje	June 1, 1763
Van Winkle Jacob	Rachel Commegaer	Joseph	May 18, 1768
Van Winkle Jacob	Rachel Commegaer	Lea	Nov. 7, 1770
Van Winkle Jacob A.	Sara Cadmus	Abraham	June 11, 1808
Van Winkle Jacob A.	Sara Cadmus	Catherine	Feb. 11, 1810
Van Winkle Jacob A.	Sara Cadmus	Jasper	May 24, 1812
Van Winkle Jacob A.	Sara Cadmus	Rachel Ann	Feb. 2, 1814
Van Winkle Jacob D.	Ann Vreeland	Michael	March 27, 1817
Van Winkle Jacob D.	Ann Vreeland	Ann W.	March 7, 1820
Van Winkle Jacob D.	Ann Vreeland	Daniel	June 27, 1822
Van Winkle Jacob D.	Ann Vreeland	Gitty	Oct. 15, 1823
Van Winkle Jacob H.	Mary Smith	Sarah Ann	Feb. 3, 1816
Van Winkle Jacob H.	Mary Smith	Fanny	Aug. 5, 1817
Van Winkle Jacob H.	Mary Smith	Gloriana	Feb. 20, 1824
Van Winkle Jacob Jacobse	Aeltje Daniels	Jacob	Sept. 19, 1676
Van Winkle Jacob Jacobse	Aeltje Daniels	Margrietje	Oct. 22, 1678
Van Winkle Jacob Jacobse	Aeltje Daniels	Daniel	July 28, 1681
Van Winkle Jacob Jacobse	Aeltje Daniels	Johannis	June 25, 1686
Van Winkle Jacob Jacobse	Aeltje Daniels	Simon	Jan. 22, 1689
Van Winkle Jacob Jacobse	Aeltje Daniels	(son)	April 10, 1692
Van Winkle Jacob Jacobse	Grietje Hendricks	Hendrick	Jan. 20, 1696

BIRTH RECORD.

FATHER.	MOTHER.	CHILD.	DATE OF BIRTH.
Van Winkle Jacob Jacobse	Grietje Hendricks	Treitje	Jan. 4, 1697
Van Winkle Jacob Jacobse	Grietje Hendricks	Teunis	Dec. 21, 1698
Van Winkle Jacob Jacobse	Grietje Hendricks	Samuel (bap)	Jan. 5, 1705
Van Winkle John	Geertje Diedricks	Antje	March 2, 1801
Van Winkle John	Geertje Diedricks	Hendrick	Feb. 26, 1802
Van Winkle John	Geertje Diedricks	Sally	April 27, 1805
Van Winkle John	Geertje Diedricks	Geertje	March 29, 1807
Van Winkle John	Geertje Diedricks	John D.	March 7, 1810
Van Winkle John	Geertje Diedricks	Jacob	Feb. 26, 1815
Van Winkle John	Geertje Diedricks	Abraham	April 6, 1818
Van Winkle John	Geertje Diedricks	Rachel	July 30, 1820
Van Winkle Jurrie	Antje Sip	Garret	Dec. 16, 1783
Van Winkle Jurrie	Antje Sip	Daniel	May 13, 1787
Van Winkle Symon Jacobse	Annetje Arianse Sip	Margrietje (bap)	———, 1676
Van Winkle Symon Jacobse	Annetje Arianse Sip	Jacob (bap)	April 18, 1682
Van Winkle Symon Jacobse	Annetje Arianse Sip	Symon (bap)	April 6, 1686
Van Winkle Symon Jacobse	Annetje Arianse Sip	Trintje (bap)	April 2, 1688
Van Winkle Symon Jacobse	Annetje Arianse Sip	Rachel (bap)	Oct. —, 1690
Van Winkle Waling Jacobse	Catrina Michielse	Michael (bap)	April 27, 1677
Van Winkle Waling Jacobse	Catrina Michielse	Trintje (bap)	March 25, 1680
Van Winkle Waling Jacobse	Catrina Michielse	Johannis (bap)	Oct. 2, 1682
Van Winkle Waling Jacobse	Catrina Michielse	Trintje (bap)	June 27, 1687
Van Winkle Waling Jacobse	Catrina Michielse	Abraham (bap)	April 22, 1690
Van Winkle Walter	Phebe Tuers	Cornelius	March 19, 1809
Veder Harmanus	Antje Hennion	Garret	Oct. 26, 1749
Veder Harmanus	Antje Hennion	Jacob	Dec. 4, 1754
Veder Harmanus	Antje Hennion	Cornelius	Feb. 27, 1758
Veder Harmanus	Antje Hennion	Maritje	Dec. 27, 1760
Veder Harmanus	Antje Hennion	Ariantje	May 12, 1763
Veder Harmanus	Antje Hennion	Cornelius	Aug. 25, 1766
Ver Meule Adrian	Christina Fredricks	Fredrick	———, 1709
Ver Meule Adrian	Christina Fredricks	Lennitje	April 8, 1712
Vernoy Cornelis	Hendrickje Jans	Dieuwer (bap)	Oct. 5, 1685
Vreeland Abraham	Margrietje Van Winckel	Enoch	March 14, 1700
Vreeland Claas	Catlyntje Sip	Michael	July 31, 1758
Vreeland Claas	Antje Bassett	Antje	Feb. 28, 1762
Vreeland Claas	Antje Bassett	Elisabet	May 30, 1764

BIRTH RECORD.

FATHER.	MOTHER.	CHILD.	DATE OF BIRTH.
Vreeland Claas	Antje Bassett	Saara	Oct. 7, 1766
Vreeland Claas	Antje Bassett	Beelitje	April 17, 1774
Vreeland Claas	Antje Bassett	Stephen	May 31, 1778
Vreeland Claas Hartmanse	Annetje Harmans	Hartman	March 10, 1698
Vreeland Cornelis	Catrina Cadmus	Michael	Nov. 24, 1757
Vreeland Cornelis	Catrina Cadmus	Dirck	May 25, 1760
Vreeland Cornelis	Catrina Cadmus	Cornelius	Sept. 20, 1762
Vreeland Cornelis Michielse	Metje Dirckse (Braecke), Aeltje (bap)		April 18, 1682
Vreeland Cornelis Michielse	Metje Dirckse (Braecke), (4th ch.)		Sept. 18, 1694
Vreeland Cornelis Michielse	Metje Dirckse (Braecke), Metje		Oct. 3, 1698
Vreeland Cornelius	Elizabeth Van Buskirk	Peter V. B.	Aug. 27, 1795
Vreeland Daniel	Cornelia Newkirk	Jane	Nov. 5, 1813
Vreeland Daniel	Cornelia Newkirk	Michael	Jan. 31, 1817
Vreeland Daniel	Cornelia Newkirk	Aaron N.	Dec. 4, 1819
Vreeland Daniel	Cornelia Newkirk	Gitty S.	April 17, 1822
Vreeland Dirck	Neesje Neiffe	Fitje	Aug. 16, 1751
Vreeland Dirck	Neesje Neiffe	Metje	Oct. 31, 1754
Vreeland Dirck	Neesje Neiffe	Leya	Sept. 17, 1758
Vreeland Elias Michielse, Grietje Jacobs		Ragel	March 8, 1676
Vreeland Elias Michielse, Grietje Jacobs		Jacob	Aug. 9, 1678
Vreeland Enoch	Keetje Kip	Joris	Aug. 16, 1771
Vreeland Enoch Michielse	Aagtje Van Hooren	(son)	March 6, 1705
Vreeland Enoch Michielse	Aagtje Van Hooren	Fitje	Feb. 2, 1707
Vreeland Enoch Michielse	Aagtje Van Hooren	Joris (bap)	Oct. 18, 1708
Vreeland Enoch Michielse	Aagtje Van Hooren	Joris	Sept. 25, 1710
Vreeland Garret	Jannetje Cadmus	Jacob	June 25, 1781
Vreeland Garret	Jannetje Cadmus	Annatje	Feb. 15, 1784
Vreeland Garret	Jannetje Cadmus	Joris	July 12, 1787
Vreeland Garret	Jannetje Cadmus	Jannetje	April 5, 1790
Vreeland Garret M.	Jane Winne	Jane V. R.	July 9, 1818
Vreeland Garret M.	Jane Winne	Gitty	Jan. 7, 1820
Vreeland Garret M.	Jane Winne	Anna Jane	Jan. 27, 1822
Vreeland George	Catherine Newkirk	Garret	Oct. 31, 1809
Vreeland George	Catherine Newkirk	Jane	April 7, 1812
Vreeland George	Catherine Newkirk	Maria	Jan. 28, 1814
Vreeland George	Catherine Newkirk	George	Oct. 8, 1816
Vreeland George	Catherine Newkirk	Margaret	July 23, 1818
Vreeland George	Catherine Newkirk	Hannah	Jan 10, 1820
Vreeland George	Catherine Newkirk	Henry	Dec. 28, 1821
Vreeland George	Catherine Newkirk	Helen	Dec. 22, 1823
Vreeland Hartman Michielse	Maritje Dirkse (Braecke)	Aeltje (bap)	Oct. 8, 1677

BIRTH RECORD.

FATHER.	MOTHER.	CHILD.	DATE OF BIRTH.
Vreeland Hartman Michielse	Maritje Dirckse (Braecke)	Michael	Dec. 31, 1678
Vreeland Hartman Michielse	Maritje Dirckse (Braecke)	Dirck	April 3, 1681
Vreeland Hartman Michielse	Maritje Dirckse (Braecke)	Fitje	Feb. 21, 1683
Vreeland Hartman Michielse	Maritje Dirckse (Braecke)	Aeltje	Oct. 19, 1685
Vreeland Hartman Michielse	Maritje Dirckse (Braecke)	Jannetje	Sept. 14, 1692
Vreeland Hartman Michielse	Maritje Dirckse (Braecke)	———	Jan. 19, 1696
Vreeland Hartman Michielse	Maritje Dirckse (Braecke)	Ariantje	July 19, 1698
Vreeland Hartman Michielse	Maritje Dirckse (Braecke)	Claas (bap)	April 6, 1675
Vreeland Helmagh	Rachel Van Buskirk	Elizabeth	Dec. 16, 1794
Vreeland Helmagh	Rachel Van Buskirk	Jannetje	May 29, 1797
Vreeland Helmigh	Neeltje Van Hoorn	Michael	Jan. 14, 1759
Vreeland Jacob	Maritje Banta	Maritje	Dec. 5, 1768
Vreeland Jacob	Wyntje Der See	Michael	Oct. 11, 1770
Vreeland Jacob	Catlyntje Blinkerhof	Henry	March 23, 1804
Vreeland Jacob	Catlyntje Blinkerhof	George	Aug. 3, 1807
Vreeland Jacob	Catlyntje Blinkerhof	John	Jan. 4, 1810
Vreeland Jacob	Catlyntje Blinkerhof	Cornelius	Aug. 26, 1812
Vreeland Jacob	Catlyntje Blinkerhof	Jacob	Sept. 29, 1817
Vreeland Johannis	Neeltje Hooglandt	Michael	April 18, 1768
Vreeland Johannis	Neeltje Hooglandt	Jannetje	June 23, 1774
Vreeland Johannis	Neeltje Hooglandt	Keetje	——— —, 1782
Veeland Johannis	Lena Garrabrants	Joris	Jan 10, 1779
Vreeland Johannis Johannissen	Annetje Diedricks	Johannis	July 30, 1731
Vreeland Johannis Michielse	Claesje Dirckse (Braecke)	Dirck (bap)	Oct. 11, 1686
Vreeland Johannis Michielse	Claesje Dirckse (Braecke)	Aegtje (bap)	April 22, 1690
Vreeland Johannis Michielse	Claesje Dirckse (Braecke)	———	June 28, 1697
Vreeland Johannis Michielse	Claesje Dirckse (Braecke)	Johannis (5th son, 10th ch.)	July 1, 1705

BIRTH RECORD. 391

FATHER.	MOTHER.	CHILD.	DATE OF BIRTH.
Vreeland John	Keetje De Maree	Neeltje	July 20, 1776
Vreeland John	Keetje De Maree	Catreintje	March 8, 1780
Vreeland John	Keetje De Maree	Jannetje	June 22, 1682
Vreeland John	Keetje De Maree	(daughter)	March 17, 1784
Vreeland, John G.	Catherine Van Houten	Jane	June 14, 1818
Vreeland John G.	Catherine Van Houten	Catalina	May 18, 1824
Vreeland Joris	Jannetje Blinkerhoff	Michael	Oct. 31, 1781
Vreeland Joris	Jannetje Blinkerhoff	Hartman	March 15, 1784
Vreeland Joris	Jannetje Blinkerhoff	Annatje	July 30, 1786
Vreeland Joris	Jannetje Blinkerhoff	Cornelius	Feb. 25, 1789
Vreeland Joris	Jannetje Blinkerhoff	John	Jan. 3, 1792
Vreeland Joris	Jannetje Blinkerhoff	Claesje	Dec. 26, 1794
Vreeland Joris	Jannetje Blinkerhoff	Hendrick	Oct. 11, 1797
Vreeland Joris	Jannetje Blinkerhoff	Jacob	Oct. 11, 1797
Vreeland Joris	Jannetje Blinkerhoff	Jacob	July 5, 1800
Vreeland Joris	Jannetje Blinkerhoff	Garret	June 26, 1803
Vreeland Joris	Jannetje Blinkerhoff	Jacob	March 9, 1809
Vreeland Joris Enochsen	Annetje Van Winkle	Aagtje	Sept. 18, 1733
Vreeland Joris Enochsen	Annetje Van Wagenen	Enoch	Sept. 22, 1737
Vreeland Joris Enochsen	Annetje Van Wagenen	Gerrit	May 18, 1739
Vreeland Joris Enochsen	Annetje Van Wagenen	Enoch	Feb. 18, 1741
Vreeland Joris Enochsen	Annetje Van Wagenen	Johannis	Sept. 21, 1749
Vreeland Joris Enochsen	Annetje Van Wagenen	Gerrit	Nov. 1, 1751
Vreeland Joris Enochsen	Annetje Van Wagenen	Jenneke	Dec. 1, 1758
Vreeland Michael	Annatje Vreeland	Joris	Jan. 31, 1762
Vreeland Michael	Annatje Vreeland	Annatje	July 19, 1764
Vreeland Michael	Annatje Vreeland	John	May 1, 1780
Vreeland Michael	Geertje Sickles	Catleyntje	Aug. 28, 1782
Vreeland Michael	Geertje Sickles	Catleyntje	Jan. 9, 1785
Vreeland Michael	Geertje Sickles	Antje	Dec. 14, 1786
Vreeland Michael	Geertje Sickles	Nicholas	Feb. 20, 1789
Vreeland Michael	Geertje Sickles	Daniel	Feb. 27, 1791
Vreeland Michael	Geertje Sickles	Gerrit	Jan. 31, 1793
Vreeland Michael	Geertje Sickles	Abraham	June 27, 1795
Vreeland Michael	Geertje Sickles	Geertruy	Feb. 23, 1805
Vreeland Michael	Annatje Garrabrants	Lybertje	Aug. 14, 1790
Vreeland Michael	Annatje Garrabrants	Johannis	——, 1792
Vreeland Michael	Annatje Garrabrants	Cornelia	Dec. 24, 1794
Vreeland Michael	Annatje Garrabrants	Annatje	March 4, 1797
Vreeland Michael	Annatje Garrabrants	Myndert	July 1, 1800
Vreeland Michael	Annatje Garrabrants	Michael	Dec. 22, 1806
Vreeland Michael	Aeltje Outwater	Joris	Jan. 25, 1802
Vreeland Michael	Aeltje Outwater	Anna	Feb. 7, 1805

FATHER.	MOTHER.	CHILD.	DATE OF BIRTH.
Vreeland Michael	Aeltje Outwater	Guilliam	Feb. 19, 1807
Vreeland Michael	Aeltje Outwater	Jacob	June 10, 1808
Vreeland Michael	Aeltje Outwater	Jane	Aug. 22, 1810
Vreeland Michael	Aeltje Outwater	Matilda	Jan. 6, 1813
Vreeland Michael	Aeltje Outwater	Cornelius	June 5, 1816
Vreeland Michael	Aeltje Outwater	Hartman	Nov. 8, 1823
Vreeland Michael Cornelise	Jenneke Helmigse Van Houten	Helmigh	Jan. 29, 1730
Vreeland Michael Cornelise	Jenneke Helmigse Van Houten	Aagtje	Feb. 14, 1732
Vreeland Michael Cornelise	Jenneke Helmigse Van Houten	Dirck	March 11, 1737
Vreeland Michael Cornelise	Jenneke Helmigse Van Houten	Jacob	March 11, 1737
Vreeland Michael Cornelise	Jenneke Helmigse Van Houten	Johannis	March 2, 1742
Vreeland Michael Hartmanse	Elysabet Gerrits	——— (bap)	March 30, 1724
Vreeland Michael Hartmanse	Elysabet Gerrits	Beeltje	March 19, 1733
Vreeland Nicholas	Hannah Winne	Nicholas	Aug. 7, 1816
Vreeland Peter	Ann Vreeland	Cornelius	June 28, 1821
Vreeland Peter	Ann Vreeland	Janet	July 31, 1823
Vreeland Stephen	Jenneke Vreeland	Antje	Feb. 4, 1799
Vreeland Stephen	Jenneke Vreeland	Cornelia	Nov. 15, 1801
Vreeland Stephen	Jenneke Vreeland	Elizabeth	May 28, 1803
Vreeland Stephen	Jenneke Vreeland	Maria	Dec. 10, 1809
Vreeland Stephen	Jenneke Vreeland	Isabella	Jan. 26, 1813
Vreeland Stephen	Jenneke Vreeland	Eliza	Feb. 18, 1816
Vreeland William	Catherine Sickles	Jane Maria	Sept. 23, 1823
Waldron Joseph	Aeffie Heilsaaken	Antje	Feb. 27, 1740
Waldron Joseph	Aeffie Heilsaaken	Sara	Jan. 14, 1742
Waldron Joseph	Aeffie Heilsaaken	Benjamin	Aug. 3, 1745
Waldron Joseph	Antje Diedricks	Geertruy	Nov. 11, 1759
Waldron Joseph	Antje Diedricks	Joseph	Jan. 25, 1764
Waldron Joseph	Antje Diedricks	Geertruy	Feb. 11, 1766
Waldron Joseph	Antje Diedricks	Johannis	Nov. 17, 1769
Waldron Joseph	Helena Ryerson	John	Aug. 19, 1792
Waldron Joseph	Helena Ryerson	Joseph	Dec. 29, 1693
Waldron Joseph	Helena Ryerson	Teunis	Aug. 10, 1795
Waldron Joseph	Helena Ryerson	Antje	March 23, 1797
Waldron Joseph	Helena Ryerson	Richard	Dec. 28, 1798
Waldron Joseph	Helena Ryerson	Martin	Jan. 4, 1800
Waldron Joseph	Helena Ryerson	Johannis	July 5, 1801

BIRTH RECORD.

FATHER.	MOTHER.	CHILD.	DATE OF BIRTH
Waldron Joseph	Helena Ryerson	Jacob	June 23, 1804
Waldron Joseph	Jacomyntje Chambers	Annatje	Oct. 20, 1808
Waldron Joseph	Jacomyntje Chambers	Daniel	Aug. 19, 1810
Waldron Joseph	Jacomyntje Chambers	Helen	Aug. 20, 1815
Wauters Merselis	Penelopa Post	Egbert	Sept. 21, 1806
Wauters Merselis	Penelope Post	Sarah P.	April 13, 1811
Wauters Merselis	Penelope Post	John	Dec. 28, 1813
Wauters Merselis	Penelope Post	Elizabeth	Sept. 6, 1821
Welsh Archer G.	Margaret Stager	Alexander F.	Dec. 1, 1824
Welsh Benjamin F.	Elizabeth Rapp	Adriana	Aug. 27, 1810
Welsh Benjamin F.	Elizabeth Rapp	Hannah	Aug. 14, 1812
Welsh Benjamin F.	Elizabeth Rapp	James	May 14, 1814
Welsh Benjamin F.	Elizabeth Rapp	Hannah	June 27, 1816
Welsh Benjamin F.	Elizabeth Rapp	Gertrude R.	Nov. 17, 1818
Welsh Benjamin F.	Isabella Lewis	John	Dec. 28, 1820
Welsh Benjamin F.	Isabella Lewis	Daniel	March 2, 1823
Welsh Daniel	Catherine Van Winkle	Mary Ann C.	July 23, 1818
Welsh Daniel	Catherine Van Winkle	Hannah	March 19, 1821
Welsh Daniel	Catherine Van Winkle	Benjamin F.	Sept. 1, 1823
Welsh Daniel	Catherine Van Winkle	Catherine W.	Sept. 30, 1824
Welsh James	Annatje Brown	Alexander	May 21, 1794
Welsh James	Annatje Brown	Mary	March 17, 1796
Welsh James	Annatje Brown	Archer G.	July 18, 1798
Welsh John	Gertrude Rapp	Elizabeth	Dec. 30, 1810
Welsh John	Gertrude Rapp	James W.	Sept. 17, 1812
Welsh John	Gertrude Rapp	Henry R.	May 23, 1814
Welsh John	Gertrude Rapp	John F.	July 21, 1816
Welsh John	Gertrude Rapp	Adam R.	April 16, 1818
Welsh John	Gertrude Rapp	Benjamin F.	Oct. 2, 1820
Welsh John	Gertrude Rapp	Abner B.	Sept. 14, 1822
Welsh John	Gertrude Rapp	Hannah M. G. L.	Nov. 19, 1824
Welsh John	Annetje Wilson	Gerrit	May 29, 1784
Williams William	Margaret Heaton	Margaret	Jan. 31, 1805
Winne Edo	Aeltje Toers	Annatje	Nov. 30, 1794
Winne Edo	Aeltje Toers	Jannetje	June 8, 1797
Winne Edo	Aeltje Toers	Antje	Dec. 17, 1799
Winne Edo	Aeltje Toers	Nicholas	Feb. 1, 1809
Winne Johannis	Aeltje Diedricks	Antje	Nov. 11, 1759
Winne Johannis	Aeltje Diedricks	Jannetje	Feb. 5, 1762
Winne Johannis	Aeltje Diedricks	Martin	Nov. 24, 1766
Winne John S.	Mary Smith	John	July 17, 1817
Winne John S.	Mary Smith	Eleanor P.	April 23, 1822
Winne Levinus	Annetje Sip	Antje	May 18, 1754
Winne Levinus	Annetje Sip	Martin	Sept. 25, 1758
Winne Levinus	Annetje Sip	Ide	May 22, 1763
Winne Levinus	Annetje Sip	Ide	May 3, 1767
Winne Martin	Jannetje Johannisen Vreeland	Antje (3d ch.)	April 15, 1723
Winne Martin	Jannetje Johannisen Vreeland	Maritje (5th ch.)	March 6, 1730

BIRTH RECORD.

FATHER.	MOTHER.	CHILD.	DATE OF BIRTH.
Winne Martin	Margrietje Banta	Johannis	July 8, 1789
Winne Martin	Margrietje Banta	Aeltje	June 18, 1792
Winne Martin	Margrietje Banta	Aeltje	June 27, 1794
Winne Martin	Geertruy Sickles	Johannis	} July 19, 1791
Winne Martin	Geertruy Sickles	Elizabeth	
Winne Martin	Geertruy Sickles	Levinus	Jan. 7, 1796
Winne Martin	Geertruy Sickles	Levinus	June 24, 1799
Winne Martin	Rachel Van Winkle	Sally	Dec. 22, 1797
Winne Martin	Rachel Van Winkle	Cornelius	Nov. 18, 1799
Winne Martin	Rachel Van Winkle	Aeltje	April 4, 1804
Winne Martin	Rachel Van Winkle	Henry	Oct. 5, 1807
Winne Martin	Rachel Van Winkle	William	June 23, 1811
Winne Martin	Rachel Van Winkle	Jacob	Feb. 20, 1813
Wood Abram	Rhenty Clendenny	Mary	July 31, 1794
Wood Abram	Rhenty Clendenny	Walter	May 3, 1796
Wood Walter	Sarah Post	Abram P.	Jan. 7, 1819
Wood Walter	Sarah Post	Jane D.	Feb. 1, 1821
Wood Walter	Sarah Post	Peter	Aug. 13, 1823
Wood William	Mary Waldron	Helen	Feb. 28, 1811
Wood William	Mary Waldron	John B.	June 15, 1815
Wood William	Mary Waldron	Anna Maria	Sept. 15, 1818
Wood William	Mary Waldron	Eliza	Aug. 13, 1820
York Jan	Elisabet Coenmoef	Hendrick	Feb. 8, 1754
York John	Ariantje Smith	John	Feb. 8, 1775
Young John	Martha De Mott	John W.	June 9, 1824
Zabriskie Albert	Catherina Van Houten	Albert	Feb. 7, 1805
Zabriskie Casparus	Annetje Vreeland	Michael	May 31, 1785
Zabriskie Jacob	Caty Van Houten	John	Aug. 28, 1807
Zabriskie John	Aegie Diedricks	Albert	July 6, 1806
Zabriskie John	Aegie Diedricks	Albert	June 21, 1811

DEATHS.

NAME.	DATE OF DEATH.
Abrahamse Cornelis, of Pemmerpook	Jan. 3, 1677
Ackerman Jacob	July 19, 1825
Ackerman Peter	May 8, 1825
Aerts Hilletje, *wife* of Bartel Claesen (?)	March 2, 1698
Airess Eliza, *daughter* of Elisha	June 16, 1805
Allen Jacob P.	July 7, 1836
Anderson Catherine	Aug. 23, 1819
Anderson Jane	May 6, 1804
Anderson John	March 24, 1837
Anderson John, *son* of William	Aug. 12, 1804
Anderson Mary	Nov. 1, 1827
Anderson Mary, *daughter* of William	Oct. 3, 1802
Andrews Joel	Dec. 16, 1835
Andries Michael	April 22, 1748

BIRTH RECORD.

NAME.	DATE OF DEATH.
Andriesen Catrina	April 8, 1735
Arabin John	June 7, 1807
Atkins John	Dec. 21, 1804
Avery Olivia	June 26, 1831
Baker Benjamin	Feb. 14, 1832
Baldwin Catreintje, *wife* of Peter Post	May 6, 1733
Baldwin Cornelia Jans, *wife* of Jan Willemse Gessiger	May 18, 1696
Baldwin Elias	Dec. 31, 1825
Baldwin Hendrick Jansen	Feb. 18, 1694
Baldwin Keetje, *wife* of John Sipper	Dec. 19, 1789
Balld Jane	Jan. 13, 1825
Bannister Joseph	April 3, 1813
Banta Aeltje	April 16, 1803
Banta Margrietje, *wife* of Martin Winne	Jan. 5, 1795
Barret James	Dec. 3, 1779
Barrow Dr. William	Aug 1, 1846
Bedle William	June 24, 182
Beekman Christopher	Sept. 26, 1799
Bell Harriet M	Nov. 8, 1825
Bend Roswell D	Aug. 3, 1835
Benson John A	Jan. 28, 1835
Benson Mary	Aug. 15, 1838
Bent Emelia	March 17, 181
Blach John	Nov. 27, 1822
Boesteen Cornelius	Jan. 26, 1807
Bokkenove Keetje	Sept. 29, 1779
Bond Joseph	Nov. 27, 1808
Bouton William	Nov. 9, 1822
Bow Geertruy, *wife* of Abraham Diedricks	June 7, 1777
Bow John	Sept. 6, 1781
Boyd Eleanor	March 21, 1840
Boyd Maria, *widow* of Andrew	Feb. 11, 1850
Boyd Thomas	Feb. 13, 1825
Boyd William	July —, 1831
Braambush William	March 18, 1797
Brant Nathan	May 14, 1837
Brestede Treintje, *wife* of Tomas Fransen	April 8, 1706
Bridget Mrs	Sept. 2, 1819
Brinkerhoff Aagtje	Feb. 20, 1761
Brinkerhoff Claesje, *wife* of Gerrit Croese	March 21, 1787
Brinkerhoff Cornelius (97 years old)	Sept. 1, 1770
Brinkerhoff Cornelius, *son* of Hartman	Dec. 9, 1772
Brinkerhoff Cornelius	June 13, 1850
Brinkerhoff Eleanor	Jan. 28, 1834
Brinkerhoff Geesje, *wife* of Cornelius Bogert	May 3, 1783
Brinkerhoff Hartman	July 15, 1832
Brinkerhoff Hendrick	Aug. 12, 1795
Brinkerhoff Henry	March 12, 1838
Brinkerhoff Jane	June 2, 1834

DEATH RECORD.

NAME.	DATE OF DEATH.
Brinkerhoff Janet	Dec. 30. 1817
Brinkerhoff Leah	July 7, 1821
Brinkerhoff Margrietje, *wife* of Mattys De Mott	Dec. 12, 1754
Brinkerhoff Walter, *son* of Hartman	Sept 22, 1805
Brinkerhoff Walter C	March 11, 1813
Britain Cornelius	Sept. 30, 1832
Brooks William	Oct. 27, 1778
Brouwer Leah, *daughter* of Jacobus	Nov. 7, 1778
Brown Daniel	Feb. 9, 1817
Brown Eliza	July 16, 1814
Brown Lawrence, *son* of Thomas	July 4, 1767
Brown Thomas	Oct. 31, 1782
Broyn John	Jan. 22, 1816
Bryant Mrs	Jan. 19, 1825
Budd Harriet	Feb. 28, 1809
Budd Joseph	May 11, 1812
Bush Ann	July 20, 1818
Bush Ellen Jane	Aug. 3, 1825
Butler Louisa A	Sept. 26, 1822
Buys Daniel, *son* of Johannis	Dec. 31, 1775
Cadmus Andrew	Aug. 27, 1832
Cadmus Catalina	Aug. 2, 1831
Cadmus Catherine	Aug. 11, 1822
Cadmus Catherine	Nov. 20, 1835
Cadmus Catreintje, *daughter* of Dirck Fredricksen	Oct. 22, 1732
Cadmus Derrick, *son* of Joris	Sept. 6, 1804
Cadmus Dirck	Oct. 5, 1746
Cadmus Dirck, *son* of Joris	July 16, 1767
Cadmus Fredrick	Nov. 8, 1745
Cadmus Fredrick (young man)	Jan. 12, 1753
Cadmus Henry	Aug. 30, 1819
Cadmus Jannetje	May 27, 1760
Cadmus Jenneke	June 29, 1795
Cadmus Johannis, *son* of Dirck	Sept. 28, 1746
Cadmus John	July 26, 1832
Cadmus Joris	April 2, 1781
Cadmus Michael	Sept. 3, 1772
Cadmus Richard	March 12, 1839
Cadmus Rutgert (buried at Tappan)	Sept. 17, 1746
Call Solomon S	March 16, 1820
Car John	Jan. 9, 1807
Carelse Carel	Jan. 5, 1684
Carmer Nicholas	May 4, 1820
Carmichael David	Aug. 22, 1747
Carpenter Theodore	July 6, 1825
Carr David	Feb. 5, 1809
Castle Mary, *daughter* of William	Sept. 5, 1803
Chay A	Aug. 10, 1822
Claes Anna, *wife* of Arent Lourens Toers	Oct. 19, 1681

DEATH RECORD.

NAME.	DATE OF DEATH.
Claes Maritje, *widow* of Gerbrand Claesen	Oct. --, 1714
Claes ——, *son* of Jan Claesen	Dec. 14, 1698
Claes Vrouwtje *wife* of Gerrit Steinmets	Nov. 8, 1686
Claesen Andries	Aug. 7, 1710
Claesen Arien, *brother* of Capt. Gerbrand Claesen	April 9, 1703
Claesen Bartel	Nov. 11, 1700
Claesen Christina	Oct. 12, 1668
Claesen Dirck (Breacke)	March 26, 1693
Claesen Capt. Gerbrand	June 19, 1703
Claesen Jan	July 9, 1705
Clark Abraham	Aug. 21, 1799
Clendenny Abraham	Dec. 2, 1813
Clendenny Aeltje, *daughter* of Walter	Nov. 6, 1786
Clendenny Claesie	Sept. 28, 1814
Clendenny Elysabet, *daughter* of Walter	June 25, 1778
Clendenny Elizabeth, *wife* of Merselis Clendenny	Jan. 28, 1807
Clendenny Hartman B.	Nov. 12, 1810
Clendenny John, *son* of Walter	Sept. 24, 1793
Clendenny Merselis	Oct. 10, 1820
Clendenny Neeltje, *daughter* of Moses	Sept. 3, 1793
Clendenny Walter	Aug. 7, 1822
Clendenny Walter J.	Dec. 31, 1818
Clintock John	Dec. 3, 1814
Coerten Geurt	Aug. 27, 1701
Cole Thomas	Jan. 13, 1815
Cole William	April 9, 1812
Coleman William	July 17, 1832
Collerd Abraham	March 5, 1831
Collerd Edward	Oct. 5, 1830
Collerd Jacob	Sept. 24, 1796
Collerd Jacob	Sept. 17, 1842
Collerd Jacobus, *son* of Jacob	Nov. 27, 1795
Collerd James	Aug. 11, 1791
Collerd John, *son* of Johannis	Sept. 27, 1792
Collerd John	Dec. 6, 1829
Collerd John A.	Feb. 9, 1826
Collerd Mary	Sept. 4, 1837
Colony Peter	July 22, 1822
Conk John	April 12, 1842
Cook Daniel	Aug. 12, 1841
Cook Margaret	Sept. 10, 1827
Cooper Ann Letitia	May —, 1835
Cooper William	Aug. 12, 1834
Cornelis Dirckje, *wife* of Hendrick Teunise Hollinge	Oct. 22, 1698
Cornelis Elysabet, *widow* of James Van Rossen	Nov. 9, 1689
Cornelis Grietje, *wife* of Jacob Lubi	May 11, 1670
Cornelise Jannetje, *daughter* of Mattheus	May 15, 1691
Cornelison Catherine C.	Sept. 15, 1821
Cornelison Helen	Oct. 18, 1836
Cornelison John, *son* of Rev. Johannis	Feb. 26, 1796

DEATH RECORD.

NAME.	DATE OF DEATH.
Cornelison Rev. John	March 20, 1828
Cornelison Mattheus	May 12, 1705
Cornelison William	May 14, 1828
Cos Claes Pieterson	Sept. 21, 1704
Coulter Catharine, *daughter* of William	Dec. 21, 1800
Coulter Charlotte	Dec. 30, 1824
Coulter Harriet	Sept. 4, 1823
Coulter Jacob	April 23, 1813
Coulter Mary	Oct. 1, 1814
Coulter Mary	Dec. 2, 1820
Coulter Mary	March 17, 1831
Coulter William	Oct. 23, 1818
Cozine Phebe	Aug. 1, 1835
Cram Rachel Ann	Sept. 1, 1811
Crane James, *son* of Morris	Aug. 17, 1809
Crane William	Aug. 7, 1818
Crosby Mrs.	Oct. 15, 1825
Cubberly John	Nov. 4, 1821
Cubberly Mary	Oct. 14, 1832
Cubberly Thomas, *son* of Isaac	Feb. 1, 1807
Cubberly Thomas	May 31, 1836
Cubberly Thomas jr	Jan. 24, 1812
Cully George	Jan. 23, 1812
Cuper Mary	Jan. 20, 1805
Curry Joseph	Dec. 20, 1814
Daken Sarah	Oct. 25, 1813
Daniels Aeltje, *wife* of Jacob Jacobse Van Winkle	June 2, 1692
Daniels John	June 1, 1846
Daniels Mrs.	Jan. 18, 1838
Darcy Augustine	June 28, 1811
Davison Elizabeth	Aug 4, 1813
Davison John	June 11, 1813
Day Hannah	July 3, 1845
Day Keziah	Nov. 22, 1836
De Graw Jacob	Aug. 17, 1831
De Graw Mayeke, *wife* of Abel	May 23, 1774
De La Grange Johannis	May 6, 1748
De La Grange Metje, *widow* of Johannis	Feb. 1, 1753
De Mott Claesje, *wife* of Cornelius Van Vorst	March 4, 1788
De Mott Elizabeth V. R.	Feb. 2, 1815
De Mott Esther G	April 4, 1840
De Mott Garret	Sept. 19, 1833
De Mott Garret G	March 30, 1822
De Mott Jane	July 14, 1826
De Mott Johannis, *son* of Mattys	Dec. 8, 1740
De Mott John, *son* of Michael	March 27, 1740
De Mott Joris	Sept. 9, 1800
De Mott Margaret E	Aug. 26, 1826
De Mott, *daughter* of Mattys [gesie (gelyd) op't Oude Kerck hos]	April 11, 1744

NAME.	DATE OF DEATH.
De Mott Mattys	March 18, 1755
De Mott Michael	Nov. 16, 1779
De Mott Michael	May 27, 1832
De Smit François	Oct. 20, 1686
De Sue John	April 12, 1820
De Witt Jan, (of N. Y.)	Oct. 14, 1747
De Witt Louis	May 18, 1837
De Witt Mary	Dec. 20, 1839
De Witt Mrs.	Jan. 6, 1834
De Young John	April 2, 1813
Dennison Elizabeth	Jan. 7, 1834
Dennison Isaac	May 13, 1834
Dennison James	March 30, 1822
Denny Elizabeth	Sept. 14, 1811
Diedricks Abraham	Feb. 6, 1799
Diedricks Aegie, *daughter* of Johannis	July 30, 1774
Diedricks Aeltje, *wife* of Johannis Winne	June 2, 1771
Diedricks Aeltje	Jan. 23, 1753
Diedricks Ann	March 1, 1816
Diedricks Annetje, *daughter* of Hendrick	Dec. 26, 1699
Diedricks Antje, *wife* of Johannis Vreeland	Sept. 19, 1780
Diedricks Antje, *daughter* of Daniel	Oct. 2, 1781
Diedricks Cornelius	Dec. 6, 1775
Diedricks Daniel	May 24, 1795
Diedricks Daniel	April 8, 1822
Diedricks Gertrude, *wife* of James Collerd	Sept. 25, 1794
Diedricks Hans	Sept. 30, 1698
Diedricks Hester, *2d wife* of Johannis	June 9, 1777
Diedricks Jacob	June 14, 1746
Diedricks Johannis	Nov. 3, 1772
Diedricks Margrietje, *wife* of Johannis	July 11, 1772
Diedricks Wander	Aug. 13, 1732
Dircks Beelitje, *wife* of Gerrit Juriansen	May 20, 1745
Dircks Elisabet	Oct. 4, 1668
Dircks Mr.	Feb. 12, 1815
Dixon Eleanor	Nov. 12, 1808
Dod Eva, *daughter* of Thomas	Aug. 5, 1767
Doegg Mrs.	March 20, 1833
Doremus Cornelius	Jan. 23, 1831
Doremus Helmigh, *son* of Hendrick	Feb. 7, 1778
Doremus Henry	Nov. 15, 1834
Doughty Ann, *wife* of Sylvester Van Buren	Aug. 22, 1800
Douglas Mr.	Feb. 27, 1822
Douglas ——, *wife* of William	Aug. 6, 1683
Druyts Lourens	Jan. 16, 1668
Dunlap Mr.	Feb. 7, 1824
Eagles Mr.	Dec. 13, 1824
Eares Samuel	Dec. 27, 1819
Earle Edward sen., of Secaucus	Dec. 15, 1711

NAME.	DATE OF DEATH.
Earle Enoch	June 12, 1803
Earle Enoch	March 8, 1849
Earle Henry	July 4, 1809
Earle James	Jan. 3, 1816
Earle Margaret	Feb. 2, 1838
Earle Mrs	Dec. 27, 1810
Earle Rynier	Sept. 21, 1834
Earle William	Dec. 5, 1815
Ebbyen Elizabeth	March 16, 1801
Edgar William	Sept. 21, 1815
Edge Fanny	Feb. 12, 1824
Edge Mary	Feb. 10, 1815
Eiderstein Styntje, *wife* of Johannis Everse	July 19, 1781
Ellis Mrs	Oct. 30, 1810
Elsworth Mr	Dec. 13, 1824
Eustis Mary	Jan. 28, 1841
Everse Barbara, 2d *wife* of Johannis	Sept. 13, 1766
Everse Barent, *son* of Barent	April 7, 1783
Everse Barent, *son* of Barent	March 7, 1788
Everse Barent	Jan. 16, 1793
Everson Catherine, *widow* of Jacob	Oct. 9, 1842
Everson Helen	Dec. 27, 1830
Everson Jacob	Aug. 15, 1832
Everson James	Sept. 7, 1832
Everson Johannis, *son* of Johannis	Oct. 26, 1780
Everson Johannis	Sept. 18, 1802
Everson Sarah	Jan. 8, 1834
Everson Scytje	Dec. 1, 1795
Fanshaw Mr	Feb. 10, 1842
Farr John	Aug. 25, 1819
Farr Mrs	Feb. 16, 1826
Fielding Effie	Feb. 24, 1813
Fielding Henry	Oct. 3, 1779
Fleishman Mary Ann	July 1, 1825
Floyd Dr. Samuel	Aug. 18, 1822
Foster John	Feb. 2, 1825
Franse Dirck	Oct. 25, 1691
Fransen Gerrit, *son* of Geertruyt Gerrits of Pemerpo	May 8, 1679
Fuhr Mrs	July 29, 1840
Garrabrants Caterina	July 31, 1803
Garrabrants Cornelius	Feb. 20, 1774
Garrabrants Cornelius, *son* of Peter	Feb. 25, 1802
Garrabrants Cornelius	June 21, 1814
Garrabrants Cornelius	March 22, 1845
Garrabrants Cornelius P	May 5, 1841
Garrabrants Garrabrant, *son* of Gerbrand Claesen	Sept. 7, 1697
Garrabrants Garrabrant	March 29, 1791
Garrabrants Garrabrant, *son* of Cornelius	Dec. 29, 1786

DEATH RECORD.

NAME.	DATE OF DEATH.
Garrabrants James	Aug. 9, 1816
Garrabrants James	Sept. 10, 1822
Garrabrants Jane	Jan. 1, 1812
Garrabrants Jane	April 9, 1826
Garrabrants Jannetje, *wife* of Cornelius	Nov. 26, 1771
Garrabrants Jannetje, *wife* of Cornelius	Oct. 28, 1772
Garrabrants John, *son* of Myndert	Aug. 28, 1804
Garrabrants Lybertje	May 3, 1803
Garrabrants Maritje	March 6, 1794
Garrabrants Myndert	May 5, 1781
Garrabrants Myndert	Sept. 20, 1814
Garrabrants Myndert	July 29, 1825
Garrabrants Myndert	Sept. 3, 1846
Garrabrants Myndert jr.	May 1, 1837
Garrabrants Neeltje, *daughter* of Cornelius	Aug. 3, 1776
Garrabrants Peter	Jan. 13, 1807
Garrabrants Peter	Dec. 24, 1825
Garrabrants Tunis	May 15, 1760
Garrabrants Trintje, *wife* of Myndert	July 21, 1753
Garretson Garret	July 28, 1811
Garretson Hessel	Jan. 19, 1831
Garretson Ren S.	Sept. 11, 1833
Garretson Stephen J	Sept. 13, 1841
Garrit William	Oct. 14, 1836
Gerrits Elisabet, *widow* of Peter Heselse	Feb. —, 1728
Gerrits Geertruy, *widow* of Cornelius Abrahamse	Oct. 11, 1680
Gerrits Geesje, *wife* of Jan Straatmaker	Feb. 11, 1700
Gerrits Jannetje, *wife* of Casper Steinmets.	Jan. 12, 1670
Gerrits Jurian	July 29, 1739
Gerrits Lysbet, *widow* of Gerrit Gerrits, of Bergen	Jan. 24, 1707
Gerritse Gerrit	Feb. 28, 1697
Gerritsen Gerrit, *widower* of Annetje Herman	April 6, 1703
Gerritsen Gerrit jr	Dec. 4, 1803
Gerritsen Hessel	Aug. 23, 1803
Greenlief Joseph	Nov. 6, 1840
Griffin Engeltje	Sept. 29, 1800
Griffin Mary Ann	Sept. 2, 1824
Grimes Elizabeth	Nov. 24, 1795
Hansem Annetje, *wife* of Claas Hartmansen Vreeland	Dec. —, 1698
Harmanse Hans	Oct. 26, 1700
Harpis Mary, *wife* of Michael Dirckse, *son* of Dirck Teunise and Jannetje Michielse Vreelant	July 22, 1690
Harrison Hannah E	Sept. 2, 1839
Hartmans Fitze, *widow* of Michiel Jansen	Oct. 17, 1697
Harvey Capt.	July 7, 1819
Hasket Elizabeth	Jan. 29, 1817
Heath Mary Ann	Jan. 22, 1837
Hedden Barney	Jan. 4, 1815
Hendrick Cornelia, *wife* of Isaac Van Giesen	Sept. 7, 1707

DEATH RECORD.

NAME.	DATE OF DEATH.
Hendrickse Joris, *son* of Hendrick Jorise	Feb. 5, 1692
Hendrickse Samuel	Jan. 24, 1694
Hendricksen Maritje Arianse, *widow* of Thomas	Dec. 10, 1702
Hendricksen Thomas	May 19, 1702
Hennell John	March 5, 1830
Hennion Cathelina	July 22, 1832
Hennion David	June 30, 1819
Hennion Garret	Oct. 9, 1795
Herman Annetje, *wife* of Gerrit Gerritsen	Sept. 7, 1696
Herrington Phebe Ann	Aug. 16, 1813
Hesselse Pieter	Aug. 30, 1688
Hine Effie	Oct. 27, 1819
Hines Mr.	Dec. 29, 1832
Holmes Catherine	Oct. 10, 1843
Holmes Martha	Aug. 30, 1829
Holmes Patty	Feb. 5, 1826
Holmes Samuel	Nov. 15, 1812
Hoogland Fitje	Jan. 20, 1796
Hopper Catrina, *wife* of Fredrick Thomasen	May 8, 1716
Hornblower Elizabeth, *wife* of Thomas B. Gautier	May 29, 1844
Hornblower James	June 21, 1828
Hornblower John	Nov. 8, 1833
Hornblower Merselis Henry	Aug. 8, 1814
Hornblower Dr. Josiah	May 7, 1848
Hornblower Dr Josiah jr	Jan. 24, 1824
Howland John C	Sept. 1, 1817
Hudson Harriet, *daughter* of George	Sept. 28, 1805
Huff George	Nov. 23, 1820
Hyre Walter	Sept. 23, 1813
Jackson Abram	Aug. 20, 1831
Jackson Ann	May 3, 1810
Jackson Annatje, *daughter* of Rev. William	Sept. 30, 1767
Jackson Annatje, *wife* of Patrick	Sept. 13, 1779
Jackson Annatje	Jan. 13, 1758
Jackson Eva, *daughter* of Rev. William	Sept. 27, 1774
Jackson Fernandus, *son* of Rev. William	Jan. 7, 1772
Jackson Jemima	July 11, 1813
Jackson Patrick	July —, 1829
Jackson Robert, *son* of Rev. William	May 1, 1779
Jackson Rev. William	July 25, 1813
Jacobs Aeltje, *wife* of Poulus Douweson	June 8, 1698
Jacobs Neesje, *wife* of Dirck Claesen Braecke	Dec. 23, 1668
Jacobs Tryntje, *wife* of Casper Steinmets	May 11, 1677
Jacobus George	Aug. 21, 1836
Jacobus Mary	Aug. 15, 1819
Jans Catrina, *daughter* of Jan Lubbertse	April 11, 1695
Jans Hilletje, *widow* of Cornelis Van Vorst	July 18, 1705
Jans Metje, *wife* of Jan Janse Van Blerrekom	Oct. 22, 1706
Janse Maddaleentje, *widow* of Hendrick Janse Spier	June 12, 1679

DEATH RECORD. 403

NAME.	DATE OF DEATH.
Jansen Joris, *son* of Jannetje Jansen	Aug. 17, 1776
Jerolamon Anna	Aug. 18, 1834
Jerolamon James	Aug. 24, 1834
Jerolamon Leonora	April 18, 1832
Johnson Isabella	July 21, 1836
Johnson Joan	Aug. 11, 1822
Jones Abraham	Nov. 10, 1810
Jones David	Nov. 25, 1821
Juriansen Aeltje, *daughter* of Gerrit	Sept. 30, 1710
Juriansen Aeltje	May 13, 1746
Juriansen Beelitje, *daughter* of Margrietje	Sept. 8, 1748
Kear Charlotte	Jan. 3, 1804
Kear Cornelius, *son* of David	Sept. 10, 1803
Kells Elizabeth, *widow* of James	May 25, 1844
Kells James, *son* of James	June 9, 1796
Kells James	Aug. 20, 1824
Kells John	Jan. 15, 1835
Kells Susanna, *daughter* of James	Aug. 2, 1795
Kells Susanna	May 16, 1808
Kelly Lea	Sept. 26, 1800
Kiersted Cornelius	Aug. 23, 1757
Kip Abraham, *son* of Peter	Nov. 8, 1802
Kuyper Annetje, *widow* of Claas Jansen	Jan. 12, 1725
Kuyper Claas Jansen	Nov. 30, 1688
Kuyper Dirck Claesen, *son* of Claas Jansen	Jan. 28, 1692
Kuyper Hendrick	March 16, 1755
Kuyper Jannetje, 2d *wife* of Hendrick	April 1, 1772
Kuyper Sarah, *wife* of Johannis Jurianse	July 2, 1741
Lamb Samuel	Feb. 7, 1825
Lamar Anna	Sept. 15, 1799
Lary John	May 25, 1832
Layman George	Sept. 17, 1822
Layman Maria	Feb. 26, 1834
Le Grange Margrietje, 2d *wife* of Jacobus Van Buskirk	Jan. 6, 1774
Lewis Timothy	June 13, 1777
Linderman Alexander	Aug. 20, 1818
Linzi Ballje, *wife* of John Van Derhoof	Dec. 10, 1789
Little Joseph	Nov. 5, 1814
Lozier Albert, *son* of Dirck	Jun 10, 1777
Lozier Christopher	June 3, 1848
Lozier Maritje	Aug. 29, 1797
Lozier Moses	Oct. 9, 1839
Lubbertse Jan, *son* of Lubbert Lubbertse of New York	Aug. 23, 1674
Lubi Anna, *wife* of Mattheus Cornelise	Dec. 20, 1685
Lubi Jacob	June 11, 1691
Luttje Antje, *daughter* of Hendrick	Jan. 10, 1779
Lyon Joseph W	Dec. 13, 1825
Lyon Levi	Nov. 23, 1817

DEATH RECORD.

NAME.	DATE OF DEATH.
Lyon Richard	Dec. 9, 1821
Mack Edwin, *son* of Daniel	Oct. 9, 1805
Maertens Trintje, *wife* of Polus Pietersen	May 19, 1702
Maltby John	June 3, 1848
Mandeville Catherine Jane	Aug. 25, 1832
Mandeville Diadame	Aug 9, 1832
Mandeville Garret	Aug. 21, 1846
Mandeville John	March 28, 1815
Mandeville John V. W	June 22, 1814
Mandeville Nicholas	Aug. 5, 1832
Mattheuse Cornelis, *son* of Mattheus Cornelise	June 7, 1691
McCall Robert	June 9, 1805
McCalvy Abby	Aug. 2, 1822
McCrindle Eliza	May 9, 1834
McCuberry Mary	Feb. 9, 1822
McCuberry Robert	Jan. 12, 1821
Mc Cuen Mr	Sept. 4, 1836
McDonald David, *son* of Thomas	Nov. 3, 1806
McDonald Thomas	Aug. 29, 1813
McDonnell Hannah	Aug. 29, 1823
McDonnell Jane	Oct. 7, 1815
McDonnell Mrs	Jan. 14, 1826
McElvoy John	Sept. 23, 1824
McFarlane Robert	March 21, 1847
McLoughlin Mary C	Aug. 6, 1841
McWilliams Thomas	July 4, 1818
Meach Elisha	Feb. 16, 1839
Meeker Caroline	June 1, 1825
Merselis Altje	Dec. 15, 1827
Merselis Altje, *daughter* of Merselis Merselis	Aug. 10, 1776
Merselis Catharine	Feb. 10, 1825
Merselis Eliza	Nov. 18, 1812
Merselis Elizabeth	Feb. 16, 1823
Merselis Elizabeth, *daughter* of John	June 23, 1786
Merselis John	Aug. 26, 1804
Merselis Merselis	Oct. 28, 1800
Merselis J. Merselis	March 21, 1837
Merselise Annatje, *daughter* of Pieter	Aug. 6, 1746
Merselise Catrina	June 16, 1747
Merselise Jenneke, *2d wife* of Pieter	Oct. 3, 1779
Merselise Pieter	Sept. 4, 1681
Merselise Pieter	April 1, 1770
Merselise —— *wife* of Pieter	Aug. 1, 1680
Mersereau Abram	Nov. 4, 1811
Mersereau Ann	Sept. 17, 1829
Mesker Jacob	Aug. 20, 1841
Meyers Cornelis, *son* of John	Oct. 12, 1699
Meyers Dircksje, *wife* of Enoch Michielse Vreeland	Oct. 5, 1688
Meyner Elizabeth, *daughter* of Stephen	Aug. 5, 1797

DEATH RECORD.

NAME.	DATE OF DEATH.
Monday Mrs	Oct. 25, 1805
Moore William	May 13, 1818
Moore William	April 18, 1819
Morehouse Chauncey	Dec. 25, 1823
Morgan Mr	Aug. 30, 1819
Morrison Peter	Sept. 18, 1811
Mulford Calvin	Dec. 19, 1847
Mulford David	Feb. 15, 1811
Nafie Hannah	Nov. 9, 1814
Needham Catherine	Dec. 28, 1816
Needham William	March 2, 1807
Neefie Elizabeth	Aug. 7, 1805
Newkirk Aaron	April 1, 1849
Newkirk Ann	Aug. 14, 1821
Newkirk Caroline	Aug. 22, 1819
Newkirk Catrina, *wife* of Gerrit	Sept. 12, 1751
Newkirk Catrina (young woman)	Sept. 18, 1759
Newkirk Catrintje, *daughter* of Garret	Sept. 17, 1779
Newkirk Cornelius	Sept. 10, 1781
Newkirk Fitje	Jan. 23, 1808
Newkirk Garret	April 23, 1785
Newkirk Garret	Aug. 29, 1832
Newkirk Garret J	Aug. 22, 1818
Newkirk Gertrude	March 5, 1828
Newkirk Helena	April 6, 1801
Newkirk Hendrick	July 8, 1795
Newkirk Jacob	Dec. 5, 1796
Newkirk Jacob	June 9, 1818
Newkirk Jane	June 4, 1830
Newkirk Jane, *daughter* of Joris	April 17, 1806
Newkirk Jannetje, *daughter* of Barent	Nov. 10, 1779
Newkirk Jannetje, *daughter* of Garret	Sept. 17, 1779
Newkirk John	Dec. 28, 1847
Newkirk Lea, *wife* of Cornelius	March 17, 1757
Newkirk Lena, *daughter* of Jacob	July 25, 1776
Newkirk Maria	Oct. 8, 1833
Newkirk Maritje, *daughter* of Jacob	Aug. 1, 1776
Newkirk Mattheus, *son* of Arent	Nov. 10, 1799
Newkirk Matthew	May 29, 1812
Newkirk Matthew	Nov. 12, 1818
Newkirk Matthew G	July 10, 1811
Newkirk Poulus	Feb 5, 1763
Newkirk Poulus, *son* of Jacob	Nov. 1, 1772
Newkirk Poulus, *son* of Jacob	Aug. 27, 1776
Newkirk Rachel	Dec. 1, 1835
Newkirk Sally, *daughter* of Garret	Dec. 9, 1794
Newkirk Sally, *daughter* of Garret	Aug. 15, 1797
Newkirk Sophia	Feb. 14, 1815
Nicol Eleanor	Oct. 7, 1802

NAME.	DATE OF DEATH.
Osborn Allen D	Oct. 3, 1839
Osborn Ann D	June 16, 1825
Osborn Maria, *widow* of Samuel	April 30, 1844
Osborn Samuel	Oct. 26, 1834
Outwater Ann	Nov. 23, 1809
Outwater Garret	June 2, 1829
Outwater Guilliam	Aug. 17, 1811
Outwater Jacob	Nov. 28, 1829
Outwater Maria	July 1, 1829
Parine Samuel	April 30, 1812
Parks Aletta Jane	Aug. 13, 1839
Parks John	Aug. 27, 1839
Parks John H	Aug. 12, 1839
Patchen Andrew	Sept. 29, 1802
Paulinson John Henry	Sept. 15, 1837
Phillips Willem	March 14, 1790
Pieterse Antje	July 15, 1737
Pieterse Marcelis (91 years old)	Oct. 23, 1747
Pietersen Gerrit, *son* of Pieter Hesselsen	Aug. 7, 1695
Pietersen Johannis	April 29, 1733
Pietersen Poulus, *widower* of Trintje Maertens	Dec. 18, 1702
Piper Gysbert	Jan. 18, 1707
Post Capt. Adrian	Feb. 28, 1677
Post Adrian	Sept. 22, 1787
Post Adrian	March 19, 183
Post Catherine	May 28, 1815
Post Cornelius, *son* of Adrian	Dec. 31, 1802
Post Cornelius, *son* of Egbert	Nov. 8, 1780
Post Cornelius, *son* of Peter	Sept. 5, 1804
Post Egbert	March 3, 1822
Post Elizabeth	Jan. 29, 1824
Post Henry	Aug. 13, 1823
Post Jacob	April 10, 1827
Post Jane	Nov. 17, 1818
Post Jane	Dec. 22, 1819
Post Jane	Aug. 2, 1823
Post Jannetje, *daughter* of Peter	Sept. 2, 1804
Post John	March 12, 1840
Post Peter	March 26, 1824
Post Phebe Ann	Sept. 28, 1841
Post Pryntje, *daughter* of Egbert	May 14, 1775
Post Rachel	May 1, 1839
Post Samuel, *son* of Pieter	March 30, 1732
Post Sara	July 9, 1821
Potter Mrs	Feb. 26, 1823
Preyer Abraham	Oct. 29, 1800
Preyer Altje, *daughter* of Jacob	Oct. 25, 1800
Preyer Andries	Nov. 16, 1696
Preyer Andries	March 4, 1792

DEATH RECORD.

NAME.	DATE OF DEATH.
Preyer Andries, *son* of Hartman	Dec. 8, 1787
Preyer Ariantje, *daughter* of Abraham	Feb. 3, 1786
Preyer Casparus	Feb. 26, 1755
Preyer Casper	May 6, 1733
Preyer Geertruy, *wife* of Andries	Dec. 14, 1783
Preyer Hester	Sept. 14, 1795
Preyer Jacob, of Constapels Hoeck (young man)	Jan. 30, 1705
Preyer Jacob, *son* of Casparus	Oct. 15, 1741
Preyer Johannis	Sept. 28, 1763
Preyer Maritje, *wife* of Abraham	March 12, 1777
Preyer Sara, *2d wife* of Casparus	Aug. 25, 1774
Preyer Zacharias, *son* of Andries	Sept. 4, 1772
Prine Catherine Ann	Jan. 19, 1831
Prine Jacob V. W	Nov. 3, 1826
Prior Abraham	Sept. 18, 1830
Prior Adriana, *widow* of Adam Rapp	Oct. 9, 1842
Prior Ann	Feb. 7, 1837
Prior Ann V. W	Dec. 28, 1822
Prior Ann, *widow* of Casparus	Nov. 16, 1843
Prior Catherine	Oct. 12, 1841
Prior Charity	Oct. 15, 1819
Prior Jacob	Feb. 8, 1826
Prior Jacob	Oct. 2, 1830
Prior Jasper	March 30, 1828
Prior Col. Jasper	Sept. 8, 1832
Prior John	April 18, 1820
Prior Martha	May 11, 1826
Prior Nicholas	May 22, 1840
Prior Pietertje	Jan. 6, 1814
Prior Sarah	April 20, 1833
Provost James	Jan. 24, 1842
Provost Mary C	June 3, 1841
Provost Sophia, *wife* of James	July 11, 1845
Puffer Adeline	Aug. 19, 1811
Rapp Adam	Oct. 3, 1820
Rapp Daniel	Aug. 14, 1819
Rapp Elizabeth	Oct. 6, 1791
Rapp John A	Aug. 18, 1819
Rapp John A	Jan. 30, 1850
Rappleye Joris, Jr	May 28, 1787
Ray Daniel, Jr	May 24, 1813
Ray George	Feb. 27, 1815
Ray William	Aug. 26, 1820,
Read Henry, *son* of Henry	Jan. 12, 1804
Reddenhaus Fitje, *daughter* of Abel	Oct. 14, 1703
Reddenhaus Hendrick, *son* of Abel	Nov. 24, 1703
Reed Maeking	Aug. 27, 1803
Reeder Ursula	March 25, 1827
Richardson Mrs	March 2, 1816

NAME.	DATE OF DEATH.
Riker Henry	Sept. 21, 1834
Riker John	May 25, 1826
Roelofs Fitje, *widow* of Joost Van Derlinden	March 3, 1681
Roll Jan (of Constable's Hook)	Feb. 2, 1761
Roos Antje, *wife* of Cornelises Diedricks	June 29, 1702
Roos Gerrit	Sept. 10, 1779
Roos Johannis, *son* of Garrite	Sept. 30, 1780
Roos Judith, *wife* of Garrit	Oct. 8, 1748
Roos Peter	June 26, 1787
Rossman Ann	Aug. 22, 1832
Rowley John	Feb. 14, 1814
Rummel Frances	Sept. 30, 1822
Rummel John C. F.	July 4, 1832
Rummel Joseph B.	July 10, 1832
Saegaerd Fitje	Feb. 28, 1801
Salter Mary M	Sept. 10, 1819
Samuels Grietje, *wife* of Hendrick Tunise Hollinge	Oct. 22, 1698
Schofield John (young man from Connecticut)	Feb. 16, 1753
Schoonmaker Ellen, *wife* of Stephen Vreeland	Feb. 14, 1849
Schuyler Eliot	Sept. 22, 1821
Selyns Rev. (Saturday, P. M.)	July 19, 1701
Shepherd Catherine	Sept. 15, 1835
Shepherd Fanny	Aug. 25, 1832
Shepherd George	March 26, 1843
Shepherd Hannah	Aug. 30, 1818
Shepherd Jacob G.	Aug. 18, 1832
Shepherd John	March 17, 1828
Shepherd Joseph	Jan. 5, 1831
Shepherd Lea, *daughter* of George	Aug. 28, 1799
Shepherd Margaret Jane	April 15, 1837
Shepherd Peggy, *daughter* of George	Sept. 13, 1799
Shepherd Samuel	Jan 10, 1817
Shepherd Samuel	Sept. 16, 1834
Shepherd Thomas, *son* of George	Sept. 2, 1799
Shields Elizabeth	Oct 30, 1810
Sickles Abraham	Feb. 16, 1804
Sickles Abraham	March 2, 1836
Sickles Aegie	Oct 3, 1802
Sickles Antje, *daughter* of Abraham	Nov. 8, 1803
Sickles Antje D.	Oct 19, 1808
Sickles Antje P.	April 19, 1807
Sickles Ariantje, *daughter* of Robert	Oct. 18, 1775
Sickles Daniel	Oct. 23, 1813
Sickles Effie	Aug. 10, 1826
Sickles Elizabeth, *wife* of Casparus Zabriskie	Nov. 10, 1790
Sickles Frederick	Nov. 19, 1781
Sickles Geertruy	Feb. 13, 1754
Sickles Geertruy, *wife* of Hendrick	Oct. 27, 1731
Sickles Geertruyt, *daughter* of Robert	Oct. 7, 1703

DEATH RECORD.

NAME.	DATE OF DEATH.
Sickles Hartman	Oct. 8, 1807
Sickles Helena	Oct. 30, 1805
Sickles Hendrick	Jan. 20, 1777
Sickles Hendrick	April 29, 1795
Sickles Henry	Jan. 15, 1839
Sickles Jenny, *wife* of Hendrick	March 28, 1781
Sickles Johannis	March 11, 1734
Sickles Johannis	Sept. 26, 1784
Sickles John	May 2, 1822
Sickles Martin, *son* of Robert	May 24, 1772
Sickles Mary	May 11, 1835
Sickles Matilda	Jan. 17, 1823
Sickles Rachel, *wife* of Zacharias	Oct. 1, 1778
Sickles Rachel	May 8, 1816
Sickles Robert	Dec. 27, 1729
Sickles Robert	Sept. 24, 1802
Sickles Sara, *2d wife* of Hendrick	April 22, 1783
Sickles Sarah	April 30, 1819
Sickles Zacharias, *son* of Robert	Aug. 18, 1775
Sickles Zacharias, *son* of Daniel	Aug. 3, 1776
Sickles Zacharias	Aug. 13, 1776
Simkins Aaron	May 2, 1813
Simkins Elizabeth	Jan. 16, 1825
Simmons Aaron, *son* of Michael	Dec. 12, 1793
Simmons Eleanor	Oct. 6, 1841
Simmons Isaac, *son* of Joseph	July 12, 1804
Simmons John	March 14, 1845
Simmons Michael	Sept. 23, 1831
Simmons Rachel	Sept. 7, 1832
Simmons Stephen	March 2, 1827
Simmons Susan	Sept. 16, 1833
Simmons William	Sept. 28, 1830
Simonson Jane	Dec. 3, 1839
Simonson Stephen	Aug. 31, 1842
Sip Antje, *wife* of Ide	Jan. 25, 1749
Sip Antje, *daughter* of Cornelius	July 3, 1763
Sip Catlyntje, *wife* of Claas Vreeland	Sept. 25, 1759
Sip Cornelius	May 9, 1793
Sip Elizabeth	March 2, 1827
Sip Gerrit	Oct. 1, 1775
Sip Ide	Feb. 26, 1762
Sip Ide, *son* of Cornelius	May 23, 1772
Sip Jan	Aug. 12, 1729
Sip Jenneke, *wife* of Cornelius Vreeland	Dec. 5, 1788
Sip Maritje, *daughter* of Peter	March 5, 1797
Sip Neeltje Adrianse, *widow*	March 17, 1691
Skidmore John	Sept. 29, 1819
Sloat Mrs	Sept. 9, 1832
Slot Eva, *wife* of Jacob Brouwer	May 3, 1776
Smith Ann	Sept. 17, 1834

NAME.	DATE OF DEATH.
Smith Benjamin	March 17, 1820
Smith Cobus	Dec. 21, 1778
Smith Cornelius	Feb. 1, 1835
Smith Jane	March 25, 1828
Smith John	July 25, 1814
Smith John	Feb. 7, 1843
Smiht Lea	Nov. 10, 1792
Smith Mareya, *daughter* of Cornelius	Oct. 27, 1798
Smith Prudence	Feb. 13, 1849
Smith Sarah	Nov. 15, 1796
Smith Thomas	Sept. 2, 1819
Solder Annatje, *daughter* of Daniel	May 9, 1775
Solder Daniel	May 6, 1775
Solder Sara, *daughter* of Daniel	May 10, 1775
Speer Ellen	Aug. 8, 1816
Speer Ellen Anna	March 5, 1842
Speer Hannah	Nov. 22, 1820
Speer John	May 21, 1827
Speer Maria	July 13, 1833
Spior Abraham	July 27, 1788
Spier Catlyna, *daughter* of Geertruy	Sept. 8, 1748
Spier Catlyntje, *wife* of Barent (91 years old)	Dec. 16, 1767
Spier Catrina (?)	April 27, 1748
Spier Johannis	July 2, 1746
Spier Rachel	April 7, 1748
Stager Jane	Aug. 12, 1827
Stager Rachel	April —, 1828
Stager William Henry	Nov. 21, 1811
Steinmets Gerrit	Nov. 9, 1736
Steinmets Joanna, *widow* of Andries Preyer	Sept. 18, 1702
Stevens Isabella	Sept. 2, 1825
Stewart Cornelia Ann	April 7, 1843
Stivers Peter	Dec. 23, 1821
Story Merselis W	Feb. 16, 1843
Straatmaker Gerrit Dirckse, *son* of Jan Dirckse	Sept. 23, 1686
Straatmaker Rachel, *wife* of Daniel Van Winckel	March 12, 1708
Strange Mary	July 31, 1818
Strange Mary	April 28, 1837
Sturge Joseph	Nov. 11, 1825
Stuyvesant Catrintje, *wife* of Jacob Van Hooren	June 21, 1780
Stuyvesant Janneka, *wife* of Hendrick Sickles	Feb. 13, 1774
Stuyvesant John, *son* of Peter	March 6, 1777
Stuyvesant Ned, *son* of Casparus	Sept. 20, 1779
Stuyvesant Pieter	Aug. 10, 1770
Stuyvesant Pryntje, *wife* of Pieter	June 22, 1763
Stuyvesant Sara, *daughter* of Casparus	Feb. 26, 1774
Swords John, *son* of Thomas	Dec. 3, 1778
Tades Katje, *wife* of Morgan Smith	Feb. 21, 1743
Tallman James	Feb. 4, 1837

DEATH RECORD.

NAME.	DATE OF DEATH.
Tallman Mrs	May 9, 1833
Taylor Anna Maria V	Feb. 24, 1836
Taylor Anna R	Jan. 20, 1842
Taylor Catherine	Oct. 22, 1821
Taylor Charles	June 28, 1825
Taylor Harriet	Sept. 15, 1840
Taylor Mary	Aug. 2, 1825
Tallyon Molly	Feb. 14, 1804
Thomasen Arien	Oct. 11, 1689
Thompkins Abraham	Aug. 17, 1819
Thompkins Elizabeth	July 7, 1818
Thompkins George	Nov. 9, 1816
Thompkins Radbridge	Sept. 8, 1819
Thorp Garret	July 9, 1823
Thorp Mary	Nov. 10, 1814
Thorp Thomas	Feb. 2, 1822
Tise Abraham	Oct. 6, 1835
Tise George jr	Sept. 6, 1826
Toers Anna, *daughter* of Claas Arentse	June 28, 1702
Toers Arent, *son* of Claas Arentse	May 26, 1694
Toers Catelyntje, *daughter* of Claas Arentse	June 7, 1702
Toers Claas Arentse	Oct, 10, 1724
Toers Jacomyntje	Dec. 10, 1742
Toers Jan A	Aug. 14, 1729
Toers Johannis, *son* of Lourens Arentse	Oct. 10, 1686
Toers Nicholas Arentse (young man)	Nov. 13, 1829
Toers Thomas Lourens, *son* of Lourens Arentse	Oct. 1, 1686
Tomasen Arien	May 25, 1702
Tomasen Jurian	Sept. 12, 1695
Town John	May 7, 1812
Trail Mary	May 22, 1813
Traphagen Eleanor	March 4, 1823
Treadwell David	Oct. 5, 1816
Tucker John	April 6, 1831
Tucker Mrs	May 17, 1830
Tuers Aaron	Sept. 17, 1835
Tuers Abraham C	Sept. 3, 1825
Tuers Annatje	June 6, 1796
Tuers Annetje, *2d wife* of Arent	Sept. 7, 1781
Tuers Arent, Sen	Sept. 17, 1779
Tuers Esther	June 2, 1822
Tuers Jacomyntje, *wife* of Hendrick Solders	May 5, 1790
Tuers Jane	March 27, 1834
Tuers Nicholas	Feb. 26, 1815
Tuttle Havens	March 24, 1848
Tuttle Joel	May 7, 1849
Tuttle Walter	May 8, 1845
Tuxbury Moses	Feb. 17, 1701
Van Blercom Jan Lubbertsen's *wife*, Maddaleena	Sept. 4, 1711

DEATH RECORD.

NAME.	DATE OF DEATH.
Van Buren Layton	Sept. 22, 1822
Van Buren Mary	Sept. 26, 1839
Van Buren Mrs	Jan. 12, 1834
Van Buren Sylvester	July 3, 1836
Van Buren William, *son* of Sylvester	July 27, 1800
Van Buskirk Andries	Aug. 25, 1761
Van Buskirk Ann	Aug. 24, 1825
Van Buskirk Cornelius	Feb. 4, 1753
Van Buskirk Cornelius	March 2, 1814
Van Buskirk Elizabeth	Sept. 10, 1814
Van Buskirk Geertruy, *wife* of Pieter Corsen	Jan. 10, 1774
Van Buskirk Jacobus	Jan. 3, 1767
Van Buskirk Jane, *wife* of Jacob Van Hoorn	Jan. 10, 1792
Van Buskirk Jane	Oct. 24, 1736
Van Buskirk Jenneke	Sept. 20, 1711
Van Buskirk Lourens	Dec. 13, 1752
Van Buskirk Lucas	March 20, 1831
Van Buskirk Margrietje, *wife* of Andries	June 3, 1775
Van Buskirk Trintje, *wife* of Pieter	Nov. 7, 1736
Van Clief Arie	July 16, 1831
Van Clief Daniel jr	Aug. 3, 1831
Van Clief Eliza	July 28, 1831
Van Clief Fitje, *daughter* of John	Oct. 14, 1796
Van Clief Gertrude	Feb. 6, 1810
Van Clief Jacob	Sept. 22, 1827
Van Clief Jane, *daughter* of John	May 4, 1805
Van Clief John	May 16, 1826
Van Dalson Henry jr	May 10, 1816
Van de Voorst Cornelis (buried in New York)	Dec. 28, 1683
Van Derbeek Abraham jr	July 6, 1811
Van Derbeek Hannah	July 15, 1815
Van Derbilt Aaron	Oct. 3, 1831
Van Derbilt Garret	April 15, 1813
Van Derbilt Jan Arentse, of Bergen	Feb. 2, 1705
Van Derbilt John, *son* of Jacob	Aug. 15, 1776
Van Derhaen Metje	May 10, 1802
Van Derhoof Gerrit	Oct. 4, 1797
Van Derhoof Hendrick	Jan. 20, 1747
Van Derhoof Hendrick, *son* of Gerrit	Sept. 3, 1777
Van Derhoof Petrus	Dec. 25, 1783
Van Derhoof Sarah	May 9, 1825
Van Deusen Hester	Oct. 7, 1778
Van Giesen Isaac, *son* of Rynier	March 26, 1703
Van Giesen Jacob	April 17, 1704
Van Emburgh John T	March 14, 1838
Van Giesen Bastiaense	May 15, 1707
Van Giesen Rynier	May 18, 1693
Van Hooren Jan	May 19 1750
Van Hooren Rut	May 15, 1741
Van Hoorn Barent	Oct. 22, 1779

DEATH RECORD.

NAME.	DATE OF DEATH.
Van Hoorn Cornelius, *son* of John	July 27, 1776
Van Hoorn Eva, *2d wife* of Barent	May 25, 1781
Van Hoorn Jacob	April 14, 1757
Van Hoorn Jan	Dec. 12, 1757
Van Hoorn Jannetje, *daughter* of Jan	Dec. 3, 1777
Van Hoorn John	Oct. 10, 1786
Van Hoorn Marjrietje, *daughter* of Jan	May 14, 1753
Van Hoorn Raegel, *daughter* of Jacob	Oct. 6, 1777
Van Horne Ann	Sept. 21, 1823
Van Horne Beelitje, *daughter* of Garret	Dec. 25, 1807
Van Horne Belina	Feb. 20, 1826
Van Horne Cornelius jr	Aug. 10, 1819
Van Horne Cornelius C	Dec. 9, 1822
Van Horne Cornelius J	Feb. 28, 1841
Van Horne Daniel, *son* of John	April 24, 1795
Van Horne Eliza	July —, 1831
Van Horne Eliza	Aug. 21, 1835
Van Horne Garret	April 7, 1809
Van Horne Garret	Sept. 22, 1838
Van Horne Garret J	Nov. 28, 1826
Van Horne Jacob	Oct. 4, 1813
Van Horne Jane C	Dec. 14, 1836
Van Horne John	Aug 29, 1843
Van Horus Margaret	Dec. 27, 1828
Van Horne Peter	Nov. 21, 1841
Van Houten Aegie	Sept. 26, 1803
Van Houten Aeltje	May 6, 1796
Van Houten Cornelius, *son* of Helmigh	Oct. 4, 1748
Van Houten Garret	Sept. 8, 1832
Van Houten Hannah	Jan. 17, 1846
Van Houten Helmigh	Oct. 23, 1803
Van Houten Helmigh	March 4, 1822
Van Houten Helmigh Roelofsen	Oct 7, 1729
Van Houten Jenneke	Nov. 24, 1795
Van Houten Johannis	Dec. 18, 1768
Van Houten John, *son* of Helmigh	Oct. 31, 1807
Van Houten John	Aug. 10, 1814
Van Houten John	July 19, 1840
Van Houten John jr	Feb. 17, 1837
Van Houten John H	Aug. 5, 1818
Van Houten Joseph	Sept. 15, 1831
Van Houten Michael	June 1, 1803
Van Houten Mortimer	March 4, 1822
Van Houten Rachel, *widow* of John	Feb. 11, 1843
Van Kleeck Pieter, *son* of Baltus Barentsen	July 8, 1688
Van Nes Grietje Cornelis, *wife* of Jacob Lubi	Sept. 11, 1689
Van Norman Oliver	May 26, 1817
Von Orden John, *son* of Abraham	March 24, 1807
Van Rypen Aeltje	Feb. 10, 1796
Van Rypen Aletta, *widow* of Cornelius	July 2, 1846

DEATH RECORD.

NAME.	DATE OF DEATH.
Van Rypen Alexander	Aug. 30, 1817
Van Rypen Ann	July 20, 1813
Van Rypen Antje, *daughter* of Jurrie	July 29, 1796
Van Rypen Benjamin	Oct. 7, 1821
Van Rypen Catherine	Sept. 10, 1819
Van Rypen Catherine	March 28, 1833
Van Rypen Celia	Feb. 27, 1842
Van Rypen Christopher	March 8, 1840
Van Rypen Cornelius, *son* of Cornelius	Aug. 30, 1767
Van Rypen Cornelius	Jan. 17, 1771
Van Rypen Cornelius	Jan. 6, 1842
Van Rypen Daniel	July 23, 1818
Van Rypen Derrick	Jan. 11, 1777
Van Rypen Derrick, *son* of Cornelius	Aug 31, 1803
Van Rypen Effie	Aug. 27, 1836
Van Rypen Elizabeth, *daughter* of Derrick	Sept. 3, 1796
Van Rypen Elizabeth	May 6, 1813
Van Rypen Elizabeth Ann	Dec. 3, 1824
Van Rypen Garret	Aug. 31, 1837
Van Rypen Garret J	Oct. 3, 1833
Van Rypen Gerrit	Aug. 30, 1795
Van Rypen Gerrit, *son* of Cornelius	Aug. 24, 1796
Van Rypen Harman	Aug. 23, 1828
Van Rypen Harriet E	Oct. 9, 1824
Van Rypen Helen	May 6, 1813
Van Rypen Henry C	April 15, 1849
Van Rypen Jannetje, *2d wife* of Johannis	July 21, 1783
Van Rypen Jannetje, *wife* of Gerrit	Oct. 13, 1784
Van Rypen Jannetje, *daughter* of Gerrit jr	Sept. 14, 1793
Van Rypen Jasper	Oct. 25, 1849
Van Rypen Jeremiah	April 4, 1826
Van Rypen Johannis	Aug. 24, 1776
Van Rypen John	May 14, 1828
Van Rypen Margrietje, *daughter* of Gerrit	July 26, 1776
Van Rypen Margrietje, *daughter* of Gerrit	May 31, 1781
Van Rypen Metje	Sept. 20, 1899
Van Rypen Neeltje	Oct. 28, 1801
Van Rypen Richard M	March 9, 1819
Van Rypen Thomas	May 26, 1846
Van Rypen Vrouwtje	Feb. 19, 1806
Van Tassel Rachel	Dec. 2, 1846
Van Varick Richard	July 7, 1794
Van Vechten Neeltje, *wife* of Rut. Van Hooren	June 15, 1738
Van Voorhesen Nancy	Feb. 8, 1806
Van Voorst Hillegont, *daughter* of Cornelius	Jan. 31, 1710
Van Vorst Annatje	Jan. 20, 1804
Van Vorst Claesje, *daughter* of Cornelius	Oct. 9, 1773
Van Vorst Cornelius	Dec. 25, 1760
Van Vorst Cornelius, *son* of Johannis	Oct. 7, 1761
Van Vorst Cornelius	Sept. 30, 1818

DEATH RECORD.

NAME.	DATE OF DEATH.
Van Vorst Hannah	March 24, 1821
Van Vorst Hannah	March 14, 1822
Van Vorst John J	Jan. 6, 1820
Van Vorst Pietertje *wife* of Merselis Pieterse,	Sept. —, 1744
Van Vorst Susanna	March 26, 1815
Van Wagenen Aeltje, *wife* of Wander Diedricks	Dec, 22, 1754
Van Wagenen Annatje, *dauhgter* of Jacob	March 20, 1778
Van Wagenen Annetje, *wife* of Joris Vreeland	Feb. 23, 1782
Van Wagenen Catlyntje, *daughter* of Jacob	Aug. 11, 1748
Van Wagenen Catlyntje, *wife* of Gerrit Van Rypen	Oct. 22, 1775
Van Wagenen Catlyntje, *wife* of Johannis	Sept. 6, 1777
Van Wagenen Effie	Jan. 6, 1820
Van Wagenen Fitje Gerrits, *wife* of Cornelius Van Voorst	May 19, 1734
Van Wagenen Gerrit, *son* of Johannis	Aug. 24, 1738
Van Wagenen Helmigh	July 19, 1747
Van Wagenen Jacob	Sept. 23, 1775
Van Wagenen Jacob	Jan. 27, 1783
Van Wagenen Jacob	June 14, 1839
Van Wagenen Johannis	March 29, 1797
Van Wagenen Johannis Gerritse	Oct. 6, 1756
Van Wagenen John	Sept. 7, 1827
Van Wagenen Lea, *2d wife* of Jacob	Dec. 19, 1775
Van Wagenen Neeltje	May 24, 1810
Van Wagening Gerrit Gerritsen	Oct. 9, 1732
Van Wart Betsey, *daughter* of Abraham	Aug 29, 1776
Van Wart Isaac	June 2, 1825
Van Wart Jacob	Sept. 28, 1813
Van Wart Sara	Jan. 18, 1783
Van Winkle Abraham	Nov. 4, 1823
Van Winkle Abraham jr	Aug. 8, 1832
Van Winkle Altje	July 19, 1776
Van Winkle Altje, *daughter* of Hendrick	Oct. 1, 1801
Van Winkle Ann	Nov. 28, 1817
Van Winkle Ann, *widow* of Daniel	Aug. 25, 1843
Van Winkle Antje, *wife* of Jacob Diedricks	Nov. 11, 1744
Van Winkle Ann C	Feb. 25, 1822
Van Winkle Asa T	Nov. 7, 1834
Van Winkle Catherine Amelia	Oct. 21, 1835
Van Winkle Catrintje	Sept. 8, 1793
Van Winkle Cornelia	July 26, 1826
Van Winkle Cornelius	Sept. 29, 1821
Van Winkle Cornelius J	Jan 22, 1837
Vna Winkle Cornelius T	July 5, 1822
Van Winkle Daniel	Jan. 10, 1757
Van Winkle Daniel, *son* of Jurrie	July 3, 1798
Van Winkle Daniel, *son* of Hendrick	Oct. 1, 1801
Van Winkle Daniel	Dec. 19, 1823
Van Winkle Daniel	June 24, 1830
Van Winkle Daniel jr	April 24, 1818
Van Winkle Garret	Aug. 30, 1814

DEATH RECORD.

NAME.	DATE OF DEATH.
Van Winkle Garret G	July 9, 1839
Van Winkle Geertje	Jan. 1, 1796
Van Winkle Geertruy, *wife* of Johannis Diedricks	Aug. 22, 1736
Van Winkle George L	Dec. 18, 1837
Van Winkle Gitty, *wife* of John	Oct. 24, 1843
Van Winkle Hannah	Oct. 4, 1811
Van Winkle Hendrick	May 28, 1767
Van Winkle Henry	Dec. 19, 1827
Van Winkle Henry D	Dec. 13, 1848
Van Winkle Jacob	Dec. 17, 1778
Van Winkle Jacob H	Aug. 17, 1819
Van Winkle Jacob Jacobsen	Nov. 20, 1724
Van Winkle Jocob Jacobsen's *widow*	Sept. 20, 1732
Van Winkle Jacob V. N	Nov. —, 1837
Van Winkle Jane	June 4, 1840
Van Winkle Jane, *widow* of Joseph	June 28, 1847
Van Winkle Jannetje	April 12, 1769
Van Winkle Jeremiah	May 3, 1837
Van Winkle John, *son* of Daniel	Aug. 1, 1801
Van Winkle John C	March 14, 1835
Van Winkle John G	Jan. 8, 1846
Van Winkle John J	June 15, 1840
Van Winkle Joseph, *son* of Hendrick (de erste op het nieuwe kerk hos)	Nov. 22, 1738
Van Winkle Joseph, *son* of Jacob	Jan. 27, 1775
Van Winkle Joseph	Aug. 4, 1809
Van Winkle Joseph	Nov. 28, 1827
Van Winkle Joseph jr	Oct. 27, 1810
Van Winkle Larry	Nov. 26, 1830
Van Winkle Lea, *daughter* of Jacob	Sept. 18, 1772
Van Winkle Margrietje	Oct. 10, 1814
Van Winkle Mary, *wife* of Johannis Jurianse	Sept. 18, 1754
Van Winkle Mary	Aug. 15, 1831
Van Winkle Michael	July 22, 1829
Van Winkle Phebe	March 12, 1826
Van Winkle Rachel, *wife* of Jacob	Sept. 18, 1772
Van Winkle Rachel	Jan. 12, 1815
Van Winkle Rachel	Oct. 20, 1821
Van Winkle Sally	Dec. 6, 1827
Van Winkle Samuel	May 2, 1754
Van Winkle Sarah	Aug. 18, 1814
Van Winkle Stephen	Sept. 17, 1813
Van Winkle Susan Ann	Nov. 19, 1835
Van Winkle Walter, *son* of Abraham	Sept. 18, 1783
Vasher Frances	April 29, 1824
Vasher Mrs	Dec. 20, 1833
Veeder Cornelius, *son* of Harmanus	Sept. 10, 1763
Veeder Jacob, *son* of Harmanus	Sept. 2, 1767
Vincent Benjamin	July 23, 1818
Vincent Mrs	Sept. 7, 1832

DEATH RECORD.

NAME.	DATE OF DEATH.
Vliereboom Geertruy, of Constable's Hook	April 22, 1759
Vreeland Aagtje, *wife* of Roelof Helmigsen	Aug. 14, 1708
Vreeland Altje, *wife* of Stephen	March 4, 1846
Vreeland Ann	Feb. 28, 1819
Vreeland Annatje	March 11, 1803
Vreeland Antje, *daughter* of Gerrit	April 8, 1788
Vreeland Ariantje Hartmanse, *wife* of Zacharias Sickles	Dec. 2, 1731
Vreeland Beelitje, *wife* of Cornelius Sip	Oct. 26, 1789
Vreeland Benjamin, *son* of Enoch	Aug. 26, 1736
Vreeland Catharine	Oct. 22, 1835
Vreeland Catherine, *daughter* of Myndert	Oct. 12, 1840
Vreeland Charity	July 2, 1814
Vreeland Claesje	March 29, 1748
Vreeland Cornelia, *daughter* of Stephen	May, 23, 1802
Vreeland Cornelia	Sept. 24, 1822
Vreeland Cornelius	Jan. 16, 1813
Vreeland Cornelius Michielse's *wife*	Aug. 17, 1724
Vreeland Effie	Sept. 19, 1822
Vreeland Elias	April 2, 1748
Vreeland Elizabeth	Feb. 21, 1816
Vreeland Elizabeth	Dec. 17, 1827
Vreeland Elizabeth, *wife* of Michael Hartmanse	Nov. 18, 1767
Vreeland Elizabeth, *wife* of Cornelius Van Rypen	April 8, 1788
Vreeland Enoch Michielse	Aug. 17, 1714
Vreeland Fitje, *daughter* of Johannis Michielse	Jan. 27, 1710
Vreeland Garret	Feb. 13, 1825
Vreeland Geertje, *daughter* of Michael	Oct. —, 1806
Vreeland George	July 19, 1824
Vreeland Gerrit, *son* of Joris	Jan. 26, 1751
Vreeland Gerrit	Feb. 8, 1784
Vreeland Guilliam, *son* of Michael	March 30, 1807
Vreeland Hannah	July 9, 1833
Vreeland Hartman Michielse	Jan. 18, 1707
Vreeland Helen (88 years old)	March 7, 1846
Vreeland Helena, *wife* of Johannis Van Houten	March 15, 1774
Vreeland Hessel	Dec. 8, 1804
Vreeland Jacob, *son* of Gerrit	Nov. 7, 1786
Vreeland Jacob, *son* of Joris	Dec. 9, 1797
Vreeland Jacob, *son* of Joris	Sept. 11, 1804
Vreeland Jacob Enochsen	March 6, 1732
Vreeland Jacob G.	Feb. 1, 1811
Vreeland Jacob Henry	March 8, 1835
Vreeland Jane	Aug. 16, 1816
Vreeland Jane	Jan. 16, 1827
Vreeland Jane T.	Aug. 16, 1819
Vreeland Janet	Sept. 17, 1823
Vreeland Jannetje, *wife* of Joris Cadmus	Nov. 12, 1766
Vreeland Johannis, *son* of Johannis	Jan. 25, 1753
Vreeland Johannis	Feb. 11, 1783
Vreeland Johannis Michielse	June 26, 1713

NAME.	DATE OF DEATH.
Vreeland John	March 22, 1797
Vreeland John	July 31, 1823
Vreeland John G	Oct. 27, 1824
Vreeland John G	July 16, 1832
Vreeland John M	April 1, 1832
Vreeland Joris	June 21, 1795
Vreeland Michael, son of Johannis Michielse	Jan. 27, 1710
Vreeland Michael	Dec. 5, 1804
Vreeland Michael	March 10, 1825
Vreeland Michael	Nov. 29, 1827
Vreeland Michael A	March 19, 1849
Vreeland Michael G	April 10, 1823
Vreeland Michael Hartmanse	April 6, 1766
Vreeland Nicholas	Feb. 9, 1802
Vreeland Nicholas jr	Aug 15, 1817
Vreeland Nicholas	March 18, 1837
Vreeland Nicholas	Feb. 14, 1847
Vreeland Nicholas	Sept. 17, 1847
Vreeland Pryntje Michielse, widow of Andries Claesen	April 21, 1711
Vreeland Richard A	Sept. 3, 1818
Vreeland William M	July 31, 1837
Wade Matthias	July 28, 1803
Waernaerse Willemtje, wife of Hans Harmans	Oct. 28, 1697
Wakeman Mr	June 4, 1841
Waldron Aegie	Oct. 4, 1792
Waldron Antje	Sept. 30, 1756
Waldron Helena	Jan. 3, 1805
Waldron Jacob	July 23, 1822
Waldron James	Aug. 17, 1834
Waldron Jemima	May 31, 1824
Waldron Joseph	Oct. 14, 1779
Waldron Joseph	Jan. 4, 1838
Waldron Joseph	July 4, 1795
Waldron Marlin, son of Joseph	July 25, 1800
Waldron Richard	Sept. 25, 1805
Waldron Sarah	July 3, 1839
Waldron Tunis	Feb. 9, 1832
Walker William	July 6, 1814
Wannamaker Richard Abraham	March 25, 1843
Ward Matilda	Sept. 4, 1820
Weart Polly	Dec. 6, 1771
Weaver Mrs	March 7, 1839
Weere Ann	Aug. 8, 1820
Welsch James	March 13, 1807
Welsh Abner, son of James	Dec. 16, 1801
Welsh Abner B	Sept. 3, 1817
Welsh Elizabeth	Nov. 12, 1819
Welsh Hannah B	July 24, 1813
Welsh Isabella	Feb. 2, 1829

NAME.	DATE OF DEATH.
Welsh John jr	Oct. 28, 1834
Welsh John B	April 21, 1831
Welsh Mary	April 17, 1832
Wessels Grietje, *wife* of Enoch Michielse Vreeland	Nov. 20, 1697
Westervelt John C	July 17, 1843
Westervelt Susanna, *wife* of Jacob Van Winkle	April 23, 1787
Wiley Thomas P	July 28, 1820
Wilks Catherine	Oct. 18, 1810
Wilmouth William	July 6, 1814
Winne Aeltje, *daughter* of Martin	Oct. 6, 1794
Winne Claesje, *2d wife* of Michael De Mott	Oct. 27, 1787
Winne Elizabeth, *daughter* of Martin	Sept. 23, 1806
Winne Hannah	Nov. 17, 1811
Winne Ide, *son* of Levinus	Oct. 27, 1765
Winne Jannetje	Sept. 11, 1762
Winne Levinus, *son* of Martin	Feb. 6, 1790
Winne Levinus	May 31, 1802
Winne Levinus, *son* of Martin	Oct. 2, 1805
Winne Martin	July 8, 1737
Winne Martin L	Aug. 10, 1808
Winner Aletta	April 30, 1823
Winner Edo	Dec. 23, 1829
Winner Eleanor V. P., *daughter* of John S	May 17, 1843
Winner Gitty	Jan. 14, 1837
Winner Jacob	Sept. 27, 1813
Winner John	July 19, 1813
Wood Catherine	April 16, 1817
Wood Egbert	July 29, 1831
Wood Jane	April 19, 1832
Wood Nancy	Feb. 28, 1822
Wood Rebecca	Oct. 19, 1819
Wood Ruth	Feb. 24, 1817
Wright Asa	July 19, 1846
Wright John, *son* of John	Aug. 12, 1807
Yokeham Daniel	Jan. 21, 1821
Zabriskie Albert	Sept. 1, 1801
Zabriskie Albert	Aug. 31, 1819
Zabriskie Catherine	Dec. 21, 1821
Zabriskie Charity	June 5, 1813
Zabriskie John	Sept. 14, 1848

INDEX.

THE REFERENCES IN THE INDEX ARE TO THE FOLIO-PAGING.

	PAGE.
Abeel John, sells Paulus Hook	45
Ackerman Jacob	61, 62
Ackerman Morris	298
Ackerman William A	202, 208
Ackland John	318
Acres, number of patented	15
Acres, number of lying in common	15
Act relating to Secaucus Commons	285
Act relating to the common lands	18
Adolph Peter	105
Adriaensen Maryn	36
Aeschman Albert	232
Aeschman John A	222
Allen Henry	143
Allen Moses	146
Alsop Thomas	295
Anderson Thomas	63
Anderson William	62
Andriesen Loarens	60
Anness John	87
Annett Robert	129
Anthony Allerd	129
Arch Bridge Lot	231
Armstrong Matthew	59, 61, 63
Arsenal property	317
Assembly of X†X, 1, encourage settlements	2
Associates of the Jersey Company	45
Aukins Douwe	70
Ayres Abigail	142
Baker's Patent, history of	50
Baldwin Daniel	152, 153
Baldwin David	71
Banker Evert	296
Banta Siba Epsa	79
Barclay Henry A. W	129
Barclay John	131
Bard James	140

	PAGE.
Bard John	295
Bayard Balthazar	108
Bayard John	141
Bayard Nicholas	37, 129
Bayard Robert	38
Bayard Samuel	38, 39, 104
Bayard Stephen	38, 39
Bayard William	38, 40, 136, 138, 144, 151, 197, 264
Beach Marcus	321
Beacon Race-course	157
Becker Abraham	59
Becker Louis	253
Bocket Claudius C.	222
Bedell Abraham	140
Benson Garret	119
Bentley Peter	76, 81, 169
Bergen, bounds of in Carteret's Charter	14
Bergen Church	88
Bergen lots	151
Bergen, map of lost	8
Bergen, owners of lots in to perform guard duty	9
Bergen, patents to be taken out for lots in	9
Bergen Point Lot, history of	136
Bergen, the Freeholders of own the common land under the Dutch	7
Bergen Township, lands within purchased of the Indians	5
Bergen, when, how, and by whom laid out	8
Bergen Woods	151
Berrien John, one of the Commissioners	32, 137, 139, 193
Berry's Patent, history of	112
Bertholf Abraham	207
Betts Frederick F.	140
Bidwell Albert G.	200, 205
Biggs Thomas	199
Block House	228
Board of Chosen Freeholders of Hudson County	131, 149, 321
Bogert Cornelius	202, 208
Bon Sejours	142
Booraem Henry Augustus	41
Booraem Toler	155
Bostwick Samuel	58, 126
Botts, Alexander L.	175
Boudinot Elisha	135
Bramhall Edmond C.	58, 142, 160, 205, 209, 313
Bramhall Moses B.	126, 260
Branker William	232
Bray Thomas E.	149, 321
Brinkerhoff Cornelius	50, 53, 60, 76, 160, 201, 203, 211, 221, 232
Brinkerhoff Eleanor C.	51, 160
Brinkerhoff Garret	53

INDEX. 423

	PAGE.
Brinkerhoff Hartman	50, 138, 305
Brinkerhoff Hendrick	50, 53, 138, 160, 305
Brinkerhoff Hendrick Joris	50
Brinkerhoff Henry	50, 53, 160, 203
Brinkerhoff Jacob	56
Brinkerhoff Jacob H.	202, 208
Brinkerhoff John	50, 160, 203, 305
Brower Ann	257
Brower Jacob	234
Brower John	228
Brown Albert A. (in text Edwin J.)	63
Brown Edwin J.	146
Brown Jack	55
Brown James	153, 163, 225
Brown Lawrence	210, 216
Brown Thomas	55, 60, 61, 79, 136, 140, 144, 209, 217, 224
Brown's Ferry Lot	231
Browning Cyrus S.	46, 154, 157, 230, 248
Bruen Alexander M.	140
Bruen George W.	140, 141, 218
Buchanan Adele	213
Budd Nathaniel	135, 371
Bull Michael	228
Burger Elias	141, 142, 143
Burnet John	318
Butler John	141
Cadmus Andrew	70, 219
Cadmus Andrew L.	149, 184
Cadmus Dederick	70
Cadmus Elizabeth	213
Cadmus George	70, 136, 138, 140, 144, 169, 215, 220
Cadmus Jasper	65, 67, 70, 140, 141, 169, 213, 218, 219, 220, 296, 306
Cadmus John	169, 218
Cadmus Michael	65
Cadmus Richard	46, 70, 306
Cadmus William	169
Campbell Simeon	202, 208
Cantello William J.	153
Carle John, Commissioner for Secaucus Commons	309
Carling Michael	129, 190, 199
Carnes John H.	87
Carragan John	213
Carragan Sidney L.	213
Carsebom Jan Everse	127
Cary Thomas	61
Castle Hill	228
Cavan Point	56
Central Railroad Company of N. J.	48, 62

	PAGE.
Centre Hill	236
Carter from Carteret	14
Carter from Queen Anne	15
Christian's Patent, history of	72
Church Lots, history of	145, 146
Claesen Bartel	68, 69
Claesen Dirck	54, 56
Claesen's First Patent, history of	56
Claesen's Second Patent, history of	57
Clark Abraham, one of the Commissioners	32, 137, 139, 193, 309
Clark Daniel	105
Clausen Klip	231
Clendenny Walter	55, 105, 107, 144, 173, 231, 248, 316
Clerk Andrew	55, 67
Clinton Charles, one of the Commissioners	29, 137, 139, 193
Clinton George, Surveyor to the Commissioners	34, 193
Close Joseph B	219
Coerten Geurt	83, 313
Coerten's First Patent, history of	82
Coerten's Second Patent, history of	85
Coerten's Third Patent, history of	86
Coghill George	148
Cole Henry L	320, 321
Cole Peter	216, 320
Coles John B	134, 316, 317
Colgate William	123
Collerd Abraham	87, 157, 235, 251
Collerd Ann	313
Collerd Jacob	235, 251
Collerd Jacobus	235
Collerd James	55, 56, 206
Collerd John	206, 251
Columbia Academy	147
Commissioners of Bergen County Loan Office	152
Common Lands	151
Common Lands, agreement among the freeholders, concerning	16
Common Lands, survey and allotment of	18
Communipaw—Gemoenepan, 7; Communican, 48; Comunipan, 48; Communipan, 48; Gamoenepaen, 52; Gemoenepaen, 56; Gemoenepa	56
Communipaw in Pauw's Colonie	5, 54
Condit Silas	309
Constable's Hook Patent, history of	73
Cook Martin R	211
Cooper William	164, 207, 208, 254
Corbin Abel R	121
Corey Ashbel W	123
Cornelison Dr. John M	149
Cornelison Rev. John	107

	PAGE.
Cos Claas Pietersen	47
Cos's Patent, history of	47
Coster John G	40
Cottenet Francis	202
Cottinal Charles	142
Coulter William	316
Court House, on what lot standing	321
Contant Ebun H	219
Crane Jasper	325
Crary Peter	140
Crips Thomas C	213
Cubberly Thomas	61
Culver Delos E	232
Culver Delos E., observations on terrestrial magnetism	24
Culver Isaac B	232
Cummings John N	143, 144
Currie James	64, 65
Dally William	173
Danforth Nicholas D	61
Danielson David	133
Danielson Joseph	147, 163, 164, 177, 199, 202, 205, 225, 253
Danielson William	254
Darcy John S	123
Davis Thomas E	73
Davison Thomas	68
Davison's First Patent, history of	66
Davison's Second Patent, history of	68
Day David	307
Day William	91, 101, 228
De Cuyper's Patent, history of	94
De Forest Isaac	68
De Forest John	109
De Groot John	155
De Hart Catherine	303
De Kay George C	257
De Mott Edward	158
De Mott Garrett	111, 158, 226
De Mott George	111, 155, 158, 177, 184, 224, 225, 226, 237, 238, 242, 252, 312
De Mott George V	112, 158, 198
De Mott Henson	158
De Mott Henry	158
De Mott Huyler	158
De Mott James	87, 158
De Mott John H	111
De Mott Joris	46, 81, 119
De Mott Josephine H	111
De Mott Mattys	46, 79, 91, 94, 101, 110
De Mott Michael	46, 79, 81, 110, 119, 158, 177, 184, 198, 224–6, 237–8, 242, 252, 312

54

	PAGE.
De Mott Thomas	158
De Nemours John Henry Beaureaux Pusey	142, 144, 145
De Nemours Peter Samuel du Pont	142
De Nemours Victor du Pont	142, 143
Deas David	153
Deas Ebenezer	202
Deas James	153
Decker Levi	202
Deed of Indians for Ahasimus	5
Deed of Indians for Aressick	4
Deed of Indians for Hoboken	3
Deed of Indians to Gov. Stuyvesant	5
Deeds from the Dutch respected by the English	13
Deeds, where recorded	13
Demarest David M	91, 140, 141, 218
Detwiller Jacob J	61
Devoe Aaron	308
Dey Anthony purchases Poulus Hook	45
Dey John	42, 127, 156, 157, 190
Dezarmauld Louis	155
Diedricks Abraham	87, 118, 138, 232, 246, 257
Diedricks Cornelius	87, 118, 234, 246, 256
Diedricks Daniel	87, 91, 118, 138, 233, 234, 235, 237, 319
Diedricks Garret	118
Diedricks Hans	117
Diedricks Johannis	118, 138, 240, 246, 256, 319
Diedricks John	233
Diedricks Wander	91, 118
Diedricks' Patent, history of	117
Dilloway George W	62
Dobbs William	304
Dole Nathaniel	129
Donnaldson William, one of the Commissioners	30, 137, 139, 193
Doremus Cornelius	222, 298, 300
Douglas George	143
Douglas William	66
Douwesse Paul	53
Drake Robert	63
Drayton Henry	202
Du Bois Edward	255
Du Pont Charles H. L. Preudhomme	140, 141, 144
Duke of York conveys New Jersey to Berkeley and Carteret	10
Duke of York obtains grant from Charles II	10
Duke's Farm, history of	132
Dunham Azariah, one of the Commissioners,	30, 136, 137, 139, 193, 309
Duplanty Raphael	142
Durar Enoch	153
Dutch grants without pecuniary consideration	10
Dyckman Jacob G	207

	PAGE.
Earle Anthebe	131, 299
Earle Daniel	243, 306
Earle Edward	131, 138, 299, 300, 306
Earle Edward jr	130, 304
Earle Elias	146
Earle Enoch	303
Earle Henry	304
Earle John	131, 296
Earle Justus E.	199
Earle Nathaniel	304, 306
Earle Philip	131, 138, 152, 306
Earle Richard	131, 254
Earle Sarah E	141
East Newark, named " Petersborough "	328
East Newark, named " Santfort "	327
Edsall Samuel	69, 73, 74
Edward Harman	95, 317
Edwards William W	53
Ellingwood Nathan Dale	232, 257
Elsworth ——	72
Emot William	305
Enyard Elias	143
Enyard John M	143
Enyard Nicholas	143
Evans Evan	318
Everson Jacob	126, 261 322
Faber Conrad W	232
Fanshaw Daniel	184
Fanshaw Samuel	294
Field-Books and Maps, history of	24
Field-Book, title page of	27
Fielding Henry	66, 138, 213, 214
Fish Jonathan	304
Fish Nicholas	303
Fisher Michael	253
Fleming James	63
Forfeited Estates, act providing for	38
Freedoms and Exemptions	2
Freeman Stephen	325
Freemason's Island	155
French Philip	88, 176, 231
Frogtown	253
Frost William	213
Gafney John J	149
Gardner Charles E	153
Gardner Elijah	153
Gardner James	153, 177

	PAGE.
Gardner James F.	153
Gardner John	187, 225, 242, 253
Gardner Robert	153, 177, 187, 225, 253
Garrabrants Cornelius	48, 55, 136, 138, 142, 190, 199, 200, 206
Garrabrants Myndert	48, 49, 138, 199, 200, 313
Garrabrants Peter	48, 54, 55, 190, 199, 206
Garrabrants Smith	112, 184
Garretse's (Dirck) Patent, history of	101, *vide* also 317
Garretson Hermanns	144, 210
Garretson Jasper	143, 210
Garretson Stephen	55, 146
Garritse's (Geurt) Patent, history of	97
Gautier Andrew	61, 140, 144, 210
Gautier Daniel	61
Gautier Francis	6, 112
Gautier Samuel T.	55, 61, 224
Gautier Thomas B.	61, 140, 184, 210, 224, 316, 318
Gerritse's (Geurt) Patent, history of	120
Gifford George	83
Gilbert Hiram	46, 154, 157, 230
Gilbert John C.	123
Gilbert William S.	123
Gilbertse's Patent, history of	62
Godyn and Blommaert at Cape May, etc.	3
Goodstay	142
Gould David	160
Graves Jared W.	148
Graves Roswell	219
Greenlief Jacob	295
Greenlief Robert	303
Gregory Dudley S.	129, 155
Grier James	153
Grosclaude Frederick	255
Grove Reformed Church	225
Gruman Ichabod	144
Grunti Robert	308
Guillame Samuel	222
Guttenbergh, village of	207, 208, 254
Hall Willis	135
Halladay John R.	48, 49, 170
Halliard John	317
Halsey William	328
Hampton Jonathan, surveyor	34, 66
Hanna James	153
Harding Elizabeth	91
Haring Cornelius, agent for forfeited estates	38, 40
Harmanse Hans	75
Harmense Douwe	110

	PAGE.
Harmense's Patent, history of	110
Harriman Elizabeth G	59
Harriman William	170
Harrington William	141
Harrison James	321
Harrison Mortimer A. T	320
Harrison Stephen D	76, 81
Harsimus, 40; Ahasimus, 4; Haasemus, 40; Hassemus, 41; Harsimus, 41; Ahasymus, 42; Haassemus, 42; Aharsimus, 45; Hahasemes, 47; Hossemus	48
Harsimus, Indian deed for	4
Hartman's First Patent, history of	51
Hartman's Second Patent, history of	54
Hawkins Joseph	76, 222, 299
Haynes John	318
Hazard Thomas	75
Heavenor John	316
Hedden Job	303
Helm George W	102
Hennion David	133, 152, 294
Hespe Charles	222
Hexamer William	236
Hickman Robert sells Hoboken	39
Hillyer George	294
Hillyer Maurice	232
Hoboken (Hobocan-Hacking, 3; Hooboocken, 39; Hoboocken,	42
Hoboken, Indian deed for	3
Hoboken Land Improvement Company	152, 154
Hoboken Patent, history of	39
Hoboken sold by Haring to Stevens	40
Hoboken sold by Hickman to Bayard	39
Hopkins Samuel	325
Hornblower Josiah	173, 248, 297, 316
Howe George W	58, 59
Hudson County Land Improvement Co	62, 67
Hudson County Real Estate Co	153
Humphreys Solon	166, 170, 211
Huyler Abraham	155, 179, 208, 244
Huyler Cornelius	154, 155, 191
Inch William Spencer	203
Indian Ratification of Stuyvesant's Deed	7
Indian Spring Lot	225
Ingham Samuel D	140, 219
Inness George B	248
Isaacs Moses	152
Jackson Henry	153, 154, 318
Jackson Jeremiah	56

INDEX.

	PAGE.
Jackson John	62
Jackson John F.	153
Jackson Patrick	318, 321
Jackson Thomas	62
Jackson William	153, 154
Jaclard Sebastian	213
Jacobs Bartel	68, 69
Jacobs John	61
Jan de Lacher's Hook	41
Jenkins Matthew C.	140, 219
Jessup Silas H.	149
Jones Mary	255
Jones Thomas J.	164
Jurianse Johannis	137, 138, 139
Keeny William	48, 49, 170
Kelly John	55
Kennedy Archibald	133, 134, 190, 328
Kennedy John	134, 328
Kennedy Robert	134, 328
Kennedy's Farm	328
Kennel John	61
Kerrigan James	313
King James G.	152, 153
King of England claims the country	10
King of England grants to the Duke of York	10
Kingsland Edmund	131, 296, 326
Kingsland Isaac	131, 304, 326
Kingsland John	300, 327
Kingsland Nathaniel	324, 325
Kingsland Roger	131
Kingsland William Edmund	131, 294, 327
Klinck Leonard G.	222, 225
Kuyper Claas Jansen	42, 127
Kuyper Cornelius	127
Kuyper Hendrick	42, 127, 136, 137, 138, 139, 140, 144, 156, 190, 191, 198, 263
La Grange Johannis	60
La Rosa Peter	144
La Tourette David	142, 144, 166, 211
La Tourette House	142
Laidlaw Marian B. and Isabel F.	157
Lane Nehemiah B.	166
Laurens Patent, history of	64
Laurense Arent	123
Laurense's Patent, history of	123
Lawrence Richard	141
Leake John George	125, 131, 179, 244, 300, 306
Leake Robert	125, 131, 261, 308

	PAGE.
Leake Robert William	125, 131
Leary David	140
Leavitt John W.	163, 202
Leavitt Samuel	163
Lee William P.	141
Leslie George	131, 297
Lester John P.	154, 157
Lienau Michael	41
Lignot Peter Julius	61
Lilliendahl Gustavus A.	62
Lindertz Paulus	128
Lockwood Daniel	141
Lockwood Frederick M.	61
Lodi	328
Lombard poplar, origin of in America	302
Long Bridge Lot	160
Loosdregh Jan	68
Loss's Map of Hoboken	40
Loubat Joseph Alphonse	202
Lozier Abraham	298
Lozier David	202, 209
Lozier Leah	202, 208
Lubertse Jan	105
Lubertse's Patent, history of	105
Luby Jacob	102, 104, 109
Luby's Patent, history of	102
Ludlam Henry	153
Ludlam Matthias	153
Lutchie	316
Mabon Rev. William V.	177
Mackie Robert	142, 143
Macpelah Cemetery	301
Magaw Dr.	83
Mandeville Henry J.	75
Marins Peter Jacobse	326
Marion Building Company	111
Marsh Daniel	309
Masons' Land	231
Masters Joseph	242
McCarter Arthur	129
McDonald John	234
McDonald Matthias	228
McDonald Thomas	213, 244
McFarland Robert	105
McGregor Coll.	128
McGuinness Benjamin	318
McIntyre George	143, 144
McKnight Andrew	53

	PAGE
McPherson John R	149
Mead John	102
Mechanics' Lot, history of	135
Mechaux André	302
Meeks John	228, 234, 257
Mellick Andrew D	142, 143, 164
Mellick Elizabeth D	143
Melyn Jacob	325
Merselis Cornelius	316
Merselis Edo	183
Merselis Jacob	63, 83, 173
Merselis M	63, 126, 260
Merselis John	173, 248, 250, 316
Merselis Merselis	107, 138, 173, 248, 316
Merselis Merselis J	49, 63, 123
Merselis Peter	78, 87, 106, 138, 173, 224, 231, 248
Mersereau John	136, 141
Michielsen Tadeus	109
Midmer John H	63
Miegs Henry	166
Mighgecticock, aboriginal name of New Barbadoes Neck	323
Miller J. Dickinson	41
Minack Thomas	228
Minnit Peter, Director-General	2
Mitchell Abraham	155
Mompesson Roger	131
Montague Ebenezer	157
Montgomery James	251
Moore Mary	295
Moore Samuel T	199
Mordainis Meadow	129
Morgan John	225
Morgen, a land measure	26
Morrell Abraham	160
Morrell Agnes	62
Morris Charles	166
Morris Gerard W	318
Morton John W	183
Mosher Nathan R	219
Mott Dr. Valentine	56
Mulford Alexander C	102
Mullany James R	141, 142, 166
Mullany John R. B	141
Murtha Peter J	222
Musgrove Thomas	61
Myerhoff Francis	153
Najacksick	58
Neil Robert	153, 154

	PAGE.
Nelson Samuel C.	61, 227
New Barbadoes Neck	324
New Field-Book	312
New Jersey conveyed to Berkeley and Carteret, 11 ; recaptured by the Dutch, 11 ; Berkeley conveys to Billinge, 11 ; divided into East and West Jersey, 12 ; East Jersey sold, 13 ; the Twenty-four Proprietors..	13
New Jersey Harbor Company	135
New Jersey Stock Yard and Market Company	54
New York Bay Cemetery Company	59, 60
Newark owns New Barbadoes Neck	325
Newham Charles E.	91
Newkirk Aaron	87, 99, 179, 180, 213
Newkirk Abraham	149
Newkirk Abram P.	6, 180
Newkirk Cornelius	231, 238
Newkirk Garret	43, 83, 87, 99, 112, 136, 138, 148, 179, 180. 231, 235, 236, 240, 242, 252, 253, 294, 295, 318
Newkirk Garret G.	112
Newkirk Garret H.	87, 99, 109, 112, 179
Newkirk Garret J.	148
Newkirk George	87, 99, 112, 123, 148, 179, 180, 222, 231, 236, 238, 252, 253
Newkirk Hendrick	99, 109, 112, 179, 180, 231, 240, 251
Newkirk Henry	112, 231, 353
Newkirk Henry H.	112
Newkirk Jacob	42, 112, 148, 149, 157, 253, 236, 238, 295
Newkirk James M.	112
Newkirk John	112
Newkirk John J.	43, 157, 238, 253
Newkirk John M.	112, 238, 253
Newkirk Mathevis	99, 112, 138, 179, 180, 231, 240, 252, 253
Newkirk Matthew P.	157
Newkirk Poulus	112
Neyousick	58
Noble and Moore's Patent, history of	76
Norman's Patent, history of	59
Oakley Israel	75
Ogden John	325
Ogilvie Rev. John	308
Olphertz Sjoert	68, 69
Oratum, Sagamore of the Hackingsacks	74
Osborn Henry	213
Osborn Samuel	148, 149
Ostrum Hendrick	314
Oude Boomse Val	315
Outwater Guilliam	202, 208, 209
Outwater Jacob G.	56, 123, 202, 222, 259
Outwater James	296

	PAGE.
Outwater John G	202, 256
Overseers of the Poor of Bergen	131
Palmer John	133
Pamrepaw—Pembrepog, 50; Pembrepogh, 52; Najacksick, 58; Pamrepogh, 70; Pembrepock, 70; Pemmerpook, 394; Pemerpo	400
Paret Henry	140
Paret John	140
Parks Altje	87
Parmily Jahiel	142
Pasman Catherine	137
Paterson William	141
Paulus Hook (Pouwels Hook, 44; Powlus Houck)	45
Paulus Hook, Indian deed for	4
Paulus Hook Patent, history of	44
Paulus Hook sold to Van Vorst	45
Pauw Michael conveys Pavonia to the Company	5
Pauw Michael purchases Hoboken	3
Pauw Michael purchases Paulus Hook, etc	4
Pavonia, the name of Pauw's Colonie	5
Pearsall Nelson B	62
Pembrepogh	58
Perine Peter	255
Peters John Priestly	320
Petersborough, name of East Newark	328
Peterse Peter II	317
Petersen Peter	221, 223
Peterson Adrian	317
Peyton Josiah	110
Pfeffel Peter Charles	232
Phelps George D	142
Philipse Frederick	87
Philipse's Patent, history of	87
Phillips Alpha	166
Pierce Robert	163
Pierson Abraham, sen	325
Pieterse Paulus	99
Pieterse's Patent, history of	99
Pinhorne John	131
Pinhorne William	130
Planck Abraham Isaacsen	45
Platt Jacob S	155
Plummer William G	149
Poillon George W	141
Post Abraham	200
Post Adrian	81, 314
Post Egbert	66, 144, 214
Post John	67
Post John E	55, 62, 206, 208

		PAGE
Post Peter		141, 144
Post's Patent, history of		81
Powers William P		155
Price Francis		163, 199
Price Rodman M		163
Prior Abraham		123, 222, 247, 259
Prior Andries		101, 105, 247
Prior Casparus		76, 101, 126, 148, 222, 247, 259, 260
Prior Hartman		247
Prior Jacob		123, 133, 146, 209, 249, 319
Prior Jasper		76, 126, 295, 317
Prior Michael		126, 259
Prior Nicholas		101, 126, 146, 232, 243
Prosser Thomas		256
Provost James		148, 236, 253
Pusy John Xavier Bureaux		142, 143, 144
Quit Rents, lands in East Jersey subject to		13, 14, 15
Rabineau Jacob		145
Raccocus (Reckpokus, 56; Regpokes, 57; Right-Coakkuss, 57; Rackpokus)		57
Rapp Adam		247
Rapp Conrad		357
Rapp Henry		254
Rapp John		254, 257
Reed William B		140, 141, 219
Richardson, J. P		154
Rod, as used in the patents		26
Roll John		60, 61
Romaine John		105, 246
Romeyn Simon Jansen		69
Rosencamp Henry		61
Rowe Norman L.		226
Rowe Peter		62, 226
Roy Jacob Jacobsen		73
Rummel John C. F		321
Ryerson Garrabrant		213
Sacket Augustus		301
Sacket James		300
Sacket Joseph		300, 304
Sacket Samuel		301
Sacket William		300, 301
Salter David		67
Salter Paul		61, 65, 67
Sanford Peregrine		328
Sandford William		324, 327, 328
Sands George W		141

	PAGE.
Saunier Michael	163, 164, 199, 202, 203, 205
Saunier Paul	301
Schneider Henry	222
School Lots, history of	147, 149
Schuyler Arent	327
Schuyler Jacob R	166, 328
Schuyler John	328
Schuyler Peter	328
Secaucus— Siskakes, 0 ; Sickakus	130
Secaucus Commons	291
Secaucus Patent, history of	130
Seely John	154
Segaerd Andries	138
Segaerd Fitje	61, 62, 210, 216
Serrel John	72
Sewell Robert	155
Seymour Julia A	61
Shepherd Joseph	116
Sherman Charles A	142, 143
Sherwood Luman	146
Showhank Brook	40, 157
Sickles Abraham	54, 138, 202, 209, 233, 236, 240, 312
Sickles Daniel	55
Sickles Derrick	234
Sickles Hendrick	91, 138, 234, 236
Sickles John	91, 234, 251
Sickles Peter	123, 184, 259
Sickles Robert	261
Sickles Zacharias	138, 184, 221, 251
Simmons Michael	125, 248, 316
Simmons William	248
Simonson Cornelius	140
Simonson Daniel	91, 251
Simonson James L	140, 144
Simonson Joseph	148, 320, 321
Simonson Stephen	234, 251
Sip Cornelius, 87, 97, 122, 138, 183, 187, 188, 221, 232, 238, 241, 243, 249, 251, 258, 261, 322	
Sip Garret..81, 87, 97, 112, 138, 146, 183, 187, 187, 188, 221, 232, 238, 241, 243, 249, 251, 258, 261, 322	
Sip Ide	88, 122
Sip Jan Adrian	81, 83, 91, 102, 109, 122
Sip Peter	114, 122, 126, 183, 296
Sip Richard	109, 122, 126, 183
Sisson Benjamin	320
Sisson Mary Elizabeth	49
Sistare Delia A	232
Slaight Nathaniel C	87
Slaugh's Meadow Patent, history of	128

	PAGE.
Slonga	40, 49, 50, 57, 152
Slot's Patent, history of	69
Smith Abel J	83, 131, 321
Smith Cornelius	304
Smith Cortlandt	61
Smith Daniel	144, 452, 223, 294
Smith Enoch	299, 300, 303, 304
Smith Gilbert C	61
Smith Job	83, 131, 138, 141, 223, 298
Smith John	141
Smith John E	144
Smith Philip	138, 298
Smith Robert L	56
Snake Hill	130
Somerindyke John	129
Southmayd Henry	123
Speer Abraham	119
Speer Henry	321
Speer John	238
Speer William H	51, 160
Spengeman Conrad C	222
Spicer Jacob, one of the Commissioners	29, 137, 159, 193
Spier Hendrick Jansen	65
Spiers Patent, history of	65
Stager Richard	148, 149
Stainer Edward	232
Staten Island belonged to Pauw	5
Steenhuysen Englebert	91
Steenhuysen's Patent, history of	91
Steenwyck Cornelis	68, 69, 81
Steinmets Caspar	46, 78, 79, 133
Steinmets Garret	133
Steinmets Johannis	317
Steinmets John	133
Stevens James	53
Stevens John	38, 40, 42, 128, 131, 154, 308
Stockholme Charity	142
Stoffelsen's Catharine Patent, history of	71
Stoffelsen Jacob	46
Stoffelsen's Jacob Patent, history of	46
Stolz Jacob	200, 205
Story Rufus	141
Straatmaker's Creek	58
Stringham James R	141
Stringham William	140, 141
Stringham Winfield	141
Sturge John	296
Stuyvesant Peter	125, 126, 135
Stuyvesant Petrus	198, 260, 316

	PAGE.
Stuyvesant's Patent, history of	47
Stuyvesant's purchase from the Indians	5
Subdivision of the Common Lands	195
Suckley George	234, 257
Suckley Rutzen	228
Sutphen John S	102
Swartwout Samuel	40
Sycan Dirck	58, 66
Sycan's First Patent, history of	58
Sycan's Second Patent, history of	65
Syms John	61, 248
Taylor Rev. Benjamin C	183
Taylor Isaac S	146
Taylor Noah D	63
Taylor Thomas	63, 183
Tead Andrew	131, 308
Terhune Michael B	75, 166
Terhune Stephen	75, 169
Teunisse Dirck's Patent, history of	149
Teunisse Hendrick's Patent, history of	114
Vide also	318
Thorp Benjamin	321
Thomas William	149
Thompson Robert	65
Tise George	135
Tise John	148, 321
Tise Richard	148
Timson Charles J	183
Toers Arent .91, 92, 102, 105, 109, 118, 123, 125, 138, 181, 236, 239, 244, 246, 247, 249, 256, 258, 262, 315, 320	
Toers Claas Arentse	91, 102
Toers Laurent Arentse	91, 315
Toers Nicholas	91, 92, 125, 245, 250, 321
Tonele John	157
Townsend William R	129
Traphagen Henry	43, 154
Tucker Reuben D	318
Tuttle John S	227
Tysen Esther	254
United Netherland Company	1
United States Watch Company	121
Urianse Altje	230
Van Ame Moses	144
Van Blarcom Gysbert	105, 247
Van Blarcom John	105, 310
Van Borsum Cornelius	129

	PAGE.
Van Buskirk Abraham	71, 75, 213
Van Buskirk Andries	60, 75, 219
Van Buskirk Cornelius	60, 65, 71, 144, 166, 169, 211, 213, 216, 217
Van Buskirk David	71
Van Buskirk Effie, *wife* of James	49
Van Buskirk Jacobus	75, 76, 213, 295
Van Buskirk James	71, 76, 166, 218
Van Buskirk Johannis	75, 138
Van Buskirk John	76, 108, 218
Van Buskirk John J	141
Van Buskirk Laurens Andriesen	60
Van Buskirk Lawrence	60, 66, 75
Van Buskirk Nicholas	76, 218
Van Clief Daniel	160
Van Dalson John	136, 144
Van Derbilt Aaron	123, 222, 259
Van Derhoof Garret	222, 259
Van Derhoof Jacobus	138, 222, 224
Van Derhoof Sarah	123
Van der Linden Jan	69, 74
Van der Linden Joost	69
Van Gelder Jesse	244
Van Giesen Isaac	307
Van Giesen John	102
Van Giesen Rynier	66, 138
Van Glahn Henry	173
Van Glahn Lawrence	53, 55
Van Horne Andrew	62, 75, 144
Van Horne Cornelius	48, 55, 71, 72, 126, 145, 199, 200, 206, 213
Van Horne David L	62, 126
Van Horne Garret	48, 43, 200, 203, 205
Van Horne Henry	144
Van Horne Jacob	54, 60, 136, 144, 171, 213, 215, 217, 220
Van Horne Jacob Barentzen	71
Van Horne James	152
Van Horne John	48, 53, 54, 55, 71, 138, 142, 170, 203, 205, 215
Van Horne John G	49, 52, 53, 76, 108, 166, 170, 200, 203, 205
Van Horne John J	173, 203, 205
Van Horne Mindert	49, 53, 57, 170, 200, 203, 205
Van Horne Peter	170, 200, 203, 205
Van Horne Rutgert	52, 53, 68, 69, 71
Van Horne Stephen	203
Van Houten Abraham	244
Van Houten Helmigh	49, 137, 138, 139, 156, 249, 259, 295, 297, 313, 320
Van Houten Johannis	79, 102, 108, 123, 225, 239, 244, 249, 252, 253, 259
Van Houten John	49, 138, 157, 225, 244, 249, 259
Van Houten Roelof	66, 76
Van Iderstein	320
Van Kleek Bultus Barentsen	101

	PAGE.
Van Nieuwkerck Mattheus Cornelise	109
Van Nostrand Henry D	59
Van Nukirk Matthewwis	138
Van Ostrum's Patent, history of	127
Van Purmerant Claas Jansen	42, 66, 127
Van Purmerant's Patent, history of	42, 127
Van Rensselaer Kiliaen, takes up land at Fort Orange	3
Van Ruyven Cornelius	128
Van Rypen Christopher	245
Van Rypen Cornelius	81, 83, 213, 227, 228, 242, 318
Van Rypen Cornelius C	85, 227, 228, 242
Van Rypen Cornelius G	79, 81, 83, 85, 97, 108, 227, 250
Van Rypen Cornelius R	227
Van Rypen Daniel	76, 81, 83, 101, 108, 138, 227, 228, 242, 250, 259, 313, 317, 321
Van Rypen Daniel R	227
Van Rypen Derrick	228
Van Rypen Garret	76, 81, 83, 126, 138, 227, 228, 230, 234, 242, 250, 261
Van Rypen Garret J	294
Van Rypen George	81, 83, 228
Van Rypen Johannis	76, 85, 97, 108, 183, 230, 241, 250, 251
Van Rypen Michael	227
Van Rypen Richard	76, 83, 101, 148, 227, 228, 242, 318
Van Rypen Thomas Jurianse	83
Van Schalckwyck's Patent, history of	70
Van Tuyl Abraham	143
Van Tuyl Andrew	143
Van Tuyl Michael	143
Van Vleck Isaac	254
Van Vleck Tielman	114, 122
Van Vleck's Patent, history of	114
Van Vorst Cornelius	40, 45, 122, 136, 138, 143, 154, 155, 156, 157, 197, 198, 224, 241, 245, 319
Van Vorst Garret	224, 241, 245
Van Vorst Ide Cornelison	40, 114
Van Vorst John	40, 155
Van Vorst William B	155
Van Vorst's Patent at Harsimus, history of	40
Van Vorst's Patent at Bergen, history of	122
Van Wagenen Cornelius	121
Van Wagenen Gerrit G. jr	64, 81, 123, 322
Van Wagenen Hartman	81, 87, 99, 119, 121, 123, 180, 187, 231, 260
Van Wagenen Jacob	63, 64, 65, 91, 97, 120, 121, 136, 138, 141, 166, 167, 187, 212, 226, 247, 260, 295
Van Wagenen Johannis	53, 91, 119, 120, 138, 187, 202, 226, 235, 253, 258, 260
Van Wagenen John	121
Van Wart Isaac	206
Van Wart Philip	140
Van Winkle Abraham	116, 255
Van Winkle Altje	83

	PAGE.
Van Winkle Cornelia	213
Van Winkle Cornelius	76, 108, 255, 257
Van Winkle Daniel	66, 109, 116, 149, 213, 214, 229, 230, 234, 245, 251, 257, 321
Van Winkle Daniel G.	116
Van Winkle Garret	148
Van Winkle Garret S.	116
Van Winkle Hendrick	91, 116, 138, 186, 235, 238, 255
Van Winkle Henry	116
Van Winkle Henry D.	83, 116, 149, 230, 318
Van Winkle Jacob	83, 116
Van Winkle Jacob D.	107, 116, 248, 257
Van Winkle Jacob Jacobse	81, 91, 116, 318
Van Winkle Jeremiah	83, 109, 116, 183, 230
Van Winkle John	233, 246, 320
Van Winkle John D.	107, 116
Van Winkle John G.	116
Van Winkle Joseph	61, 116, 235, 238, 255, 304
Van Winkle Samuel	116
Van Zyle James	140
Varick Abraham	45, 143
Varick Richard	45, 143
Varlet Nicholas	39, 127
Varlet's Patent, history of	125
Varlet and Bayard's Patent, history of	108
Varlet and Bayard's Patent (Secaucus), history of	130
Veeder Hermanus	138, 232
Ver Bruggen Johannis	129
Vetterlein Bernhard	51
Vinge Jan	128
Vinge's Patent, history of	128
Voorhis Charles F.	123
Vreeland Abraham	146, 227, 232
Vreeland Claas	54, 57, 136, 141, 144
Vreeland Cornelius Michielse	52, 53, 56, 57, 66
Vreeland Cornelius	62, 75, 105, 140, 141, 218
Vreeland Cornelius M.	87, 99
Vreeland Daniel	55, 113
Vreeland Elias Michielse	52, 79
Vreeland Enoch Michielse	52, 58
Vreeland Garret	54, 55, 56, 59, 60, 63, 67, 92, 164, 170, 200, 222
Vreeland Garret J.	75
Vreeland Garret M.	54
Vreeland George	59, 60, 61, 62, 67, 136, 138, 142, 148, 164, 205, 209, 211, 213, 216, 236, 253
Vreeland Hartman	67, 140, 141, 208, 218
Vreeland Hartman Michielse	52, 54, 56
Vreeland Helmus	105, 140, 219
Vreeland Henry	62, 75, 219
Vreeland Jacob	59, 60, 226

	PAGE.
Vreeland Janetje Michielse	52
Vreeland Johannis	53, 118, 138, 202, 205, 207, 208
Vreeland Johannis Michielse	52, 56, 57
Vreeland John	59, 60, 67, 105, 136, 142, 164, 211, 213, 226, 295
Vreeland John M.	58, 162, 163
Vreeland Michael	49, 53, 54, 55, 57, 58, 66, 67, 105, 138, 162, 163, 164, 183, 200, 205, 208, 214, 219
Vreeland Michael Cornelise	136, 162, 201, 204, 209, 212, 214
Vreeland Michael G.	65, 202, 208, 209
Vreeland Michael Hartmanse	116, 138, 202, 204, 207, 208, 255
Vreeland Mindert	58, 162, 163
Vreeland Nicholas	54, 55, 222, 295
Vreeland Nicholas S.	57, 62, 208
Vreeland Peter	140, 141, 218
Vreeland Peter V. B.	53
Vreeland Pryntje Michielse	52
Vreeland Richard	46, 58, 59, 61, 114, 164
Vreeland Stephen	57, 62, 141, 170, 179, 202, 204, 207, 208, 213
Vreeland Stephen B.	57, 63, 208
Vreeland Thomas	138
Vreeland William	75, 140, 141, 218
Vreeland William C.	67, 75, 166
Wade Nathaniel	304
Waldron Charles	155
Waldron Joseph	55, 206
Waldron Joseph J.	155
Ward John	325
Ward Jonas	153, 154
Warman Richard	131
Warner Abraham B.	211
Warren Sir Peter	128, 263
Watts Charles	152, 294
Wauters Egbert	227
Wauters Garret	214
Wauters John	62
Wauters Merselis	67
Weehawken (Wiehacken, 6; Awiehaken, 36; Wiehaken)	151
Weehawken Patent, history of	36
Weldon Walter	224
Welsh Benjamin F.	55, 102
Welsh Daniel	54
Welsh James W.	102
Welsh John	102
Wescott Samuel	62, 126
West Bergen	232
West Hoboken Land Association, No. 2	236
West India Company incorporated	1
West India Company's Farm, history of	42, 46, 132

	PAGE.
Westerfield Benjamin C.	254
Westerfield Elizabeth	254
Westerfield Henry	254
Westervelt Albert A.	131
Westervelt Jasper B.	254
Wetherby Mrs.	244
White Anthony	136, 141, 144
White Samuel C.	140
Willard Edward A.	213
Willemer Adolphus	222
Williams John J.	305, 306
Williams Philip	316
Williamson James A.	141
Wilson Blakely	112, 149
Wilson Peter	296
Winfield Charles H.	62, 140
Winfield Harriet M.	62
Winne Edo	92, 245
Winne John	46, 135, 138, 146, 234
Winne John S.	114, 244, 254
Winne Levinus	46, 105, 114, 138, 183, 245, 254, 294
Winne Martin	105, 114, 245, 257
Winner Nicholas T.	222
Wolvern William H.	141
Woods Martin	141
Woods Walter	62
Woolmington John	173
Woolsey Benjamin F.	143
Wright Edwin R. V.	157
Wright William	126
Wyman Aaron	153
Young Edward F. C.	87
Youmans Jonathan	257
Zabriskie Albert	69, 227
Zabriskie Albert M.	140, 141, 142, 219, 313
Zabriskie Benjamin	219
Zabriskie David	142
Zabriskie family	143
Zabriskie Jacob	152, 210, 225, 313
Zabriskie Jasper	141, 142, 143, 210, 219
Zabriskie John	222, 232, 246, 313
Zabriskie John H.	92
Zabriskie Michael	140, 141, 142, 166, 210
Zabriskie Peter	152
Zule John	153